INSIDE
MAD ®

Edited by John Ficarra

Designed by Patricia Dwyer

Time
HOME ENTERTAINMENT

MAD Magazine

VICE PRESIDENT & EXECUTIVE EDITOR John Ficarra
ART DIRECTOR Sam Viviano
SENIOR EDITORS Charlie Kadau, Joe Raiola
EDITOR Dave Croatto
ASSOCIATE EDITOR Jacob Lambert
ASSOCIATE ART DIRECTOR Ryan Flanders
ASSISTANT ART DIRECTOR Doug Thomson
PRODUCTION ARTIST Lana Limón

MAD THANKS

Special thanks to Al Feldstein and Nick Meglin, who originally edited many of the articles in this book, and to John Putnam and Lenny Brenner, who art directed them. Thanks to writer/editor Vic Arkoff, for her untiring work in obtaining the celebrity appreciations for this book. Thanks to Doug Gilford and Mike Slaubaugh for their always handy and accurate MAD fan sites, and to Grant Geissman for foolishly trusting us with his pristine Alfred Pop Art poster. An extra special thanks to Bill Gaines, who started it all and whose spirit lives on in the MAD offices, to all the "Usual Gang of Idiots" past and present and, of course, to Max Korn. Lastly, we would be remiss if we didn't say thanks to Time Home Entertainment's Steve Sandonato, though what exactly we're thanking him for remains unclear.

Time Home Entertainment

PUBLISHER Jim Childs
VICE PRESIDENT, BRAND & DIGITAL STRATEGY Steven Sandonato
EXECUTIVE DIRECTOR, MARKETING SERVICES Carol Pittard
EXECUTIVE DIRECTOR, RETAIL & SPECIAL SALES Tom Mifsud
EXECUTIVE PUBLISHING DIRECTOR Joy Butts
EDITORIAL DIRECTOR Stephen Koepp
DIRECTOR, BOOKAZINE DEVELOPMENT & MARKETING Laura Adam
FINANCE DIRECTOR Glenn Buonocore
ASSOCIATE PUBLISHING DIRECTOR Megan Pearlman
ASSOCIATE GENERAL COUNSEL Helen Wan
ASSISTANT DIRECTOR, SPECIAL SALES Ilene Schreider
DESIGN & PREPRESS MANAGER Anne-Michelle Gallero
BRAND MANAGER Katie McHugh Malm
ASSOCIATE PREPRESS MANAGER Alex Voznesenskiy
ASSOCIATE PRODUCTION MANAGER Kimberly Marshall

SPECIAL THANKS

Katherine Barnet, Jeremy Biloon, Susan Chodakiewicz, Rose Cirrincione, Jacqueline Fitzgerald, Christine Font, Jenna Goldberg, Hillary Hirsch, David Kahn, Mona Li, Amy Mangus, Nina Mistry, Dave Rozzelle, Ricardo Santiago, Adriana Tierno, Vanessa Wu

Published by Time Home Entertainment Inc.
135 West 50th Street • New York, NY 10020

ISBN 10: 1-61893-089-3
ISBN 13: 978-1-61893-089-7
Library of Congress Control Number: 2013936688

We welcome your comments and suggestions about Time Home Entertainment Books. Please write to us at:
Time Home Entertainment Books, Attention: Book Editors, P.O. Box 11016,
Des Moines, IA 50336-1016

If you would like to order any of our hardcover Collector's Edition books,
please call us at 1-800-327-6388, Monday through Friday, 7 a.m. to 8 p.m.,
or Saturday, 7 a.m. to 6 p.m., Central Time.

Please send any glowing comments and flattering letters to:
MAD 1700 Broadway New York, NY 10019
Please send any cheap shots, nasty complaints or thinly-veiled threats to Time Home Entertainment Books at the address above.

To subscribe to MAD, visit madmagazine.com
Download the MAD app for the iPad at the iTunes store

Table of Contents

5 Foreword by John Ficarra

6 Introduction by Judd Apatow

8 A MAD Peek Behind the Scenes at Apatow Productions

10 Bob Staake: Crime Foilers for the Average Citizen

16 Paul Coker: Horrifying Clichés

18 MAD's Career-Oriented Mother Goose

21 More Fairy Tales Scenes We'd Like to See – The Princess in the Tower

22 Essay by Roseanne Barr

24 "Grossanne"

30 Butch D'Ambrosio: Baseball at the Bat

32 Editor's Pick: Don't Be Fooled

34 Matt Lassen: The Knockout

35 Rick Tulka: Tomorrow's Parents

38 Scott Maiko: Will Success Spoil Charlie Brown?

42 Essay by Todd McFarlane

43 MAD Cover Super Special #83

44 Dave Croatto: The Shadow Knows

46 Doug Thomson: You're a Great Pageant Mom if…

48 Essay by Whoopi Goldberg

50 Angelo Torres: "Popicorn"

56 Jacob Lambert: A MAD Look at the Moment Before The Disaster

59 Kit Lively: MAD Cover #229

60 Jack Davis: "Three of My Favorite Artists"

62 Drew Friedman: Louis Farrakhan Christmas Carols

66 Essay by Dane Cook

68 A Day in the Life of Dane Cook

71 Editor's Pick: "God Save Us from the Catholic League"

72 Mort Drucker: "Put*on"

79 Hermann Mejia: MAD Marginals

80 Jeff Kruse: The Pet Peddler

82 Editor's Pick: "Canadian Club and Pink Elephants"

83 James Warhola: MAD Cover #105

84 Essay by Ken Burns

85 One Fine Day During the Civil War

86 Dick DeBartolo: Stoppa-Da-Sneezin'

88 Editor's Pick: The Museum of Monkey Art

90 Teresa Burns Parkhurst: How to Draw a Monkey

91 Mark Fredrickson: MAD Cover #501

92 Anthony Barbieri: Songs of Food

95 Desmond Devlin: An Architectural Triumph

97 Scott Nickel: MAD Cover #89

98 Frank Santopadre: Dr. Kevorkian's Children's Book Club

99 Essay by John Stamos

100 "America's Phoniest Home Videos Visits Fool House"

105 Editor's Pick: "Tom Bunk and the Mayan Calendar"

106 David Shayne: Cheap Foreign Ripoffs of American Cartoons

108 Richard Williams: MAD Cover #242

109 Charlie Kadau: Charade Magazine

113 Michael Gallagher: The History of Communication

114 Essay by Tony Hawk

115 One Afternoon While Running an Errand

116 Al Jaffee: Planned Obsolescence in Everyday Products

121 Essay by Ice-T

122 "Lewd & Disorder: It's P.U."

127 Frank Jacobs: Presenting the Bill

128 Sergio Aragonés' A MAD Historical Look at the MAD Offices: Special Deluxe Foldout Insert (Big Deal!)

129 Tom Cheney: At the Academy of Electric Fan Repair

130 MAD in Movies

132 Sergio Aragonés: A MAD Look at Other Uses for Live Lobsters

135 Darren Johnson: Rumbaflex 2000

139 Slash: "A Letter from Slash"

140 Irving Schild: MAD's Great Moments in Advertising

142 Essay by Penn Jillette

143 "Totally Recalled"

147 Barry Liebmann: MAD School Songs for Everyday Activities

150 Rick Geary: MAD #49

152 Essay by Jeff Probst

154 "Survivoyeur"

160 Mike Snider: James Bond Villains' Pet Peeves

163 Editor's Pick: Why George W. Bush is in Favor of Global Warming – A MAD Exposé

166 Tom Bunk: Spy vs. Spy Poster

168 Editor's Pick: MAD Cover #505

169 Patrick Merrell: "The Lost Marginals"

170 Lou Silverstone: "Clodumbo"

177 Christopher Baldwin: One Fine Day in the Middle Ages

178 Essay by Pendleton Ward

179 MAD's Do-It-Yourself "Adventure Time" Episode

180 Harry North: "Correspondence with Al Jaffee"

182 MAD on TV

184 Tim Carvell: The Rejection Slip

187 Jonathan Bresman: The MAD Strip Club

190 Arnie Kogen: "Henna and Her Sickos"

195 Joe Raiola: When Other Comic Strips Start Using The "Far Side" Formula

198 Essay by Harry Hamlin

200 Dennis Snee: MAD Cover #171

201 Tom Richmond: The MAD "Comic" Opera

207 Editor's Pick: The Banana Republican Catalog

211 Peter Kuper: When Johnny Comes Marching Home Again

212 Spy vs. Spy

214 Ward Sutton: "Gulf Wars, Episode II — Clone of the Attack"

215 Leonard Brenner: "Jerkules & Zima"

221 Essay by David Lynch

222 John Caldwell: The Ventriloquist Priest

224 Ryan Flanders: Kanye West's Most Moronic Tweets

226 Annie Gaines: America, the Beautiful — Revisited

229 Essay by Matthew Weiner

230 "Sad Men"

236 Essay by John Slattery

237 Stan Sinberg: Concertina Expanding Can

238 Andrew J. Schwartzberg: How to Tell You've Selected a Bad HMO

240 Nick Meglin: "Thirtysuffering"

245 Larry Siegel: Up-To-Date Safety Songs for Children

248 Essay by George Lopez

249 Spy vs. Spy

250 Scott Bricher: Season's Greetings from the NRA

252 Sam Sisco: The Jedi Bunch

253 Editor's Pick: Airport Maps Reveal What Cities are Really Famous For

256 Essay by Paul Feig

Celebrity Caricatures Artist: Rick Tulka
"Drawn Out Dramas" throughout by Sergio Aragonés

The idea for a book in which MAD contributors write about their favorite MAD articles was first suggested by longtime MAD editor Nick Meglin back in the 1980s. But for a reason that escapes me at the moment, we just never pulled that book together. Wait, now I remember why. We went to lunch instead.

Fast forward to January of this year. I was sitting in my office with MAD Art Director Sam Viviano along with Katie McHugh Malm and Megan Pearlman from Time Home Entertainment. We were brainstorming ideas for a follow-up to *Totally MAD*, our inexplicably successful book of 2012.

Sensing an opportunity to self-promote, I immediately jumped on Meglin's idea and offered it up as my own. Everyone loved it! (A first for a Meglin idea, I believe.)

By the end of day, I had sent out emails to many of MAD's contributors, something to the effect of, "Pick your all-time favorite MAD article and write a short essay about it or you'll never work for MAD again!"

It was a strong threat, I know. While most of MAD's writers and artists claim they would love nothing better than to never work for the magazine again, in reality they keep coming back issue after issue after issue. They obviously love working for low rates and abusive editors. (We don't call them "The Usual Gang of Idiots" for nothing.)

Their essays started rolling in.

But with little faith that the MAD contributors would come through with anything worthwhile, I also contacted L.A.-based writer/editor Vic Arkoff and asked for her help in getting a celebrity to write an essay for the book. I figured one well-written essay by a big-name Hollywood star would counterbalance whatever questionable junk I received from MAD's contributors. Ever the overachiever, Vic didn't get just one celebrity essay; she got 17.

Suddenly, we had a book.

Inside MAD offers a rare look into the twisted minds of the writers and artists who have produced the magazine for the past 61 years. I would like to say it's illuminating and insightful, but unfortunately I can't — I've read it.

It's now abundantly clear to me that a book featuring essays by MAD contributors was an ill-conceived project that never should have been green-lit. Did I mention it was Meglin's idea?

John Ficarra
May 2013

Introduction by

Judd Apatow

My young mind was shaped by MAD Magazine, Bill Cosby records and Steve Martin SNL appearances.

MAD Magazine has asked me to write the intro to this very prestigious anthology (how many anthologies can they make? Talk about cashing in!).

I guess I was chosen because they respect me (or because J.J. Abrams already did one). I am a longtime fan of MAD Magazine (especially in the years when they tried to make it funny). My young mind was shaped by MAD Magazine, Bill Cosby records and Steve Martin *SNL* appearances (when I didn't fall asleep before it came on). I could not have loved Don Martin more (possibly because I look like his characters, nose-wise).

In fact, when I was a kid, my friend Brande Eigen lived next door to the great MAD artist Mort Drucker (only nerds know his name — hello, nerds). One day when we were 10 or 11 years old we worked up the nerve to knock on his door and say hello. He was very nice to us. (He had to be. Who is gonna be cruel to a comedy nerd who knocks on your door?) He gave us a tour of his office and showed us the next week's MAD Magazine before its release date, which felt like a big deal (it kind of isn't).

Mort taught me that it is important to always be kind to your fans, even when they invade your privacy (don't invade my privacy or I will have one of my goons take you apart).

One of the great achievements I cherish is that my work has been so perfect that MAD Magazine has never parodied it (due to lack of interest). I guess when your films and TV series are so hilarious and insightful, there is no way to goof on them. They are too pure (or so corny one can't even write a corny spoof of them). That and the fact that *Freaks and Geeks* never jumped the shark are my career highlights (how can you jump the shark when you are canceled instantly?).

So I toast MAD for 60 brilliant years (well, maybe 18 of the 60) and here's hoping we get 60 more (or just another good 18 — leaving out the 42 hit-and-miss years). I would not be who I am today without you (a man who desperately seeks attention by shocking people with graphic representations of other people's private parts).

God bless you, MAD Magazine. (Really.)

Mr. Apatow is correct. MAD never did a spoof of any of his movies or TV shows. So he demanded we do one in this book on the next two pages. Just what we need — more work! Thanks, Judd!

A MAD Peek Behind the Scenes

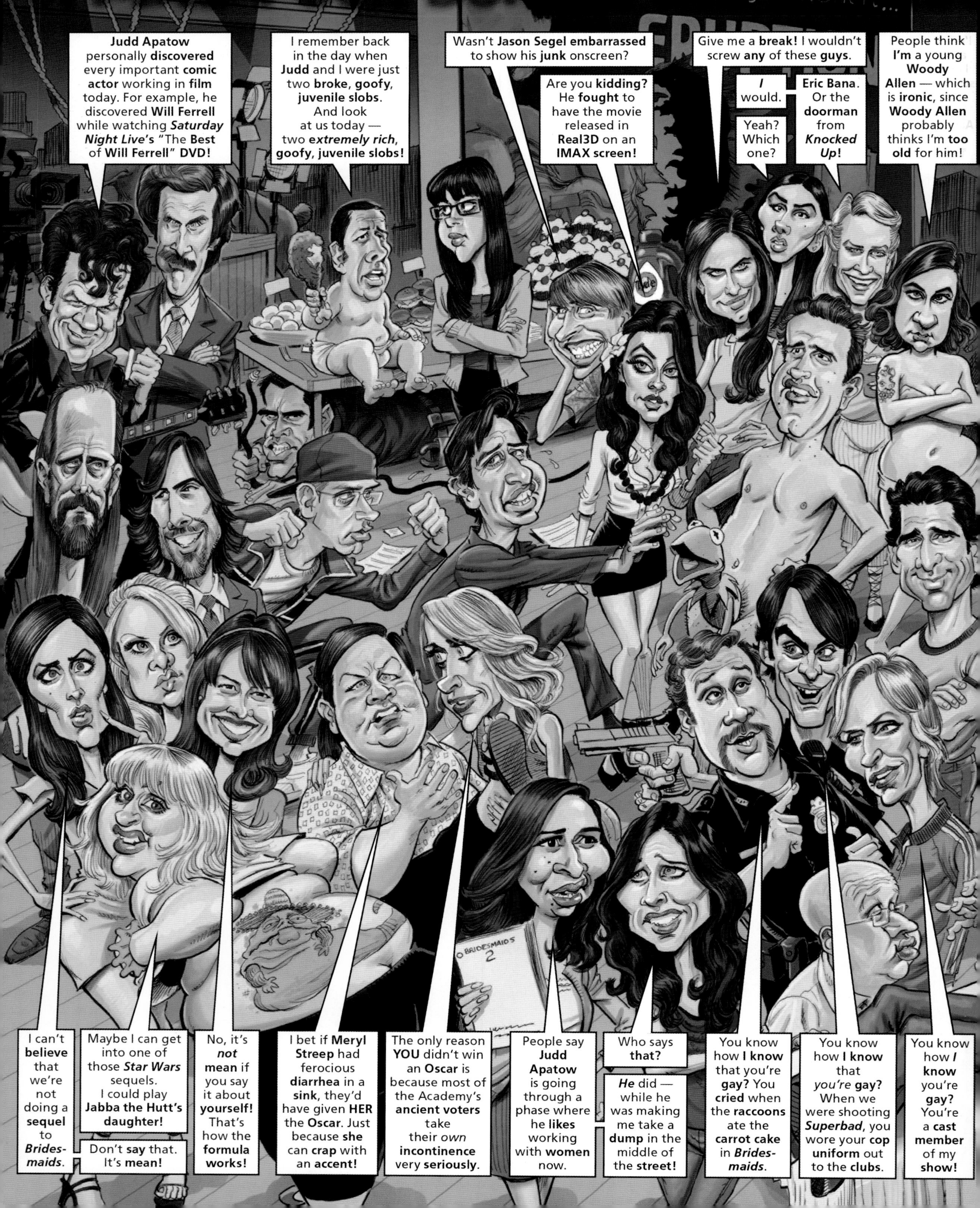
Judd Apatow personally discovered every important comic actor working in film today. For example, he discovered Will Ferrell while watching *Saturday Night Live*'s "The Best of Will Ferrell" DVD!
I remember back in the day when Judd and I were just two broke, goofy, juvenile slobs. And look at us today — two *extremely rich*, goofy, juvenile slobs!
Wasn't Jason Segel embarrassed to show his junk onscreen?
Are you kidding? He fought to have the movie released in Real3D on an IMAX screen!
Give me a break! I wouldn't screw any of these guys.
I would.
Yeah? Which one?
Eric Bana. Or the doorman from *Knocked Up*!
People think I'm a young Woody Allen — which is ironic, since Woody Allen probably thinks I'm too old for him!
I can't believe that we're not doing a sequel to *Bridesmaids*.
Maybe I can get into one of those *Star Wars* sequels. I could play Jabba the Hutt's daughter!
Don't say that. It's mean!
No, it's *not* mean if you say it about yourself! That's how the formula works!
I bet if Meryl Streep had ferocious diarrhea in a sink, they'd have given HER the Oscar. Just because she can crap with an accent!
The only reason YOU didn't win an Oscar is because most of the Academy's ancient voters take their *own* incontinence very seriously.
People say Judd Apatow is going through a phase where he likes working with women now.
Who says that?
He did — while he was making me take a dump in the middle of the street!
You know how I know that you're gay? You cried when the raccoons ate the carrot cake in *Bridesmaids*.
You know how I know that *you're* gay? When we were shooting *Superbad*, you wore your cop uniform out to the clubs.
You know how *I* know you're gay? You're a cast member of my show!
BRIDESMAIDS 2

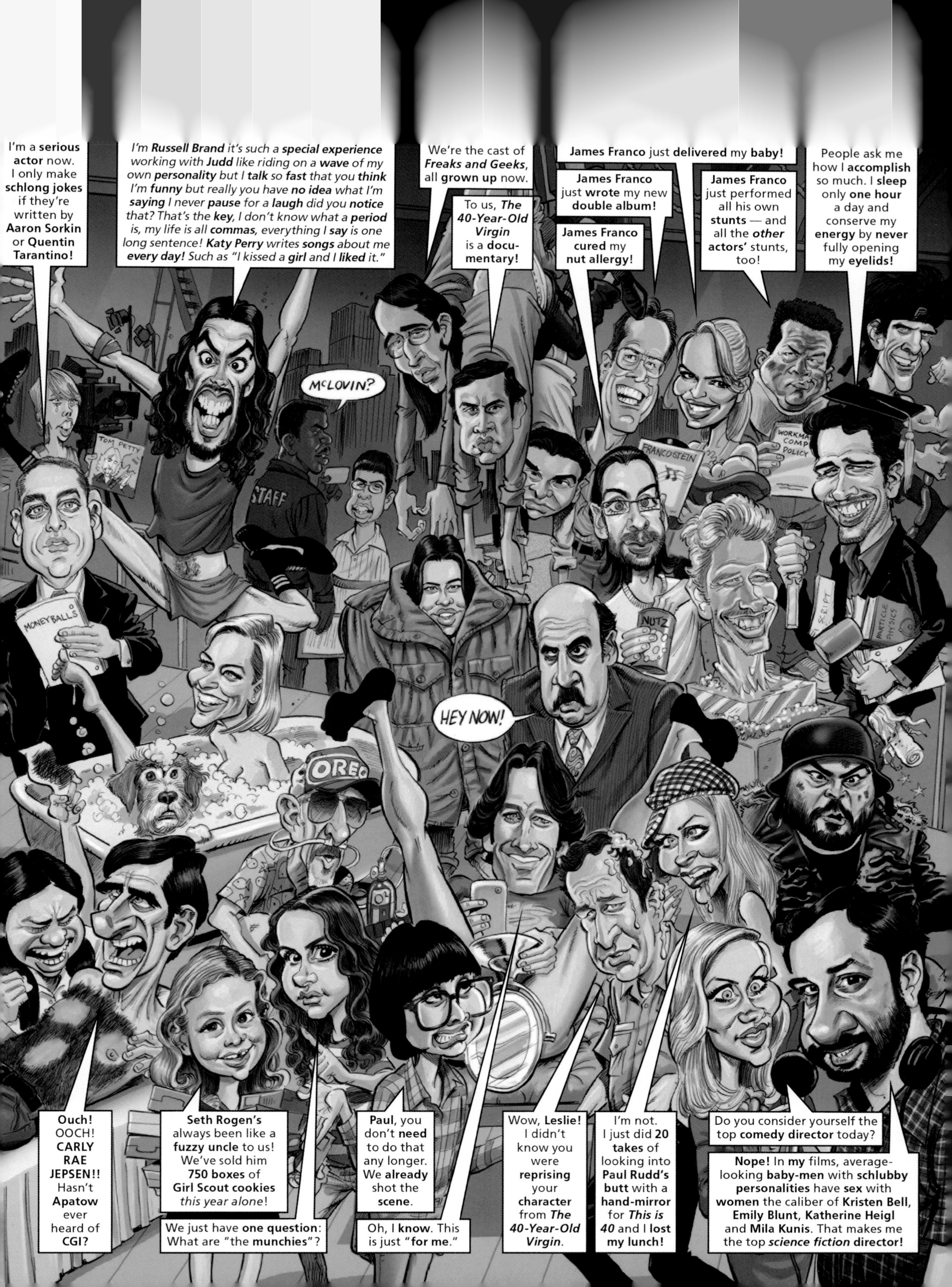

I'm a **serious actor** now. I only make **schlong jokes** if they're written by **Aaron Sorkin** or **Quentin Tarantino!**
*I'm **Russell Brand** it's such a **special experience** working with **Judd** like riding on a **wave** of my own **personality** but I **talk** so **fast** that you **think** I'm **funny** but really you have **no idea** what I'm **saying** I never **pause** for a **laugh** did you **notice** that? That's the **key**, I don't know what a **period** is, my life is all **commas**, everything I **say** is one long sentence! **Katy Perry** writes **songs** about me **every day!** Such as "I kissed a **girl** and I **liked** it."*
We're the cast of ***Freaks and Geeks***, all **grown up** now.
To us, ***The 40-Year-Old Virgin*** is a **documentary!**
James Franco just **delivered** my **baby!**
James Franco just **wrote** my new **double album!**
James Franco cured my **nut allergy!**
James Franco just performed all his own **stunts** — and all the ***other* actors'** stunts, too!
People ask me how I **accomplish** so much. I **sleep** only **one hour** a day and conserve my **energy** by **never** fully opening my **eyelids!**
McLOVIN?
TOM PETTY
STAFF
MONEYBALLS
FRANCOSTEIN
WORKMAN'S COMP POLICY
NUTZ
SCRIPT
PARTICLE PHYSICS
HEY NOW!
OREO
Ouch! OOCH! **CARLY RAE JEPSEN!!** Hasn't **Apatow** ever heard of **CGI?**
Seth Rogen's always been like a **fuzzy uncle** to us! We've sold him **750 boxes** of **Girl Scout cookies** *this year alone*!
We just have **one question**: What are "the **munchies**"?
Paul, you don't **need** to do that any longer. We **already** shot the **scene**.
Oh, I **know**. This is just "**for me**."
Wow, **Leslie!** I didn't know you were **reprising** your **character** from ***The 40-Year-Old Virgin***.
I'm not. I just did **20 takes** of looking into **Paul Rudd's butt** with a **hand-mirror** for ***This is 40*** and I **lost my lunch!**
Do you consider yourself the top **comedy director** today?
Nope! In **my** films, average-looking **baby-men** with **schlubby personalities** have **sex** with **women** the caliber of **Kristen Bell**, **Emily Blunt**, **Katherine Heigl** and **Mila Kunis**. That makes me the top ***science fiction*** **director!**

PROPS AND ROBBERS DEPT.

Street crime is rising at an alarming rate. Every day, people are mugged, robbed and beaten. The police would like to help, but Heaven knows they have their hands full with gamblers, illegal parkers and Sunday Blue Law violators. Nor can anyone expect help from his neighbor. Nobody wants to get involved. Alarms, whistles and sundry

CRIME FOILERS FOR T

MUGGINGS, HOLD-UPS, PURSE-SNATCHINGS

THE PHONY FRONT

BUS STOP
WANTED

Almost all muggers count on the element of surprise. They attack from behind to avoid tangling with anyone who can fight back. This costume prevents all that. It consists of a two-way suit and shirt. Phony shoe fronts complete the ensemble. No matter which way mugger approaches, he always thinks he's facing you, and you're watching him.

THE SPINY ATTACHE CASE

Pushbutton trigger in handle instantly releases dozens of porcupine-like telescoping barbed steel spines. Warning "attacker" that spine tips are coated with curare poison guarantees safety . . . if he hasn't run into them already.

by Bob Staake
ARTIST

I distinctly remember an afternoon in 1973 when I was feeling, you know, not so fresh.

Maybe I sucked in some particularly bad smog or ate an iffy fish taco, but whatever it was had begun roiling my stomach, and Mom said I'd feel better if I got rid of it.

I tried, but forcing myself to vomit always felt like cheating — or worse, I was afraid I'd do it all wrong and everything would come out of my nose. Mom,

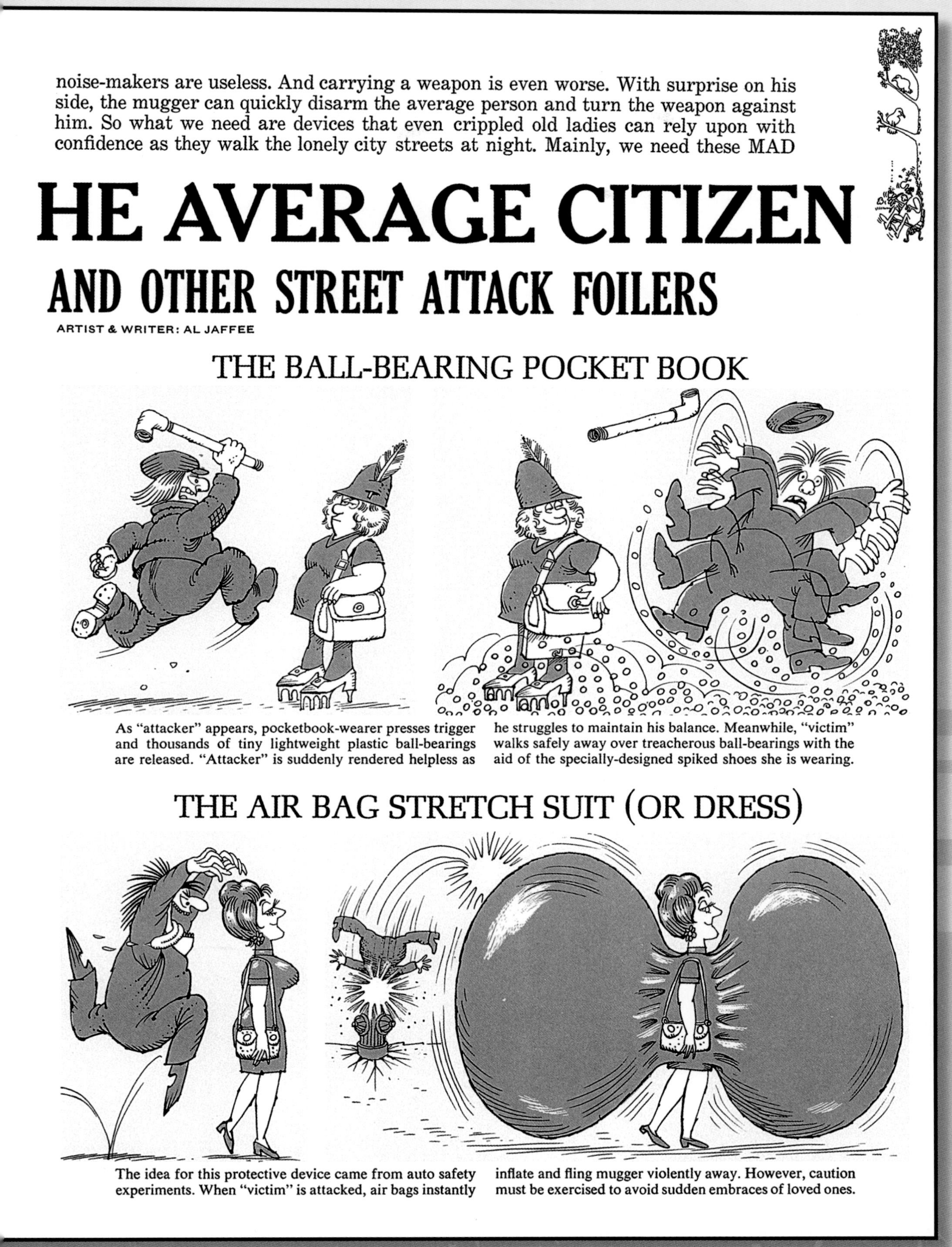

noise-makers are useless. And carrying a weapon is even worse. With surprise on his side, the mugger can quickly disarm the average person and turn the weapon against him. So what we need are devices that even crippled old ladies can rely upon with confidence as they walk the lonely city streets at night. Mainly, we need these MAD

HE AVERAGE CITIZEN

AND OTHER STREET ATTACK FOILERS

ARTIST & WRITER: AL JAFFEE

THE BALL-BEARING POCKET BOOK

As "attacker" appears, pocketbook-wearer presses trigger and thousands of tiny lightweight plastic ball-bearings are released. "Attacker" is suddenly rendered helpless as he struggles to maintain his balance. Meanwhile, "victim" walks safely away over treacherous ball-bearings with the aid of the specially-designed spiked shoes she is wearing.

THE AIR BAG STRETCH SUIT (OR DRESS)

The idea for this protective device came from auto safety experiments. When "victim" is attacked, air bags instantly inflate and fling mugger violently away. However, caution must be exercised to avoid sudden embraces of loved ones.

MAD #161/SEPTEMBER 1973

however, was insistent, so she went to Sav-on and returned with a small bottle of ipecac syrup and, much to my surprise, a copy of MAD.

She handed me the magazine and I flipped through it. I drooled over Mort Drucker's bikini-clad women, counted the holes in the soles of Jack Davis' characters' shoes, and eventually focused on a simple Al Jaffee line drawing showing a robber being triple-skewered by a spring-loaded anti-burglary device.

It wasn't an overtly gross image — in fact it showed no blood at all — yet there

THE SMOKESCREEN SUITCASE

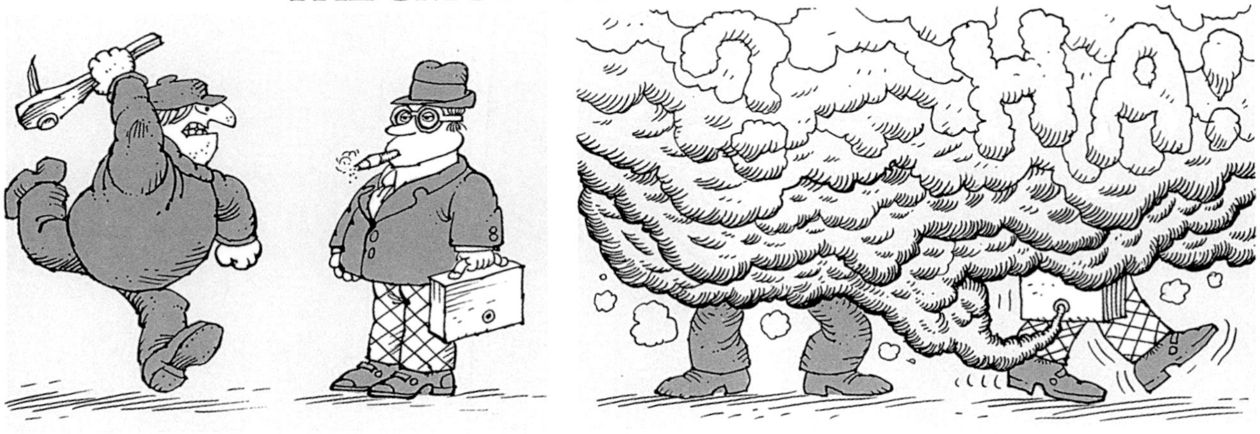

Potential "victim" presses handle and releases huge smoke cloud. Special eyeglasses permit clear vision through the chemical smoke, and "victim" can take off without fear of bumping into "attacker," or any other unpleasant object.

THE MAGNETIC VEST

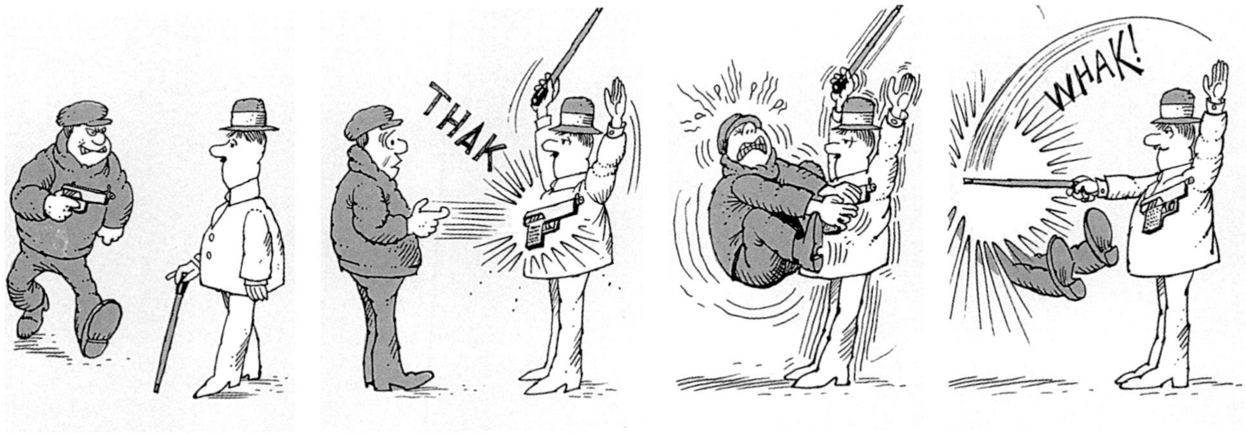
THAK
WHAK!

This garment looks like any ordinary vest but is actually lined with powerful magnets. Anyone approaching magnetic field with metal weapon (gun, knife, ice pick, etc.) is immediately rendered weaponless. However, caution must be exercised by wearer in everyday situations, such as when approaching metal object like a car, fence, lampost, etc.

THE GUSHING HANDBAG

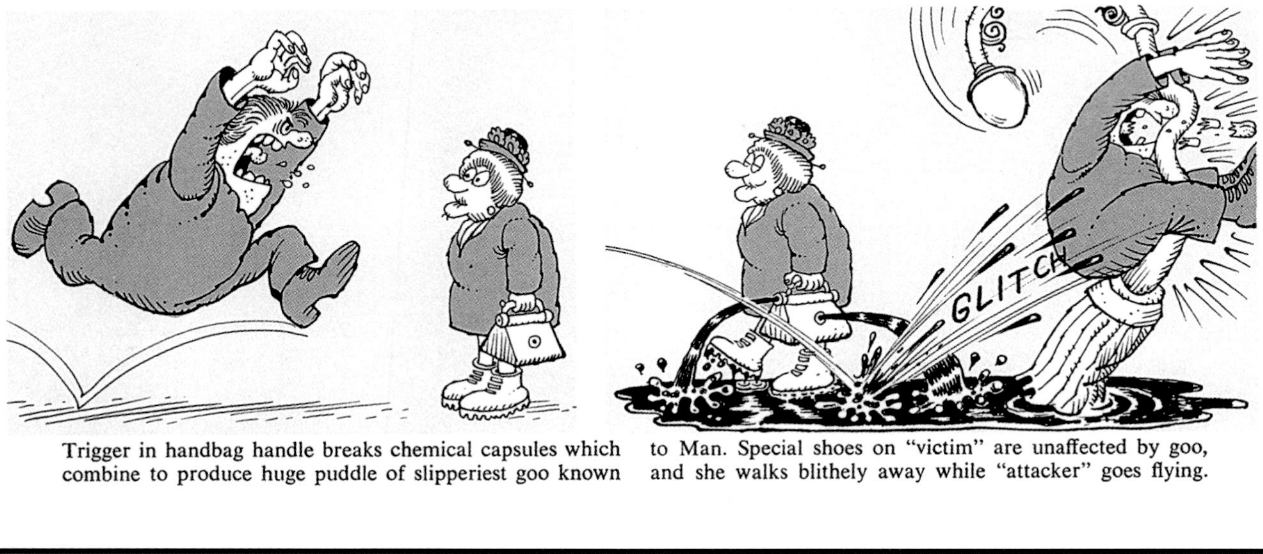
GLITCH

Trigger in handbag handle breaks chemical capsules which combine to produce huge puddle of slipperiest goo known to Man. Special shoes on "victim" are unaffected by goo, and she walks blithely away while "attacker" goes flying.

was something so oddly unsettling about it that as I stared at the drawing it initiated in me the sudden and violent elimination of whatever was in my stomach, launching it into the tin trash can emblazoned with the Los Angeles Rams logo that sat next to my bed.

Mom turned to me, a spoonful of the now unnecessary ipecac in her hand. She smiled, poured the syrup back into the little amber bottle and said, "Honey, I feel the same way about that damn magazine."

THE VISE-GRIP PURSE

C
A
B

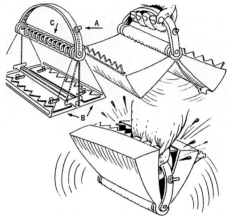

As purse-snatcher grabs purse away, handle-button (A) is released and trigger (B) unlocks two separate bag-halves. Powerful bear trap spring (C) whips bag halves around at lightning speed and bone-crushing force onto muggers hand.

THE EXPLODING HAT NET

BOOM
THWOOP
PD
NET
EXPLOSIVE
HEAD SHIELD
COLLAR TRIGGER

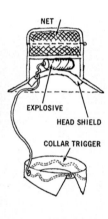

Net, woven of extremely fine but strong synthetic fibers, is carefully packed into hat. When "victim" is grabbed at throat, special collar triggers an explosive device which sends net billowing out over both "victim" and "attacker." Since they are both trapped until help comes, "attacker" will not hurt "victim" and risk more serious punishment.

THE BONE-CRUSHING KNAPSACK

Innocent-looking knapsack contains spring-mounted flatiron which is released by any violence directed at wearer from the rear. Delivers a blow equal to being hit by a 5-pound weight dropped from the top of the Empire State Building.

BURGLARIES, BREAK-INS, THEFTS, ROBBE

THE TRAP DOOR WELCOME MAT

WELCOME
WELC

Special lock on door is calibrated to accept special key. Any other device such as a jimmy, screwdriver, hairpin or foreign key sets off mechanism that opens trap door. If homeowner intends to be away for an extended period, it is advisable to leave some food and water in the trap. Otherwise, disgusting sight will greet him on his return.

THE SPRING LOADED WINDOW

When burglar lifts lower (inner) sash, it hits mechanism (A) which releases spring (B). Upper (outer) sash comes down with thrust equal to two tons of weight, trapping thief in the act. Too bad if he's a moonlighting pianist.

THE FEROCIOUS ANIMAL

ROWWRRRR
A
B
C
D
E

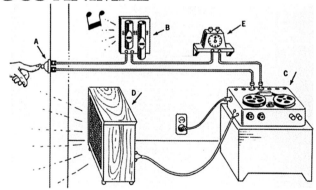

Since burglar always rings doorbell first to make sure no one is home, this simple set-up effectively discourages him. When bell-button (A) is pressed, it rings chimes (B) and starts tape (C) which emits thunderous animal roars through loudspeaker (D). Timer switch (E) stops the tape after 5 minutes. If another burglar comes, it starts all over again. Set-up can accommodate 6 or 7 burglars, which should just about cover one night's supply in most cities.

RIES AND OTHER HOUSE CRIME FOILERS

THE AUTOMATIC WINDOW BARS

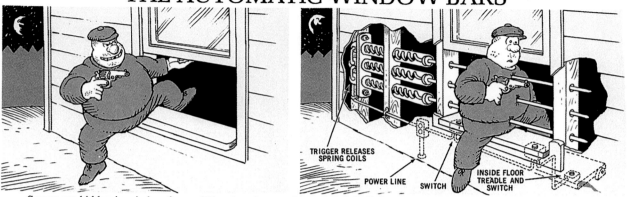

TRIGGER RELEASES SPRING COILS

POWER LINE **SWITCH** **INSIDE FLOOR TREADLE AND SWITCH**

Spears are hidden in window frame. When burglar puts his weight on window sill, switch is activated and spears are released which effectively bar entry to thief. Too bad—

heh-heh—if he's caught in the middle! Note: floor treadle safety feature (A) which cuts current to spring switch so that a person opening window from the inside is protected.

THE SLAMMING SHUTTERS

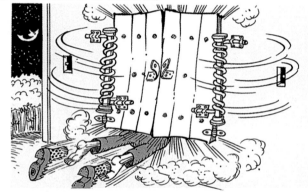

Innocent-looking shutters are hooked up so that lifting window releases spring-hinges and they crash on un-

suspecting intruder. Naturally, window panes are made of shatterproof glass to avoid cuts and bloodshed and—ecch.

THE GUILLOTINE WINDOW

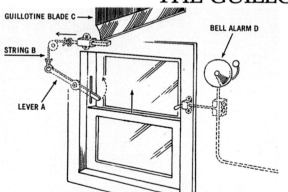

GUILLOTINE BLADE C

BELL ALARM D

STRING B

LEVER A

When intruder raises window beyond a certain point, it pushes lever (A). Lever (A), in turn, pulls string (B). String (B) releases razor sharp guillotine blade (C) which is concealed in the wall above the window. When

guillotining blade (C) drops, it presents a steel shield, blocking entry to the thief, and also setting off a bell alarm (D). And if the intruder is slow getting out of the way, it also sets off another alarm...a scream (E).

SPOOKING FROM PICTURES DEPT.

Hey, gang! It's time once again for MAD'S new game. Here's how it works: Take any familiar phrase or colloquial expression, give it an eerie setting so you come up with a new-type monster, and you're playing it. Mainly, you're

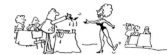

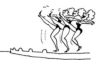

HORRIFYING CLICHÉS

ARTIST: PAUL COKER JR. WRITER: PHIL HAHN

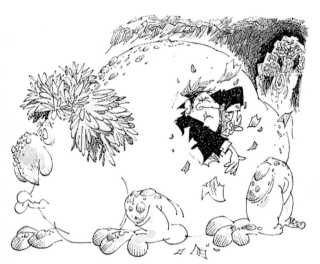

Breaking out of a SLUMP

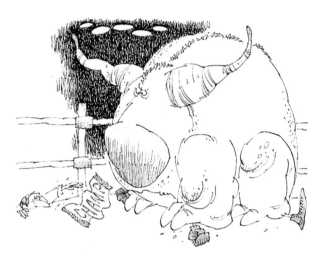

Giving in to a WHIM

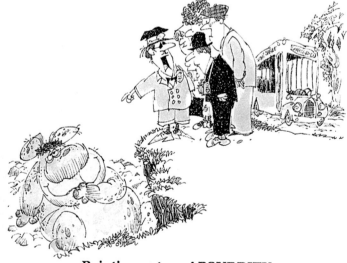

Pointing out an ABSURDITY

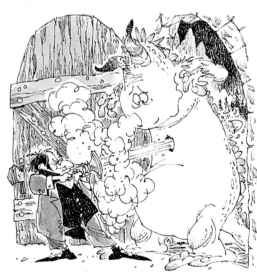

Plugging a LEAK

by Paul Coker
ARTIST

This assignment gives me a chance to express my gratitude to the writers who have kept me cartooning all these years. Without them I would, no doubt, be sitting at my drawing board just sucking air.

I especially want to thank my old friend and fellow Kansan, Phil Hahn, who many years ago wrote a funny script for MAD and encouraged me to illustrate it. My lifetime association with MAD began as a result of Phil's idea.

Laying out a PLAN

Covering up a SCANDAL

Feeding one's EGO

Couching a PHRASE

Working out your HOSTILITIES

Hitting the NAIL on the head

RE: VERSE PSYCHOLOGY DEPT.

Parents love reading "Mother Goose" to their kids. The problem is that those old Nursery Rhymes don't prepare youngsters for their future careers. Wouldn't it be great idea if career-oriented mothers and fathers we

MAD'S CAREER-ORI MOTHER GO

ARTIST: PAUL COKER, JR. WRITER: FRANK JACOBS

MARY HAD AN LTD
as told by an
AUTO MECHANIC

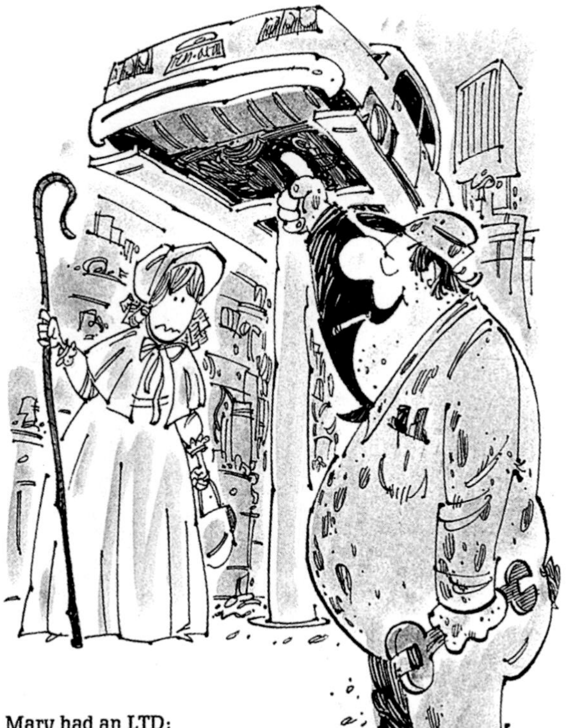

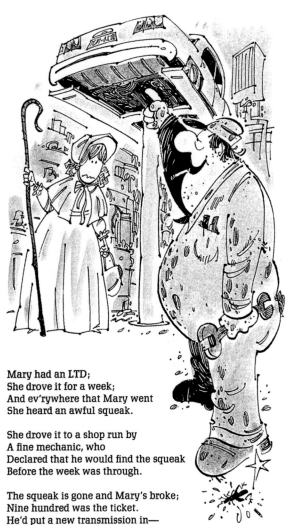

Mary had an LTD;
She drove it for a week;
And ev'rywhere that Mary went
She heard an awful squeak.

She drove it to a shop run by
A fine mechanic, who
Declared that he would find the squeak
Before the week was through.

The squeak is gone and Mary's broke;
Nine hundred was the ticket.
He'd put a new transmission in—
And taken out the cricket!

JACK AND JILL
as told by an
ECONOMIST

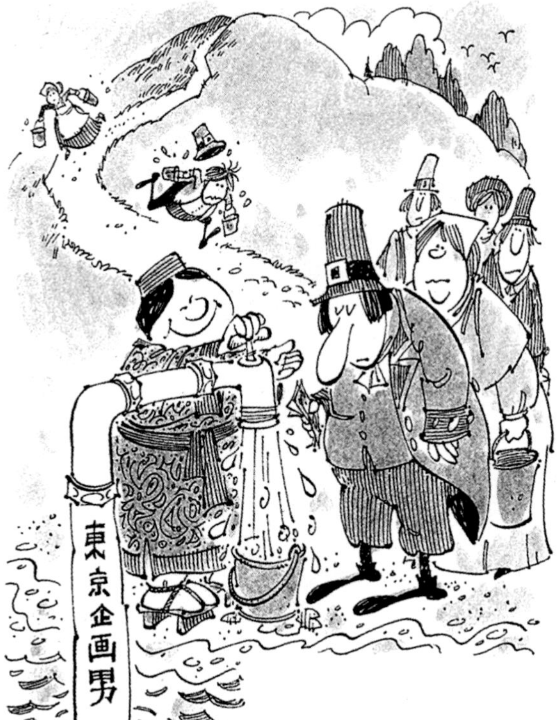
東京企画男

Jack and Jill
Climb down their hill
With water for the nation;
Already, twice,
They've raised their price
To keep up with inflation.

Jack and Jill
More buckets fill;
They work until they totter;
But though they're beat,
They can't compete
With cheap, imported water!

Frank Jacobs is another MAD writer to whom I owe many thanks. His clever, witty verses in the manner of Mother Goose, Shakespeare, Francis Scott Key, etc., are not only entertaining but also great fun to illustrate.

applied with verses dealing with their particular jobs
d professions? Then they could inspire their kids with

NTED
OSE

AS I WAS GOING TO ST. IVES
as told by a
DOCTOR

As I was going to St. Ives
I met a man who had the hives,
A woman with a fractured hip,
A dozen children with the grippe,
Two cyclists in a head-on crash,
A tourist with a dreadful rash,
Six barefoot girls with broken toes,
A shepherd with a twisted nose;

How many people did I tell to call my nurse
for an appointment during office hours after
I returned from playing golf at St. Ives?

LITTLE MISS MUFFET
as told by a
GOSSIP COLUMNIST

Little Miss Muffet
    Is sharing her tuffet
With Bo-Peep and Solomon Grundy;
    They say Georgie Porgie
    Was seen at an orgy
With Old Mother Hubbard last Sunday.

    Seems Little Boy Blue
    Gets it on in the shoe
"Cause he's heard the Old Woman is kinky;
    And as for Jack Sprat,
    Well, his wife left him flat
And is living with Wee Willie Winkie.

TOM, TOM, THE PIPER'S SON
as told by a
PSYCHIATRIST

Tom, Tom, the piper's son,
Stole a pig and away he run;
His parents sent him here to me
To get intensive ther-a-py.

Tom, Tom, it's very clear,
Shows great progress in just a year;
I'm pleased to say that now he feels
Much more at peace each time he steals!

MAD #225/SEPTEMBER 1981

HUMPTY DUMPTY

as told by a
LAWYER

Humpty Dumpty sat on a wall;
Humpty Dumpty had a great fall;
"The bricks of the wall," said his lawyer,
  "were loose;"
"We've got a good case, so we'll sue
  Mother Goose!"

Humpty's lawyer got a big trial;
Humpty's lawyer won it with style,
Took Mother Goose for a million, did he,
Of which he got half, which is not a bad fee!

LITTLE BOY BLUE

as told by a
BOOKIE

Little Boy Blue,
Come bet the Rams;
They're playing the Cowboys,
Put down 50 clams!

Little Boy Blue,
The Chiefs will win;
They'll murder Miami,
So send it all in!

Little Boy Blue,
The Bears are hot;
They'll ruin the Raiders;
It's sure worth a shot!

Little Boy Blue,
You lost your bets;
Do you want the spread
Monday night on the Jets?

TWEEDLE-DUM AND TWEEDLE-DEE

as told by a
FASHION DESIGNER

Tweedle-Dum and Tweedle-Dee
  Created women's clothes;
And ev'ry fashion they designed
  The women always chose.

They introduced a seaweed belt,
  A skirt of styrofoam;
They fashioned fancy dresses made
  Of hamster fur and chrome.

They came out with a burlap blouse,
  A yak coat long and shaggy,
A pair of slacks made out of straw,
  A gown shaped like a Baggie.

"It's plain to see," said Tweedle-Dum,
  "We've got the magic touch!"
"It's also clear," said Tweedle-Dee,
  "We don't like women much!"

TAFFY WAS A HITMAN

as told by a
MAFIA DON

Taffy was a hitman;
Taffy made good bread;
Taffy pulled a double-cross
And killed his Capo dead.

Taffy had an alibi,
But his mob could tell
Taffy's tale was full of holes;
Now Taffy is, as well!

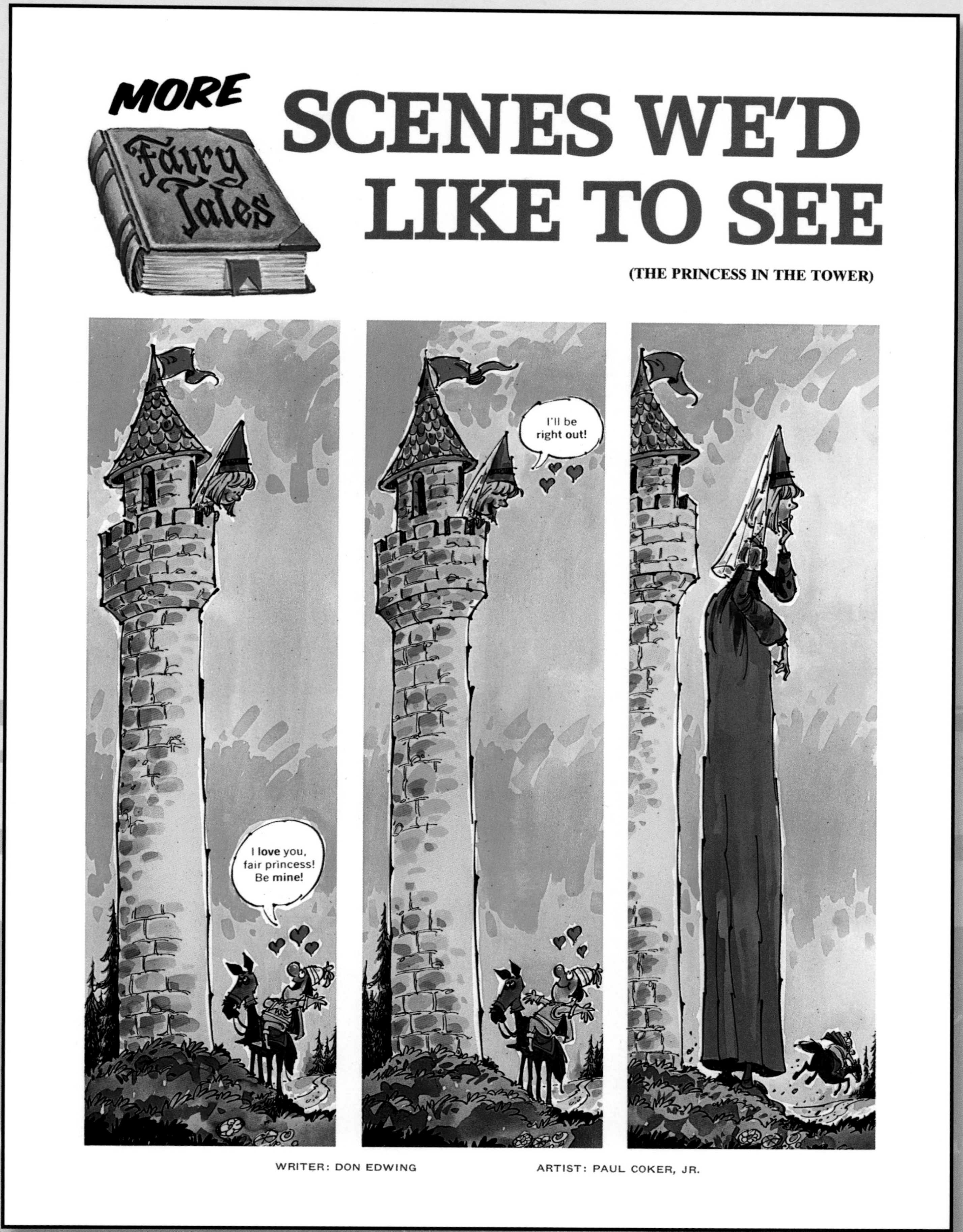
MORE
Fairy Tales
SCENES WE'D LIKE TO SEE
(THE PRINCESS IN THE TOWER)
I love you, fair princess! Be mine!
I'll be right out!
WRITER: DON EDWING
ARTIST: PAUL COKER, JR.

MAD #183/JUNE 1976

The third person I want to acknowledge is Don "Duck" Edwing. He's a MAD writer and artist whose wildly imaginative and zany ideas I have enjoyed illustrating for many years and, I hope, many more to come.

Too often, the idea person does not get the recognition he or she deserves, simply because the drawing is so much more showy and obvious. I hope this brief acknowledgement will help remedy the long-overdue credit the writers deserve.

My dad and I used to walk down to the Rexall Drug store on the corner by our house in SLC, Utah for fun. We would first buy an ice cream cone and then browse the magazine racks while eating, spilling ice cream all over the pages, leaving fingerprints on the covers, without a second thought, until one particular week when we came in, and there was a new sign: "NO BROWSING." My dad complained to the clerk, who told us that people were no longer allowed to eat in their store, either. My dad got angry, and told me that we would never come back there again, as the owners were Anti-Semites (he also told me that Santa was an Anti-Semite too, and that's why he never came to our house on Christmas). I remember that he then walked over and tore the subscription card out of a copy of MAD, without buying the magazine, because he was very cheap. But, he told me we were going to "subscribe" to it instead and that it would come to our home in the mail. It came to our mailbox sometime later, and my dad was quite proud of himself, as it was the first and only magazine he ever received in the mail.

Roseanne Barr

MAD Magazine was the first and only magazine my dad ever received in the mail.

My dad explained the "satire" of MAD Magazine to me by proudly stating that it was the handiwork of Jews from New York, whose job it was to make fun of the ridiculous things in the world! I remember asking where New York was located, and if it was in the USA. He assured me that it was not foreign at all, and that Madison Avenue itself was a large hangout of the Jewish people. I was astounded, as I recall, used to being the only Jewish student from the only Jewish family for miles and miles.

Man, the idea that Jews could be something besides the occasional comedian on TV, helpless victims, or just generally neurotic outcasts who avoided pork and athletics, planted a large seed in my brain. Making fun of everything seemed like the type of career I wanted; I just HAD to get to New York, somehow, someday!

Well, I didn't get there till I was famous, and while New York was pretty exciting, I don't know if any of the perks that come with fame and fortune could rank up there with finally being the target of the genius MADmen who inflicted their maniacal magic on me and my TV show. I mean, working with brilliant actors and writers, ruling the airwaves on Wednesday nights, season after season, was a dream come true for that little working-class girl from Utah, but being thoroughly roasted by the wiseguys at MAD was something above and beyond.

"Grossanne" was hilarious, in the tradition of the best of the MAD hatchet jobs on big TV shows, movies and anything else that needed a good poke in the ribs and the naked emperor treatment. I bought my dad dozens of copies and had it framed, too. My dad was very proud, though upset at what he called the "Anti-Semitic fat jokes" at my expense. I still have that issue on a wall in my house and it brings a grin every time I walk by.

Well, MAD and I have turned 60 at about the same time and it's my sincere wish that we continue to roll along, both MADLY in love with our mission to mock and scorn everything and everybody who needs it. Happy 60th Birthday, MAD, from one of your biggest fans ever!

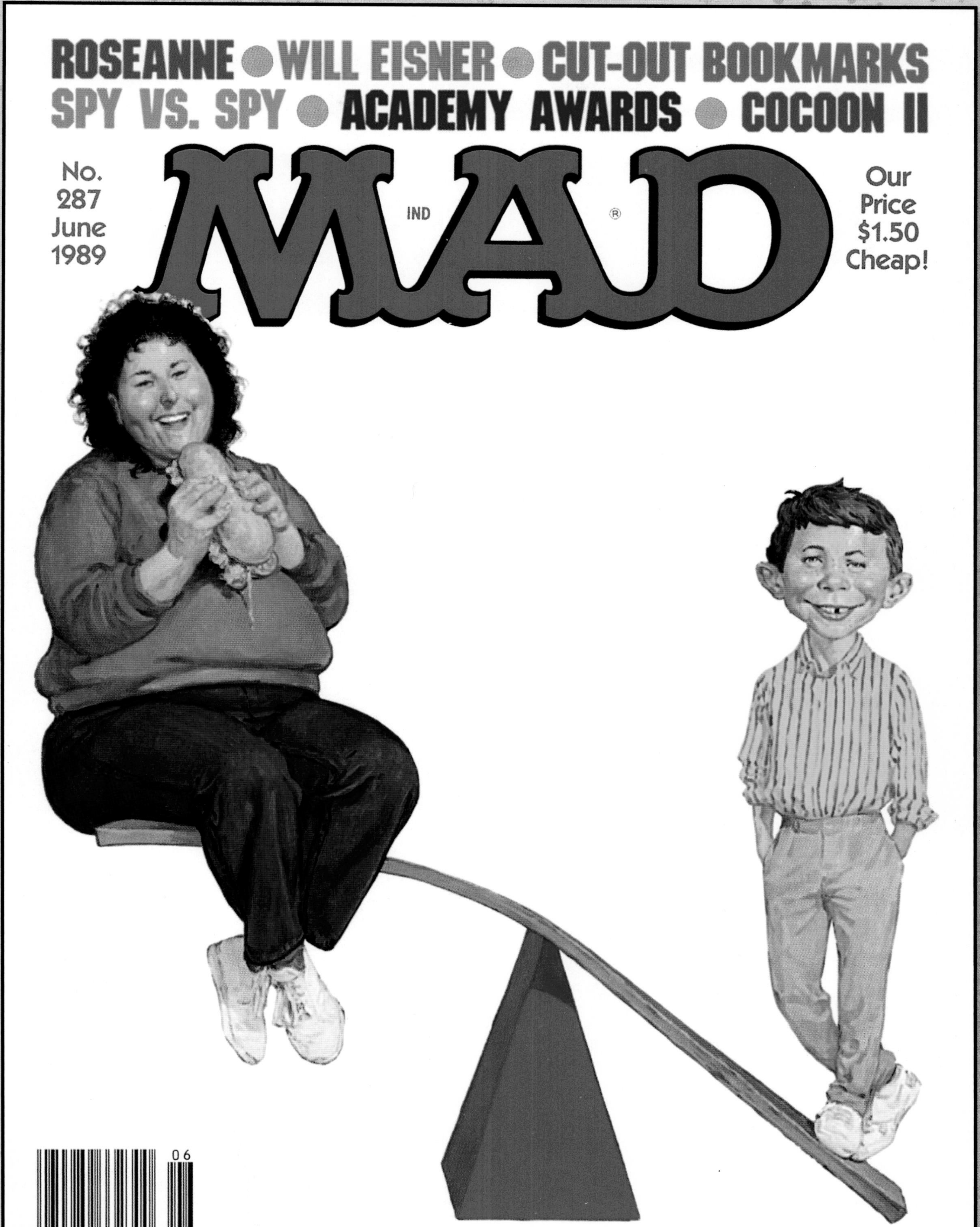
ROSEANNE • WILL EISNER • CUT-OUT BOOKMARKS
SPY VS. SPY • ACADEMY AWARDS • COCOON II
No. 287 June 1989
MAD
Our Price $1.50 Cheap!

ARTIST: RICHARD WILLIAMS

MAD #287/JUNE 1989

THE FATS OF LIFE DEPT.

So, you couldn't wait for the Writer's Strike to be over so you could see the new season's television shows. Well now, don't you feel like the prize idiot, expecting the new programs to be worth waiting for? However...among the bombs scattered around your TV dial, one show seems to stand out as a heavyweight hit. It's about a sarcastic woman who keeps zinging her family with one-liners and... aw, hell, you've waited long enough as it is! Here she is now...

GRO

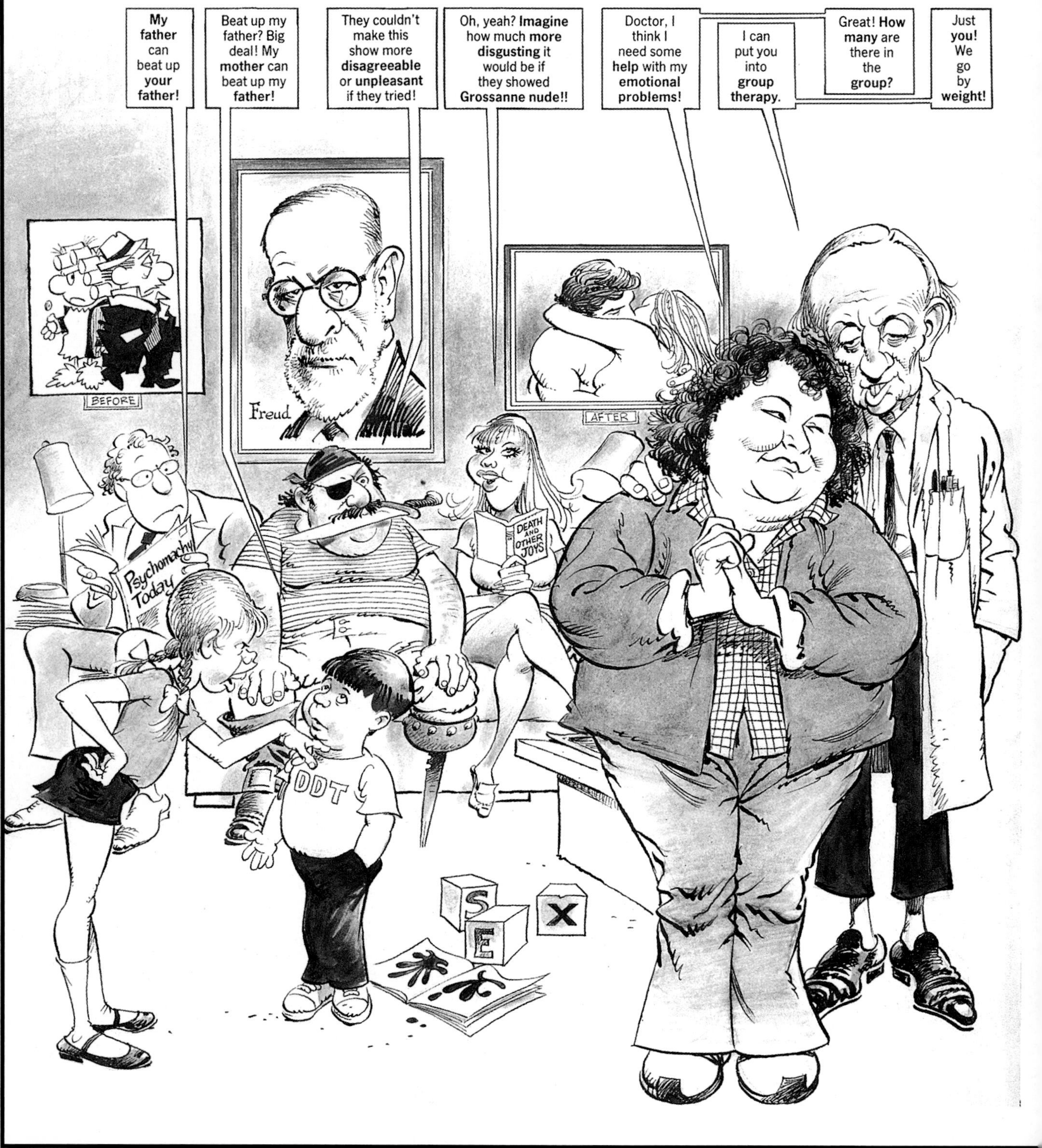
My father can beat up your father!
Beat up my father? Big deal! My mother can beat up my father!
They couldn't make this show more disagreeable or unpleasant if they tried!
Oh, yeah? Imagine how much more disgusting it would be if they showed Grossanne nude!!
Doctor, I think I need some help with my emotional problems!
I can put you into group therapy.
Great! How many are there in the group?
Just you! We go by weight!
BEFORE
Freud
AFTER
Psychomachy Today
DEATH AND OTHER JOYS
DDT
S
E
X

SSANNE

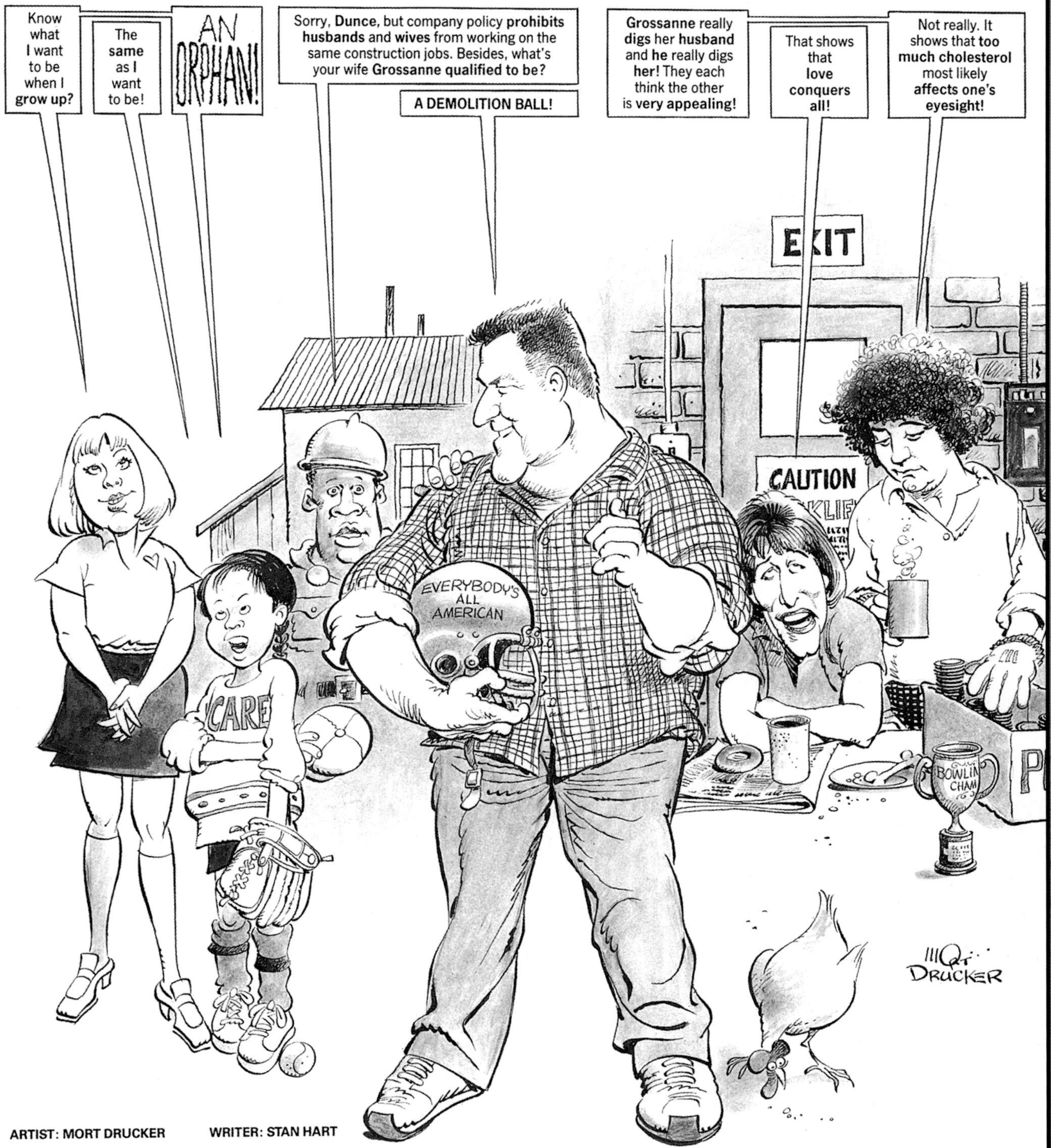

Know what I want to be when I grow up?
The same as I want to be!
AN ORPHAN!
Sorry, Dunce, but company policy prohibits husbands and wives from working on the same construction jobs. Besides, what's your wife Grossanne qualified to be?
A DEMOLITION BALL!
Grossanne really digs her husband and he really digs her! They each think the other is very appealing!
That shows that love conquers all!
Not really. It shows that too much cholesterol most likely affects one's eyesight!
EXIT
CAUTION
EVERYBODY'S ALL AMERICAN
CARE
BOWLIN CHAM
DRUCKER

ARTIST: MORT DRUCKER WRITER: STAN HART

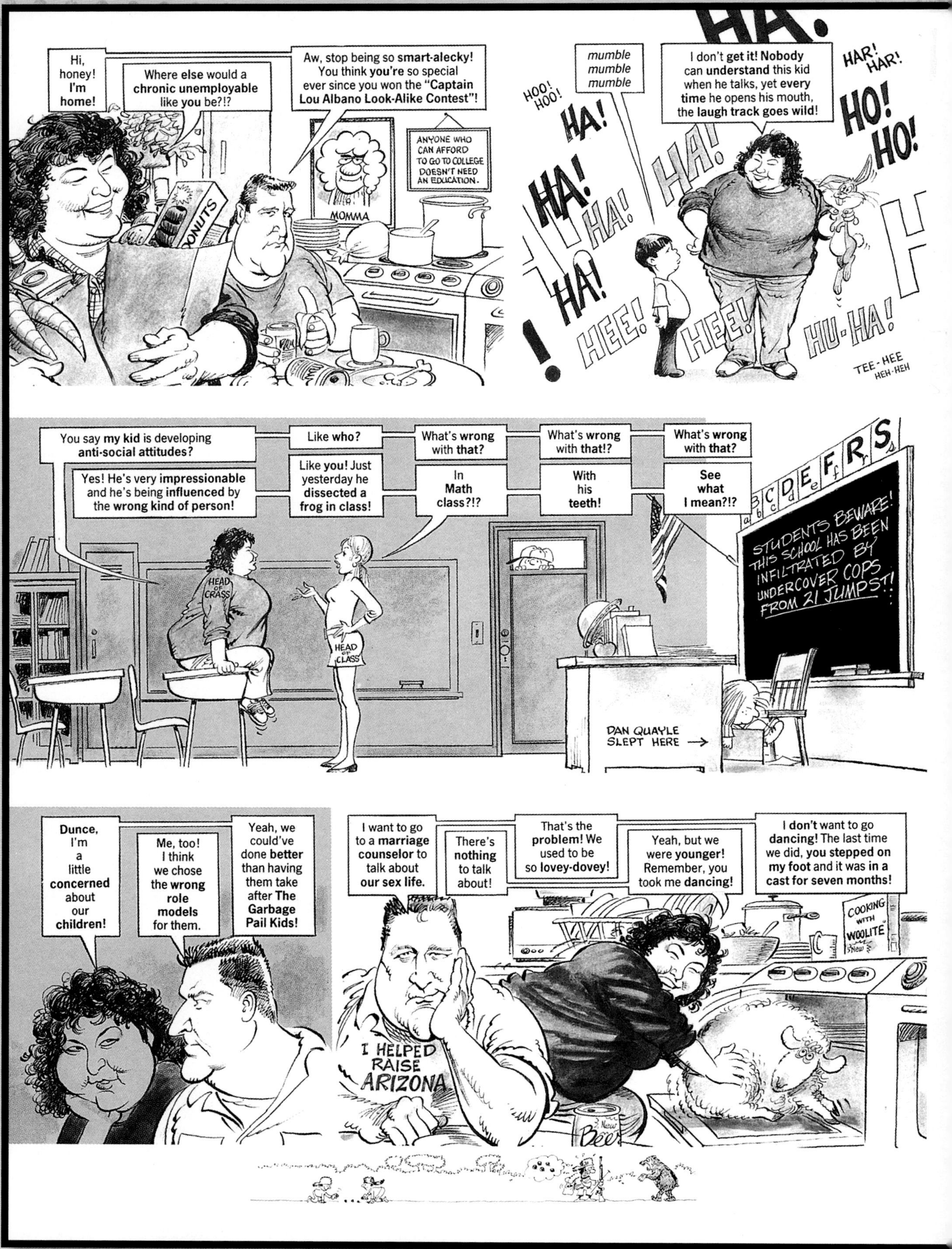
Hi, honey! I'm home!
Where else would a chronic unemployable like you be?!?
Aw, stop being so smart-alecky! You think you're so special ever since you won the "Captain Lou Albano Look-Alike Contest"!
MOMMA
ANYONE WHO CAN AFFORD TO GO TO COLLEGE DOESN'T NEED AN EDUCATION.
ONUTS
mumble mumble mumble
I don't get it! Nobody can understand this kid when he talks, yet every time he opens his mouth, the laugh track goes wild!
HA!
HOO! HOO!
HA!
HAR! HAR!
HO! HO!
HA!
HA!
HA!
HA!
HEE!
HEE!
HU-HA!
TEE-HEE HEH-HEH
You say my kid is developing anti-social attitudes?
Yes! He's very impressionable and he's being influenced by the wrong kind of person!
Like who?
Like you! Just yesterday he dissected a frog in class!
What's wrong with that?
In Math class?!?
What's wrong with that!?
With his teeth!
What's wrong with that?
See what I mean?!?
HEAD OF CRASS
HEAD OF CLASS
STUDENTS BEWARE! THIS SCHOOL HAS BEEN INFILTRATED BY UNDERCOVER COPS FROM 21 JUMPST!
DAN QUAYLE SLEPT HERE →
Dunce, I'm a little concerned about our children!
Me, too! I think we chose the wrong role models for them.
Yeah, we could've done better than having them take after The Garbage Pail Kids!
I want to go to a marriage counselor to talk about our sex life.
There's nothing to talk about!
That's the problem! We used to be so lovey-dovey!
Yeah, but we were younger! Remember, you took me dancing!
I don't want to go dancing! The last time we did, you stepped on my foot and it was in a cast for seven months!
COOKING WITH WOOLITE
I HELPED RAISE ARIZONA
Beer

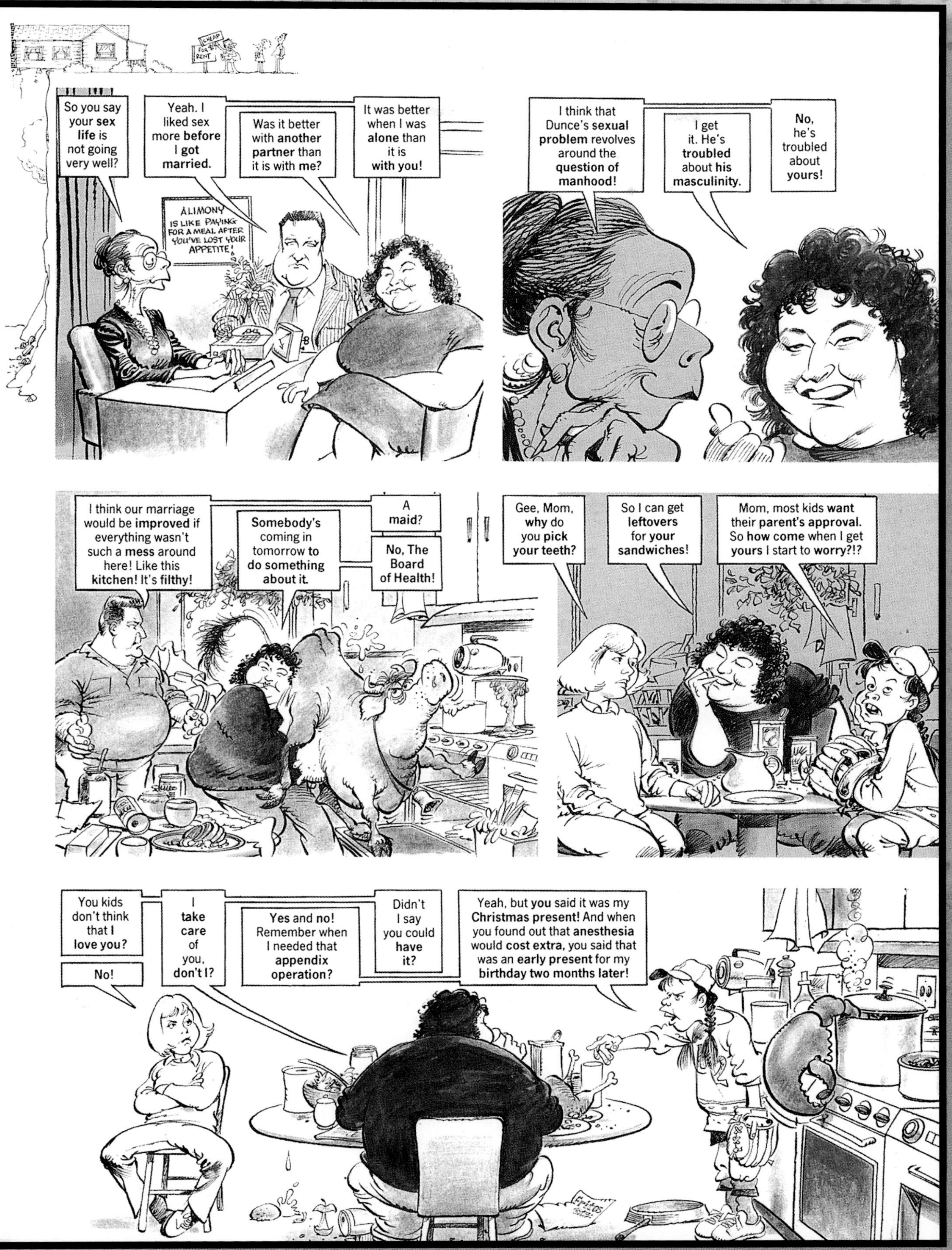
So you say your **sex life** is not going very well?
Yeah. I liked sex more **before** I **got married.**
Was it better with **another partner** than it is with **me?**
It was better when I was **alone** than it is **with you!**
ALIMONY IS LIKE PAYING FOR A MEAL AFTER YOU'VE LOST YOUR APPETITE!
I think that Dunce's **sexual problem** revolves around the **question of manhood!**
I get it. He's **troubled** about **his masculinity.**
No, he's troubled about **yours!**
I think our marriage would be **improved** if everything wasn't such a **mess** around here! Like this **kitchen!** It's **filthy!**
Somebody's coming in tomorrow **to do something about it.**
A **maid?**
No, The Board of Health!
Gee, Mom, **why** do you **pick your teeth?**
So I can get **leftovers** for **your sandwiches!**
Mom, most kids **want** their **parent's approval.** So **how come** when I get **yours** I start to **worry?!?**
You kids don't think that **I love you?**
No!
I **take care** of you, **don't I?**
Yes and **no!** Remember when I needed that **appendix operation?**
Didn't I say you could **have it?**
Yeah, but **you** said it was my **Christmas present!** And when you found out that **anesthesia** would **cost extra,** you said that was an **early present** for my **birthday two months later!**

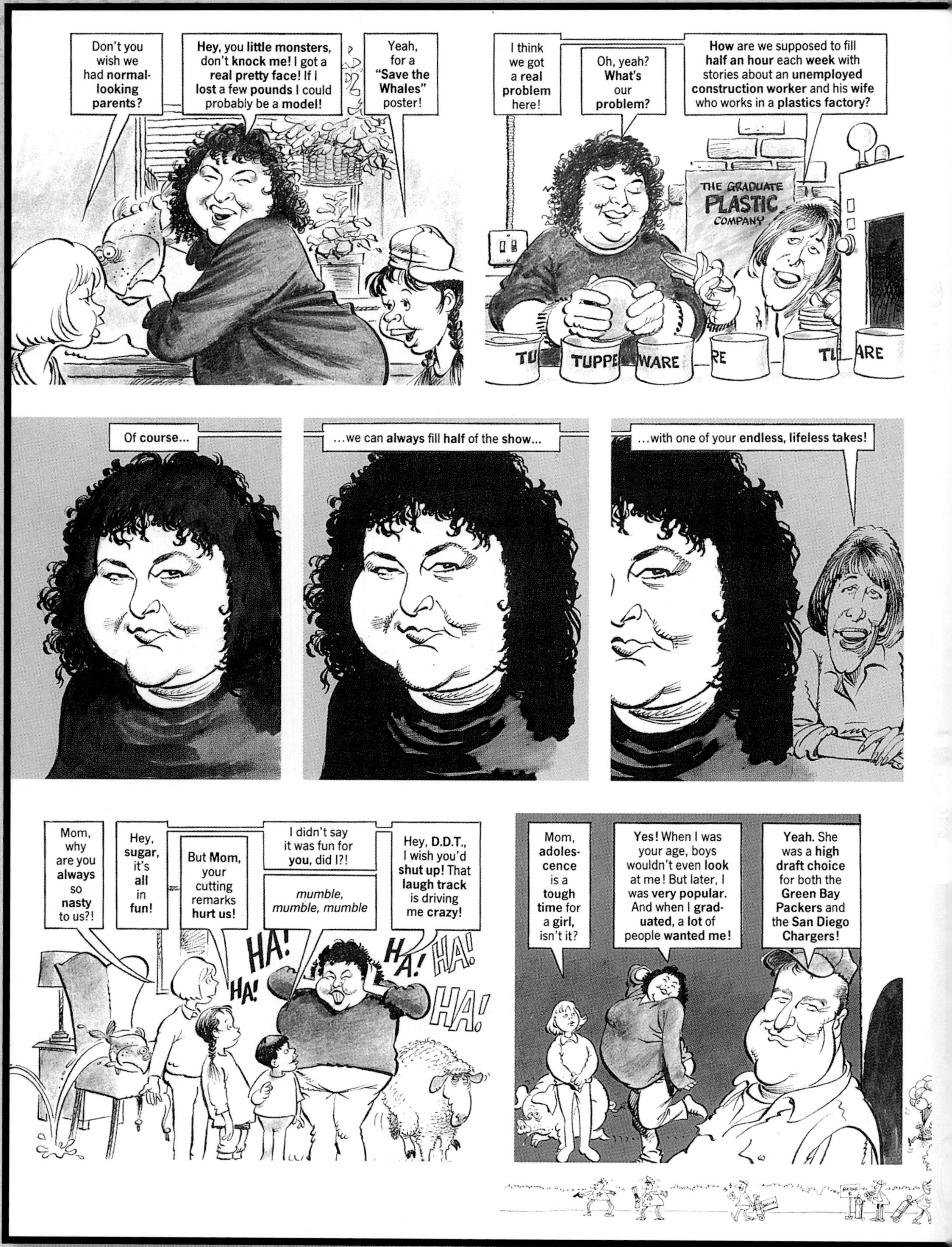
Don't you wish we had normal-looking parents?
Hey, you little monsters, don't knock me! I got a real pretty face! If I lost a few pounds I could probably be a model!
Yeah, for a "Save the Whales" poster!
I think we got a real problem here!
Oh, yeah? What's our problem?
How are we supposed to fill half an hour each week with stories about an unemployed construction worker and his wife who works in a plastics factory?
THE GRADUATE PLASTIC COMPANY
TUPPE WARE
Of course...
...we can always fill half of the show...
...with one of your endless, lifeless takes!
Mom, why are you always so nasty to us?!
Hey, sugar, it's all in fun!
But Mom, your cutting remarks hurt us!
I didn't say it was fun for you, did I?!
mumble, mumble, mumble
Hey, D.D.T., I wish you'd shut up! That laugh track is driving me crazy!
HA! HA! HA! HA! HA!
Mom, adolescence is a tough time for a girl, isn't it?
Yes! When I was your age, boys wouldn't even look at me! But later, I was very popular. And when I graduated, a lot of people wanted me!
Yeah. She was a high draft choice for both the Green Bay Packers and the San Diego Chargers!

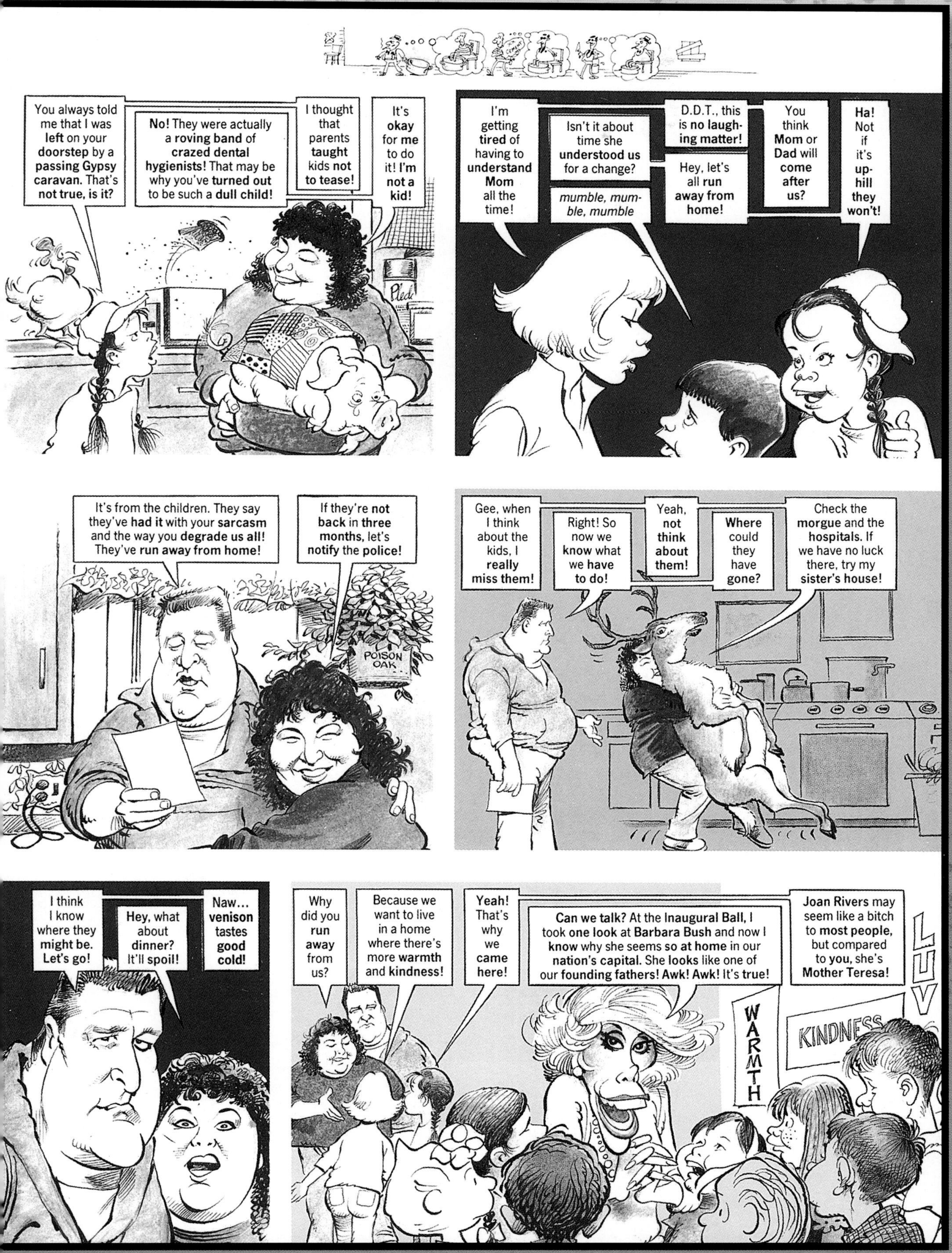

You always told me that I was left on your doorstep by a passing Gypsy caravan. That's not true, is it?
No! They were actually a roving band of crazed dental hygienists! That may be why you've turned out to be such a dull child!
I thought that parents taught kids not to tease!
It's okay for me to do it! I'm not a kid!
I'm getting tired of having to understand Mom all the time!
Isn't it about time she understood us for a change?
mumble, mumble, mumble
D.D.T., this is no laughing matter!
Hey, let's all run away from home!
You think Mom or Dad will come after us?
Ha! Not if it's uphill they won't!
It's from the children. They say they've had it with your sarcasm and the way you degrade us all! They've run away from home!
If they're not back in three months, let's notify the police!
POISON OAK
Gee, when I think about the kids, I really miss them!
Right! So now we know what we have to do!
Yeah, not think about them!
Where could they have gone?
Check the morgue and the hospitals. If we have no luck there, try my sister's house!
I think I know where they might be. Let's go!
Hey, what about dinner? It'll spoil!
Naw... venison tastes good cold!
Why did you run away from us?
Because we want to live in a home where there's more warmth and kindness!
Yeah! That's why we came here!
Can we talk? At the Inaugural Ball, I took one look at Barbara Bush and now I know why she seems so at home in our nation's capital. She looks like one of our founding fathers! Awk! Awk! It's true!
Joan Rivers may seem like a bitch to most people, but compared to you, she's Mother Teresa!
WARMTH
KINDNESS
LUV

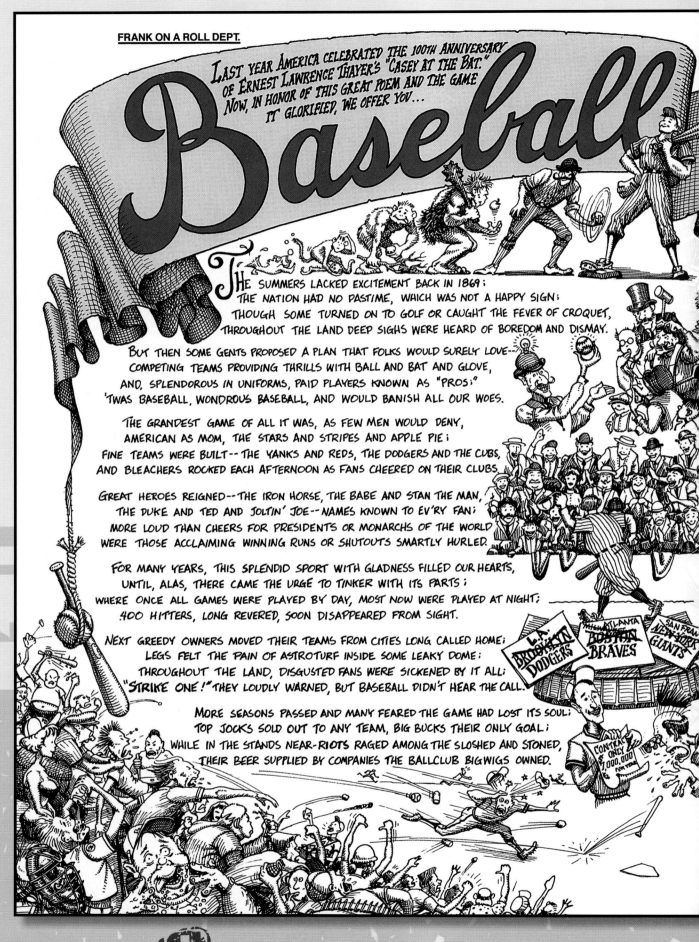

LAST YEAR AMERICA CELEBRATED THE 100th ANNIVERSARY OF ERNEST LAWRENCE THAYER'S "CASEY AT THE BAT." NOW, IN HONOR OF THIS GREAT POEM AND THE GAME IT GLORIFIED, WE OFFER YOU...

Baseball

THE SUMMERS LACKED EXCITEMENT BACK IN 1869;
THE NATION HAD NO PASTIME, WHICH WAS NOT A HAPPY SIGN;
THOUGH SOME TURNED ON TO GOLF OR CAUGHT THE FEVER OF CROQUET,
THROUGHOUT THE LAND DEEP SIGHS WERE HEARD OF BOREDOM AND DISMAY.

BUT THEN SOME GENTS PROPOSED A PLAN THAT FOLKS WOULD SURELY LOVE--
COMPETING TEAMS PROVIDING THRILLS WITH BALL AND BAT AND GLOVE,
AND, SPLENDOROUS IN UNIFORMS, PAID PLAYERS KNOWN AS "PROS;"
'TWAS BASEBALL, WONDROUS BASEBALL, AND WOULD BANISH ALL OUR WOES.

THE GRANDEST GAME OF ALL IT WAS, AS FEW MEN WOULD DENY,
AMERICAN AS MOM, THE STARS AND STRIPES AND APPLE PIE;
FINE TEAMS WERE BUILT-- THE YANKS AND REDS, THE DODGERS AND THE CUBS,
AND BLEACHERS ROCKED EACH AFTERNOON AS FANS CHEERED ON THEIR CLUBS.

GREAT HEROES REIGNED--THE IRON HORSE, THE BABE AND STAN THE MAN,
THE DUKE AND TED AND JOLTIN' JOE--NAMES KNOWN TO EV'RY FAN;
MORE LOUD THAN CHEERS FOR PRESIDENTS OR MONARCHS OF THE WORLD
WERE THOSE ACCLAIMING WINNING RUNS OR SHUTOUTS SMARTLY HURLED.

FOR MANY YEARS, THIS SPLENDID SPORT WITH GLADNESS FILLED OUR HEARTS,
UNTIL, ALAS, THERE CAME THE URGE TO TINKER WITH ITS PARTS;
WHERE ONCE ALL GAMES WERE PLAYED BY DAY, MOST NOW WERE PLAYED AT NIGHT;
.400 HITTERS, LONG REVERED, SOON DISAPPEARED FROM SIGHT.

NEXT GREEDY OWNERS MOVED THEIR TEAMS FROM CITIES LONG CALLED HOME;
LEGS FELT THE PAIN OF ASTROTURF INSIDE SOME LEAKY DOME;
THROUGHOUT THE LAND, DISGUSTED FANS WERE SICKENED BY IT ALL;
"STRIKE ONE!" THEY LOUDLY WARNED, BUT BASEBALL DIDN'T HEAR THE CALL.

MORE SEASONS PASSED AND MANY FEARED THE GAME HAD LOST ITS SOUL;
TOP JOCKS SOLD OUT TO ANY TEAM, BIG BUCKS THEIR ONLY GOAL;
WHILE IN THE STANDS NEAR-RIOTS RAGED AMONG THE SLOSHED AND STONED,
THEIR BEER SUPPLIED BY COMPANIES THE BALLCLUB BIGWIGS OWNED.

L.A. BROOKLYN DODGERS · MILW. ATLANTA BOSTON BRAVES · SAN FRAN. NEW YORK GIANTS

CONTRACT ONLY 7,000,000 PER YEAR

by Butch D'Ambrosio
WRITER

Long before I ever knew what makes a great poem great, I knew that Frank Jacobs was a great poet. I've always been partial to MAD's "Casey At The Bat" parodies and, of the seven (!) the Internet tells me he wrote, this is one of the best. READ IT OUT LOUD! Seriously, I just did again. Rhythm? Rhyme? Meter? It's a master class in poetry. When I sent my first submission to MAD — a 12-year-old boy's parody of "Casey At The Bat" — I didn't know anything about scansion…prosody…stanzas…syllables…speling. I still don't, but Jacobs does. This thing sings — and it's funny. Alliteration, wordplay, unexpected rhymes: on the micro

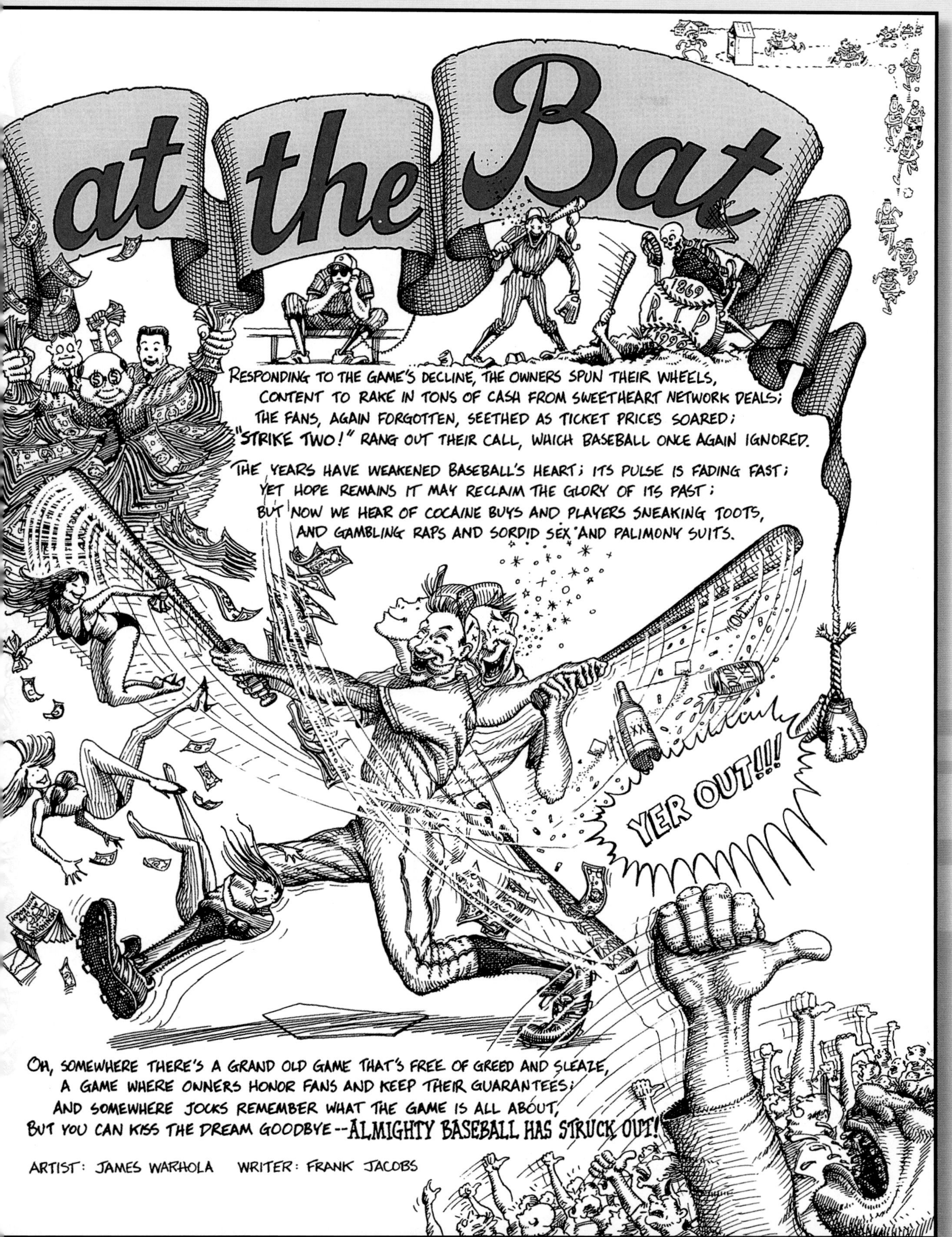
at the Bat
1869
R.I.P.
1996
RESPONDING TO THE GAME'S DECLINE, THE OWNERS SPUN THEIR WHEELS,
CONTENT TO RAKE IN TONS OF CASH FROM SWEETHEART NETWORK DEALS;
THE FANS, AGAIN FORGOTTEN, SEETHED AS TICKET PRICES SOARED;
"STRIKE TWO!" RANG OUT THEIR CALL, WHICH BASEBALL ONCE AGAIN IGNORED.
THE YEARS HAVE WEAKENED BASEBALL'S HEART; ITS PULSE IS FADING FAST;
YET HOPE REMAINS IT MAY RECLAIM THE GLORY OF ITS PAST;
BUT NOW WE HEAR OF COCAINE BUYS AND PLAYERS SNEAKING TOOTS,
AND GAMBLING RAPS AND SORDID SEX AND PALIMONY SUITS.
YER OUT!!!
OH, SOMEWHERE THERE'S A GRAND OLD GAME THAT'S FREE OF GREED AND SLEAZE,
A GAME WHERE OWNERS HONOR FANS AND KEEP THEIR GUARANTEES;
AND SOMEWHERE JOCKS REMEMBER WHAT THE GAME IS ALL ABOUT,
BUT YOU CAN KISS THE DREAM GOODBYE--ALMIGHTY BASEBALL HAS STRUCK OUT!
ARTIST: JAMES WARHOLA WRITER: FRANK JACOBS

MAD #291/DECEMBER 1989

scale it's all there. And in the big picture, the setup comes in stanzas, the transformation from past to present, all in service to the truth of the punch line — which seems, to me, as relevant now as it did in 1989. But then, I'm not really a baseball fan; I just love the idea of taking these iconic poems that sound incredible and making them MAD poems that sound incredible. (You did read it out loud, right?) I love that the poem concludes with "has struck out," as in the original, and that this is not a constraint, but a target, skillfully hit, just as a "sturdy batsman" slams "the leather covered sphere come hurtling through the air." In this case, one might say that our Poet Laureate has hit it out of the park.

A tip of the cap, also, to James Warhola's art, which shares that classic look-close-and-keep-looking visual-gag-after-gag characteristic that I always knew was a given whenever I submitted a piece with the words "funny picture here."

EDITOR'S PICK

THE KING IS BLED DEPT.

Elvis Presley died in 1977. At least, that's what most people believe. But there's still a bunch of kooks who think he faked his death and is really alive. Not to mention the fast-buck hucksters living off the Presley legend. Which makes us ask: "What would Elvis say about all this?" Most likely, he'd pick up his guitar and sing...

"DON

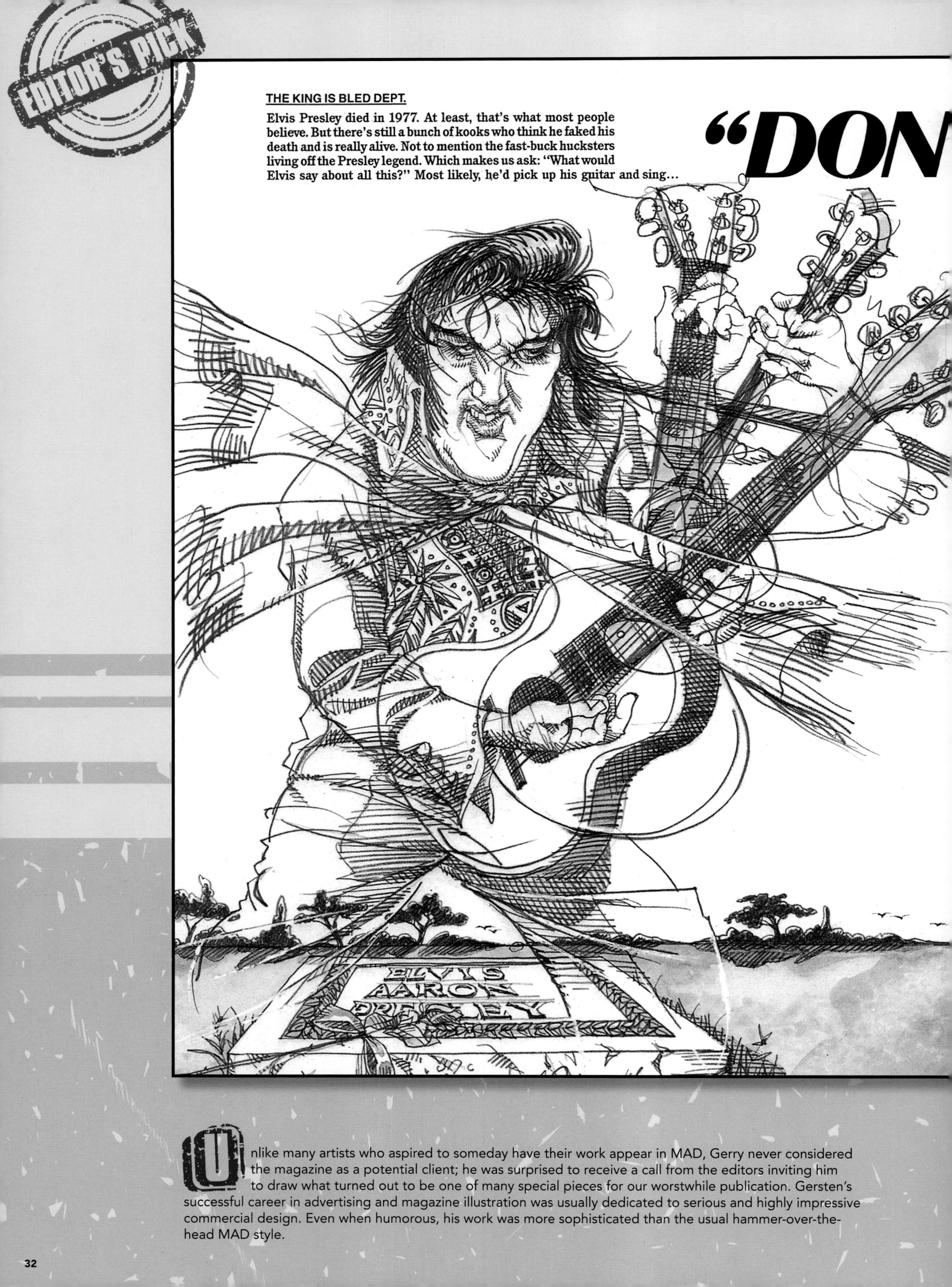
ELVIS
AARON
PRESLEY

Unlike many artists who aspired to someday have their work appear in MAD, Gerry never considered the magazine as a potential client; he was surprised to receive a call from the editors inviting him to draw what turned out to be one of many special pieces for our worstwhile publication. Gersten's successful career in advertising and magazine illustration was usually dedicated to serious and highly impressive commercial design. Even when humorous, his work was more sophisticated than the usual hammer-over-the-head MAD style.

'T BE FOOLED"

(sung to the tune of "Don't Be Cruel")

There's a *number* folks..are..cal-lin'
(and you know it's *not..toll-free*)
With a *tape* of *some guy..drawl-in'*,
Who is *claim-in'* to..*be..me*.
DON'T BE FOOLED!
'Cause it just ain't true!

There's a *girl* in *San..Di-e-go*,
Who's convinced that *I..ain't..dead;*
Says I *drive* a *Win-ne-ba-go*
With a *para-keet..named..Fred.*
DON'T BE FOOLED!
That's a rip-off too!

They're just *play-in'* with..*your..head;*
Ev'rybody..knows
The *King* is dead!

There's a *load* of *im-i-tat-ors*
Comin' off as *El-vis..clones*—
Mainly *crum-my second..rat-ers.*
Makin' *mon-ey* off..*my..bones.*
DON'T BE FOOLED!
That ain't noth-in' new!

Makes no *diff-rence* how..*they..sound;*
I'm still bur-ied
Six feet underground!

There's a *book* by an..*ad-mir-er,*
Says I live in *Mam-moth..Cave,*
And she *swears* in..the.."*En-quir-er*"
Jimmy Hoffa's *in..my..grave.*
DON'T BE FOOLED!
Not a word is true!

You can tell the *tab-loid..press,*
The King's got no
Fowarding address!

If you *want* an *ex-plan-a-tion*
For the *stor-ies* they..*contrive,*
Check the *rise* in..*cir-cu-la-tion*
Ev'ry time I'm "*proved*"..*a-live.*
DON'T BE FOOLED!
They're all conning you!

Don't let it *break..your..heart;*
Where..I've..gone
There's no Top Forty Chart!

Yes, I'm *push-in'* up..the..*dai-sies,*
But the *uproar* just..*won't..cease,*
'Cause the *world* is *full of..cra-zies*
Who won't *let me rest..in..peace!*
DON'T BE FOOLED!
This I'm tellin' you!
DON'T BE FOOLED!
What they say ain't true!

ARTIST: GERRY GERSTEN　　**WRITER: FRANK JACOBS**

MAD #285/MARCH 1989

But a different approach to caricature was exactly what MAD was seeking at the time in its quest to expand and grow its own style. Gersten provided that in spades. He employed a unique process of drawing and redrawing with pencil on tracing paper until he reached his visual goal — as opposed to the traditional pen, brush and ink style that had served the cartooning field since its earliest days.

Gersten's end result was vital and distinctive, and it paired well with poem and song-lyric parodies, such as this spoof of the Elvis Presley hit "Don't Be Cruel." — *Nick Meglin*

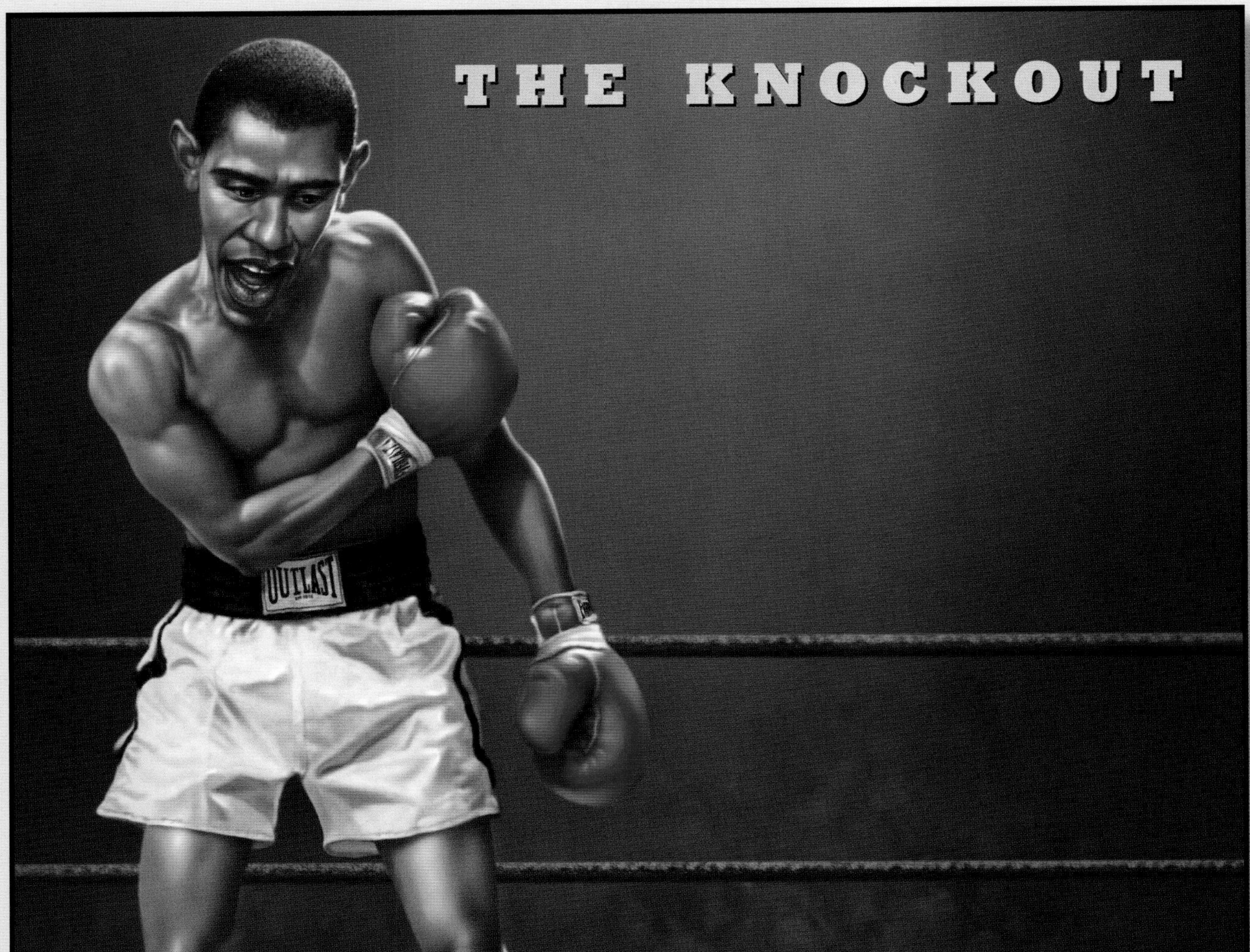
THE KNOCKOUT
OUTLAST
A MAD POLITICAL POSTER
ARTIST: MARK FREDRICKSON

MAD #492/AUGUST 2008

by Matt Lassen
WRITER

MAD is great at cementing the emotions of a time period in a funny, satirical way. "The Knockout" is a perfect example. During my first week as an intern at MAD in 2008, Barack Obama had just sealed the Democratic Presidential nomination. Almost immediately, someone on staff had the great idea to parody the famous photograph of Muhammad Ali knocking out Sonny Liston, with Obama knocking out Hillary Clinton. I was amazed at being a part of the staff discussion of the pros and cons of the piece and who should do the art, and I even remember [editor] John Ficarra acting out how Bill Clinton should be in the front row!

As the weeks went by, we saw draft after draft until the final piece appeared in print. It was amazing to see the whole process. Years later, I was interviewing for a job at an advertising agency. They had nothing on any of the walls. It was crazy to me! I went into the boss' office and the walls were empty too — except for a big poster of "The Knockout." That was the best moment of my life, since I realized people actually liked something I had been a tiny part of. It was deemed the only thing good enough to be on the wall!

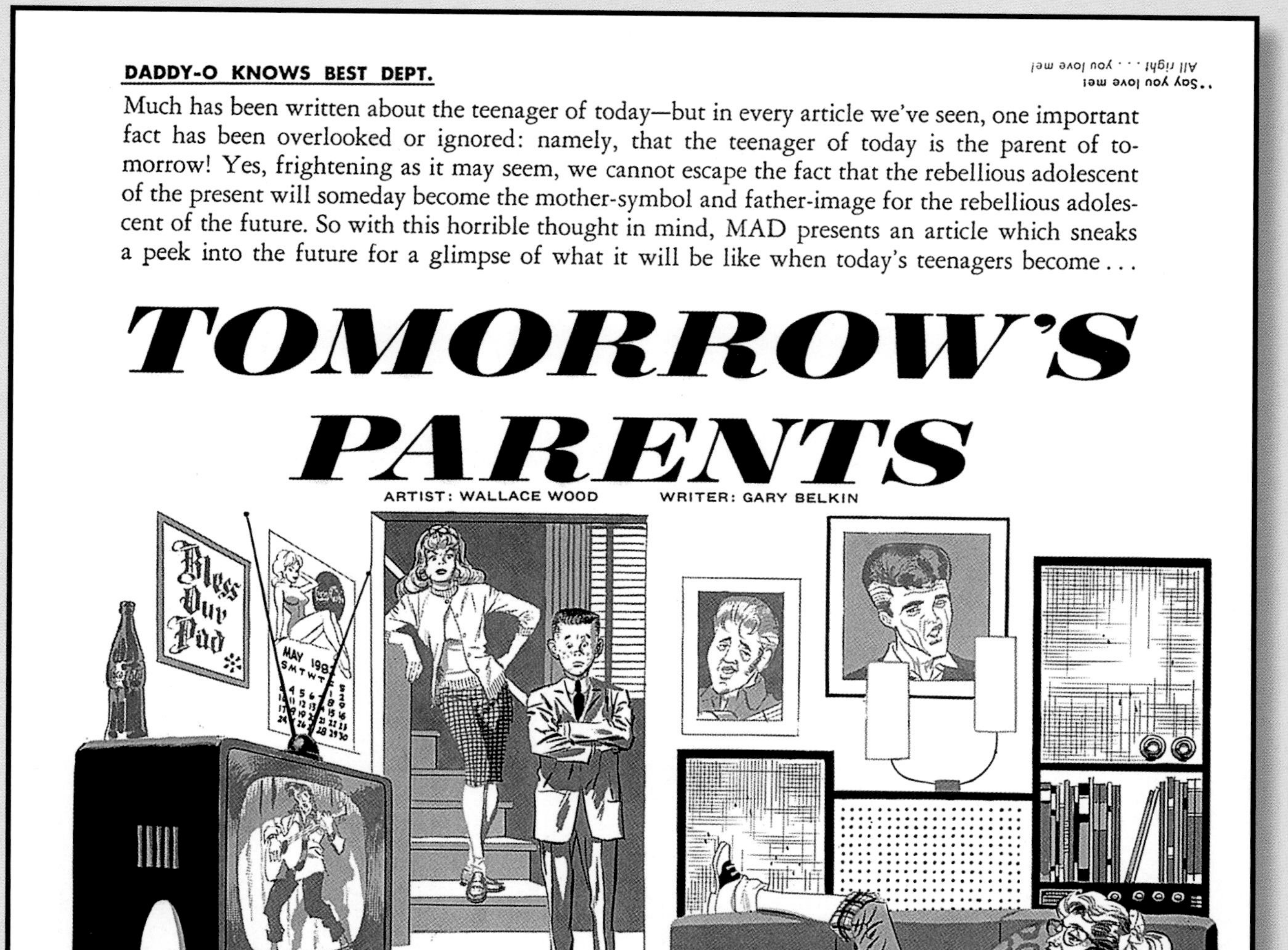
DADDY-O KNOWS BEST DEPT.

'Say you love me!
All right . . . you love me!

Much has been written about the teenager of today—but in every article we've seen, one important fact has been overlooked or ignored: namely, that the teenager of today is the parent of tomorrow! Yes, frightening as it may seem, we cannot escape the fact that the rebellious adolescent of the present will someday become the mother-symbol and father-image for the rebellious adolescent of the future. So with this horrible thought in mind, MAD presents an article which sneaks a peek into the future for a glimpse of what it will be like when today's teenagers become . . .

TOMORROW'S PARENTS

ARTIST: WALLACE WOOD WRITER: GARY BELKIN

MAD #62/APRIL 1961

by Rick Tulka
ARTIST

On the summer of 1962, when I was seven years old, my neighbor gave me an old copy of MAD Magazine (April 1961, Issue # 62). It was all torn and tattered and missing its cover. This was the first time I ever saw one. Since I already knew that I wanted to be an artist (yes, that is true) the visuals I saw, page after page, just astounded me! I never read it. I just looked at the pictures over and over. The one article that really stood out for me was "Tomorrow's Parents," by artist Wallace (Wally) Wood and writer Gary Belkin. I couldn't get over Wood's drawings. The characters, details and scenes just blew me away. I didn't have to read the piece to understand the story. His drawings were enough for me. I also knew that after that first viewing, I was addicted and needed to see more of this magazine. I happily bought issue after issue, and eventually I got a subscription and had my young brain melted by MAD's insanity. For the record, I still have that first tattered magazine that was given to me way back when.

MATERNITY WARD
LIKE QUIET
CLODS
LIKE IT'S A CHICK
DO NO
FEED TH

By the 1970's, today's young people will have found the answer to their respective teenage prayers, and many of them will have gotten married and become parents. As all parents do, they will name their children after their own personal idols. The most popular names for boys in 1970 will be Fabian, Frankie, Frankenstein, Bobby, Darin and Elvis. The most popular names for girls in 1970 will be Sandra, Tuesday, Wednesday, Annette, Funicello and Elvis.

Here are two typical parents of 1975 — Fred and Ginger (named after their own parent's idols) Typical — proudly posing behind their two children: five-year-old Tuesday Sandra Typical, and six-year-old Kingston Trio Typical.

When Tuesday and Kingston reach their teens, they've got all the things Fred and Ginger's parents refused to give them: their own rooms, their own phones, monogrammed bongos, subscriptions to MAD, and a fifth-rate education.

ALFRED E. NEUMAN
MORE ELVIS
MAD

Yet, despite all these advantages, Fred and Ginger sense that their children are not turning out "right." Tuesday and Kingston keep their rooms neat and clean, never leave clothes lying around, read books, drink milk, watch only Educational TV, hate Rock 'n Roll, don't go steady (even though both are well past 12), and actually enjoy school.

ROCK
PROUST
MILK
CHOPIN
BACH

Sincerely worried about the strange behavior of their two teenage children, Fred and Ginger seek professional help. Reluctantly, they discuss the problem with a psychiatrist:

Temporarily relieved, Fred and Ginger resume their normal lives, hoping for the day when their children's rebellious phase will pass. But one day, that hope is shattered . . .

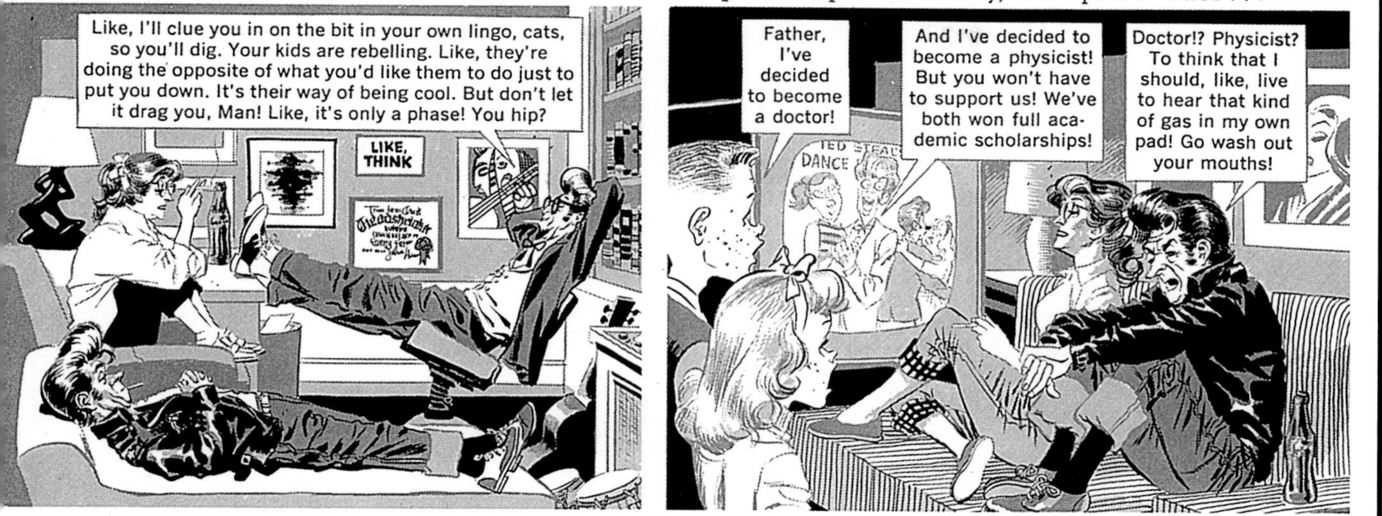

Like, I'll clue you in on the bit in your own lingo, cats, so you'll dig. Your kids are rebelling. Like, they're doing the opposite of what you'd like them to do just to put you down. It's their way of being cool. But don't let it drag you, Man! Like, it's only a phase! You hip?
LIKE, THINK
Father, I've decided to become a doctor!
And I've decided to become a physicist! But you won't have to support us! We've both won full academic scholarships!
Doctor!? Physicist? To think that I should, like, live to hear that kind of gas in my own pad! Go wash out your mouths!
DANCE

**Where can I get in touch with you?
No place! I'm ticklish!

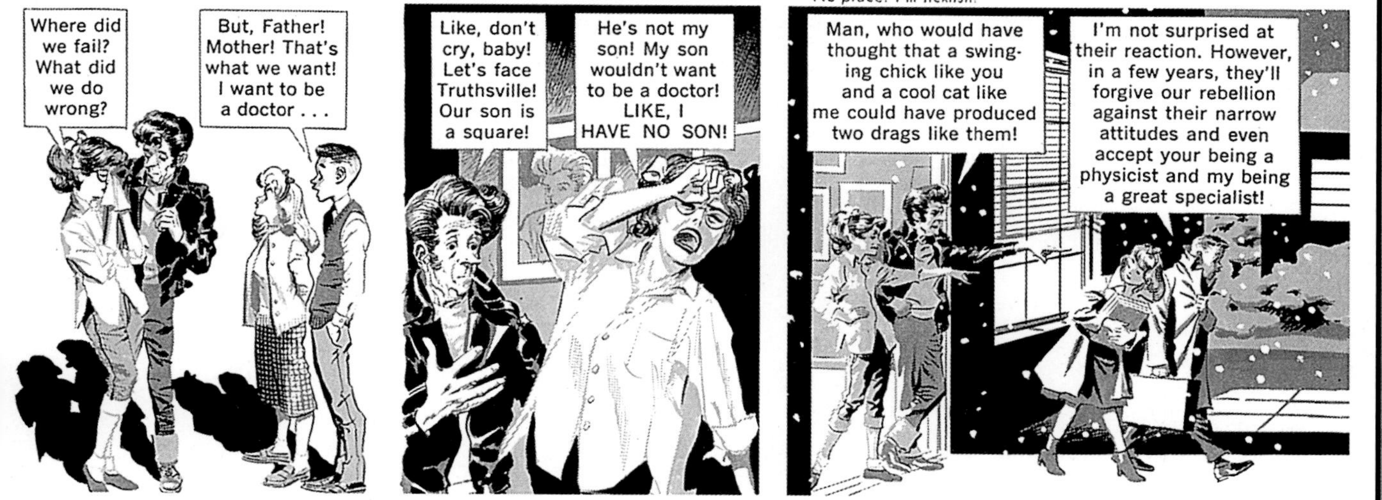

Where did we fail? What did we do wrong?
But, Father! Mother! That's what we want! I want to be a doctor . . .
Like, don't cry, baby! Let's face Truthsville! Our son is a square!
He's not my son! My son wouldn't want to be a doctor! LIKE, I HAVE NO SON!
Man, who would have thought that a swinging chick like you and a cool cat like me could have produced two drags like them!
I'm not surprised at their reaction. However, in a few years, they'll forgive our rebellion against their narrow attitudes and even accept your being a physicist and my being a great specialist!

Kingston's remarks are prophetic. In years to come, Fred and Ginger will forgive and accept their children for what they are. However, having failed as doting parents, they will achieve astonishing success as doting grandparents. Because, just as their own children rebelled against them, their grandchildren will rebel against their own parents.

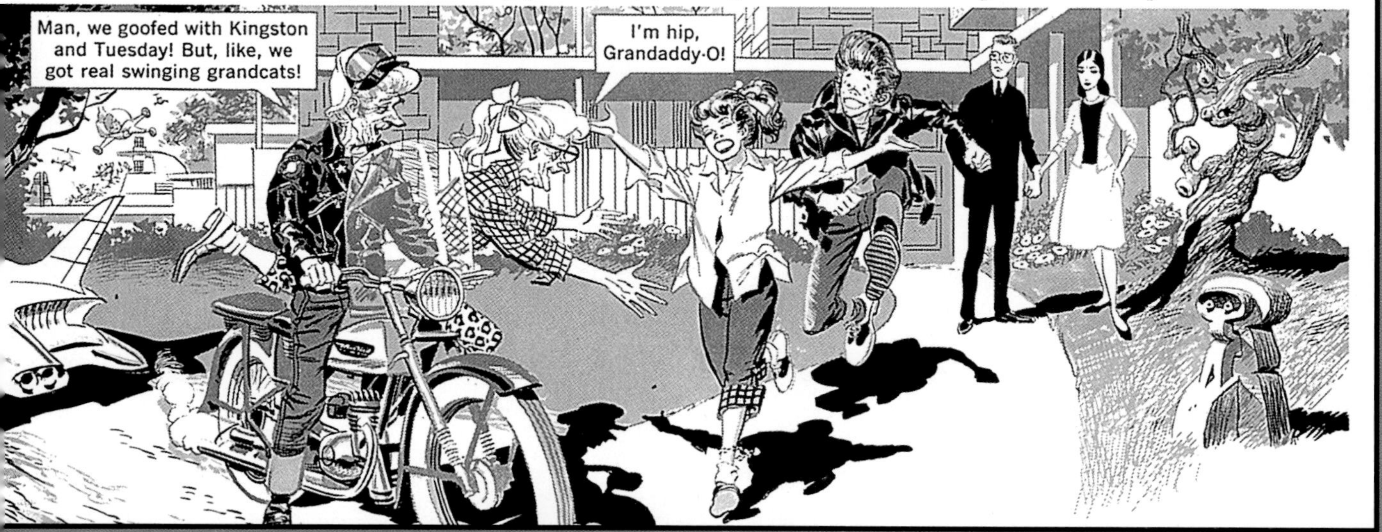

Man, we goofed with Kingston and Tuesday! But, like, we got real swinging grandcats!
I'm hip, Grandaddy-O!

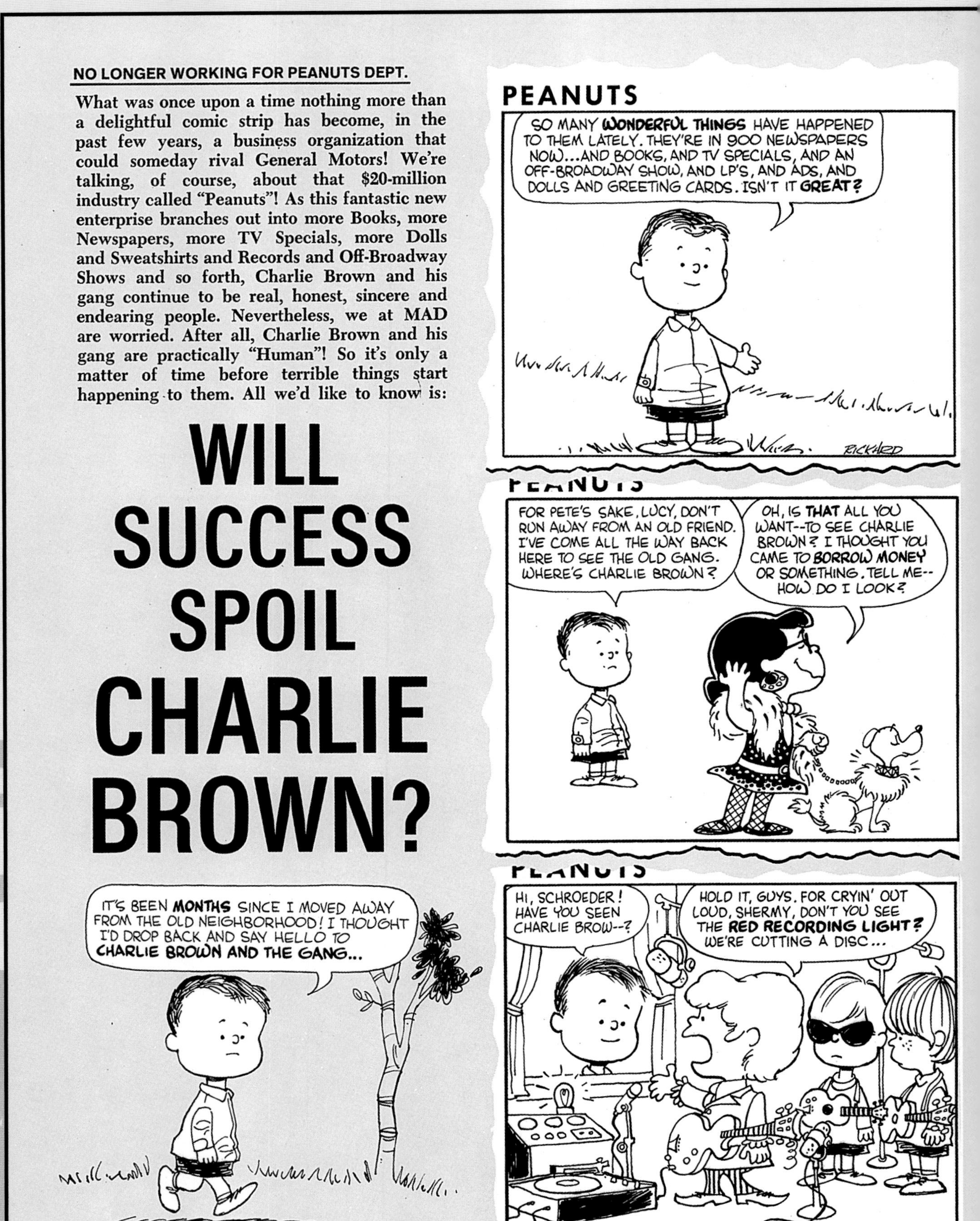

NO LONGER WORKING FOR PEANUTS DEPT.

What was once upon a time nothing more than a delightful comic strip has become, in the past few years, a business organization that could someday rival General Motors! We're talking, of course, about that $20-million industry called "Peanuts"! As this fantastic new enterprise branches out into more Books, more Newspapers, more TV Specials, more Dolls and Sweatshirts and Records and Off-Broadway Shows and so forth, Charlie Brown and his gang continue to be real, honest, sincere and endearing people. Nevertheless, we at MAD are worried. After all, Charlie Brown and his gang are practically "Human"! So it's only a matter of time before terrible things start happening to them. All we'd like to know is:

WILL SUCCESS SPOIL CHARLIE BROWN?

IT'S BEEN MONTHS SINCE I MOVED AWAY FROM THE OLD NEIGHBORHOOD! I THOUGHT I'D DROP BACK AND SAY HELLO TO CHARLIE BROWN AND THE GANG...
PEANUTS
SO MANY WONDERFUL THINGS HAVE HAPPENED TO THEM LATELY. THEY'RE IN 900 NEWSPAPERS NOW...AND BOOKS, AND TV SPECIALS, AND AN OFF-BROADWAY SHOW, AND LP'S, AND ADS, AND DOLLS AND GREETING CARDS. ISN'T IT GREAT?
RICKARD
FOR PETE'S SAKE, LUCY, DON'T RUN AWAY FROM AN OLD FRIEND. I'VE COME ALL THE WAY BACK HERE TO SEE THE OLD GANG. WHERE'S CHARLIE BROWN?
OH, IS THAT ALL YOU WANT--TO SEE CHARLIE BROWN? I THOUGHT YOU CAME TO BORROW MONEY OR SOMETHING. TELL ME-- HOW DO I LOOK?
HI, SCHROEDER! HAVE YOU SEEN CHARLIE BROW--?
HOLD IT, GUYS. FOR CRYIN' OUT LOUD, SHERMY, DON'T YOU SEE THE RED RECORDING LIGHT? WE'RE CUTTING A DISC...

ARTIST: JACK RICKARD WRITER: LARRY SIEGEL

by Scott Maiko
WRITER

My copy of 1981's Super Special #36, "A MAD Look At The Comics," eventually fell apart due to my excessive re-re-re-reading of it (or from the cheap glue and substandard staples MAD used to bind it). My favorite article: "Will Success Spoil Charlie Brown?"

Today (in a world where SpongeBob Pop-Tarts exist), aggressive and all-encompassing merchandising blitzes for popular properties are the norm. In 1968 (when the piece first ran), it must have been something of a novelty (or annoyance)

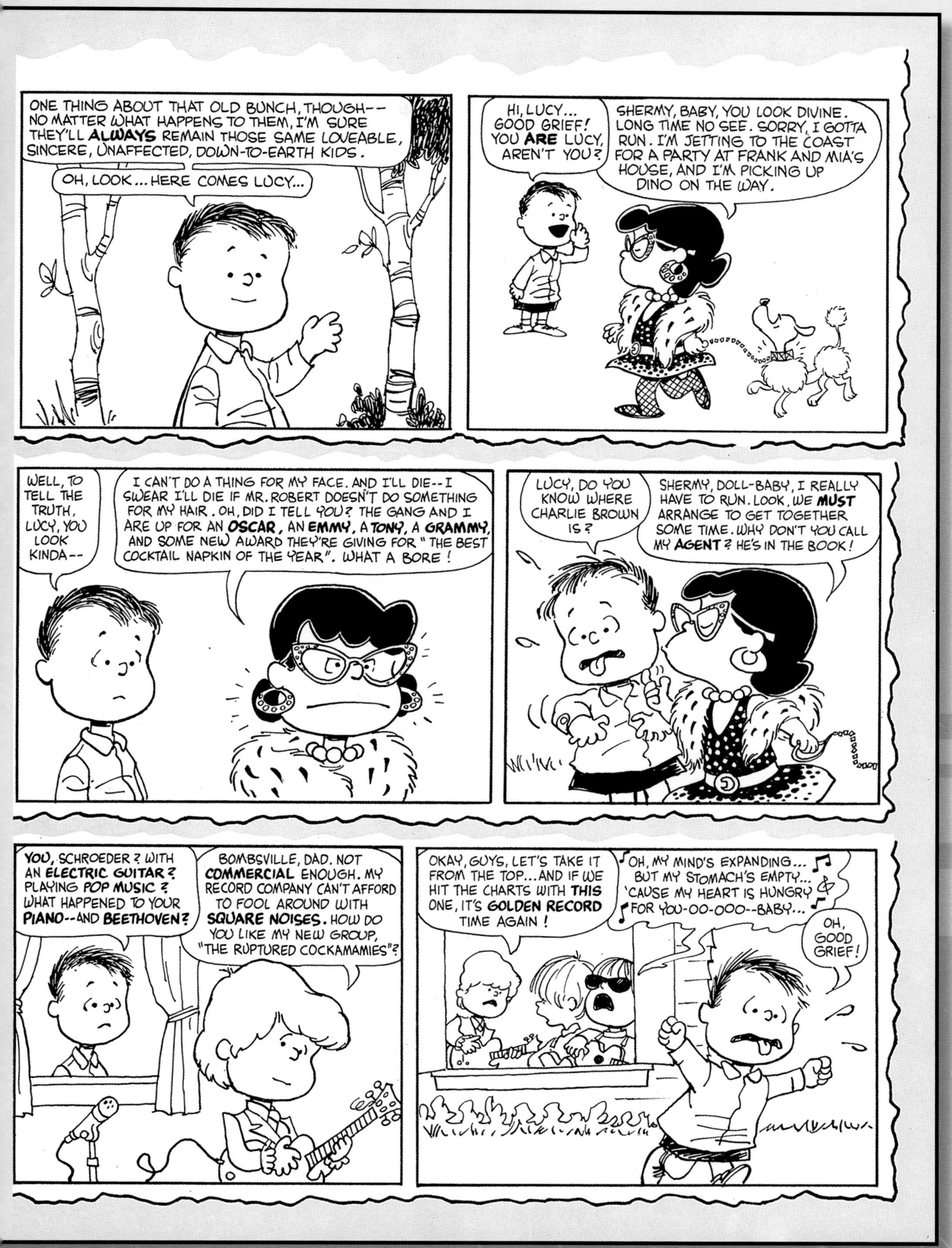

ONE THING ABOUT THAT OLD BUNCH, THOUGH-- NO MATTER WHAT HAPPENS TO THEM, I'M SURE THEY'LL **ALWAYS** REMAIN THOSE SAME LOVEABLE, SINCERE, UNAFFECTED, DOWN-TO-EARTH KIDS.
OH, LOOK... HERE COMES LUCY...
HI, LUCY... GOOD GRIEF! YOU **ARE** LUCY, AREN'T YOU?
SHERMY, BABY, YOU LOOK DIVINE. LONG TIME NO SEE. SORRY, I GOTTA RUN. I'M JETTING TO THE COAST FOR A PARTY AT FRANK AND MIA'S HOUSE, AND I'M PICKING UP DINO ON THE WAY.
WELL, TO TELL THE TRUTH, LUCY, YOU LOOK KINDA--
I CAN'T DO A THING FOR MY FACE. AND I'LL DIE--I SWEAR I'LL DIE IF MR. ROBERT DOESN'T DO SOMETHING FOR MY HAIR. OH, DID I TELL YOU? THE GANG AND I ARE UP FOR AN **OSCAR**, AN **EMMY**, A **TONY**, A **GRAMMY**, AND SOME NEW AWARD THEY'RE GIVING FOR "THE BEST COCKTAIL NAPKIN OF THE YEAR". WHAT A BORE!
LUCY, DO YOU KNOW WHERE CHARLIE BROWN IS?
SHERMY, DOLL-BABY, I REALLY HAVE TO RUN. LOOK, WE **MUST** ARRANGE TO GET TOGETHER SOME TIME. WHY DON'T YOU CALL MY **AGENT**? HE'S IN THE BOOK!
YOU, SCHROEDER? WITH AN **ELECTRIC GUITAR**? PLAYING **POP MUSIC**? WHAT HAPPENED TO YOUR **PIANO**--AND **BEETHOVEN**?
BOMBSVILLE, DAD. NOT **COMMERCIAL** ENOUGH. MY RECORD COMPANY CAN'T AFFORD TO FOOL AROUND WITH **SQUARE NOISES**. HOW DO YOU LIKE MY NEW GROUP, "THE RUPTURED COCKAMAMIES"?
OKAY, GUYS, LET'S TAKE IT FROM THE TOP... AND IF WE HIT THE CHARTS WITH **THIS** ONE, IT'S **GOLDEN RECORD** TIME AGAIN!
OH, MY MIND'S EXPANDING... BUT MY STOMACH'S EMPTY... 'CAUSE MY HEART IS HUNGRY FOR YOU-OO-OOO--BABY...
OH, GOOD GRIEF!

MAD #117/MARCH 1968

to see Peanuts merchandise everywhere, inspiring writer Larry Siegel to pen this comic masterpiece.

Over a week's worth of strips, Siegel brilliantly exposes the Peanuts gang for the spoiled brats he'd envisioned they'd become — as seen through the eyes of Shermy, a character Peanuts cartoonist Charles Schulz had by then dropped from the strip. Who better to bring back to the neighborhood to witness the unfortunate consequences of the comic's rampant popularity?

Jack Rickard's illustrations mimic, near-perfectly, the strip's style, and even the lettering

PEANUTS

Panel 1: HERE COMES LINUS. HEY, LINUS, HAVE YOU SEEN CHARL-- LINUS, WHAT'S THAT? A **MINK BLANKET**?!

Panel 2: WHAT'S **HAPPENING** HERE? LUCY'S GONE "HOLLYWOOD", SHROEDER'S PLAYING ROCK 'N' ROLL, AND LINUS HAS A "MINK BLANKET"...

Panel 3: THERE'S PIG PEN. HI, PIG PEN... WELL, THANK GOODNESS **YOU** HAVEN'T CHANGED. — WHAT ARE YOU TALKING ABOUT? THIS IS **IMPORTED DUST**.

Panel 4: SMELL THAT BOUQUET. IT'S GENUINE ITALIAN ANTIQUE. 50 B.C. WAS A **GREAT YEAR** FOR DIRT. — WHERE'S CHARLIE BROWN!?

PEANUTS

Panel 1: LINUS, HAVE YOU SEEN CHARLIE BROWN? — SORRY, I CAN'T TALK. SNOOPY'S **CAVIAR** WILL DRY OUT.

Panel 2: HI, VIOLET, HAVE YOU SEEN-- OH, NO--THAT'S NOT FOR SNOOPY **TOO**, IS IT? — HE'S GOING TO **KILL** ME. WE'RE ALL OUT OF **ROQUEFORT DRESSING**.

Panel 3: FOR SNOOPY, I SUPPOSE. — I HOPE HE'S NOT UPSET. THE **PHEASANT** IS JUST RIGHT, BUT THE **GLASS** IT'S UNDER IS CRACKED.

Panel 4: OH, NO. IT'S NOT **HAPPENING**. MAYBE IF I CLOSE MY EYES IT'LL ALL **GO AWAY**.

PEANUTS

Panel 1: SHERMY, I **FOUND** CHARLIE BROWN. — GREAT. WHERE IS HE?

Panel 2: THIS WAY. HIS TEAM IS **PLAYING** TODAY. — MAYBE **I** CAN PLAY, TOO. I ALWAYS WAS THE BEST SHORTSTOP ON CHARLIE BROWN'S TEAM.

Panel 3: **POLO**?? CHARLIE BROWN IS PLAYING **POLO**? — **SHERMY**, OLD PAL, IT'S GRAND **SEEING** YOU AGAIN. WE **MUST** SIT DOWN FOR A BUDDY-BUDDY TALK. CALL MY SECRETARY. I THINK I CAN GIVE YOU 5 MINUTES NEXT TUESDAY.

looks like it flowed from Schulz's pen. The piece ends with a Sunday strip where Good Ol' Charlie Brown's featured role has been upgraded to a "fabulous" starring turn; he dons a toupee, hits on Violet, insults Shermy and rats out Mary Worth as a Communist. Success spoiled Charlie Brown magnificently.

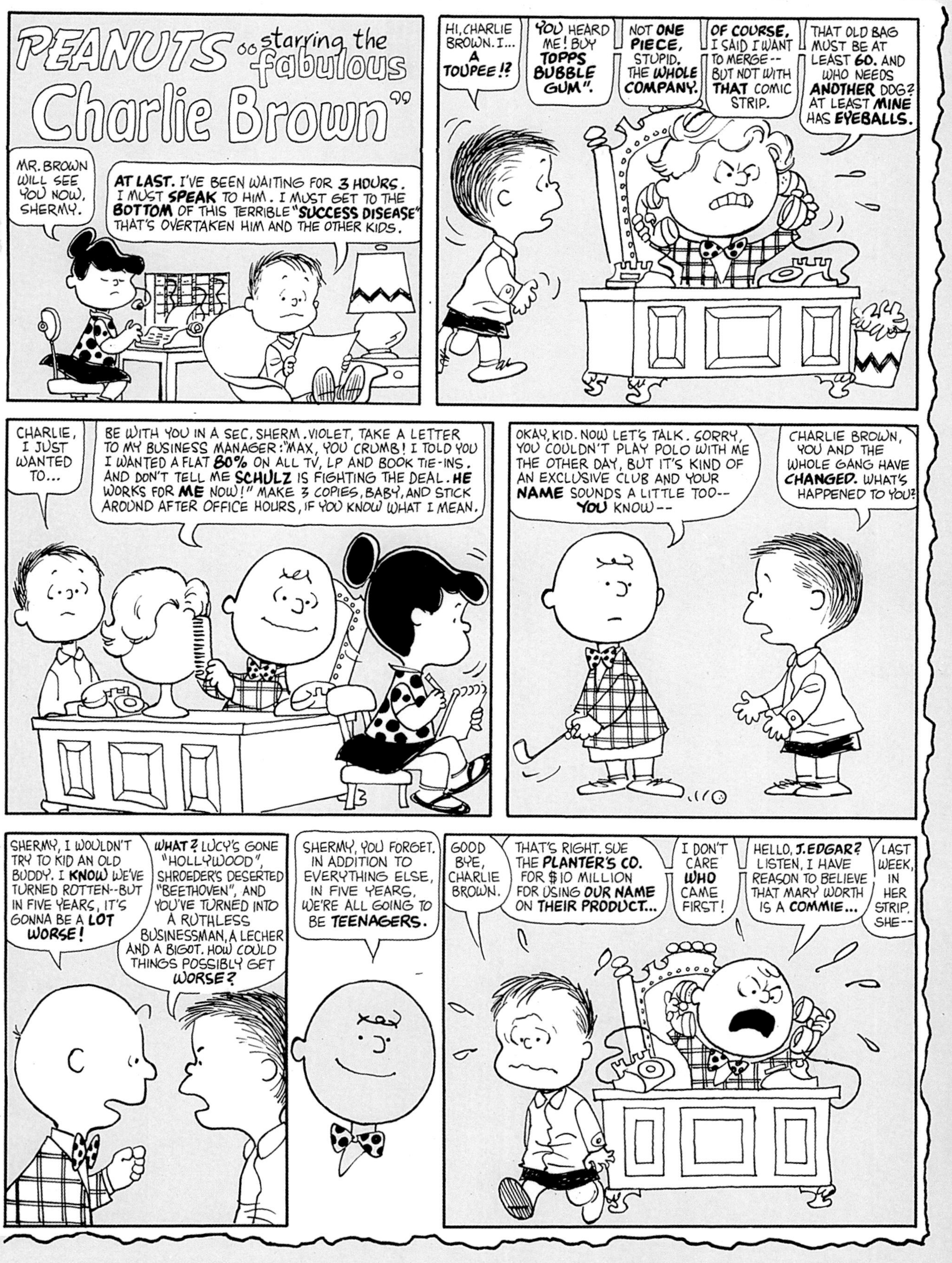
PEANUTS .. starring the "fabulous Charlie Brown"
MR. BROWN WILL SEE YOU NOW, SHERMY.
AT LAST. I'VE BEEN WAITING FOR 3 HOURS. I MUST SPEAK TO HIM. I MUST GET TO THE BOTTOM OF THIS TERRIBLE "SUCCESS DISEASE" THAT'S OVERTAKEN HIM AND THE OTHER KIDS.
HI, CHARLIE BROWN. I... A TOUPEE!?
YOU HEARD ME! BUY TOPPS BUBBLE GUM".
NOT ONE PIECE, STUPID. THE WHOLE COMPANY.
OF COURSE, I SAID I WANT TO MERGE-- BUT NOT WITH THAT COMIC STRIP.
THAT OLD BAG MUST BE AT LEAST 60. AND WHO NEEDS ANOTHER DOG? AT LEAST MINE HAS EYEBALLS.
CHARLIE, I JUST WANTED TO...
BE WITH YOU IN A SEC, SHERM. VIOLET, TAKE A LETTER TO MY BUSINESS MANAGER: "MAX, YOU CRUMB! I TOLD YOU I WANTED A FLAT 80% ON ALL TV, LP AND BOOK TIE-INS. AND DON'T TELL ME SCHULZ IS FIGHTING THE DEAL. HE WORKS FOR ME NOW!" MAKE 3 COPIES, BABY, AND STICK AROUND AFTER OFFICE HOURS, IF YOU KNOW WHAT I MEAN.
OKAY, KID. NOW LET'S TALK. SORRY YOU COULDN'T PLAY POLO WITH ME THE OTHER DAY, BUT IT'S KIND OF AN EXCLUSIVE CLUB AND YOUR NAME SOUNDS A LITTLE TOO-- YOU KNOW--
CHARLIE BROWN, YOU AND THE WHOLE GANG HAVE CHANGED. WHAT'S HAPPENED TO YOU?
SHERMY, I WOULDN'T TRY TO KID AN OLD BUDDY. I KNOW WE'VE TURNED ROTTEN--BUT IN FIVE YEARS, IT'S GONNA BE A LOT WORSE!
WHAT? LUCY'S GONE "HOLLYWOOD", SHROEDER'S DESERTED "BEETHOVEN", AND YOU'VE TURNED INTO A RUTHLESS BUSINESSMAN, A LECHER AND A BIGOT. HOW COULD THINGS POSSIBLY GET WORSE?
SHERMY, YOU FORGET. IN ADDITION TO EVERYTHING ELSE, IN FIVE YEARS, WE'RE ALL GOING TO BE TEENAGERS.
GOOD BYE, CHARLIE BROWN.
THAT'S RIGHT. SUE THE PLANTER'S CO. FOR $10 MILLION FOR USING OUR NAME ON THEIR PRODUCT...
I DON'T CARE WHO CAME FIRST!
HELLO, J. EDGAR? LISTEN, I HAVE REASON TO BELIEVE THAT MARY WORTH IS A COMMIE...
LAST WEEK, IN HER STRIP, SHE--

I didn't really start collecting comic books until I was 16, but I started reading MAD long before that. Maybe I didn't think it was a comic book because it was magazine size. I didn't know I was going to be a true artist at that point, but I was a doodler. I was always fascinated looking at people's art and seeing how they drew. The Mort Drucker stuff was, to me, mind-numbing because even as a young kid — at eight, nine, 10, 11 — in a heartbeat I could tell who each one of his characters were. Wow! It's William Shatner! MAD was sometimes parodying the shows I was watching, too, but at no time did I ever not know who every one of those guys were in Mort Drucker's drawings. To this day, I'm jealous of political cartoonists who do the same thing. They lampoon people and you go, "Yep. That's them." They somehow know how to play up the characteristics.

So to me, Drucker was the guy who was the king of that book. And then of course, after that there was Sergio Aragonés' stuff in the margins. "Spy vs. Spy" was always filled with fun, goofy stuff, and I think every kid went to the newsstands — and I know we shouldn't have — and folded in the back cover and left damaged magazines on the rack. Two MAD spoofs that really stood out for me were both by Mort Drucker: his *Star Trek* spoof — I have a clear recollection of how he really nailed both Shatner and Nimoy — and then *Batman,* which was really powerful to me when I was a kid, especially because of the way he drew some of the villains. And *Planet of the Apes*, of course. I was a big *Planet of the Apes* fan. Not *Star Wars*. It was all about *Planet of the Apes* for me.

Todd McFarlane

It's not by accident that some of Mort's work rubbed off on me.

When you're a kid, you just swallow stuff because you like it, so I gobbled up MAD. It was like six flavors of Skittles to me, and it all tasted great. I didn't know it at the time, but what I got out of MAD Magazine was that everybody didn't have to have the same look, or the same artistic style, to still be in the same comedic arena. Some guys did it with a very simple style, as with "Spy vs. Spy," and Mort did it with his super-intricate style — but you still knew that you were in "Funland." It opened my eyes to the fact that you can have a variety of looks and still be there, because I know at the time, I was still trying to find my way as an artist with any style! I have a clear recollection that I would try 10 different styles — not comic book styles, because I hadn't gotten bit by that bug yet — from landscape drawing to realism; then I'd go draw silly cartoons and dumb stuff. I was all over the map, trying to figure out, "Do any of these fit me personally?" At some point I decided to concentrate and teach myself to draw superhero comic books. Knowing what MAD taught me, I saw the same thing was true about comics: it's a genre in a medium where some guys had a super-clean look, but I could have a complex look. It's not by accident that some of Mort's work rubbed off on me. I do a lot of cross-hatch and a lot of line work too, like he does. It's not good for deadlines, but we eventually get there.

Mort also sometimes liked to throw unrelated or random things into the background for extra interest. When I started taking off and took over the "Amazing Spiderman" books, I started hiding spiders on the cover; then, depending on the number of spiders, I would sign it with a number under my name. People would come up to me and ask "Why's it say 'McFarlane 4?'" Because of the spiders. "What?" Then they had to look at it. Really look at it. Also, I had a buddy who had been in the Vietnam War. He was a little shell-shocked and would walk around town all day with a Felix the Cat stuffed toy, so I started hiding Felix in there, just for that one guy.

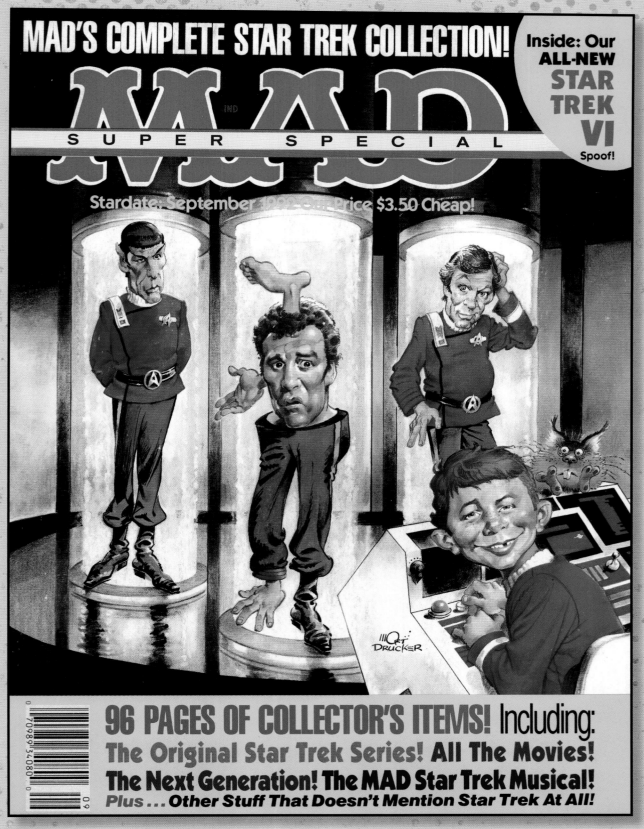

MAD'S COMPLETE STAR TREK COLLECTION!

Inside: Our **ALL-NEW STAR TREK VI** Spoof!

MAD
SUPER SPECIAL

Stardate: September 1992 • Price $3.50 Cheap!

96 PAGES OF COLLECTOR'S ITEMS! Including:
The Original Star Trek Series! All The Movies!
The Next Generation! The MAD Star Trek Musical!
Plus ... Other Stuff That Doesn't Mention Star Trek At All!

ARTIST: MORT DRUCKER   MAD SUPER SPECIAL #83/SEPTEMBER 1992

I also took a page from MAD's schtick book — I would do my equivalent of MAD Magazine by making up false headlines in newspapers that characters were reading. I was a big sports nut, still am, so I would stack all the baseball teams by trading the best players to my favorite teams, or if someone beat one of my teams I'd make a headline saying he retired. Goofy stuff. I'd mess with the logos for different sports teams on clothes just to have a little bit of fun. They have to be wearing something, right? We all have a tendency to wear stuff, so that was my way of dressing up the pages just like

Mort did in his backgrounds.

I was born in 1961 and became aware of MAD probably when I was seven or eight. And now, all these years later, it's funny because I became friends with Sergio, one of the guys who got me into the groove to appreciate the wonder of comic books. It's also strange to come full circle when MAD makes a reference to my comics. You get to the point, I guess, where you appreciate it anytime anyone pays attention to you, good, bad or indifferent. It makes me smile knowing I did something worthy of MAD making fun of.

WE GOT YOUR PENUMBRA DEPT.

Who Knows What Evils Lurk In THE SHADOW

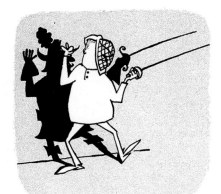

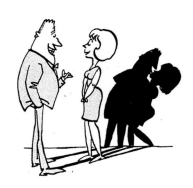

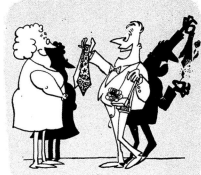

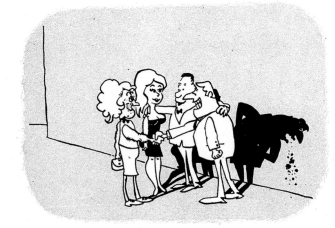

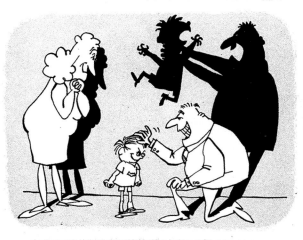

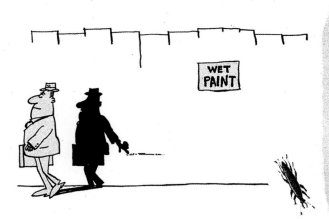

WET PAINT

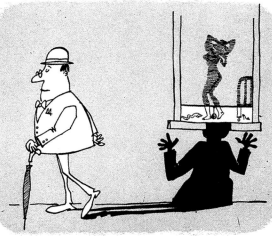

by Dave Croatto
WRITER

"The Shadow Knows" is one of the greatest MAD features of all time — it's clever and funny and completely original. (At least, that's what Editor John Ficarra said when he rejected my feature "The Silhouette Comprehends.") But the true honor (and I'm sure Sergio will agree with me on this) is that it was also the first MAD piece I ever read. I was sleeping over a friend's house in the 4th grade, and his parents came in to tell us that it was lights out. Within a minute of his bedroom door closing behind them, my friend had pulled out a flashlight and a small stack of MAD paperbacks for us to read. I wound up grabbing "The

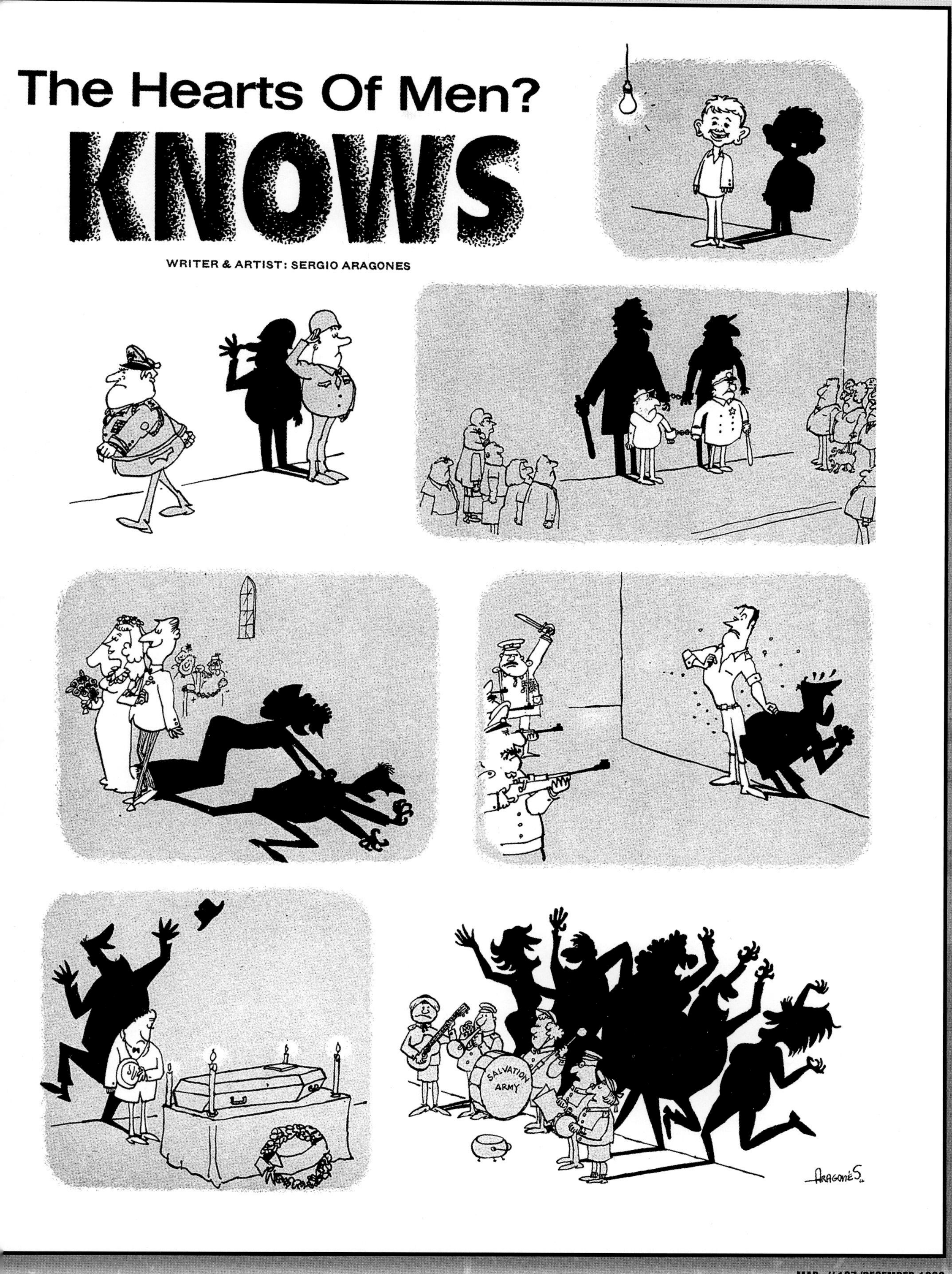
The Hearts Of Men?
KNOWS
WRITER & ARTIST: SERGIO ARAGONES
SALVATION ARMY
ARAGONÉS

MAD #107/DECEMBER 1966

Shadow Knows" and it immediately blew my sleep-deprived, Pepsi-addled mind. At that age, I devoured comic strips — from Family Circus to Garfield to Calvin & Hobbes — but I had never seen anything like this before. There were gags about husbands who were ashamed of their ugly wives! And drunk drivers whose cars' shadows were shaped like coffins! Coffins! It was fun and accessible, but also dark and moral — it was a crazy, intoxicating combo. I felt like I had stumbled into a world that straddled childhood and adulthood — and I've pretty much been there ever since. In his five decades working with MAD, Sergio has enjoyed many well-deserved accolades, but his greatest accomplishment (and I'm sure Sergio will also agree with me on this) is the huge and lasting impact he had on my grade-school brain.

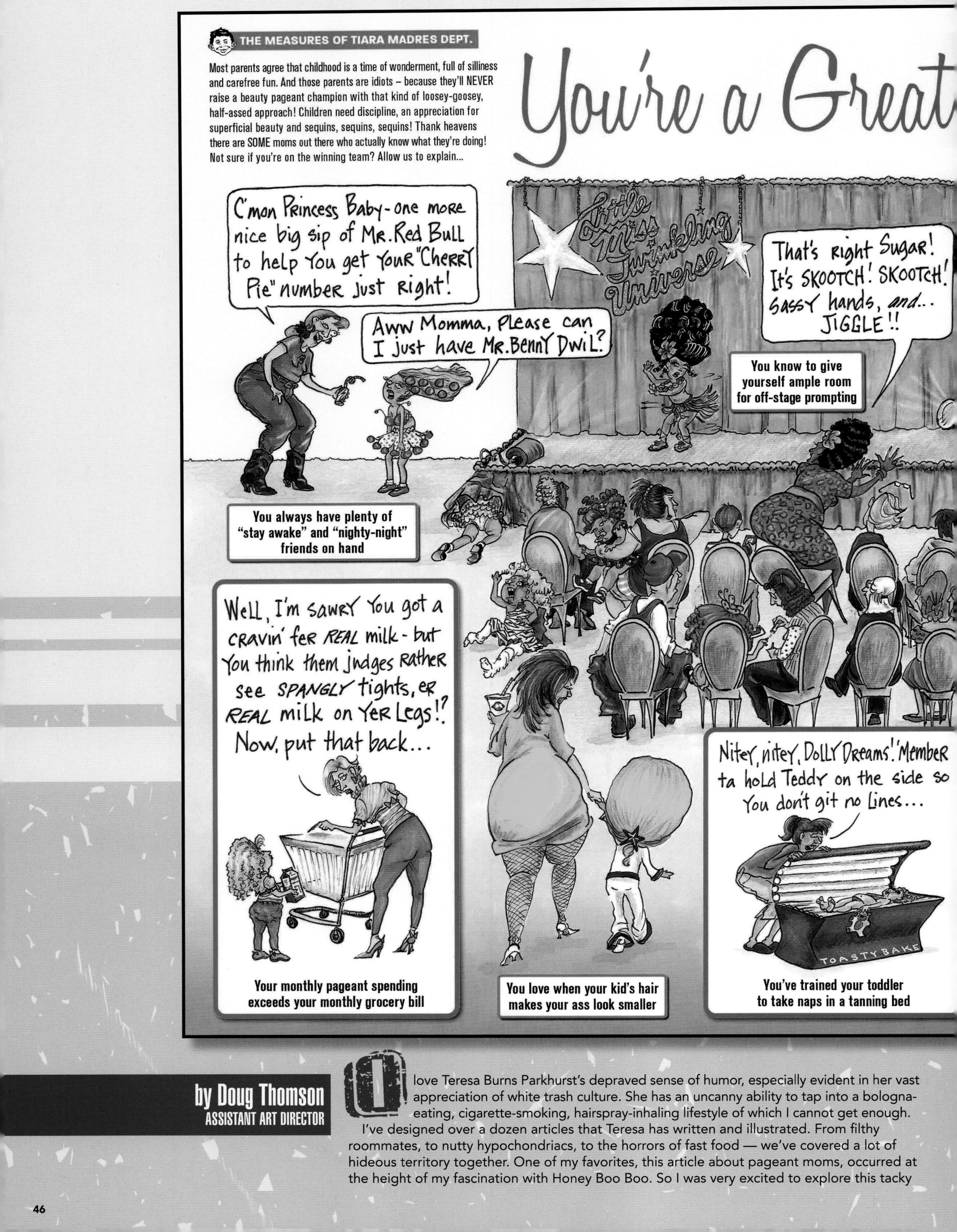
THE MEASURES OF TIARA MADRES DEPT.
Most parents agree that childhood is a time of wonderment, full of silliness and carefree fun. And those parents are idiots – because they'll NEVER raise a beauty pageant champion with that kind of loosey-goosey, half-assed approach! Children need discipline, an appreciation for superficial beauty and sequins, sequins, sequins! Thank heavens there are SOME moms out there who actually know what they're doing! Not sure if you're on the winning team? Allow us to explain...
You're a Great
Little Miss Twinkling Universe
C'mon Princess Baby - one more nice big sip of Mr. Red Bull to help You get Your "Cherry Pie" number just right!
Aww Momma, Please can I just have Mr. Benny Dwil?
You always have plenty of "stay awake" and "nighty-night" friends on hand
That's right Sugar! It's SKOOTCH! SKOOTCH! Sassy hands, and... JIGGLE!!
You know to give yourself ample room for off-stage prompting
Well, I'm sawry You got a cravin' fer REAL milk - but You think them judges rather see SPANGLY tights, er REAL milk on Yer Legs!? Now, put that back...
Your monthly pageant spending exceeds your monthly grocery bill
You love when your kid's hair makes your ass look smaller
Nitey, nitey, Dolly Dreams! 'Member ta hold Teddy on the side so You don't git no Lines...
TOASTY BAKE
You've trained your toddler to take naps in a tanning bed

by Doug Thomson
ASSISTANT ART DIRECTOR

I love Teresa Burns Parkhurst's depraved sense of humor, especially evident in her vast appreciation of white trash culture. She has an uncanny ability to tap into a bologna-eating, cigarette-smoking, hairspray-inhaling lifestyle of which I cannot get enough.

I've designed over a dozen articles that Teresa has written and illustrated. From filthy roommates, to nutty hypochondriacs, to the horrors of fast food — we've covered a lot of hideous territory together. One of my favorites, this article about pageant moms, occurred at the height of my fascination with Honey Boo Boo. So I was very excited to explore this tacky

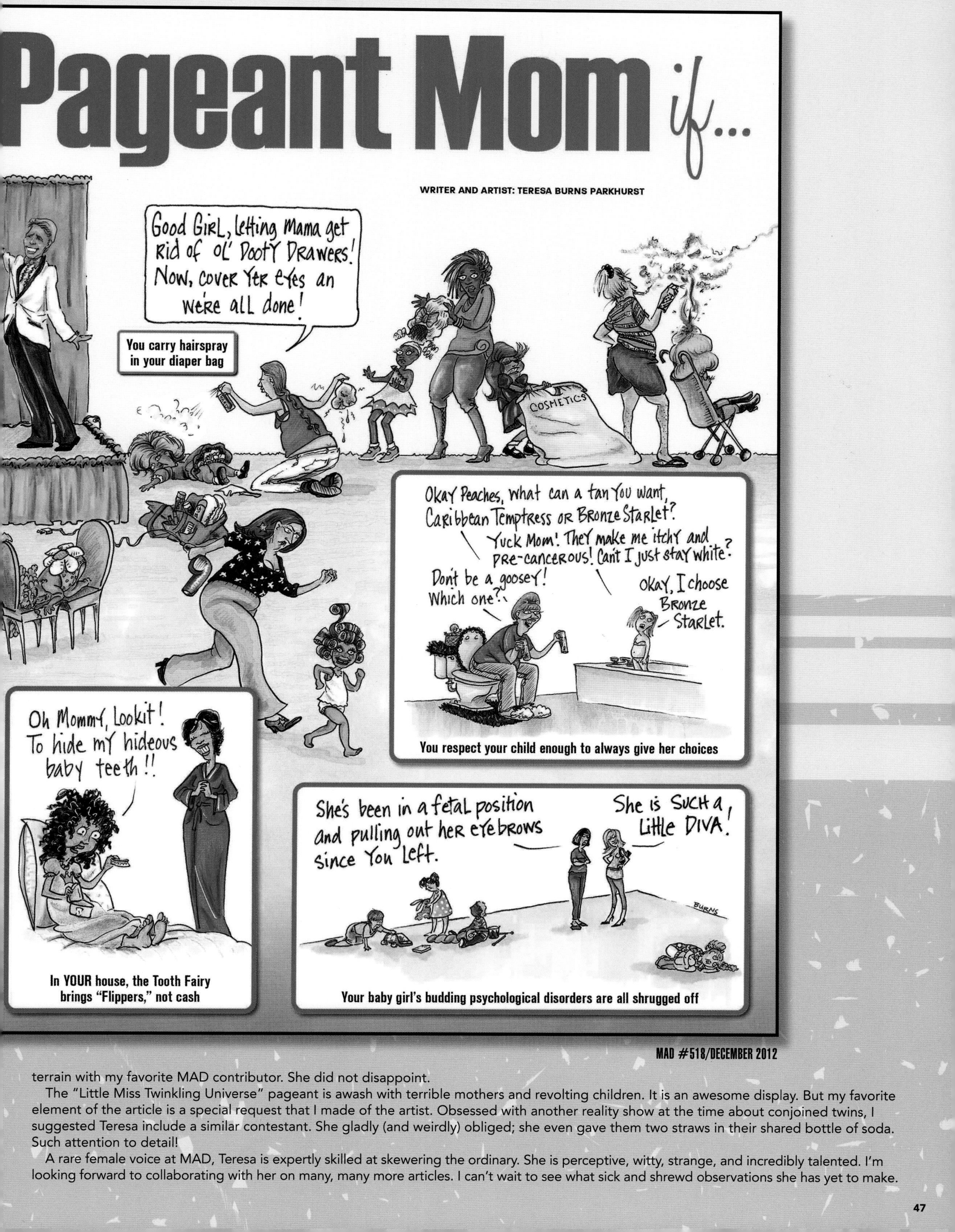
Pageant Mom if...
WRITER AND ARTIST: TERESA BURNS PARKHURST
Good GiRL, letting Mama get Rid of OL' DooTY DRawers! Now, coveR YeR eYes an we're all done!
You carry hairspray in your diaper bag
COSMETICS
Okay Peaches, what can a tan You want, Caribbean Temptress oR Bronze StarLet?
Yuck Mom! They make me itchY and pre-cancerous! Can't I just stay white?
Don't be a goosey! Which one?
Okay, I choose Bronze StarLet.
You respect your child enough to always give her choices
Oh Mommy, Lookit! To hide my hideous baby teeth!!
In YOUR house, the Tooth Fairy brings "Flippers," not cash
She's been in a fetal position and pulling out her eyebrows since You Left.
She is SUCH a Little DIVA!
BURNS
Your baby girl's budding psychological disorders are all shrugged off

MAD #518/DECEMBER 2012

terrain with my favorite MAD contributor. She did not disappoint.

The "Little Miss Twinkling Universe" pageant is awash with terrible mothers and revolting children. It is an awesome display. But my favorite element of the article is a special request that I made of the artist. Obsessed with another reality show at the time about conjoined twins, I suggested Teresa include a similar contestant. She gladly (and weirdly) obliged; she even gave them two straws in their shared bottle of soda. Such attention to detail!

A rare female voice at MAD, Teresa is expertly skilled at skewering the ordinary. She is perceptive, witty, strange, and incredibly talented. I'm looking forward to collaborating with her on many, many more articles. I can't wait to see what sick and shrewd observations she has yet to make.

Whoopi Goldberg

*M*AD Magazine was such a huge part of my life growing up. It all started when my mother gave me a subscription for one of my birthdays (she liked reading them, too). My mom liked "Spy vs. Spy," my brother liked the parodies and I liked EVERYTHING. I liked the back page where, with a fold here and there, things were not as they seemed. I liked the artwork, which gave me some of the best times, and frankly, I wished that one day I would be immortalized in MAD Magazine...and it happened. Being in MAD Magazine and getting an Oscar — two very high notes for me.

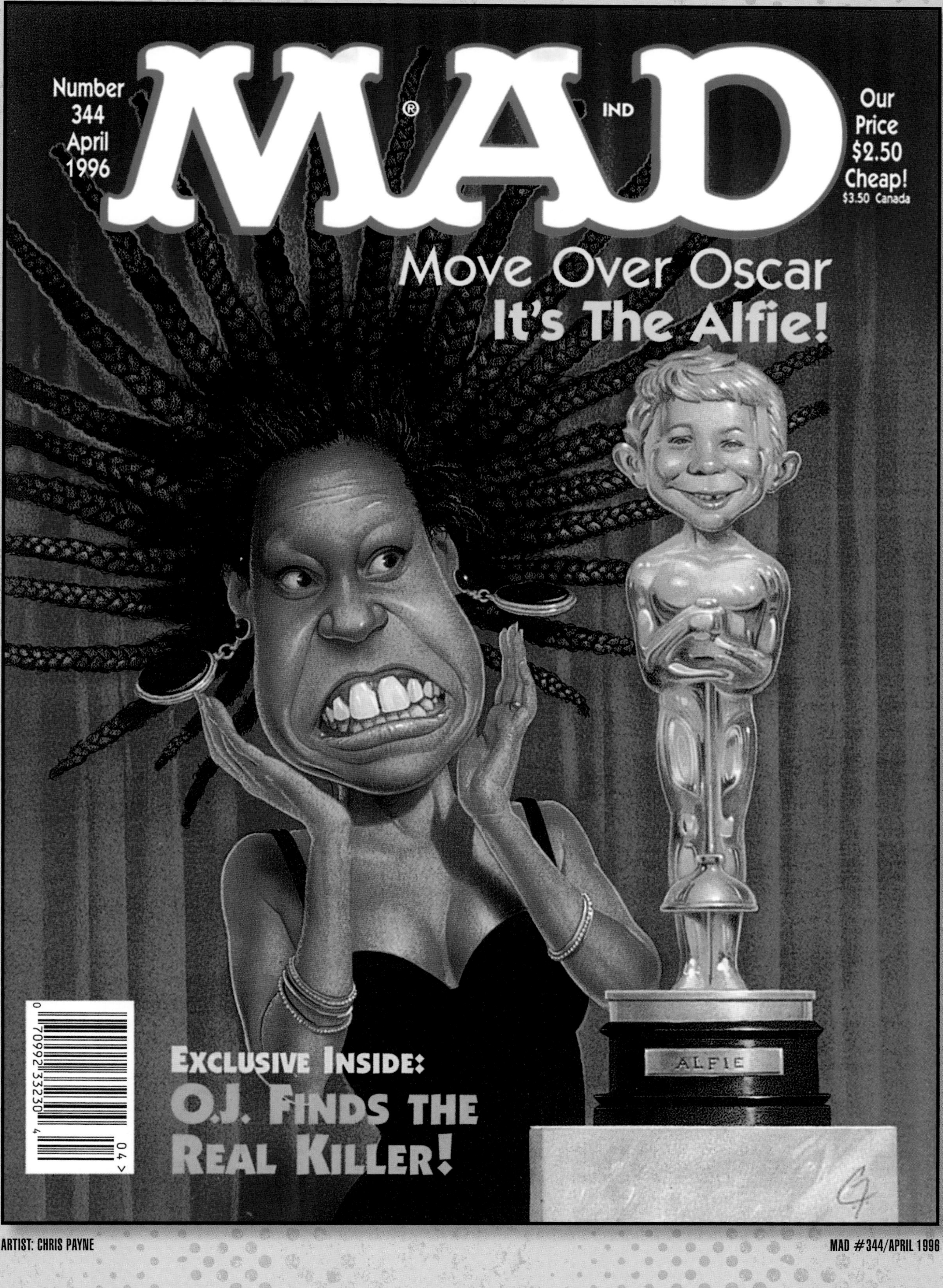
Number
344
April
1996
MAD®
IND
Our
Price
$2.50
Cheap!
$3.50 Canada
Move Over Oscar
It's The Alfie!
ALFIE
EXCLUSIVE INSIDE:
O.J. FINDS THE
REAL KILLER!

ARTIST: CHRIS PAYNE

MAD #344/APRIL 1996

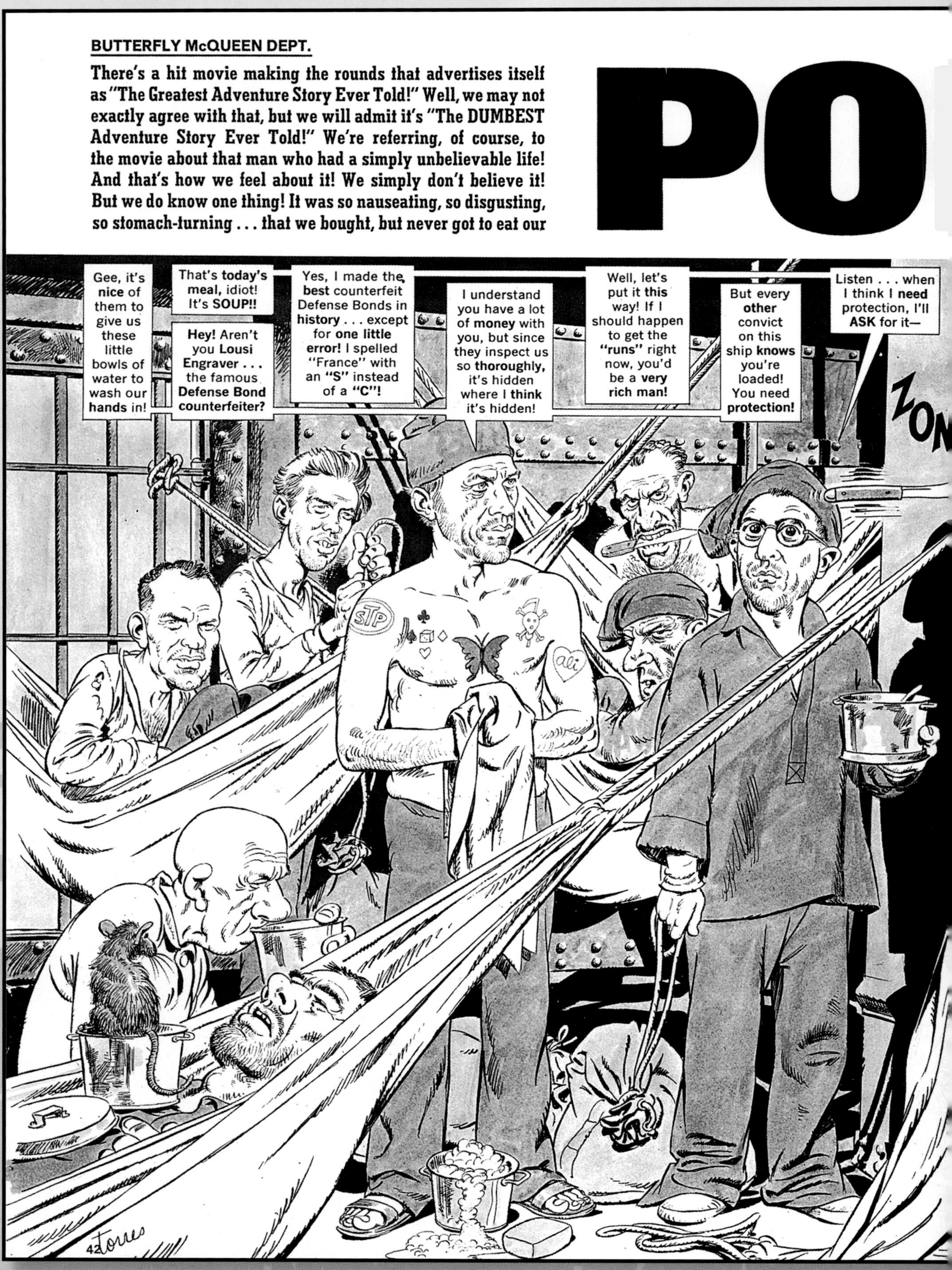

BUTTERFLY McQUEEN DEPT.
There's a hit movie making the rounds that advertises itself as "The Greatest Adventure Story Ever Told!" Well, we may not exactly agree with that, but we will admit it's "The DUMBEST Adventure Story Ever Told!" We're referring, of course, to the movie about that man who had a simply unbelievable life! And that's how we feel about it! We simply don't believe it! But we do know one thing! It was so nauseating, so disgusting, so stomach-turning . . . that we bought, but never got to eat our
PO
Gee, it's nice of them to give us these little bowls of water to wash our hands in!
That's today's meal, idiot! It's SOUP!!
Hey! Aren't you Lousi Engraver . . . the famous Defense Bond counterfeiter?
Yes, I made the best counterfeit Defense Bonds in history . . . except for one little error! I spelled "France" with an "S" instead of a "C"!
I understand you have a lot of money with you, but since they inspect us so thoroughly, it's hidden where I think it's hidden!
Well, let's put it this way! If I should happen to get the "runs" right now, you'd be a very rich man!
But every other convict on this ship knows you're loaded! You need protection!
Listen . . . when I think I need protection, I'll ASK for it—
ZON

by Angelo Torres
ARTIST

The second job I ever did for MAD Magazine was a movie. It was early in 1969 and I had just become the newest member of the Usual Gang of Idiots. I had never expected to get a movie to do so soon, if at all. I had been hired by MAD primarily to illustrate TV spoofs and whatever other assignments they felt I could handle. The movies were to be done by Mort Drucker, because, like James Bond, nobody did it better.

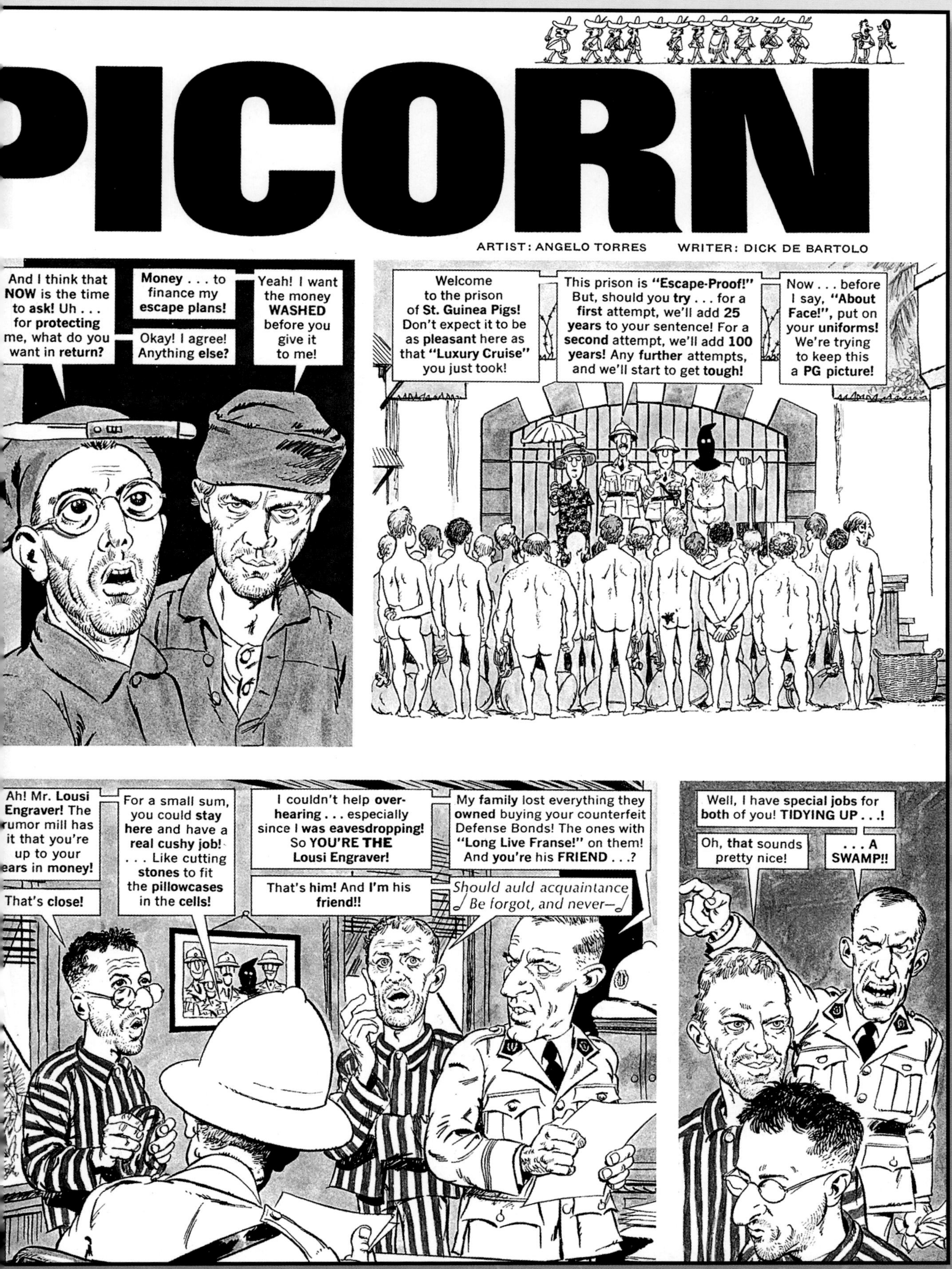

PICORN
ARTIST: ANGELO TORRES WRITER: DICK DE BARTOLO
And I think that NOW is the time to ask! Uh . . . for protecting me, what do you want in return?
Money . . . to finance my escape plans!
Okay! I agree! Anything else?
Yeah! I want the money WASHED before you give it to me!
Welcome to the prison of St. Guinea Pigs! Don't expect it to be as pleasant here as that "Luxury Cruise" you just took!
This prison is "Escape-Proof!" But, should you try . . . for a first attempt, we'll add 25 years to your sentence! For a second attempt, we'll add 100 years! Any further attempts, and we'll start to get tough!
Now . . . before I say, "About Face!", put on your uniforms! We're trying to keep this a PG picture!
Ah! Mr. Lousi Engraver! The rumor mill has it that you're up to your ears in money!
That's close!
For a small sum, you could stay here and have a real cushy job! . . . Like cutting stones to fit the pillowcases in the cells!
I couldn't help over-hearing . . . especially since I was eavesdropping! So YOU'RE THE Lousi Engraver!
That's him! And I'm his friend!!
My family lost everything they owned buying your counterfeit Defense Bonds! The ones with "Long Live Franse!" on them! And you're his FRIEND . . .?
Should auld acquaintance Be forgot, and never—
Well, I have special jobs for both of you! TIDYING UP . . .!
Oh, that sounds pretty nice!
. . . A SWAMP!!

MAD #170/OCTOBER 1974

During those first few years at MAD, I found myself doing one movie a year at best, and they were a welcome break from illustrating TV sitcoms and dramas — which were fun to do, but, let's face it, *Conan the Barbarian* they weren't (Don Martin would draw that one some years later).

So it was in 1974 when I got a call from MAD telling me to go see the movie *Papillon* — my next assignment. I had not yet seen the movie but was familiar with the story about

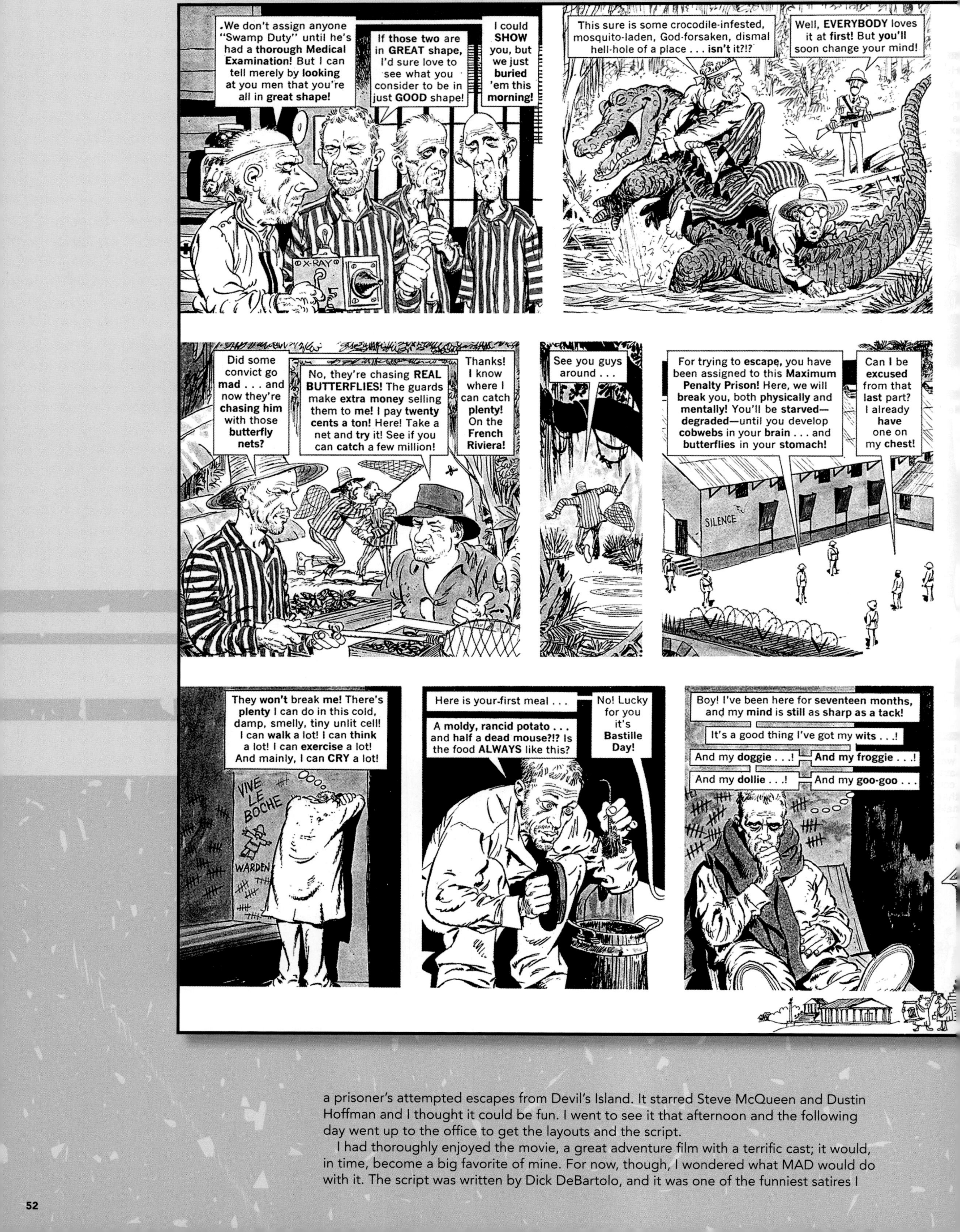
We don't assign anyone "Swamp Duty" until he's had a thorough Medical Examination! But I can tell merely by looking at you men that you're all in great shape!
If those two are in GREAT shape, I'd sure love to see what you consider to be in just GOOD shape!
I could SHOW you, but we just buried 'em this morning!
X-RAY
This sure is some crocodile-infested, mosquito-laden, God-forsaken, dismal hell-hole of a place . . . isn't it?!?
Well, EVERYBODY loves it at first! But you'll soon change your mind!
Did some convict go mad . . . and now they're chasing him with those butterfly nets?
No, they're chasing REAL BUTTERFLIES! The guards make extra money selling them to me! I pay twenty cents a ton! Here! Take a net and try it! See if you can catch a few million!
Thanks! I know where I can catch plenty! On the French Riviera!
See you guys around . . .
For trying to escape, you have been assigned to this Maximum Penalty Prison! Here, we will break you, both physically and mentally! You'll be starved—degraded—until you develop cobwebs in your brain . . . and butterflies in your stomach!
Can I be excused from that last part? I already have one on my chest!
SILENCE
They won't break me! There's plenty I can do in this cold, damp, smelly, tiny unlit cell! I can walk a lot! I can think a lot! I can exercise a lot! And mainly, I can CRY a lot!
VIVE LE BOCHE
WARDEN
Here is your first meal . . .
A moldy, rancid potato . . . and half a dead mouse?!? Is the food ALWAYS like this?
No! Lucky for you it's Bastille Day!
Boy! I've been here for seventeen months, and my mind is still as sharp as a tack!
It's a good thing I've got my wits . . .!
And my doggie . . .!
And my froggie . . .!
And my dollie . . .!
And my goo-goo . . .

a prisoner's attempted escapes from Devil's Island. It starred Steve McQueen and Dustin Hoffman and I thought it could be fun. I went to see it that afternoon and the following day went up to the office to get the layouts and the script.

I had thoroughly enjoyed the movie, a great adventure film with a terrific cast; it would, in time, become a big favorite of mine. For now, though, I wondered what MAD would do with it. The script was written by Dick DeBartolo, and it was one of the funniest satires I

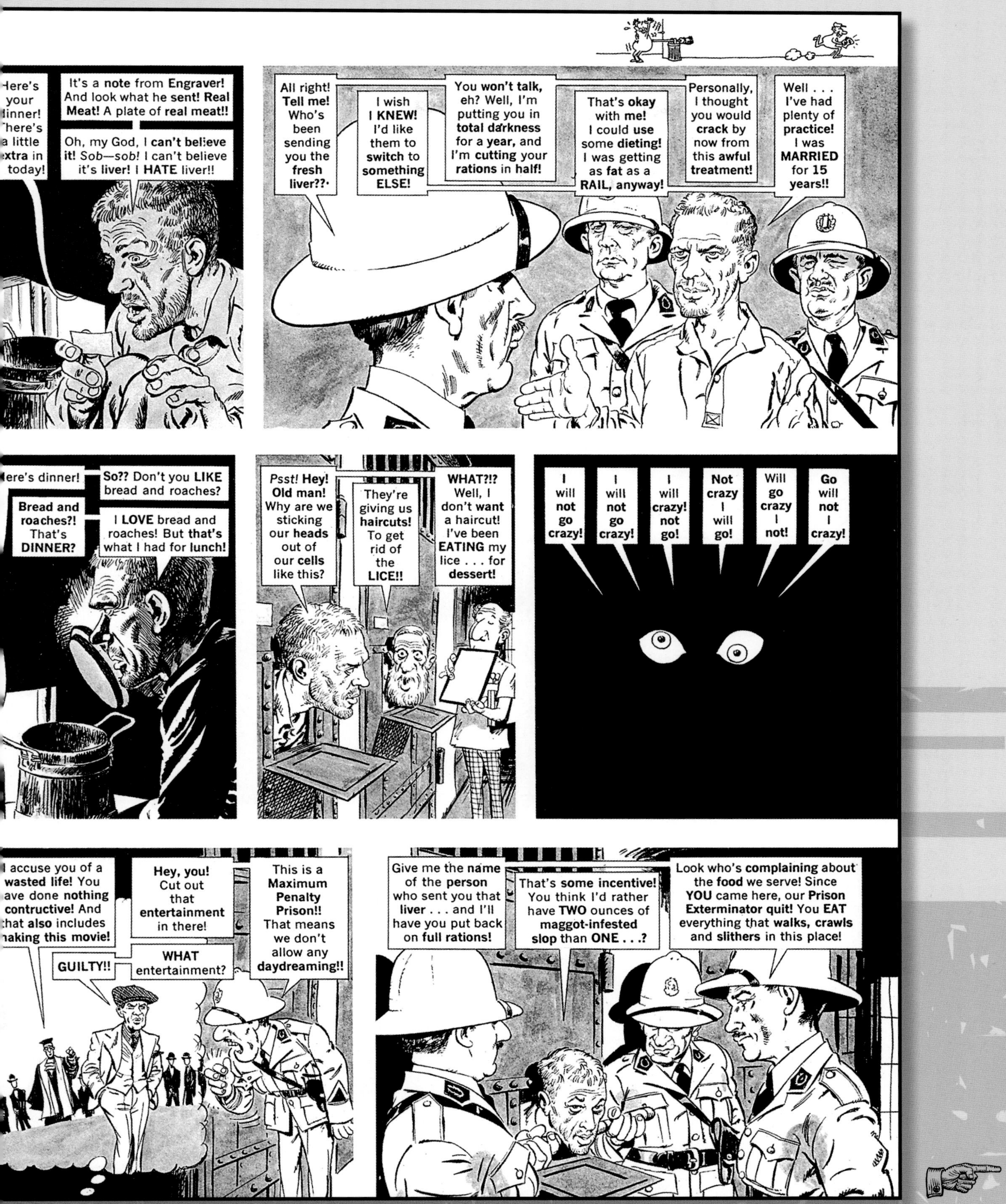

Here's your dinner! There's a little extra in today!
It's a note from Engraver! And look what he sent! Real Meat! A plate of real meat!!
Oh, my God, I can't believe it! Sob—sob! I can't believe it's liver! I HATE liver!!
All right! Tell me! Who's been sending you the fresh liver??
I wish I KNEW! I'd like them to switch to something ELSE!
You won't talk, eh? Well, I'm putting you in total darkness for a year, and I'm cutting your rations in half!
That's okay with me! I could use some dieting! I was getting as fat as a RAIL, anyway!
Personally, I thought you would crack by now from this awful treatment!
Well . . . I've had plenty of practice! I was MARRIED for 15 years!!
ere's dinner!
So?? Don't you LIKE bread and roaches?
Bread and roaches?! That's DINNER?
I LOVE bread and roaches! But that's what I had for lunch!
Psst! Hey! Old man! Why are we sticking our heads out of our cells like this?
They're giving us haircuts! To get rid of the LICE!!
WHAT?!? Well, I don't want a haircut! I've been EATING my lice . . . for dessert!
I will not go crazy!
I will not go crazy!
I will crazy! not go!
Not crazy I will go!
Will go crazy I not!
Go will not I crazy!
I accuse you of a wasted life! You ave done nothing contructive! And hat also includes naking this movie!
GUILTY!!
Hey, you! Cut out that entertainment in there!
WHAT entertainment?
This is a Maximum Penalty Prison!! That means we don't allow any daydreaming!!
Give me the name of the person who sent you that liver . . . and I'll have you put back on full rations!
That's some incentive! You think I'd rather have TWO ounces of maggot-infested slop than ONE . . .?
Look who's complaining about the food we serve! Since YOU came here, our Prison Exterminator quit! You EAT everything that walks, crawls and slithers in this place!

would ever do for MAD. When I read it, with the movie still fresh in my mind, I busted out laughing. The job called for me to draw filthy, ragged convicts, a vile prison run by sadistic guards, a leper colony, rotten teeth, vermin and a treacherous Mother Superior. I never had more fun with a story, thanks to Dick's outrageously funny script.

It was renamed "Popicorn," and after all these years and after the many movies and TV shows I would do later, it's still my all-time favorite MAD job.

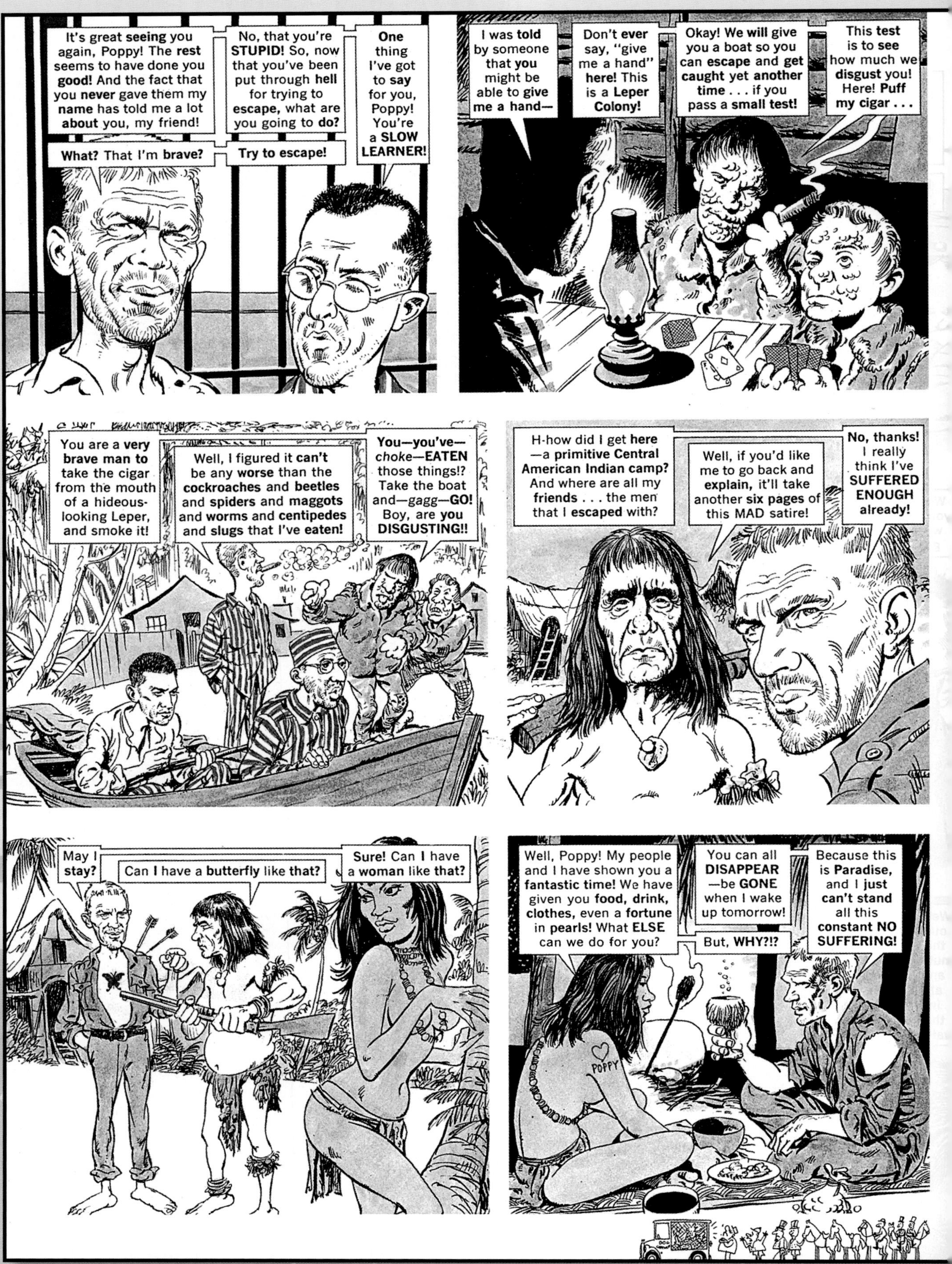
It's great seeing you again, Poppy! The rest seems to have done you good! And the fact that you never gave them my name has told me a lot about you, my friend!
What? That I'm brave?
No, that you're STUPID! So, now that you've been put through hell for trying to escape, what are you going to do?
Try to escape!
One thing I've got to say for you, Poppy! You're a SLOW LEARNER!
I was told by someone that you might be able to give me a hand—
Don't ever say, "give me a hand" here! This is a Leper Colony!
Okay! We will give you a boat so you can escape and get caught yet another time . . . if you pass a small test!
This test is to see how much we disgust you! Here! Puff my cigar . . .
You are a very brave man to take the cigar from the mouth of a hideous-looking Leper, and smoke it!
Well, I figured it can't be any worse than the cockroaches and beetles and spiders and maggots and worms and centipedes and slugs that I've eaten!
You—you've—choke—EATEN those things!? Take the boat and—gagg—GO! Boy, are you DISGUSTING!!
H-how did I get here—a primitive Central American Indian camp? And where are all my friends . . . the men that I escaped with?
Well, if you'd like me to go back and explain, it'll take another six pages of this MAD satire!
No, thanks! I really think I've SUFFERED ENOUGH already!
May I stay?
Can I have a butterfly like that?
Sure! Can I have a woman like that?
Well, Poppy! My people and I have shown you a fantastic time! We have given you food, drink, clothes, even a fortune in pearls! What ELSE can we do for you?
You can all DISAPPEAR—be GONE when I wake up tomorrow!
But, WHY?!?
Because this is Paradise, and I just can't stand all this constant NO SUFFERING!
POPPY

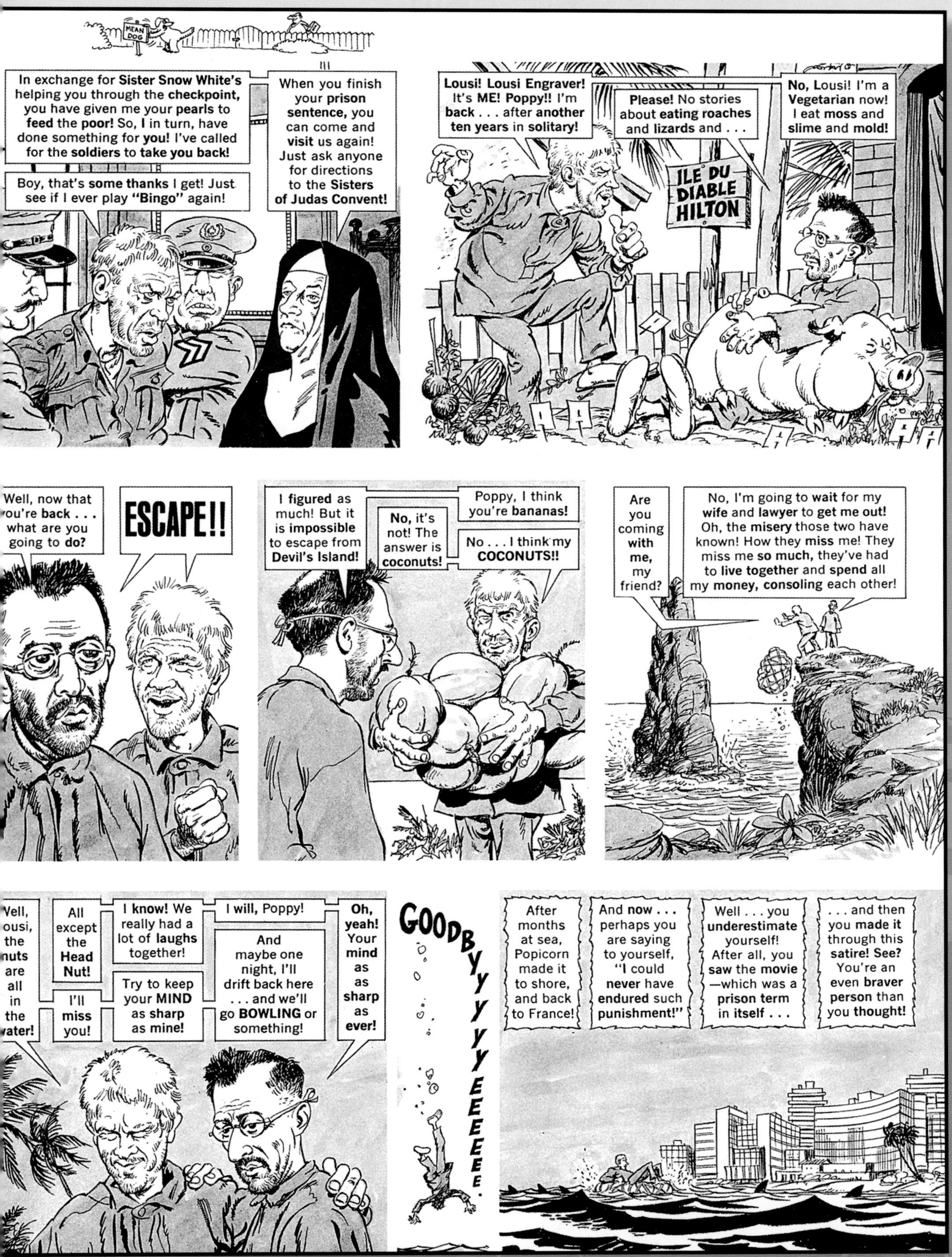

MEAN DOG
In exchange for Sister Snow White's helping you through the checkpoint, you have given me your pearls to feed the poor! So, I in turn, have done something for you! I've called for the soldiers to take you back!
Boy, that's some thanks I get! Just see if I ever play "Bingo" again!
When you finish your prison sentence, you can come and visit us again! Just ask anyone for directions to the Sisters of Judas Convent!
Lousi! Lousi Engraver! It's ME! Poppy!! I'm back . . . after another ten years in solitary!
Please! No stories about eating roaches and lizards and . . .
No, Lousi! I'm a Vegetarian now! I eat moss and slime and mold!
ILE DU DIABLE HILTON
Well, now that ou're back . . . what are you going to do?
ESCAPE!!
I figured as much! But it is impossible to escape from Devil's Island!
Poppy, I think you're bananas!
No, it's not! The answer is coconuts!
No . . . I think my COCONUTS!!
Are you coming with me, my friend?
No, I'm going to wait for my wife and lawyer to get me out! Oh, the misery those two have known! How they miss me! They miss me so much, they've had to live together and spend all my money, consoling each other!
Vell, ousi, the nuts are all in the vater!
All except the Head Nut!
I'll miss you!
I know! We really had a lot of laughs together!
Try to keep your MIND as sharp as mine!
I will, Poppy!
And maybe one night, I'll drift back here . . . and we'll go BOWLING or something!
Oh, yeah! Your mind as as sharp as ever!
GOODBYYYYYYEEEEEEE.
After months at sea, Popicorn made it to shore, and back to France!
And now . . . perhaps you are saying to yourself, "I could never have endured such punishment!"
Well . . . you underestimate yourself! After all, you saw the movie—which was a prison term in itself . . .
. . . and then you made it through this satire! See? You're an even braver person than you thought!

ZINGS TO COME DEPT.

A MAD LOO

Moment Before

KEEP OFF THE GRASS

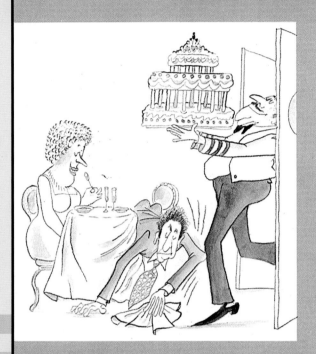

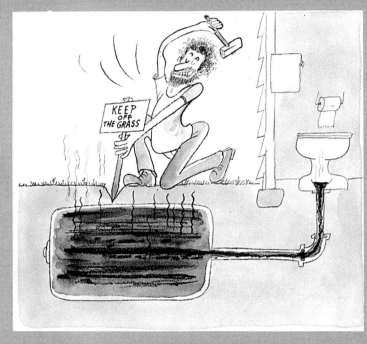

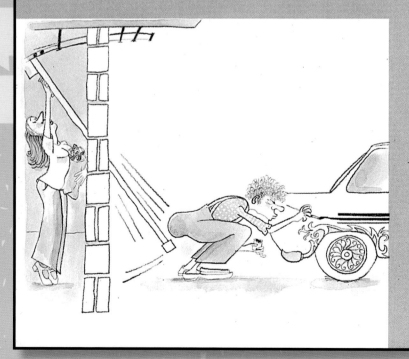

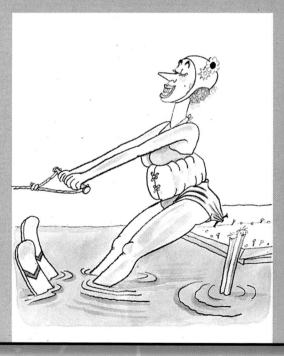

by Jacob Lambert
WRITER

I was nine years old when my father brought Super Special #60 (Fall 1987) home for me from the newsstand. It was my second issue — he'd bought me my first when I was home sick from school the previous month — and I was already becoming obsessed with this chaotic, vaguely dangerous-seeming magazine. It made the adult world seem absurd and hopeless in a joyful, mischievous way, and made me feel a part of some knowing secret society. I'd never experienced anything like it.

K AT THE
The Disaster

ARTIST & WRITER: PAUL PETER PORGES

MAD #200/JULY 1978

"A MAD Look at the Moment Before the Disaster" from that Super Special seemed to me a pure distillation of the gleefully bleak MAD outlook: panel after panel of impending doom, played out by a cast of mute grotesques, all for my amusement. Everything about those three pages was horrible — the situations, the sheer ugliness of the people trapped in them — yet I couldn't look away. I read it over and over, playing out the ensuing disasters — the aging hippie being pummeled by his tough-guy neighbor; the little boy being dragged off by his giant dog — in my mind: my own comical cinema of pain. Thanks, Mr. Porges. Thanks, Dad.

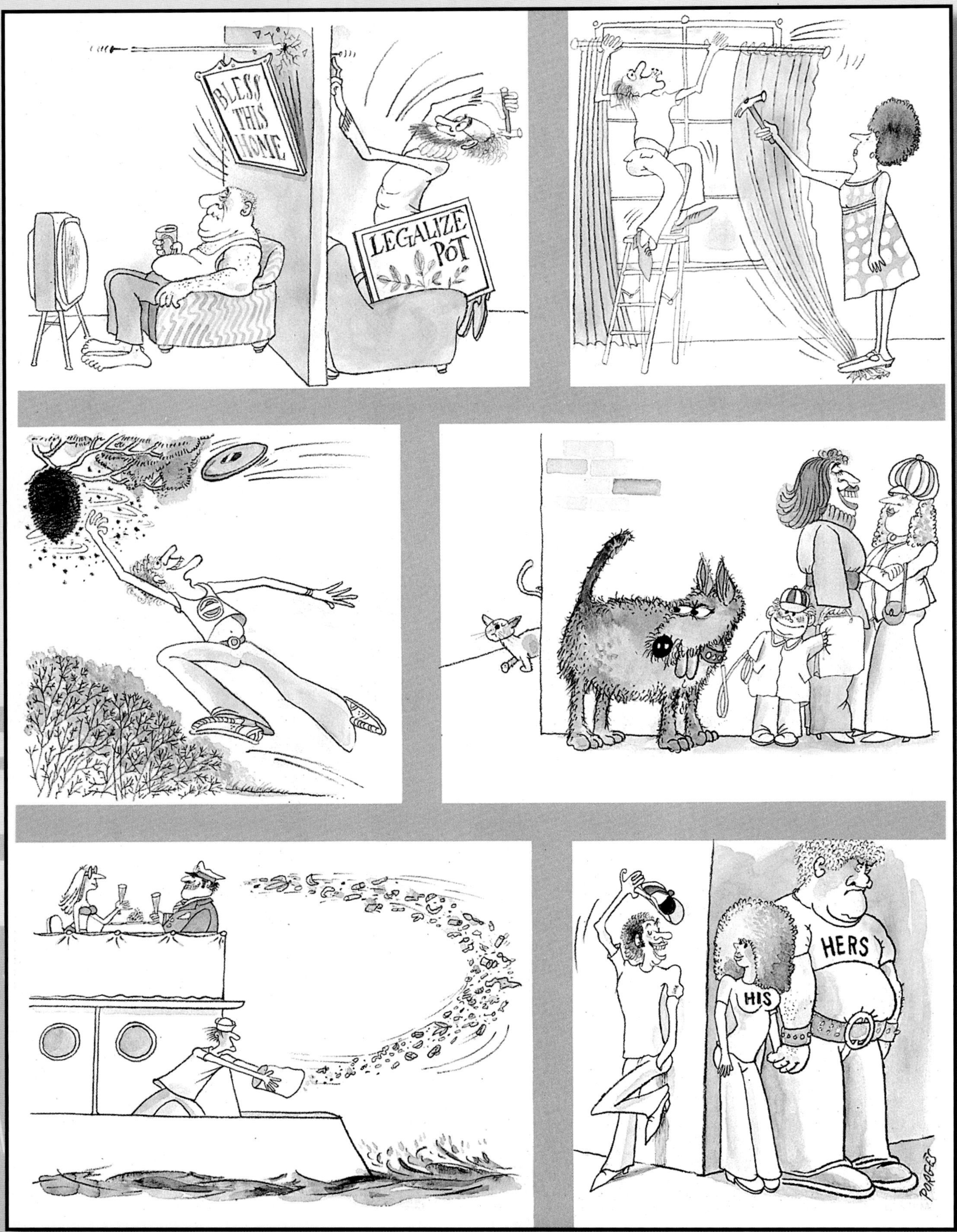
BLESS THIS HOME
LEGALIZE POT
HIS
HERS
PORGES

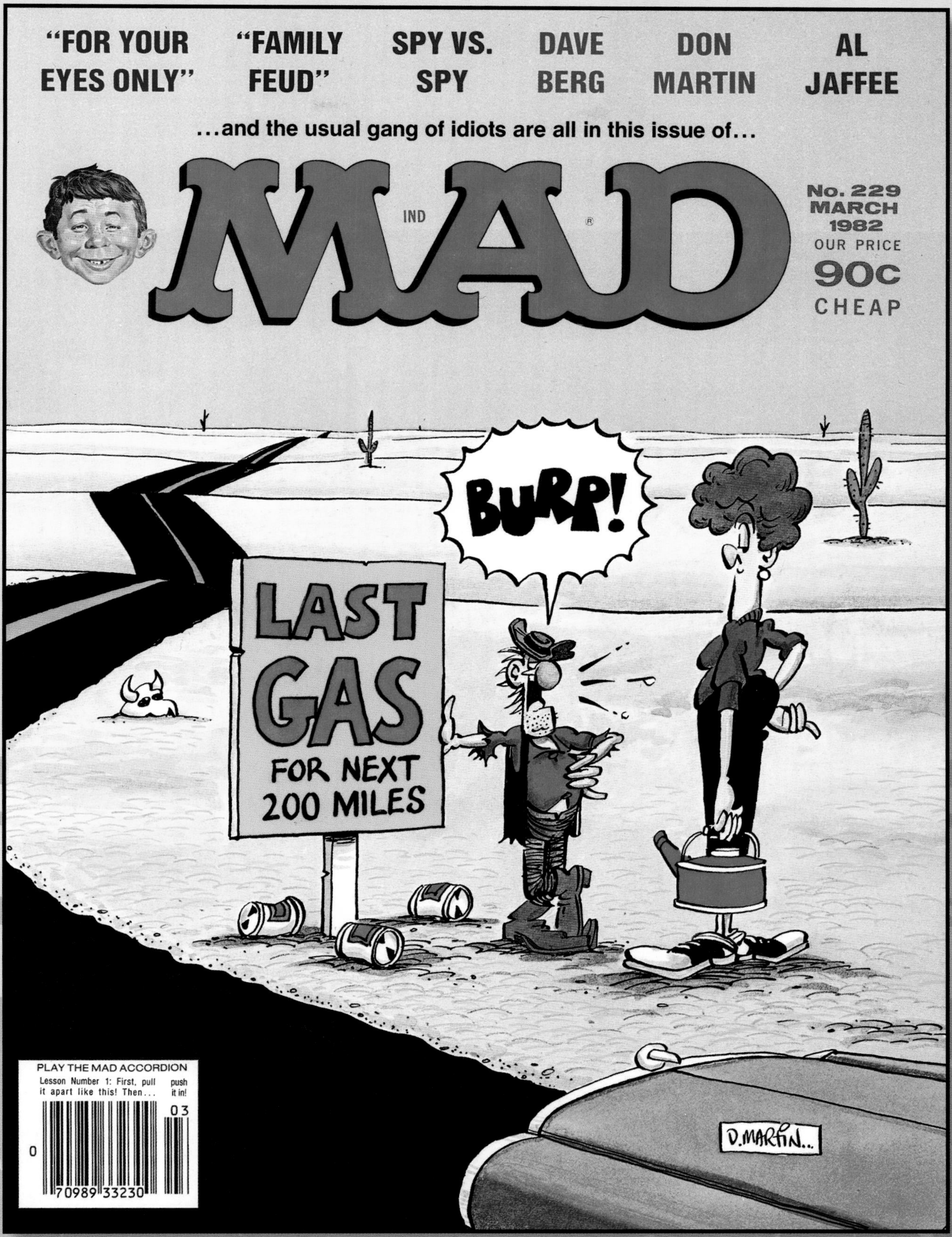
"FOR YOUR EYES ONLY"
"FAMILY FEUD"
SPY VS. SPY
DAVE BERG
DON MARTIN
AL JAFFEE
...and the usual gang of idiots are all in this issue of...
MAD
IND
No. 229 MARCH 1982
OUR PRICE 90c CHEAP
BURP!
LAST GAS FOR NEXT 200 MILES
PLAY THE MAD ACCORDION
Lesson Number 1: First, pull it apart like this! Then... push it in!
D.MARTIN..

ARTIST: DON MARTIN

MAD #229/MARCH 1982

by Kit Lively
WRITER/ARTIST

The cover of MAD #229 from March of 1982 is not only a great Don Martin gag, but also something of substantial sentimental value to me. As a teen — and like most MAD Magazine contributors, I suspect — I didn't have any friends. And certainly no girlfriend. When prom rolled around, my first impulse was to simply skip it. But a rare case of gumption took over, and I decided to go with my head held high, a copy of MAD Magazine on my arm. I selected issue #229 due to the fact that I was at the time unsure of my sexual preference, and the cover featured both a man and a woman. After a magical, whirlwind evening, the MAD and I found ourselves a nice room at the Holiday Inn. We were finally alone, and I was able to do the Fold-In, something I'd been aching to do all night. And even though I haven't seen this particular copy in years, and I'm sure many others have done the Fold-In since, I'll always know that I was the first.

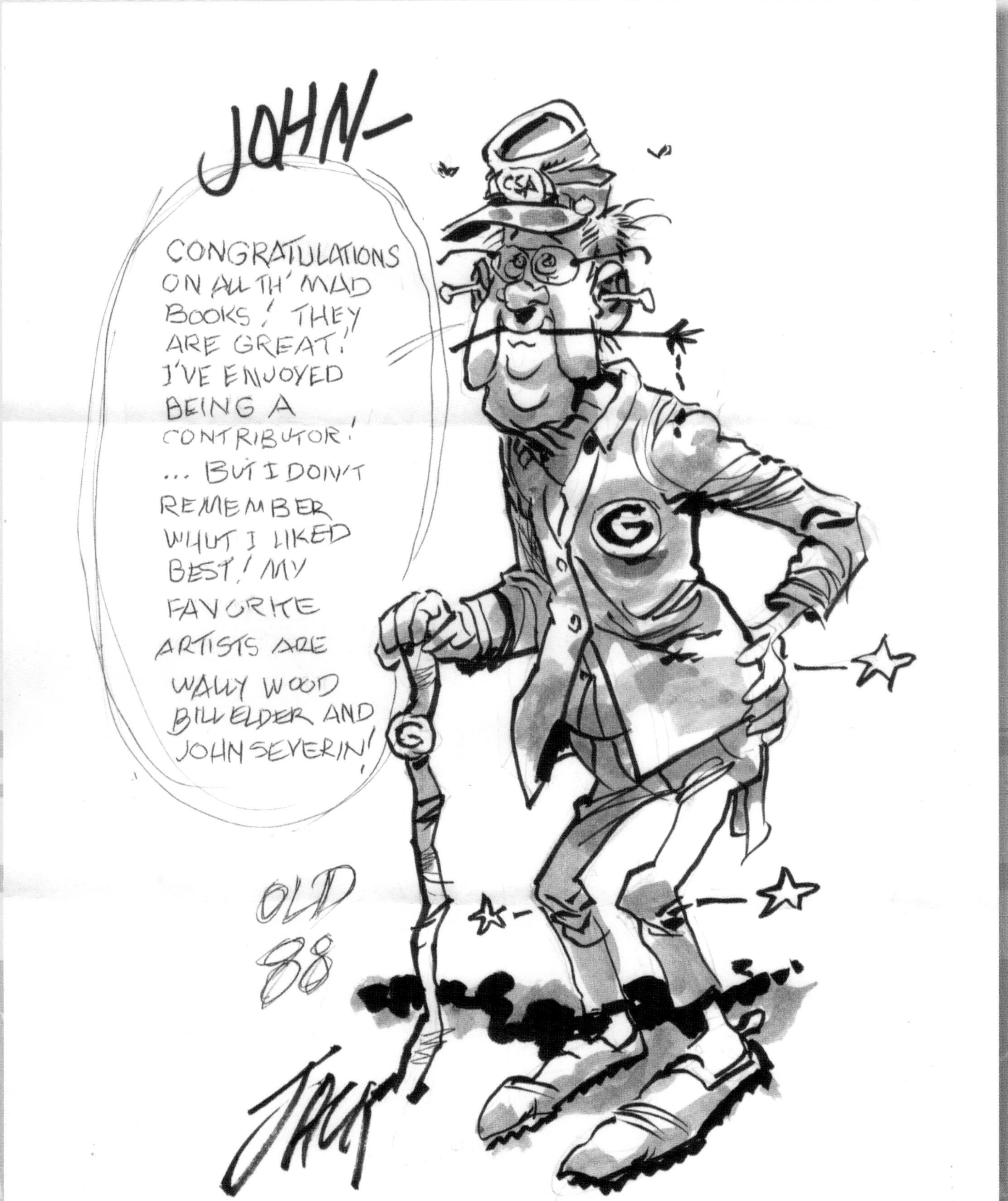
JOHN-
CONGRATULATIONS ON ALL TH' MAD BOOKS! THEY ARE GREAT! I'VE ENJOYED BEING A CONTRIBUTOR! ... BUT I DON'T REMEMBER WHUT I LIKED BEST! MY FAVORITE ARTISTS ARE WALLY WOOD BILL ELDER AND JOHN SEVERIN!
CSA
G
OLD 88
JACK

by Jack Davis
ARTIST

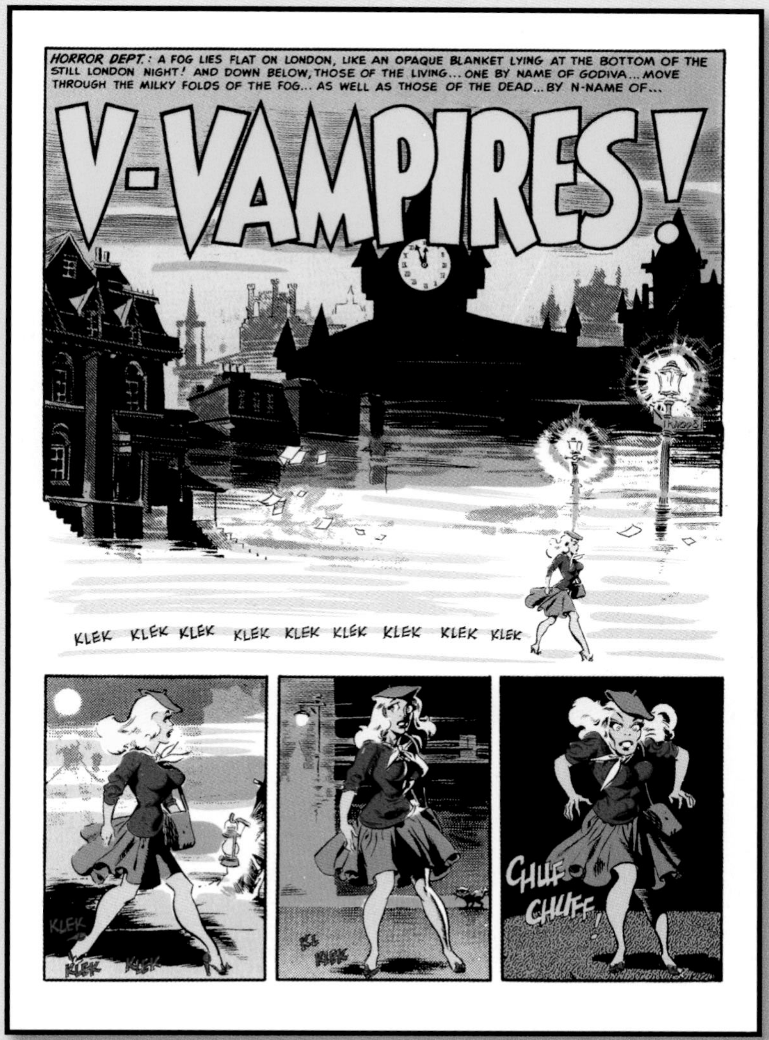
HORROR DEPT.: A FOG LIES FLAT ON LONDON, LIKE AN OPAQUE BLANKET LYING AT THE BOTTOM OF THE STILL LONDON NIGHT! AND DOWN BELOW, THOSE OF THE LIVING... ONE BY NAME OF GODIVA... MOVE THROUGH THE MILKY FOLDS OF THE FOG... AS WELL AS THOSE OF THE DEAD... BY N-NAME OF...
V-VAMPIRES!
KLEK KLEK KLEK KLEK KLEK KLEK KLEK KLEK KLEK
KLEK
KLEK KLEK
KLEK
CHUF CHUFF

ARTIST: WALLY WOOD MAD #3/JANUARY-FEBRUARY 1953

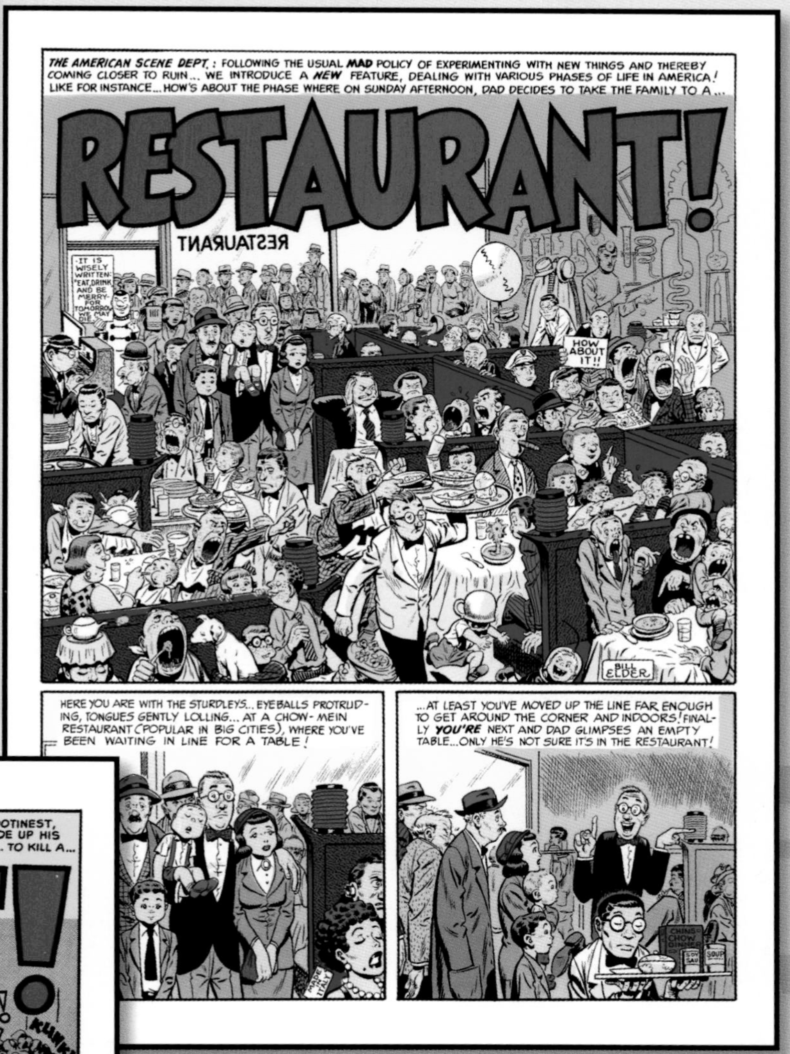
THE AMERICAN SCENE DEPT.: FOLLOWING THE USUAL MAD POLICY OF EXPERIMENTING WITH NEW THINGS AND THEREBY COMING CLOSER TO RUIN... WE INTRODUCE A NEW FEATURE, DEALING WITH VARIOUS PHASES OF LIFE IN AMERICA! LIKE FOR INSTANCE... HOW'S ABOUT THE PHASE WHERE ON SUNDAY AFTERNOON, DAD DECIDES TO TAKE THE FAMILY TO A...
RESTAURANT!
RESTAURANT
HOW ABOUT IT!!
BILL ELDER
HERE YOU ARE WITH THE STURDLEYS... EYEBALLS PROTRUDING, TONGUES GENTLY LOLLING... AT A CHOW-MEIN RESTAURANT (POPULAR IN BIG CITIES), WHERE YOU'VE BEEN WAITING IN LINE FOR A TABLE!
...AT LEAST YOU'VE MOVED UP THE LINE FAR ENOUGH TO GET AROUND THE CORNER AND INDOORS! FINALLY YOU'RE NEXT AND DAD GLIMPSES AN EMPTY TABLE... ONLY HE'S NOT SURE IT'S IN THE RESTAURANT!

ARTIST: BILL ELDER MAD #16/OCTOBER 1954

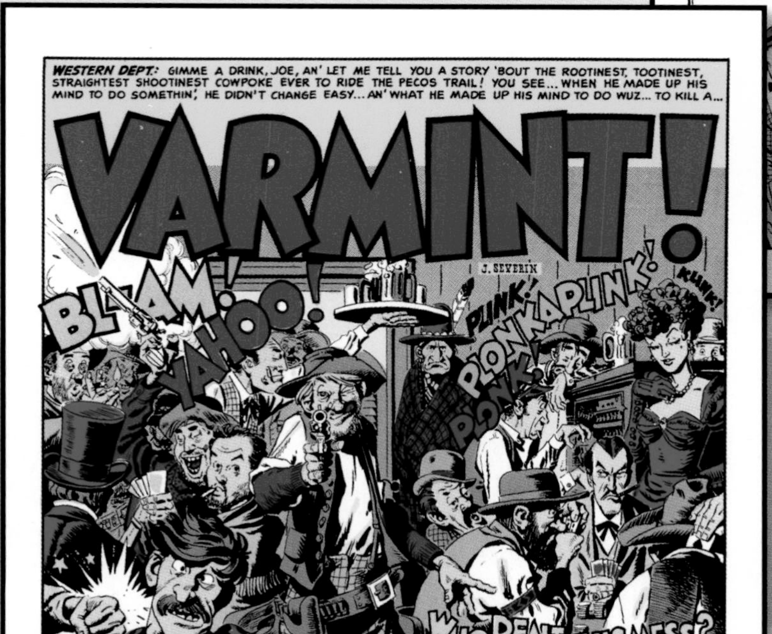
WESTERN DEPT.: GIMME A DRINK, JOE, AN' LET ME TELL YOU A STORY 'BOUT THE ROOTINEST, TOOTINEST, STRAIGHTEST SHOOTINEST COWPOKE EVER TO RIDE THE PECOS TRAIL! YOU SEE... WHEN HE MADE UP HIS MIND TO DO SOMETHIN' HE DIDN'T CHANGE EASY... AN' WHAT HE MADE UP HIS MIND TO DO WUZ... TO KILL A...
VARMINT!
J. SEVERIN
BLAM!
YAHOO!
PLINK! PLONKAPLINK!
KLUNK!
WHO DEALT THIS MESS?
SWE HAW HAW! -DADA LINE
PLINKAPLINK
YAHOO!
PLINK! PLINK!
BLAM!
MYAD-DALINE!
WHOHA! YIIII HA!
POW!
PLINK-PLINK!
BLONGABLONG PLINK!

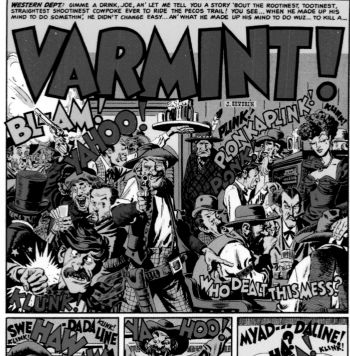

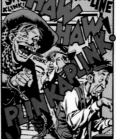

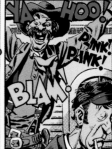

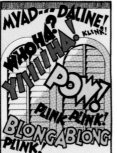

ARTIST: JOHN SEVERIN MAD #1/OCTOBER-NOVEMBER 1952

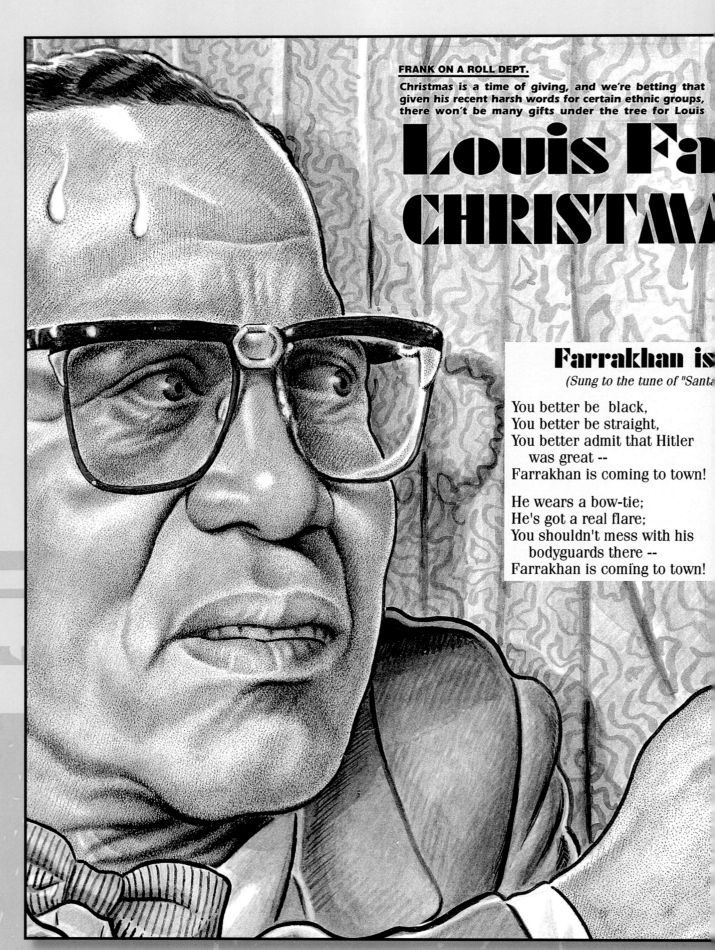

Christmas is a time of giving, and we're betting that given his recent harsh words for certain ethnic groups, there won't be many gifts under the tree for Louis

Louis Fa
CHRISTMA

Farrakhan is

(Sung to the tune of "Santa

You better be black,
You better be straight,
You better admit that Hitler
    was great --
Farrakhan is coming to town!

He wears a bow-tie;
He's got a real flare;
You shouldn't mess with his
    bodyguards there --
Farrakhan is coming to town!

by Drew Friedman
ARTIST

ick my favorite MAD article? That's like asking me to pick my favorite Jerry Lewis movie...or my favorite Wayne Newton song. Impossible! Oh all right... *The Big Mouth* and "Danke Schoen." Happy?
Still..."Louis Farrakhan Christmas Carols" looms pretty large...very large... OK, largest. This was the fourth piece I illustrated for MAD, and if my early MAD contributions were perhaps a bit tentative, it was no doubt due to my still feeling somewhat in awe that my art was actually being published alongside my heroes —

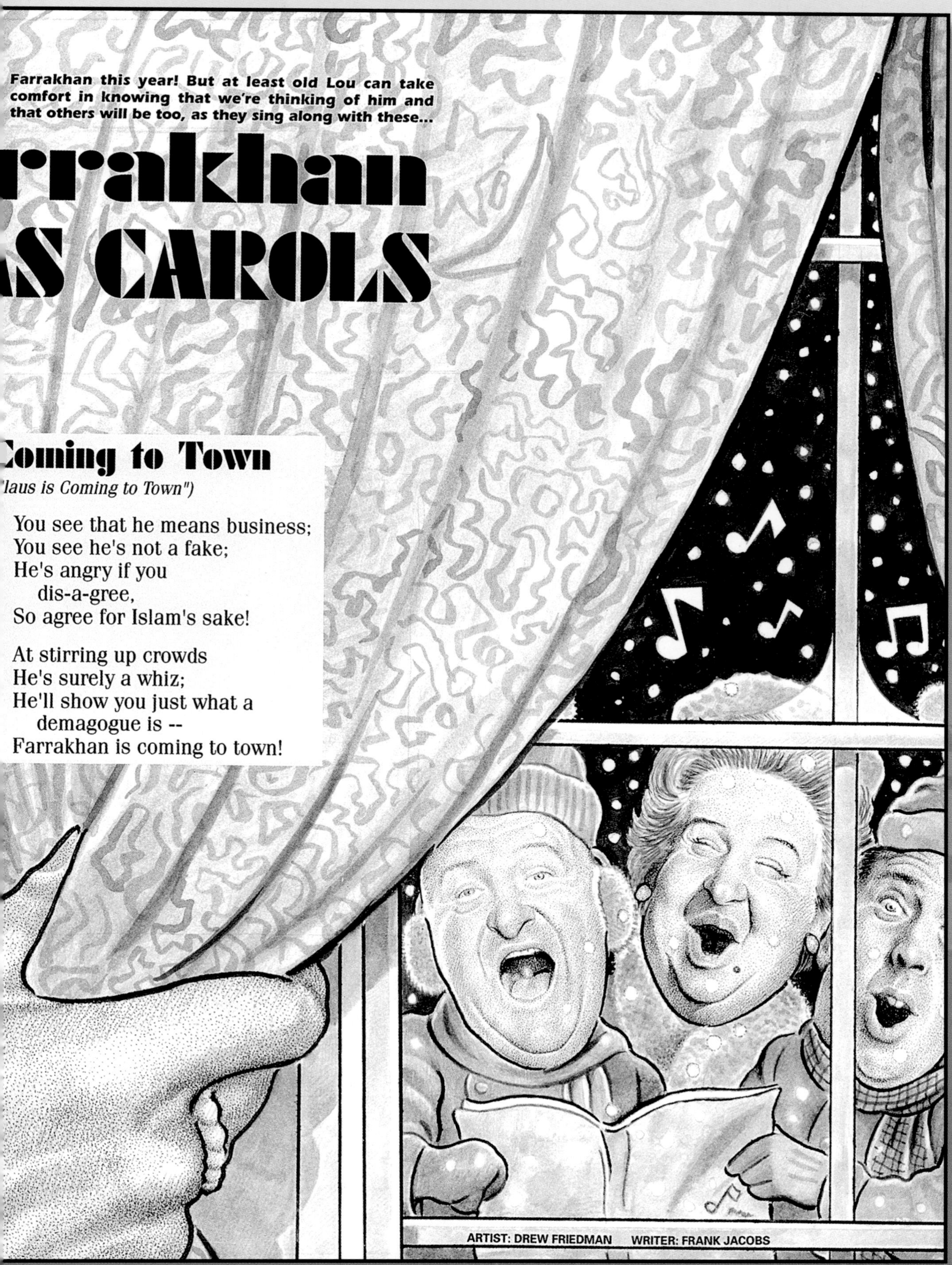
Farrakhan this year! But at least old Lou can take comfort in knowing that we're thinking of him and that others will be too, as they sing along with these...
rrakhan
AS CAROLS
Coming to Town
'laus is Coming to Town")
You see that he means business;
You see he's not a fake;
He's angry if you
dis-a-gree,
So agree for Islam's sake!
At stirring up crowds
He's surely a whiz;
He'll show you just what a
demagogue is --
Farrakhan is coming to town!
ARTIST: DREW FRIEDMAN WRITER: FRANK JACOBS

MAD #332/DECEMBER 1994

legends like Al Jaffee...Dave Berg...Mort Drucker...Andrew J. Schwartzberg...the "Usual Gang of Idiots." Was I really worthy to join such a gang?

Then I was assigned "Louis Farrakhan Christmas Carols," written by the MAD poet laureate Frank Jacobs. Oy vey, what to do? This: I calmed myself down, showered, had a Tofu Pup, and decided to rise to the occasion and create artwork that would (hopefully) compliment the piece and well-serve the brilliant "Jacobs-ian" Christmas/ Farrakhan song parodies. I think I succeeded. Validation came when I was told that

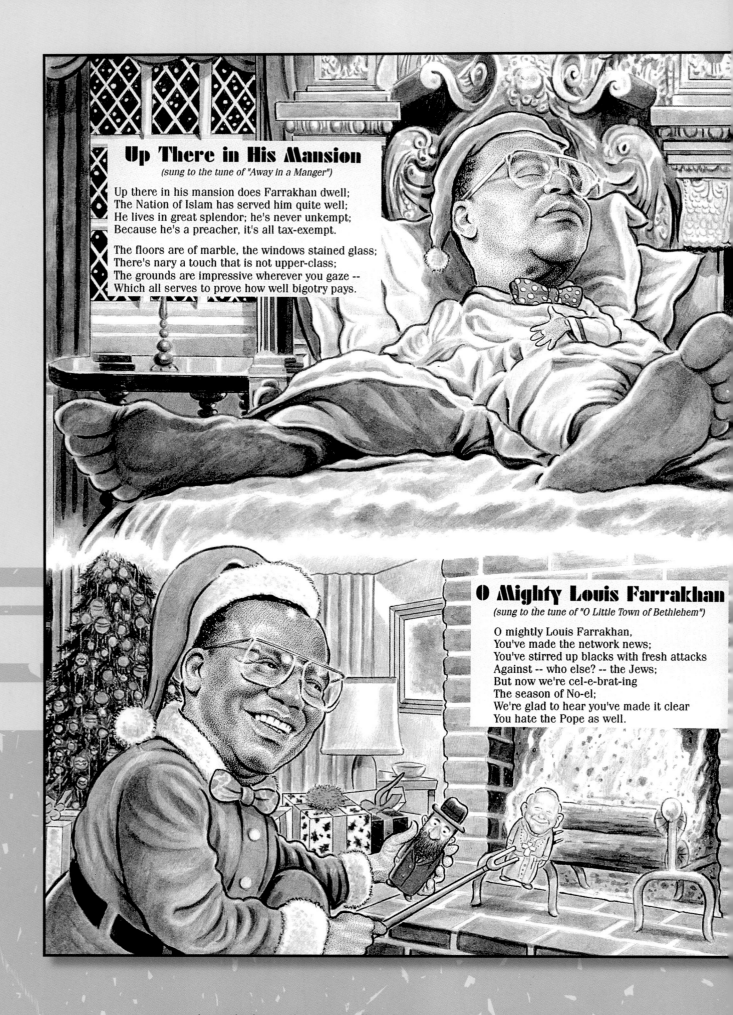

Up There in His Mansion
(sung to the tune of "Away in a Manger")

Up there in his mansion does Farrakhan dwell;
The Nation of Islam has served him quite well;
He lives in great splendor; he's never unkempt;
Because he's a preacher, it's all tax-exempt.

The floors are of marble, the windows stained glass;
There's nary a touch that is not upper-class;
The grounds are impressive wherever you gaze --
Which all serves to prove how well bigotry pays.

O Mighty Louis Farrakhan
(sung to the tune of "O Little Town of Bethlehem")

O mightly Louis Farrakhan,
You've made the network news;
You've stirred up blacks with fresh attacks
Against -- who else? -- the Jews;
But now we're cel-e-brat-ing
The season of No-el;
We're glad to hear you've made it clear
You hate the Pope as well.

angry letters had arrived at MAD's offices from several Nation of Islam members condemning Mr. Jacobs and myself — one stating that we would both surely "Burn in Hell" for mocking their leader, the honorable (Jew-baiter) Minister Farrakhan. Hearing this really didn't bother me much, though — mainly because I was delighted to learn that even members of the Nation of Islam read MAD.

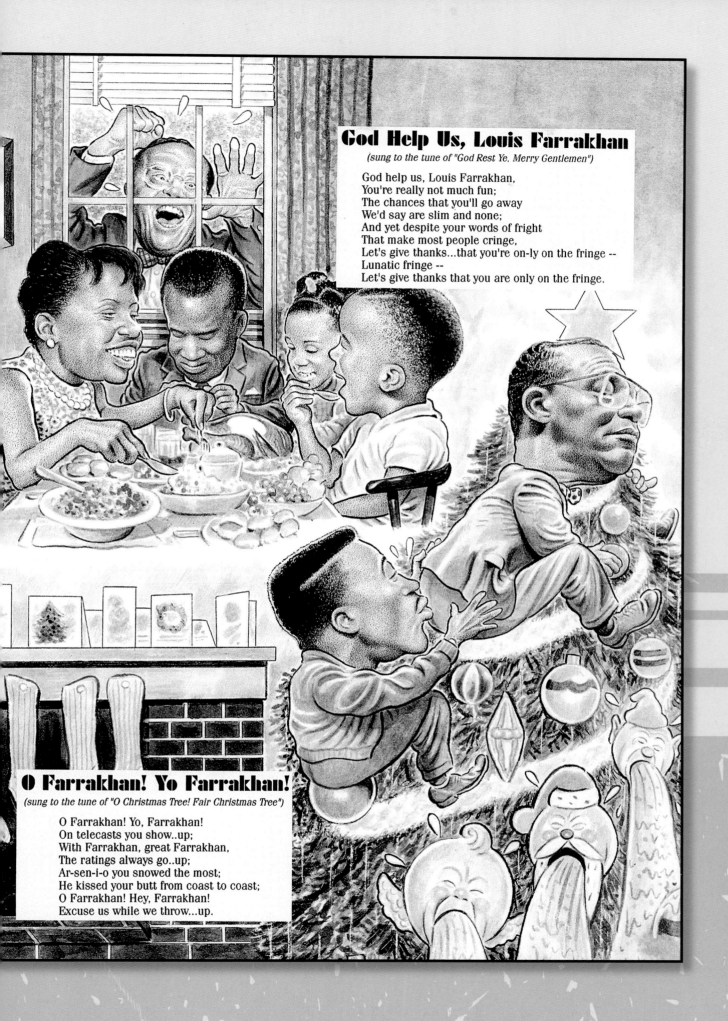

God Help Us, Louis Farrakhan

(sung to the tune of "God Rest Ye, Merry Gentlemen")

God help us, Louis Farrakhan,
You're really not much fun;
The chances that you'll go away
We'd say are slim and none;
And yet despite your words of fright
That make most people cringe,
Let's give thanks...that you're on-ly on the fringe --
Lunatic fringe --
Let's give thanks that you are only on the fringe.

O Farrakhan! Yo Farrakhan!

(sung to the tune of "O Christmas Tree! Fair Christmas Tree")

O Farrakhan! Yo, Farrakhan!
On telecasts you show..up;
With Farrakhan, great Farrakhan,
The ratings always go..up;
Ar-sen-i-o you snowed the most;
He kissed your butt from coast to coast;
O Farrakhan! Hey, Farrakhan!
Excuse us while we throw...up.

When I was a young boy, protected from the ways of this cruel world, seeking out what's mine, I quickly discovered and started to collect MAD Magazine. I kept them tucked underneath my mattress. At night I would rifle through the pages and wonder who was behind all of this scattered dumb insanity. It bothered me that it existed because in some ways it seemed to just rip people apart unnecessarily without due diligence. You were chosen, convicted and sentenced by a jury of who?

MAD Magazine was the drunk uncle of my home. It walked in with its pants down, danced in front of your best friends, spilled something stain-related on the new rug and then blamed you. It made me cringe for years until I finally understood why I had this love/loathe relationship with it. I believed that someday MAD would pounce on me. I would be tried by a jury of no one and my mug shot would appear on its cover with that weird looking freak Alfred E. Neuman. As I got older and more recognized for my contributions to the creative arts society (haha) it dawned on me that the monster under my bed would be coming for me soon. Yup, some young aspiring nobodies dream of winning an Oscar, but I was mulling over the idea of being discovered inside the pages of this well-crafted, beautifully illustrated drivel.

Dane Cook

MAD Magazine was the drunk uncle of my home.

Then it happened. Wednesday, February 21st, 2007. My big head staring right back at me from what I thought must be a fake mock-up version of MAD.
I was overjoyed and also weirded out. It signaled my arrival to success and my departure from respect. Wow. Wow. Sh*t.

I've never opened the pages of my issue. I won't look. I know what lurks in there and it ain't good. My issue of MAD Magazine (damn that's wild to write and read back aloud) is sealed shut forever. Laminated not to preserve its shiny coat but to lock away the demons that dwell somewhere in between my doppelgänger and the Fold-In.

It's tucked underneath my mattress* where it will remain forever.

*It's not actually underneath my mattress. I just thought that sounded cooler. I think it's in storage or was stolen by some workers that I hired to refinish my floors.

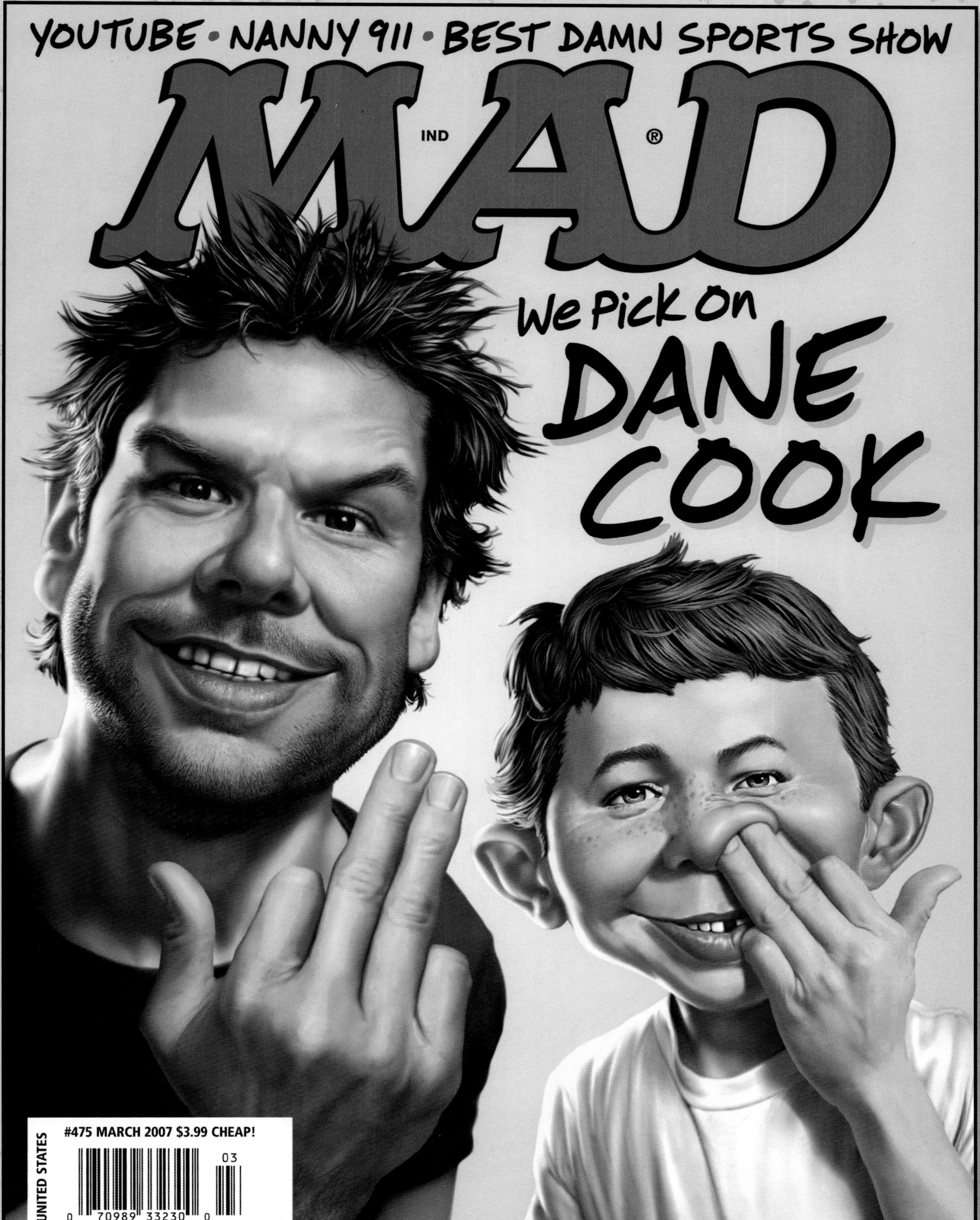
YOUTUBE • NANNY 911 • BEST DAMN SPORTS SHOW
MAD
IND
We Pick On
DANE
COOK
#475 MARCH 2007 $3.99 CHEAP!
UNITED STATES
madmag.com

ARTIST: MARK FREDRICKSON

MAD #475/MARCH 2007

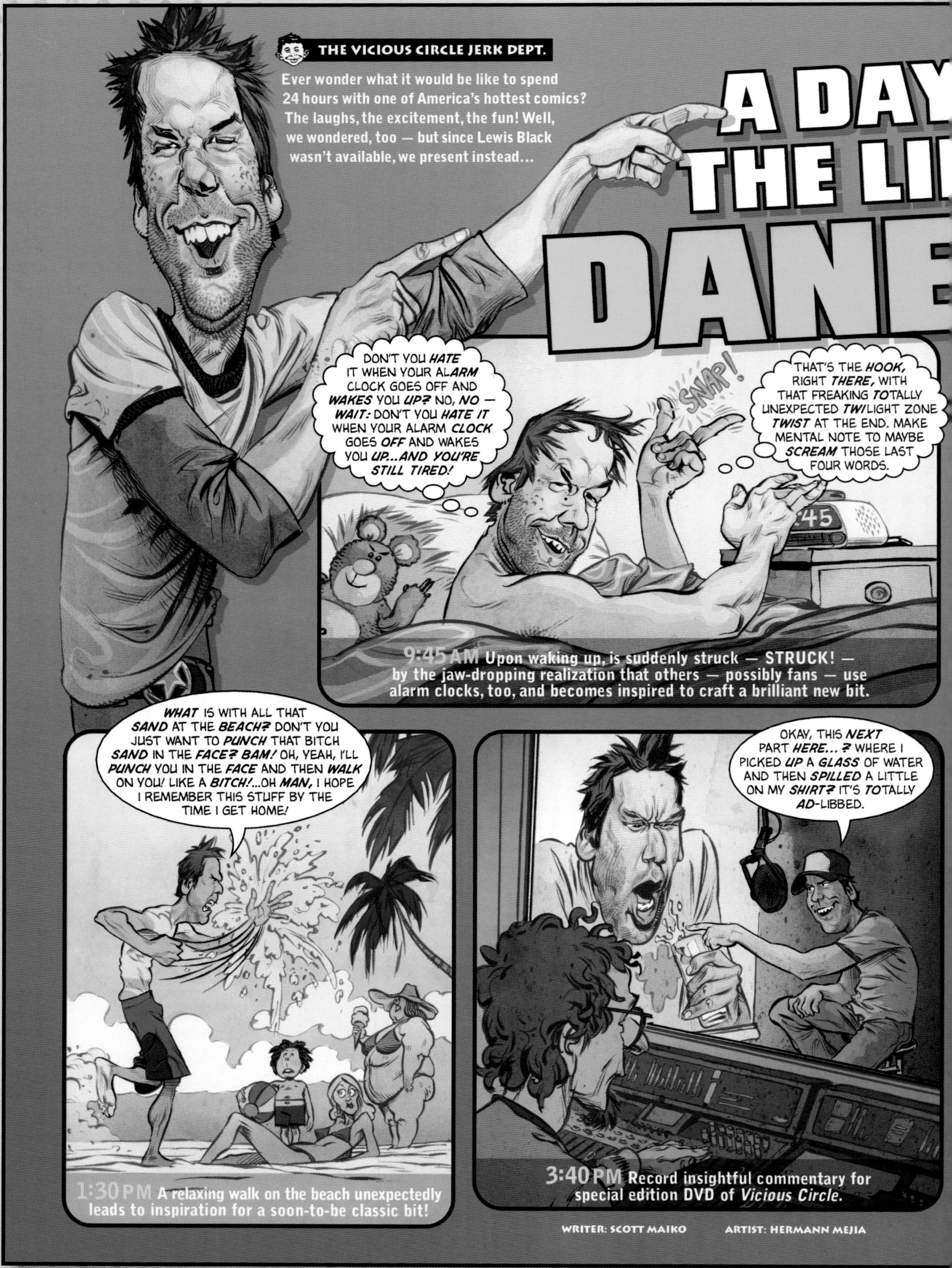
THE VICIOUS CIRCLE JERK DEPT.
Ever wonder what it would be like to spend 24 hours with one of America's hottest comics? The laughs, the excitement, the fun! Well, we wondered, too — but since Lewis Black wasn't available, we present instead...
A DAY THE LI DANE
DON'T YOU HATE IT WHEN YOUR ALARM CLOCK GOES OFF AND WAKES YOU UP? NO, NO — WAIT: DON'T YOU HATE IT WHEN YOUR ALARM CLOCK GOES OFF AND WAKES YOU UP...AND YOU'RE STILL TIRED!
SNAP!
THAT'S THE HOOK, RIGHT THERE, WITH THAT FREAKING TOTALLY UNEXPECTED TWILIGHT ZONE TWIST AT THE END. MAKE MENTAL NOTE TO MAYBE SCREAM THOSE LAST FOUR WORDS.
9:45 AM Upon waking up, is suddenly struck — STRUCK! — by the jaw-dropping realization that others — possibly fans — use alarm clocks, too, and becomes inspired to craft a brilliant new bit.
WHAT IS WITH ALL THAT SAND AT THE BEACH? DON'T YOU JUST WANT TO PUNCH THAT BITCH SAND IN THE FACE? BAM! OH, YEAH, I'LL PUNCH YOU IN THE FACE AND THEN WALK ON YOU! LIKE A BITCH!...OH MAN, I HOPE I REMEMBER THIS STUFF BY THE TIME I GET HOME!
1:30 PM A relaxing walk on the beach unexpectedly leads to inspiration for a soon-to-be classic bit!
OKAY, THIS NEXT PART HERE...? WHERE I PICKED UP A GLASS OF WATER AND THEN SPILLED A LITTLE ON MY SHIRT? IT'S TOTALLY AD-LIBBED.
3:40 PM Record insightful commentary for special edition DVD of Vicious Circle.
WRITER: SCOTT MAIKO
ARTIST: HERMANN MEJIA

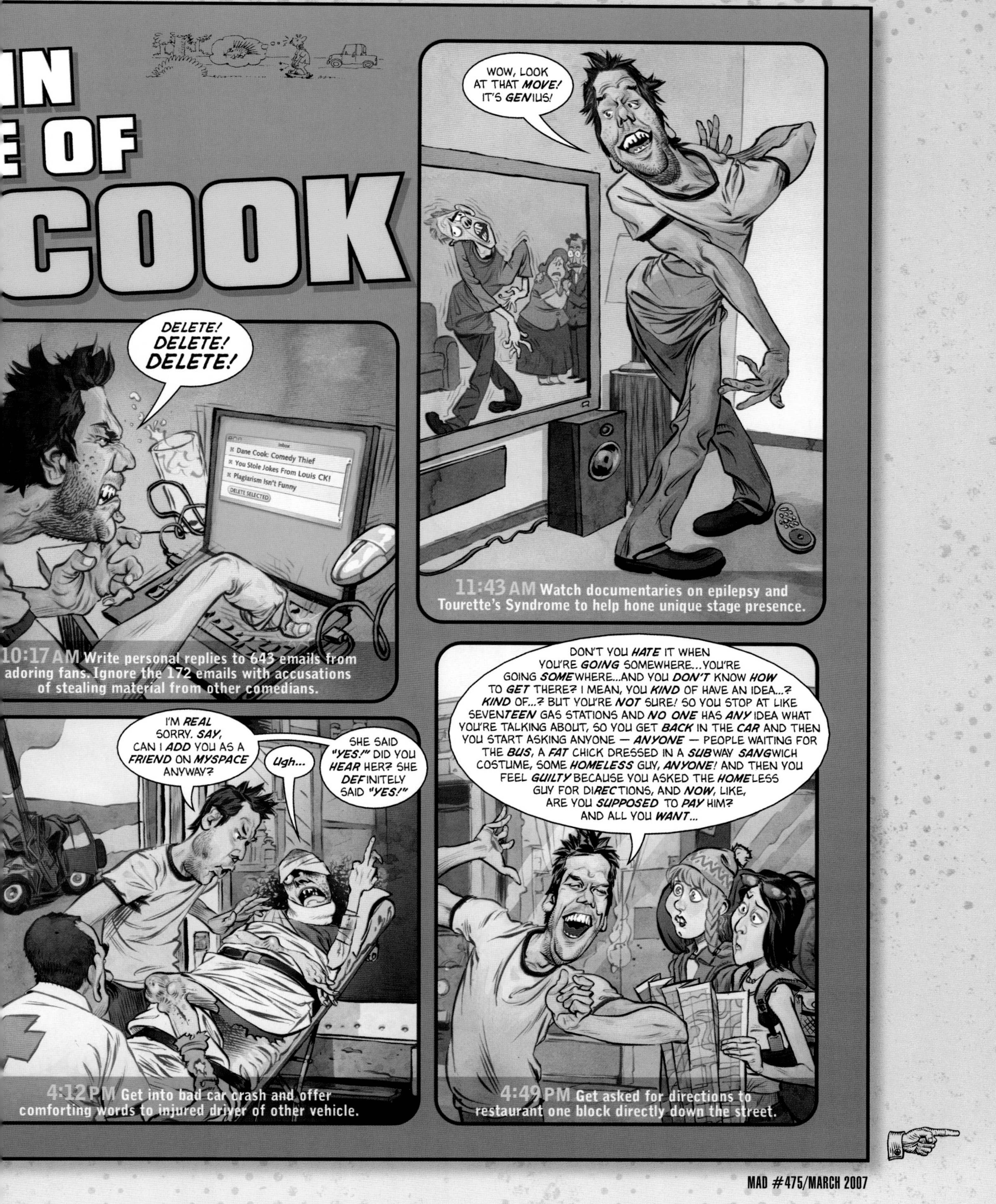

IN
E OF
COOK
WOW, LOOK AT THAT MOVE! IT'S GENIUS!
11:43 AM Watch documentaries on epilepsy and Tourette's Syndrome to help hone unique stage presence.
DELETE! DELETE! DELETE!
Inbox
Dane Cook: Comedy Thief
You Stole Jokes From Louis CK!
Plagiarism Isn't Funny
DELETE SELECTED
10:17 AM Write personal replies to 643 emails from adoring fans. Ignore the 172 emails with accusations of stealing material from other comedians.
I'M REAL SORRY. SAY, CAN I ADD YOU AS A FRIEND ON MYSPACE ANYWAY?
Ugh...
SHE SAID "YES!" DID YOU HEAR HER? SHE DEFINITELY SAID "YES!"
4:12 PM Get into bad car crash and offer comforting words to injured driver of other vehicle.
DON'T YOU HATE IT WHEN YOU'RE GOING SOMEWHERE...YOU'RE GOING SOMEWHERE...AND YOU DON'T KNOW HOW TO GET THERE? I MEAN, YOU KIND OF HAVE AN IDEA...? KIND OF...? BUT YOU'RE NOT SURE! SO YOU STOP AT LIKE SEVENTEEN GAS STATIONS AND NO ONE HAS ANY IDEA WHAT YOU'RE TALKING ABOUT, SO YOU GET BACK IN THE CAR AND THEN YOU START ASKING ANYONE — ANYONE — PEOPLE WAITING FOR THE BUS, A FAT CHICK DRESSED IN A SUBWAY SANGWICH COSTUME, SOME HOMELESS GUY, ANYONE! AND THEN YOU FEEL GUILTY BECAUSE YOU ASKED THE HOMELESS GUY FOR DIRECTIONS, AND NOW, LIKE, ARE YOU SUPPOSED TO PAY HIM? AND ALL YOU WANT...
4:49 PM Get asked for directions to restaurant one block directly down the street.

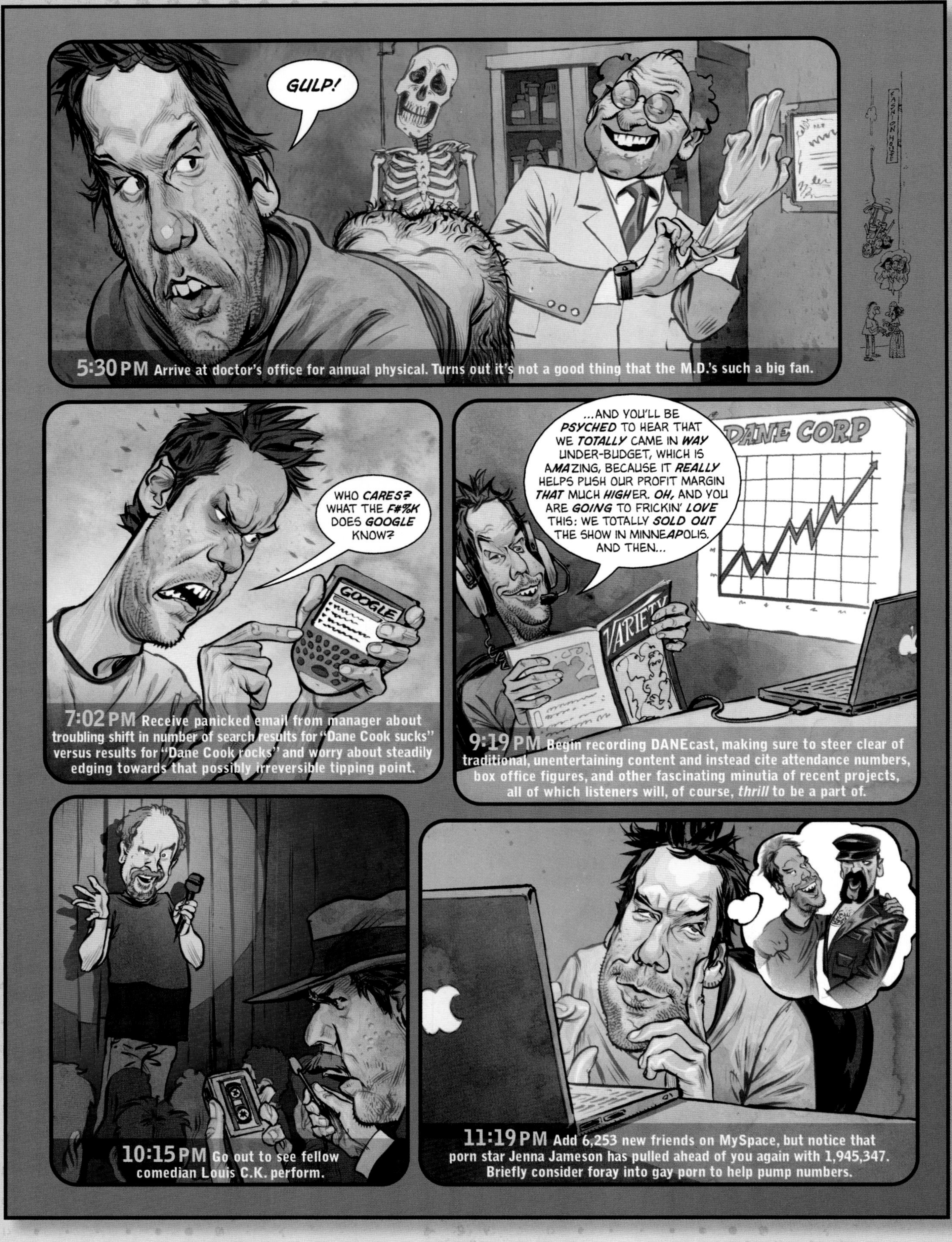
GULP!
5:30 PM Arrive at doctor's office for annual physical. Turns out it's not a good thing that the M.D.'s such a big fan.
WHO CARES? WHAT THE F#%K DOES GOOGLE KNOW?
GOOGLE
7:02 PM Receive panicked email from manager about troubling shift in number of search results for "Dane Cook sucks" versus results for "Dane Cook rocks" and worry about steadily edging towards that possibly irreversible tipping point.
...AND YOU'LL BE PSYCHED TO HEAR THAT WE TOTALLY CAME IN WAY UNDER-BUDGET, WHICH IS AMAZING, BECAUSE IT REALLY HELPS PUSH OUR PROFIT MARGIN THAT MUCH HIGHER. OH, AND YOU ARE GOING TO FRICKIN' LOVE THIS: WE TOTALLY SOLD OUT THE SHOW IN MINNEAPOLIS. AND THEN...
DANE CORP
VARIETY
9:19 PM Begin recording DANEcast, making sure to steer clear of traditional, unentertaining content and instead cite attendance numbers, box office figures, and other fascinating minutia of recent projects, all of which listeners will, of course, thrill to be a part of.
10:15 PM Go out to see fellow comedian Louis C.K. perform.
11:19 PM Add 6,253 new friends on MySpace, but notice that porn star Jenna Jameson has pulled ahead of you again with 1,945,347. Briefly consider foray into gay porn to help pump numbers.

EDITOR'S PICK

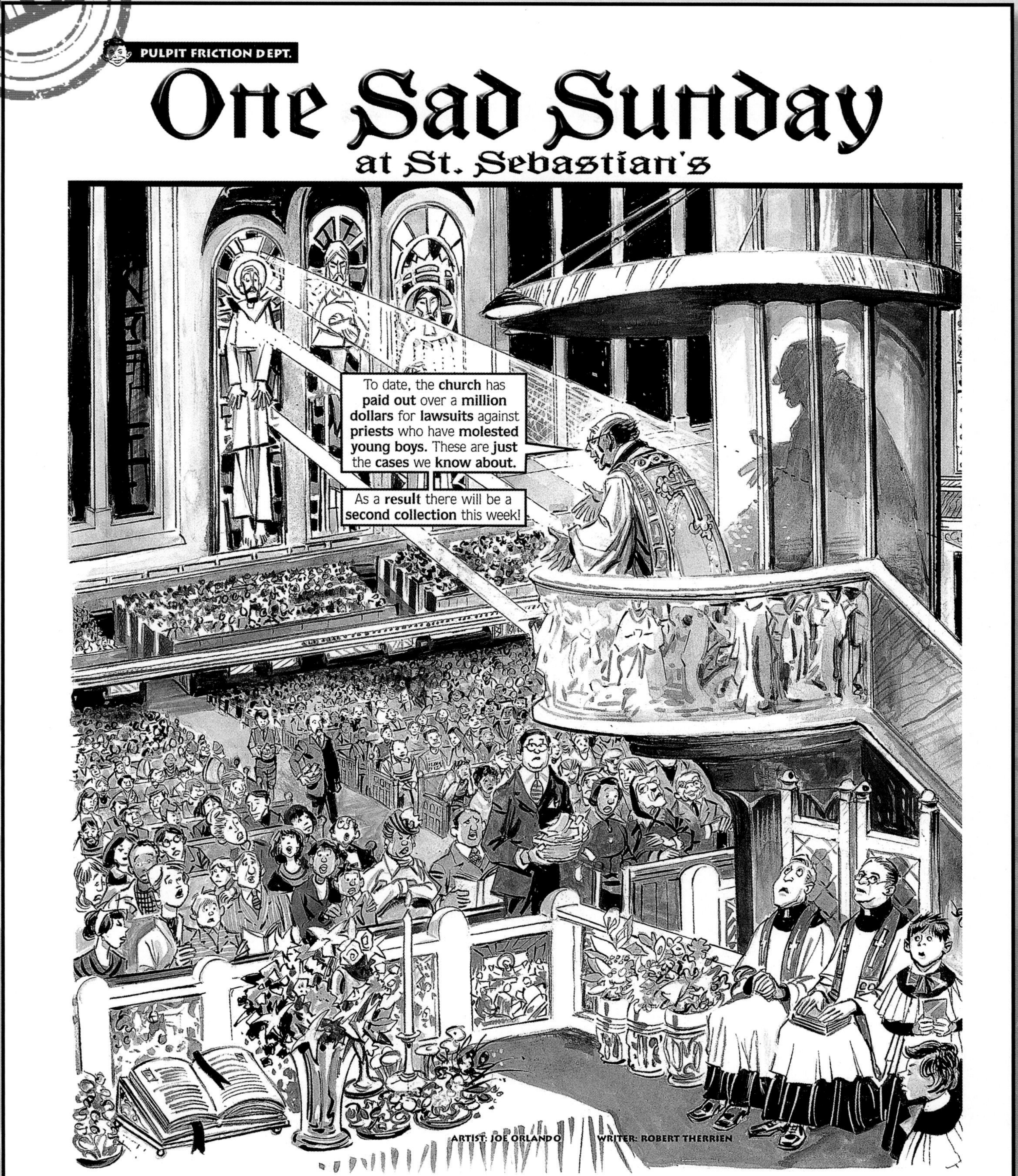
PULPIT FRICTION DEPT.
One Sad Sunday
at St. Sebastian's
To date, the church has paid out over a million dollars for lawsuits against priests who have molested young boys. These are just the cases we know about.
As a result there will be a second collection this week!
ARTIST: JOE ORLANDO
WRITER: ROBERT THERRIEN

MAD #356/APRIL 1997

We ran this rather benign (in my view) one-pager back in 1997, just as news was breaking of sexual abuse lawsuits being settled by the Catholic Church (but well before it was known just how widespread the abuse was). Almost immediately after it was published, the Catholic League issued a blistering press release accusing the magazine, and me personally, of "Catholic bashing." I keep a copy of the press release tacked on the bulletin board in my office as a badge of honor. — *John Ficarra*

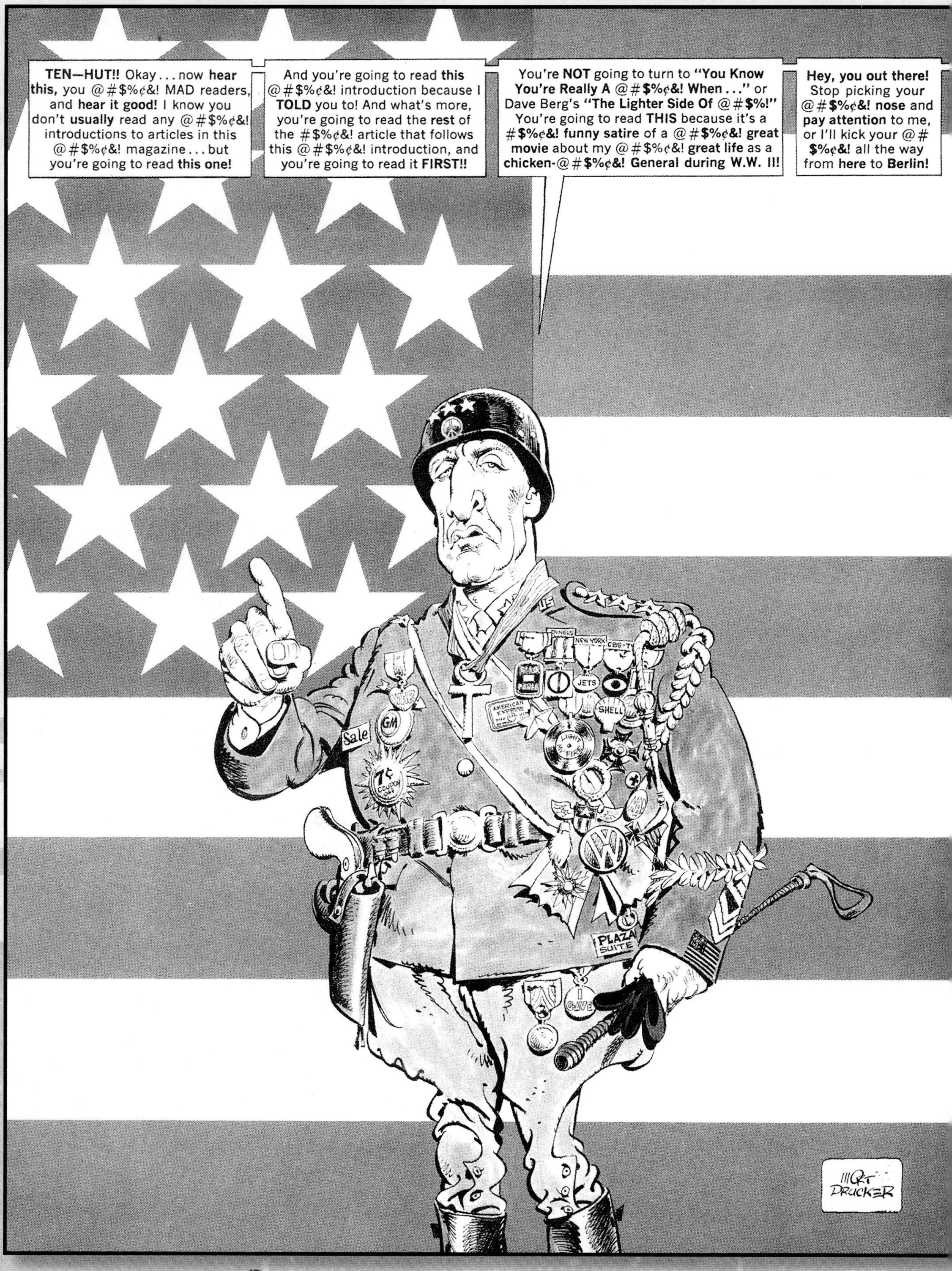
TEN—HUT!! Okay . . . now hear this, you @#$%¢&! MAD readers, and hear it good! I know you don't usually read any @#$%¢&! introductions to articles in this @#$%¢&! magazine . . . but you're going to read this one!
And you're going to read this @#$%¢&! introduction because I TOLD you to! And what's more, you're going to read the rest of the #$%¢&! article that follows this @#$%¢&! introduction, and you're going to read it FIRST!!
You're NOT going to turn to "You Know You're Really A @#$%¢&! When . . ." or Dave Berg's "The Lighter Side Of @#$%!" You're going to read THIS because it's a #$%¢&! funny satire of a @#$%¢&! great movie about my @#$%¢&! great life as a chicken-@#$%¢&! General during W.W. II!
Hey, you out there! Stop picking your @#$%¢&! nose and pay attention to me, or I'll kick your @#$%¢&! all the way from here to Berlin!
Sale
GM
JETS
SHELL
PLAZA SUITE
I GAVE
MORT DRUCKER

by Mort Drucker
ARTIST

While my best satirical work doesn't necessarily come from films that I personally enjoy — there have been times when a movie I didn't like turned out very well, and vice-versa — it certainly gets my energy flowing when the film has great faces that I know I can have fun with.

Such was the case with *Patton* ("Put*On"), starring George C. Scott and Karl Malden, which the editors jokingly called "The War of the Noses" when they saw the last panel on page four of the finished art.

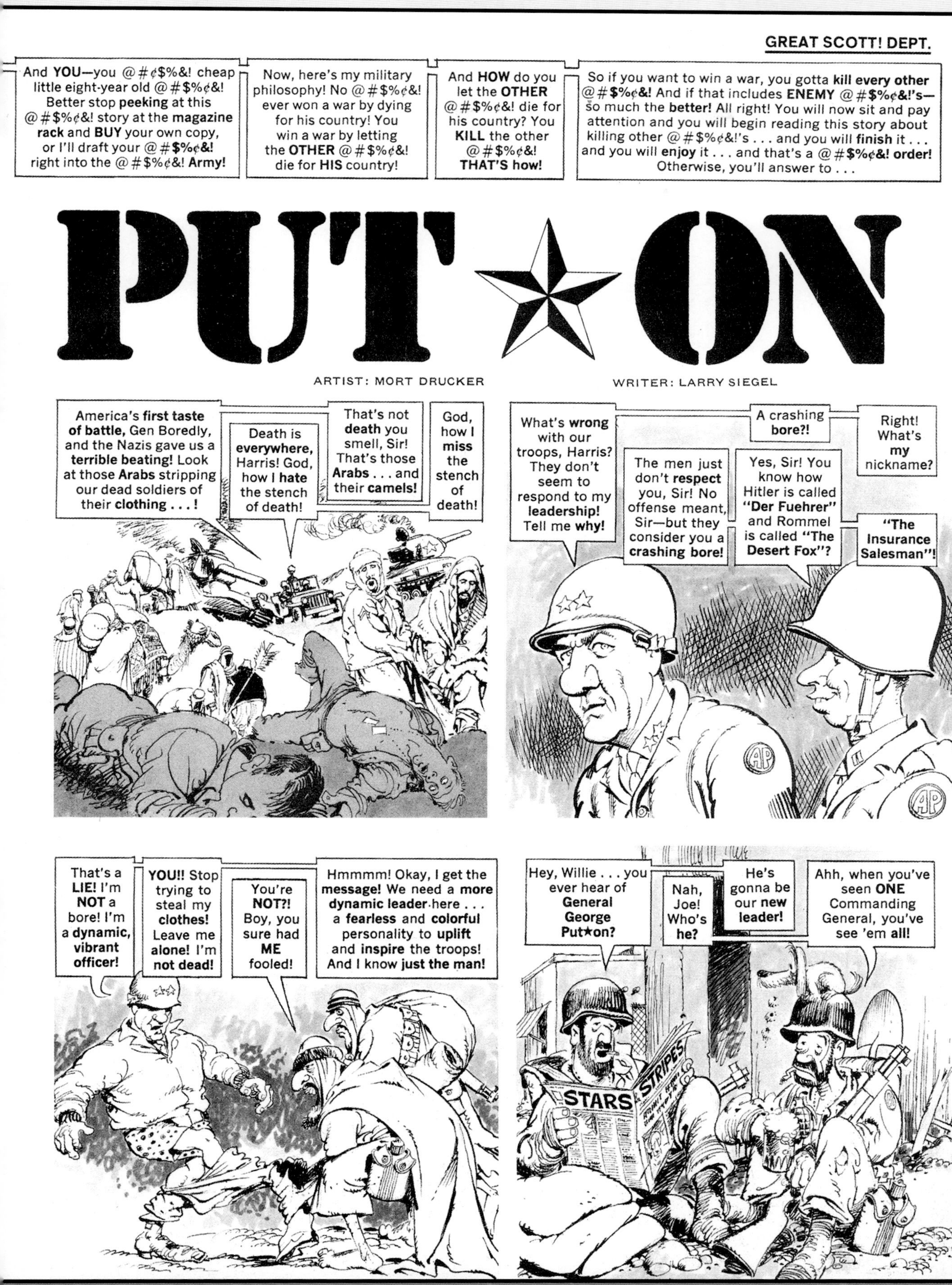
GREAT SCOTT! DEPT.
And YOU—you @#¢$%&! cheap little eight-year old @#$%¢&! Better stop peeking at this @#$%¢&! story at the magazine rack and BUY your own copy, or I'll draft your @#$%¢&! right into the @#$%¢&! Army!
Now, here's my military philosophy! No @#$%¢&! ever won a war by dying for his country! You win a war by letting the OTHER @#$%¢&! die for HIS country!
And HOW do you let the OTHER @#$%¢&! die for his country? You KILL the other @#$%¢&! THAT'S how!
So if you want to win a war, you gotta kill every other @#$%¢&! And if that includes ENEMY @#$%¢&!'s—so much the better! All right! You will now sit and pay attention and you will begin reading this story about killing other @#$%¢&!'s . . . and you will finish it . . . and you will enjoy it . . . and that's a @#$%¢&! order! Otherwise, you'll answer to . . .
PUT★ON
ARTIST: MORT DRUCKER
WRITER: LARRY SIEGEL
America's first taste of battle, Gen Boredly, and the Nazis gave us a terrible beating! Look at those Arabs stripping our dead soldiers of their clothing . . . !
Death is everywhere, Harris! God, how I hate the stench of death!
That's not death you smell, Sir! That's those Arabs . . . and their camels!
God, how I miss the stench of death!
What's wrong with our troops, Harris? They don't seem to respond to my leadership! Tell me why!
The men just don't respect you, Sir! No offense meant, Sir—but they consider you a crashing bore!
A crashing bore?!
Yes, Sir! You know how Hitler is called "Der Fuehrer" and Rommel is called "The Desert Fox"?
Right! What's my nickname?
"The Insurance Salesman"!
That's a LIE! I'm NOT a bore! I'm a dynamic, vibrant officer!
YOU!! Stop trying to steal my clothes! Leave me alone! I'm not dead!
You're NOT?! Boy, you sure had ME fooled!
Hmmmm! Okay, I get the message! We need a more dynamic leader here . . . a fearless and colorful personality to uplift and inspire the troops! And I know just the man!
Hey, Willie . . . you ever hear of General George Put★on?
Nah, Joe! Who's he?
He's gonna be our new leader!
Ahh, when you've seen ONE Commanding General, you've see 'em all!
STARS STRIPES

MAD #140/JANUARY 1971

Drawing for MAD has always been very different from most commercial accounts in that MAD's editors encouraged my visual gags as opposed to restricting my flights of whimsy. Why not? Wasn't that a contributing factor in MAD's initial success? I still chuckle at the memory of the background gags Will Elder, Jack Davis and Wally Wood used to delight readers with. I'll often add visual gags that are apropos to the story, as well as silly-looking animals and creatures and inside gags. Lots of inside gags. In "Put*On," I included an homage to graphic icons of military themes and characters:

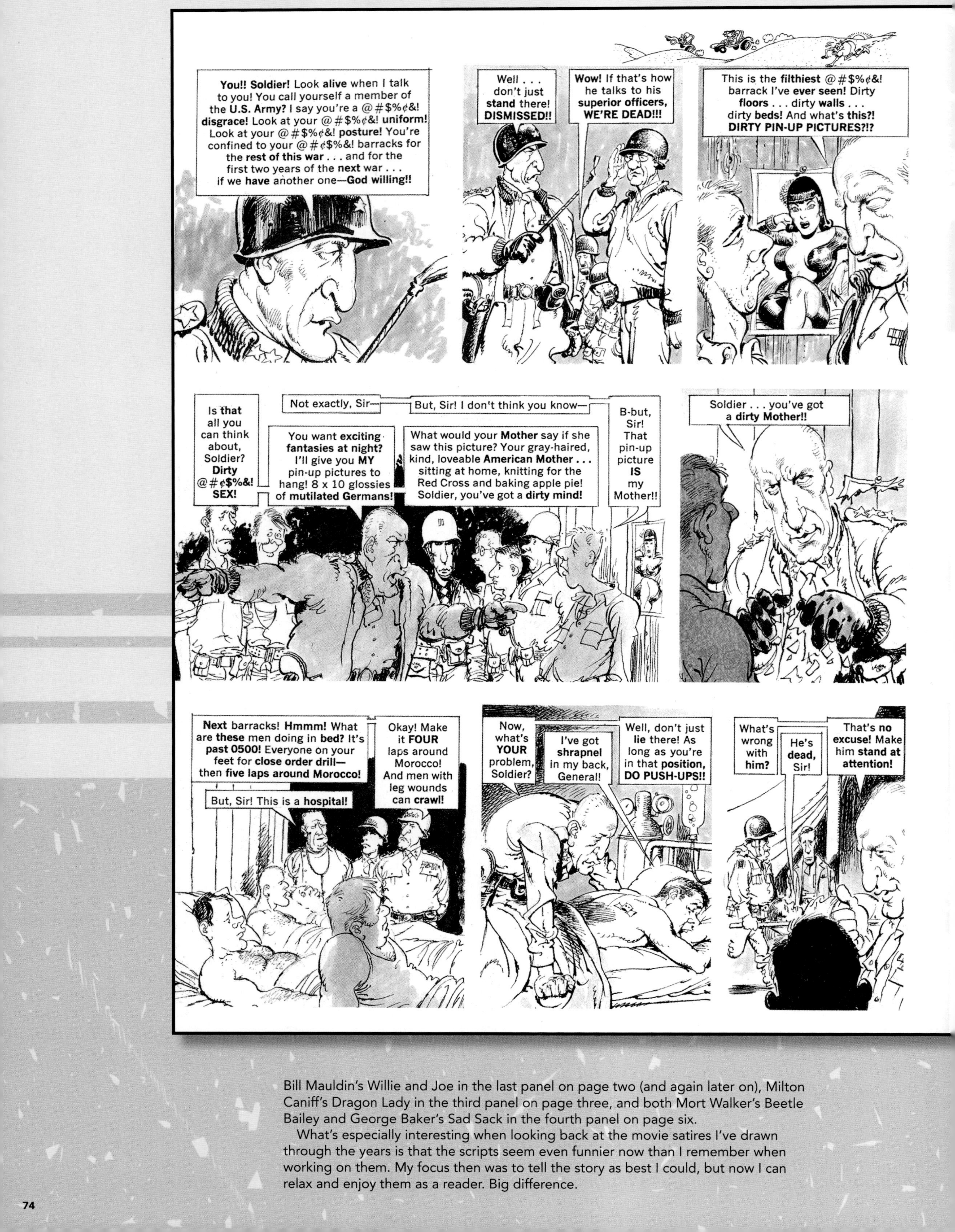
You!! Soldier! Look alive when I talk to you! You call yourself a member of the U.S. Army? I say you're a @#$%¢&! disgrace! Look at your @#$%¢&! uniform! Look at your @#$%¢&! posture! You're confined to your @#¢$%&! barracks for the rest of this war . . . and for the first two years of the next war . . . if we have another one—God willing!!
Well . . . don't just stand there! DISMISSED!!
Wow! If that's how he talks to his superior officers, WE'RE DEAD!!!
This is the filthiest @#$%¢&! barrack I've ever seen! Dirty floors . . . dirty walls . . . dirty beds! And what's this?! DIRTY PIN-UP PICTURES?!?
Is that all you can think about, Soldier? Dirty @#¢$%&! SEX!
Not exactly, Sir—
You want exciting fantasies at night? I'll give you MY pin-up pictures to hang! 8 x 10 glossies of mutilated Germans!
But, Sir! I don't think you know—
What would your Mother say if she saw this picture? Your gray-haired, kind, loveable American Mother . . . sitting at home, knitting for the Red Cross and baking apple pie! Soldier, you've got a dirty mind!
B-but, Sir! That pin-up picture IS my Mother!!
Soldier . . . you've got a dirty Mother!!
Next barracks! Hmmm! What are these men doing in bed? It's past 0500! Everyone on your feet for close order drill—then five laps around Morocco!
But, Sir! This is a hospital!
Okay! Make it FOUR laps around Morocco! And men with leg wounds can crawl!
Now, what's YOUR problem, Soldier?
I've got shrapnel in my back, General!
Well, don't just lie there! As long as you're in that position, DO PUSH-UPS!!
What's wrong with him?
He's dead, Sir!
That's no excuse! Make him stand at attention!

Bill Mauldin's Willie and Joe in the last panel on page two (and again later on), Milton Caniff's Dragon Lady in the third panel on page three, and both Mort Walker's Beetle Bailey and George Baker's Sad Sack in the fourth panel on page six.

What's especially interesting when looking back at the movie satires I've drawn through the years is that the scripts seem even funnier now than I remember when working on them. My focus then was to tell the story as best I could, but now I can relax and enjoy them as a reader. Big difference.

Ach! Zis mission should be a piece of kuchen, Hermann! Ve come in low over ze town, ve shpray them mit machine gun fire, und zen ve bomb zem—
Turn back, Carl! It's a trap! Ve're outnumbered!
Outnumbered?! Ze Americans haf no planes, no anti-aircraft guns, nuttink! All I see is zat dumkopf in ze middle of ze road firing two pistols at us!
Zat iss vot I mean! Zat iss General George Put★on! Take it from me—ve're outnumbered!!
Take that, you #¢$%&! Kraut! And that . . . and that!!
Mein Gott! He's a madman! But now ve get him! He ran out of bullets!
Turn back, Carl! Please! He'll find OTHER weapons!!
Gott in Himmel! Now, he's throwink rocks at us!
Vit vot . . . ?
Turn back! You don't know zis idiot! He'll destroy you vit anythink! He killed by brother Vilhelm in ze desert a few weeks ago!
You von't believe zis, but he BIT him to death!!
Hah! NOW, ve get him! He ran out of bullets und he ran out of rocks!
Ach du lieber! He got me right in ze eyes! I can't see! Zis iss it! Ve're goink to crash!
Carl! Vot happened to us?!
YOU'RE not goink to believe ZIS, Hermann—but a bomber in Der Fuehrer's Luftvaffe vas just shot down mit SHPIT!
Brilliant, George! One of the greatest single-handed feats of this war! One of the greatest feats of this century!
You call this a WAR?! You call this a CENTURY!?
BLAM
They don't make wars like they used to! Gee I miss the Spanish Inquisition! The water torture! The cutting out of tongues! Why don't we cut out tongues anymore? And who remembers what's-his-name? Attila The Hun!? What a wild, crazy nut . . . with his pillage and rapine! What ever became of pillage and rapine?
And what about that Oriental kook, Ghengis Khan, and his lovable Hordes? Gee, I'd love to slaughter with my own Horde! And what about those goofy Crusaders with their torture racks for Pagans—burning heretics in the name of God? What's become of us? Why aren't we religious anymore?
The old man going down Memory Lane again?
Shhh! Don't disturb an old soldier and his dreams!

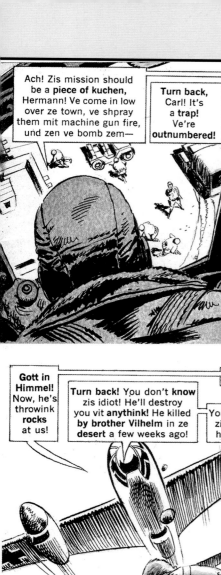

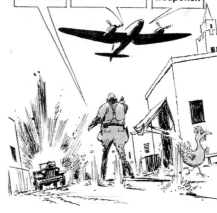

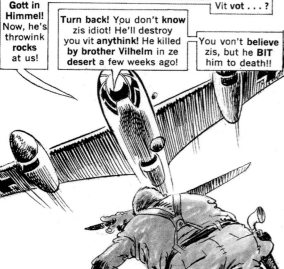

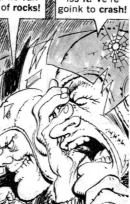

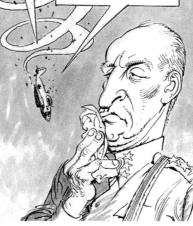

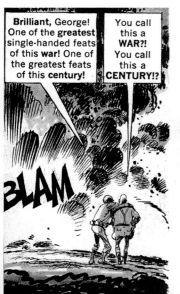

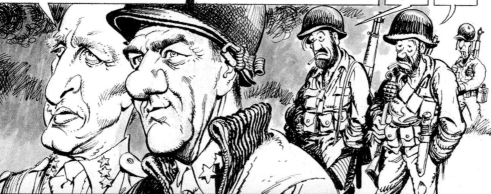

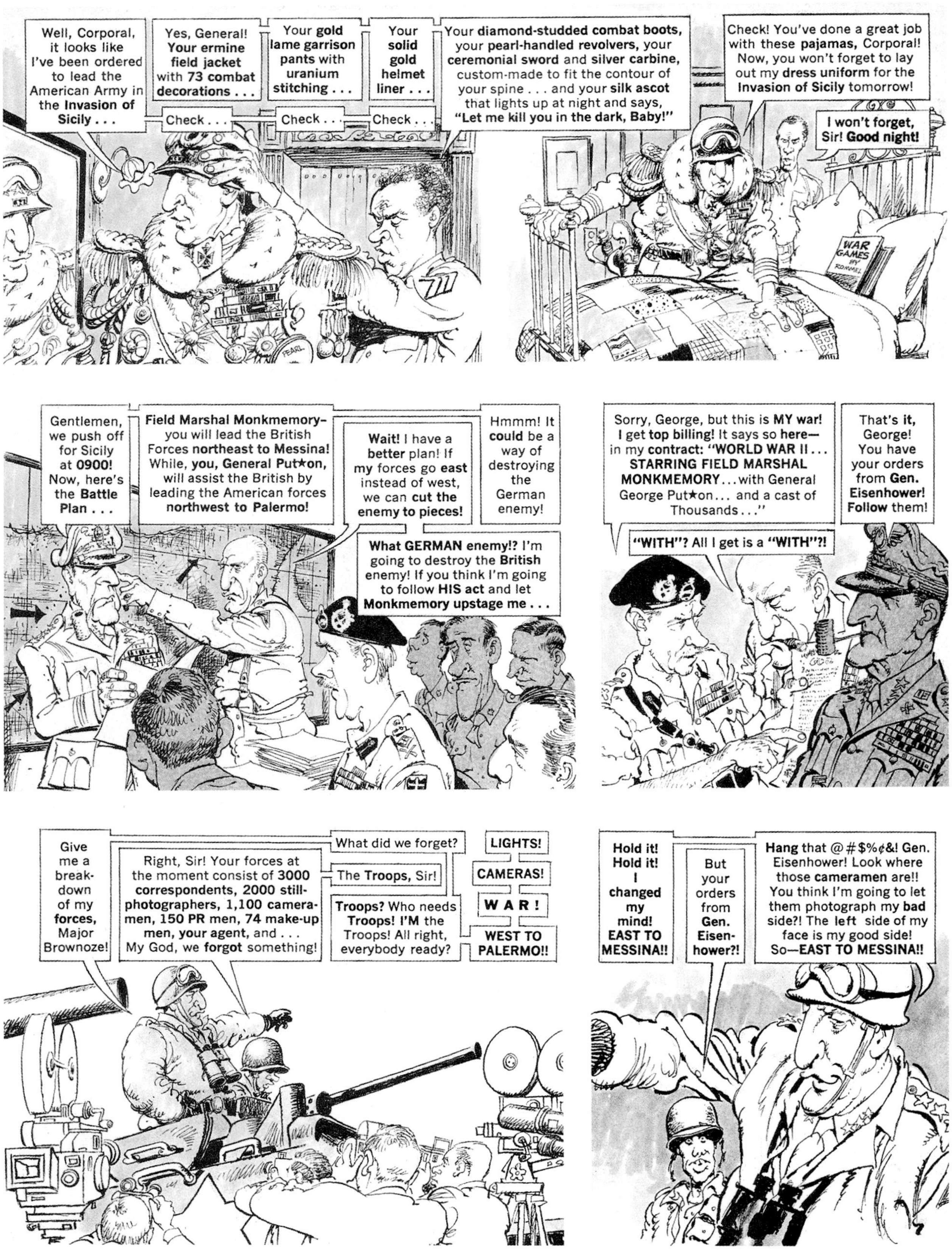
Well, Corporal, it looks like I've been ordered to lead the American Army in the Invasion of Sicily . . .
Yes, General! Your ermine field jacket with 73 combat decorations . . .
Check . . .
Your gold lame garrison pants with uranium stitching . . .
Check . . .
Your solid gold helmet liner . . .
Check . . .
Your diamond-studded combat boots, your pearl-handled revolvers, your ceremonial sword and silver carbine, custom-made to fit the contour of your spine . . . and your silk ascot that lights up at night and says, "Let me kill you in the dark, Baby!"
Check! You've done a great job with these pajamas, Corporal! Now, you won't forget to lay out my dress uniform for the Invasion of Sicily tomorrow!
I won't forget, Sir! Good night!
WAR GAMES
Gentlemen, we push off for Sicily at 0900! Now, here's the Battle Plan . . .
Field Marshal Monkmemory– you will lead the British Forces northeast to Messina! While, you, General Put★on, will assist the British by leading the American forces northwest to Palermo!
Wait! I have a better plan! If my forces go east instead of west, we can cut the enemy to pieces!
Hmmm! It could be a way of destroying the German enemy!
What GERMAN enemy!? I'm going to destroy the British enemy! If you think I'm going to follow HIS act and let Monkmemory upstage me . . .
Sorry, George, but this is MY war! I get top billing! It says so here— in my contract: "WORLD WAR II . . . STARRING FIELD MARSHAL MONKMEMORY . . . with General George Put★on . . . and a cast of Thousands . . ."
That's it, George! You have your orders from Gen. Eisenhower! Follow them!
"WITH"? All I get is a "WITH"?!
Give me a breakdown of my forces, Major Brownnoze!
Right, Sir! Your forces at the moment consist of 3000 correspondents, 2000 still-photographers, 1,100 cameramen, 150 PR men, 74 make-up men, your agent, and . . . My God, we forgot something!
What did we forget?
The Troops, Sir!
Troops? Who needs Troops! I'M the Troops! All right, everybody ready?
LIGHTS!
CAMERAS!
WAR!
WEST TO PALERMO!!
Hold it! Hold it! I changed my mind! EAST TO MESSINA!!
But your orders from Gen. Eisenhower?!
Hang that @#$%¢&! Gen. Eisenhower! Look where those cameramen are!! You think I'm going to let them photograph my bad side?! The left side of my face is my good side! So—EAST TO MESSINA!!

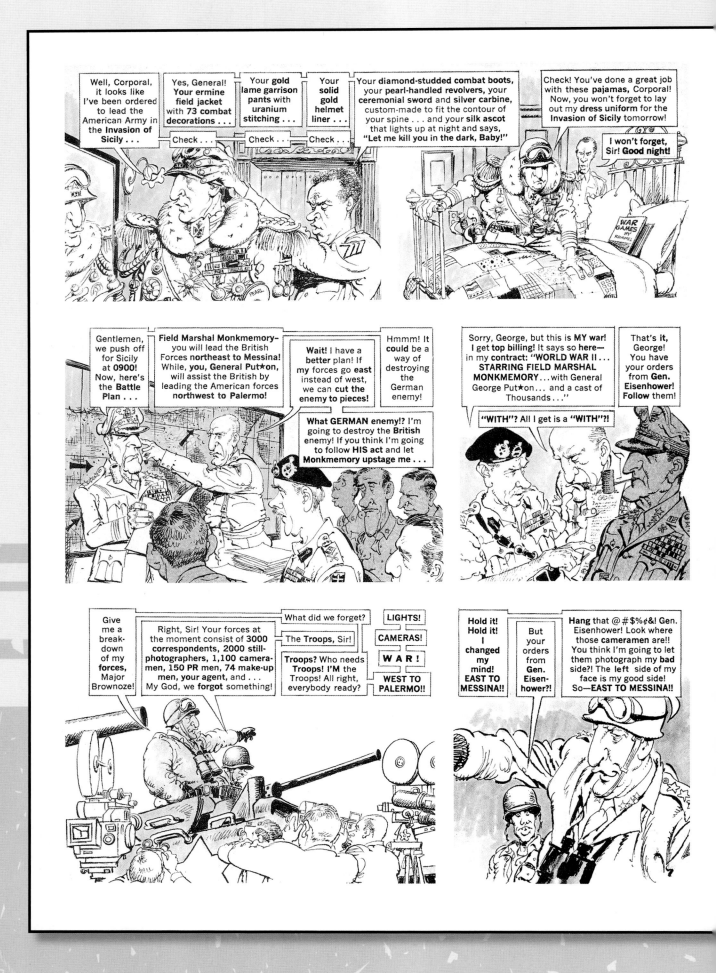

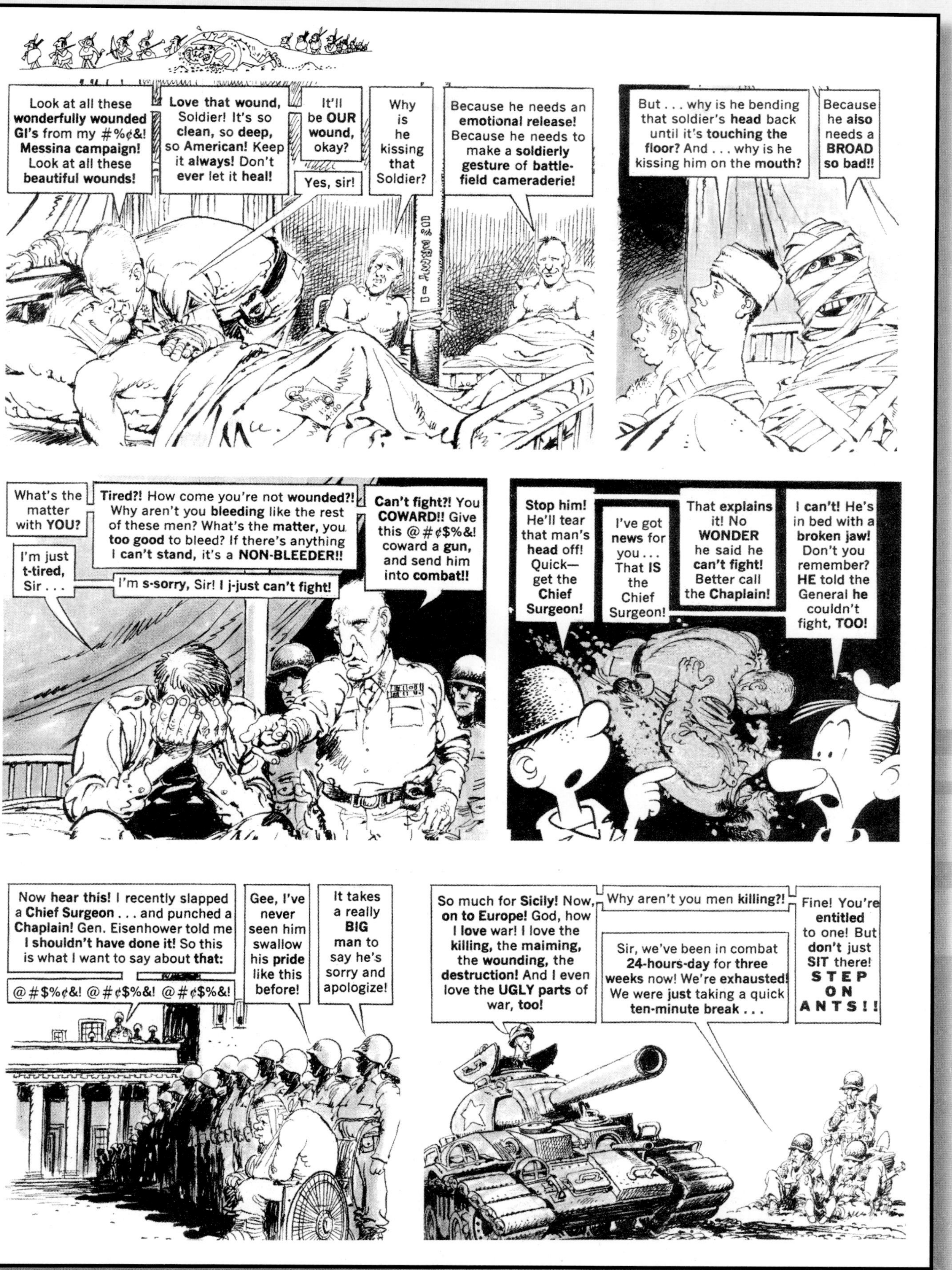

Look at all these wonderfully wounded GI's from my #%¢&! Messina campaign! Look at all these beautiful wounds!
Love that wound, Soldier! It's so clean, so deep, so American! Keep it always! Don't ever let it heal!
It'll be OUR wound, okay?
Yes, sir!
Why is he kissing that Soldier?
Because he needs an emotional release! Because he needs to make a soldierly gesture of battle-field cameraderie!
But . . . why is he bending that soldier's head back until it's touching the floor? And . . . why is he kissing him on the mouth?
Because he also needs a BROAD so bad!!
What's the matter with YOU?
I'm just t-tired, Sir . . .
Tired?! How come you're not wounded?! Why aren't you bleeding like the rest of these men? What's the matter, you too good to bleed? If there's anything I can't stand, it's a NON-BLEEDER!!
I'm s-sorry, Sir! I j-just can't fight!
Can't fight?! You COWARD!! Give this @#¢$%&! coward a gun, and send him into combat!!
Stop him! He'll tear that man's head off! Quick— get the Chief Surgeon!
I've got news for you . . . That IS the Chief Surgeon!
That explains it! No WONDER he said he can't fight! Better call the Chaplain!
I can't! He's in bed with a broken jaw! Don't you remember? HE told the General he couldn't fight, TOO!
Now hear this! I recently slapped a Chief Surgeon . . . and punched a Chaplain! Gen. Eisenhower told me I shouldn't have done it! So this is what I want to say about that:
@#$%¢&! @#¢$%&! @#¢$%&!
Gee, I've never seen him swallow his pride like this before!
It takes a really BIG man to say he's sorry and apologize!
So much for Sicily! Now, on to Europe! God, how I love war! I love the killing, the maiming, the wounding, the destruction! And I even love the UGLY parts of war, too!
Why aren't you men killing?!
Sir, we've been in combat 24-hours-day for three weeks now! We're exhausted! We were just taking a quick ten-minute break . . .
Fine! You're entitled to one! But don't just SIT there! STEP ON ANTS!!

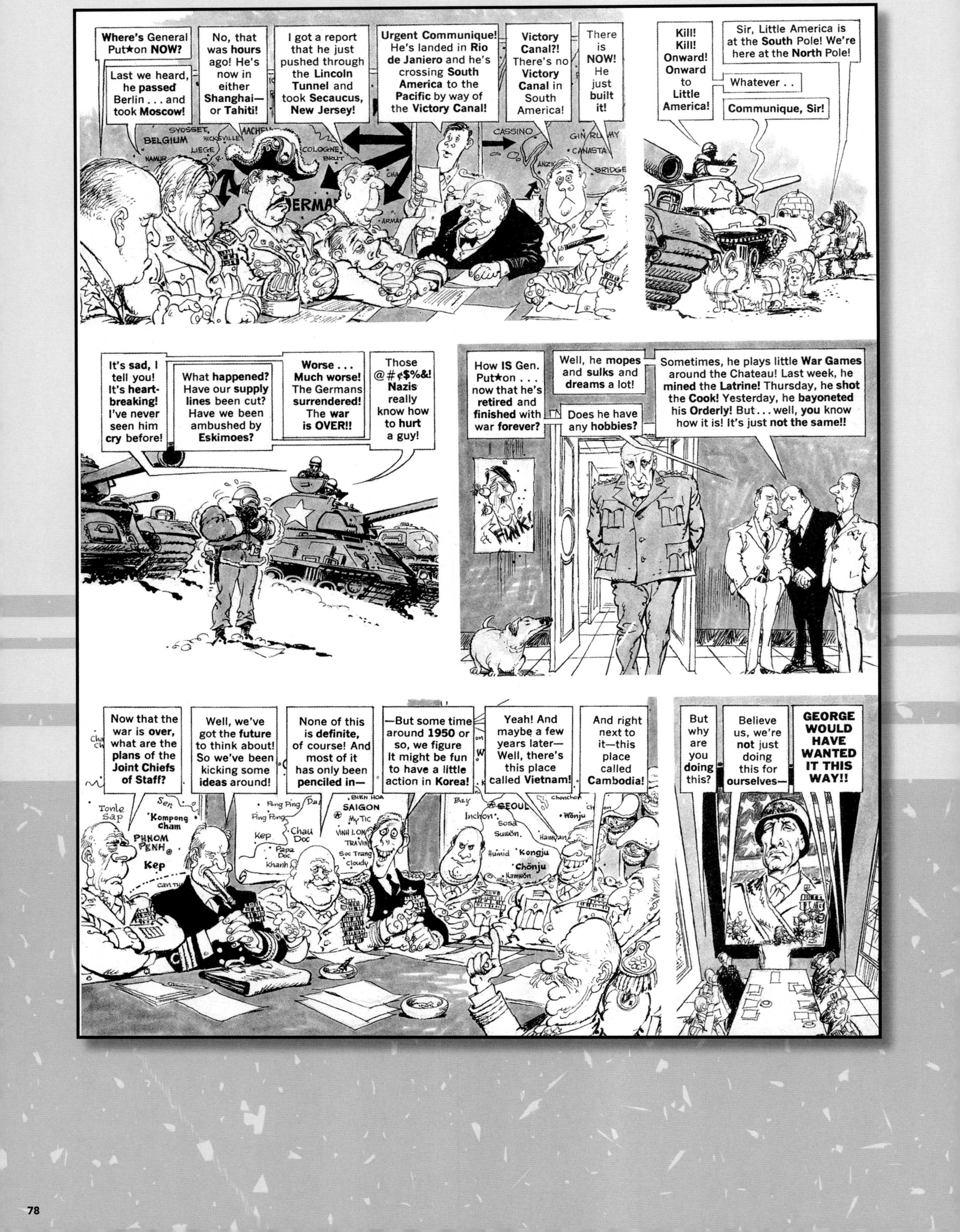

Where's General Put★on NOW?
Last we heard, he passed Berlin . . . and took Moscow!
No, that was hours ago! He's now in either Shanghai— or Tahiti!
I got a report that he just pushed through the Lincoln Tunnel and took Secaucus, New Jersey!
Urgent Communique! He's landed in Rio de Janiero and he's crossing South America to the Pacific by way of the Victory Canal!
Victory Canal?! There's no Victory Canal in South America!
There is NOW! He just built it!
Kill! Kill! Onward! Onward to Little America!
Sir, Little America is at the South Pole! We're here at the North Pole!
Whatever . .
Communique, Sir!
It's sad, I tell you! It's heart-breaking! I've never seen him cry before!
What happened? Have our supply lines been cut? Have we been ambushed by Eskimoes?
Worse . . . Much worse! The Germans surrendered! The war is OVER!!
Those @#¢$%&! Nazis really know how to hurt a guy!
How IS Gen. Put★on . . . now that he's retired and finished with war forever?
Well, he mopes and sulks and dreams a lot!
Does he have any hobbies?
Sometimes, he plays little War Games around the Chateau! Last week, he mined the Latrine! Thursday, he shot the Cook! Yesterday, he bayoneted his Orderly! But . . . well, you know how it is! It's just not the same!!
FINK!
Now that the war is over, what are the plans of the Joint Chiefs of Staff?
Well, we've got the future to think about! So we've been kicking some ideas around!
None of this is definite, of course! And most of it has only been penciled in—
—But some time around 1950 or so, we figure it might be fun to have a little action in Korea!
Yeah! And maybe a few years later— Well, there's this place called Vietnam!
And right next to it—this place called Cambodia!
But why are you doing this?
Believe us, we're not just doing this for ourselves—
GEORGE WOULD HAVE WANTED IT THIS WAY!!

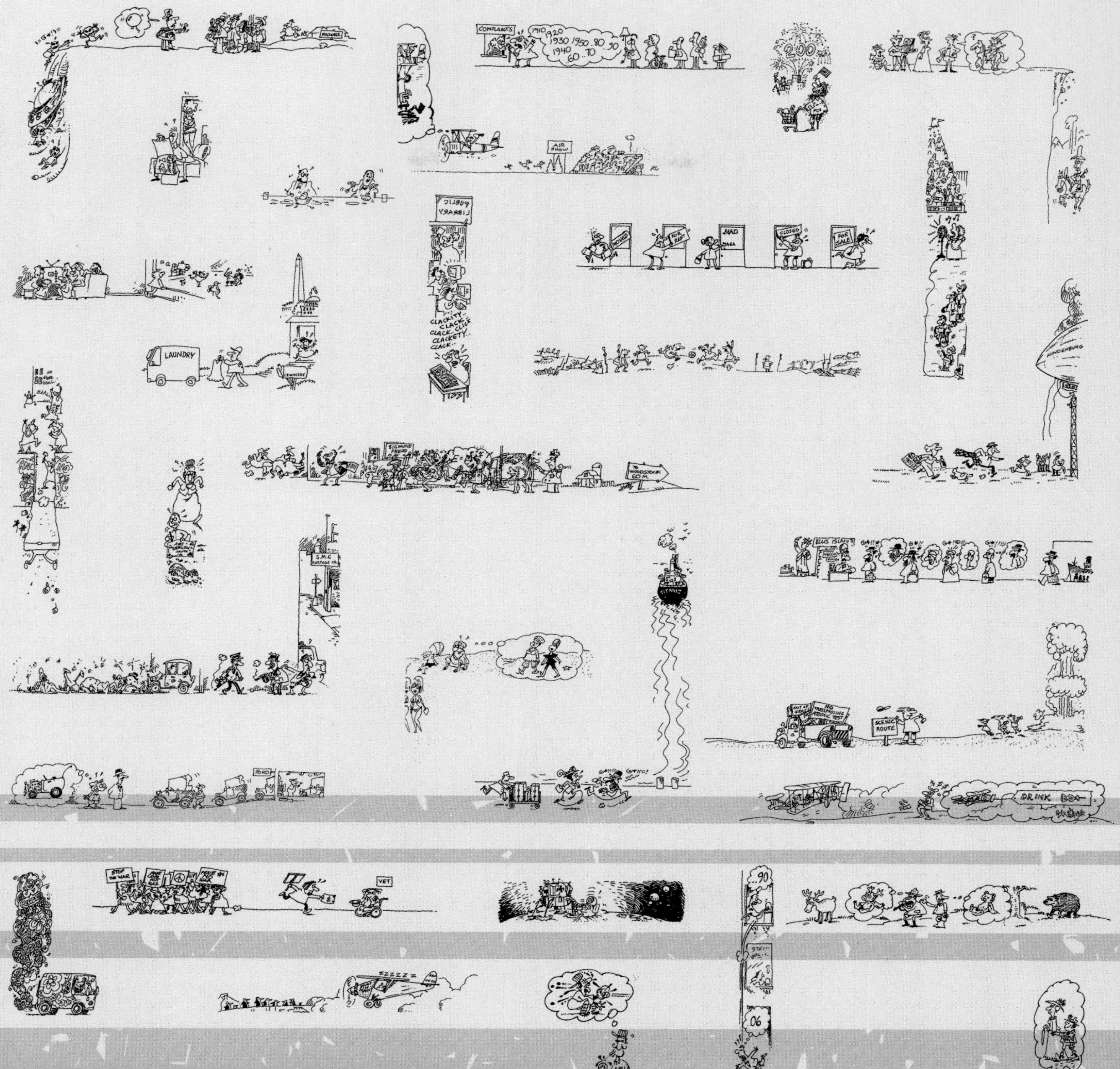
COMPLAINTS
AIR SHOW
PUBLIC LIBRARY
MAD
CLOSED
FOR SALE
LAUNDRY
HINDENBURG
TO WOODSTOCK
TITANIC
SCENIC ROUTE
DRINK
STOP THE WAR
VET
.90
.06

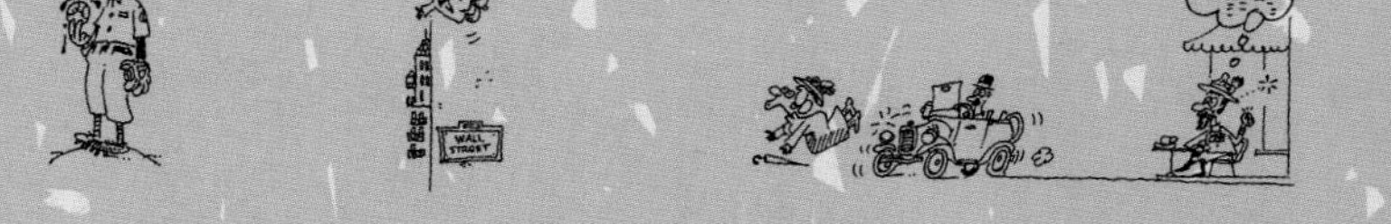

by Hermann Mejia
ARTIST

Mi primera MAD la encontré a los 30 años sobre un banco a la salida del colegio, era el principio de las decada de los 80. Fue amor a primera vista. Todo me inspiraba y hacia reir. Explorándola detalladamente, descubrí lo que a mi entender eran bromas ocultas para niños espías: las viñetas del gran Sergio Aragonés. A partir de ese momento la revista pasó a ser una isla de terosos ocultos; mis ojos hurgaban milimetro a milimetro cada uno de los rincones de las páginas en busca de estas joyas que me desternillaban de risa y maravillaban con su buen dibujo.

La publicación estaba en inglés...Casí todo en inglés; el trabajo del señor Aragones era diferente, era humor de mimos, mudo, universal, blanco y negro...

¡Viva Sergio!

I found my first MAD 30 years ago on a bench outside of my school; it was the beginning of the '80s. It was love at first sight. Everything inspired me and made me laugh. Exploring it in detail, I discovered what I thought were hidden jokes for kid spies: the cartoons of the great Sergio Aragonés. From that moment on, the magazine became an island of hidden treasures; my eyes scanned millimeter by millimeter each corner of the pages in search of these jewels that cracked me up and amazed me with the great drawings. The publication was in English...almost entirely in English; the work of Mr. Aragonés was different; it was mime humor, silent, universal, black and white...

Long live Sergio!

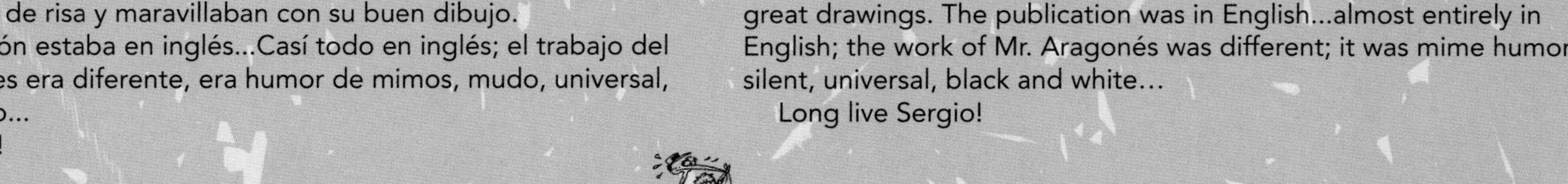

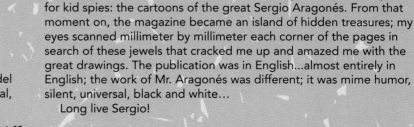

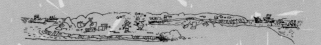

THE PET PEDDLER

YOUR ONE-STOP SOURCE FOR ADOPTING THE ANIMALS OTHER PEOPLE EVENTUALLY GOT SICK OF

IRISH SETTER, 23 No need to care for him 24/7, since he tends to wander off for days at a time. Not much of a "pet," really. Answers to the name of "Get your butt off the couch, you worthless mongrel." 555-4567

LORIKEET, WAS 15 Excellent taxidermy job. Makes no mess, doesn't squawk at night. Great for recreating that Monty Python "Pet Shop" skit with your geek friends. 555-8008

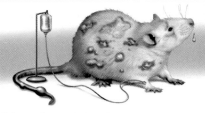

FORMER LAB RAT, 2 Has five different types of lesions. Loves NutriSweet, aspartame, MSG. Must have special medical procedures each week. 555-6954

RODEO BRONCO, 3 So your whining little daughter wants a pony, does she? She'll shut up real quick after a ride on Ol' Rowdy! 1-853-555-8000

POT-BELLIED PYTHON, 6 We don't know what sort of pet is in his stomach, but we will throw it in for free! 555-6294.

HELPER CHIMP, 8 Has served the disabled for five years. Can prepare meals and operate a standard VCR (though, unfortunately, has great love for Steven Seagal films). Dabbles in playwriting, currently working on Shakespearean tragedy with 999 other chimp collaborators. 1-800-555-9008

SHEEPDOG, 5 Loving and diligent. Favorite foods include mutton and lamb chops. 555-0345

ARTIST: SCOTT BRICHER   WRITER: JEFF KRUSE

JACK RUSSELL TERRIER, 5 Can do an amazing assortment of tricks: fetch ball, roll over, make Statue of Liberty disappear, etc. 555-0033

FREE-RANGE LAWN FLAMINGO Sturdy aluminum, has had all shots and been spayed. Free to good home. 555-0011

COCKATIEL, 7 Highly intelligent, approx. 10,000 word vocab. Stubby can't actually *speak* any of the words, but he does know them. Trust me. 555-4381

---

by Jeff Kruse
WRITER

ike most people, I've always hated TV ads, and my favorite MAD piece was "Advertising Makes You Wonder..." in issue #218. Sadly, I didn't write that one, so I'll focus on one that I did.

For several years, I'd had a cockatiel, Stubby, who was able to whistle a few tunes, but never spoke a word. One day a weird thought occurred to me: maybe he knows words, but just doesn't feel like talking. That's when I got the idea to do an article of

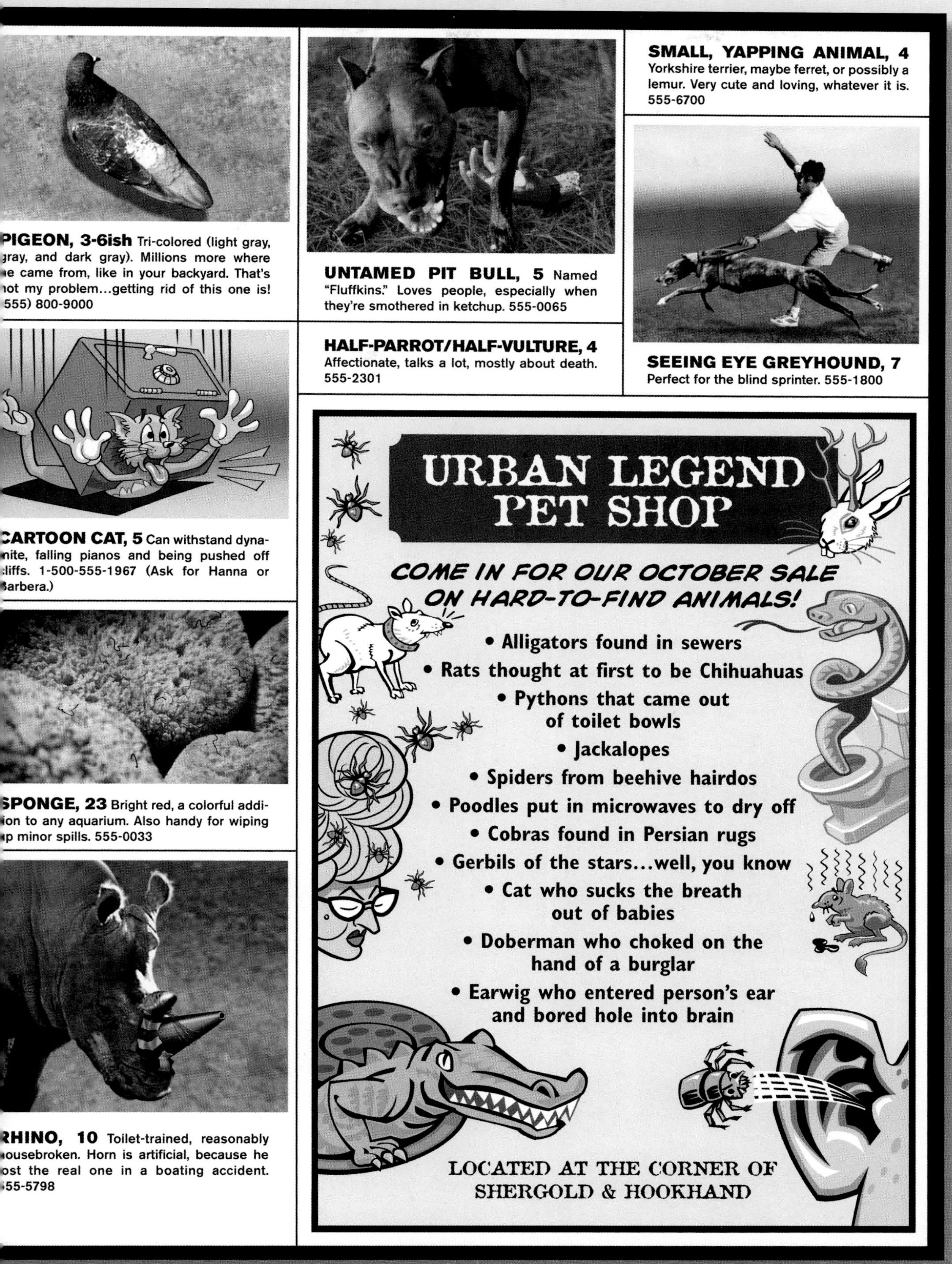

PIGEON, 3-6ish Tri-colored (light gray, gray, and dark gray). Millions more where e came from, like in your backyard. That's ot my problem...getting rid of this one is! 555) 800-9000

UNTAMED PIT BULL, 5 Named "Fluffkins." Loves people, especially when they're smothered in ketchup. 555-0065

SMALL, YAPPING ANIMAL, 4 Yorkshire terrier, maybe ferret, or possibly a lemur. Very cute and loving, whatever it is. 555-6700

HALF-PARROT/HALF-VULTURE, 4 Affectionate, talks a lot, mostly about death. 555-2301

SEEING EYE GREYHOUND, 7 Perfect for the blind sprinter. 555-1800

CARTOON CAT, 5 Can withstand dyna-nite, falling pianos and being pushed off liffs. 1-500-555-1967 (Ask for Hanna or arbera.)

SPONGE, 23 Bright red, a colorful addi-ion to any aquarium. Also handy for wiping p minor spills. 555-0033

RHINO, 10 Toilet-trained, reasonably ousebroken. Horn is artificial, because he ost the real one in a boating accident. 55-5798

URBAN LEGEND PET SHOP

COME IN FOR OUR OCTOBER SALE ON HARD-TO-FIND ANIMALS!

- Alligators found in sewers
- Rats thought at first to be Chihuahuas
- Pythons that came out of toilet bowls
- Jackalopes
- Spiders from beehive hairdos
- Poodles put in microwaves to dry off
- Cobras found in Persian rugs
- Gerbils of the stars...well, you know
- Cat who sucks the breath out of babies
- Doberman who choked on the hand of a burglar
- Earwig who entered person's ear and bored hole into brain

LOCATED AT THE CORNER OF SHERGOLD & HOOKHAND

MAD #411/NOVEMBER 2001

pet classified ads. I started with the real-life bird and added a bunch of fictional pets, hoping MAD would see fit to give Stubby his chance at the big time.

They did, and "The Pet Peddler" appeared in issue #411, which MAD fans will remember for its poignant post-9/11 cover. Scott Bricher did an amazing job of drawing all the animals, including one of a certain intelligent nine-year-old cockatiel reading a book. I don't need to tell you that Stubby never even said thank you.

EDITOR'S PICK

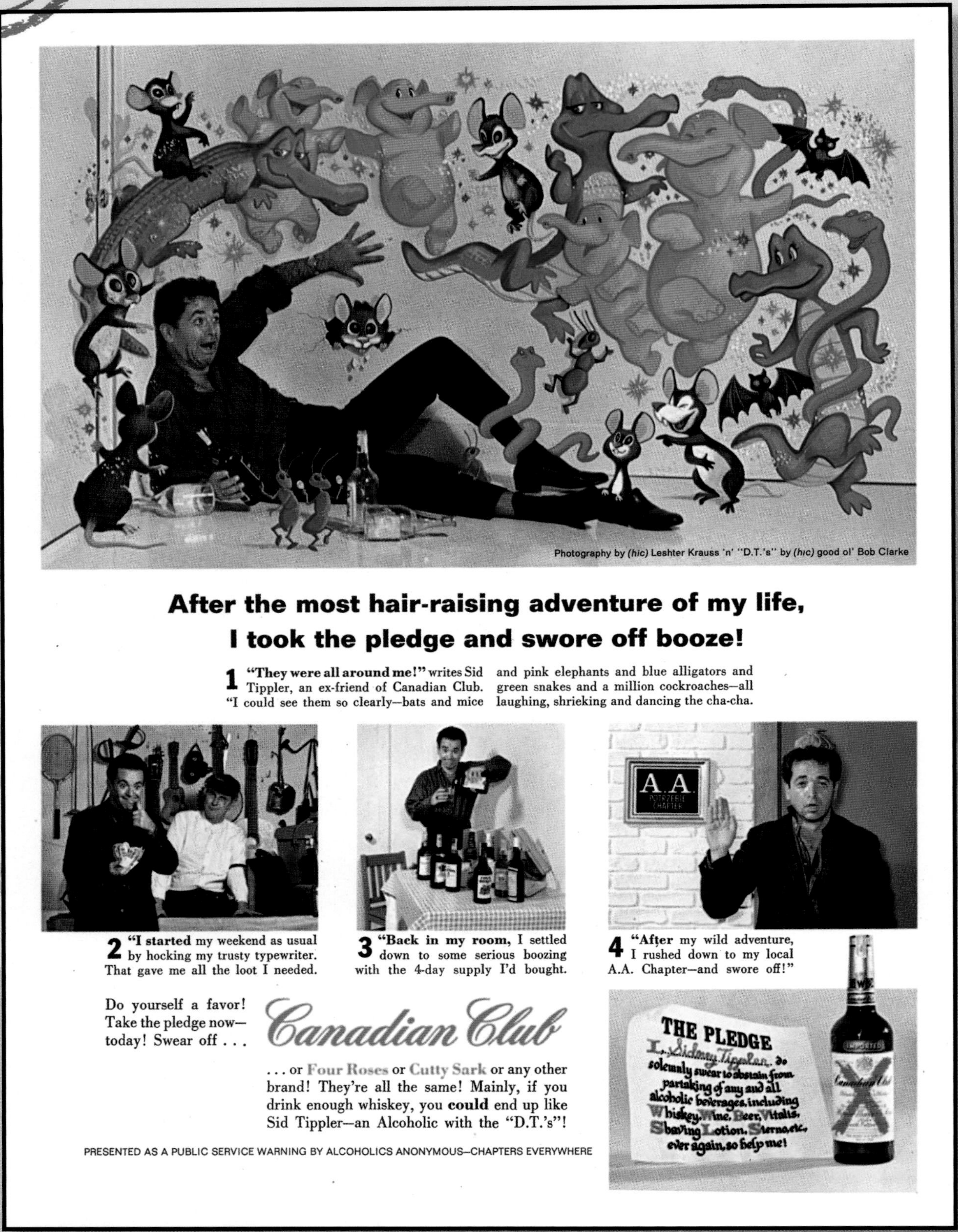
Photography by (hic) Leshter Krauss 'n' "D.T.'s" by (hic) good ol' Bob Clarke
After the most hair-raising adventure of my life, I took the pledge and swore off booze!
1 "They were all around me!" writes Sid Tippler, an ex-friend of Canadian Club. "I could see them so clearly—bats and mice and pink elephants and blue alligators and green snakes and a million cockroaches—all laughing, shrieking and dancing the cha-cha.
A.A.
POTZREBIE CHAPTER
2 "I started my weekend as usual by hocking my trusty typewriter. That gave me all the loot I needed.
3 "Back in my room, I settled down to some serious boozing with the 4-day supply I'd bought.
4 "After my wild adventure, I rushed down to my local A.A. Chapter—and swore off!"
Do yourself a favor! Take the pledge now—today! Swear off . . .
Canadian Club
. . . or Four Roses or Cutty Sark or any other brand! They're all the same! Mainly, if you drink enough whiskey, you could end up like Sid Tippler—an Alcoholic with the "D.T.'s"!
THE PLEDGE
I, Sidney Tippler, do solemnly swear to abstain from partaking of any and all alcoholic beverages, including Whiskey, Wine, Beer, Vitalis, Shaving Lotion, Sterno, etc. ever again, so help me!
PRESENTED AS A PUBLIC SERVICE WARNING BY ALCOHOLICS ANONYMOUS—CHAPTERS EVERYWHERE

MAD #94/APRIL 1965

Since Bob Clarke had an active career in advertising, whenever an ad parody came in, his name was always on the short list for an artist who could handle the assignment. We loved the fact that one of Madison Avenue's own would be biting the hand that fed it. Bob rose to MAD's challenge again and again over his long and illustrious career, thoroughly enjoying himself along the way.

One of Bob's most memorable assignments was the Canadian Club "pink elephants" liquor ad. Back then the procedure wasn't a digital process as it is now. The work had to be done on paper with plastic sheet tracings crafted in special colored dyes and paints that were placed over the background, be it photograph or art (as was this one) in order to create a "reality" of the combined images when reproduced.

In the end, the Canadian Club spoof allowed Bob to do a personal take in the style of the legendary Walt Disney who surely served as inspiration for cartoonists the world over. As, of course, did Bob Clarke himself. — *Nick Meglin*

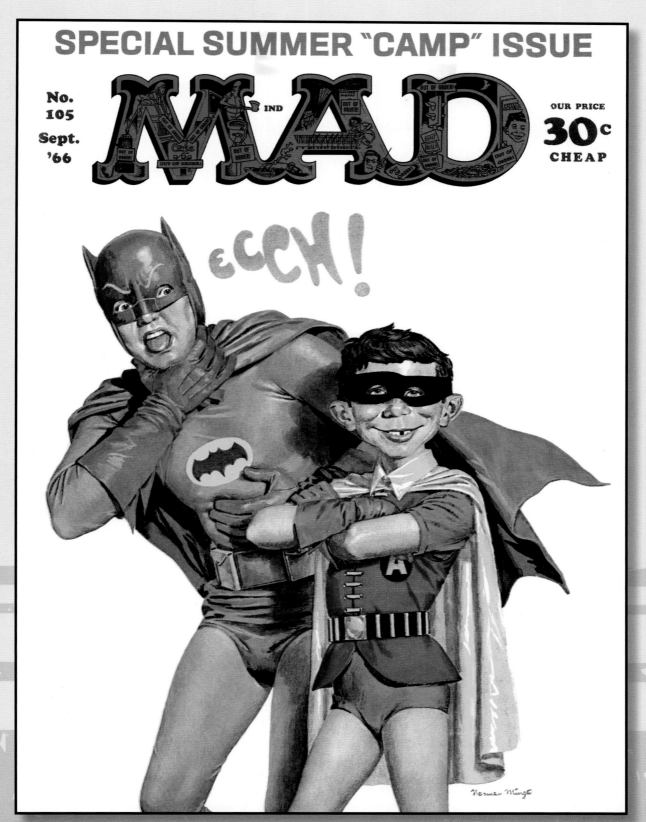

SPECIAL SUMMER "CAMP" ISSUE

MAD

No. 105 Sept. '66

IND

OUR PRICE 30¢ CHEAP

ECCH!

ARTIST: NORMAN MINGO

MAD #105/SEPTEMBER 1966

by James Warhola
ARTIST

I discovered MAD in the 1960's when I was a very impressionable young lad of about seven. In our household my mom forbade me from reading Dr. Seuss — thinking he was just too weird for my delicate brain — but with MAD she was okay. So to her I am grateful for making the right choice, because MAD certainly influenced my life's path.

The old adage "One shouldn't judge a book by its cover" is WRONG! MAD delivered gut-wrenching humor, starting with its covers. They were over-the-top clever and brilliant. *The Saturday Evening Post* had Norman Rockwell but MAD had Rembrandt — or, I mean, Norman Mingo. Mingo found his niche at MAD in the 1950's and helped shape its destiny. Being the veteran "old-school"

illustrator that he was, he gave Alfred personality and portrayed him in bizarre situations that kids like myself could identify with. The purely visual covers enticed us to read on. May I say genius? Okay, yes, Mingo's covers were pure genius! A big favorite that I distinctly remember was MAD #105, featuring Batman gagging at the sight of his trusty sidekick, who was none other than the imposter — "Robin E. Neuman." What kid wouldn't want to be Robin at the time? Alfred became our proud stand-in, thanks to Norman Mingo.

Little did I know that I would hop on board with "The Usual Gang of Idiots" and have a crack at a few covers myself about 20 years later. This was a dream come true, but wow — what an unbelievably high standard Mr. Mingo set for all cover artists. His covers are forever great inspirations to aspiring artists and will always reflect the American culture of a bygone era.

Ken Burns

I grew up reading MAD, loving every chapter, remembering always to watch for what's going on in the margins. I learned irony, how to spot a fraud and what's the best way to drop 19 stories.

DON MARTIN DEPT. PART II

ONE FINE DAY DURING THE CIVIL WAR

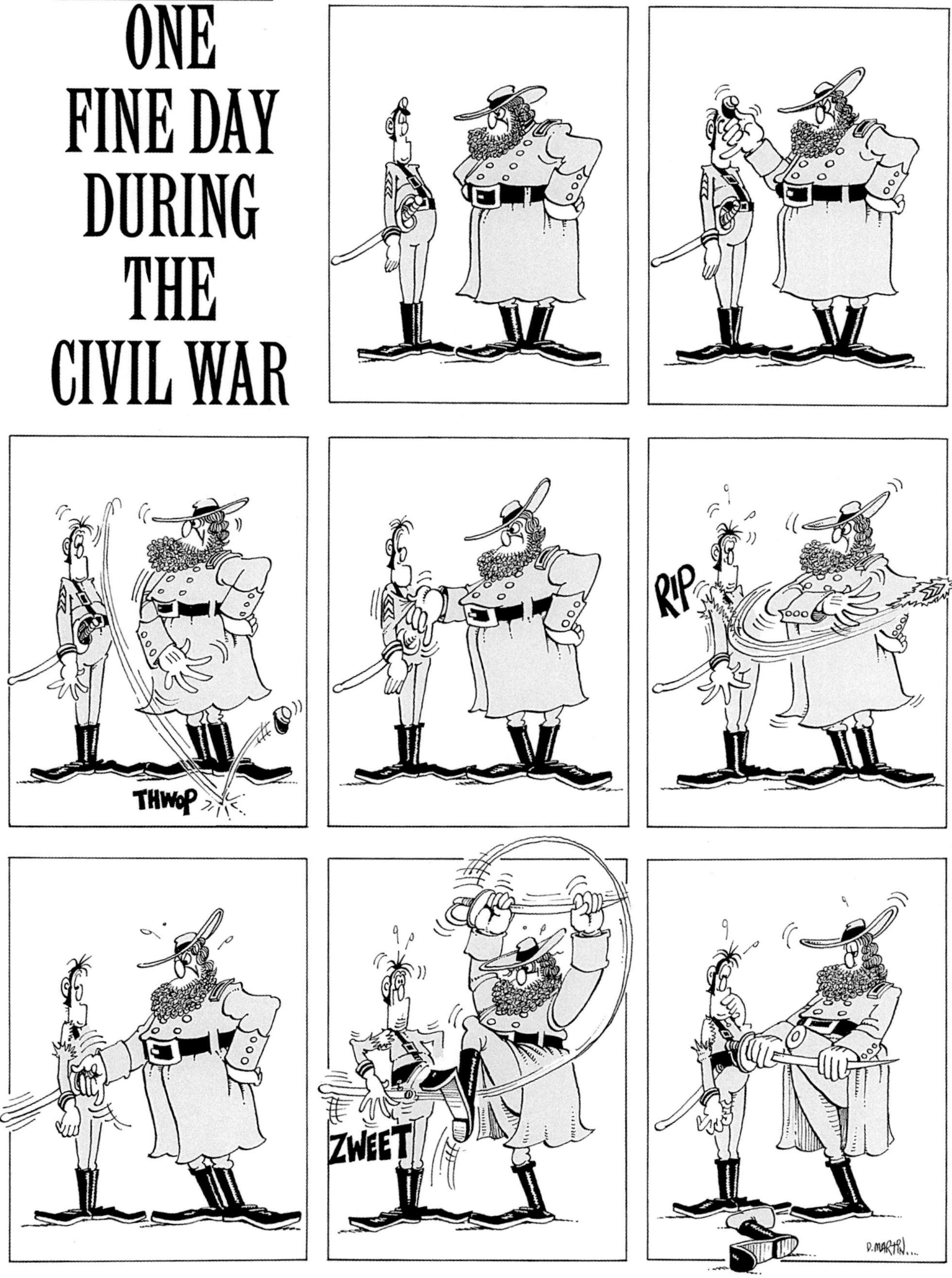
THWOP
RIP
ZWEET
D. MARTIN...

I CAN'T BREATHE!!

THANK YOU, *STOPPA-DA-SNEEZIN'®* !

STOPPA-DA-SNEEZIN'®: *WHAT IT DOES*

*_Stoppa-Da-Sneezin'®_ stops wheezing, coughing, snoring, crying, chafing, itching, burning, scratching, and, in some cases, breathing. It has not proven to be an effective remedy for sneezing.

*_Stoppa-Da-Sneezin'®_ should not be used to treat ACUTE symptoms. It is mildly effective on very mild symptoms, and 100% effective on no symptoms.

***Success Rate:** More than 90% of the 2% that survived till the end of the controlled clinical study reported that they experienced something.

*42 patients were given _Stoppa-Da-Sneezin'®_ and 42 patients were given a placebo. Some felt better and some didn't. Tests would have been more conclusive if we had kept track of who got the real pills and who got the placebo.

by Dick DeBartolo
WRITER

Outside of MAD movie satires, my favorite things to write are ad parodies; the first thing I ever sold to MAD, 50 years ago, was an advertisement take-off. My all-time favorite MAD ad was for a cold pill I called "STOPPA-DA-SNEEZIN'." Those two-page drug ads are just ripe for satire. They start out with one page of total puffery that promises to cure anything from toe fungus to a bad accent, followed by another page that basically tells you that taking just one of the advertised

STOPPA-DA-SNEEZIN'®: *WHAT YOU NEED TO KNOW*

Before use: Check with your doctor and your pharmacist. Also, your pharmacist's doctor and your doctor's pharmacist. Boy, you'll be busy!

24-Hour Relief: Should occur over a 30-day period, averaging about 49 minutes of relief a day.

Drug Use and Dependence: There is no indication that ***Stoppa-Da-Sneezin'®*** is addictive or habit forming. Scientists in our marketing department are now working to try to correct that.

Stoppa-Da-Sneezin'® is not a substitute for other drugs. It IS however a substitute for MOP & GLO, Heavy Duty Lysol, WD-40 and Lo-Cal Cool Whip Topping.

This product is available ONLY by prescription. However some unscrupulous pharmacies have been known to sell it under the counter. For a list of unscrupulous pharmacies, please contact us.

STOPPA-DA-SNEEZIN'®: *IS IT RIGHT FOR YOU?*

Ask your doctor. If your doctor recommends ***Stoppa-Da-Sneezin'®***, begin immediately. If your doctor does not recommend our product, tell him to call our Doctor's Gift Incentive Program immediately.

This drug has been approved by the FDA (Fiendish Drug Administration).

Are there any side effects?

There are no known side effects, but your entire body may become numb, hot, cold, lukewarm and insensitive to pain. If you are able to drive nails into a cement wall with your forehead and not feel a stinging sensation, you might consider reducing the number of pills you're taking. **Body Shrinkage:** Fingernails and toenails may shrink and fall off. At the very least, they will become soft and may melt. Wear cheap socks while taking this drug. **Impairment of Fertility:** Studies with laboratory mice indicate no reduced sexual drive, therefore the patient should not experience any adverse reaction if he/she is sexually attracted to laboratory mice. **Adverse Reactions:** Nasal burning, bruising, irritation, redness, soreness, infection, and, in very few cases (less than 71%), complete blockage of oxygen to the brain. **Cardiovascular:** May cause heart to slow down, speed up, stop, reverse direction, palpitate, skip or relocate. In rare cases, heart will start to operate as a second liver. **Vision:** Blurry vision, watery eyes, conjunctivitis, peripheral edema and glaucoma can occur. If you experience temporary blindness while driving, pull over to the side of the road for a few minutes. If blindness persists, re-read product dosage instructions carefully. **Nervous System:** Paresthesia, confusion, hyperkinesia, hypertonia, vertigo and the desire to burrow underground and live in a hole are other possible side effects. Also Axolotl may occur. **Gastrointestinal:** Hysopedsia, abdominal pain, diarrhea, flatulence, constipation, vomiting, ulcerative stomatitis, aggravated tooth caries, gastritis, rectal hemorrhaging, hemorrhoids and melanoma may occur in "cry baby type" patients. **Hair:** May turn gray, curl, loosen, fall out, move, thicken, thin, recede or start growing on the inside of the scalp. Hair growing on the inside is not particularly harmful, but it will make shaving and haircuts slightly more difficult. **RHINITIS** and **IDIOPATHIC URTICARIA** can occur, but only people who know what these words mean need be concerned. **Blood Pressure:** This drug should not be taken by patients with high blood pressure or low blood pressure. Or normal blood pressure. There are no adverse effects for people with no blood pressure. **Dosage:** Two pills every four hours. If symptoms persist, try four pills every two hours. Don't take more than 48 pills in 181 hours 20 minutes, or at one time, unless of course ***Stoppa-Da-Sneezin'®*** is near the end of its shelf life and you have to use it up quickly. **Interaction with Food and Other Drugs:** For best results we recommend you do not eat 24 hours before, or 24 hours after taking **Stoppa-Da-Sneezin'®**. If you are taking other drugs, triple the recommended dosage of ***Stoppa-Da-Sneezin'®*** so your body knows it's in there! **Explosion Hazard:** While recommended dosages are nonvolatile (in general), excessive use in a confined area near an open flame can result in a small explosion, estimated to be less than the equivalent of five sticks of dynamite, or 200 cherry bombs.

This is a brief copy of the side effects. For a copy of ALL the side effects, call 1-800-212-ACHOO and ask for publication SDS-a7, volumes 1 through 26.

STOPPA-DA-SNEEZIN'®

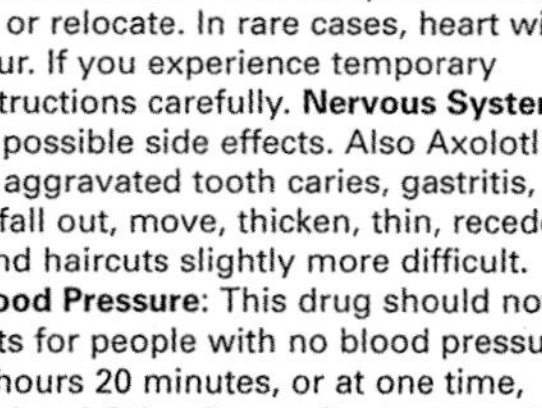
STOPPA-DA-SNEEZIN'®

PHOTO: IRVING SCHILD WRITER: DICK DEBARTOLO

MAD #354/FEBRUARY 1997

pills could kill you instantly.

I had the most fun writing the STOPPA-DA-SNEEZIN' side effects, which, as you can see, takes up a solid paragraph of tiny type. It was one of the few times I wrote something really fast, then read it, and actually broke myself up laughing. Hopefully it will make you laugh too. If it doesn't, may I suggest a new companion product from STOPPA-DA-SNEEZIN'. It's called STARTA-DA-LAUGHIN'. Please.

MOMA

The Art of Monkeyangelo
September 1 - December 15, 1982

THE MUSEUM OF MONKEY ART

DAVID
BY
MONKEYANGELO

ARTIST: HERMANN MEJIA

MOMA

Gorilla With a Pearl Earring
Banannas Vermeer's Masterpiece on loan
June 6, 1990 - January 8, 1991

THE MUSEUM OF MONKEY ART

ARTIST: ROBERTO PARADA

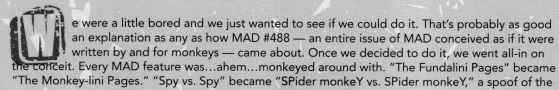

e were a little bored and we just wanted to see if we could do it. That's probably as good an explanation as any as how MAD #488 — an entire issue of MAD conceived as if it were written by and for monkeys — came about. Once we decided to do it, we went all-in on the conceit. Every MAD feature was…ahem…monkeyed around with. "The Fundalini Pages" became "The Monkey-lini Pages." "Spy vs. Spy" became "SPider monkeY vs. SPider monkeY," a spoof of the

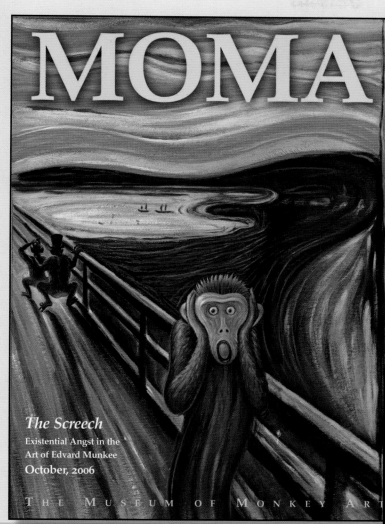

MOMA

The Screech
Existential Angst in the
Art of Edvard Munkee
October, 2006

THE MUSEUM OF MONKEY ART

ARTIST: JAMES WARHOLA

Whistler's Monkey
Simian Art at the Fin de Siècle
March 27 - September 3, 1999

MOMA

THE MUSEUM OF MONKEY ART

ARTIST: RICHARD WILLIAMS

dating website "eHarmony" became "eHarmonkey" and a Banana Republic catalog became, what else, "Bananas Republic." But my personal favorite article featured classic works of art in a catalog from MoMA —The Museum of Monkey Art. In the end, the issue proved two things: first, there is no limit to how far the MAD staff will go to prove its stupidity and, secondly, there is a surprisingly high number of ways you can turn flinging poop at humans into a punch line. — *John Ficarra*

How to Draw a Monkey

By Noted Artist Skittles O'Shea

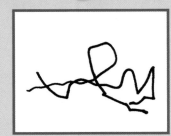

1. Begin by drawing a circle. Don't worry if it's not perfectly round.

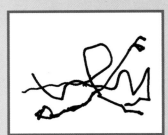

2. Now add a nose right in the middle of the circle. Be careful not to make it too big. We're not drawing a mandrill here. (They're much too hard to draw.)

3. Next, just above the nose we add two eyes. Make them small and sort of monkeylike.

4. On both sides of the circle we add the ears. Chimps have big ears and rhesus monkeys have tiny ears. Let's make this fellow a chimp.

5. Okay. Now it's time to give our monkey a mouth. Let's give him a big smile.

6. Hey. Don't forget to add his deadly sharp monkey teeth.

7. Now just above the eyes, we add his furrowed brow. Because, despite his great big smile, there's plenty of turmoil in the world to fret about. Even for a monkey. What am I saying? *Especially* for a monkey.

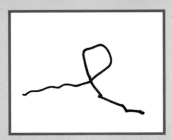

8. Okay. Just below his left eye (that's the eye on your right), add a tiny teardrop tattoo. This indicates that he may have killed another monkey in prison. Hey, it happens.

9. Finally we put the finishing touches on his monkey facial features by adding scars, blemishes, wrinkles, or shaved medical testing patches. And there you have it. A monkey drawing you can be proud of. Well done.

WRITER AND ARTIST: JOHN "ZIG ZAG" CALDWELL

MAD #488/APRIL 2008

by Teresa Burns Parkhurst
WRITER/ARTIST

Chances are, I may not be the only contributor to choose a John Caldwell piece, because we all know what happens when Caldwell doesn't get any attention, and frankly, I don't have the time, energy, or stockpile of Rust-Oleum to resurface my Corolla yet again. However, I think I am the only contributor who refers to him by his baptismal name of Helen. So, there's that.

Truth is, if not for Helen, I'd still have my TV table and cigar box set up down at the corner trying to hawk cartoons and tiny Play-Doh pies and cakes. He's the one who took me by the collar and then forgot what he was going to say and then quickly made up something else using his cheesy mob voice, but I knew what he meant. And it changed the direction of my life. And my collar.

Sure, we all know this isn't representative of his true skill and expertise when it comes to, say, drawing an epileptic monk gone bad, but, it's funny as hell (personal fave: "Let's make this fellow a chimp." Kills me), he barely had to do anything, and, HELLO, he got paid for it. Genius.

So thank you, Helen, and all of the comical powers-that-be who have led me to my own scribblings on the legendary pages of MAD, thus affording this cartoonist much happiness, and, when necessary, the random case of Rust-Oleum.

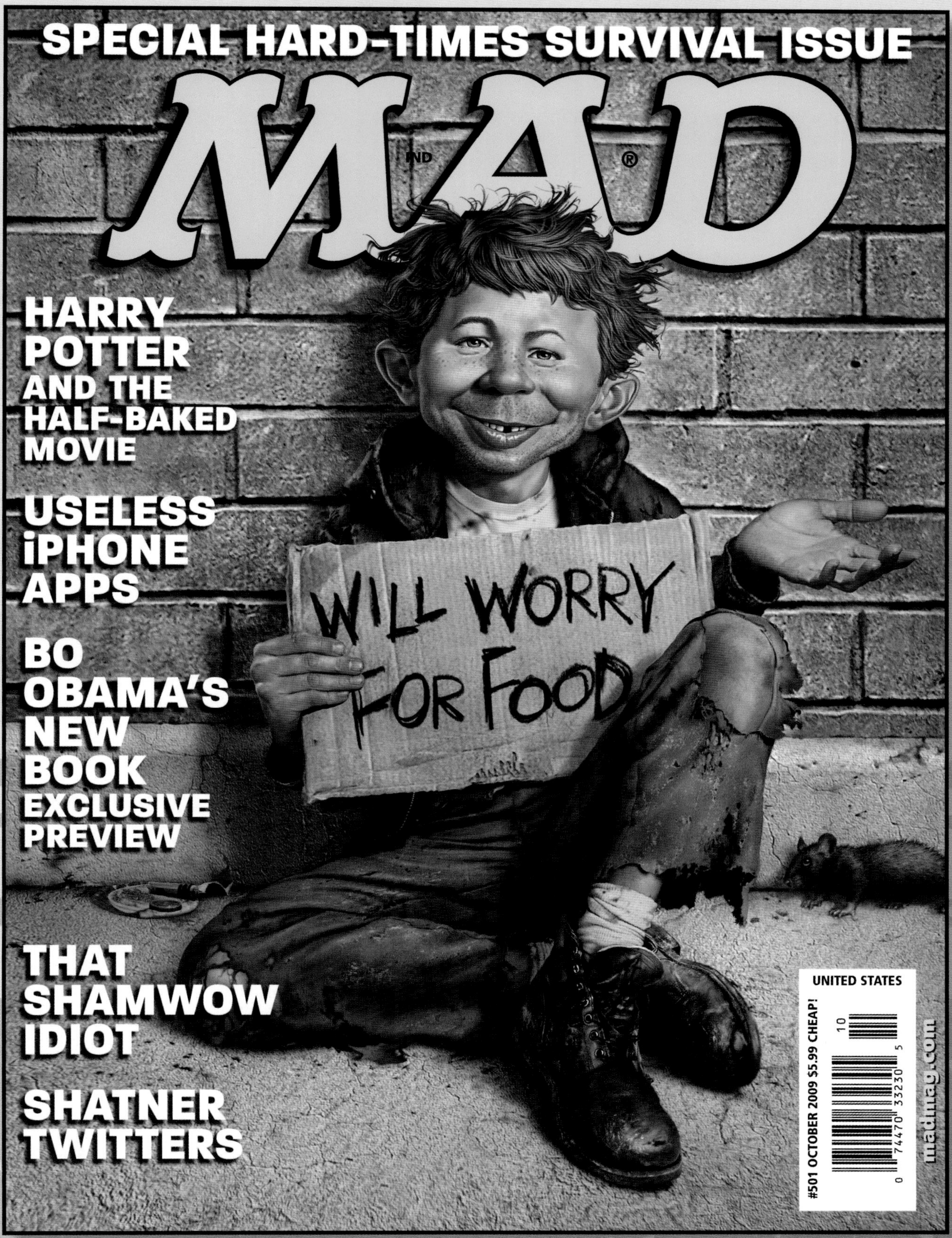
SPECIAL HARD-TIMES SURVIVAL ISSUE
MAD
HARRY POTTER AND THE HALF-BAKED MOVIE
USELESS iPHONE APPS
BO OBAMA'S NEW BOOK EXCLUSIVE PREVIEW
THAT SHAMWOW IDIOT
SHATNER TWITTERS
WILL WORRY FOR FOOD
UNITED STATES
#501 OCTOBER 2009 $5.99 CHEAP!
madmag.com
MAD #501/OCTOBER 2009

by Mark Fredrickson
ARTIST

A personal favorite of mine from MAD is my own cover of a homeless Alfred with his cardboard "Will Worry for Food" sign. This cover was featured on a few financial blogs that dealt with the stock market. Ironically, the image was seen as a contrarian Wall Street indicator — when Wall Street is bearish, contrarians say it's time to buy stocks. Strangely enough, the cover presaged a huge rally in the stock market that's still going strong. Yes, you can make money by reading MAD. The cover was also memorable for the type on the sign. My favorite art director, MAD's extraordinarily talented Sam Viviano, gave me his usual goofy doodle to get me going on the cover art. His roughly sketched type for the sign was impossible to improve upon, so it appears as he sketched it on Alfred's piece of cardboard.

Nearly all Popular Songs these days are written about "love" . . . falling in love, falling out of love, two-faced love, lost love, unrequited love, etc. But love is only a small part of our lives. What's really important is food! Not only does eating food take up a great deal of our time, but it's also absolutely vital to our survival. After all, you can't live on love alone!

SONGS OF

ARTIST: PAUL COKER, JR.

THE DELICATESSEN CANTATA
(Sung to the tune of "Hello, Dolly")

Hello, Delly!
This is Joe, Delly!
Would you please send up a
    nice corned beef on rye!
A box of Ritz, Delly!
And some Schlitz, Delly!
Some chopped liver and a
    sliver of your apple pie!

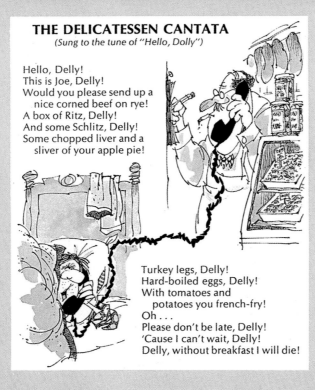

Turkey legs, Delly!
Hard-boiled eggs, Delly!
With tomatoes and
    potatoes you french-fry!
Oh . . .
Please don't be late, Delly!
'Cause I can't wait, Delly!
Delly, without breakfast I will die!

THE HOT PIZZA SERENADE
(Sung to the tune of "There's A Small Hotel")

There's a strange new dye
On my fav-rite tie—
I got it when I ate
Hot Pizza!

There's a glob of goo
On my new suede shoe—
I got it when I ate
Hot Pizza!

Each time that I eat it
    I am dripping Mozzerella!
I need an umbrella—
    Sloppy fella!

When my clothes have spots
Thick as polka dots,
I scrape the greasy stuff
From my collar, shirt and cuff,
And know I've had enough
Hot Pizza!

THE AIRLINE ANTHEM
(Sung to the tune of "Tonight")

In flight!
In flight!
They serve great food in flight!
The sirloins are so tasty and rare!

In flight!
In flight!
I try to eat in flight!
But it just doesn't work in the air!

In flight!
Those headwinds we are bucking!
And soon I am upchucking!
Oh, what a sorry sight!

I'm white
With fright
From trying to hold down every bite
In . . . flight!

by Anthony Barbieri
WRITER

Since I was about six, I've known Frank Jacobs' fake songs more than the real ones they're based on. It started when the platoon of old ladies who sat on the stoop outside my Brooklyn apartment demanded entertainment. I immediately busted out with MAD's hot new tune, "Bad Breath Ballad" (...to the tune of "Moon River"). Chopped liver! Onions on the side.... It killed (the charges were later dropped). From that moment on, it was all about MAD. "Dave Berg this" and "Snappy Answers that." But Frank Jacobs

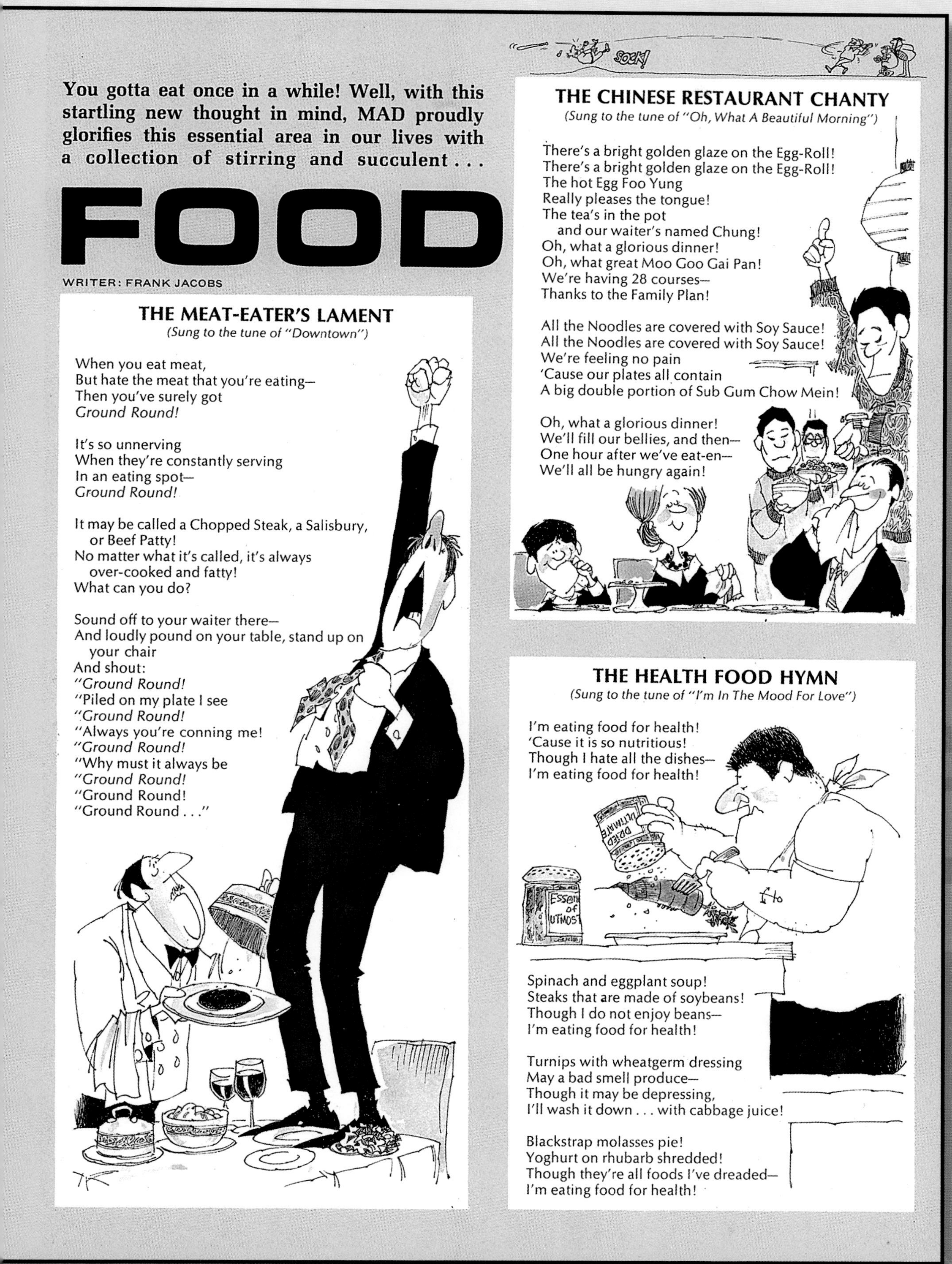

You gotta eat once in a while! Well, with this startling new thought in mind, MAD proudly glorifies this essential area in our lives with a collection of stirring and succulent . . .

FOOD

WRITER: FRANK JACOBS

THE MEAT-EATER'S LAMENT

(Sung to the tune of "Downtown")

When you eat meat,
But hate the meat that you're eating—
Then you've surely got
Ground Round!

It's so unnerving
When they're constantly serving
In an eating spot—
Ground Round!

It may be called a Chopped Steak, a Salisbury,
or Beef Patty!
No matter what it's called, it's always
over-cooked and fatty!
What can you do?

Sound off to your waiter there—
And loudly pound on your table, stand up on
your chair
And shout:
"Ground Round!
"Piled on my plate I see
"Ground Round!
"Always you're conning me!
"Ground Round!
"Why must it always be
"Ground Round!
"Ground Round!
"Ground Round . . ."

THE CHINESE RESTAURANT CHANTY

(Sung to the tune of "Oh, What A Beautiful Morning")

There's a bright golden glaze on the Egg-Roll!
There's a bright golden glaze on the Egg-Roll!
The hot Egg Foo Yung
Really pleases the tongue!
The tea's in the pot
and our waiter's named Chung!
Oh, what a glorious dinner!
Oh, what great Moo Goo Gai Pan!
We're having 28 courses—
Thanks to the Family Plan!

All the Noodles are covered with Soy Sauce!
All the Noodles are covered with Soy Sauce!
We're feeling no pain
'Cause our plates all contain
A big double portion of Sub Gum Chow Mein!

Oh, what a glorious dinner!
We'll fill our bellies, and then—
One hour after we've eat-en—
We'll all be hungry again!

THE HEALTH FOOD HYMN

(Sung to the tune of "I'm In The Mood For Love")

I'm eating food for health!
'Cause it is so nutritious!
Though I hate all the dishes—
I'm eating food for health!

Spinach and eggplant soup!
Steaks that are made of soybeans!
Though I do not enjoy beans—
I'm eating food for health!

Turnips with wheatgerm dressing
May a bad smell produce—
Though it may be depressing,
I'll wash it down . . . with cabbage juice!

Blackstrap molasses pie!
Yoghurt on rhubarb shredded!
Though they're all foods I've dreaded—
I'm eating food for health!

SOCK!
DRIED ULTIMATE
ESSENCE of UTMOST

MAD #110/APRIL 1967

was something special. He wrote over 575 Articles for the magazine, more than anyone. So blame him, folks.

He was THE song parody pioneer. For an aspiring comedy kid, Frank was like Bruce. Vilanch. He was my Dylan. McDermott. I can keep going with this...

A few years back, I got a chance to meet him at Nick Meglin's retirement party, hosted by fellow MAD legend Arnie Kogen. The wine and cheesy jokes were flowing. Starstruck, I introduced myself to Frank just as someone knocked over a

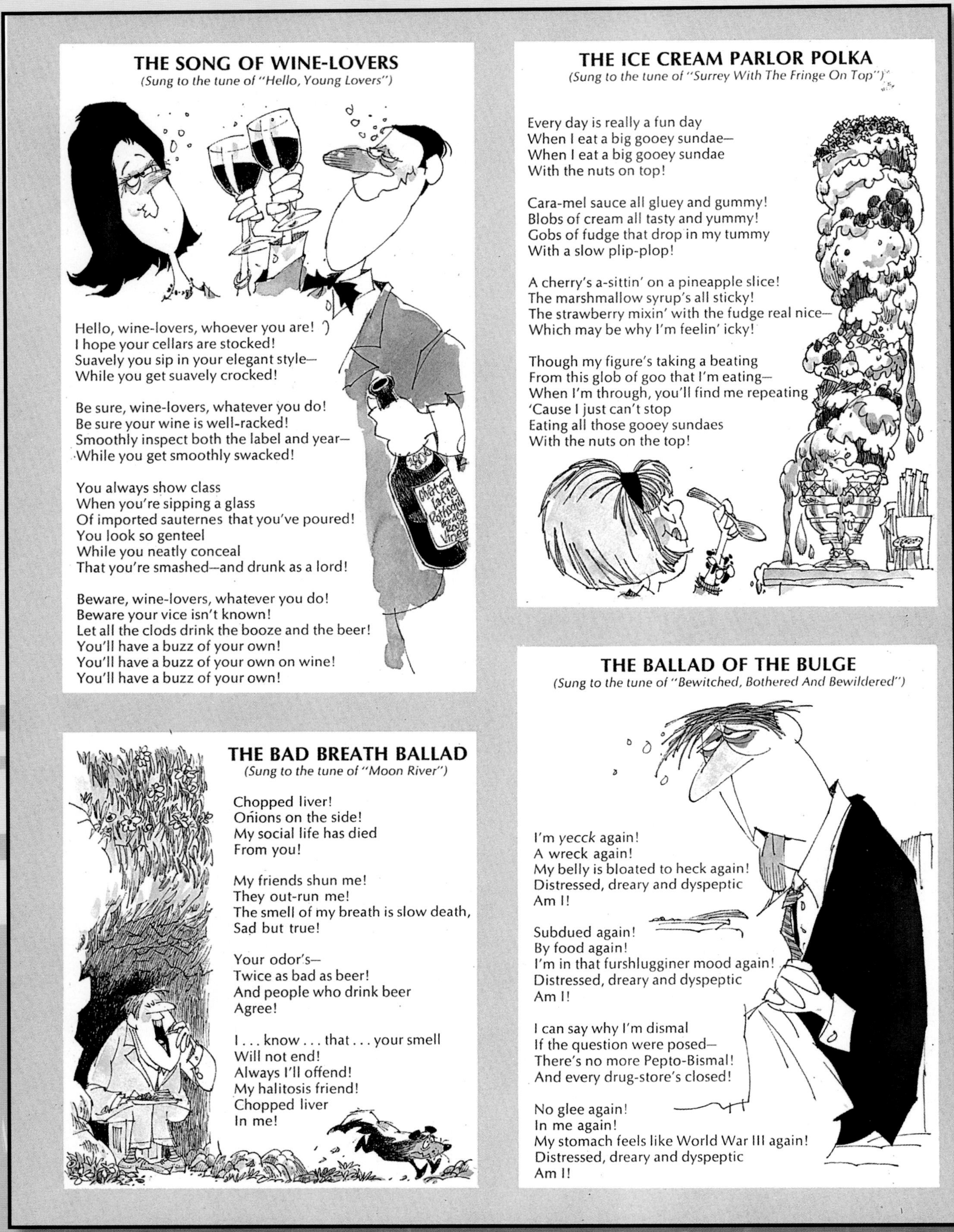

THE SONG OF WINE-LOVERS

(Sung to the tune of "Hello, Young Lovers")

Hello, wine-lovers, whoever you are!
I hope your cellars are stocked!
Suavely you sip in your elegant style—
While you get suavely crocked!

Be sure, wine-lovers, whatever you do!
Be sure your wine is well-racked!
Smoothly inspect both the label and year—
While you get smoothly swacked!

You always show class
When you're sipping a glass
Of imported sauternes that you've poured!
You look so genteel
While you neatly conceal
That you're smashed—and drunk as a lord!

Beware, wine-lovers, whatever you do!
Beware your vice isn't known!
Let all the clods drink the booze and the beer!
You'll have a buzz of your own!
You'll have a buzz of your own on wine!
You'll have a buzz of your own!

THE ICE CREAM PARLOR POLKA

(Sung to the tune of "Surrey With The Fringe On Top")

Every day is really a fun day
When I eat a big gooey sundae—
When I eat a big gooey sundae
With the nuts on top!

Cara-mel sauce all gluey and gummy!
Blobs of cream all tasty and yummy!
Gobs of fudge that drop in my tummy
With a slow plip-plop!

A cherry's a-sittin' on a pineapple slice!
The marshmallow syrup's all sticky!
The strawberry mixin' with the fudge real nice—
Which may be why I'm feelin' icky!

Though my figure's taking a beating
From this glob of goo that I'm eating—
When I'm through, you'll find me repeating
'Cause I just can't stop
Eating all those gooey sundaes
With the nuts on the top!

THE BAD BREATH BALLAD

(Sung to the tune of "Moon River")

Chopped liver!
Onions on the side!
My social life has died
From you!

My friends shun me!
They out-run me!
The smell of my breath is slow death,
Sad but true!

Your odor's—
Twice as bad as beer!
And people who drink beer
Agree!

I . . . know . . . that . . . your smell
Will not end!
Always I'll offend!
My halitosis friend!
Chopped liver
In me!

THE BALLAD OF THE BULGE

(Sung to the tune of "Bewitched, Bothered And Bewildered")

I'm *yecck* again!
A wreck again!
My belly is bloated to heck again!
Distressed, dreary and dyspeptic
Am I!

Subdued again!
By food again!
I'm in that furshlugginer mood again!
Distressed, dreary and dyspeptic
Am I!

I can say why I'm dismal
If the question were posed—
There's no more Pepto-Bismal!
And every drug-store's closed!

No glee again!
In me again!
My stomach feels like World War III again!
Distressed, dreary and dyspeptic
Am I!

glass of vino behind him. Frank mumbled that he'll "probably get blamed for this" and bolted. That was that.

A magical moment.

There will only ever be one Frank Jacobs but, sadly, there will be a ton of his songs.

Thanks, Frank.

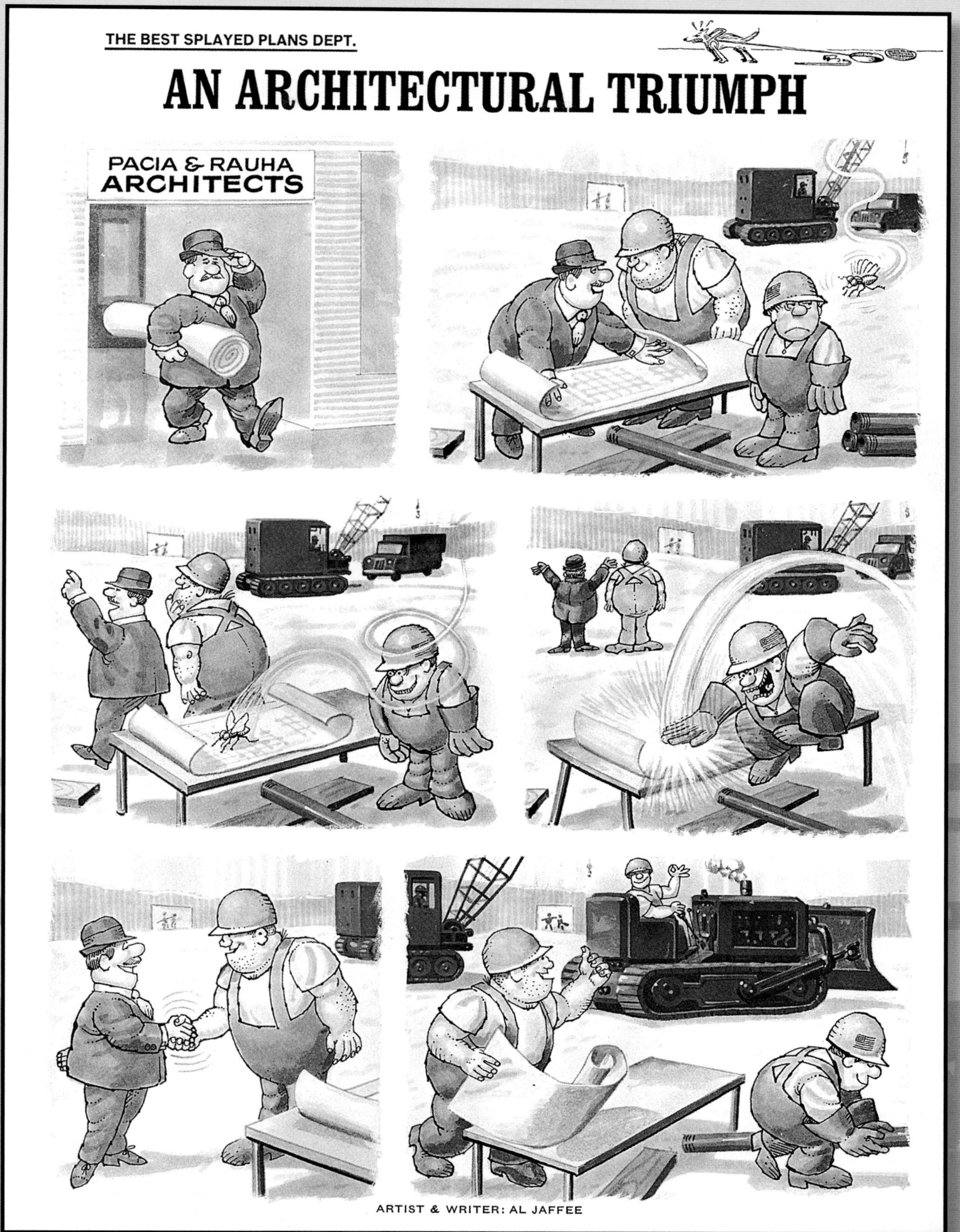
THE BEST SPLAYED PLANS DEPT.
AN ARCHITECTURAL TRIUMPH
PACIA & RAUHA ARCHITECTS
ARTIST & WRITER: AL JAFFEE

MAD #164/JANUARY 1974

by Desmond Devlin
WRITER

Al Jaffee is the man. He's the man who writes sharp, ingenious jokes about a slew of serious subjects, from consumerism to repressed rage to political malfeasance to environmental decay to childhood angst. He's also the man who draws funny pictures about 12-foot cigarettes and magic tricks and people forever puking up chicken bones and fish skeletons. He's the irreplaceable embodiment of MAD Magazine's range: smart but silly, angry but understanding, sophisticated but gross, upbeat but hopeless.

When you spend a lifetime reading him, and I have, you see that he's uncommonly interested in figuring out how things work, and exasperated because things NEVER work. The piece I picked is Al's "An Architectural Triumph." Just look at that second page. It's one of the greatest, most astonishing "reveal" gags ever. What's

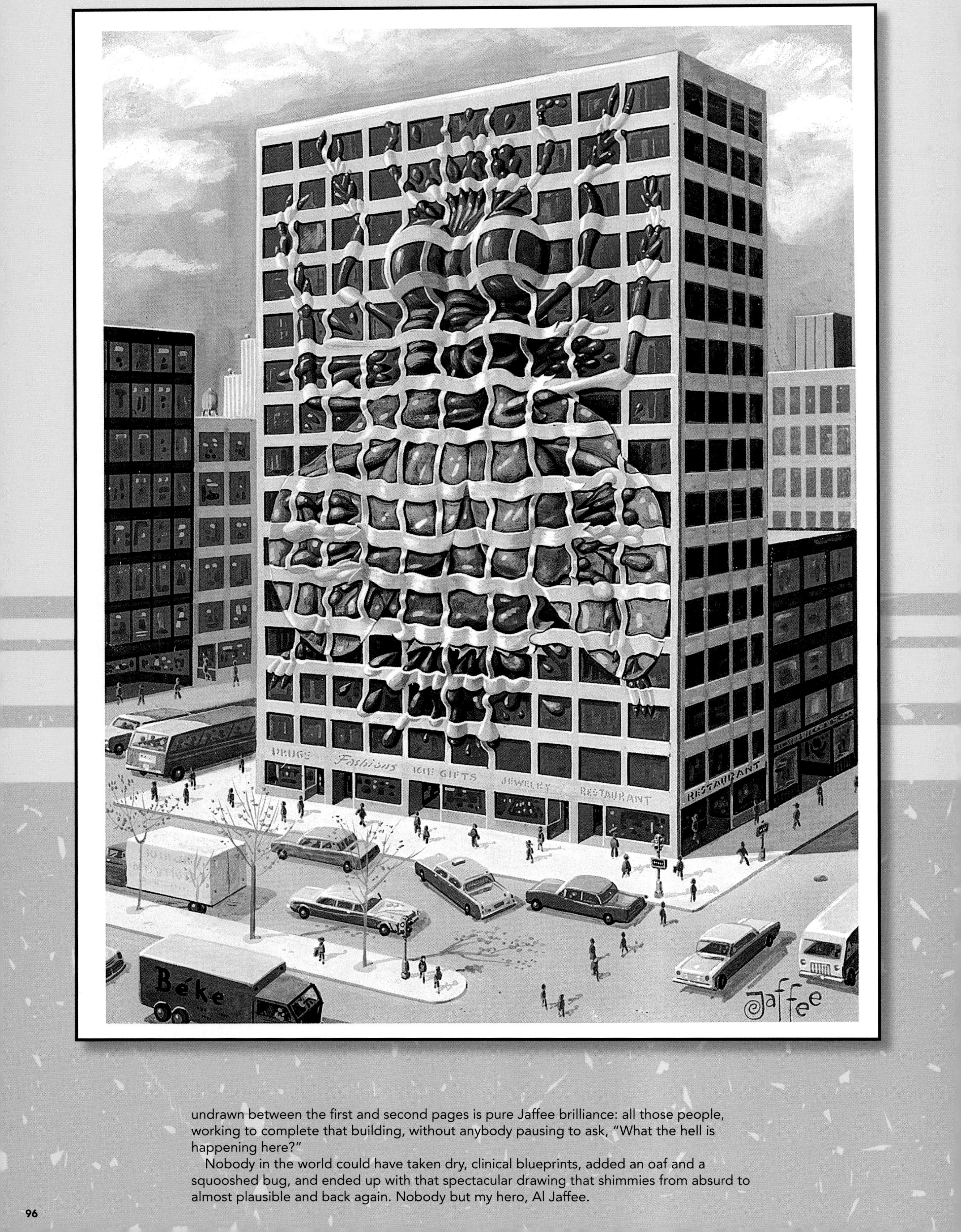
DRUGS
Fashions
GIFTS
JEWELRY
RESTAURANT
RESTAURANT
Béke
Jaffee

undrawn between the first and second pages is pure Jaffee brilliance: all those people, working to complete that building, without anybody pausing to ask, "What the hell is happening here?"

Nobody in the world could have taken dry, clinical blueprints, added an oaf and a squooshed bug, and ended up with that spectacular drawing that shimmies from absurd to almost plausible and back again. Nobody but my hero, Al Jaffee.

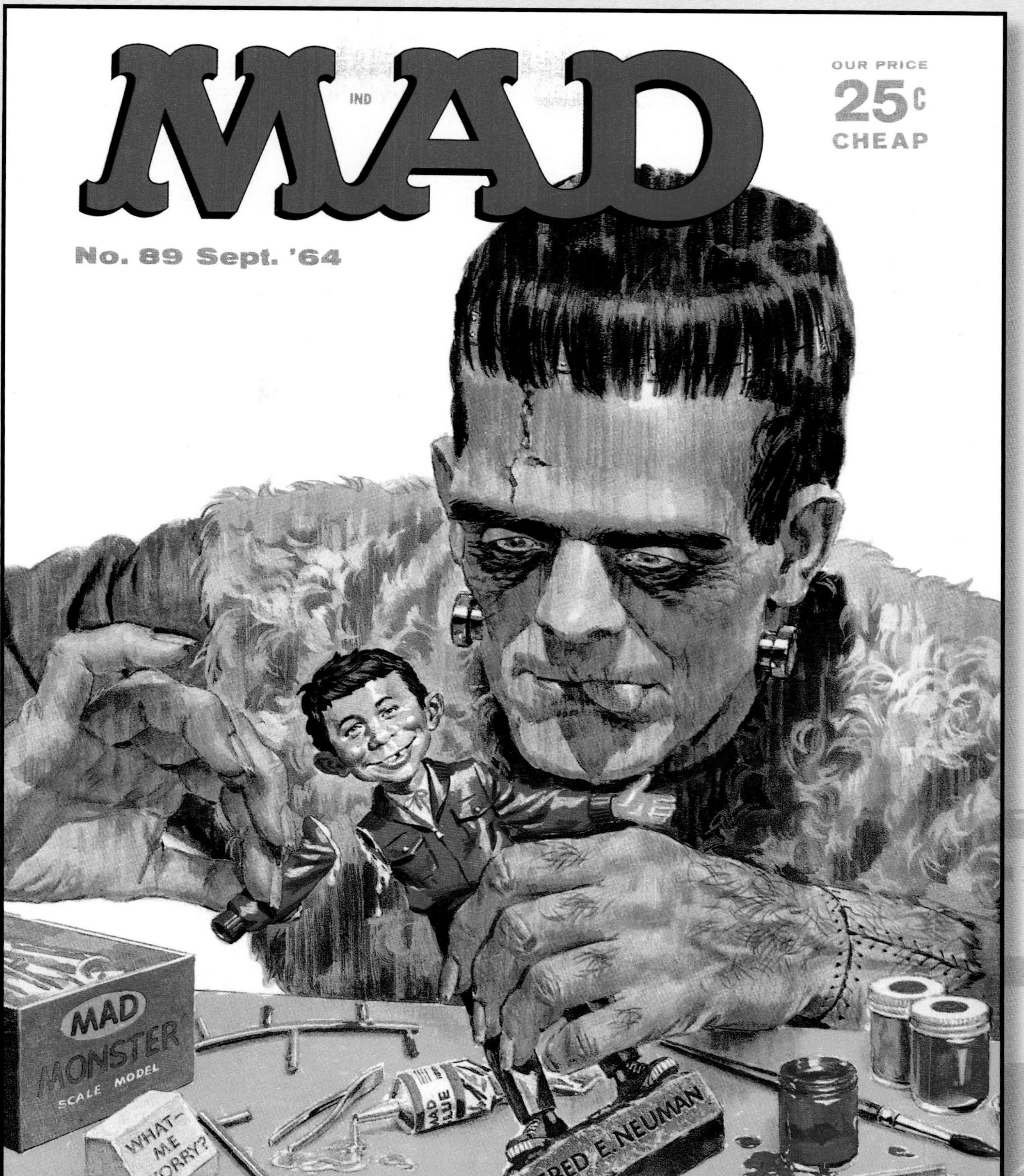
MAD
IND
OUR PRICE
25¢
CHEAP
No. 89 Sept. '64
MAD
MONSTER
SCALE MODEL
WHAT—
ME
WORRY?
MAD
GLUE
ALFRED E. NEUMAN
Norman Mingo

ARTIST: NORMAN MINGO

MAD #89/SEPTEMBER 1964

by Scott Nickel
WRITER/ARTIST

The cover of MAD #89, painted by the inimitable Norman Mingo, features three of my favorite things: Frankenstein, plastic model kits, and Alfred E. Neuman.

I discovered classic Universal monster movies, models, and MAD Magazine at about the same time. I was just a wee lad, and I would spend hours watching movies on TV, building monster kits and laughing hysterically at the pages of MAD. The incredible work of Mort Drucker, Jack Davis, Al Jaffee, Don Martin, Frank Jacobs, Larry Siegel, Dick DeBartolo, Sergio Aragonés and the rest of the Usual Gang of Idiots permanently warped my brain…or maybe it was all that model glue I accidentally inhaled while putting together Frankenstein, Dracula, and their plastic pals.

Hard to say.

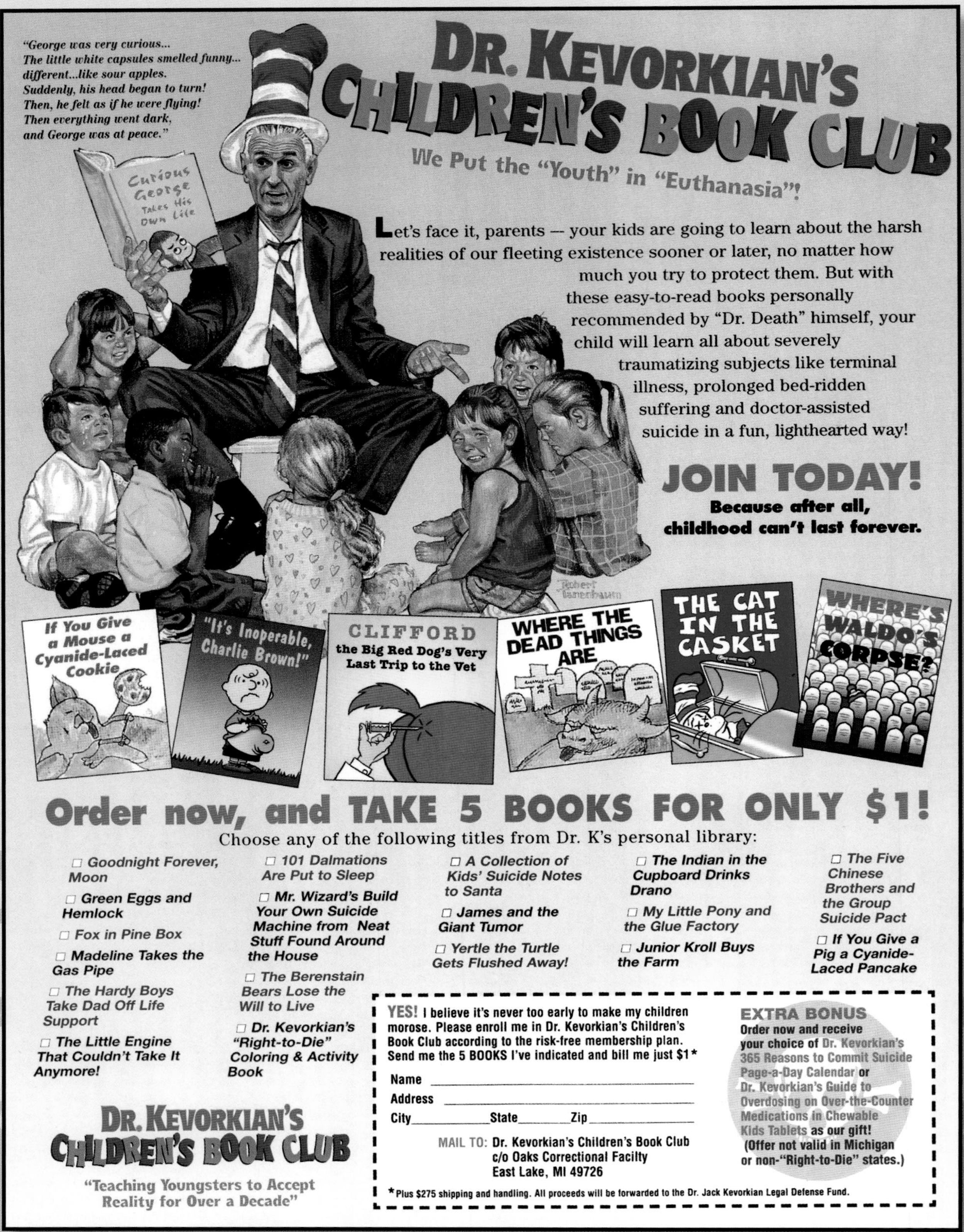
"George was very curious...
The little white capsules smelled funny...
different...like sour apples.
Suddenly, his head began to turn!
Then, he felt as if he were flying!
Then everything went dark,
and George was at peace."
DR. KEVORKIAN'S CHILDREN'S BOOK CLUB
We Put the "Youth" in "Euthanasia"!
Curious George Takes His Own Life
Let's face it, parents — your kids are going to learn about the harsh realities of our fleeting existence sooner or later, no matter how much you try to protect them. But with these easy-to-read books personally recommended by "Dr. Death" himself, your child will learn all about severely traumatizing subjects like terminal illness, prolonged bed-ridden suffering and doctor-assisted suicide in a fun, lighthearted way!
JOIN TODAY!
Because after all, childhood can't last forever.
If You Give a Mouse a Cyanide-Laced Cookie
"It's Inoperable, Charlie Brown!"
CLIFFORD the Big Red Dog's Very Last Trip to the Vet
WHERE THE DEAD THINGS ARE
THE CAT IN THE CASKET
WHERE'S WALDO'S CORPSE?
Order now, and TAKE 5 BOOKS FOR ONLY $1!
Choose any of the following titles from Dr. K's personal library:
□ Goodnight Forever, Moon
□ Green Eggs and Hemlock
□ Fox in Pine Box
□ Madeline Takes the Gas Pipe
□ The Hardy Boys Take Dad Off Life Support
□ The Little Engine That Couldn't Take It Anymore!
□ 101 Dalmations Are Put to Sleep
□ Mr. Wizard's Build Your Own Suicide Machine from Neat Stuff Found Around the House
□ The Berenstain Bears Lose the Will to Live
□ Dr. Kevorkian's "Right-to-Die" Coloring & Activity Book
□ A Collection of Kids' Suicide Notes to Santa
□ James and the Giant Tumor
□ Yertle the Turtle Gets Flushed Away!
□ The Indian in the Cupboard Drinks Drano
□ My Little Pony and the Glue Factory
□ Junior Kroll Buys the Farm
□ The Five Chinese Brothers and the Group Suicide Pact
□ If You Give a Pig a Cyanide-Laced Pancake
DR. KEVORKIAN'S CHILDREN'S BOOK CLUB
"Teaching Youngsters to Accept Reality for Over a Decade"
YES! I believe it's never too early to make my children morose. Please enroll me in Dr. Kevorkian's Children's Book Club according to the risk-free membership plan. Send me the 5 BOOKS I've indicated and bill me just $1*
Name
Address
City State Zip
MAIL TO: Dr. Kevorkian's Children's Book Club
c/o Oaks Correctional Facilty
East Lake, MI 49726
EXTRA BONUS
Order now and receive your choice of Dr. Kevorkian's 365 Reasons to Commit Suicide Page-a-Day Calendar or Dr. Kevorkian's Guide to Overdosing on Over-the-Counter Medications in Chewable Kids Tablets as our gift!
(Offer not valid in Michigan or non-"Right-to-Die" states.)
*Plus $275 shipping and handling. All proceeds will be forwarded to the Dr. Jack Kevorkian Legal Defense Fund.

ARTIST: ROBERT TANENBAUM

MAD #386/OCTOBER 1999

by Frank Santopadre
WRITER

Sometimes a comedy piece starts with the most basic jumping-off point. In this case, it was a rather tenuous Dr. Seuss-Dr. Kevorkian connection (since they both went by the title "Dr."). From there, it was a short step to an actual premise: satirizing the glut of celebrity-authored kids' books by juxtaposing children's literature and physician-assisted suicide. Once the MAD editors signed off on the idea of Kevorkian hawking his own line of death-centric kiddie lit, the challenge was coming up with enough titles to flesh out the piece.

The first few came quickly: *Green Eggs and Hemlock...It's Inoperable, Charlie Brown!* When ideas ran dry, I invited an ex-bookstore clerk and TV writer pal, Mike Dobkins, to team up with me. We met at a Hollywood deli and began tossing titles at each other until we had enough jokes.

I laughed out loud when I saw Robert Tanenbaum's brilliant illustration of Dr. Jack reading to a small group of horrified schoolkids while sporting a Cat in the Hat-type hat. The moment you see your writing fully executed by an artist is always a thrill — I'd only imagined what something so bizarre might look like, but Robert's art actually brought it to life.

The crowning achievement, however, would come months later in the form of a reader's letter to MAD: "Dear Editors: the back cover of issue #386, 'Dr. Kevorkian's Children's Book Club,' was cruel. You have stepped over the line between comedic naughtiness and just plain tastelessness. You should realize that killing animals (even cartoon ones) is not funny." (Interestingly, not a word about poor Charlie Brown or Mr. Hardy; only harm coming to the cartoon animals disturbed her.)

Keep those letters coming, readers. If I can deeply offend even one person, I know I've done my job.

John Stamos

I grew up with MAD Magazine, so I knew to be afraid of the day when they'd inevitably spoof *Full House* — which they called "Fool House." Oh, God. You destroyed us! But it was so funny. You got Bob Saget's face about right. Dave Coulier was so excited he took all the pages out and had them framed perfectly, to hang in his house. I think the running gag was that the thing *Full House* really needed was more laugh-track. Ha! We always had that terrible laugh-track where we would say the stupidest joke and it would get such a big laugh. Well, once again, MAD Magazine got it right!

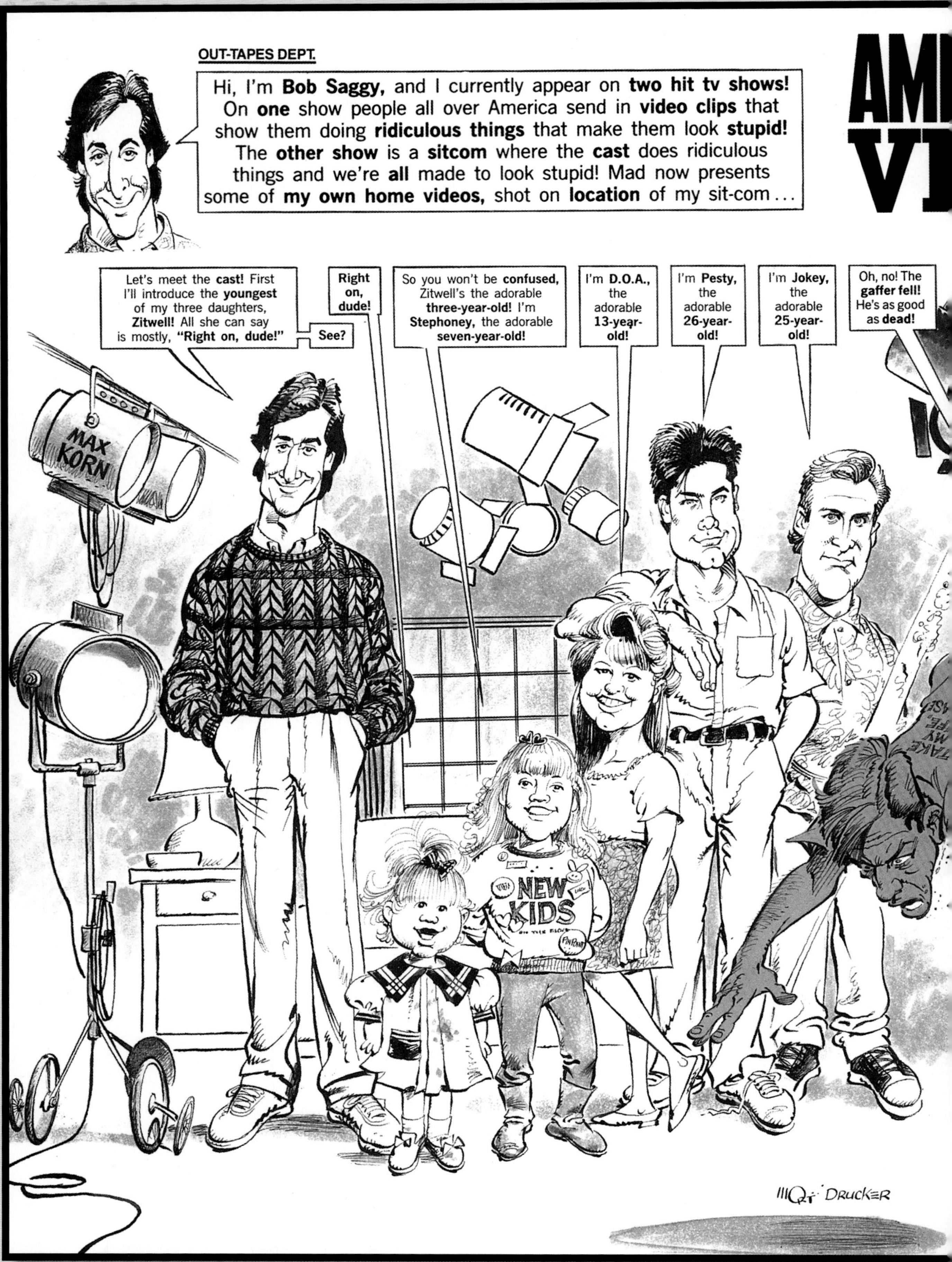
OUT-TAPES DEPT.
Hi, I'm Bob Saggy, and I currently appear on two hit tv shows! On one show people all over America send in video clips that show them doing ridiculous things that make them look stupid! The other show is a sitcom where the cast does ridiculous things and we're all made to look stupid! Mad now presents some of my own home videos, shot on location of my sit-com...
Let's meet the cast! First I'll introduce the youngest of my three daughters, Zitwell! All she can say is mostly, "Right on, dude!"
See?
Right on, dude!
So you won't be confused, Zitwell's the adorable three-year-old! I'm Stephoney, the adorable seven-year-old!
I'm D.O.A., the adorable 13-year-old!
I'm Pesty, the adorable 26-year-old!
I'm Jokey, the adorable 25-year-old!
Oh, no! The gaffer fell! He's as good as dead!
MAX KORN
NEW KIDS

RICA'S PHONIEST HOME VIDEOS
SITS FOOL HOUSE

ARTIST: MORT DRUCKER WRITER: DICK DEBARTOLO

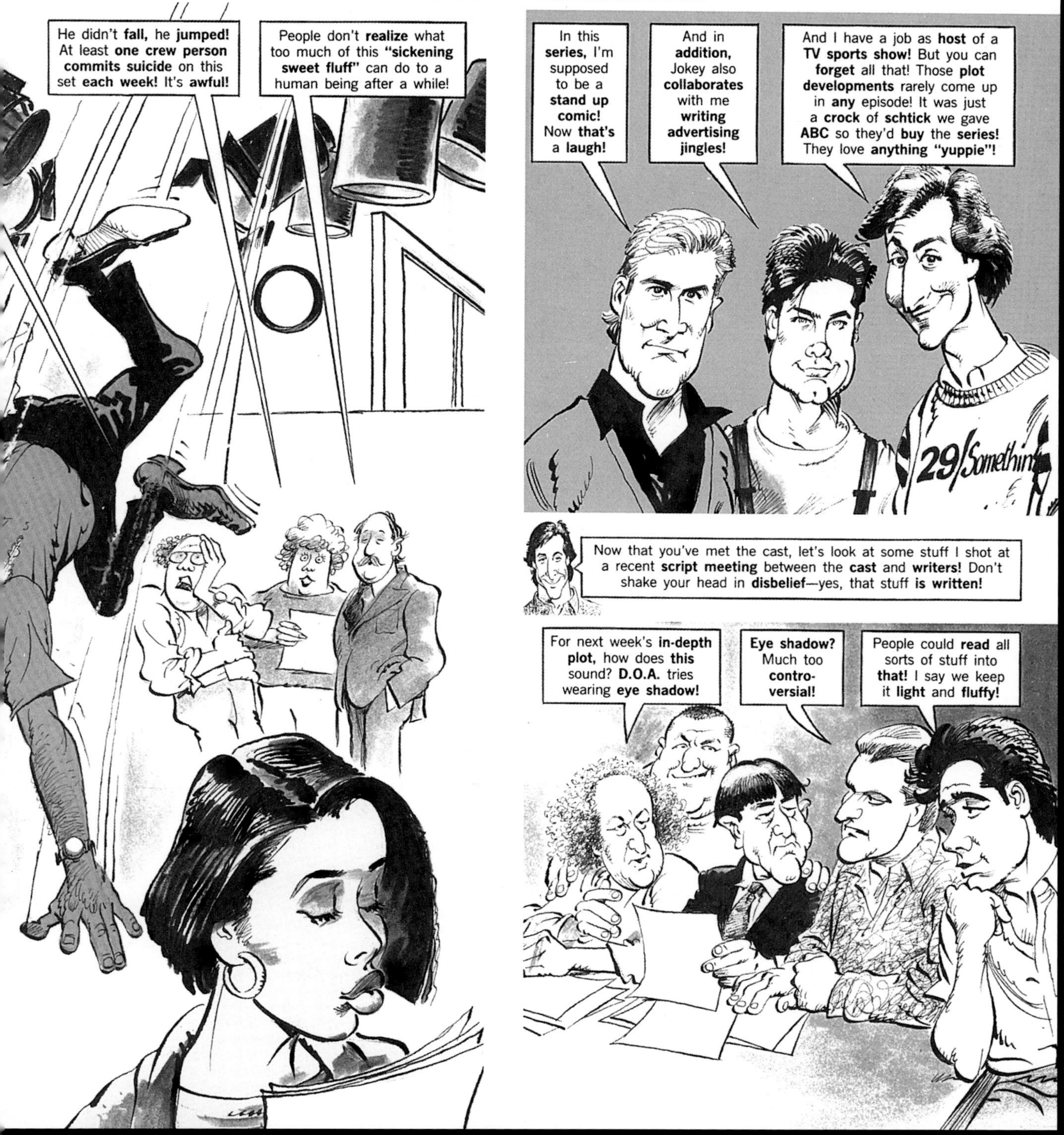

He didn't **fall,** he **jumped!** At least **one crew person commits suicide** on this set **each week!** It's **awful!**
People don't **realize** what too much of this **"sickening sweet fluff"** can do to a human being after a while!
In this **series,** I'm supposed to be a **stand up comic!** Now **that's** a **laugh!**
And in **addition,** Jokey also **collaborates** with me **writing advertising jingles!**
And I have a job as **host** of a **TV sports show!** But you can **forget** all that! Those **plot developments** rarely come up in **any** episode! It was just a **crock of schtick** we gave **ABC** so they'd **buy** the **series!** They love **anything "yuppie"!**
29/Somethin
Now that you've met the cast, let's look at some stuff I shot at a recent **script meeting** between the **cast** and **writers!** Don't shake your head in **disbelief**—yes, that stuff **is written!**
For next week's **in-depth plot,** how does **this** sound? **D.O.A.** tries wearing **eye shadow!**
Eye shadow? Much too **contro-versial!**
People could **read** all sorts of stuff into **that!** I say we keep it **light** and **fluffy!**

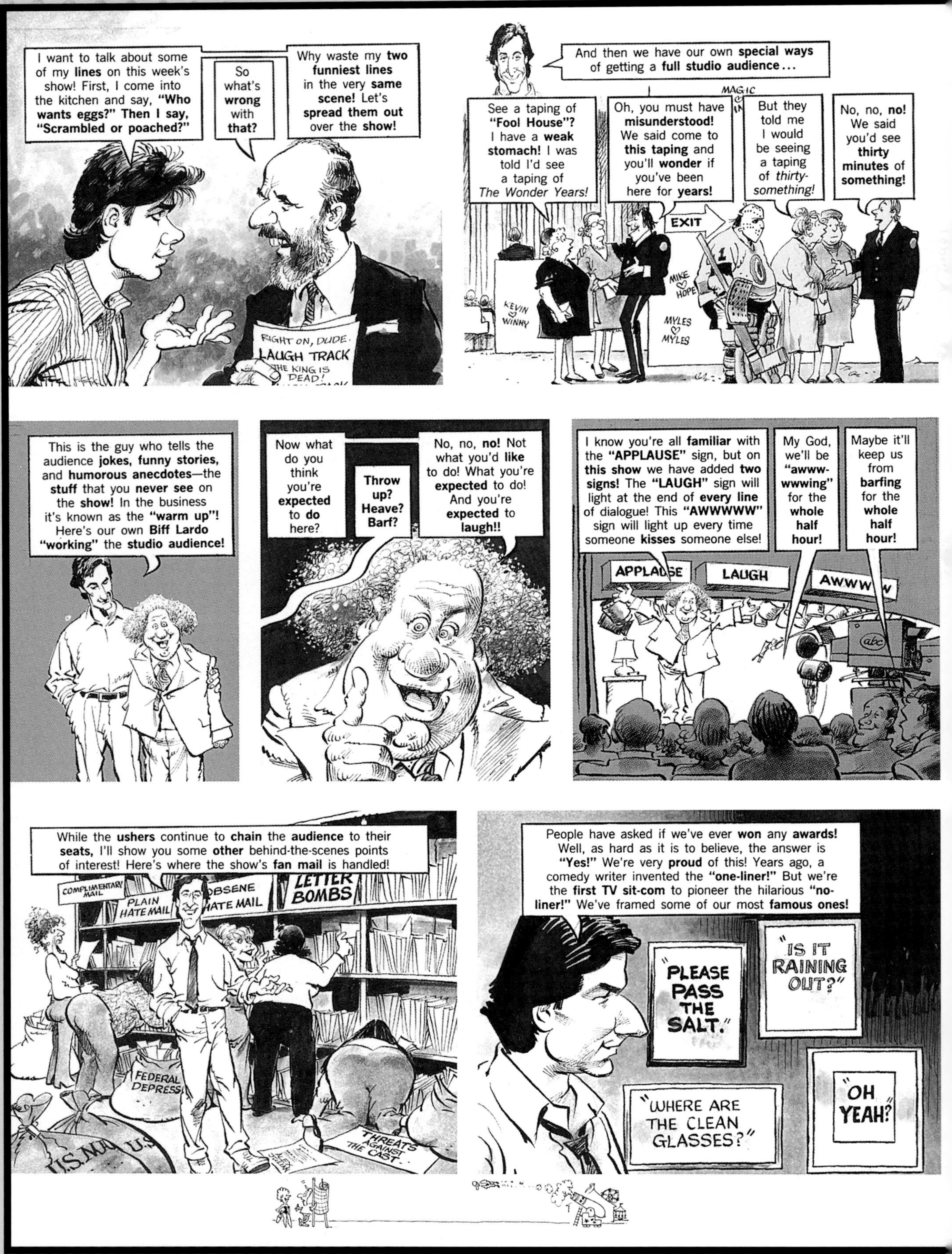

I want to talk about some of my lines on this week's show! First, I come into the kitchen and say, "Who wants eggs?" Then I say, "Scrambled or poached?"
So what's wrong with that?
Why waste my two funniest lines in the very same scene! Let's spread them out over the show!
RIGHT ON, DUDE.
LAUGH TRACK
THE KING IS DEAD!
And then we have our own special ways of getting a full studio audience...
See a taping of "Fool House"? I have a weak stomach! I was told I'd see a taping of The Wonder Years!
Oh, you must have misunderstood! We said come to this taping and you'll wonder if you've been here for years!
But they told me I would be seeing a taping of thirty-something!
No, no, no! We said you'd see thirty minutes of something!
EXIT
KEVIN ♡ WINNY
MIKE ♡ HOPE
MYLES ♡ MYLES
This is the guy who tells the audience jokes, funny stories, and humorous anecdotes—the stuff that you never see on the show! In the business it's known as the "warm up"! Here's our own Biff Lardo "working" the studio audience!
Now what do you think you're expected to do here?
Throw up? Heave? Barf?
No, no, no! Not what you'd like to do! What you're expected to do! And you're expected to laugh!!
I know you're all familiar with the "APPLAUSE" sign, but on this show we have added two signs! The "LAUGH" sign will light at the end of every line of dialogue! This "AWWWWW" sign will light up every time someone kisses someone else!
My God, we'll be "awww-wwwing" for the whole half hour!
Maybe it'll keep us from barfing for the whole half hour!
APPLAUSE
LAUGH
abc
While the ushers continue to chain the audience to their seats, I'll show you some other behind-the-scenes points of interest! Here's where the show's fan mail is handled!
COMPLIMENTARY MAIL
PLAIN HATE MAIL
LETTER BOMBS
FEDERAL DEPRESS
THREATS AGAINST THE CAST
People have asked if we've ever won any awards! Well, as hard as it is to believe, the answer is "Yes!" We're very proud of this! Years ago, a comedy writer invented the "one-liner!" But we're the first TV sit-com to pioneer the hilarious "no-liner!" We've framed some of our most famous ones!
"PLEASE PASS THE SALT."
"IS IT RAINING OUT?"
"WHERE ARE THE CLEAN GLASSES?"
"OH YEAH?"

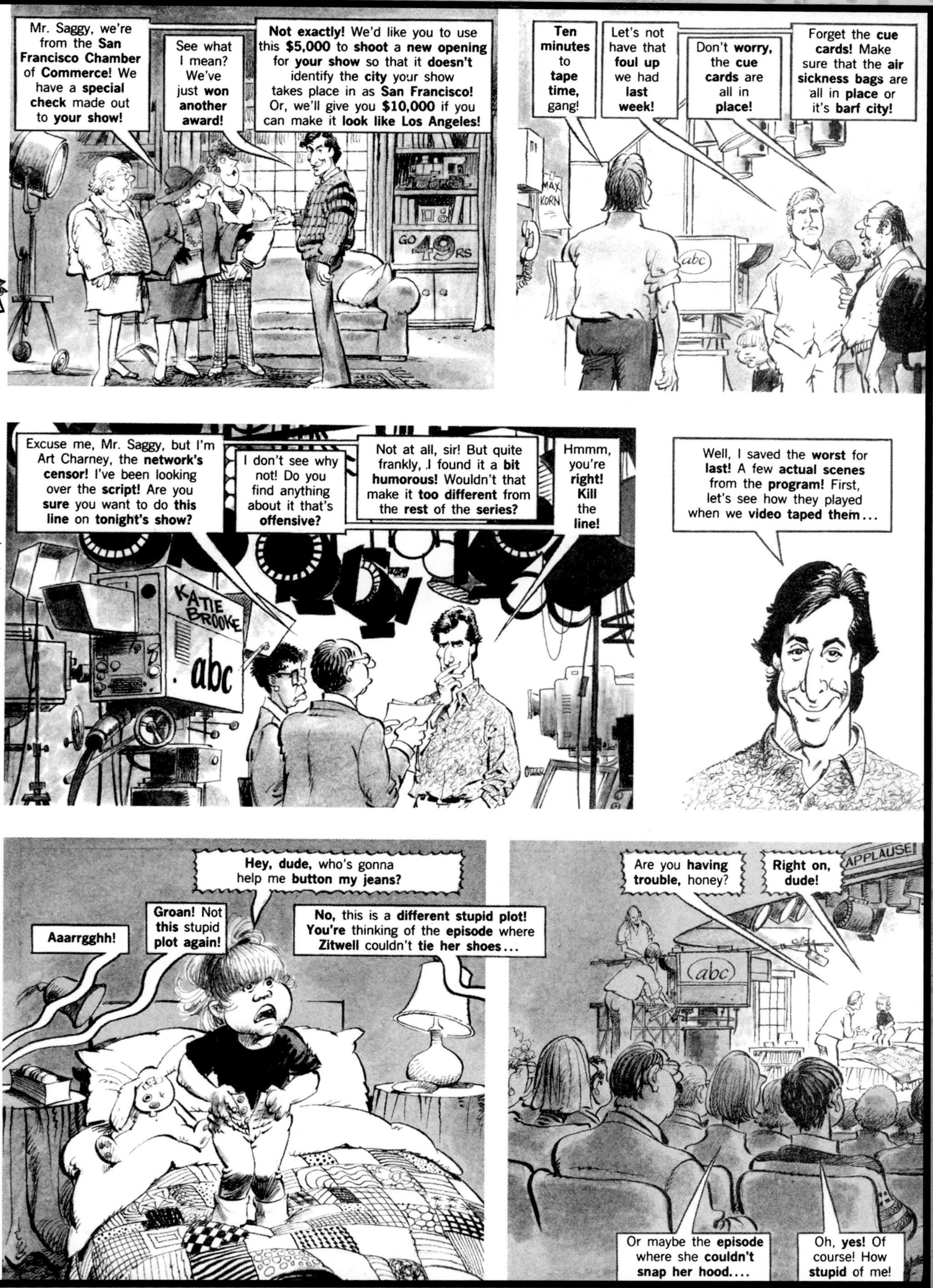

Mr. Saggy, we're from the San Francisco Chamber of Commerce! We have a special check made out to your show!
See what I mean? We've just won another award!
Not exactly! We'd like you to use this $5,000 to shoot a new opening for your show so that it doesn't identify the city your show takes place in as San Francisco! Or, we'll give you $10,000 if you can make it look like Los Angeles!
GO 49RS
Ten minutes to tape time, gang!
Let's not have that foul up we had last week!
Don't worry, the cue cards are all in place!
Forget the cue cards! Make sure that the air sickness bags are all in place or it's barf city!
MAX KORN
abc
Excuse me, Mr. Saggy, but I'm Art Charney, the network's censor! I've been looking over the script! Are you sure you want to do this line on tonight's show?
I don't see why not! Do you find anything about it that's offensive?
Not at all, sir! But quite frankly, I found it a bit humorous! Wouldn't that make it too different from the rest of the series?
Hmmm, you're right! Kill the line!
KATIE BROOKE
abc
Well, I saved the worst for last! A few actual scenes from the program! First, let's see how they played when we video taped them...
Hey, dude, who's gonna help me button my jeans?
Aaarrgghh!
Groan! Not this stupid plot again!
No, this is a different stupid plot! You're thinking of the episode where Zitwell couldn't tie her shoes...
Are you having trouble, honey?
Right on, dude!
APPLAUSE
abc
Or maybe the episode where she couldn't snap her hood....
Oh, yes! Of course! How stupid of me!

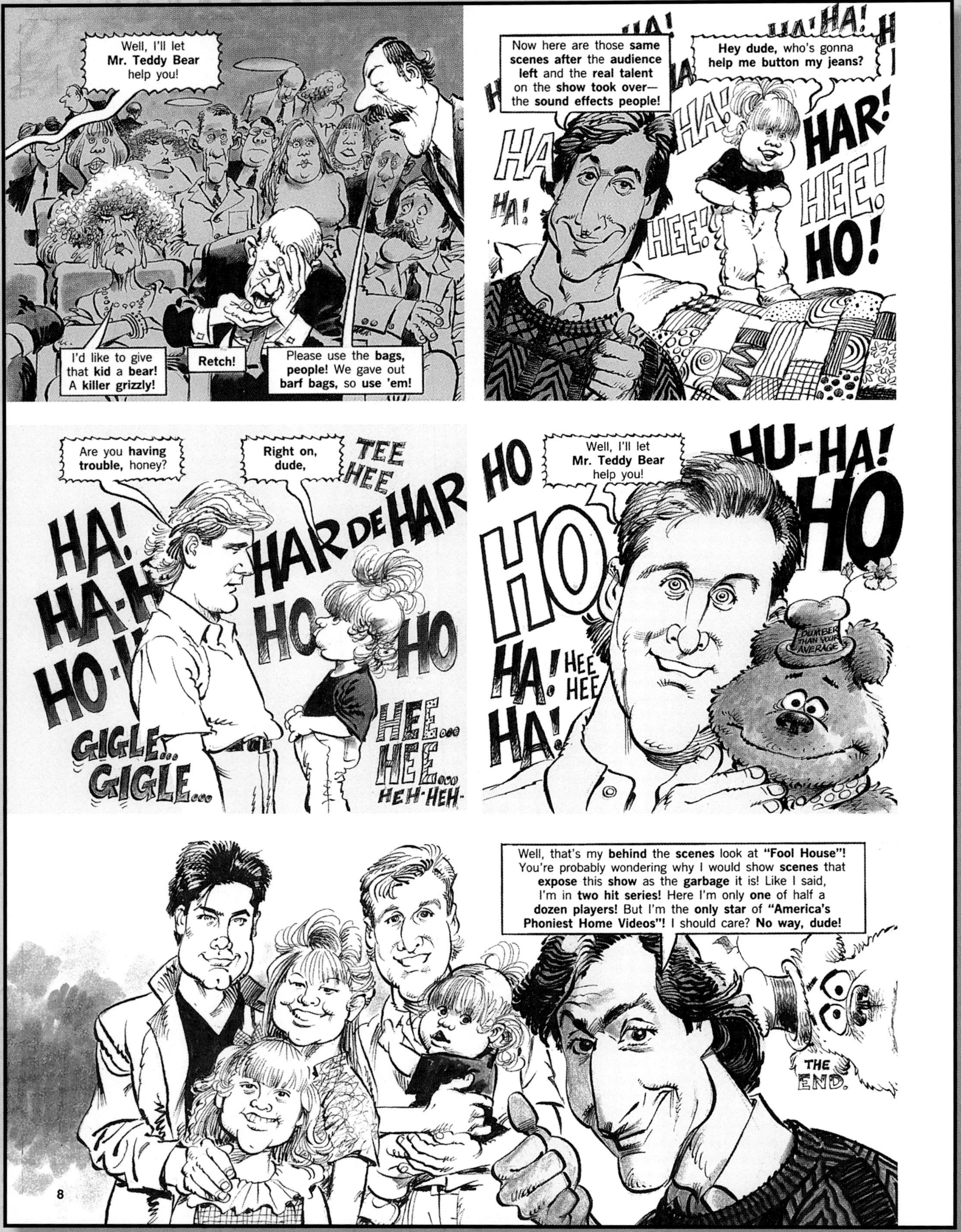
Well, I'll let Mr. Teddy Bear help you!
I'd like to give that kid a bear! A killer grizzly!
Retch!
Please use the bags, people! We gave out barf bags, so use 'em!
Now here are those same scenes after the audience left and the real talent on the show took over— the sound effects people!
HA! HA!
HA!
Hey dude, who's gonna help me button my jeans?
HA!
HA!
HAR! HEE! HO!
HEE!
Are you having trouble, honey?
Right on, dude,
TEE HEE
HA! HA-H HO-H
HAR DE HAR
HO HO
GIGLE... GIGLE...
HEE... HEE... HEH-HEH-
HO
Well, I'll let Mr. Teddy Bear help you!
HU-HA! HO
HO
HA! HA!
HEE HEE
DUMBER THAN YOUR AVERAGE
Well, that's my behind the scenes look at "Fool House"! You're probably wondering why I would show scenes that expose this show as the garbage it is! Like I said, I'm in two hit series! Here I'm only one of half a dozen players! But I'm the only star of "America's Phoniest Home Videos"! I should care? No way, dude!
THE END.
8

EDITOR'S PICK

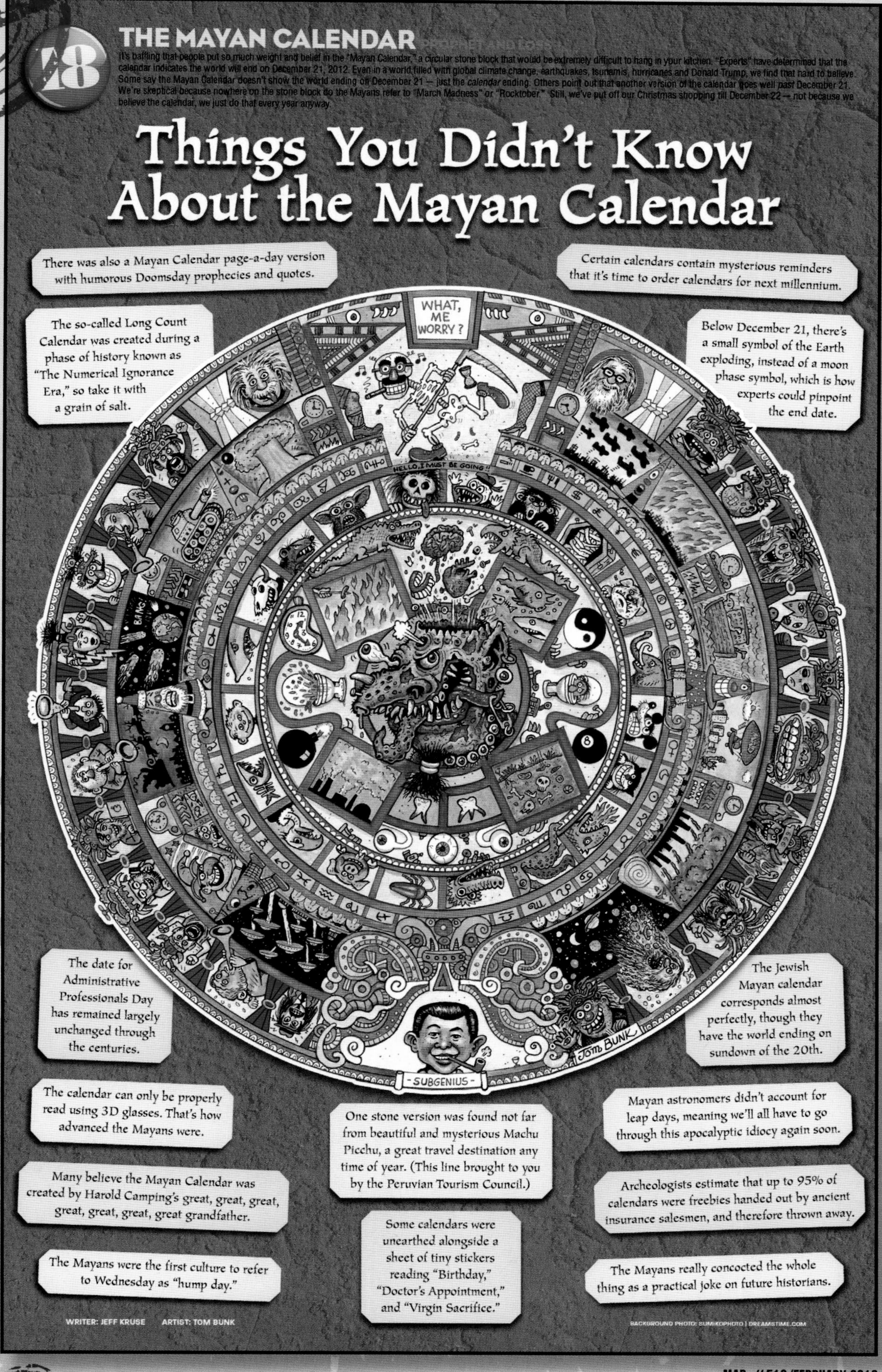
18

THE MAYAN CALENDAR PROPHET AND LOSS

It's baffling that people put so much weight and belief in the "Mayan Calendar," a circular stone block that would be extremely difficult to hang in your kitchen. "Experts" have determined that the calendar indicates the world will end on December 21, 2012. Even in a world filled with global climate change, earthquakes, tsunamis, hurricanes and Donald Trump, we find that hard to believe. Some say the Mayan Calendar doesn't show the world ending on December 21 — just the *calendar* ending. Others point out that another version of the calendar goes well *past* December 21. We're skeptical because nowhere on the stone block do the Mayans refer to "March Madness" or "Rocktober." Still, we've put off our Christmas shopping till December 22 — not because we believe the calendar, we just do that every year anyway.

Things You Didn't Know About the Mayan Calendar

There was also a Mayan Calendar page-a-day version with humorous Doomsday prophecies and quotes.

Certain calendars contain mysterious reminders that it's time to order calendars for next millennium.

The so-called Long Count Calendar was created during a phase of history known as "The Numerical Ignorance Era," so take it with a grain of salt.

Below December 21, there's a small symbol of the Earth exploding, instead of a moon phase symbol, which is how experts could pinpoint the end date.

WHAT, ME WORRY?
HELLO, I MUST BE GOING
TOM BUNK
SUBGENIUS

The date for Administrative Professionals Day has remained largely unchanged through the centuries.

The Jewish Mayan calendar corresponds almost perfectly, though they have the world ending on sundown of the 20th.

The calendar can only be properly read using 3D glasses. That's how advanced the Mayans were.

One stone version was found not far from beautiful and mysterious Machu Picchu, a great travel destination any time of year. (This line brought to you by the Peruvian Tourism Council.)

Mayan astronomers didn't account for leap days, meaning we'll all have to go through this apocalyptic idiocy again soon.

Many believe the Mayan Calendar was created by Harold Camping's great, great, great, great, great, great, great grandfather.

Some calendars were unearthed alongside a sheet of tiny stickers reading "Birthday," "Doctor's Appointment," and "Virgin Sacrifice."

Archeologists estimate that up to 95% of calendars were freebies handed out by ancient insurance salesmen, and therefore thrown away.

The Mayans were the first culture to refer to Wednesday as "hump day."

The Mayans really concocted the whole thing as a practical joke on future historians.

WRITER: JEFF KRUSE ARTIST: TOM BUNK

BACKGROUND PHOTO: SUMIKOPHOTO | DREAMSTIME.COM

MAD #519/FEBRUARY 2013

As the hubbub of the Mayan Calendar/End of the World Prophecy reached fever pitch, writer Jeff Kruse sold us a "Fast Five" for our Fundalini Pages section called "Things You Didn't Know About the Mayan Calendar." Quick and fun; we asked artist Tom Bunk for a quarter-page illustration to accompany Jeff's five lines. A few weeks later, Tom showed up at the MAD offices with this spectacular, hilariously detailed piece of artwork. Even a person with limited editing skills such as myself instantly recognized that we had comedy gold on our hands. We asked Jeff to write more lines and the little Fundalini throwaway quickly grew to a center spread in MAD's "20 Dumbest People, Events and Things of 2012" issue. Enjoy poring over Tom's artwork. And be sure to keep an eye out for Stanley, my tuxedo cat, who (totally coincidentally) pops up in most of Tom's illustrations. — *John Ficarra*

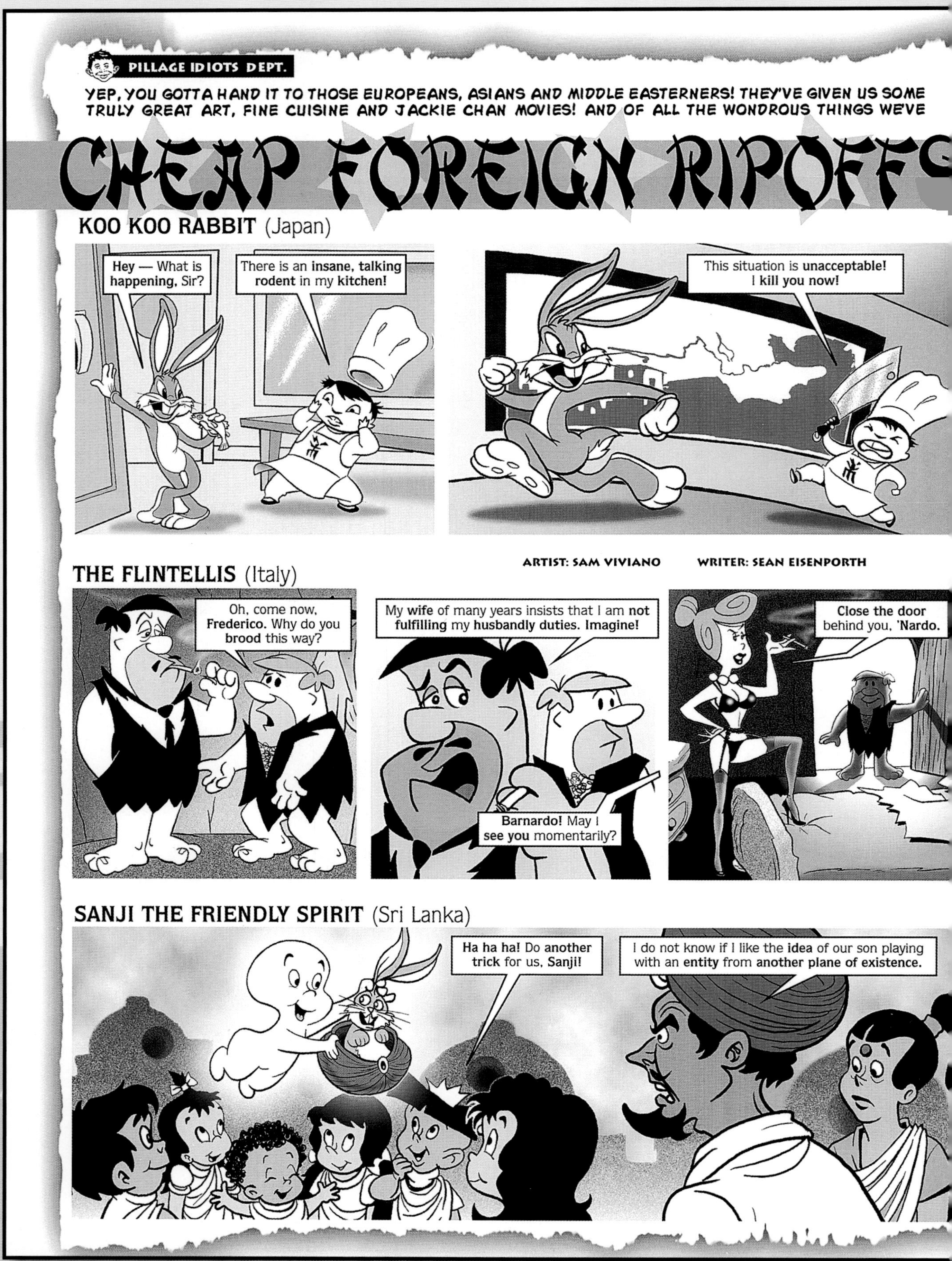
PILLAGE IDIOTS DEPT.
YEP, YOU GOTTA HAND IT TO THOSE EUROPEANS, ASIANS AND MIDDLE EASTERNERS! THEY'VE GIVEN US SOME TRULY GREAT ART, FINE CUISINE AND JACKIE CHAN MOVIES! AND OF ALL THE WONDROUS THINGS WE'VE
CHEAP FOREIGN RIPOFF
KOO KOO RABBIT (Japan)
Hey — What is happening, Sir?
There is an insane, talking rodent in my kitchen!
This situation is unacceptable! I kill you now!
ARTIST: SAM VIVIANO
WRITER: SEAN EISENPORTH
THE FLINTELLIS (Italy)
Oh, come now, Frederico. Why do you brood this way?
My wife of many years insists that I am not fulfilling my husbandly duties. Imagine!
Barnardo! May I see you momentarily?
Close the door behind you, 'Nardo.
SANJI THE FRIENDLY SPIRIT (Sri Lanka)
Ha ha ha! Do another trick for us, Sanji!
I do not know if I like the idea of our son playing with an entity from another plane of existence.

by David Shayne
WRITER

I come from a long line of former MAD interns who somehow managed to parlay a lackluster unpaid internship into a lackluster poorly-paying editorial position. Being a MAD editor means spending much of your day reading a lot of funny submissions as they're passed from office to office. (It also means reading a lot of unfunny submissions, but that's another book.) Oftentimes that initial idea is a work-in-progress: The comedic bones are there, but it'll require a rewrite or two before it's bought and passed on to the artist. But "Cheap Foreign Rip-Offs of American Cartoons" came in almost fully fleshed out, with very little altered

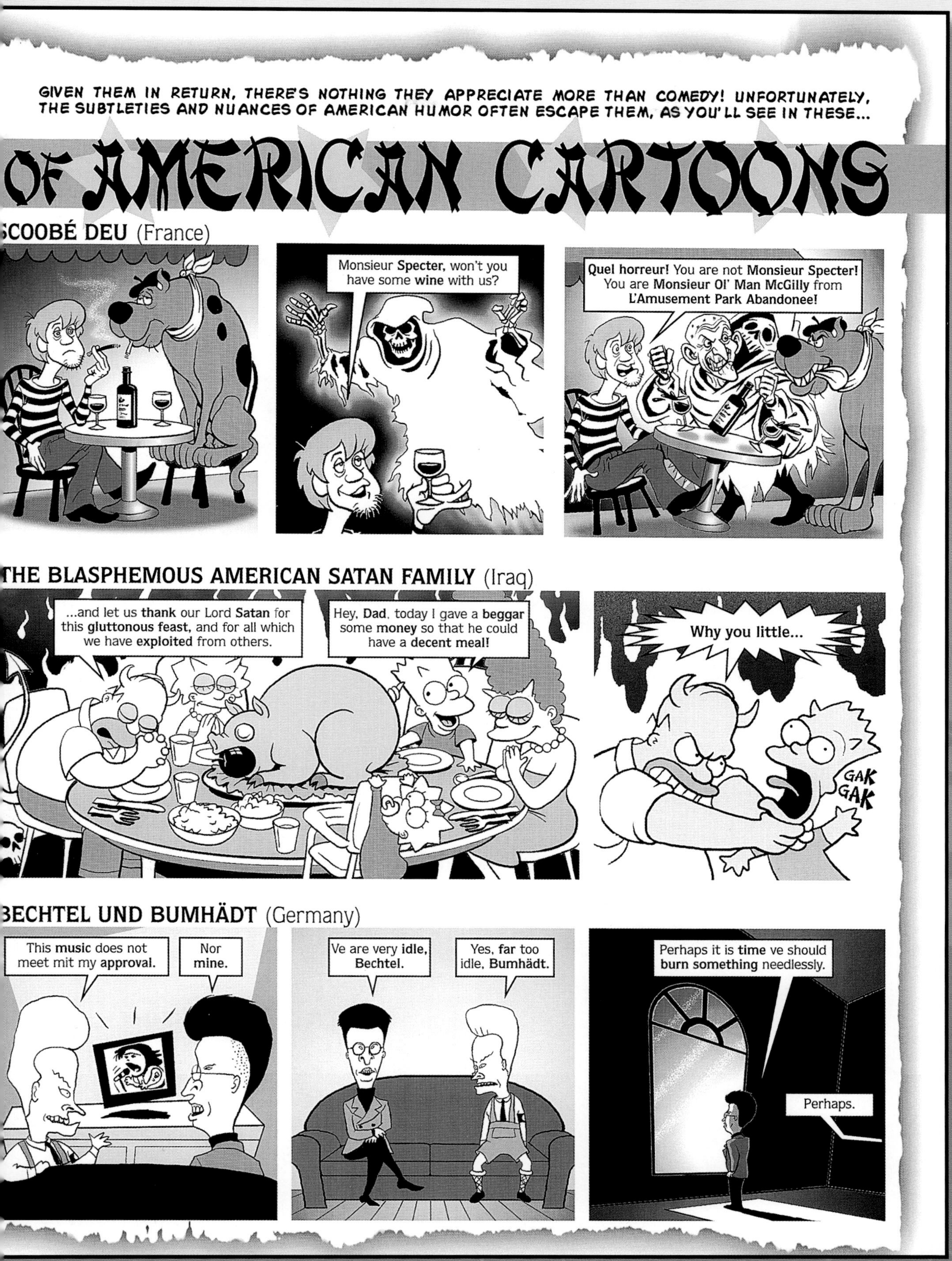
GIVEN THEM IN RETURN, THERE'S NOTHING THEY APPRECIATE MORE THAN COMEDY! UNFORTUNATELY, THE SUBTLETIES AND NUANCES OF AMERICAN HUMOR OFTEN ESCAPE THEM, AS YOU'LL SEE IN THESE...
OF AMERICAN CARTOONS
SCOOBÉ DEU (France)
Monsieur Specter, won't you have some wine with us?
Quel horreur! You are not Monsieur Specter! You are Monsieur Ol' Man McGilly from L'Amusement Park Abandonee!
THE BLASPHEMOUS AMERICAN SATAN FAMILY (Iraq)
...and let us thank our Lord Satan for this gluttonous feast, and for all which we have exploited from others.
Hey, Dad, today I gave a beggar some money so that he could have a decent meal!
Why you little...
GAK GAK
BECHTEL UND BUMHÄDT (Germany)
This music does not meet mit my approval.
Nor mine.
Ve are very idle, Bechtel.
Yes, far too idle, Bumhädt.
Perhaps it is time ve should burn something needlessly.
Perhaps.

MAD #362/OCTOBER 1997

from premise to publication. Even writer Sean Eisenporth's original rough sketches are pretty close to Sam Viviano's masterfully-drawn final illustrations. (And note how Sam successfully mimics the styles of six different cartoons, while also giving each a clever "foreign" spin.) From the moment it hit my desk, I thought the piece was laugh-out-loud funny. What can I say? It combines two of my great loves: Cartoons and xenophobia. For weeks after, whenever I passed then Co-Editor John Ficarra in the hallway (which was frequently — it was a small hallway), I'd say in my best German accent: "Perhaps it is time ve should burn something needlessly." To which he would reply with great Germanic menace, "Perhaps."

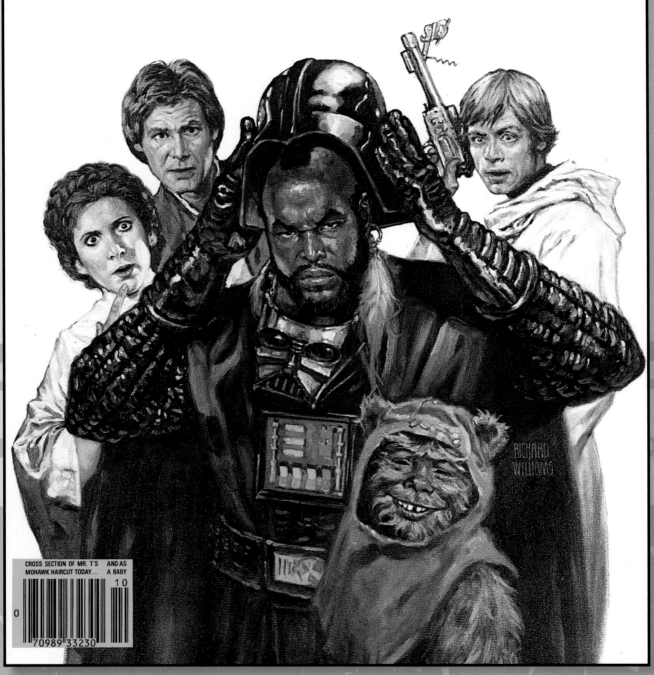

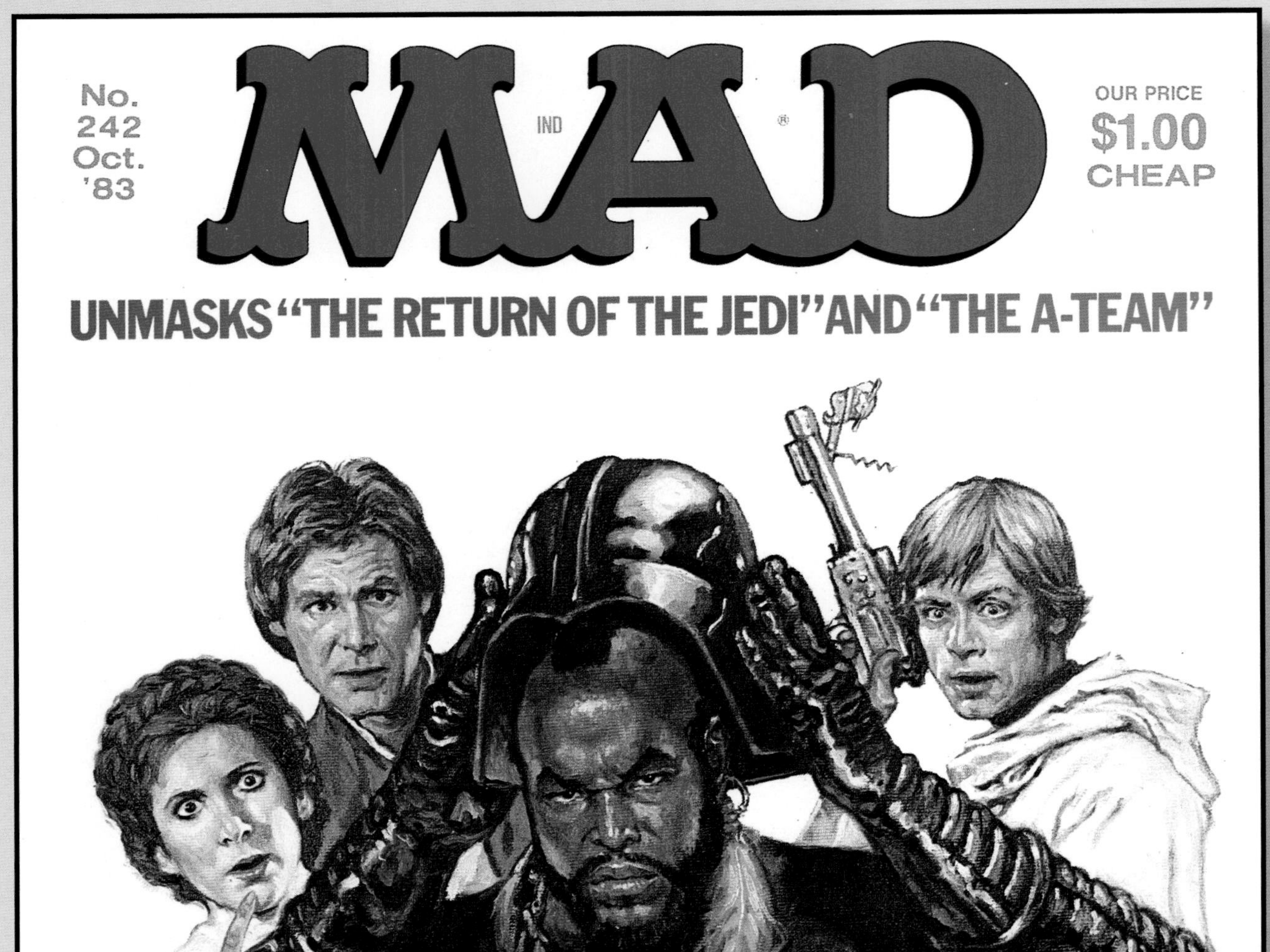
No. 242 Oct. '83
MAD
IND
OUR PRICE $1.00 CHEAP
UNMASKS "THE RETURN OF THE JEDI" AND "THE A-TEAM"
RICHARD WILLIAMS
CROSS SECTION OF MR. T'S MOHAWK HAIRCUT TODAY... AND AS A BABY

MAD #242/OCTOBER 1983

by Richard Williams

ARTIST

My favorite cover would have to be the first one I did. Of course I had read MAD as a kid, but at the time that they commissioned me to do this cover I hadn't seen the magazine for many years. I almost turned it down. I was still new to the field of illustration and this was just one of many jobs I was doing at that time. No big deal; I would get it done and move on to the next client.

But the editors kept coming back to me with new cover assignments. And I'm very glad they did! Over the years, working with everyone at MAD and getting to know them has been the highlight of my career as an illustrator. After a while they were no longer a "client," they were friends.

It has been and continues to be a wonderful experience to be associated with MAD and the people who create it. I could never claim to be a great artist but I can say I have been an extremely fortunate artist. That first cover changed the course of my life. And to think I almost passed up that fabulous opportunity.

INSERT OUCH! DEPT.

WRITERS: JOE RAIOLA AND CHARLIE KADAU

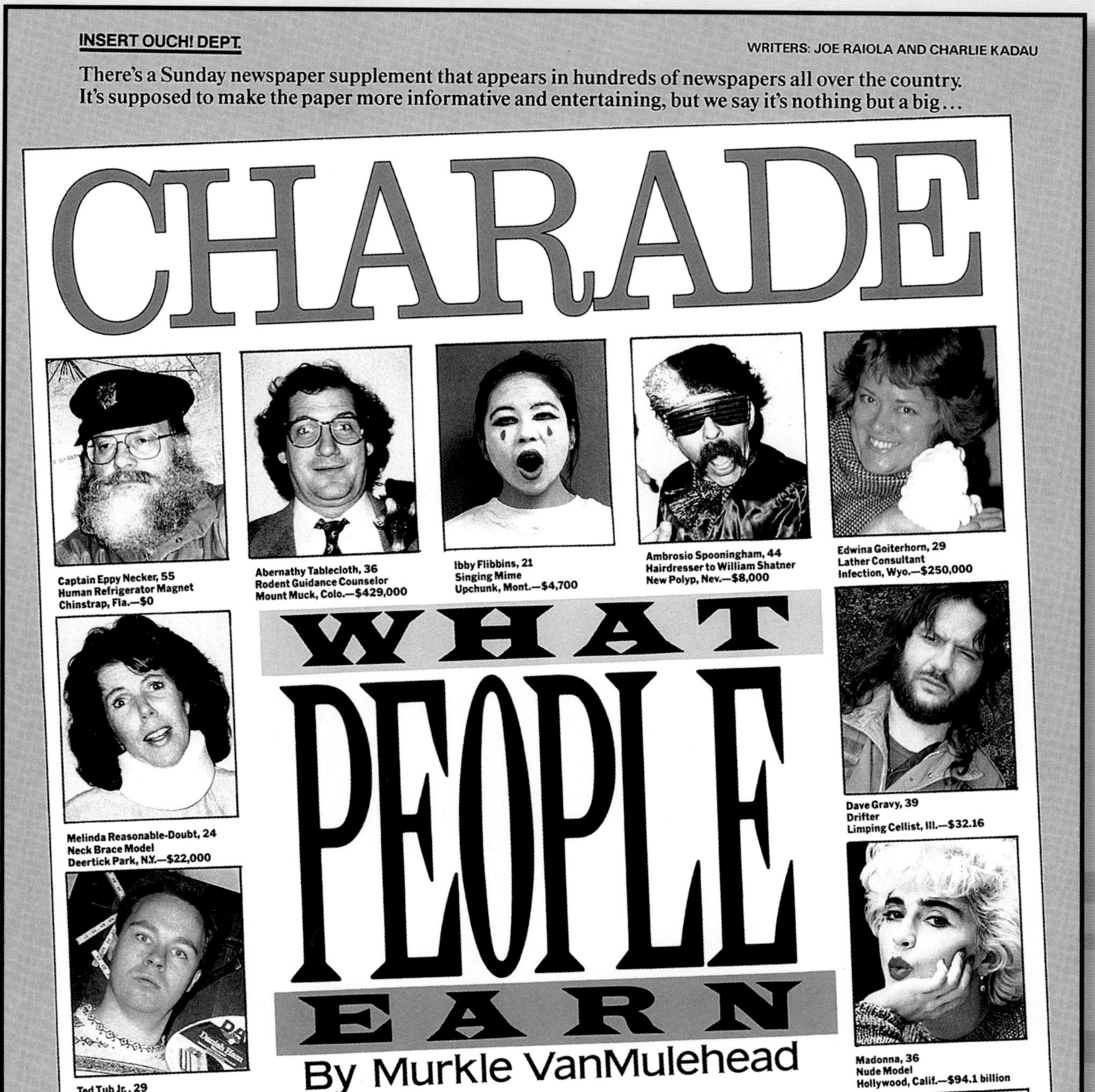

There's a Sunday newspaper supplement that appears in hundreds of newspapers all over the country. It's supposed to make the paper more informative and entertaining, but we say it's nothing but a big…

CHARADE

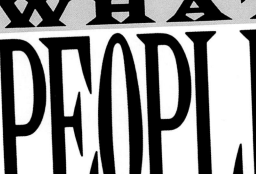

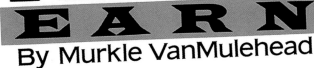

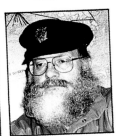

Captain Eppy Necker, 55
Human Refrigerator Magnet
Chinstrap, Fla.—$0

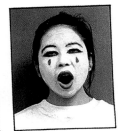

Abernathy Tablecloth, 36
Rodent Guidance Counselor
Mount Muck, Colo.—$429,000

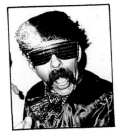

Ibby Flibbins, 21
Singing Mime
Upchunk, Mont.—$4,700

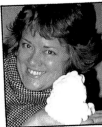

Ambrosio Spooningham, 44
Hairdresser to William Shatner
New Polyp, Nev.—$8,000

Edwina Goiterhorn, 29
Lather Consultant
Infection, Wyo.—$250,000

WHAT PEOPLE EARN

By Murkle VanMulehead

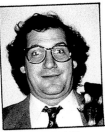

Melinda Reasonable-Doubt, 24
Neck Brace Model
Deertick Park, N.Y.—$22,000

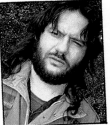

Dave Gravy, 39
Drifter
Limping Cellist, Ill.—$32.16

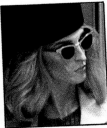

Ted Tub Jr., 29
Ham Repairman
Mallsville, Mich.—$16,000

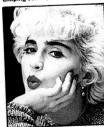

Madonna, 36
Nude Model
Hollywood, Calif.—$94.1 billion

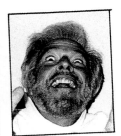

Wynette Buffington, 30
Department Store Mannequin
Repulsive Village, Tenn.—$48,000

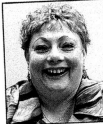

The Baffling Zincarlo, 52
Inaccurate Psychic
Wamelsdorf, Tex.—$112,000

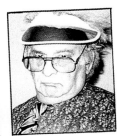

Glenda Bubblechin, 52
Voice of TV's Cleo The Skunk
Toxic Springs, W. Vir.—$1.7 million

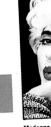

Murkle VanMulehead, 60
Hack Writer
Phlegmington, Penna.—$32.16

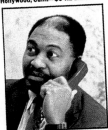

Stubby Klingsoot, 42
Owner, Midget Vacuuming Service
Gob Field, Kan.—$56,000

MAD #321/SEPTEMBER 1993

by Charlie Kadau
WRITER

The Sunday newspaper insert *Parade* was such a parody-ready publication, I had thoughts of what a spoof of it might be like even before I joined the MAD staff. Its "Personality Parade" questions that always read as fake as the letters to *Penthouse*, the uninformative "Intelligence Report," the lowest-common-denominator columns and ridiculous ads were all the ripest of fruit for a MAD send-up.

In MAD's (cheap!) tradition of not hiring professional models, office staffers, contributors and friends posed for the cover and interior features. Artist Sam Viviano (now MAD's art director) didn't take a byline credit because even though he had "aped" the styles of artists for other MAD features, he was a friend of and socialized with the artists he was spoofing in this article. (At least that's what he told us.) As for Joe Raiola, I could not ask for a better friend or collaborator. (65 articles and counting.) We both like nothing better than getting the other to laugh, and when we do, we know we have a line we can use. We did a lot of laughing while writing "Charade."

WALTER SNOTT'S

Personality Charade

Want the dirt? Innuendo? Lies? Write Walter Snott, Box 4621, New York, NY 10185. Fool's name will be used unless otherwise requested. Volume of mail makes writing phony letters a necessity.

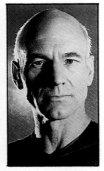

Stewart and Gorbachev: Separated at birthmark

Q. *How could a renowned world leader such as Mikhail Gorbachev demean himself by playing the captain in "Star Trek: The Next Generation." Doesn't this respected statesman realize this is a step down from bringing freedom and democracy to the former Soviet Union?—Sarita Taffy, Neckband, S.D.*

A. You are confusing Mikhail Gorbachev with the British actor Patrick Stewart who portrays Captain Jean Luc Picard on "Star Trek: The Next Generation." As of this writing, Gorbachev has no plans to appear in a syndicated science fiction series.

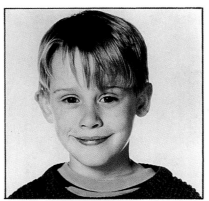

He's still single, girls

Q. *After seeing the 1991 smash "Home Alone" I've become interested in the actor Macaulay Culkin. Is he married? Does he have any children? Grandchildren? —Harry Suffocating, Sinkingfast, Wash.*

A. Despite persistent rumors, his publicist insists that Macaulay Culkin, 10, has never been married and has no children. He was the star of the 1991 smash "Home Alone."

Q. *I hear that comedian Bill Cosby, star of one of the most popular sitcoms in television history, is now a destitute homeless man, living out of dumpsters in San Diego where he must compete with rats for maggot-infested scraps of discarded food. My question is this: Whatever became of Eppy Stickel, the man who captured the hearts of America when he nearly lost his life in a freakish shampooing accident?—Cherry Oddbodkins, Dead City, Ala.*

A. Phillip "Eppy" Stickel, 54, the man who captured the hearts of America when he nearly lost his life in a freakish shampooing accident, currently resides in Tampa, Florida where he leads a reclusive life. He has not washed his hair in 27 years.

Selleck on New York corner

Q. *Is it true actor Tom Selleck has the power to make himself invisible? I need this answer to settle a bet. Might he have been in my home and I not have known it?—Jennifer Izbrick, Hopeless Junction, Ind.*

A. You lose the bet. While actor Tom Selleck, 48, does have the ability to appear and disappear at will, he assures us he has never been in your home.

Q. *Of the following three celebrities, which one would be most likely to sue you if you printed falsehoods about them in your magazine: Susan Lucci, Luke Perry, Hammer?—Barney Wagonblast, Cupenluck, N.M.*

A. There's one sure way to find out: Susan Lucci launders money for the Medellin drug cartel. Luke Perry supported Saddam Hussein during the Gulf War. Hammer is one of America's largest traffickers of pornography. We will answer your question as soon as we hear from their lawyers and let you know as soon as we receive our first subpoena.

Q. *Was The Lucy Show's Gale Gorden a homosexual? If not, why did he have a woman's name? And what about Glenn Close and Mel Harris? They're women but they have men's names. Are they lesbians? —Mabel Duck, Hangover Falls, Mass.*

A. We were very excited when your question arrived because it contains everything a good Personality Charade question should have: celebrities, sex, a hint of scandal, and the anticipation of forbidden secrets about to be revealed. That's why we're happy to print your question, even though we have absolutely no idea as to the answer. We do, however, have some juicy tidbits about Richard Gere, but since you didn't ask, too bad!

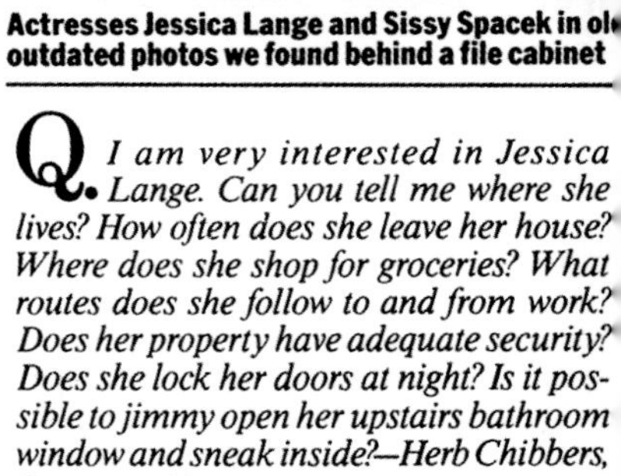

Actresses Jessica Lange and Sissy Spacek in ol outdated photos we found behind a file cabinet

Q. *I am very interested in Jessica Lange. Can you tell me where she lives? How often does she leave her house? Where does she shop for groceries? What routes does she follow to and from work? Does her property have adequate security? Does she lock her doors at night? Is it possible to jimmy open her upstairs bathroom window and sneak inside?—Herb Chibbers, Stagnant, Nev.*

A. While it is possible to jimmy open the bathroom window of two-time Academy Award winner Jessica Lange, 44, it would require a large ladder which may be too cumbersome for a lone stalker to maneuver. May we suggest the home of fellow two-time Oscar recipient Sissy Spacek, 44, who is known to leave her basement door unlocked.

Laugh Charade

CARTOONIST DREW ME WITH NO LEGS

MASSIVE MUTT©

Veterinarian

We know there's nothing wrong with him. We'd like to put him to sleep anyway.

How quaint! An old-fashioned street brawl!

Unintelligence Report

Because of volume of mail received, Charade regrets it gave out its address.

The Face Isn't Familiar

Wealth and adoring fans are two things your favorite celebrities have in common, but here's something they don't: their looks. The Philadelphia based group Celeb-Watch reports most famous people look nothing alike. "Some public figures like James Woods have bad complexions and misshapen lips," says Celeb-Watch President Vic Moron, "while others, such as Joan Rivers have beady little eyes and an oversized jaw." His group has been studying celebrities' features for the past six years. "It's surprising how many stars look nothing alike," Moron adds. "Notice the thick, scruffy beard of Wade Boggs as opposed to the smooth, creamy complexion of Kim Basinger... No one would ever mistake one for the other." Celeb-Watch named these other prominent people who do not resemble one another exclusively for Charade: Mariah Carey and Brian Dennehy, Pauly Shore and Sister Souljah, John Madden and Dick Cavett, Dick Cavett and Mariah Carey.

Three celebrities who look nothing alike.

Legal Sparring

The next time the President has to nominate a new Supreme Court Justice, don't be surprised if boxer Mike Tyson appears on his short list. Observers point out there is growing pressure to appoint a second African American to the high court, and Tyson, a political moderate, could receive both Republican and Democratic support. The former Heavyweight Champ has a reputation for being tough and he has a special understanding of men behind bars. Insiders speculate that if the Senate allows Don King to do all the talking for Tyson, as is usually the case, confirmation could be swift. As for his history with women, all agree that Tyson's record isn't much different than already appointed Justice Clarence Thomas.

Free Government Help In Determining Your Age

How old are you this year? How old were you last year? The National Age Foundation has completed a three-year, 8 billion dollar study, the results of which can be found in a comprehensive series of booklets that will assist you in calculating your correct age. For instance, if you were born in 1978 (Series 4, Book 2), this is what your age will be in each of the following years:

1993	15	2008	30
1996	18	2013	35
2001	23	2014	36

For a copy of the booklets, which were paid for with funds taken from the Health Care for the Needy Program, write to the National Age Foundation, Washington, D.C.

Ask Marilyn
BY MARILYN IDIOT SAVANT

On the same day, a train leaves Denver Station at 8:00 and another train leaves Chicago Terminal an hour later. The Denver train is pulling 15 boxcars and travels at 67 miles per hour. The Chicago train is pulling 22 boxcars and travels at 55 miles per hour. Each boxcar on the Denver train weighs four tons. Each boxcar on the Chicago train weighs 3½ tons. Both trains' destinations are St. Louis. Which will arrive first?
—Edgar Cheese, Empty Gap, Kan.

Actually, neither train would arrive first. The only trains leaving Denver Station and Chicago Terminal are Amtrak trains, and they would surely derail and catch fire soon after their departure.

Here's A Brainteaser From Me To You:

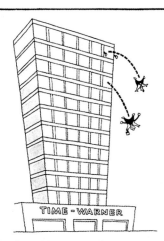

Hank and Sandy are both washing windows outside a Manhattan skyscraper. Hank is on the 96th floor and Sandy is on the 89th. In a freak accident, they both begin plummeting helplessly to earth at the same time. Sandy is clinging to his cleaning brush and failed safety harness, but Hank weighs 40 pounds more than Sandy. Who will die first? (For answer, see next week's column.)

Blight Ideas
BY LAME CIABATTERY

MEALS ON WHEELS

Do you often get hungry while driving only to discover there's not a restaurant around for miles? Try storing food in your hubcaps. Even

after driving through mud puddles, the spinning tires keep salad greens dry and crisp. Meats stored in the rear hubcaps near the exhaust take on a smoky, barbecue flavor. Bon appetit!

TICKETS? WHO NEEDS 'EM!

Sneaking into high-priced events like basketball games, rock concerts or Broadway plays is a uniquely rewarding experience that nearly anyone can enjoy. The trick is to have a friend create a diversion—say, feigning a coronary, or strangling an unsuspecting passerby. The guy at the door will probably try to help and you'll be able to slip inside unnoticed. Enjoy the show!

IDEA OF THE WEEK

Earn Extra Cash

Want to make some extra cash and liven up your weekend at the same time? Dress up as a minister and go from door to door asking people for money. If they ask what the money is for, mumble something and run away from them.

We would like you to write this column for us. Send your suggestions to "Blight Ideas," Charade, NY, NY 10017.

"Do You Know The Enervating Health Secrets of The Ages?"

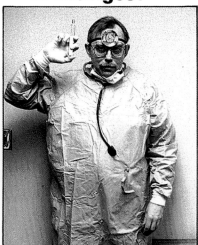

I'm Dr. Grady Pounder, and I'm revealing just a few of my little-known health secrets in this ad...that's because if I told you I'm revealing ALL of my little-known health secrets in this ad, you wouldn't buy my book!

Look at some of the amazing secrets revealed in this list

- Taunt your liver into healing itself.
- Eliminate your blisters through collective bargaining.
- Hiccup your diarrhea away.
- Poor vision? Maybe your eyes are closed.
- What your fingernails are telling you about your pancreas.
- Why your pancreas is denying what your fingernails are saying about it.
- Epilepsey...do you think we spelled it right?
- Treat your sore gums to dinner and a movie.
- Panic attacks? Maybe taking those little green pills in your medicine cabinet isn't such a bad idea.
- Are grapes following you to work? You may be hallucinating.
- Strategies to prevent hat loss.
- The vegetable that will have your big toe begging for mercy.

To order Dr. Grady Pounder's "Enervating Health Secrets of the Ages," cough into a napkin and send it along with $13.98 to: Sickness Publications, Communicable Disease, Montana 09988.

HITS AND MISSIVES DEPT.
THE HISTORY OF COMMUNICATION
ARTIST: MORT DRUCKER
WRITER: MICHAEL GALLAGHER
PRIMITIVE CAVEMEN
EARLY CIVILIZATION
1520'S
1860'S
1980'S
MAX KORN
TODAY

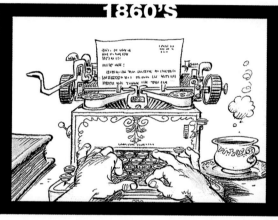

MAD #343/MARCH 1996

by Michael Gallagher
WRITER

In the early 60s, Mort Drucker had a profound influence on me as a budding teenaged cartoonist. I loved his movie parodies so much that I tore them out of my copies of MAD and kept them in a separate file to study endlessly (kudos to all the writers as well). The caricatures were overwhelming and seemed alive with self-aware, mischievous joy. Mort's compelling cartoon style, technical skill, visual storytelling and mastery of MAD's "chicken fat" backgrounds made a permanent imprint on my reptilian brain stem.

Fast-forward to the mid-90s and my first sale to MAD. I was told that Mort would be drawing my one-page article idea, "The History of Communication," in MAD #343. I hung up, smiled and shouted, "Okay, you can shoot me now!" (Fortunately, I was alone at the time.) I've met Mort several times since then and can honestly say he's one of the sweetest guys — not to mention one of the greatest MAD artists — ever.

Tony Hawk

I remember reading MAD when I was young and feeling like I was "getting away" with something that my parents didn't know about. They thought it was a comic book of some sort, but I knew it was sharp, dark and poignant humor even at a young age. I remember literally laughing out loud while reading it, when it was way past my bedtime. My parents had no idea that it would help shape my twisted sense of humor well into my adult life.

DON MARTIN DEPT. PART II

ONE AFTERNOON WHILE RUNNING AN ERRAND

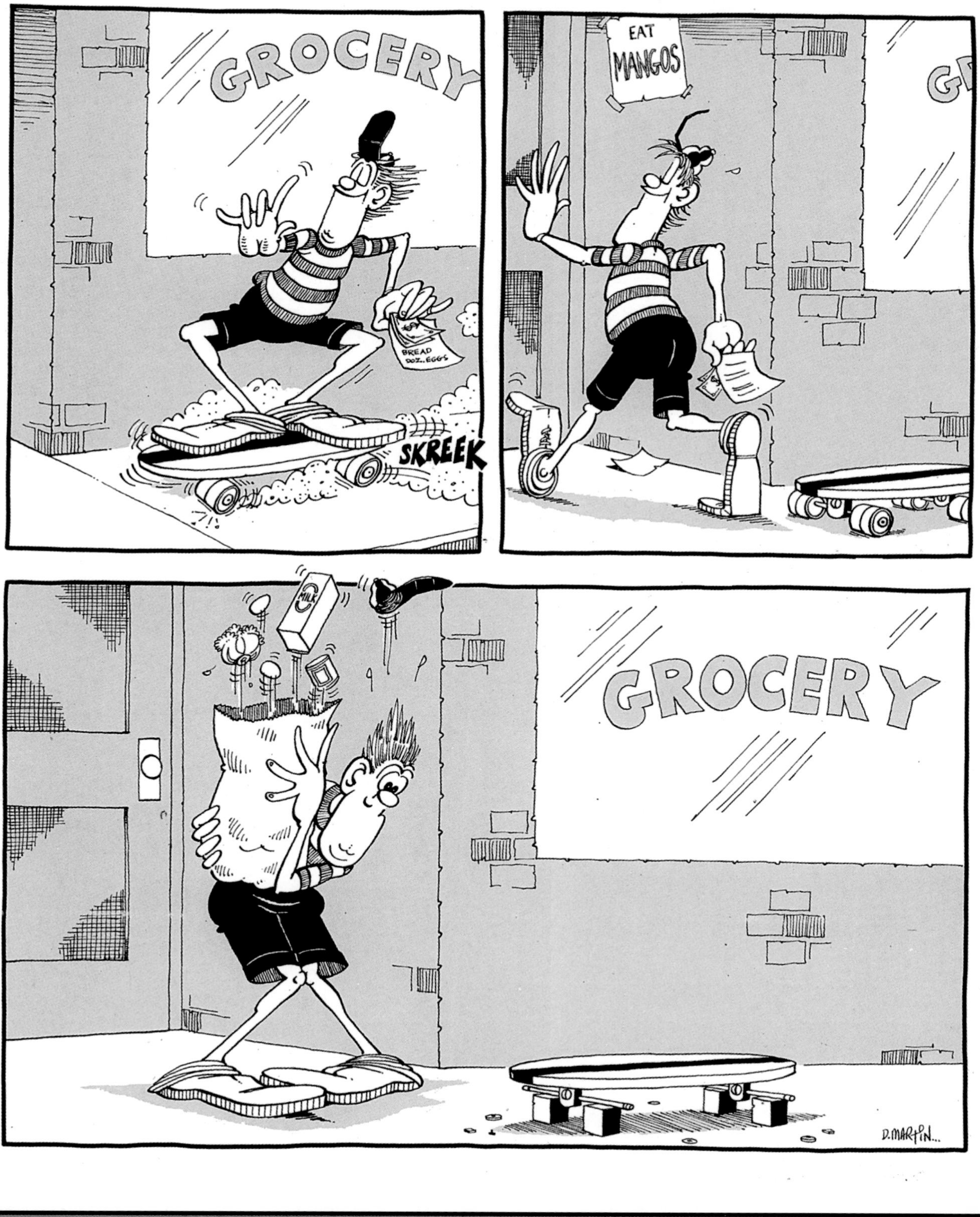
GROCERY
BREAD
DOZ. EGGS
SKREEK
EAT MANGOS
GR
MILK
GROCERY
D. MARTIN...

A WORSE MOUSETRAP DEPT.

The big corporations have always depended upon "Planned Obsolescence", the calculated rapid breakdown in acceptable design and performance of their products, to keep their coffers filled. Planned Obsolescence boosts sales and profits by insuring quick replacement of worn-out or outmoded items. Recently, consumer crusaders

PLANNED OBSOLESCENCE

TOILET PAPER

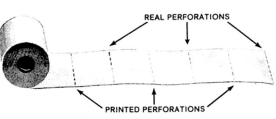

REAL PERFORATIONS
PRINTED PERFORATIONS

Careful examinations have disclosed that perforations alternate between real ones and phony ones. Phony ones are only printed on. Thus, when consumer gives normal yank, five feet of tissue cascades onto floor. Since consumer never suspects real reason, he vows time and again to be more careful next time. Of course, tissue on floor is discarded...and roll goes fast that way.

SOAP

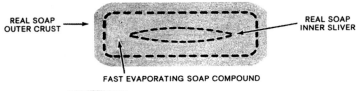

REAL SOAP OUTER CRUST
REAL SOAP INNER SLIVER
FAST EVAPORATING SOAP COMPOUND
FADE
NEWLY UNWRAPPED
2 DAYS LATER
5 DAYS LATER

Most bars of soap will turn into slivers in about 5 days whether soap is used or not. This is due to presence of "fast evaporating soap compound"—located between normal outer crust and inner sliver—which is dissolved by air.

NUTS AND BOLTS

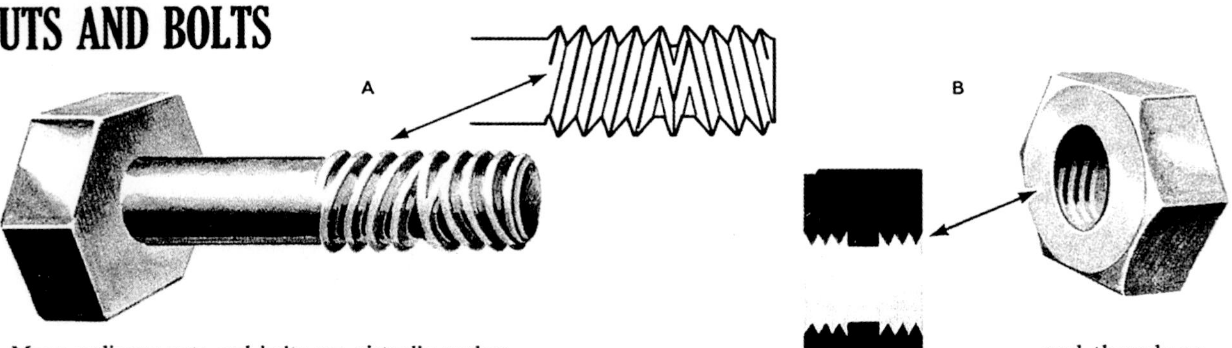

A
B

Many ordinary nuts and bolts are virtually useless. For example, threads on bolts (A) are manufactured so that they cannot work with any ordinary nuts...

...and threads on nuts (B) come to an end halfway inside.

by Al Jaffee
WRITER/ARTIST

Most of us are not aware that planned obsolescence even exists. We just take for granted that things have a short, limited life, wear out, and need to be replaced often. But that was not always the case. Years ago a young consumer crusader named Ralph Nader set out to prove that as a matter of fact, manufacturers build breakdowns into their products so their consumers have to replace and pay for new ones over and over again.

The original crusade against planned obsolescence involved major products which were expensive to buy and repair. Items such as automobiles, washing machines and television sets like Ralph Nader have been exposing the despicable practice of Planned Obsolescence in the automobile and appliance fields. But the use of Planned Obsolescence in less spectacular, but no less important products, that the average consumer cannot do without, has been totally ignored. And so, to fill the gap, here's a MAD report on

IN EVERYDAY PRODUCTS

ARTIST & WRITER: AL JAFFEE

PENCILS

Investigation shows how lead is placed in many pencils today, and the kinds of points you get when you sharpen them.

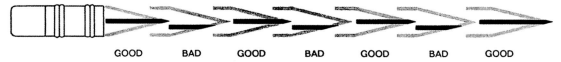

GOOD   BAD   GOOD   BAD   GOOD   BAD   GOOD

Note that every other point is bad. As a result, when the consumer sharpens pencil, he keeps doing it until he gets a good point. Thus, he uses up this pencil twice as fast as a well-made one, and the sharpener is usually blamed.

ZIPPERS

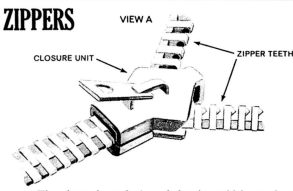

VIEW A

CLOSURE UNIT

ZIPPER TEETH

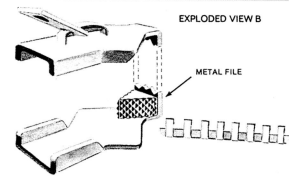

EXPLODED VIEW B

METAL FILE

The zipper is so foolproof that it could be made to last forever. But what good would that be? So, as in exploded view (B) above, we see how a carefully placed metal file in every closure unit goes to work on the zipper teeth as it moves up and down over them, wearing them out quickly. This causes gapping, jamming and—best of all—*replacing!*

ELECTRICAL UNIT PULLCHAINS

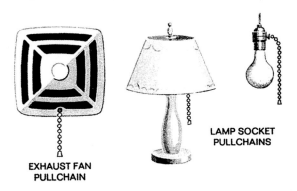

EXHAUST FAN PULLCHAIN

LAMP SOCKET PULLCHAINS

One link in almost every electrical unit pullchain has a built-in weak spot. After short period of use, pullchain breaks and entire unit must be discarded ...because the weak link is always located *inside* unit.

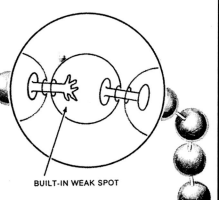

BUILT-IN WEAK SPOT

MAD #159/JUNE 1973

were in this category. Manufacturers could easily insert undetectable weak spots into these complicated devices so that when they broke down it appeared to be either normal wear and tear or the fault of the user. This scheme worked so well it created ancillary industries, like repair shops and replacement-parts manufacturers.

This attracted the attention of other manufacturers of small, uncomplicated items in everyday use who wanted to get in on this profitable new business model.

Take, for example, the original ketchup bottle. It had a cleverly designed narrow neck that prevented too much from pouring out all at once. That was good. But then came the bad part. After a while the ketchup thickened, as

ADHESIVE TAPES

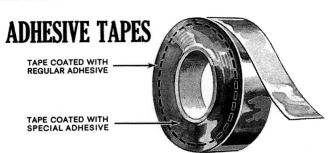

TAPE COATED WITH REGULAR ADHESIVE

TAPE COATED WITH SPECIAL ADHESIVE

First three feet of most adhesive tapes are coated with the normal adhesive and unrolled easily. But after that, a special adhesive is used which has been designed to stick best to tape itself. This makes it virtually impossible to remove more than one inch of tape at a time, and the disgusted consumer, thinking it's just old, buys new roll.

STAPLES

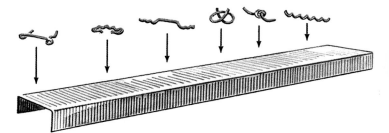

Most bars of staples look perfectly innocent. But every third staple is actually made of soft, inferior wire that can't penetrate even one sheet of paper. It simply turns into one of the grotesque shapes shown and is discarded.

CIGARETTES

Most new long cigarettes actually burn down more quickly than old shorter types, thanks to specially-developed tobacco.

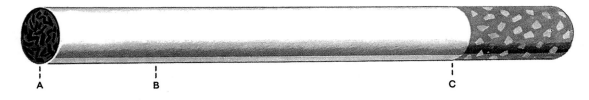

A   B   C

TOBACCO BETWEEN "A" AND "B" IS REGULAR SLOW-BURNING KIND

TOBACCO BETWEEN "B" AND "C" IS SPECIALLY-DEVELOPED NEW TYPE (IMPREGNATED WITH PARTICLES OF GUN POWDER) WHICH BURNS DOWN IN A SPLIT SECOND SO CONSUMER QUICKLY LIGHTS UP ANOTHER ONE.

FACIAL TISSUES

Alternate sheets of many brands of facial tissues have been specially die-cut to create a built-in failure feature.

TEAR·E·Z TISSUES

CENTER SECTIONS OF ALTERNATE FACIAL TISSUE SHEETS ARE HELD IN PLACE BY FOUR TINY FIBERS.

WHEN A SPECIALLY DIE-CUT SHEET IS USED, IT IS TOTALLY INEFFECTIVE AND EMBARRASSING, CAUSING CONSUMER TO QUICKLY GRAB FOR ANOTHER TISSUE.

intended by the manufacturer, and no matter how hard you shook, smacked or pounded the bottle, the remaining 10%, 20%, or more never came out and required the consumer to go out and purchase another bottle. Peanut butter manufacturers came up with a different and equally brilliant way of gaming the system. They had jars designed with attractive, intricately sculpted bottoms. Thus, when the user reaches that area inside the jar there is no instrument yet invented that can reach every bit of peanut butter that fills these nooks and crannies. All one can do is toss it and buy another jar just like it.

TEABAGS

TEA LEAVES
LEAKOUT TEA CO.
SECRET OPENING

YECCH!
LEAKOUT TEA CO.

Many teabags are made with secret openings that are cleverly concealed to prevent discovery by inspection. These openings are sealed with a non-toxic glue that dissolves in hot water. When secret opening is unsealed, tea leaves escape into the water, and unwary consumer is forced to dump it out and start all over with a new tea bag.

NAILS

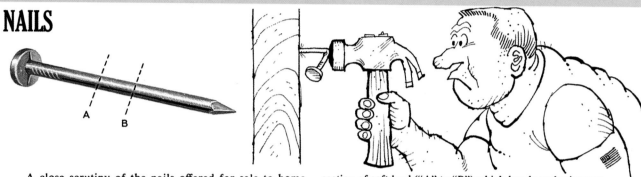

A
B

A close scrutiny of the nails offered for sale to home workshop buffs reveals that a high percentage of them may look normal but are actually manufactured with a ¼ inch section of soft lead ("A" to "B") which bends under impact of first hammer blow. Amateur carpenter naively thinks it is his bad aim, pulls out bent nail and uses another one.

MATCHES

STRIKEOUT MATCH
STRIKEOUT MATCH

NORMAL HEAD
TREATED BODY

Many matches when struck, spark, sputter and then go out. User thinks match is wet and takes another one! Actually, match has been treated with a flameproof chemical! A box of 50% bad matches like these gets used up mighty fast.

PLAYING CARDS

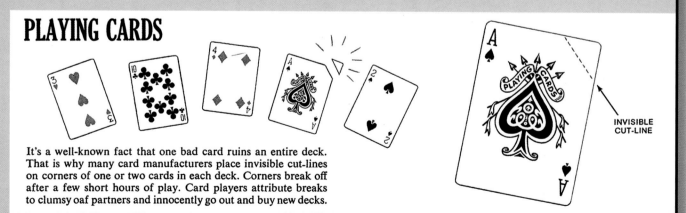

PLAYING CARDS
INVISIBLE CUT-LINE

It's a well-known fact that one bad card ruins an entire deck. That is why many card manufacturers place invisible cut-lines on corners of one or two cards in each deck. Corners break off after a few short hours of play. Card players attribute breaks to clumsy oaf partners and innocently go out and buy new decks.

Then there's the planned obsolescence in coffee shops and restaurants. We're all familiar with the little packets of sugar, ketchup, mustard, jam, etc. The food industry loves these because most of it goes to waste and must be constantly replaced. Even unopened packets have to be discarded because of health laws.

This idea was so intriguing I simply had to create an article for MAD imagining how this could be applied to all everyday products.

SCREWDRIVERS

SCREWEM BRAND
STEEL
LEAD

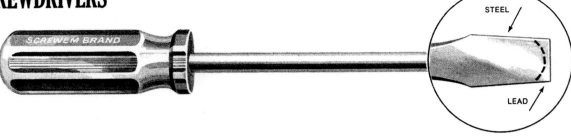

Today, many screwdrivers are made with a soft lead tip so it looks like it has a clean, square edge before use. But after one use, tip ends up looking like rounded fingernail ...and is about equally as effective for driving screws.

SANDPAPER

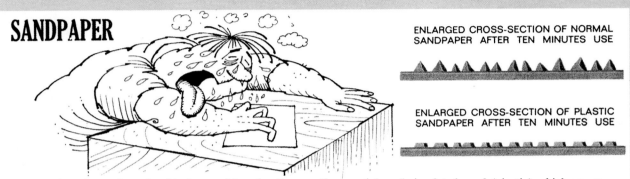

ENLARGED CROSS-SECTION OF NORMAL SANDPAPER AFTER TEN MINUTES USE
ENLARGED CROSS-SECTION OF PLASTIC SANDPAPER AFTER TEN MINUTES USE

Normal sandpaper is made with tiny particles of ordinary sand which has sharp cutting edges that last a reasonable time. Many companies are turning out sandpaper made with tiny particles of simulated sand (plastic) which wears flat in no time. Buyer must replace it or wear himself down faster than he'll ever wear down what he's sanding.

RUBBER ERASERS

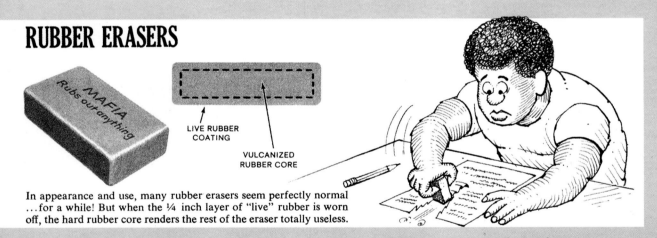

MAFIA
Rubs out anything
LIVE RUBBER COATING
VULCANIZED RUBBER CORE

In appearance and use, many rubber erasers seem perfectly normal ...for a while! But when the ¼ inch layer of "live" rubber is worn off, the hard rubber core renders the rest of the eraser totally useless.

PAPERBACK BOOKS

CLOD'S LETTERS TO MAD

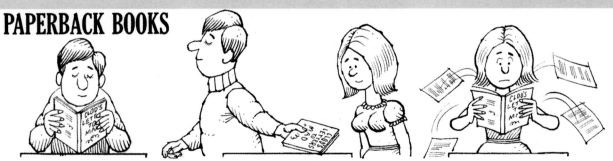

Most paperback book publishers equip their products with special "one-use" bindings made from rigid-drying glue which limit books to one reader. When buyer first opens the book and turns the pages, binding is broken half-way. When book is closed, binding is broken rest of the way. The next time the book is opened, all the pages fall out.

Ice-T

*M*AD was my favorite mag growing up! "Spy vs Spy," Don Martin, all that. I need a new subscription!

I started reading MAD in junior high. I don't really know how I got turned on to MAD back in the day, but I got turned on by "Spy vs. Spy" and Don Martin's cool sight-comedy, and those little drawings in the margins without any words. It all just looked so cool. I was into Alfred E. Neuman on the cover and the "What, me worry?" stuff. MAD's artwork was always incredible, with so much stuff going on. I would go on my own to the corner store or the comics store to get it, and I'd always do the back page Fold-In before I left.

MAD Magazine has a kind of dark humor, which triggered my imagination in a way that straightforward comedy satire like *Saturday Night Live* and *MAD TV* didn't do. The way MAD would satirize politics opened my eyes. It still catches my eye, too, whenever I pass an airport newsstand.

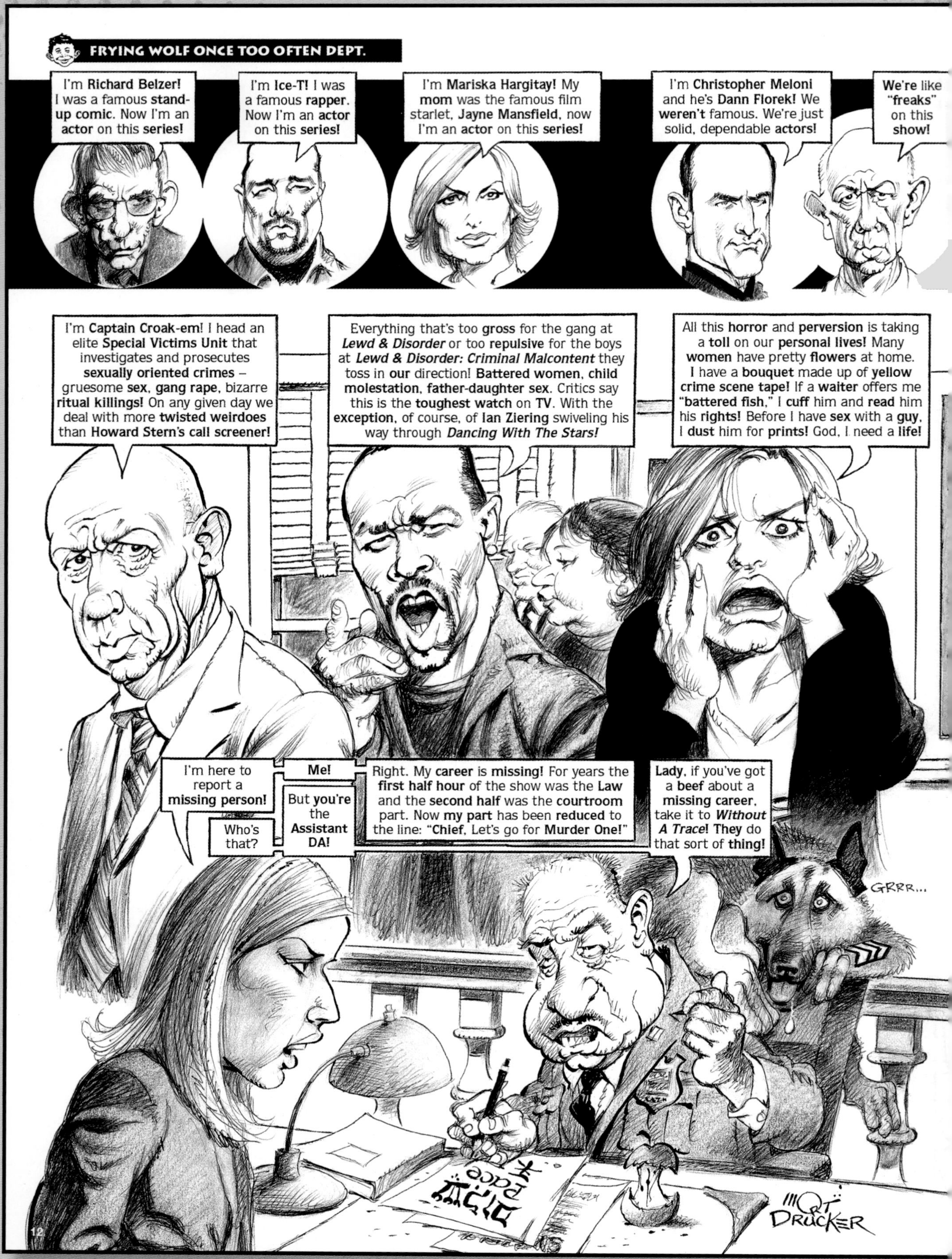
FRYING WOLF ONCE TOO OFTEN DEPT.
I'm Richard Belzer! I was a famous stand-up comic. Now I'm an actor on this series!
I'm Ice-T! I was a famous rapper. Now I'm an actor on this series!
I'm Mariska Hargitay! My mom was the famous film starlet, Jayne Mansfield, now I'm an actor on this series!
I'm Christopher Meloni and he's Dann Florek! We weren't famous. We're just solid, dependable actors!
We're like "freaks" on this show!
I'm Captain Croak-em! I head an elite Special Victims Unit that investigates and prosecutes sexually oriented crimes – gruesome sex, gang rape, bizarre ritual killings! On any given day we deal with more twisted weirdoes than Howard Stern's call screener!
Everything that's too gross for the gang at Lewd & Disorder or too repulsive for the boys at Lewd & Disorder: Criminal Malcontent they toss in our direction! Battered women, child molestation, father-daughter sex. Critics say this is the toughest watch on TV. With the exception, of course, of Ian Ziering swiveling his way through Dancing With The Stars!
All this horror and perversion is taking a toll on our personal lives! Many women have pretty flowers at home. I have a bouquet made up of yellow crime scene tape! If a waiter offers me "battered fish," I cuff him and read him his rights! Before I have sex with a guy, I dust him for prints! God, I need a life!
I'm here to report a missing person!
Who's that?
Me!
But you're the Assistant DA!
Right. My career is missing! For years the first half hour of the show was the Law and the second half was the courtroom part. Now my part has been reduced to the line: "Chief, Let's go for Murder One!"
Lady, if you've got a beef about a missing career, take it to Without A Trace! They do that sort of thing!
GRRR...
MORT DRUCKER
12

LEWD & DISORDER
IT'S P.U.

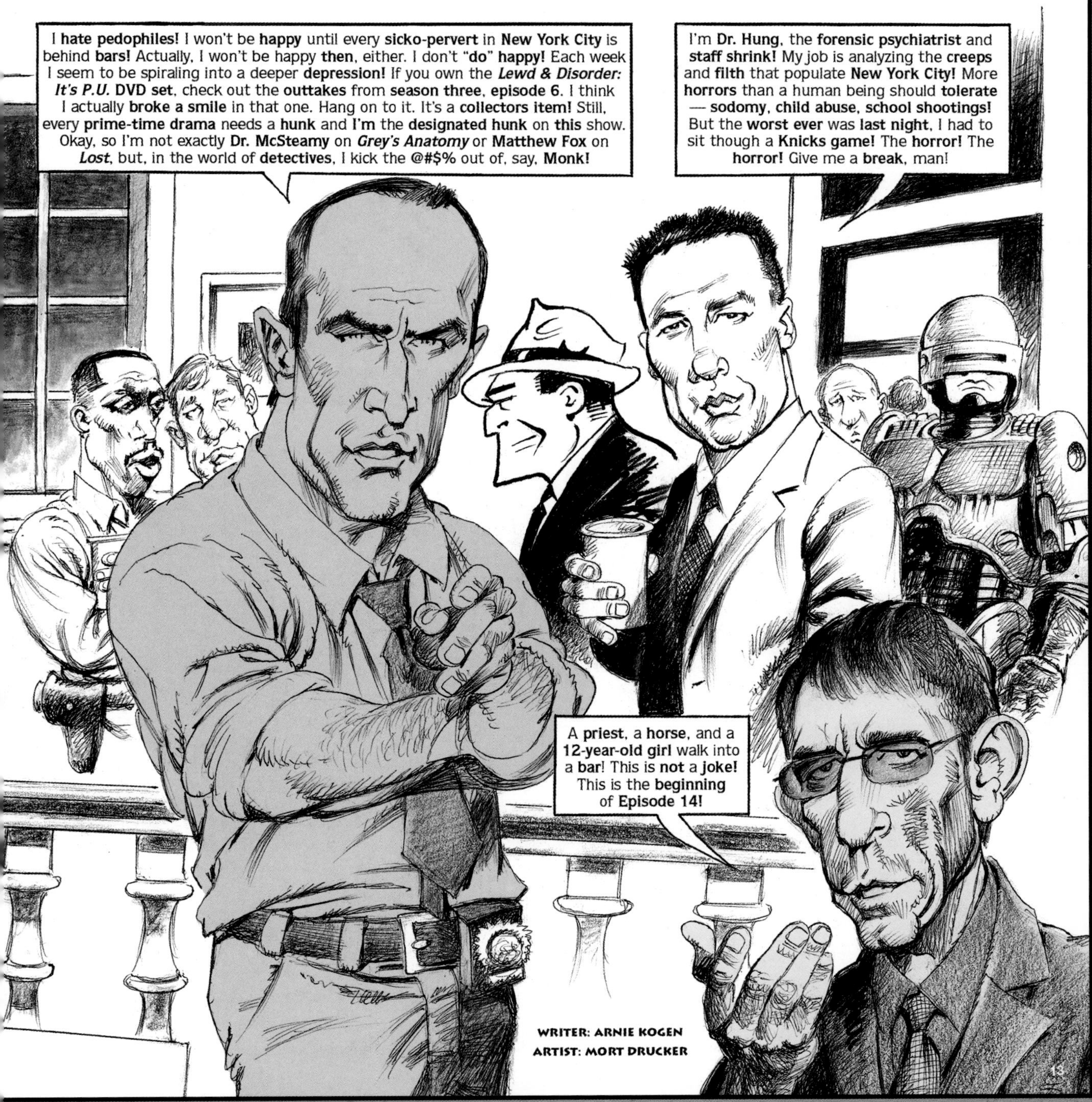
I **hate pedophiles!** I won't be **happy** until every **sicko-pervert** in **New York City** is behind **bars!** Actually, I won't be happy **then**, either. I don't "**do**" **happy!** Each week I seem to be spiraling into a deeper **depression!** If you own the ***Lewd & Disorder: It's P.U.*** **DVD set**, check out the **outtakes** from **season three**, **episode 6**. I think I actually **broke a smile** in that one. Hang on to it. It's a **collectors item!** Still, every **prime-time drama** needs a **hunk** and **I'm** the **designated hunk** on **this** show. Okay, so I'm not exactly **Dr. McSteamy** on ***Grey's Anatomy*** or **Matthew Fox** on ***Lost***, but, in the world of **detectives**, I kick the **@#$%** out of, say, **Monk!**
I'm **Dr. Hung**, the **forensic psychiatrist** and **staff shrink!** My job is analyzing the **creeps** and **filth** that populate **New York City!** More **horrors** than a human being should **tolerate** — **sodomy, child abuse, school shootings!** But the **worst ever** was **last night**, I had to sit though a **Knicks game!** The **horror!** The **horror!** Give me a **break**, man!
A **priest**, a **horse**, and a **12-year-old girl** walk into a **bar!** This is **not** a **joke!** This is the **beginning** of **Episode 14!**
WRITER: ARNIE KOGEN
ARTIST: MORT DRUCKER

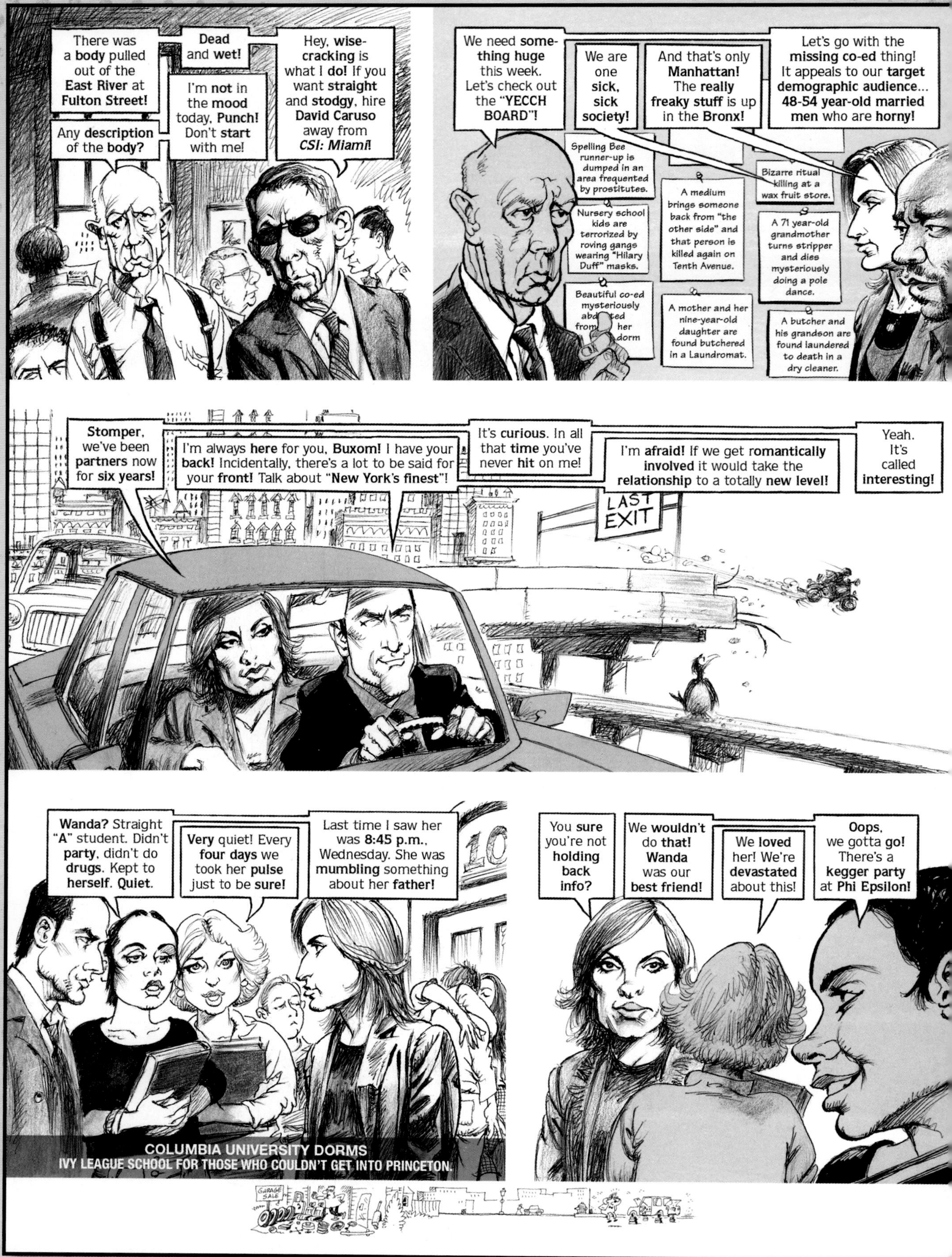
There was a **body** pulled out of the **East River** at **Fulton Street!**
Any **description** of the **body?**
Dead and **wet!**
I'm **not** in the **mood** today, **Punch!** Don't **start** with me!
Hey, **wise-cracking** is what I **do!** If you want **straight** and **stodgy**, hire **David Caruso** away from ***CSI: Miami!***
We need **some-thing huge** this week. Let's check out the "**YECCH BOARD**"!
We are one **sick, sick society!**
And that's only **Manhattan!** The **really freaky stuff** is up in the **Bronx!**
Let's go with the **missing co-ed** thing! It appeals to our **target demographic audience... 48-54 year-old married men** who are **horny!**
Spelling Bee runner-up is dumped in an area frequented by prostitutes.
Nursery school kids are terrorized by roving gangs wearing "Hilary Duff" masks.
Beautiful co-ed mysteriously
A medium brings someone back from "the other side" and that person is killed again on Tenth Avenue.
A mother and her nine-year-old daughter are found butchered in a Laundromat.
Bizarre ritual killing at a wax fruit store.
A 71 year-old grandmother turns stripper and dies mysteriously doing a pole dance.
A butcher and his grandson are found laundered to death in a dry cleaner.
Stomper, we've been **partners** now for **six years!**
I'm always **here** for you, **Buxom!** I have your **back!** Incidentally, there's a lot to be said for your **front!** Talk about "**New York's finest**"!
It's **curious**. In all that **time** you've never **hit** on me!
I'm **afraid!** If we get **romantically involved** it would take the **relationship** to a totally **new level!**
Yeah. It's called **interesting!**
LAST EXIT
Wanda? Straight "**A**" student. Didn't **party**, didn't do **drugs**. Kept to **herself**. **Quiet**.
Very quiet! Every **four days** we took her **pulse** just to be **sure!**
Last time I saw her was **8:45 p.m.**, Wednesday. She was **mumbling** something about her **father!**
You **sure** you're not **holding back** info?
We **wouldn't** do **that!** **Wanda** was our **best friend!**
We **loved** her! We're **devastated** about this!
Oops, we gotta **go!** There's a **kegger party** at **Phi Epsilon!**
COLUMBIA UNIVERSITY DORMS
IVY LEAGUE SCHOOL FOR THOSE WHO COULDN'T GET INTO PRINCETON.
GARAGE SALE

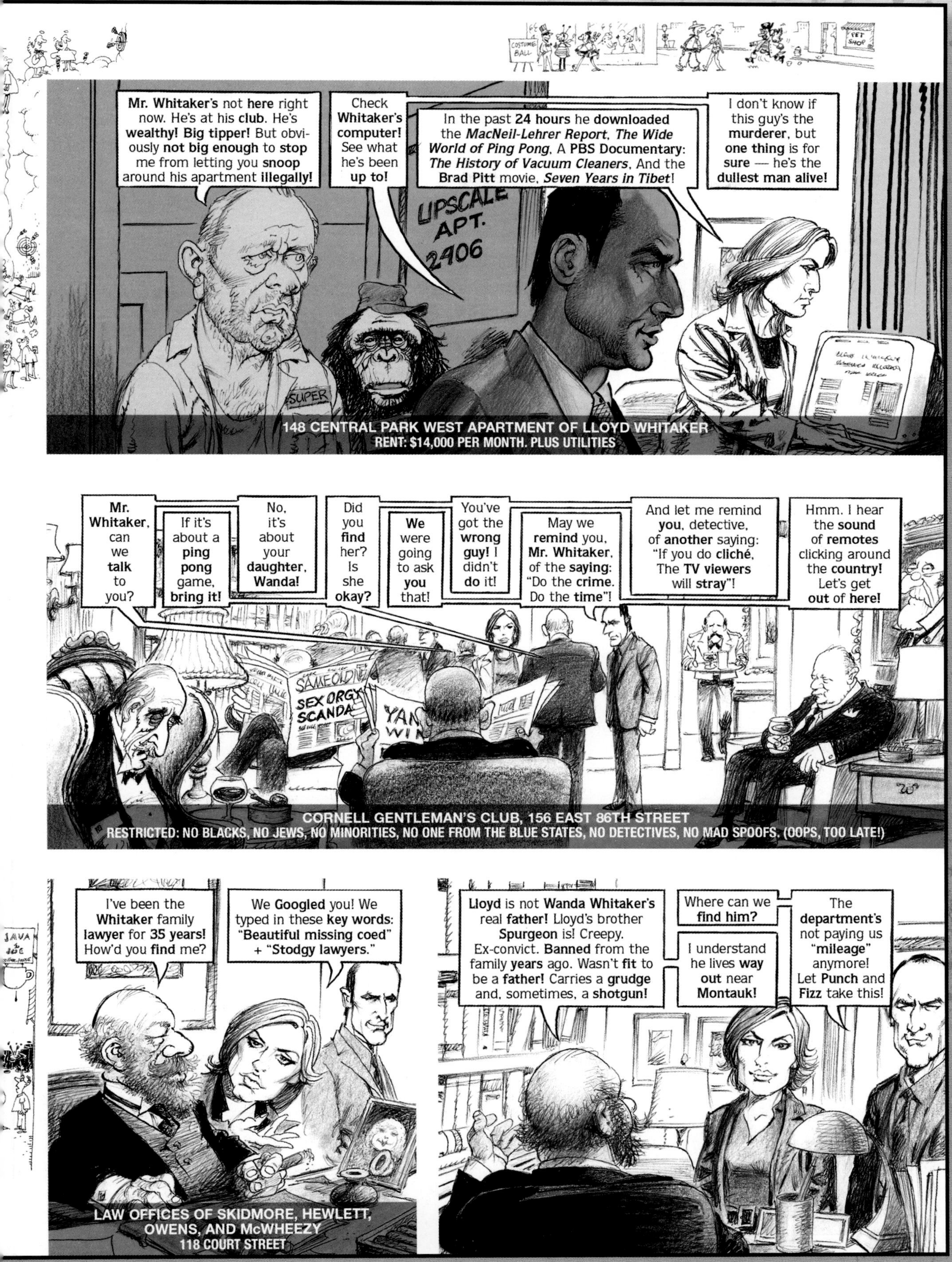
Mr. Whitaker's not here right now. He's at his club. He's wealthy! Big tipper! But obviously not big enough to stop me from letting you snoop around his apartment illegally!
Check Whitaker's computer! See what he's been up to!
In the past 24 hours he downloaded the MacNeil-Lehrer Report, The Wide World of Ping Pong, A PBS Documentary: The History of Vacuum Cleaners, And the Brad Pitt movie, Seven Years in Tibet!
I don't know if this guy's the murderer, but one thing is for sure — he's the dullest man alive!
UPSCALE APT. 2406
SUPER
148 CENTRAL PARK WEST APARTMENT OF LLOYD WHITAKER
RENT: $14,000 PER MONTH. PLUS UTILITIES
Mr. Whitaker, can we talk to you?
If it's about a ping pong game, bring it!
No, it's about your daughter, Wanda!
Did you find her? Is she okay?
We were going to ask you that!
You've got the wrong guy! I didn't do it!
May we remind you, Mr. Whitaker, of the saying: "Do the crime. Do the time"!
And let me remind you, detective, of another saying: "If you do cliché, The TV viewers will stray"!
Hmm. I hear the sound of remotes clicking around the country! Let's get out of here!
SEX ORGY SCANDA
CORNELL GENTLEMAN'S CLUB, 156 EAST 86TH STREET
RESTRICTED: NO BLACKS, NO JEWS, NO MINORITIES, NO ONE FROM THE BLUE STATES, NO DETECTIVES, NO MAD SPOOFS, (OOPS, TOO LATE!)
I've been the Whitaker family lawyer for 35 years! How'd you find me?
We Googled you! We typed in these key words: "Beautiful missing coed" + "Stodgy lawyers."
LAW OFFICES OF SKIDMORE, HEWLETT, OWENS, AND McWHEEZY
118 COURT STREET
Lloyd is not Wanda Whitaker's real father! Lloyd's brother Spurgeon is! Creepy. Ex-convict. Banned from the family years ago. Wasn't fit to be a father! Carries a grudge and, sometimes, a shotgun!
Where can we find him?
I understand he lives way out near Montauk!
The department's not paying us "mileage" anymore! Let Punch and Fizz take this!

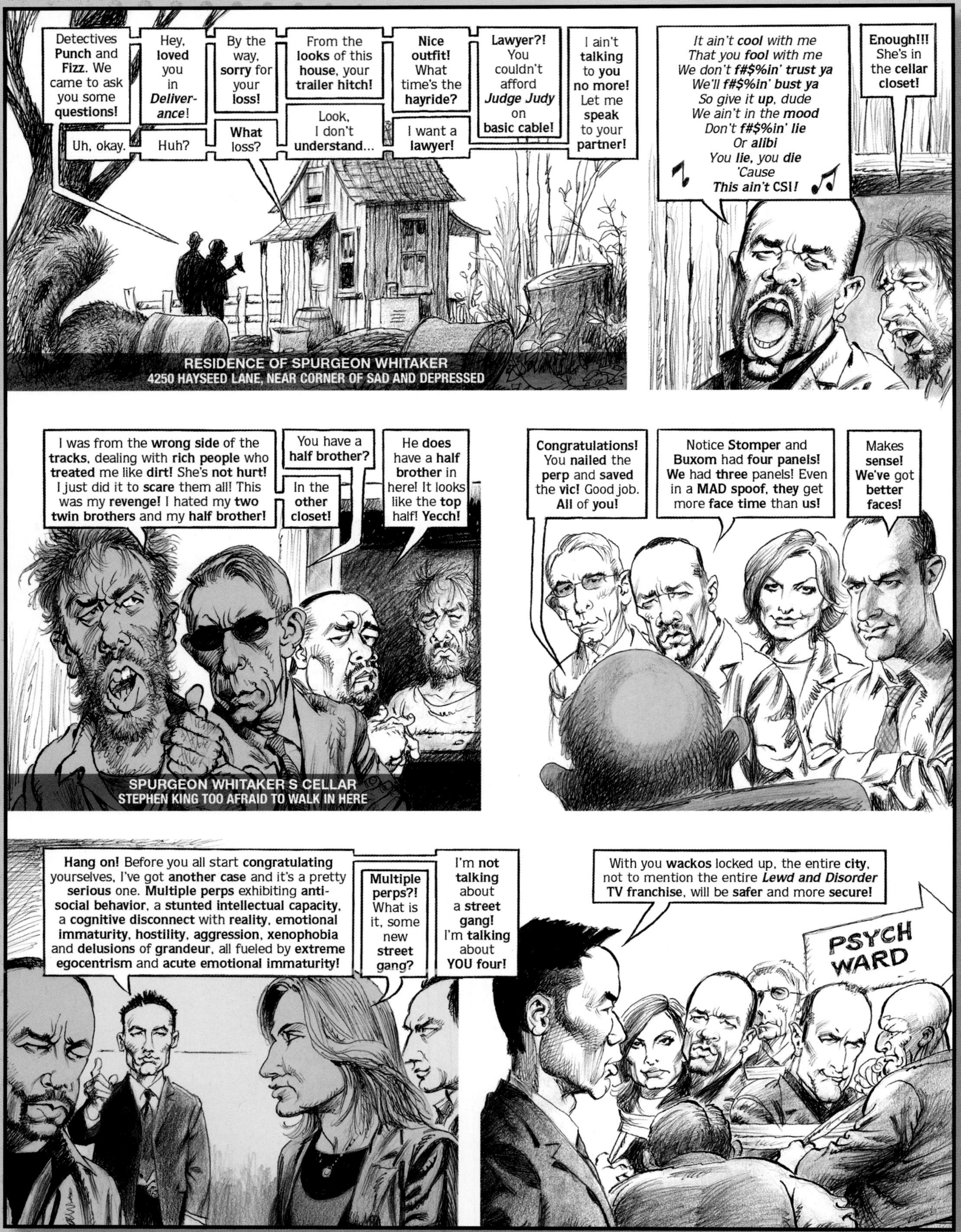

Detectives Punch and Fizz. We came to ask you some questions!
Uh, okay.
Hey, loved you in Deliverance!
Huh?
By the way, sorry for your loss!
What loss?
From the looks of this house, your trailer hitch!
Look, I don't understand...
Nice outfit! What time's the hayride?
I want a lawyer!
Lawyer?! You couldn't afford Judge Judy on basic cable!
I ain't talking to you no more! Let me speak to your partner!
RESIDENCE OF SPURGEON WHITAKER
4250 HAYSEED LANE, NEAR CORNER OF SAD AND DEPRESSED
It ain't cool with me That you fool with me We don't f#$%in' trust ya We'll f#$%in' bust ya So give it up, dude We ain't in the mood Don't f#$%in' lie Or alibi You lie, you die 'Cause This ain't CSI!
Enough!!! She's in the cellar closet!
I was from the wrong side of the tracks, dealing with rich people who treated me like dirt! She's not hurt! I just did it to scare them all! This was my revenge! I hated my two twin brothers and my half brother!
You have a half brother?
In the other closet!
He does have a half brother in here! It looks like the top half! Yecch!
SPURGEON WHITAKER S CELLAR
STEPHEN KING TOO AFRAID TO WALK IN HERE
Congratulations! You nailed the perp and saved the vic! Good job. All of you!
Notice Stomper and Buxom had four panels! We had three panels! Even in a MAD spoof, they get more face time than us!
Makes sense! We've got better faces!
Hang on! Before you all start congratulating yourselves, I've got another case and it's a pretty serious one. Multiple perps exhibiting anti-social behavior, a stunted intellectual capacity, a cognitive disconnect with reality, emotional immaturity, hostility, aggression, xenophobia and delusions of grandeur, all fueled by extreme egocentrism and acute emotional immaturity!
Multiple perps?! What is it, some new street gang?
I'm not talking about a street gang! I'm talking about YOU four!
With you wackos locked up, the entire city, not to mention the entire Lewd and Disorder TV franchise, will be safer and more secure!
PSYCH WARD

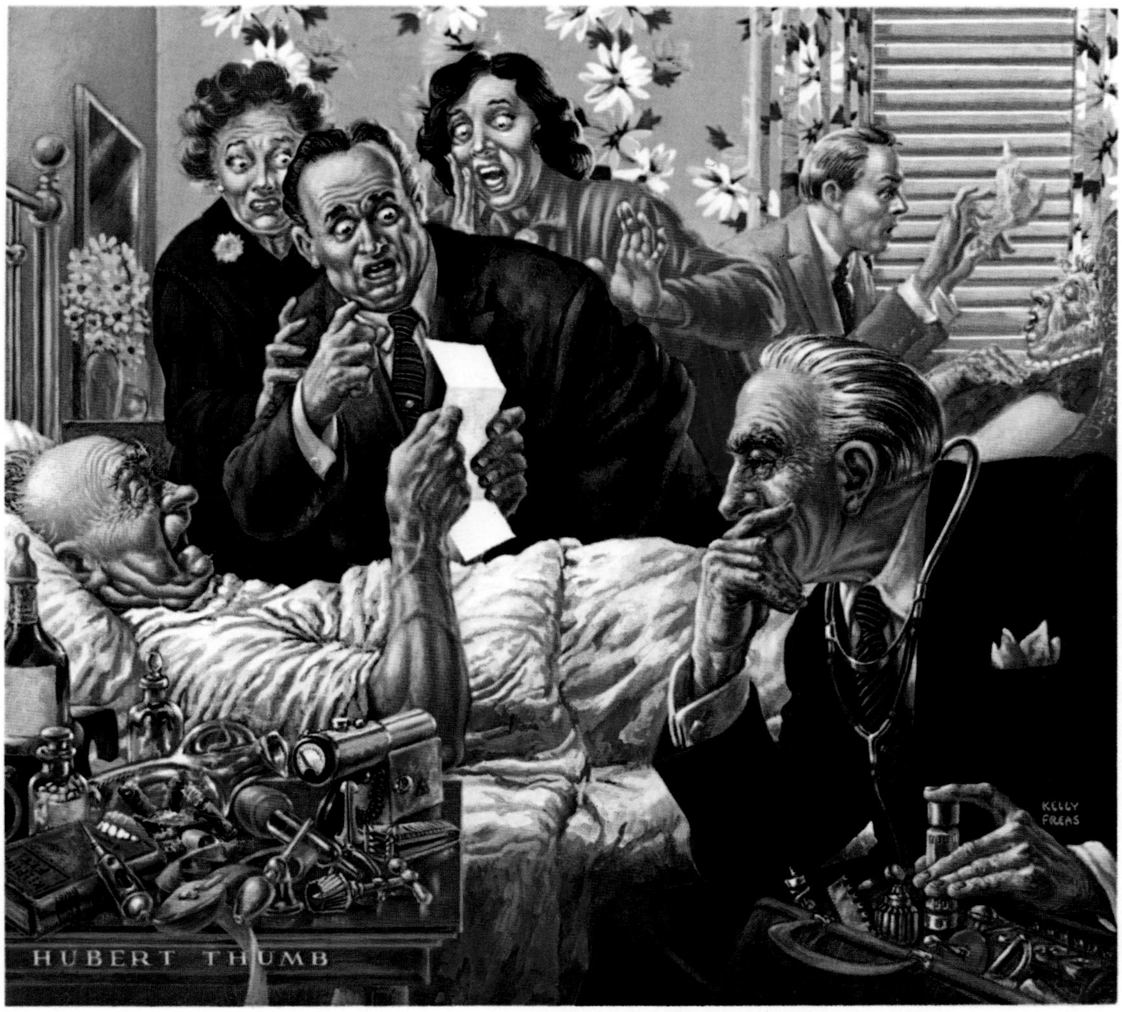
HUBERT THUMB
KELLY FREAS

PRESENTING THE BILL—reproduced here, is one of a series of original oil paintings, "Practising Medicine For Fun and Profit", commissioned by Park-David.

Great Moments in Medicine

Once the crisis has passed . . . once the patient has regained his strength . . . once the family is relieved and grateful . . . that's the time when the physician experiences one of the great moments in medicine. In fact, the *greatest moment* in medicine! Mainly, the moment when he presents his bill! That's the time when all of the years of training and study and work seem worthwhile. And there's always the chance that the shock might mean more business for him!

Park-David scientists are proud of their place in the history of practicing medicine for fun and profit, helping to provide doctors with the materials that mean higher fees and bigger incomes. For example, our latest development . . . tranquilizer-impregnated bill paper . . . designed to eliminate the shock and hysteria that comes when the patient gets a look at your bill. Not only will he remain calm when he sees what you've charged . . . now he won't even *care!*

COPYRIGHT 1959—PARK-DAVID & COMPANY, WITH THE BLESSINGS OF THE AMA

PARK-DAVID *. . . Pioneers in bigger medical bills*

ARTIST: KELLY FREAS **MAD #48/JULY 1959**

by Frank Jacobs
WRITER

Why pick this?

It remains a MAD classic. It stands out as the ideal spoof of an ad campaign. Its artwork by Kelly Freas maintains the look of the artwork in the Parke-Davis ads, albeit with typical MAD touches. But most important, I laughed out loud the first time I saw it…and still do.

After 430 Fold-Ins, It's About Time We Did a
FOLD-OUT!

As a special bonus, here's an inside look at 61 years of life in the MAD offices. And who better to take "A MAD Look at MAD" than the one and only Sergio Aragonés, who has traveled, cavorted and hobnobbed with his fellow members of "The Usual Gang of Idiots" for more than five of those six decades? On the following gatefold, Sergio (with the able assistance of colorist Tom Luth) takes us on a guided tour through MAD's history, from Harvey Kurtzman and Willie Elder back at 225 Lafayette Street, through Bill Gaines's office and John Putnam's art department at 485 MADison Avenue, to John Ficarra's current digs at 1700 Broadway — complete with the comings and goings of various writers, artists and staff members who have passed through MAD's doors through the years — all mashed together in one phantasmagorical tapestry. (Bet you never thought you'd read the word "phantasmagorical" in MAD!)

But that's not all!

For the reverse side of Sergio's masterpiece, we have unearthed a rare artifact from MAD's history: the first reprinting ever of the "Pop Art-Op Art" poster of Alfred E. Neuman which originally appeared in *More Trash From MAD #8* in 1965. Created during the heyday of Andy Warhol, Roy Lichtenstein and Bridget Riley, this hypnotic portrait was the work of longtime MAD editor Al Feldstein. Famed as an artist for EC Comics' horror and sci-fi titles (and today as a painter of Western themes), Feldstein created very little art for MAD during his 29-year stint as the magazine's editor, and most of that, like this poster, went uncredited. The poster was originally printed on two large sheets of newsprint, which had to be removed from the magazine and taped together to create a life-sized portrait of the "What — Me Worry?" kid. While it appears here at about half the size of the original, it is presented on much better paper — and without the need for you to pull out your scissors and tape to piece it together.

So there you have it — two MAD masterpieces, suitable for framing. Of course, in order to frame both, you'll need to purchase a second copy of *Inside MAD*…and then, once you've mutilated both of those books, you'll have to pony up for yet a third, so you'll have a pristine copy to display on your shelf and keep for posterity (or at least to get a better price on eBay!). It's a special bonus indeed: our sneaky way of getting you to buy multiple copies of *Inside MAD* and make it a best seller — Fa fa fa!

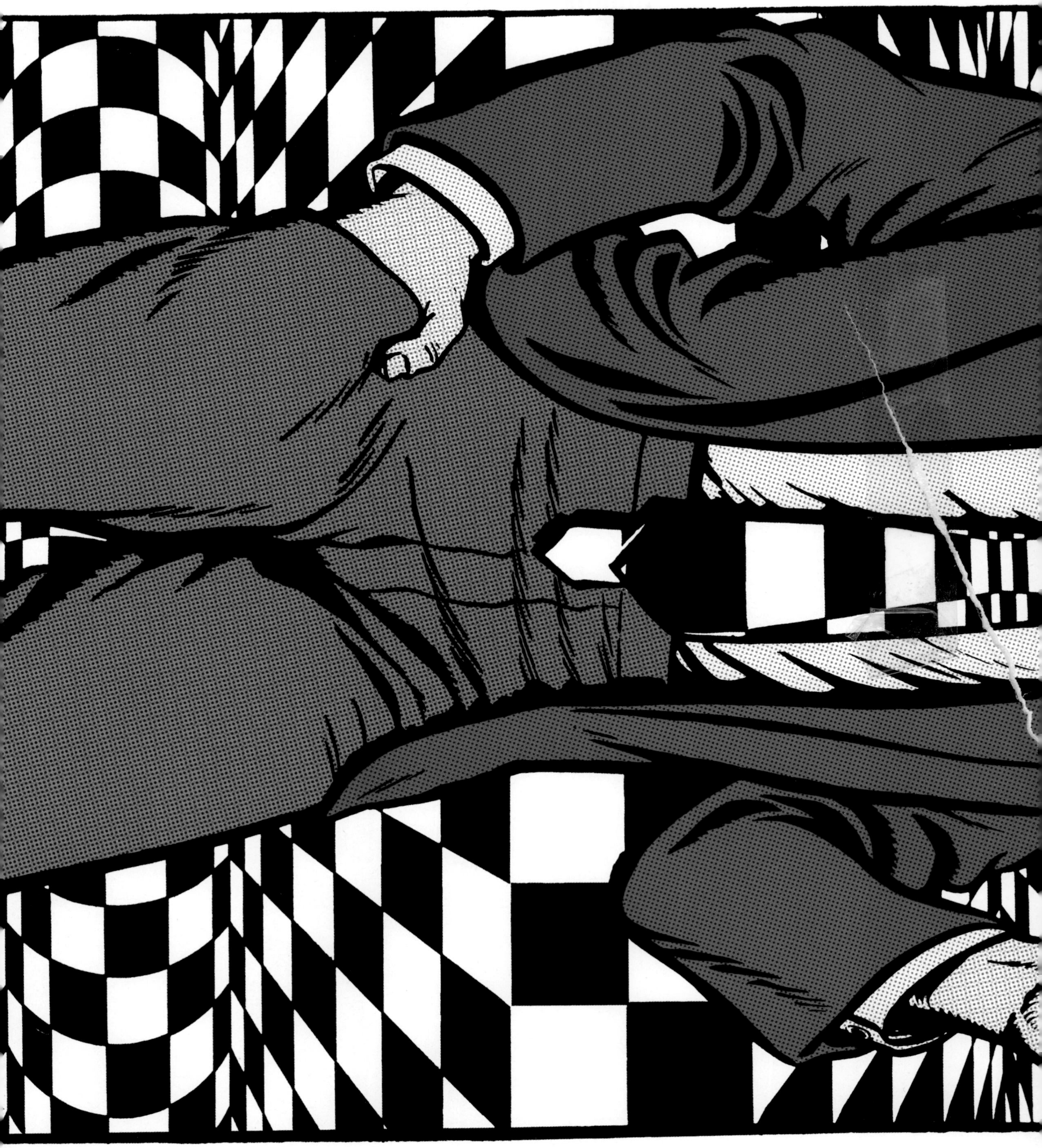

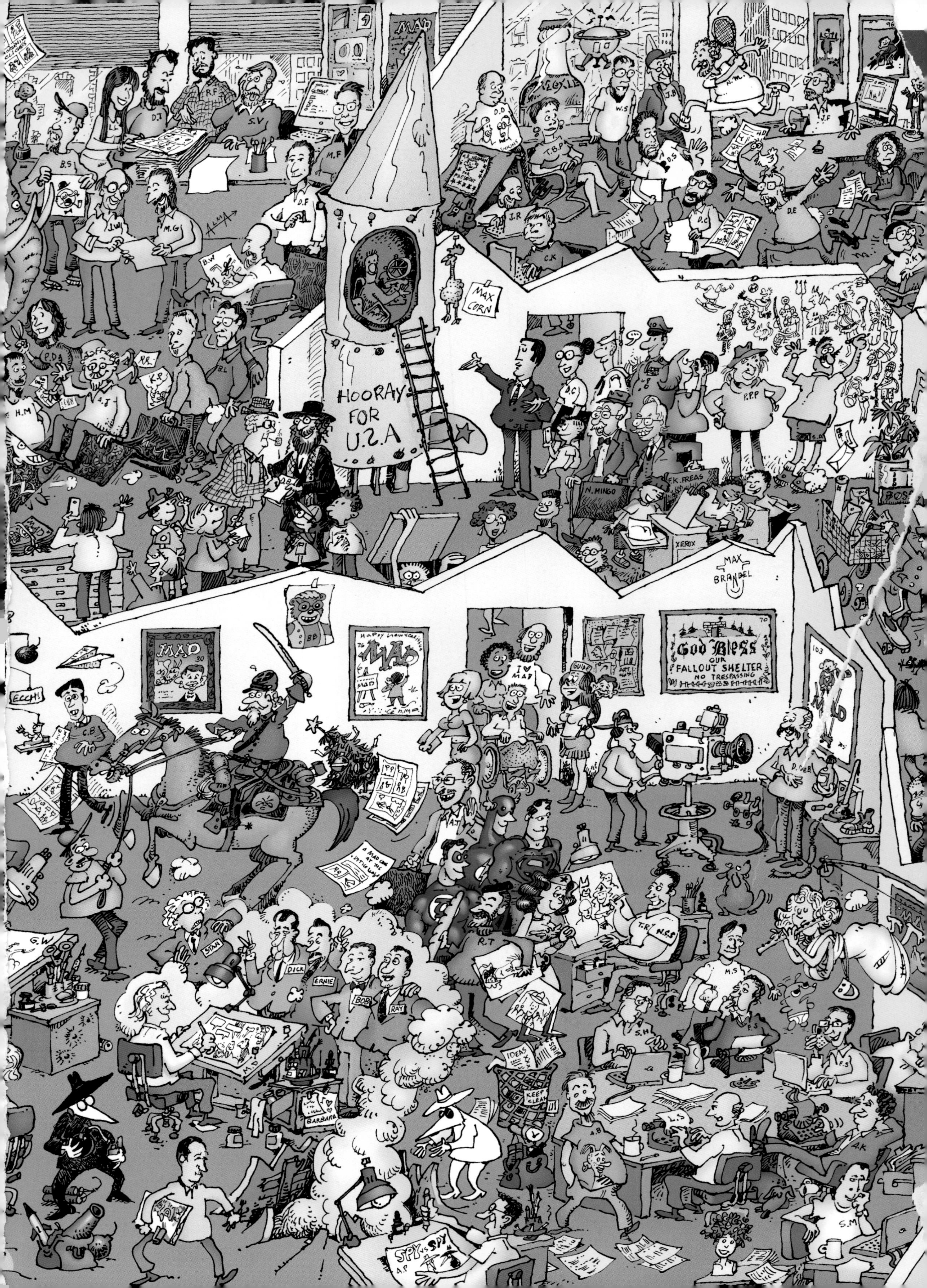
HOORAY FOR U.S.A
MAX CORN
MAX BRANDEL
GOD BLESS OUR FALLOUT SHELTER NO TRESPASSING
XEROX
N. MINGO
F.K. FREAS
ECCH!
STAN
DICK
ERNIE
BOB
RAY
IDEAS
KEEP CLEAN
BARBARA
SPY vs SPY

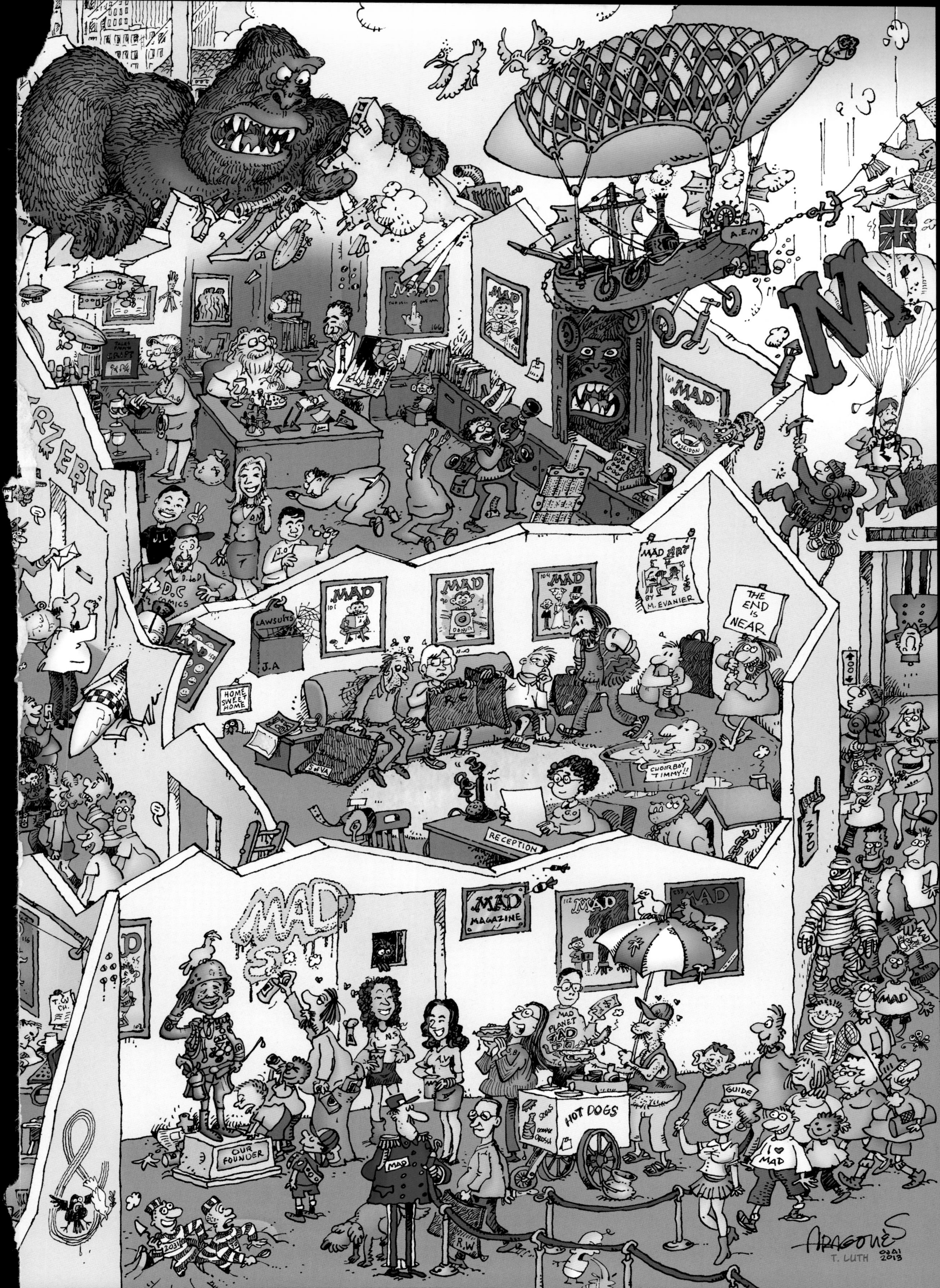

A.E.N
POSEIDON
D.C COMICS
LAWSUITS
J.A
HOME SWEET HOME
MAD ART BY M. EVANIER
THE END IS NEAR
CHOIRBOY TIMMY!!
RECEPTION
MAD MAGAZINE
OUR FOUNDER
HOT DOGS
GUIDE
MAD
ARAGONES
T. LUTH

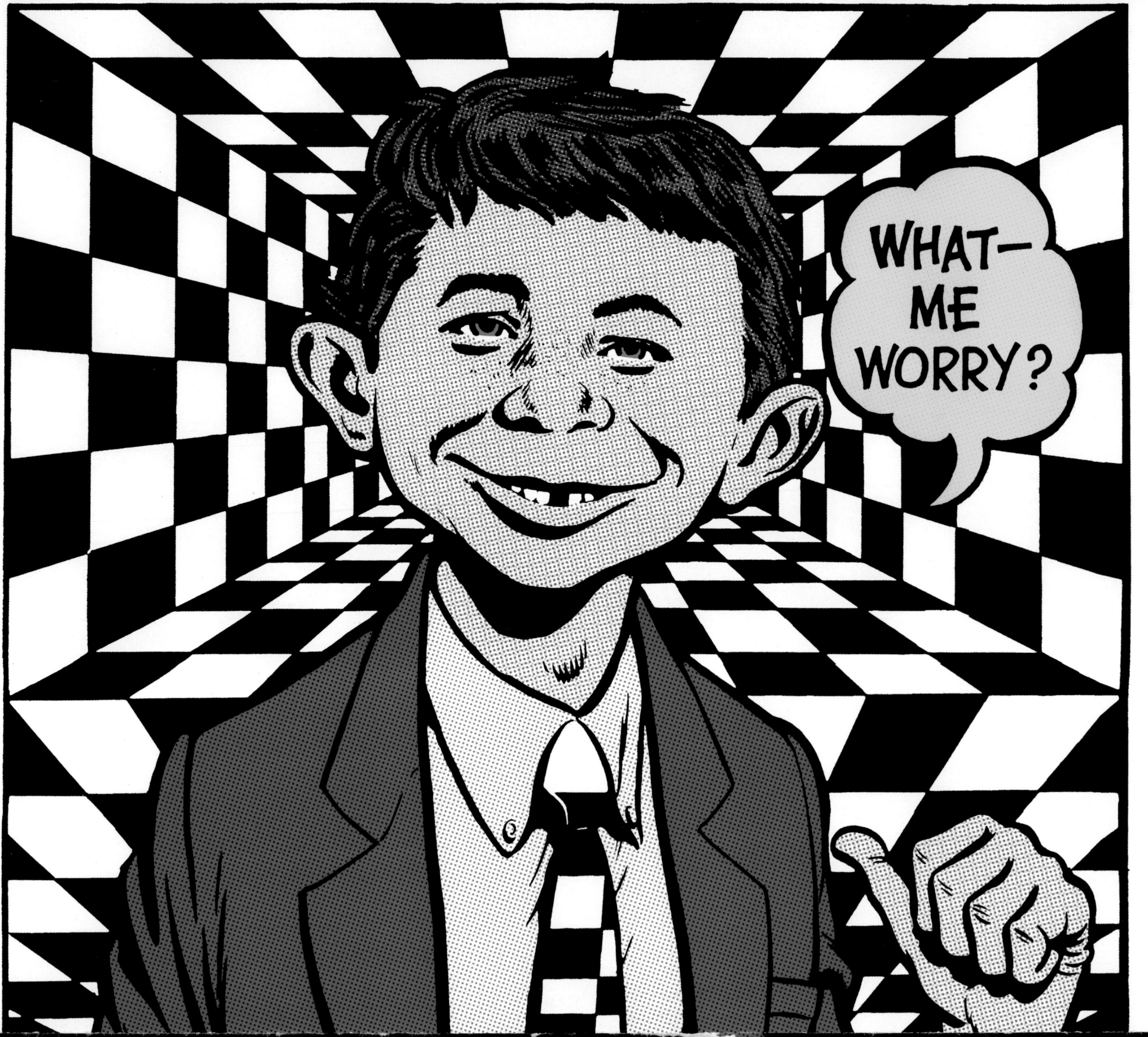
WHAT—
ME
WORRY?

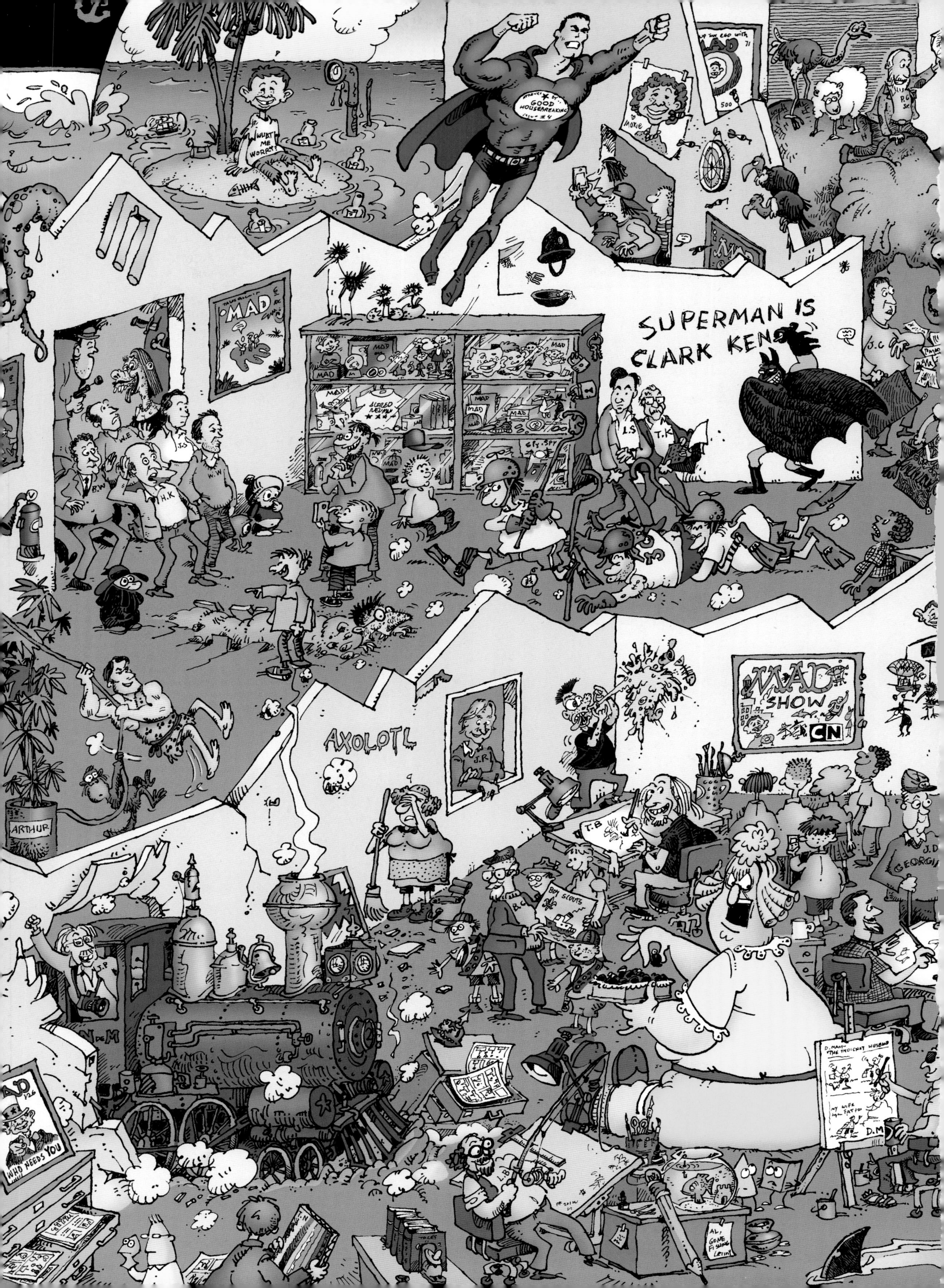
WHAT ME WORRY?
GOOD HOUSEBREAKING
MAD
SUPERMAN IS
CLARK KEN
MAD
AXOLOTL
ARTHUR
MAD SHOW
CN
BOY SCOUTS
WHO NEEDS YOU
AL GONE FISHING
D.M

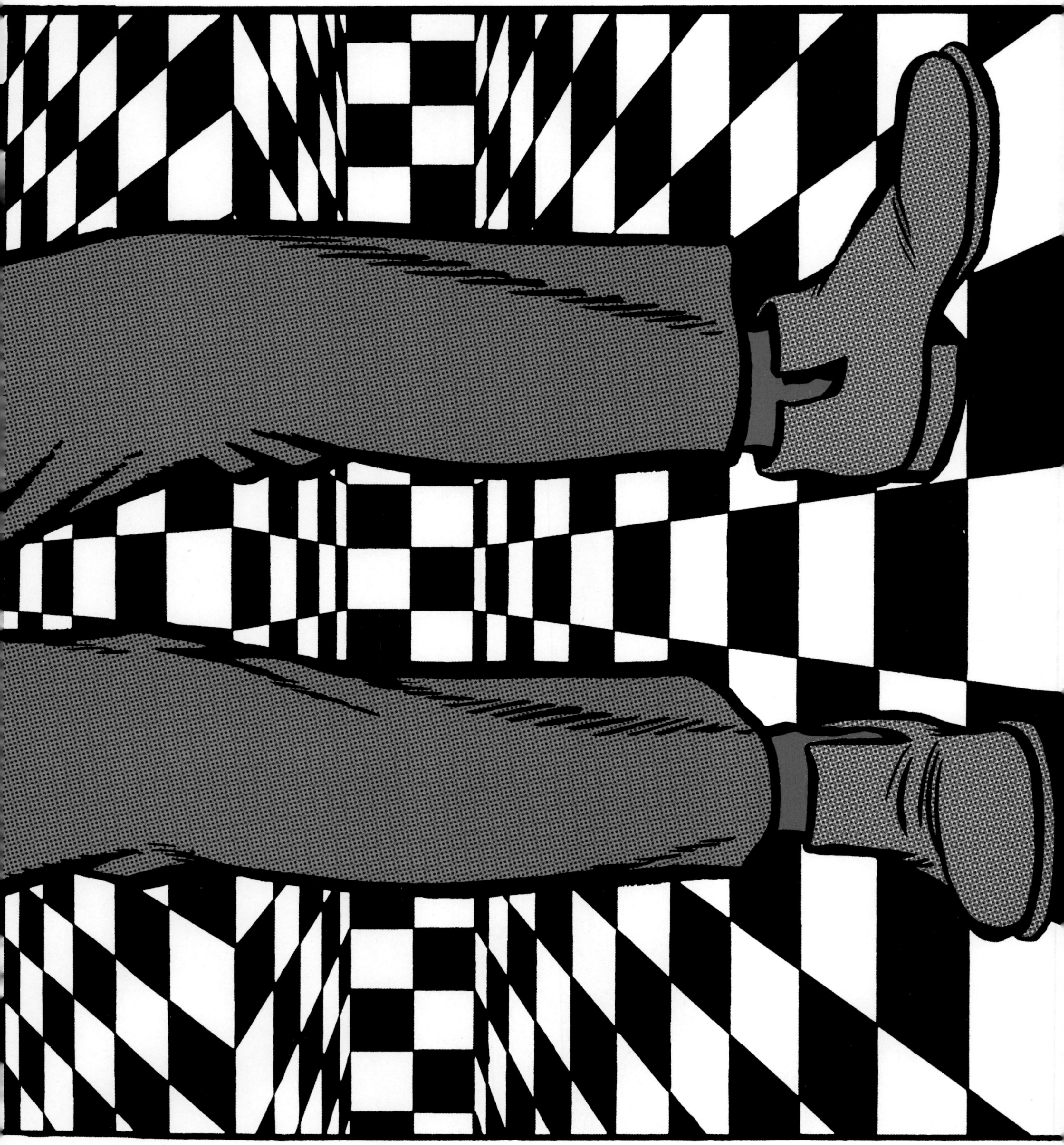

DON MARTIN DEPT. PART I

At The Academy Of Electric Fan Repair

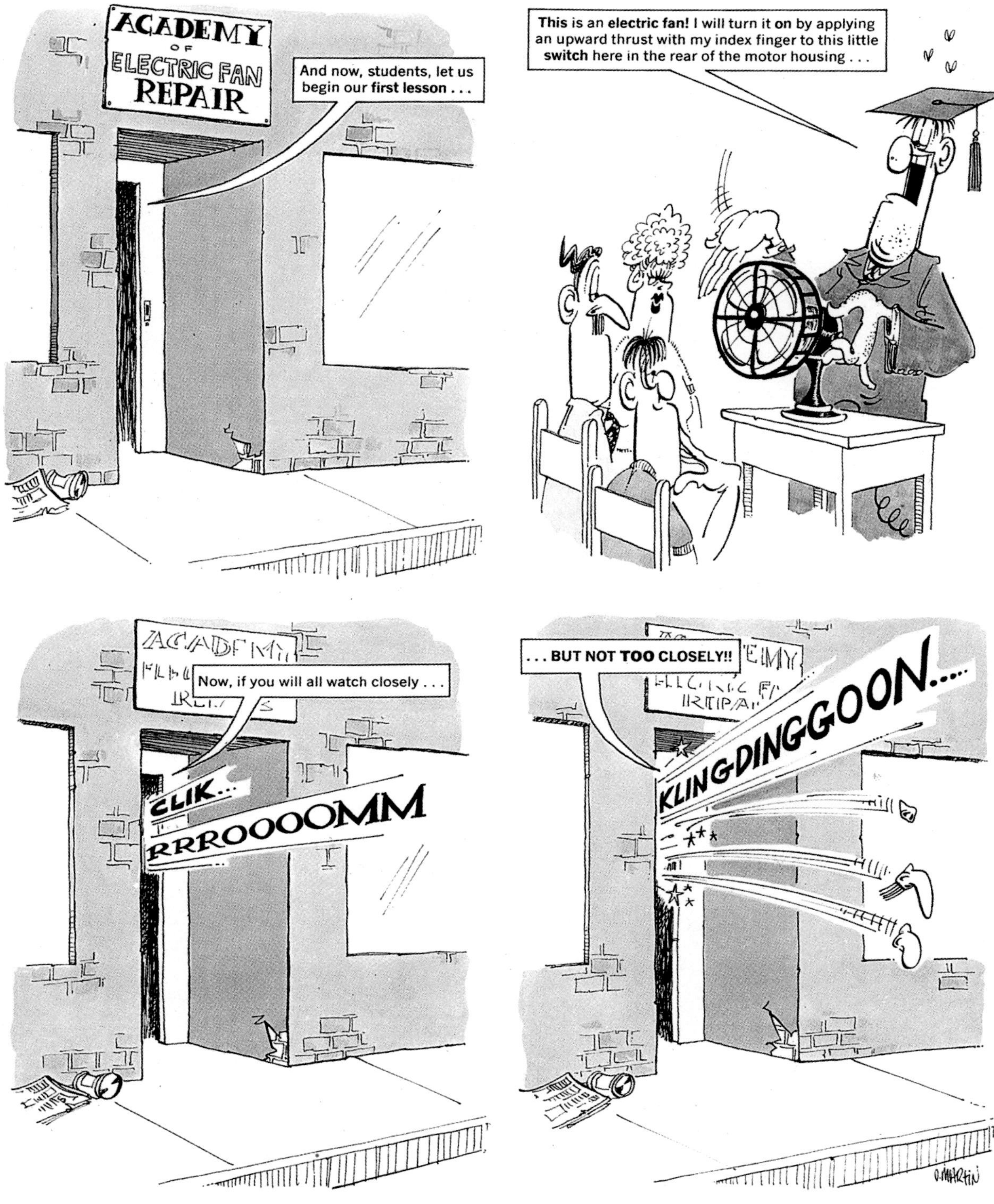
ACADEMY OF ELECTRIC FAN REPAIR
And now, students, let us begin our **first lesson** . . .
This is an **electric fan!** I will turn it **on** by applying an upward thrust with my index finger to this little **switch** here in the rear of the motor housing . . .
Now, if you will all watch closely . . .
CLIK...
RRROOOOMM
. . . BUT NOT TOO CLOSELY!!
KLING-DINGGOON.....
D. MARTIN

MAD #113/SEPTEMBER 1967

by Tom Cheney
WRITER/ARTIST

As good Catholic boys, my brother and I were forbidden to read or possess MAD. Apparently our mother perceived some sort of satanic glimmer in Alfred's eye. Thus, after being repeatedly warned about having our flesh perpetually roasted in the furnaces of hell, we regularly went over to our catholic cousin Dave's house and read his copies of MAD.

One afternoon, while the three of us were "blackening our souls" with Dave's bountiful collection of "Alfreds," my brother started laughing so hard that he fell off the porch railing he'd been sitting on. Bruised, but still giggling like Renfield, he pointed at the page he'd been reading and handed it over to Dave, who was soon gripped by a grand mal seizure of cackling. I snatched the copy away from him, read the strip, and for the next 15 minutes the three of us fed the flames of our convulsive laughter by repeating Don Martin's immortal sound effect: "KLINGDINGGOON!"

As our good Catholic mother predicted, Don Martin had, in less than five minutes, turned her good Catholic sons into complete, incurable, and perhaps eternally damned MADmen.

MAD *in Movies*

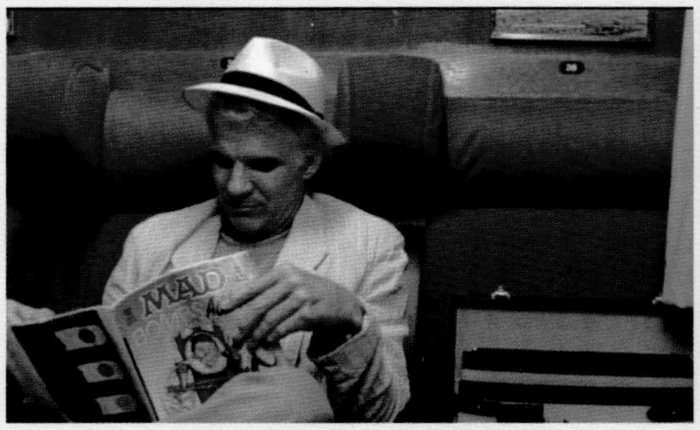
MAD

DIRTY ROTTEN SCOUNDRELS, 1988

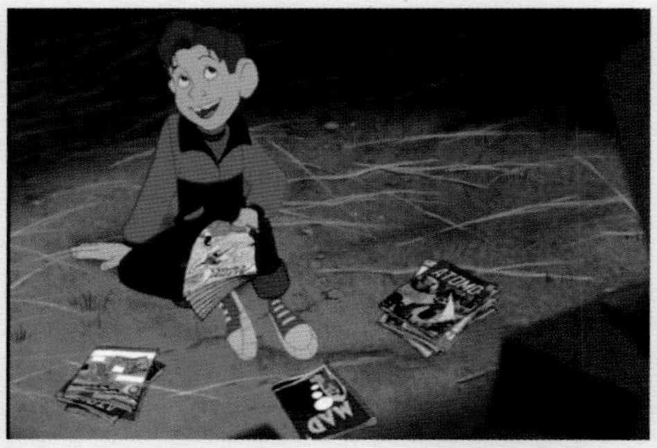

THE IRON GIANT, 1999

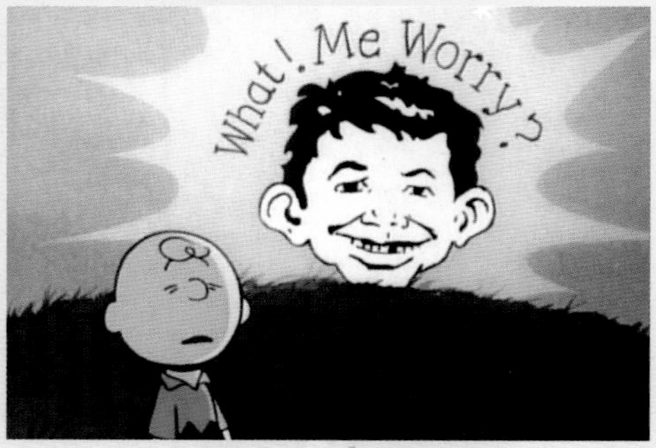
What! Me Worry?

IT'S AN ADVENTURE, CHARLIE BROWN, 1983

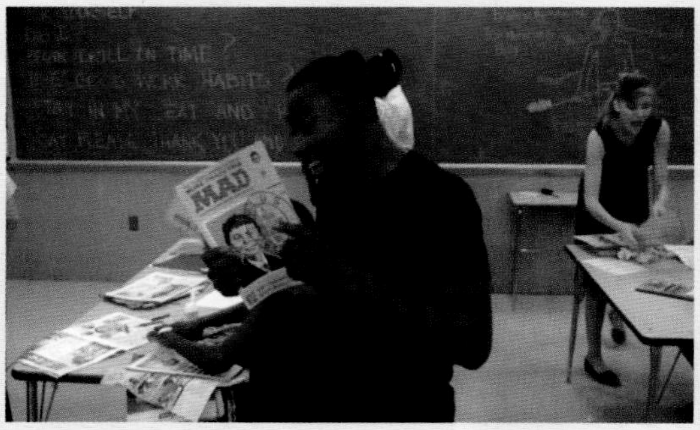
MAD

HAIRSPRAY, 1988

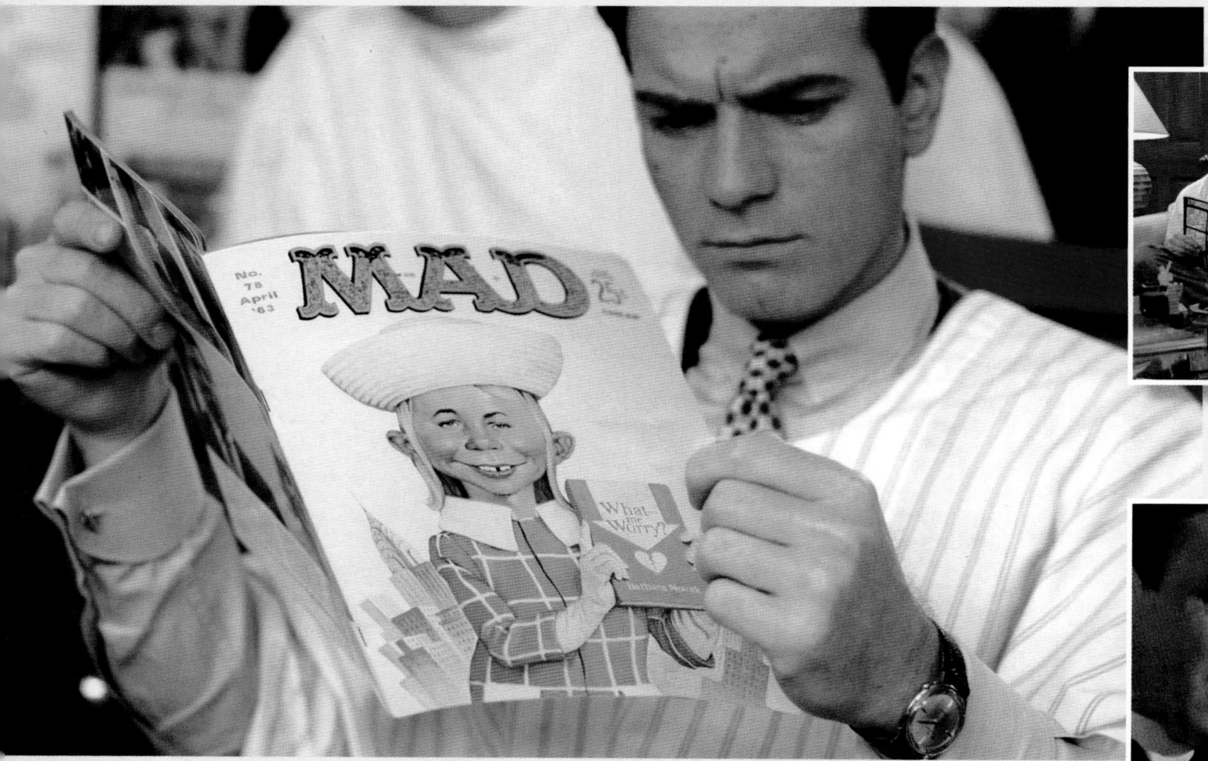
No. 78
April
'63
MAD
What— me Worry?

DOWN WITH LOVE, 2003

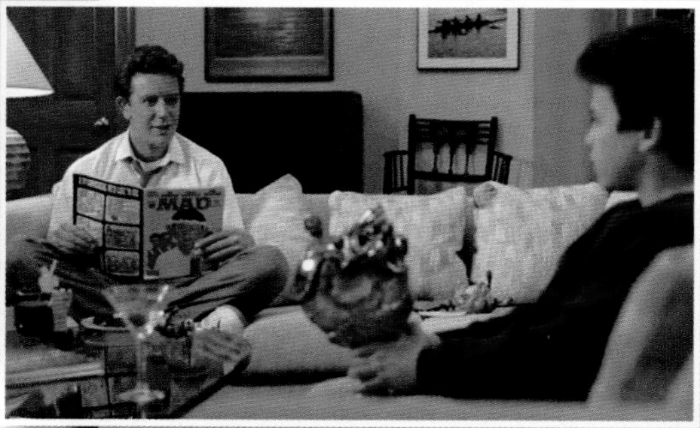
MAD

VICE VERSA, 1988

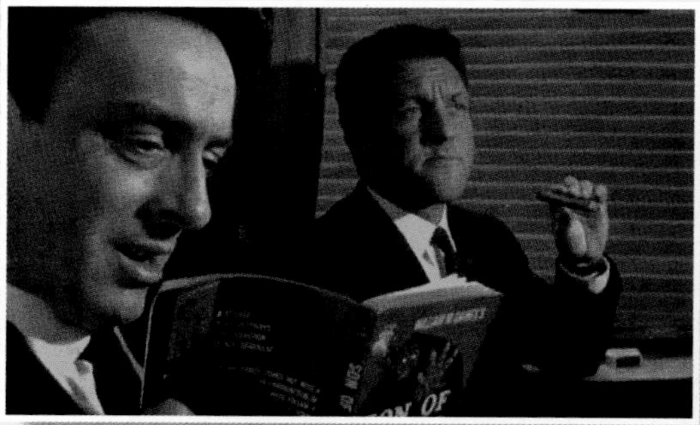

A HARD DAY'S NIGHT, 1964

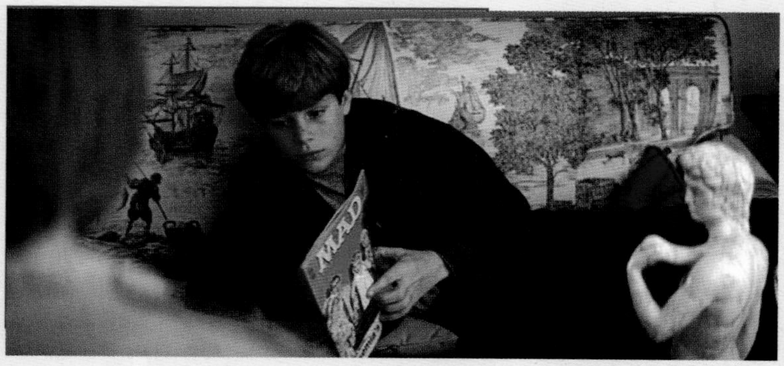
MAD

THE GOONIES, 1985

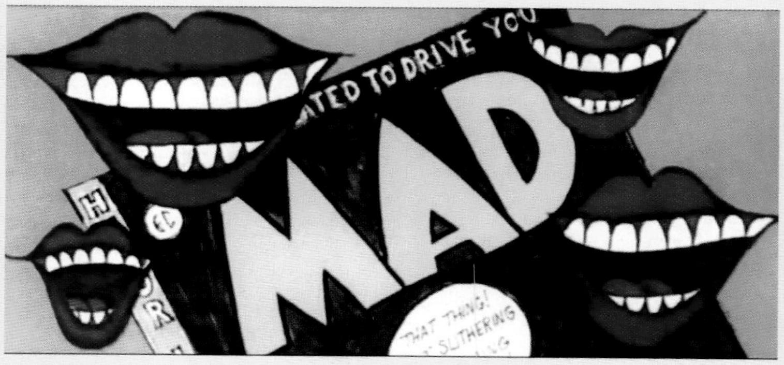
TED TO DRIVE YOU
MAD

GREASE, 1978

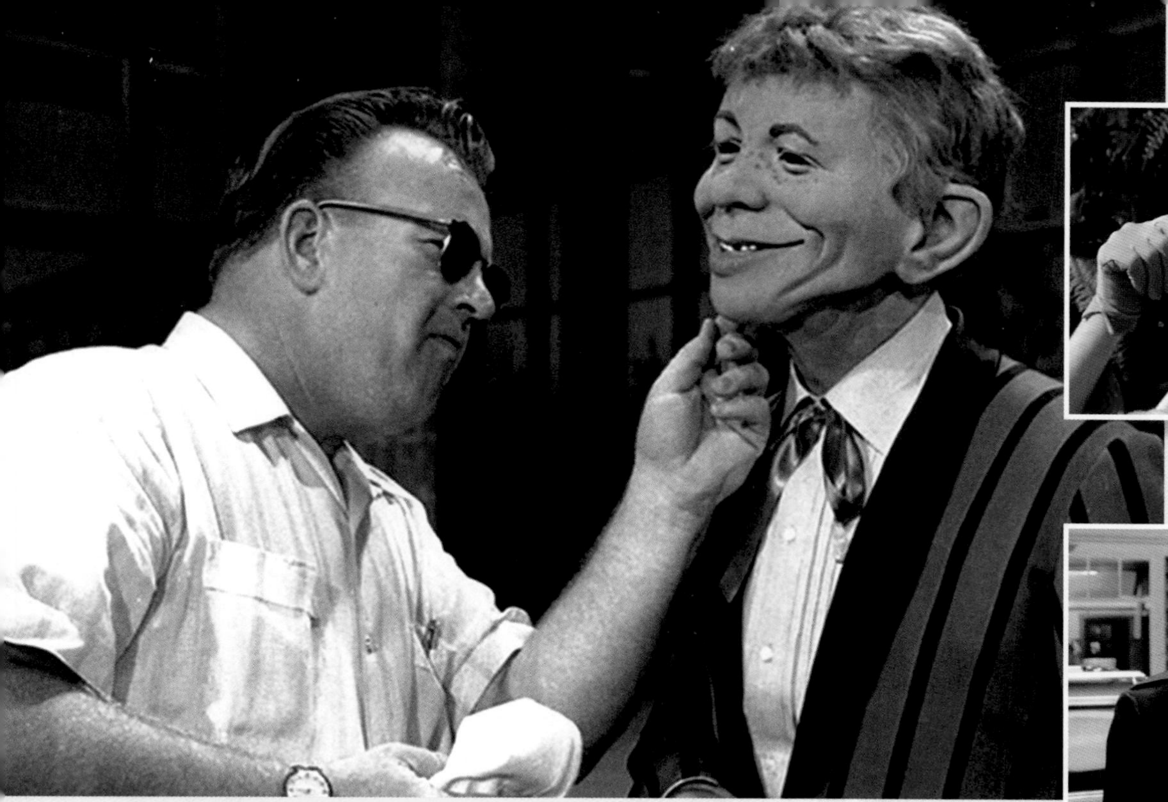

ARGO, 2012

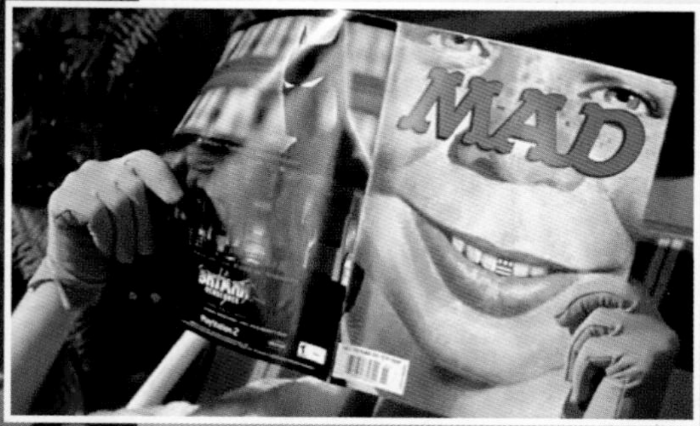
MAD

DICKIE ROBERTS: FORMER CHILD STAR, 2003

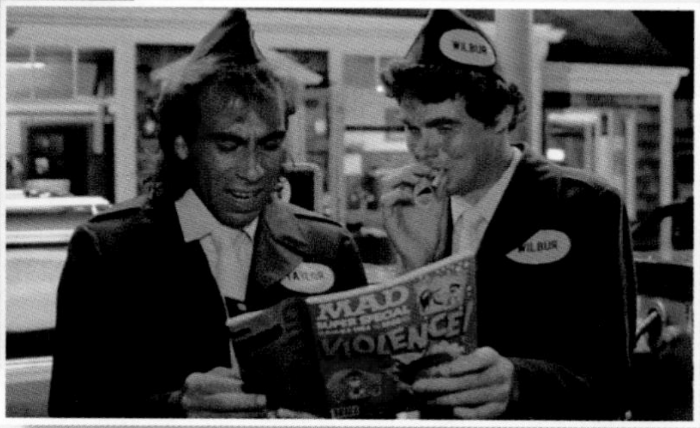
MAD
VIOLENCE

ONE CRAZY SUMMER, 1986

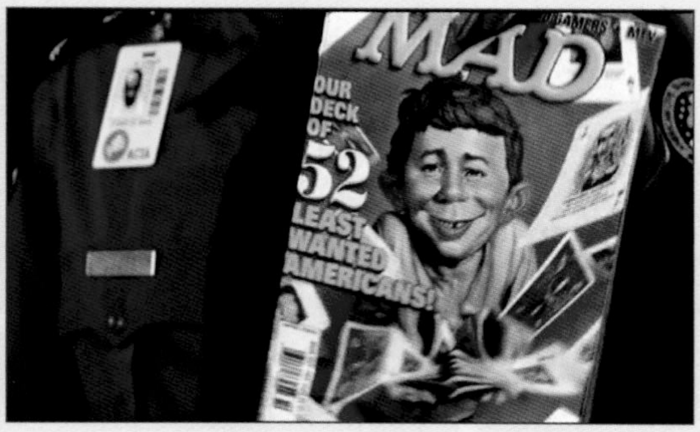
MAD
OUR DECK OF 52 LEAST WANTED AMERICANS!

DUE DATE, 2010

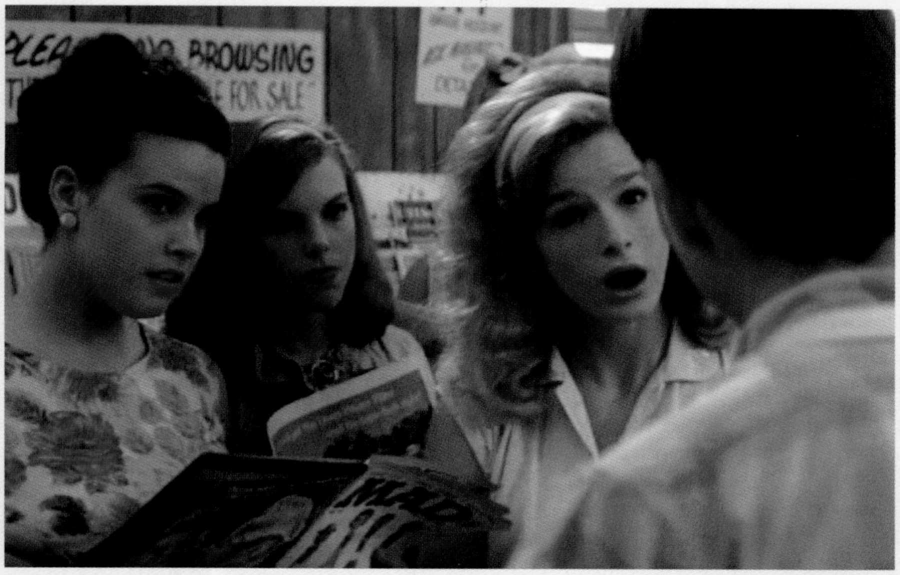
BROWSING
MAD

BORN ON THE FOURTH OF JULY, 1989

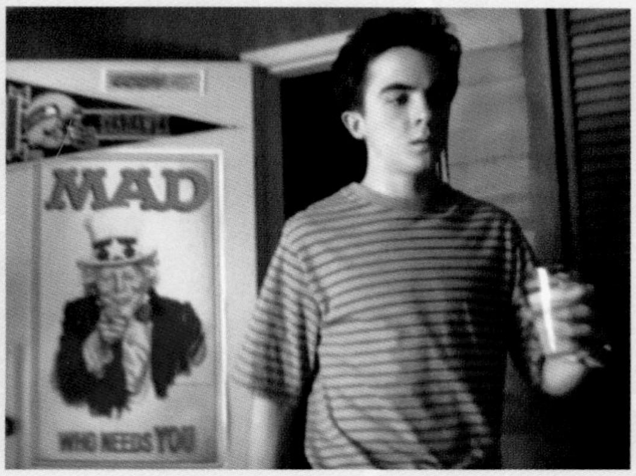
MAD
WHO NEEDS YOU

AGENT CODY BANKS, 2003

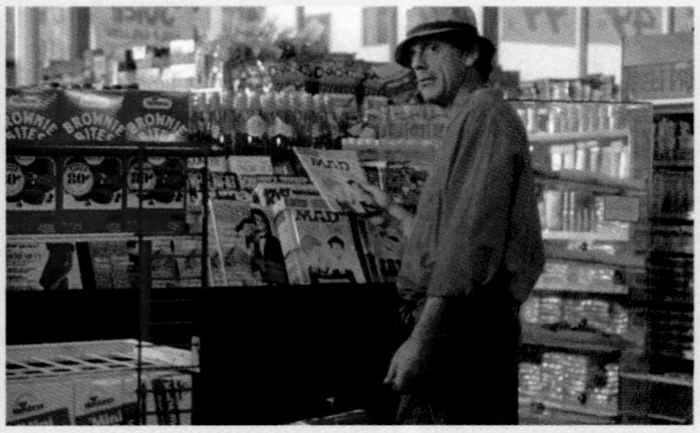
MAD

CAMP NOWHERE, 1994

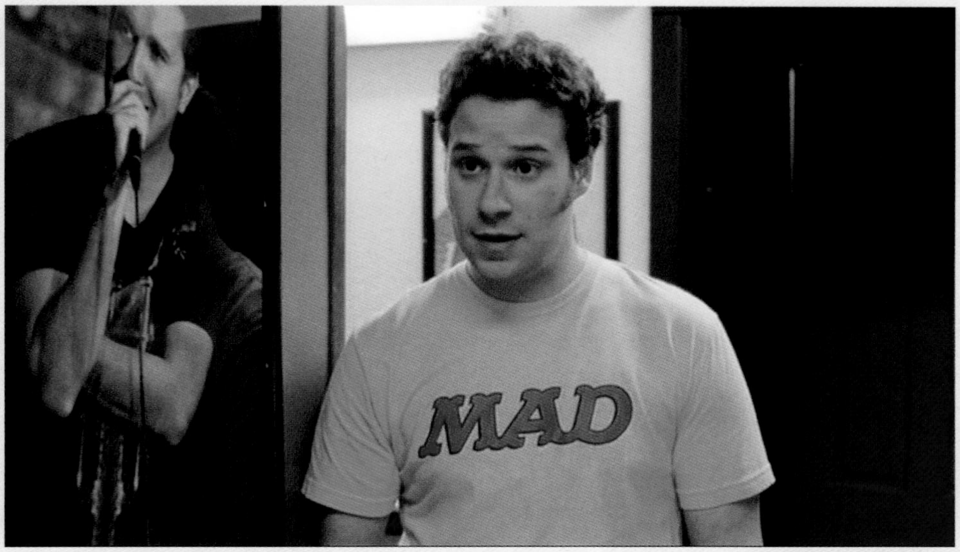
MAD

FUNNY PEOPLE, 2009

FOR ALL YOU SOFT-HEARTED CLODS WHO LOVE LIVE LOBSTERS...BUT CAN

A MAD LOOK AT OTHER USES FO

DIAPER RINSER

HIGH SHELF EXTENSION PRONGS

EARPHONES HOLDER

TURN INDICATOR

COAT & HAT RACK

by Sergio Aragonés
WRITER/ARTIST

As a dedicated fan def cartoons since my youth, I was aware of Paul Peter Porges' gag panels in *The New Yorker* before I came to the United States to become a cartoonist myself. It was a great experience for me when we met several years later as professionals at MAD. In a short time, it became obvious that his zany approach to humor was an accurate reflection of Porges himself — totally unrestricted, a willing follower of whichever path his crazy mind would take him. His gags about pets, insects, fish, fowl and creatures of every known species were

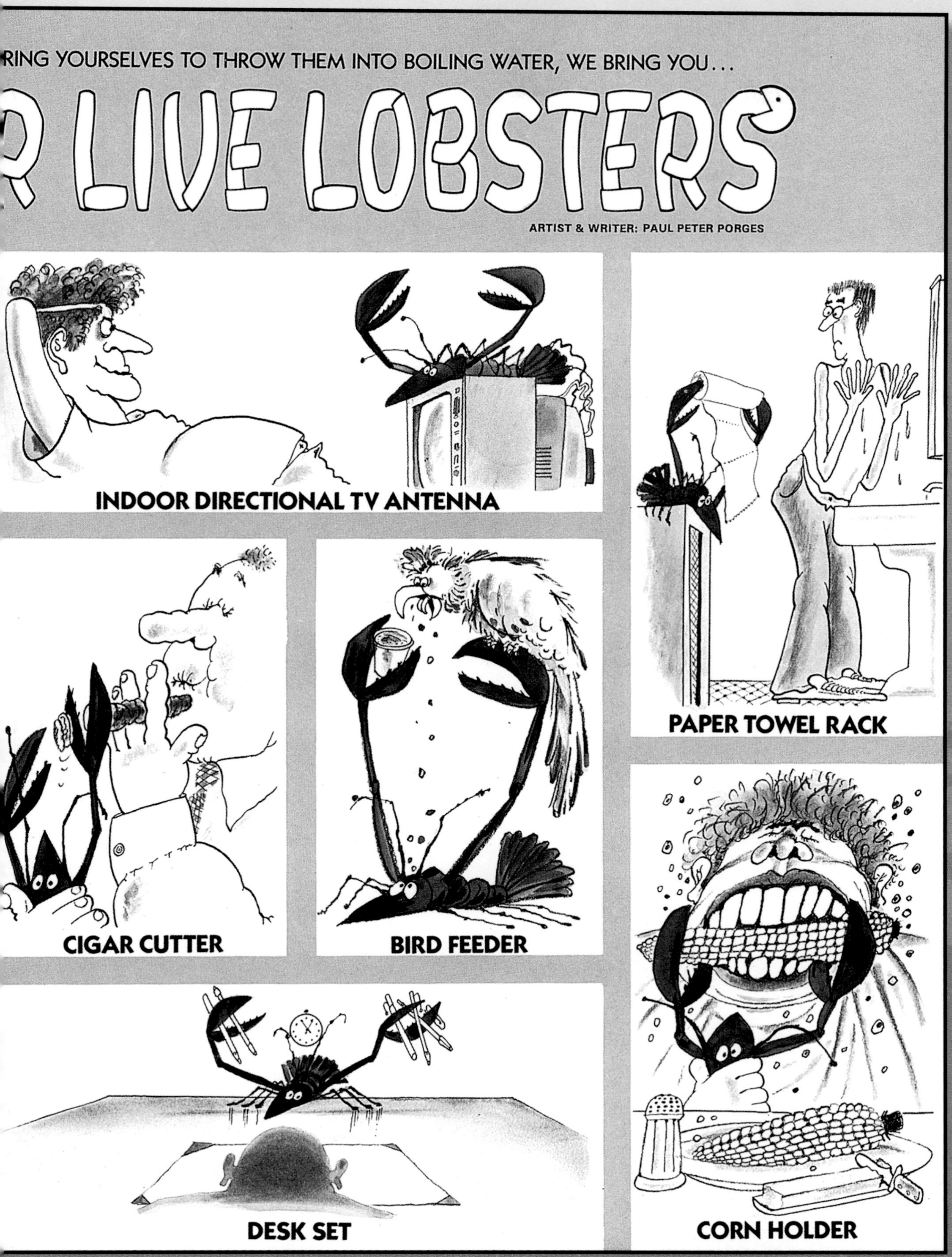
RING YOURSELVES TO THROW THEM INTO BOILING WATER, WE BRING YOU...
R LIVE LOBSTERS
ARTIST & WRITER: PAUL PETER PORGES
INDOOR DIRECTIONAL TV ANTENNA
PAPER TOWEL RACK
CIGAR CUTTER
BIRD FEEDER
DESK SET
CORN HOLDER

MAD #233/SEPTEMBER 1982

especially hysterical to me. Porges' animals were the opposite of Walt Disney's animals, which had a human layer of cuteness and charm. Porges offered the edgy side of nature in all its mischief and chaos, warts and nastiness — in other words, wildlife that was truly wild.

His "Lobster" article is one of my favorites and I smile every time I have a steamed one on a plate in front me, relieved that it is in no condition to cause the kind of damage a Porges creature is capable of.

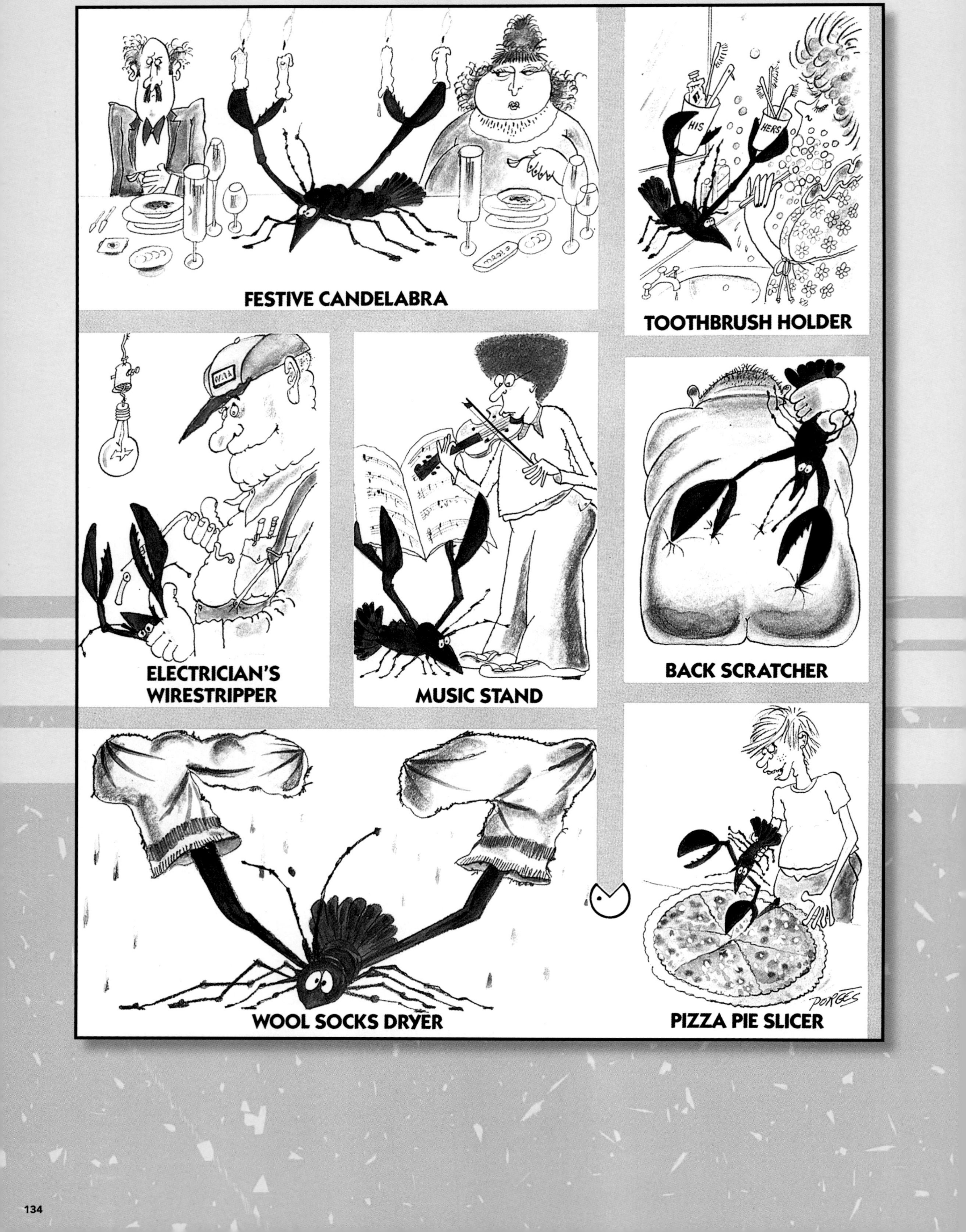
FESTIVE CANDELABRA
HIS
HERS
TOOTHBRUSH HOLDER
ELECTRICIAN'S WIRESTRIPPER
MUSIC STAND
BACK SCRATCHER
WOOL SOCKS DRYER
PORGES
PIZZA PIE SLICER

If there's an especially hot place in hell, surely it is reserved for the numbskull idiot morons who write assembly instructions. Whether you're trying to put together a child's toy, an exercise bike or storage bin, if there's a way to make the instructions impossible to understand, these beanhead writers do it with ambiguous terms, technical jargon and meaningless phrases. (Then again, maybe all these instructions are clear and it's just the entire population of the planet that is "mechanically challenged".) Nah, it's them! And we wish them a pox on their house as we present. . .

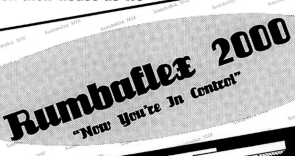

Rumbaflex 2000
"Now You're In Control"

Dear Consumer:

By purchasing the RumbaFlex 2000 you have chosen the finest, and shown you're a smart consumer. The RumbaFlex 2000 will give you years of trouble-free operation and user satisfaction. In fact, with proper maintenance you will probably never have to replace your RumbaFlex 2000.

With the RumbaFlex 2000, quality and durability are designed right in. And with our patented "snap-to" assembly, you'll be enjoying your RumbaFlex 2000 in minutes. The following simple instructions will show you how to assemble, operate and maintain your new RumbaFlex 2000.

If you're a first time Rumba user, welcome to the exciting world of Rumba products. If you're one of our loyal customers, you will find the 2000 Series much easier to assemble. (No tube inserts or daubing necessary!) and less irritating to use indoors (No more messy sponges or awkward harnesses!) than the old 1000 Series or chain-driven Rumba products. Say goodbye to the annoying grit. Say goodbye to the fuzz and drip. And say hello to that supple, saucy satisfaction.

Enjoy! With the new RumbaFlex 2000, you're in control!

ARTIST: MALINDA DUNN   WRITER: JIM BARTON

MAD #337/JULY 1995

by Darren Johnson
WRITER

I was a rookie "Idiot" with a handful of MAD sales when Jim Barton's Rumbaflex 2000 opened my eyes (tear-filled from laughter) to no-holds-barred, flat-out funny absurdity. Paired with Malinda Dunn's equally preposterous and spot-on illustrations, his riff on indecipherable owner's manuals reached levels of ludicrousness I never thought possible. The "Parts List" alone is worth the price of admission, from the "styrene winch nuggets" to the "load-bearing tongue wafers." Somehow Jim sustained this nonsensical hilarity over four pages (!) chock-full of salsa, sponges and swelling, all delivered in deadpan "instruction-ese." By eschewing pop culture references or topical humor and simply reveling in giddy gibberish, Rumbaflex 2000 remains as relevant and ridiculous today as it did in 1995.

ASSEMBLY *"Save Some Biscuits For Me!"*

Practically everything you need to assemble the RumbaFlex 2000 is included. The only additional supplies you'll need are a putty knife, a 14" orbital band saw, cotton or cheesecloth buffing mitts, a ceramic rabbit or other clamping device, a standard set of metric socket wrenches and 48oz. of luke-warm pudding.

You'll see the difference in the new RumbaFlex 2000 before you've even used it. That's because we've made assembly so easy.

The following is a list of the parts included in your RumbaFlex 2000 package:

PARTS LIST

Base Grid Chassis	2" Wood Screws (57)	Variable-Speed Goose Thongs (4)	Saf-T-Flip "Weezle" Joist
Welded Support Frame	1" Wood Screws (1)	Horizontal Clearing Blades	4lbs. Lightly-Salted Mackerel
T-Grid Access Bars (12)	4mm Locking Nuts (125)	Padded Flogging Scoops (14)	Melt-N-Smelt Pine-Scented Epoxy
Deluxe J-Clips (16)	6mm Macadamia Nuts (1)	Steam Pressure Valves (6)	Hex-Shank Implant Extensions
Gouda Cheese Wedge	Chilled Swivel "Lips" (5)	"Fenzle-koont" Leather TensionBelts	Stainless Steel Spunk Duct (3)
Soft "Comfor-T-Nozzles" (3)	Suction Arm Sockets (23)	Load-Bearing Tongue Wafers	Galvanized Flossing Fibers
Central Drive Motor	"Sure-Grip" Thigh Clamps	Two-Tone Latex Dribble Sheets (8)	Rayon Security Spats
"Roto-Reemer" Drive Shafts (24)	Velcro Chafing Pad	8' Grapple Bodice	Load-Bearing Boot Hosers
Styrene Winch Nuggets (7)	"Bald-Top" 6000V Rectal Fuse	Lubricated Busby Hook	Extruded-Flannel Pebble Flutes
Chamois Relief Tissues	Tamper-Resistant Backwash Feeder	Hydraulic Juggle Truss (2)	"Bartle Master" Octo-Beebler (7)
Centrifugal "Whir" Straps (80)	Collapsible Odor Probes (17)	Textured "Dura-Lung" (2)	Velvet Lug Bushels (84)
Suction Lugs (14)	Adhesive Racing Stripe	16" Trundle Swabs	Spec-Lunge Frazzle Snips (134)
Foam Dispenser w/Fendle Lugs	486 Computer Timing Monitor	14' Steel Treads (3)	All-Weather Radial Tires (16)

When assembling your RumbaFlex 2000, it is best to dress comfortably and avoid wearing fragrances. Also, to avoid tripping or stumbling during assembly, never wear shoes with tassels, festoons or jutting, beak-like appendages. By following these few simple steps, you will be able to quickly and easily assemble your RumbaFlex 2000, and start enjoying it right away. Here at Rumba Products, Inc., we like to say, "Rumba is so easy, and moist too!" **ENJOY!**

1) On a clean, dry surface, arrange all RumbaFlex 2000 parts in a sweeping floral pattern, making sure to weed out any with defective gaskets or pungent odors.

2) Attach all core grids, chassis, frames, bars, joists, blades and scoops using wood screws and epoxy. Soak all connections and joints in a zesty tomato-based sauce.

3) Join all valves, fuses, clamps, sockets and shafts with your choice of nuts and straps.

4) Insert all probes. (Keep that chamois cloth coming!)

5) Firmly attach housing and casing by wrapping flexi-fins around U-shaped nugget logs and crimping with your custom needle-nose "nipping grips." This is especially important for those who will be using the RumbaFlex 2000 in humid climates, during street festivals or near fishing rodeos.

6) Finally, add decorative accessories and sporty detailing. Make your RumbaFlex 2000 a reflection of your personality—racy, reserved, bright, cheerful, morose, wacky, laconic, bloated, unctuous — whatever you like! Remember...now you're in control!

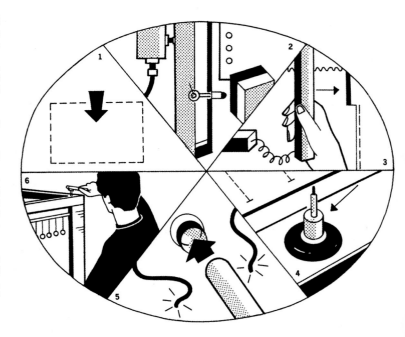

OPERATION

"Just Like Salsa...Only Square!"

Your new RumbaFlex 2000 is so easy to operate, you'll think you've just flossed. But don't worry, it's the Rumba way!

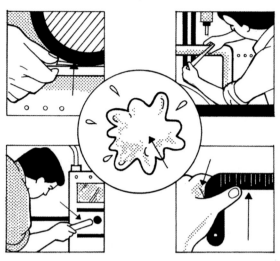

1) Start your RumbaFlex 2000 by turning the ignition key and pedaling the choke roller. On cold or cloudy mornings you may experience some hesitation or sputtering in the RumbaFlex 2000 ignition mechanism. Don't worry! Unless there's a prurient discharge, a simple shim insertion beneath the sprocket reel will restore instant starting.

2) Before engaging the RumbaFlex 2000's forward rotary units or siphon puffs (They look harmless, but have you ever had a head hickey?), make sure you have secured the colorful bunting and tightened all tarpaulin lines. (Remember, Rumba's not just a name anymore! Rumba! Rumba!)

3) Choose your operation and target coordinates. It's important to choose the operation first, before selecting target coordinates. You'll avoid messy and costly mistakes, cleanup will be easier and you'll escape the itch and swelling.

4) During operation, keep a firm grip on all backhoe levers, without neglecting the deli meats. With the RumbaFlex 2000, you no longer have to choose between a fresh hoagie and a tingling scalp. Remember, you've chosen the best. You've chosen Rumba!

5) Once you've finished the job, it's easy to secure and store your RumbaFlex 2000 for future "Rumba Tasks"! Simply fold the juice flumes back over the cabin shelves (Don't worry! The snaps are there!), zip up the forward dickey crispers, and spread a little "Hasty-Jam" paste across the injection nodes.

And that's it! Your RumbaFlex 2000 is safely stored and protected, ready to once again serve all your Rumba needs.

MAINTENANCE

"Never Too Tight! Never Too Thick!"

The RumbaFlex 2000 practically takes care of itself. And with its new "Auto-Whisk" mechanism, you'll never have to spackle again. Just make sure to follow these simple steps on a regular basis, and your new RumbaFlex will give you years and years of trouble-free operation.

1) Buff all towels at least every three weeks. You'll feel better. Your RumbaFlex 2000 will cover more ground. 2) Keep the pistons and shafts free of lint, butter and aloe build-up. This can cause sticking and chin irritation, resulting in stunted horizontal thrashing. 3) Remember to flush the tubes and valves with our special "Rumba-Wash" lubricating pepper gel. This ensures firm suction and cutting motion as smooth as toast. 4) When storing your RumbaFlex 2000, be sure to place all protective cushion-boots on the external probes and blades. Also, the snack basket and steam press should be covered to prevent rust, deterioration and grass stains. 5) Remove all beef slabs and used ointment applicators from the overhead compartment. Your RumbaFlex 2000 will smell better, and rats and opossum will stay away.

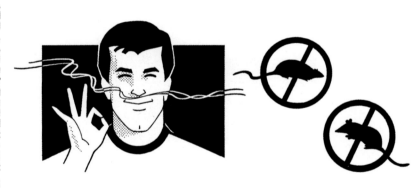

The most important thing to remember about maintaining your new RumbaFlex is to relax. We've designed durability and flexibility right in. Plus, your Rumba service representative is as close as your telephone. Just call us up and say, "It's a Rumba day! And moist too!"

TROUBLESHOOTING *"Pop If It's Blue!"*

You may experience some slight initial malfunctions or operational interruptions in your new RumbaFlex 2000. Don't worry! This is normal. Any mechanism as sensitive and complex as the RumbaFlex 2000 will experience "growing pains" as its electronics and components adjust to start-up performance and your particular user environment.

To make this breaking-in period less troublesome, here are a few troubleshooting pointers:

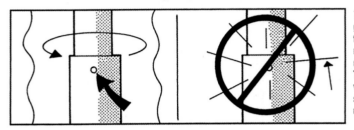

1) A low wheezing or grinding sound in the piston buffers means there is not enough silicone putty reaching the auger bits. This is easily remedied by wedging a set of wooden soup spoons between your upper thighs during use.

2) If you experience excessive horizontal vibration when switching the vinyl chipper into mulch mode, simply shift the timing sprockets two notches toward the "stick-n-sturdy" floor struts, daub a liberal amount of McComb's "SuperSalve" grooming paste on the AZ34 gel receptacle, and continue normal operation. If vibration persists, the problem could rest in the jacketed solvent seal, in which case you're screwed.

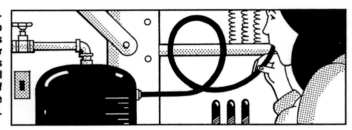

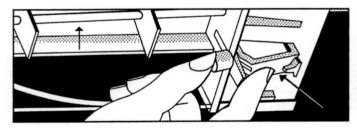

3) When using your new RumbaFlex 2000 to bore through masonry or prepare tuna side dishes, you may notice a slight burning sensation in the pelvic region. If you find this objectionable, tighten the bypass enclosure that leads from your fabric dip tanks to the bobber bins. This should quickly ease the pressure and flush out all harsh poultry residues. Say cheese!

WARNING!

Your new RumbaFlex 2000 is equipped with numerous multi-level, redundant safety systems to prevent personal injuries and foul odors. However, use of the RumbaFlex 2000 as a recreational vehicle, hygiene supplement or decorative centerpiece is extremely dangerous and strongly discouraged. Rumba, Inc. assumes no responsibility for any results or consequences stemming from such use.

Rumbaflex 2000
"Now You're In Control"

A Letter From Slash

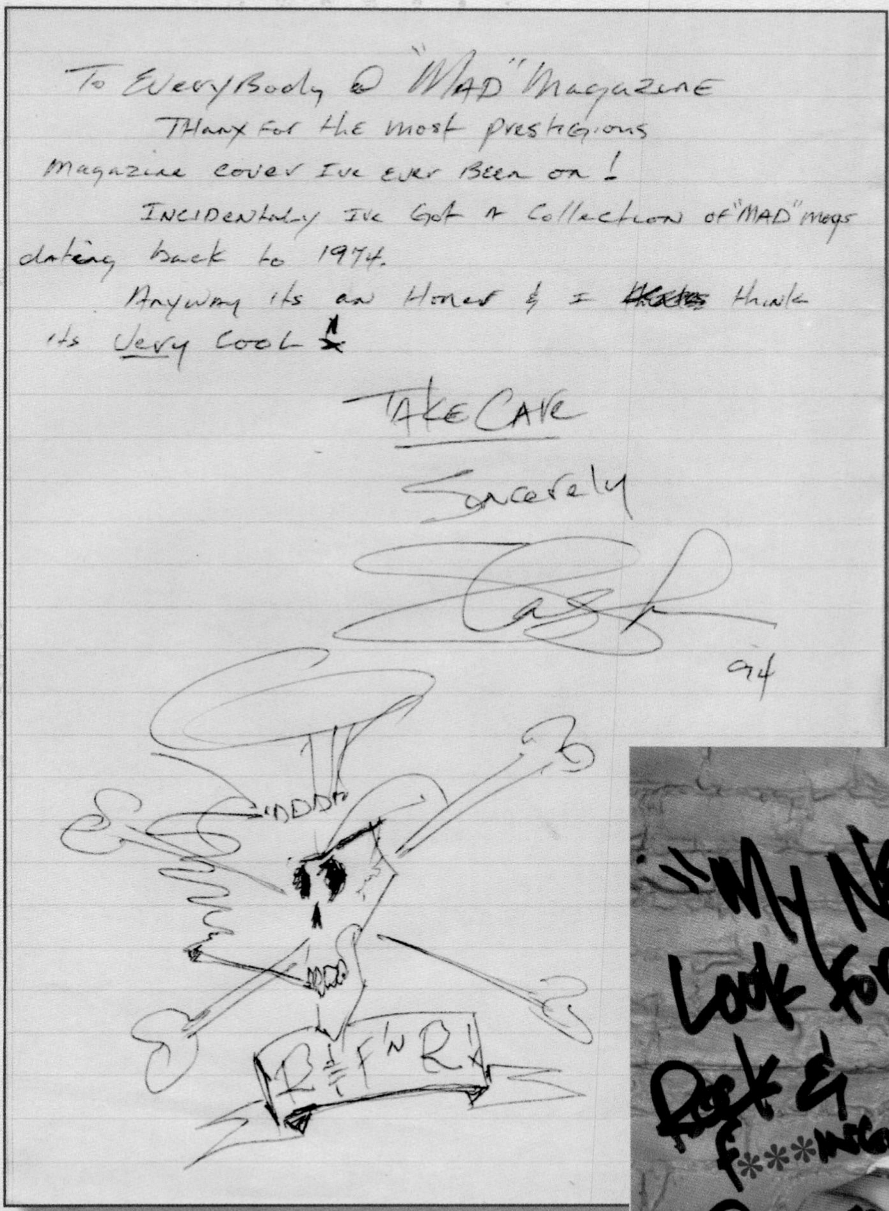
To EveryBody @ "MAD" Magazine
Thanx for the most prestigious magazine cover I've ever Been on!
Incidentally I've Got a Collection of "MAD" mags dating back to 1974.
Anyway its an Honer & I think its Very Cool!
Take Care
Sincerely
Slash
94
R&F'N'R!

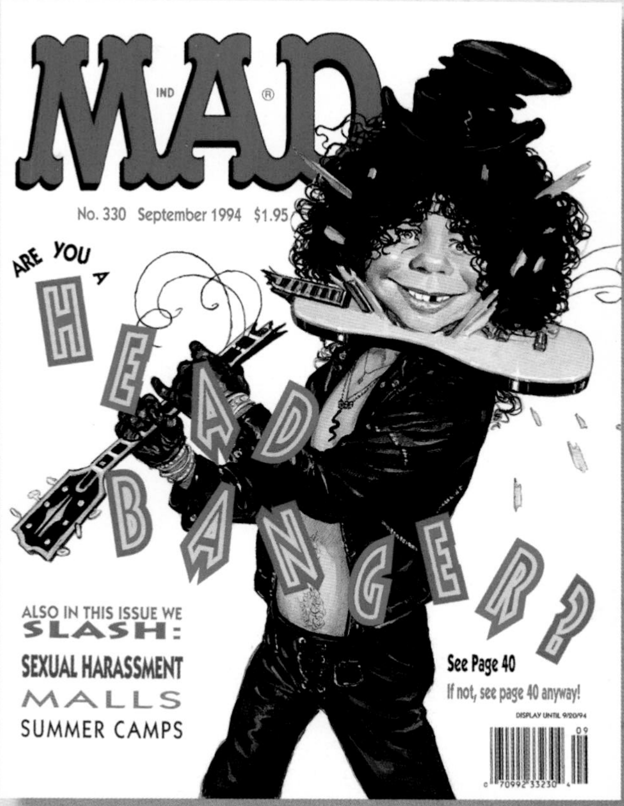
MAD
IND
No. 330 September 1994 $1.95
ARE YOU A HEADBANGER?
ALSO IN THIS ISSUE WE SLASH:
SEXUAL HARASSMENT
MALLS
SUMMER CAMPS
See Page 40
If not, see page 40 anyway!
DISPLAY UNTIL 9/20/94

ARTIST: RICHARD WILLIAMS

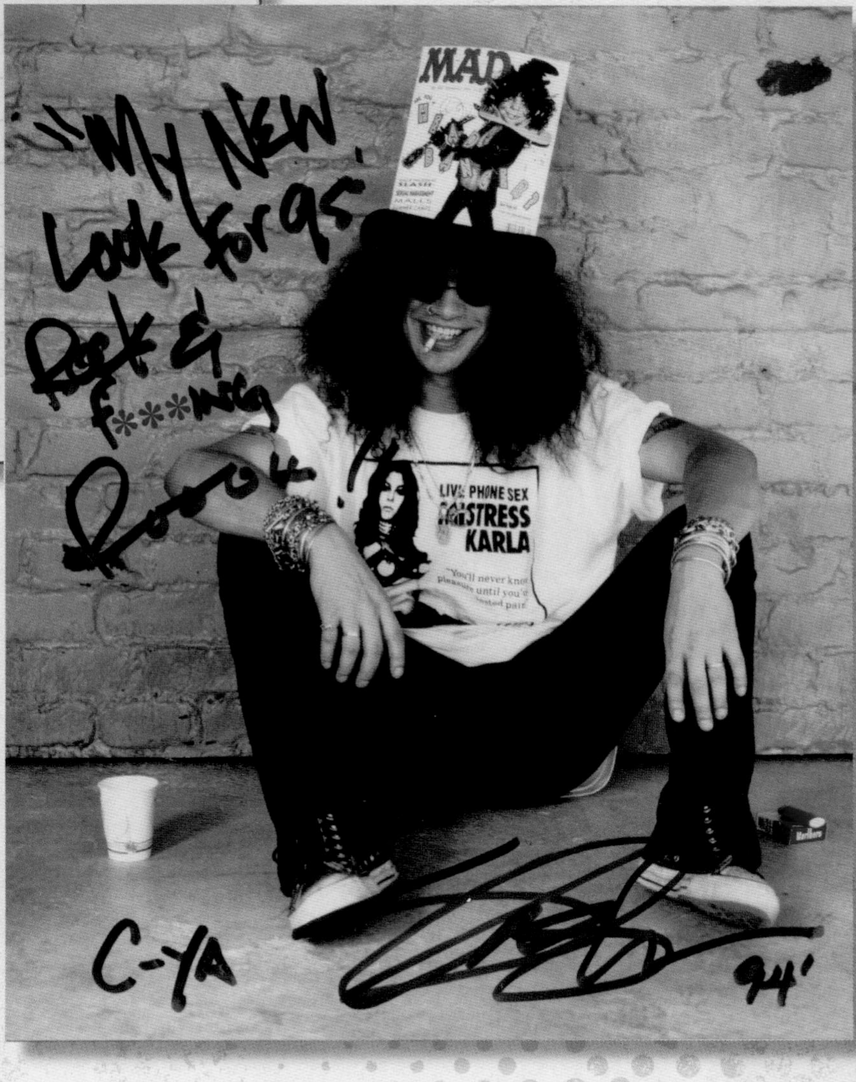
"My New Look for 95'
Rock & F***ing Roll!
LIVE PHONE SEX
MISTRESS
KARLA
C-YA
94'

MAD's
Great Moments In Advertising

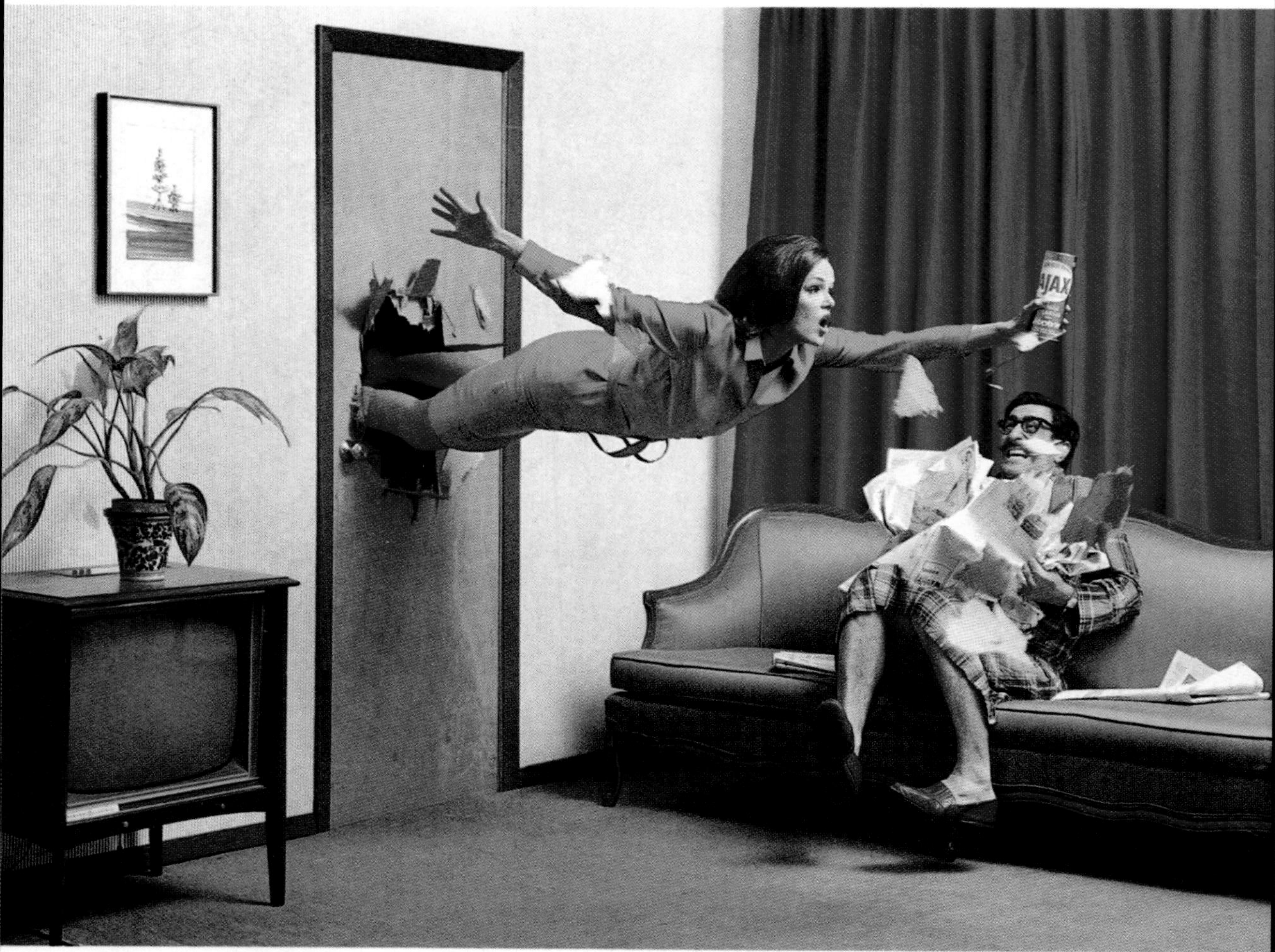
AJAX

Photography by IRVING *"Breakthrough"* SCHILD

THE DAY THAT "AJAX" GOT THE HOUSEWIFE OUT OF THE KITCHEN A LITTLE TOO FAST!

MAD #98/OCTOBER 1965

by Irving Schild
PHOTOGRAPHER

Picking a single favorite past picture I created for MAD is like picking a favorite child from a dozen precocious children. Every assignment was a creative joy to execute, rich in challenging complex logistics necessary to accomplish that perfect shot. There were the typical budget restrictions, tight time deadlines and none of the techno-graphic solutions that exist today. Every assignment meant translating MAD's zany humor — often in the form of a pencil sketch, created by Art Director John Putnam — into a real-life recreation involving lots of big sets, non-stop playful creativity, and some hilarious resulting moments.

John and Chief Editor Al Feldstein were both on board at that time. Al was extremely gifted and talented. He knew exactly what he wanted, was a perfectionist to boot, a visionary who saw MAD Magazine as bigger than LIFE, while demanding

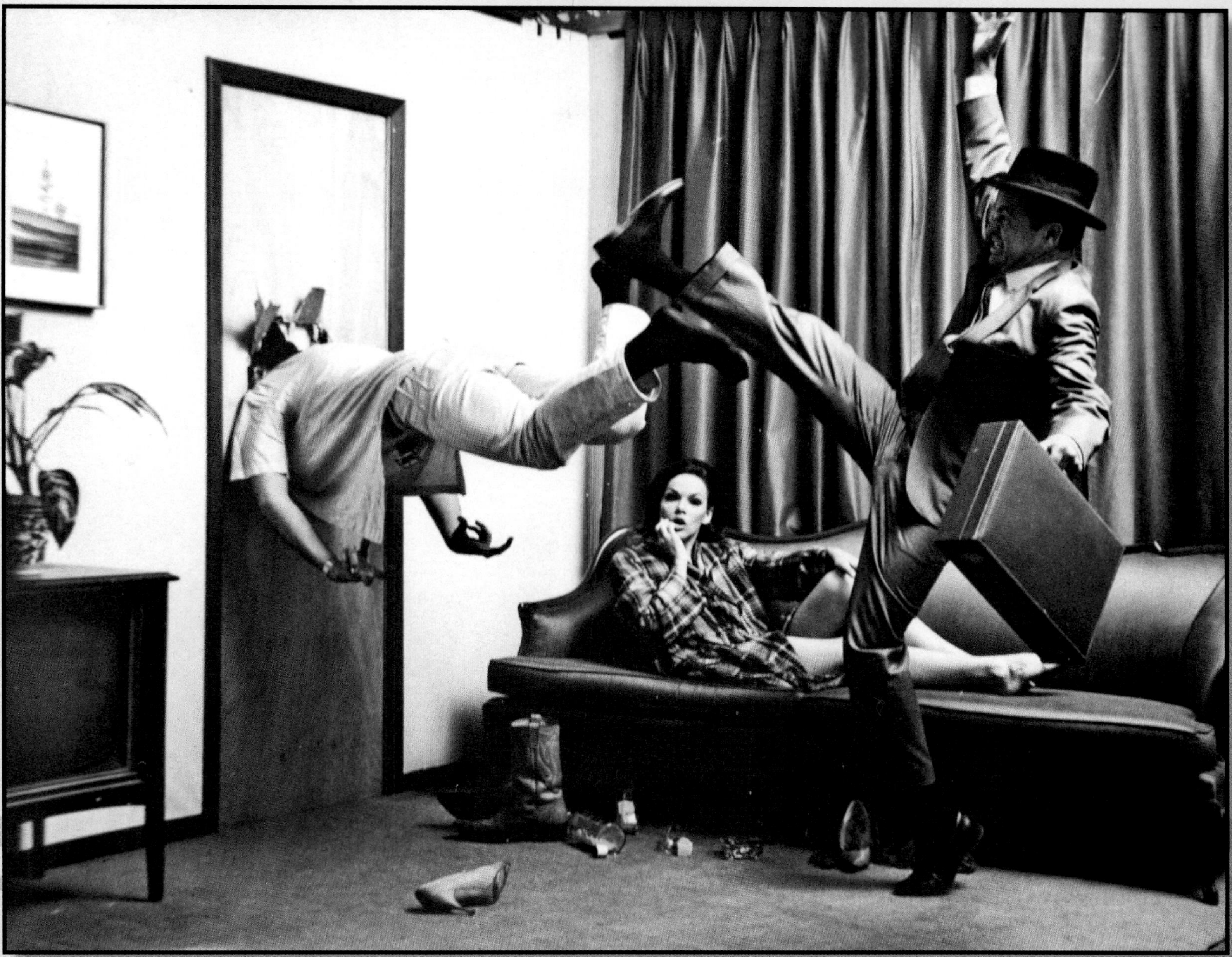

the very best; in other words, not an easy guy to work for. He was a challenge, and without programs like Photoshop, which did not yet exist, the construction of each assignment was time-consuming, belabored and required out-of-the-box thinking. I always came through though, had fun in the process and the MAD guys were happy with the results.

For their current request I picked from a special series by MAD on Great Moments In Advertising. I selected this particular image because Sergio Aragonés is in the photo; he is a very special person, a good friend, extremely talented and I will always be grateful to him for introducing me to Al Feldstein. This particular photographic assignment was given to me by Feldstein, where I was to mimic an Ajax TV commercial running at that time. It depicted a housewife flying from room to room in her home pulled by the box she was holding in her hand as her home was made instantly clean by the product.

Feldstein said: "We are going to do an Ajax ad. I want you to create a living room setting with a closed door and a woman flying through the door holding a box. We will title this ad "The Day That Ajax Got the Housewife Out of the Kitchen a Little Too Fast!" My immediate reaction was, "You must be kidding," which was a fairly common reaction to Feldstein's crazy jobs for me, to which I commonly answered: "No problem!" Then, he shared with me an equally absurd budget and timeline of three days for the shoot. My reaction again was: "You must be kidding… no problem." I returned to my studio located a block away from MAD's Manhattan headquarters and immediately began putting the components together. A furnishings rental delivered a TV, sofa, and a rug. I then headed to a local hardware store where I purchased a door, moldings and a 2x6 ft. board to brace the model. Two days later the set was ready.

Feldstein, Putnam, Sergio and Lesley — the theoretically flying Ajax model — arrived the next morning at my studio and we began the shoot. Lesley took up her position, with her right leg hiding the board and arm outstretched holding the Ajax box, just like the TV commercial had depicted. Sergio sat on the couch wearing a startled and shocked expression. For added motion illusion — while shooting — Putnam and Lenny, my assistant, threw wood chips into the set during the shots. It was a fun shoot and at the end, just for laughs, we created a reversed black and white photo where Feldstein is kicking Sergio through the door and Lesley is sitting on the couch looking startled.

Working for MAD is working in an environment of dedicated, brilliant and crazy creative artists and writers.

N RBQ — the New Rhythm and Blues Quartet — is about the grooviest band that ever was. They would go from Sun Ra, to Eddie Cochran to Sinatra without a flinch. You could listen to NRBQ and not know that people had broken music down into categories other than good and bad.

I would see NRBQ at the Bottom Line in NYC, and Keith Richards would be in the audience. Paul McCartney had them do a private show for his band. Elvis Costello carried on about them being the best live band ever.

They *were* the best live band. I saw them many times and finally became friends with them, but… I didn't feel that I really fit in. I wasn't part of their culture. They had a song called "Wacky Tobaccy" about marijuana and I felt left out. I never smoked. I cared about only the first and last parts of sex and drugs and rock and roll. I related to the music, but not really to the band. NRBQ never published their lyrics, and some of the words were garbled, so there were places, when I listened, that I had no idea what they were saying. I had listened to their song "Wacky Tobaccy" a zillion times before it hit me.

Penn Gillette

It's crackers to slip a rozzer the dropsy in snide

All of a sudden, this one time, like Kurtz's diamond bullet, I understood what he was singing in that one line of the song: "It's crackers to slip a rozzer, oh, the dropsy in snide, boys!" This wasn't dope talk. This wasn't "Waiting for my Man," or "Lucy in the Sky with Diamonds," or "Puff, the Magic Dragon." (That's marijuana, right?) This was a message coded for a Rosetta Stone that I had in my head. This was for me! I'm not a pothead, but I sure am a MAD Magazine fan. Now, I'm not saying those two are mutually exclusive; there may even be some correlation, but my life proves it's not a perfect correlation. All of a sudden NRBQ really was my band. They might be singing about dope, but they were also singing about a dope, Alfred E. Neuman, my dope from MAD Magazine.

"It's crackers to slip a rozzer, oh, the dropsy in snide, boys!" is a straightforward way of saying that it's ill-advised to bribe a peace officer with counterfeit money. The phrase is originally from Margery Allingham's mid-'30s detective story "The Fashion in Shrouds," but it was obscure Aussie slang so we all know that NRBQ got it from MAD Magazine. MAD founder Bill Gaines loved the phrase, so in the 1950s, MAD snuck it in everywhere, scattered through every issue for years. Almost no one knew what it meant, but the phrase became teenage slang for something to say when you didn't know what to say. Decades later it gave me something to say to NRBQ, backstage, when they were done talking guitar strings and amps with the Stones, because I knew they could talk MAD Magazine with me.

I'm from a dead factory town in Western Massachusetts and the first person I knew in showbiz was me. My mom and dad liked a joke, but I didn't know anyone in comedy. I didn't know anyone who thought about serious things by laughing. My subscription to MAD Magazine let me know I wasn't alone. Bob Dylan said of Woody Guthrie, "You could listen to his songs and learn how to live." I could read MAD and learn how to think.

I got older and didn't read MAD as much. My subscription ran out (I need to find someone famous reading it, take a picture, and a get a year free). I didn't think much about MAD Magazine when I was all fancy-pants and Broadway, and Letterman, and Stern and *Rolling Stone* magazine. Then someone showed

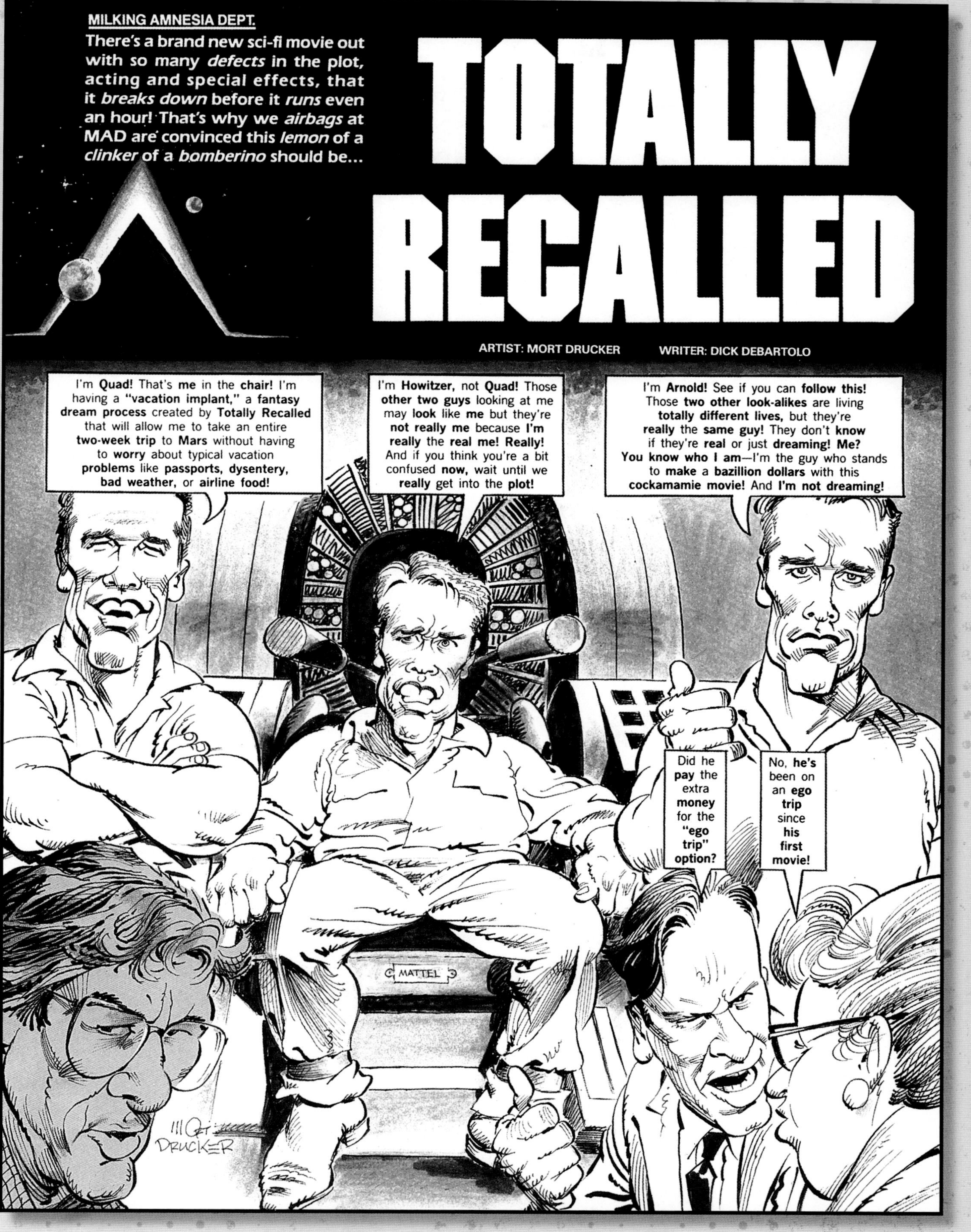
MILKING AMNESIA DEPT.
There's a brand new sci-fi movie out with so many *defects* in the plot, acting and special effects, that it *breaks down* before it *runs* even an hour! That's why we *airbags* at MAD are convinced this *lemon* of a *clinker* of a *bomberino* should be...
TOTALLY RECALLED
ARTIST: MORT DRUCKER WRITER: DICK DEBARTOLO
I'm **Quad!** That's **me** in the **chair!** I'm having a **"vacation implant,"** a **fantasy dream process** created by **Totally Recalled** that will allow me to take an entire **two-week trip** to **Mars** without having to **worry** about typical vacation **problems** like **passports, dysentery, bad weather,** or **airline food!**
I'm **Howitzer,** not **Quad!** Those **other two guys** looking at me may **look** like **me** but they're **not really me** because **I'm really the real me! Really!** And if you think you're a bit confused **now,** wait until we **really** get into the **plot!**
I'm **Arnold!** See if you can **follow this!** Those **two other look-alikes** are living **totally different lives,** but they're **really** the **same guy!** They don't **know** if they're **real** or just **dreaming! Me? You know who I am**—I'm the guy who stands to **make** a **bazillion dollars** with this **cockamamie movie!** And **I'm not dreaming!**
Did he **pay** the extra **money** for the **"ego trip"** option?
No, **he's** been on an **ego trip** since **his first movie!**
MATTEL
MORT DRUCKER

MAD #299/DECEMBER 1990

me the December 1990 MAD parody of *Total Recall*. There, on the third page, were Penn & Teller. Forgive the Chevy Chase quality of talking about myself in the third person, but... Penn & Teller in MAD was amazing. It was a level of success and acceptance that I hadn't aspired to because I had never thought it was possible.

There was my face and name in MAD Magazine. My face and my business partner's face!

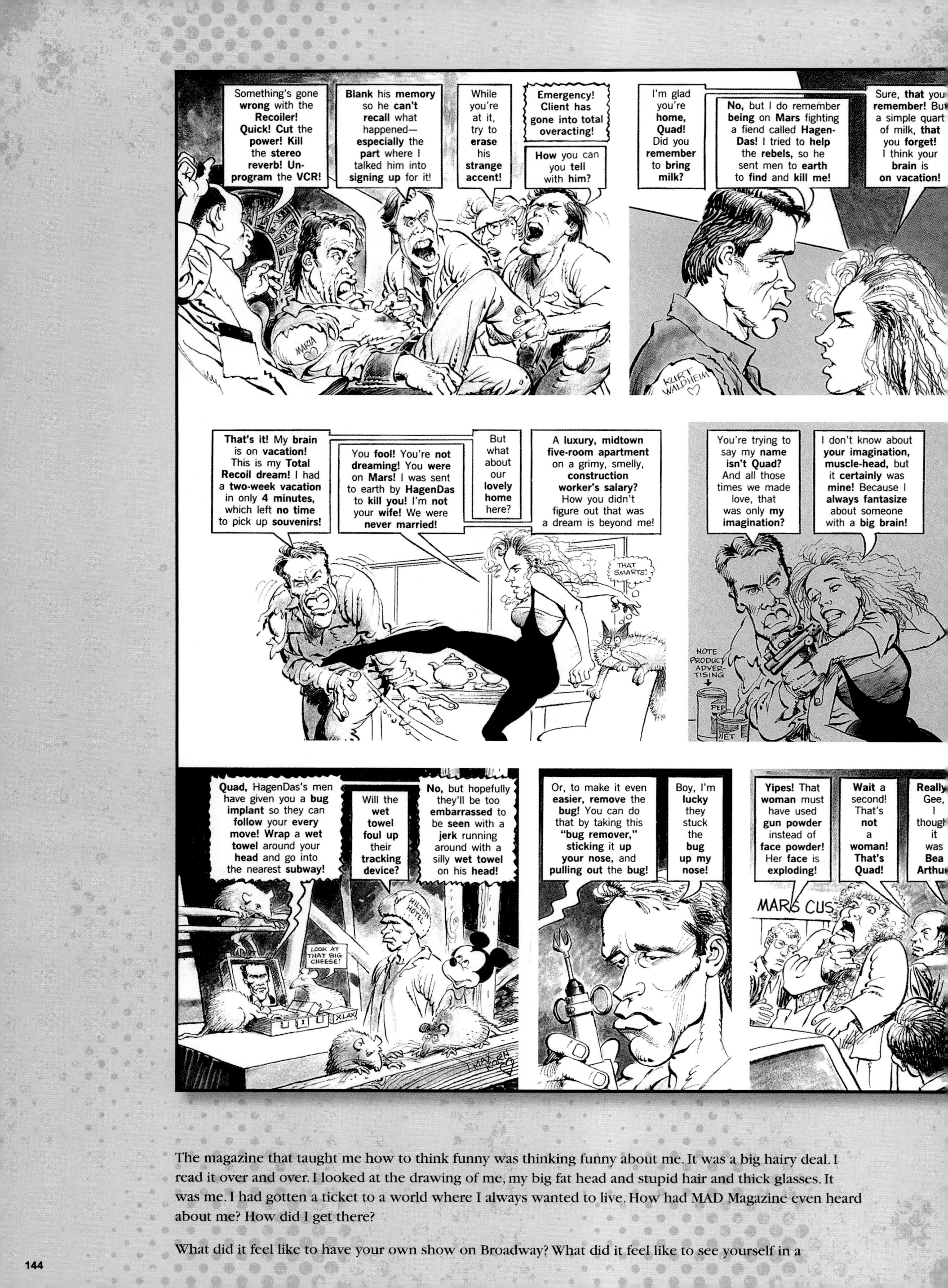
Something's gone wrong with the Recoiler! Quick! Cut the power! Kill the stereo reverb! Un-program the VCR!
Blank his memory so he can't recall what happened—especially the part where I talked him into signing up for it!
While you're at it, try to erase his strange accent!
Emergency! Client has gone into total overacting!
How you can you tell with him?
MARIA
I'm glad you're home, Quad! Did you remember to bring milk?
No, but I do remember being on Mars fighting a fiend called Hagen-Das! I tried to help the rebels, so he sent men to earth to find and kill me!
Sure, that you remember! Bu a simple quart of milk, that you forget! I think your brain is on vacation!
KURT WALDHEIM
That's it! My brain is on vacation! This is my Total Recoil dream! I had a two-week vacation in only 4 minutes, which left no time to pick up souvenirs!
You fool! You're not dreaming! You were on Mars! I was sent to earth by HagenDas to kill you! I'm not your wife! We were never married!
But what about our lovely home here?
A luxury, midtown five-room apartment on a grimy, smelly, construction worker's salary? How you didn't figure out that was a dream is beyond me!
THAT SMARTS!
You're trying to say my name isn't Quad? And all those times we made love, that was only my imagination?
I don't know about your imagination, muscle-head, but it certainly was mine! Because I always fantasize about someone with a big brain!
NOTE PRODUCT ADVER-TISING
Quad, HagenDas's men have given you a bug implant so they can follow your every move! Wrap a wet towel around your head and go into the nearest subway!
Will the wet towel foul up their tracking device?
No, but hopefully they'll be too embarrassed to be seen with a jerk running around with a silly wet towel on his head!
HILTON HOTEL
LOOK AT THAT BIG CHEESE!
XLAX
Or, to make it even easier, remove the bug! You can do that by taking this "bug remover," sticking it up your nose, and pulling out the bug!
Boy, I'm lucky they stuck the bug up my nose!
Yipes! That woman must have used gun powder instead of face powder! Her face is exploding!
Wait a second! That's not a woman! That's Quad!
Really Gee, I thoug it was Bea Arthu
MARS CUS

The magazine that taught me how to think funny was thinking funny about me. It was a big hairy deal. I read it over and over. I looked at the drawing of me, my big fat head and stupid hair and thick glasses. It was me. I had gotten a ticket to a world where I always wanted to live. How had MAD Magazine even heard about me? How did I get there?

What did it feel like to have your own show on Broadway? What did it feel like to see yourself in a

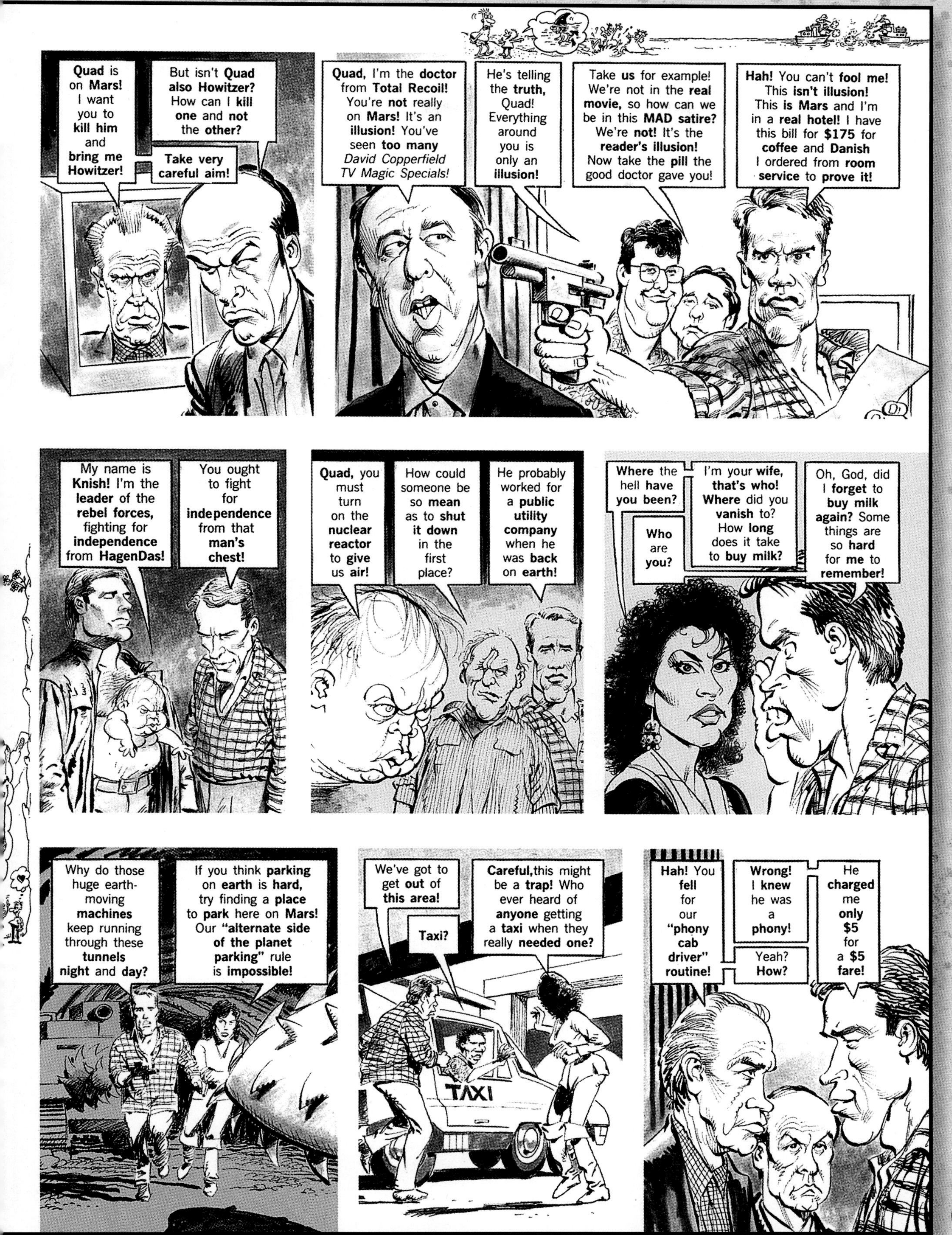

Quad is on Mars! I want you to kill him and bring me Howitzer!
But isn't Quad also Howitzer? How can I kill one and not the other?
Take very careful aim!
Quad, I'm the doctor from Total Recoil! You're not really on Mars! It's an illusion! You've seen too many David Copperfield TV Magic Specials!
He's telling the truth, Quad! Everything around you is only an illusion!
Take us for example! We're not in the real movie, so how can we be in this MAD satire? We're not! It's the reader's illusion! Now take the pill the good doctor gave you!
Hah! You can't fool me! This isn't illusion! This is Mars and I'm in a real hotel! I have this bill for $175 for coffee and Danish I ordered from room service to prove it!
My name is Knish! I'm the leader of the rebel forces, fighting for independence from HagenDas!
You ought to fight for independence from that man's chest!
Quad, you must turn on the nuclear reactor to give us air!
How could someone be so mean as to shut it down in the first place?
He probably worked for a public utility company when he was back on earth!
Where the hell have you been?
Who are you?
I'm your wife, that's who! Where did you vanish to? How long does it take to buy milk?
Oh, God, did I forget to buy milk again? Some things are so hard for me to remember!
Why do those huge earth-moving machines keep running through these tunnels night and day?
If you think parking on earth is hard, try finding a place to park here on Mars! Our "alternate side of the planet parking" rule is impossible!
We've got to get out of this area!
Taxi?
Careful, this might be a trap! Who ever heard of anyone getting a taxi when they really needed one?
TAXI
Hah! You fell for our "phony cab driver" routine!
Wrong! I knew he was a phony!
Yeah? How?
He charged me only $5 for a $5 fare!

movie? What did it feel like to have a theater named after you, and your picture on the side of a hotel in Vegas?

All of those things have happened to me, but all those things I had some control over. All those things I worked for. But being in a MAD parody, I didn't work for. I didn't even really get lucky — it just happened. All of a sudden I was sucked into a world that was full of people like me, and now I was part of it. Wow.

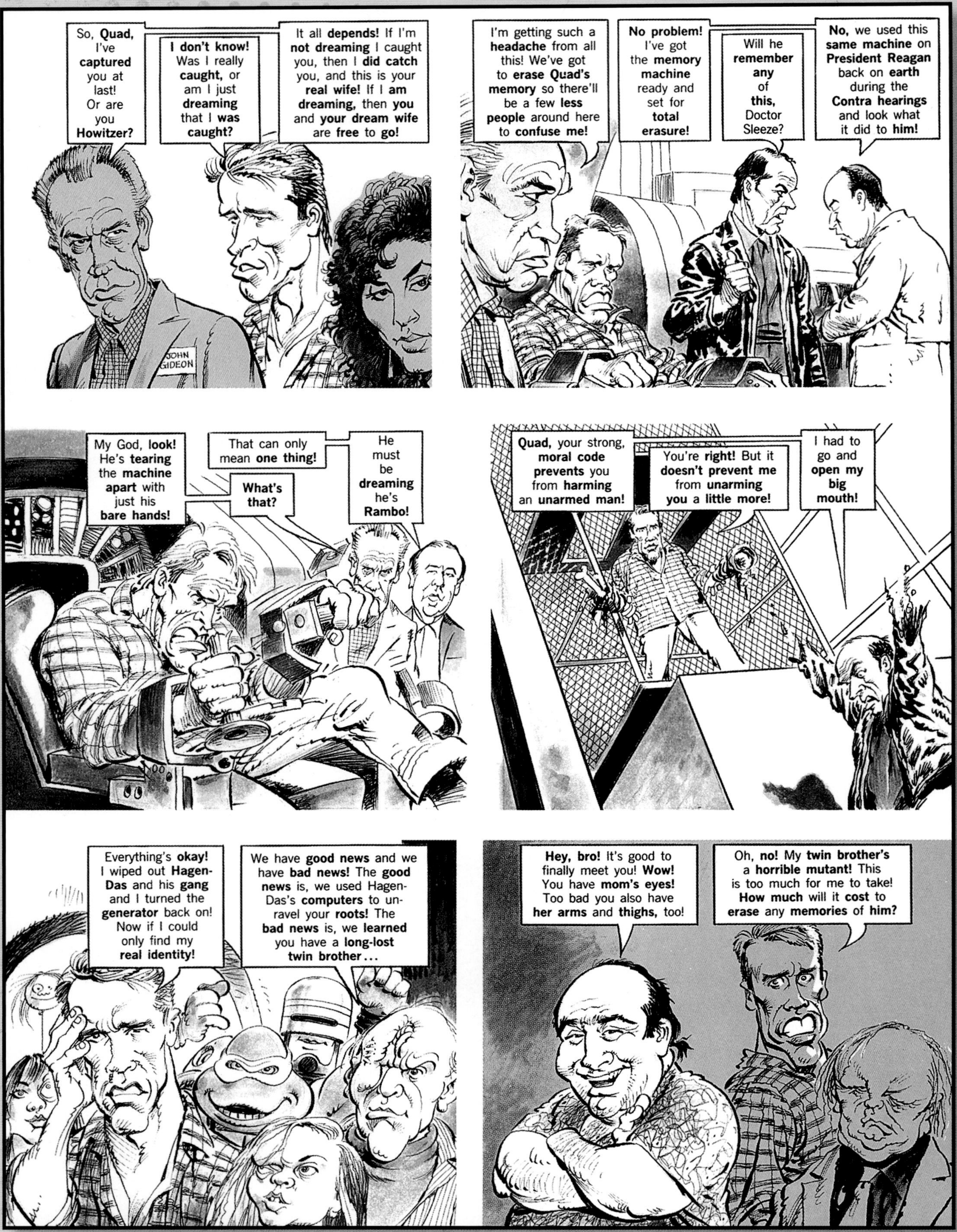
So, **Quad,** I've **captured** you at last! Or are you **Howitzer?**
I don't know! Was I really **caught,** or am I just **dreaming** that I **was caught?**
It all **depends!** If I'm **not dreaming** I caught you, then I **did catch** you, and this is your **real wife!** If I **am dreaming,** then **you** and **your dream wife** are **free** to **go!**
JOHN GIDEON
I'm getting such a **headache** from all this! We've got to **erase Quad's memory** so there'll be a few **less people** around here to **confuse me!**
No problem! I've got the **memory machine** ready and set for **total erasure!**
Will he **remember any** of **this,** Doctor Sleeze?
No, we used this **same machine** on **President Reagan** back on **earth** during the **Contra hearings** and look what it did to **him!**
My God, **look!** He's **tearing** the **machine apart** with just his **bare hands!**
That can only mean **one thing!**
What's that?
He **must** be **dreaming** he's **Rambo!**
Quad, your strong, **moral code prevents** you from **harming** an **unarmed man!**
You're **right!** But it **doesn't prevent me** from **unarming you a little more!**
I had to go and **open my big mouth!**
Everything's **okay!** I wiped out **Hagen-Das** and his **gang** and I turned the **generator** back on! Now if I could only find my **real identity!**
We have **good news** and we have **bad news!** The **good news** is, we used Hagen-Das's **computers** to unravel your **roots!** The **bad news** is, we **learned** you have a **long-lost twin brother...**
Hey, bro! It's good to finally meet you! **Wow!** You have **mom's eyes!** Too bad you also have **her arms** and **thighs,** too!
Oh, **no!** My **twin brother's** a **horrible mutant!** This is too much for me to take! **How much** will it **cost** to **erase** any **memories of him?**

Years later, Bill Gaines came to our Broadway show and I trembled as I shook his hand. He asked me out for lunch and then chose to die rather than take a chance of being stuck with the check. So I met him only that one night at our show and it was a thrill, but meeting Bill himself was not as big of a thrill as seeing my face and name in that magazine.

I was finally home. And there's only one way to sum that up: It's crackers to slip a rozzer the dropsy in snide!

SISS . . . BOOM . . . BLAH . . . DEPT.

When a kid enters school, some of the first things he learns are the School Songs. MAD has made a study of these songs, and we've discovered that they fall into two main categories:

The first type of School Song is the "Rock-'em—Sock-'em Fight Song," calculated to glorify the Football Team and fill the student body with that old "School Spirit." Here is an example of a typical Rock-'em—Sock-'em Fight Song:

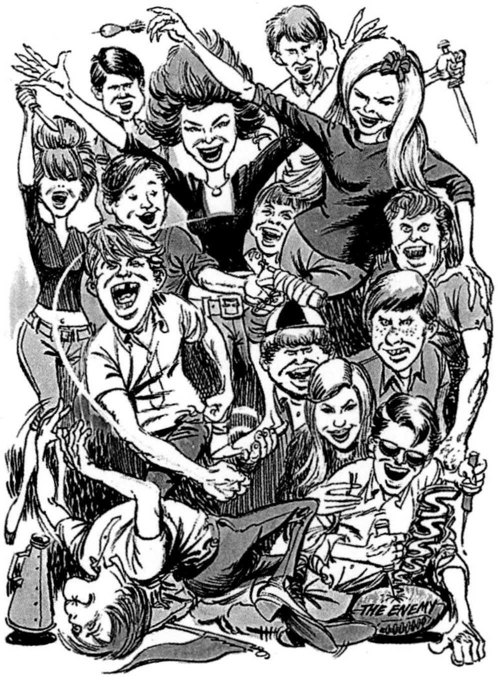
THE ENEMY

The Black And The Blue

(to the tune of **"The Notre Dame Fight Song"**)

Cheer, cheer the Black and the Blue!
You're gonna win 'cause we are for you!
Push their faces in the mud!
Punch out their teeth and draw their blood!
Stomp on their stomachs! Break all their bones!
We wanna hear their screams and their moans!
If you follow our advice,
You'll win a clean vic-tor-y!

The second type of Song is written in praise of the School itself. It's sung mainly at Graduation Exercises, and it's supposed to evoke deep emotional feelings and bring a lump to everyone's throat. Here's an example of this type song:

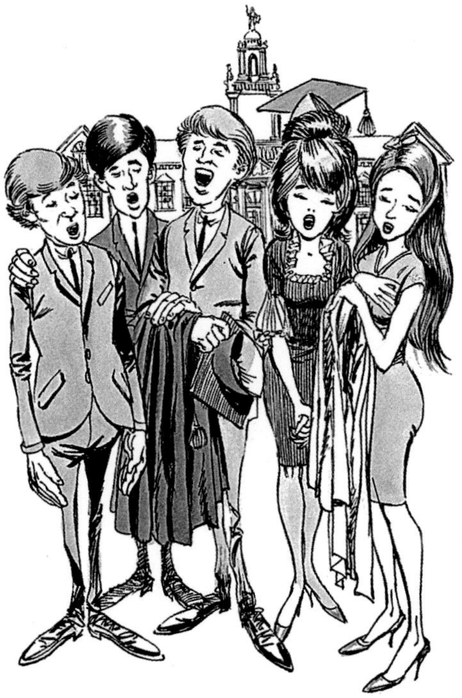

Hail To Thee, Oh Frisbee High!

(to the tune of **"High Above Cayuga's Waters"**)

Hail to thee, oh Frisbee High School—
Faithful, good and true!
If you spoke, you'd say you love us
Like we all love you!
Frisbee High School, when we've left you,
And the days seem long—
We will think back how they made us
Sing this stupid song!

Now these songs are okay for special occasions, but they don't have much value in the long, humdrum hours of ordinary school life. Kids spend most of that time sitting in classrooms, going to lunch, and trying to pass surprise quizzes. To this dull existence, we dedicate:

MAD SCHOOL SONGS FOR EVERYDAY ACTIVITIES

ARTIST: GEORGE WOODBRIDGE WRITER: FRANK JACOBS

MAD #109/MARCH 1967

by Barry Liebmann
WRITER

When I was in junior high school I memorized "The Lunchroom March" from "MAD School Songs For Everyday Activities" with greater skill and speed than any of my school assignments. (Of course, it had a lot more significance to me.) Eventually a friend and I created our own variation of this parody… with much raunchier lyrics. Lennon and McCartney we were not! I can't say that this one no-hit blunder was what eventually inspired me to write for MAD. But it was a constructive alternative to the anti-social, juvenile delinquent-types of activities other kids were into… Though if you heard it, you might not agree!

The Early Morning Rouser
(to the tune of "I've Been Working On The Railroad")

I am getting up at seven,
So I won't be late!
I am getting up at seven,
So I'll get to school by eight!
Can't you hear the 'larm clock ringing:
"Rise up and hurry on your way!"
Can't you hear my mother shouting:
"You fool! It's Saturday!"

The Failure's Hymn
(To the tune of "From The Halls Of Montezuma")

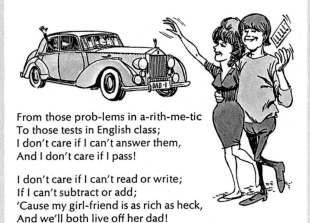

From those prob-lems in a-rith-me-tic
To those tests in English class;
I don't care if I can't answer them,
And I don't care if I pass!

I don't care if I can't read or write;
If I can't subtract or add;
'Cause my girl-friend is as rich as heck,
And we'll both live off her dad!

The Emergency Bathroom Chant
(to the tune of "Over There")

Catch her eye!
Catch her eye!
  Wave and shout!
  Yell right out!
Catch her eye!

For your need is growing,
And you are knowing
If you don't leave the room,
  you'll die!

You must try!
Don't be shy!
  Make her look!
  Throw a book!
Scream and cry!

O O O O P S !

It's too late now!
You couldn't wait now!
Boy, you're really sunk
'Cause you didn't catch her eye!

The Lunchroom March
(to the tune of "The Air Force Song")

Off we go—
Into the lunch-room yonder,
Pushing girls
Out of the way!

Forward, boys!
Start moving down the counter!
Grab your grub!
Fill up your tray!
(Clankity-Clank)

Try the beans—
They were prepared last Friday!
And the meat's
Tough as a mule!
The soup is cold!
The bread's got mold!
    Yecch!
Anything beats our lunchroom at school!

The March Of The Hell-Raisers

(to the tune of **"Stout Hearted Men"**)

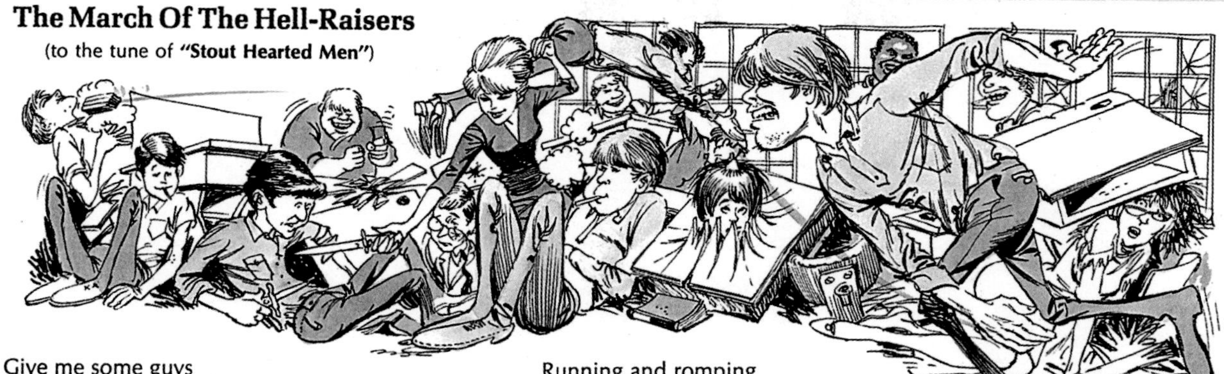

Give me some guys
Who are hell-raising guys
Who can shake up and break up a class!
Guys who don't care,
Who will stand on their chair,
Who will shout and give out with the sass! **Yeah!**
Running and romping
And screaming and stomping,
We brawl like it's all just a gas!
When—
The teacher fin'lly sees
That we don't give a hoot!
Then—
We'll start again!
Because she's just a substitute!

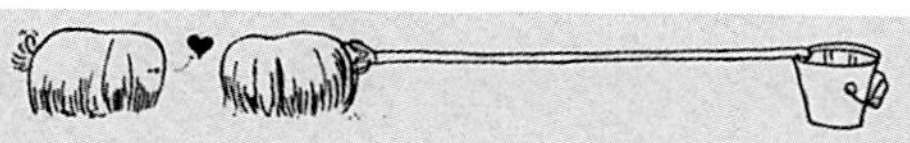

The Cheater's Chant

(to the tune of **"Bless 'em All"**)

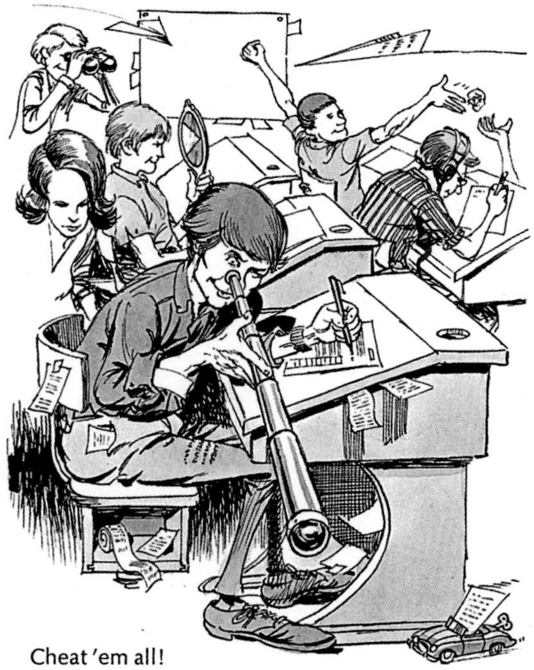

Cheat 'em all!
Cheat 'em all!
In Springtime, in Winter and Fall!
Those Lincoln quotations we hide in our fist!
That Longfellow verse written on our left wrist!
If you find that your mind can't recall
The date when the Romans took Gaul—
A glance at your knee-cap
Will help you to recap!
So why take a chance?
Cheat 'em all!

The Goof-Off's Anthem

(to the tune of **"Over Hill, Over Dale"**)

In a test
For a class
That we know that we can't pass—
See the goof-offs go faking along!

Start to heave;
Fake a chill;
Anything so you'll look ill;
As the goof-offs go faking along!

For it's hi-hi-hoo!
Let's all fake the Asian flu!
Call out your symptoms loud and strong—
"Blah! Ecch!"
We will feel enthused
When the teachers says "Excused!"
As the goof-offs go faking along!

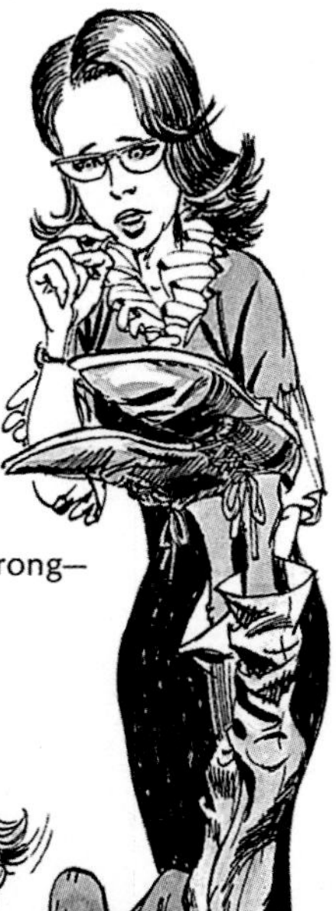

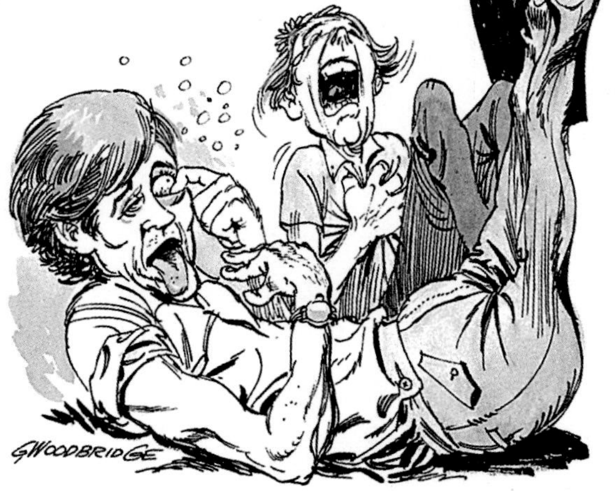
GWOODBRIDGE

WANT TO COOL OFF? SIT ON THIS COPY OF...
MAD
IN THIS ISSUE: SID CAESAR
MAD LOOKS AT BOOK CLUBS
FUNCTIONAL ARCHITECTURE
FAMILY MAGAZINES
AMERICA'S DREAM CAR
MAD MEDALS FOR EVERYDAY HEROES
A Best Seller Hits The COMMERCIAL TRAIL
VIC TINNY GYMS
THE NEW VIC TINNY METHOD
SPECIAL PROBLEMS
THE BUSINESS END
THE ULTIMATE DREAM

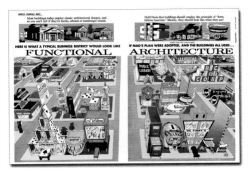

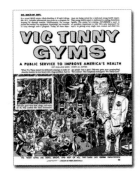

by Rick Geary
ARTIST

This is a tribute to a single issue of MAD: my first one, which I discovered in the summer of 1959, at age 13. It was the September issue, with a big block of ice on the cover, painted, of course, by Frank Kelly Freas. Inside was my introduction to the art of George Woodbridge, Bob Clarke, Don Martin, Wally Wood and especially Mort Drucker, as well as to strange and exotic (to a midwestern WASP) words like Potrzebie, Fershlugginer and Cowsnofsky. I read it cover-to-

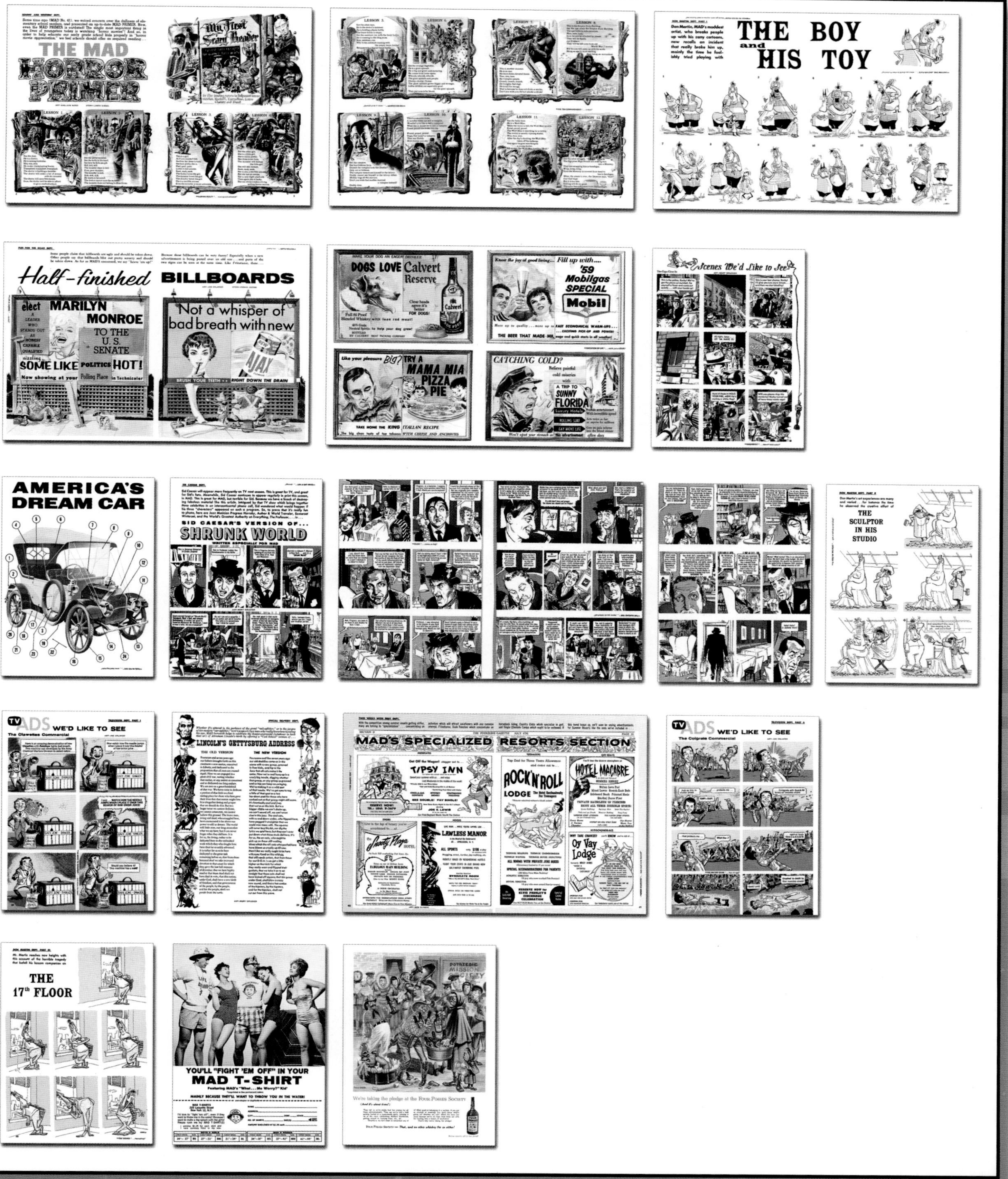
THE MAD HORROR PRIMER
My First Scary Reader
THE BOY and HIS TOY
Half-finished BILLBOARDS
elect MARILYN MONROE TO THE U.S. SENATE
SOME LIKE POLITICS HOT!
Not a whisper of bad breath with new AJAX
DOGS LOVE Calvert Reserve
'59 Mobilgas SPECIAL
Mobil
MAMA MIA PIZZA PIE
CATCHING COLD?
A TRIP TO SUNNY FLORIDA
Scenes We'd Like to See
AMERICA'S DREAM CAR
SID CAESAR'S VERSION OF...
SHRUNK WORLD
THE SCULPTOR IN HIS STUDIO
TV ADS WE'D LIKE TO SEE
LINCOLN'S GETTYSBURG ADDRESS
MAD'S SPECIALIZED RESORTS SECTION
TIPSY INN
ROCK'N'ROLL LODGE
HOTEL MACABRE
LAWLESS MANOR
Oy Vay Lodge
THE 17th FLOOR
YOU'LL "FIGHT 'EM OFF" IN YOUR MAD T-SHIRT

MAD #49/SEPTEMBER 1959

cover and back again until it was ragged. I also copied certain faces and figures in fruitless attempts to capture the styles of my favorite artists. At that time, I just loved to draw. A career in art was very far from my mind, let alone actually contributing to MAD. In the months to come, I picked up new issues whenever I found them, until my parents finally sprung for a subscription.

Jeff Probst

I grew up on MAD Magazine and would read each issue over and over. I did the Fold-In so many times, the back cover would finally tear apart. I didn't realize it at the time, but MAD's unique sense of humor gave me permission to think outside the lines.

Years later, I achieved a childhood dream when I was put on the cover for a *Survivor* issue! It's a cherished possession to this day! By the way, if you go to page five of that issue, in the "Mad Celebrity Snaps," you'll see a photo of a guy posing with me while holding a copy of MAD. We said he was an out-of-work carpenter who met me at a party and you gave him a free subscription for sending in the photo. We lied. He is the *Survivor Challenge* producer and he just wanted to be in the magazine!

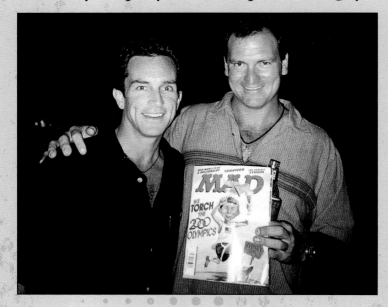

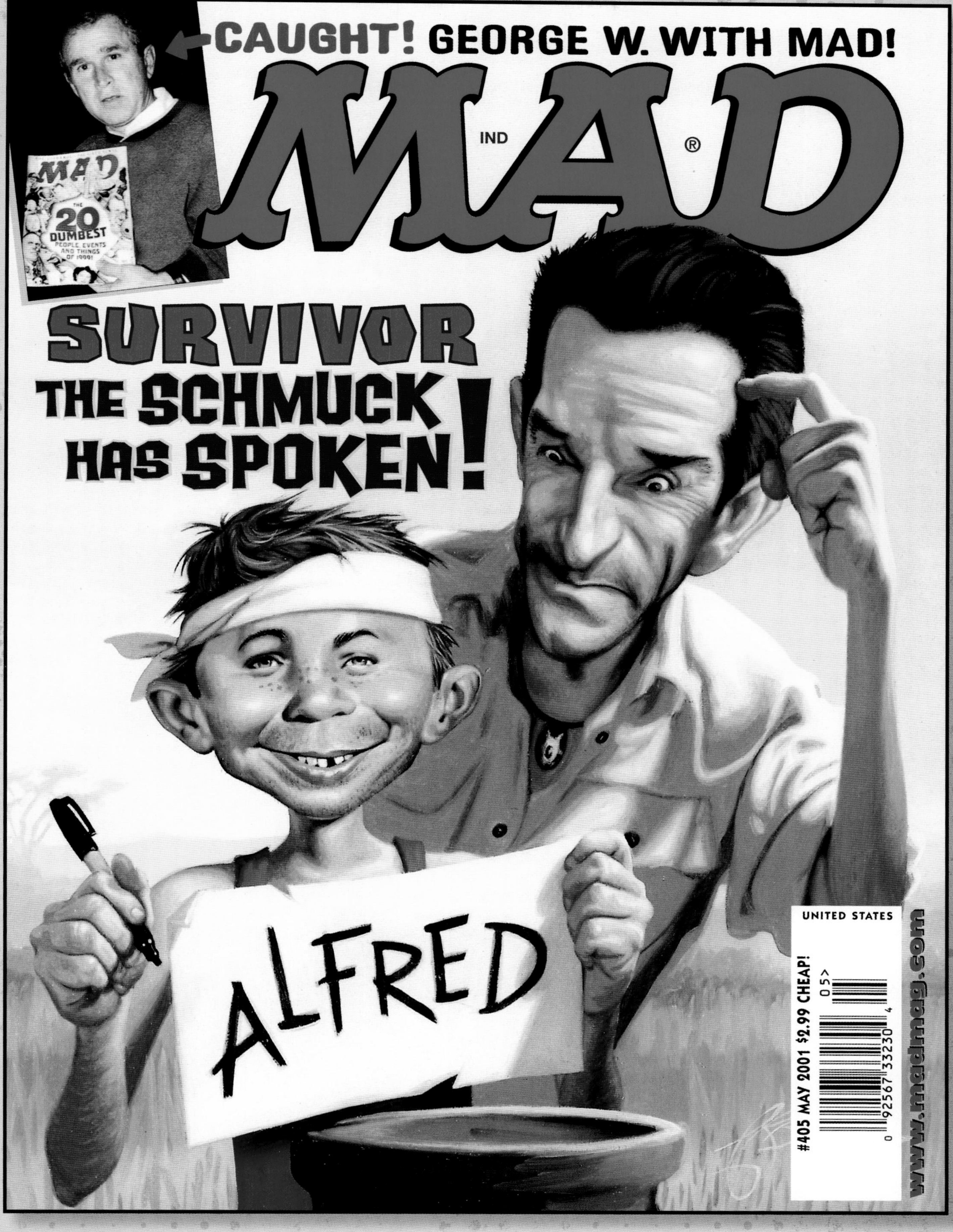
CAUGHT! GEORGE W. WITH MAD!
MAD
IND
®
MAD
THE
20
DUMBEST
PEOPLE, EVENTS AND THINGS OF 1999!
SURVIVOR
THE SCHMUCK HAS SPOKEN!
ALFRED
UNITED STATES
#405 MAY 2001 $2.99 CHEAP!
www.madmag.com

ARTIST: JAMES BENNETT

MAD #405/MAY 2001

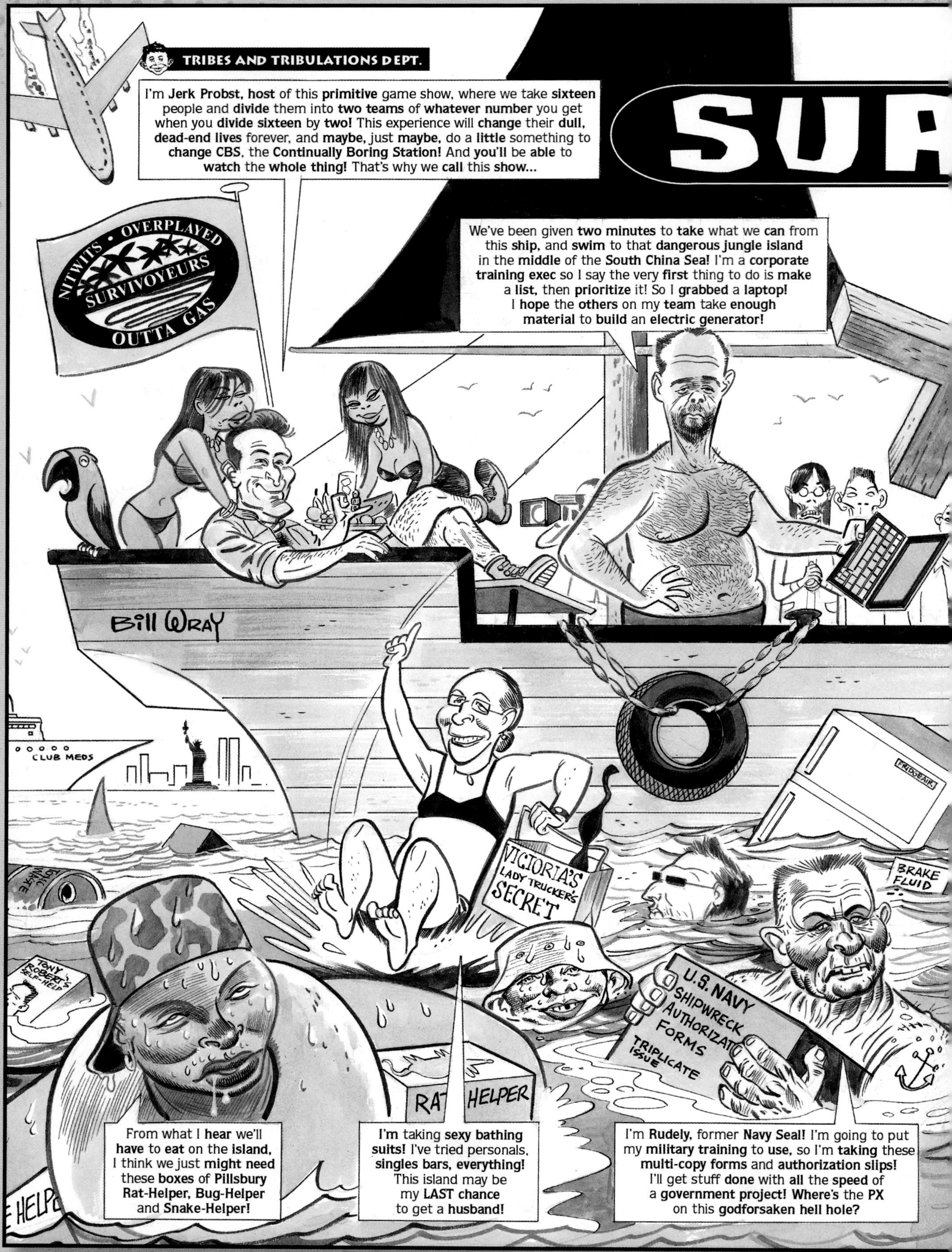

TRIBES AND TRIBULATIONS DEPT.
I'm Jerk Probst, host of this primitive game show, where we take sixteen people and divide them into two teams of whatever number you get when you divide sixteen by two! This experience will change their dull, dead-end lives forever, and maybe, just maybe, do a little something to change CBS, the Continually Boring Station! And you'll be able to watch the whole thing! That's why we call this show...
SUR
NITWITS • OVERPLAYED
SURVIVOYEURS
OUTTA GAS
We've been given two minutes to take what we can from this ship, and swim to that dangerous jungle island in the middle of the South China Sea! I'm a corporate training exec so I say the very first thing to do is make a list, then prioritize it! So I grabbed a laptop! I hope the others on my team take enough material to build an electric generator!
BILL WRAY
CLUB MEDS
VICTORIA'S LADY TRUCKER'S SECRET
BRAKE FLUID
U.S. NAVY SHIPWRECK AUTHORIZAT FORMS
TRIPLICATE ISSUE
RAT HELPER
From what I hear we'll have to eat on the island, I think we just might need these boxes of Pillsbury Rat-Helper, Bug-Helper and Snake-Helper!
I'm taking sexy bathing suits! I've tried personals, singles bars, everything! This island may be my LAST chance to get a husband!
I'm Rudely, former Navy Seal! I'm going to put my military training to use, so I'm taking these multi-copy forms and authorization slips! I'll get stuff done with all the speed of a government project! Where's the PX on this godforsaken hell hole?

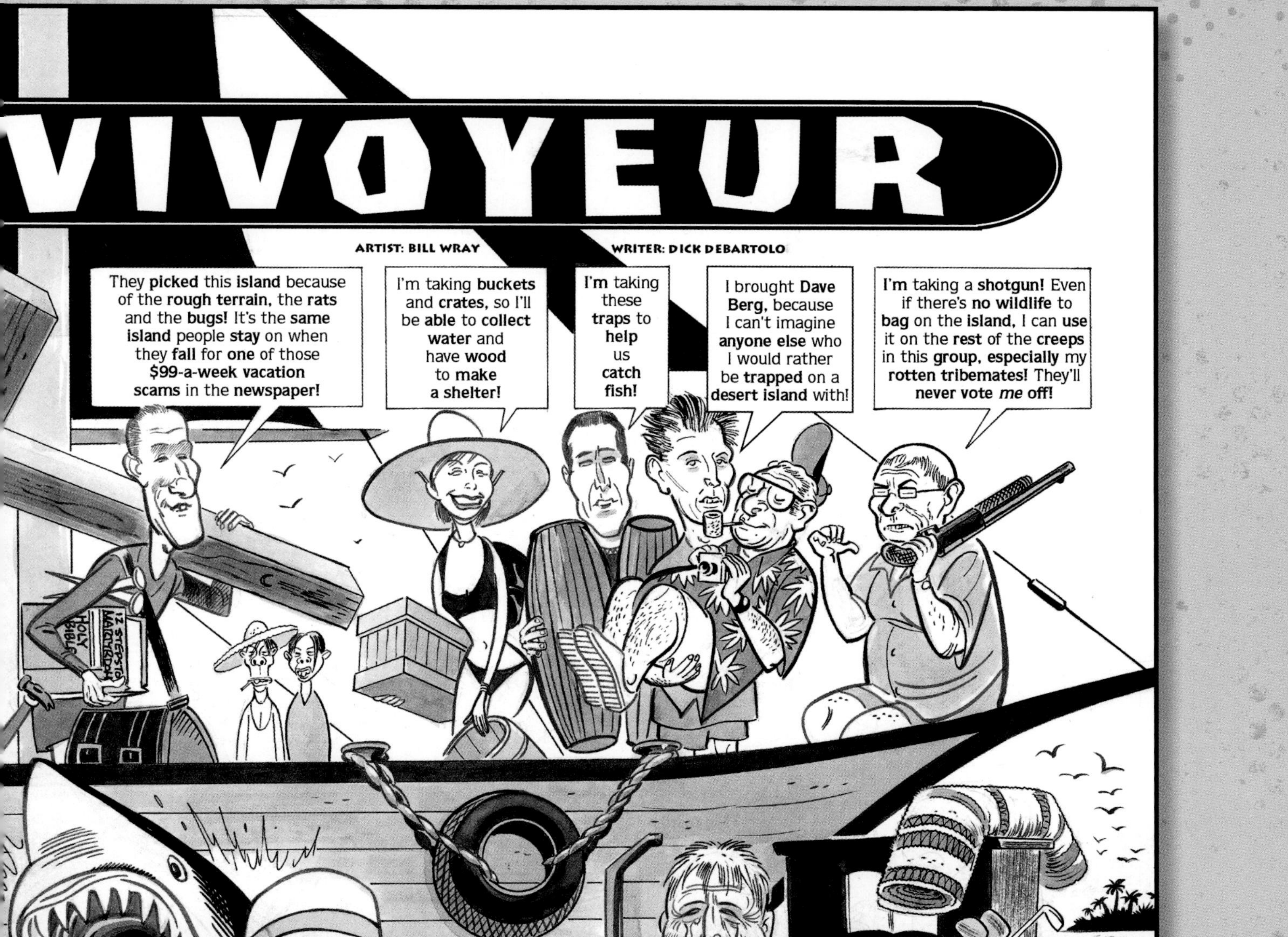
VIVOYEUR
ARTIST: BILL WRAY
WRITER: DICK DEBARTOLO
They picked this island because of the rough terrain, the rats and the bugs! It's the same island people stay on when they fall for one of those $99-a-week vacation scams in the newspaper!
I'm taking buckets and crates, so I'll be able to collect water and have wood to make a shelter!
I'm taking these traps to help us catch fish!
I brought Dave Berg, because I can't imagine anyone else who I would rather be trapped on a desert island with!
I'm taking a shotgun! Even if there's no wildlife to bag on the island, I can use it on the rest of the creeps in this group, especially my rotten tribemates! They'll never vote *me* off!
HOLY BIBLE
HOOVER 2000
PLUNK PLUNK PLUNK
NITROUS OXIDE
FRESH FOOT KITTY LITTER 50 LBS
LIFE RAFT
Those other survivors are idiots! I'm taking this chest with the million bucks and flagging down the next ship heading back to America!
I want out now! This is inhumane! Flesh packed against flesh! The lack of food, the way people smell, the crappy way we're treated!
What are you talking about? You're not even on the island yet!
I'm not talking about the island! I'm talking about that horrible flight down here! Flying coach is worse than ever!

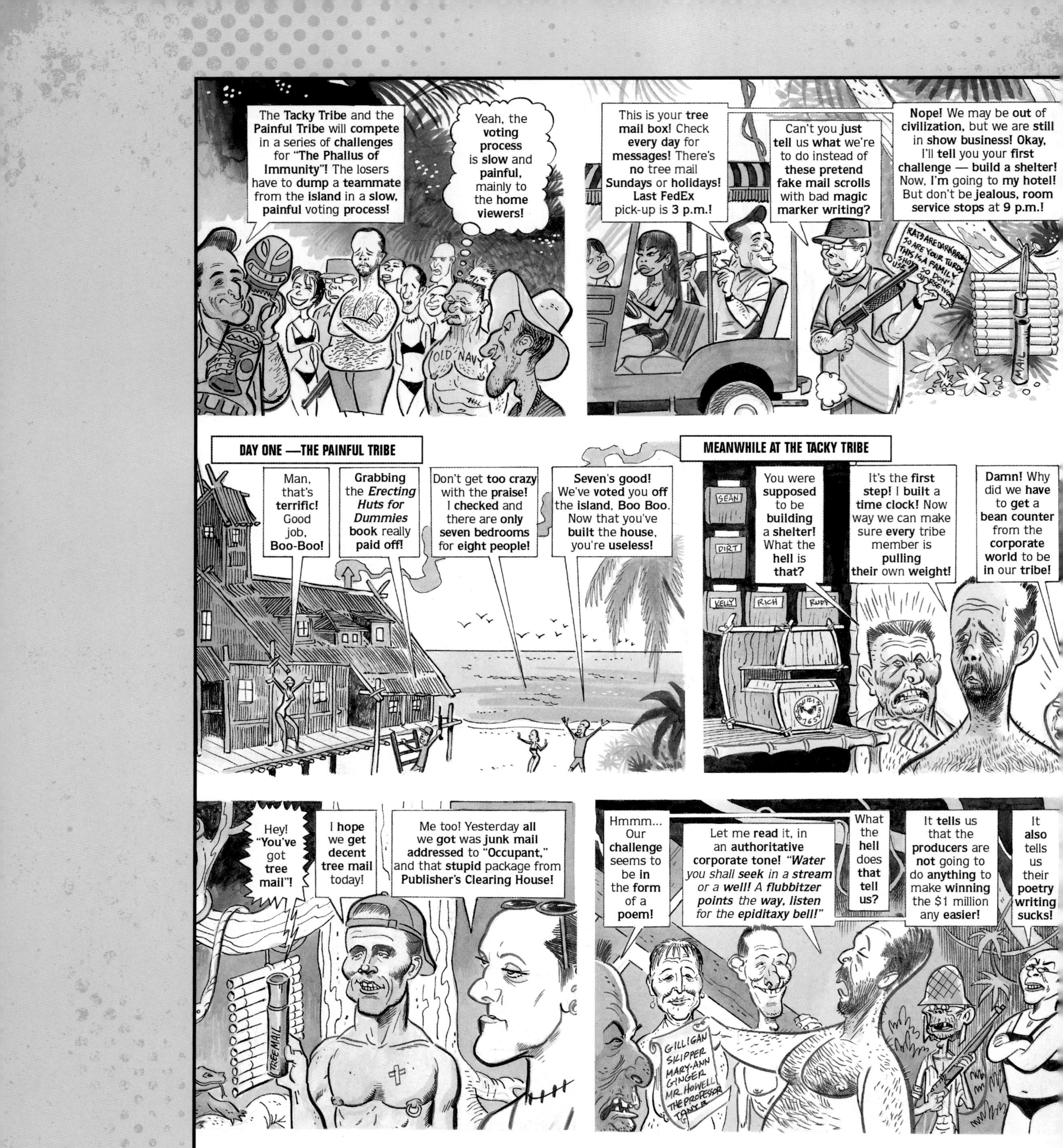
The Tacky Tribe and the Painful Tribe will compete in a series of challenges for "The Phallus of Immunity"! The losers have to dump a teammate from the island in a slow, painful voting process!
Yeah, the voting process is slow and painful, mainly to the home viewers!
OLD NAVY
This is your tree mail box! Check every day for messages! There's no tree mail Sundays or holidays! Last FedEx pick-up is 3 p.m.!
Can't you just tell us what we're to do instead of these pretend fake mail scrolls with bad magic marker writing?
Nope! We may be out of civilization, but we are still in show business! Okay, I'll tell you your first challenge — build a shelter! Now, I'm going to my hotel! But don't be jealous, room service stops at 9 p.m.!
MAIL
DAY ONE —THE PAINFUL TRIBE
Man, that's terrific! Good job, Boo-Boo!
Grabbing the Erecting Huts for Dummies book really paid off!
Don't get too crazy with the praise! I checked and there are only seven bedrooms for eight people!
Seven's good! We've voted you off the island, Boo Boo. Now that you've built the house, you're useless!
MEANWHILE AT THE TACKY TRIBE
SEAN
DIRT
KELLY
RICH
RUDY
You were supposed to be building a shelter! What the hell is that?
It's the first step! I built a time clock! Now way we can make sure every tribe member is pulling their own weight!
Damn! Why did we have to get a bean counter from the corporate world to be in our tribe!
Hey! "You've got tree mail"!
TREE MAIL
I hope we get decent tree mail today!
Me too! Yesterday all we got was junk mail addressed to "Occupant," and that stupid package from Publisher's Clearing House!
Hmmm... Our challenge seems to be in the form of a poem!
Let me read it, in an authoritative corporate tone! "Water you shall seek in a stream or a well! A flubbitzer points the way, listen for the epiditaxy bell!"
What the hell does that tell us?
It tells us that the producers are not going to do anything to make winning the $1 million any easier!
It also tells us their poetry writing sucks!
GILLIGAN
SKIPPER
MARY-ANN
GINGER
MR. HOWELL
THE PROFESSOR

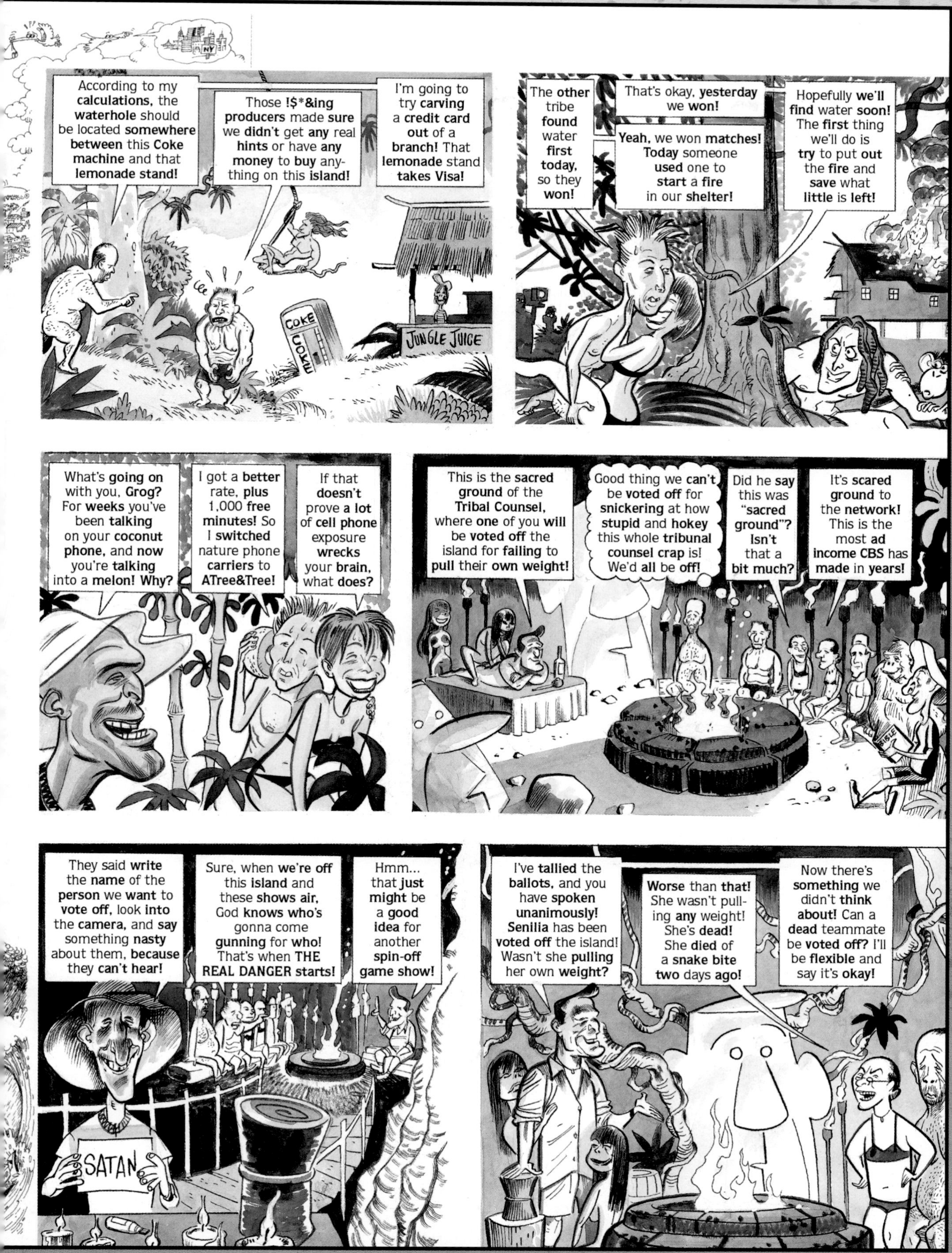

According to my calculations, the waterhole should be located somewhere between this Coke machine and that lemonade stand!
Those !$*&ing producers made sure we didn't get any real hints or have any money to buy any-thing on this island!
I'm going to try carving a credit card out of a branch! That lemonade stand takes Visa!
COKE
COKE
JUNGLE JUICE
The other tribe found water first today, so they won!
That's okay, yesterday we won!
Yeah, we won matches! Today someone used one to start a fire in our shelter!
Hopefully we'll find water soon! The first thing we'll do is try to put out the fire and save what little is left!
What's going on with you, Grog? For weeks you've been talking on your coconut phone, and now you're talking into a melon! Why?
I got a better rate, plus 1,000 free minutes! So I switched nature phone carriers to ATree&Tree!
If that doesn't prove a lot of cell phone exposure wrecks your brain, what does?
This is the sacred ground of the Tribal Counsel, where one of you will be voted off the island for failing to pull their own weight!
Good thing we can't be voted off for snickering at how stupid and hokey this whole tribunal counsel crap is! We'd all be off!
Did he say this was "sacred ground"? Isn't that a bit much?
It's scared ground to the network! This is the most ad income CBS has made in years!
They said write the name of the person we want to vote off, look into the camera, and say something nasty about them, because they can't hear!
Sure, when we're off this island and these shows air, God knows who's gonna come gunning for who! That's when THE REAL DANGER starts!
Hmm... that just might be a good idea for another spin-off game show!
SATAN
I've tallied the ballots, and you have spoken unanimously! Senilia has been voted off the island! Wasn't she pulling her own weight?
Worse than that! She wasn't pull-ing any weight! She's dead! She died of a snake bite two days ago!
Now there's something we didn't think about! Can a dead teammate be voted off? I'll be flexible and say it's okay!

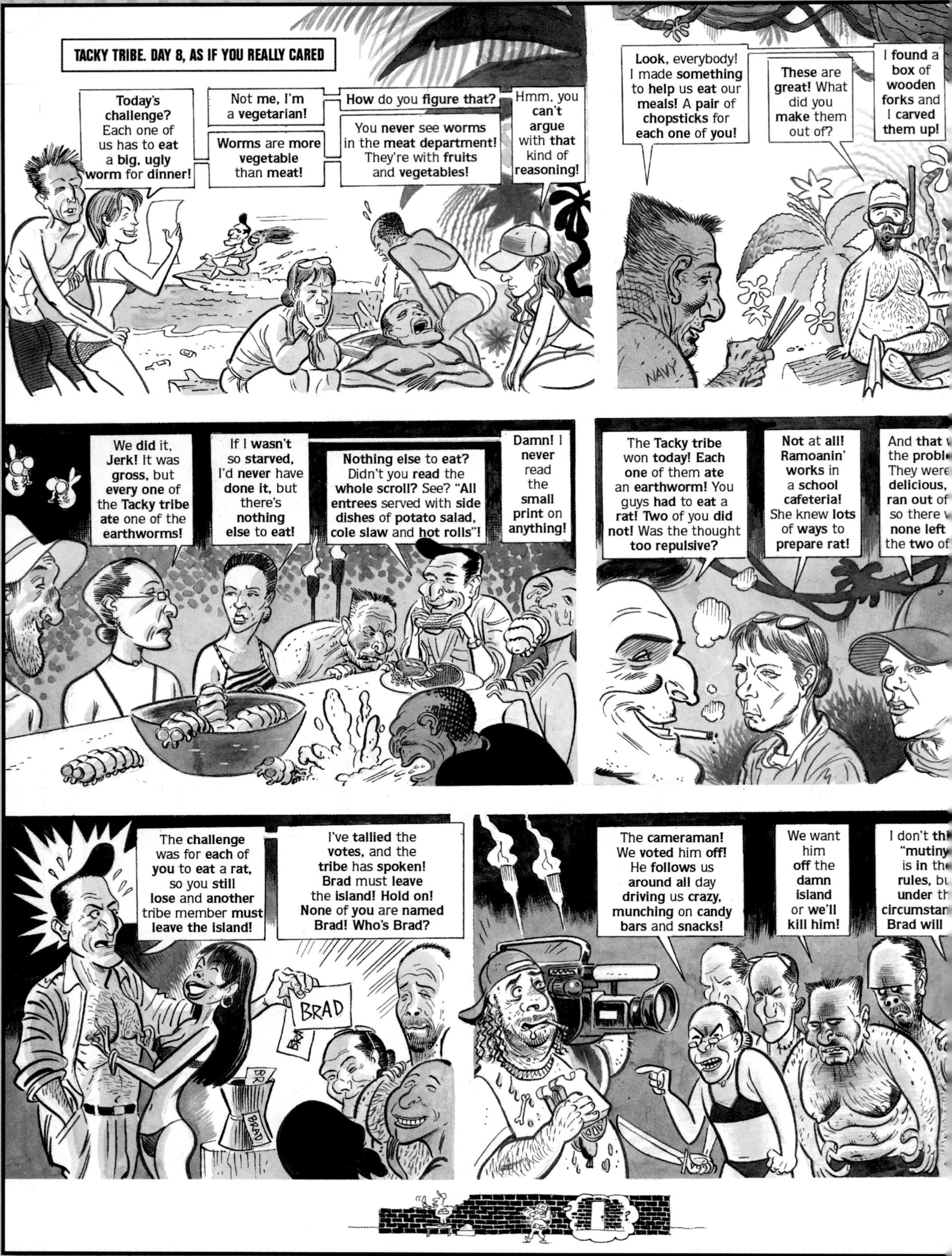
TACKY TRIBE. DAY 8, AS IF YOU REALLY CARED
Today's challenge? Each one of us has to eat a big, ugly worm for dinner!
Not me, I'm a vegetarian!
Worms are more vegetable than meat!
How do you figure that?
You never see worms in the meat department! They're with fruits and vegetables!
Hmm, you can't argue with that kind of reasoning!
Look, everybody! I made something to help us eat our meals! A pair of chopsticks for each one of you!
These are great! What did you make them out of?
I found a box of wooden forks and I carved them up!
NAVY
We did it, Jerk! It was gross, but every one of the Tacky tribe ate one of the earthworms!
If I wasn't so starved, I'd never have done it, but there's nothing else to eat!
Nothing else to eat? Didn't you read the whole scroll? See? "All entrees served with side dishes of potato salad, cole slaw and hot rolls"!
Damn! I never read the small print on anything!
The Tacky tribe won today! Each one of them ate an earthworm! You guys had to eat a rat! Two of you did not! Was the thought too repulsive?
Not at all! Ramoanin' works in a school cafeteria! She knew lots of ways to prepare rat!
And that the probl They were delicious, ran out of so there none left the two of
The challenge was for each of you to eat a rat, so you still lose and another tribe member must leave the island!
I've tallied the votes, and the tribe has spoken! Brad must leave the island! Hold on! None of you are named Brad! Who's Brad?
BRAD
BRAD
The cameraman! We voted him off! He follows us around all day driving us crazy, munching on candy bars and snacks!
We want him off the damn island or we'll kill him!
I don't th "mutiny is in th rules, bu under th circumstan Brad will

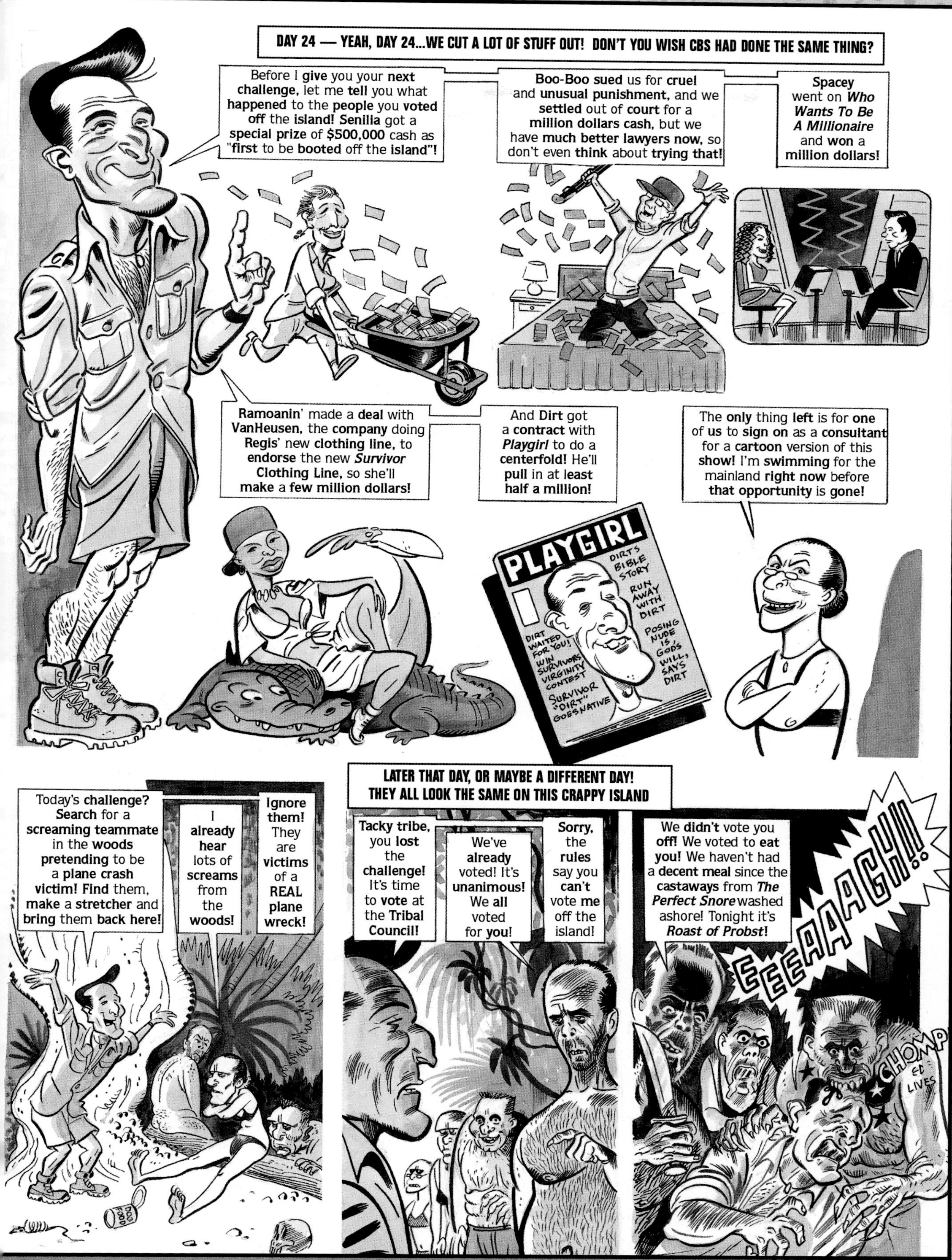

DAY 24 — YEAH, DAY 24...WE CUT A LOT OF STUFF OUT! DON'T YOU WISH CBS HAD DONE THE SAME THING?
Before I give you your next challenge, let me tell you what happened to the people you voted off the island! Senilia got a special prize of $500,000 cash as "first to be booted off the island"!
Boo-Boo sued us for cruel and unusual punishment, and we settled out of court for a million dollars cash, but we have much better lawyers now, so don't even think about trying that!
Spacey went on Who Wants To Be A Millionaire and won a million dollars!
Ramoanin' made a deal with VanHeusen, the company doing Regis' new clothing line, to endorse the new Survivor Clothing Line, so she'll make a few million dollars!
And Dirt got a contract with Playgirl to do a centerfold! He'll pull in at least half a million!
The only thing left is for one of us to sign on as a consultant for a cartoon version of this show! I'm swimming for the mainland right now before that opportunity is gone!
PLAYGIRL
DIRT'S BIBLE STORY
RUN AWAY WITH DIRT
POSING NUDE IS GOD'S WILL, SAYS DIRT
DIRT WAITED FOR YOU! WIN SURVIVOR'S VIRGINITY CONTEST
SURVIVOR "DIRT" GOES NATIVE
LATER THAT DAY, OR MAYBE A DIFFERENT DAY! THEY ALL LOOK THE SAME ON THIS CRAPPY ISLAND
Today's challenge? Search for a screaming teammate in the woods pretending to be a plane crash victim! Find them, make a stretcher and bring them back here!
I already hear lots of screams from the woods!
Ignore them! They are victims of a REAL plane wreck!
DOG FOOD
Tacky tribe, you lost the challenge! It's time to vote at the Tribal Council!
We've already voted! It's unanimous! We all voted for you!
Sorry, the rules say you can't vote me off the island!
We didn't vote you off! We voted to eat you! We haven't had a decent meal since the castaways from The Perfect Snore washed ashore! Tonight it's Roast of Probst!
EEEAAAGH!!
CHOMP
ED LIVES

LET'S GET READY TO GRUMBLE! DEPT.

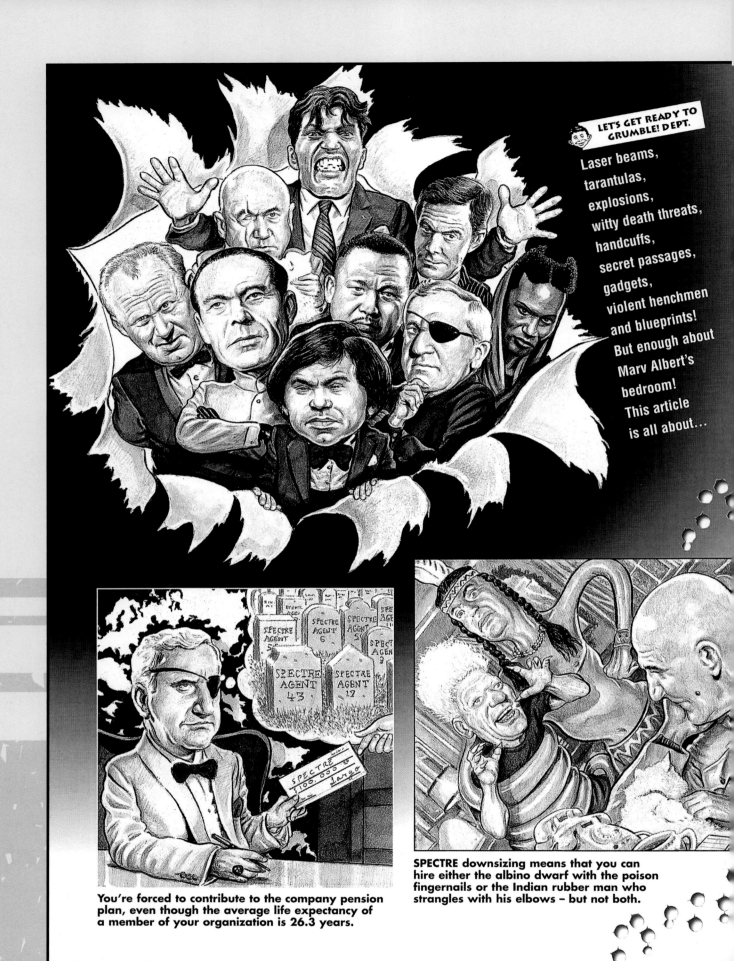

Laser beams, tarantulas, explosions, witty death threats, handcuffs, secret passages, gadgets, violent henchmen and blueprints! But enough about Marv Albert's bedroom! This article is all about...

SPECTRE AGENT 5
SPECTRE AGENT 6
SPECTRE AGENT 5
SPECTRE AGENT 9
SPECTRE AGENT 43
SPECTRE AGENT 17
SPECTRE
$100,000.00
Largo

You're forced to contribute to the company pension plan, even though the average life expectancy of a member of your organization is 26.3 years.

SPECTRE downsizing means that you can hire either the albino dwarf with the poison fingernails or the Indian rubber man who strangles with his elbows – but not both.

by Mike Snider
WRITER

To me, writing for MAD from about 1980 onward was like the world's weirdest scavenger hunt: searching through the "Land of MAD Topsy-Turvy" already carved out by the "O.G.'s" (the "Original Gang" of Idiots — Frank, Dick, Stan, et al.), looking high and low for new ideas and premises that were different...or at least different enough to be not-so-obvious rip-offs of prior articles... but not SO different as to wind up in the editors' reject pile!

One of my fellow "scavenger-hunters" who came a few years after me, Desmond

JAMES BOND VILLAINS' PET PEEVES

Should have spent the extra $50,000 for the off-shore hideaway WITHOUT the "Destroy Entire Island" button.

ARTIST: DREW FRIEDMAN   WRITER: DESMOND DEVLIN

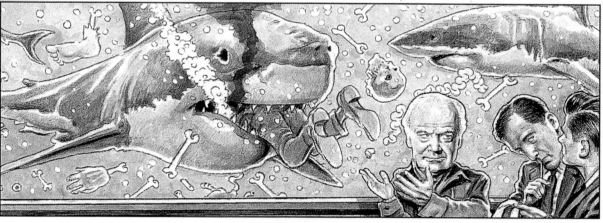

Before they'll allow the deduction, the IRS demands proof that you use your 1,800 foot shark tank exclusively for business purposes.

Every time you and your criminal organization finally learn to recognize 007 on sight, they send a new James Bond with a totally different face!

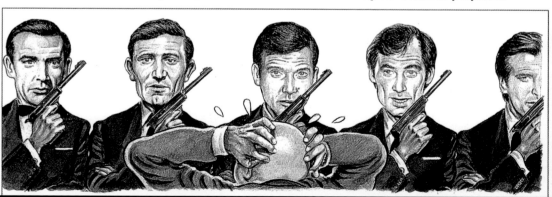

MAD #365/JANUARY 1998

Devlin, is an uncommonly funny and clever guy whose work has sometimes made me laugh out loud...and sometimes made me jealous as hell! Take this article of Desmond's from 1998, "James Bond Villains' Pet Peeves." When I first read it, my initial reaction was, "Damn! He beat me to another good idea! And I'd already been searching in those areas of Premise-ville just last week!" The out-loud laughter came next, at two of his gag-lines that I never would've come up with myself! (All MAD writers are "bent," but each at his own angle!)

JAMES BOND VILLAINS' PET PEEVES

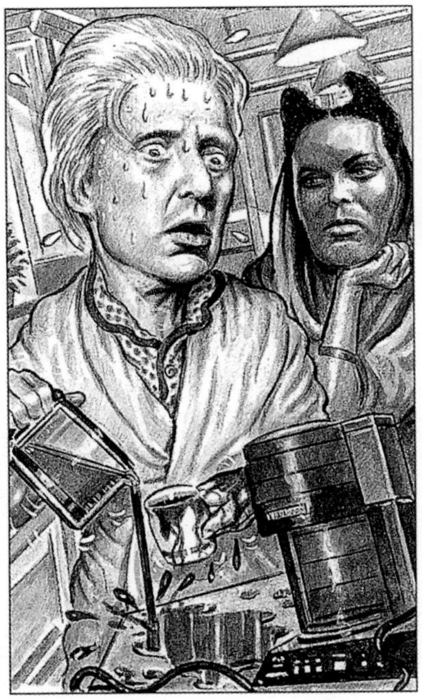

With all of Bond's hidden devices and micro-gadgets, you're too paranoid to work the friggin' coffee machine in the morning!

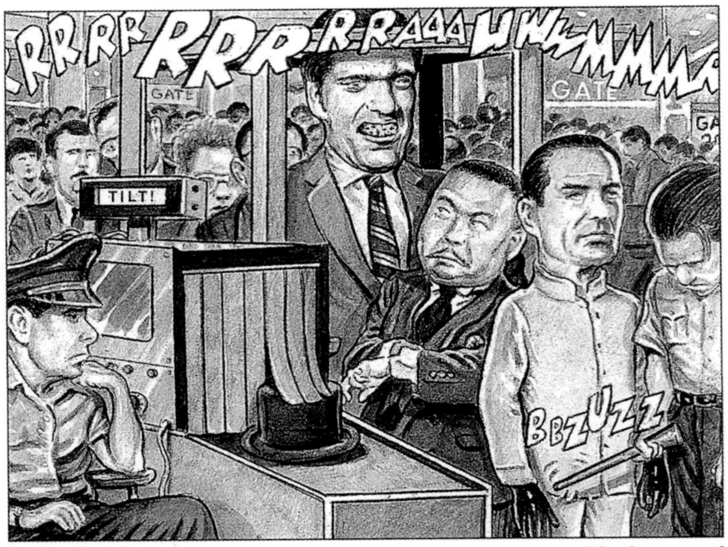

TILT!
GATE
BBZUZZ

Between the guy with the metal teeth, the guy with the metal hands and the guy with the metal hat, it takes absolutely forever for you and your henchmen to get past airport security!

Your psychiatrist has told you and told you that always keeping Bond alive so you can tell him your secret plans is "a spiraling self-destructive pattern," but you just can't help it!

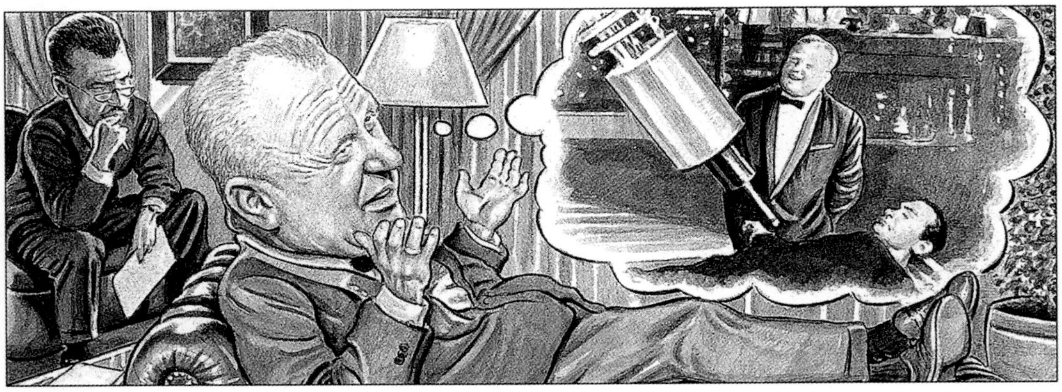

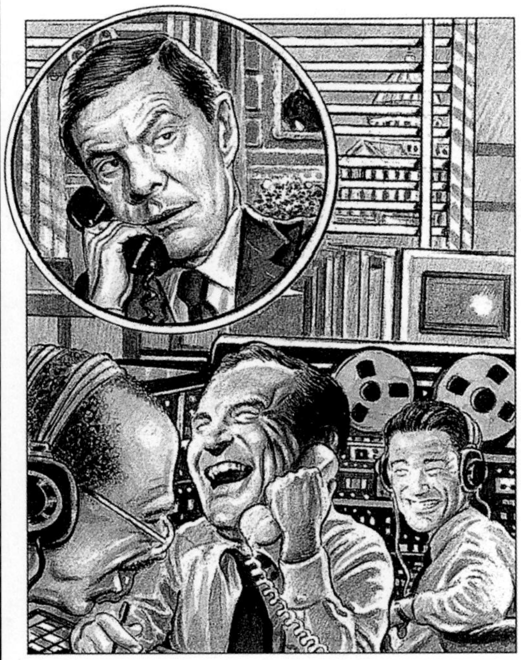

Nowadays, when you threaten to detonate a 15-megaton bomb in Washington D.C., the FBI tells you to "get in line."

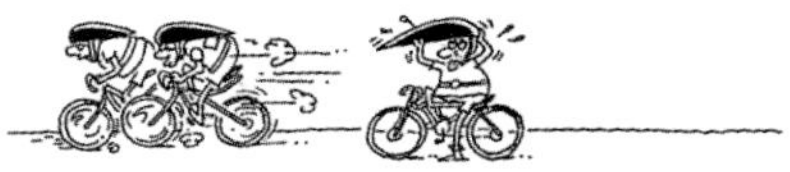

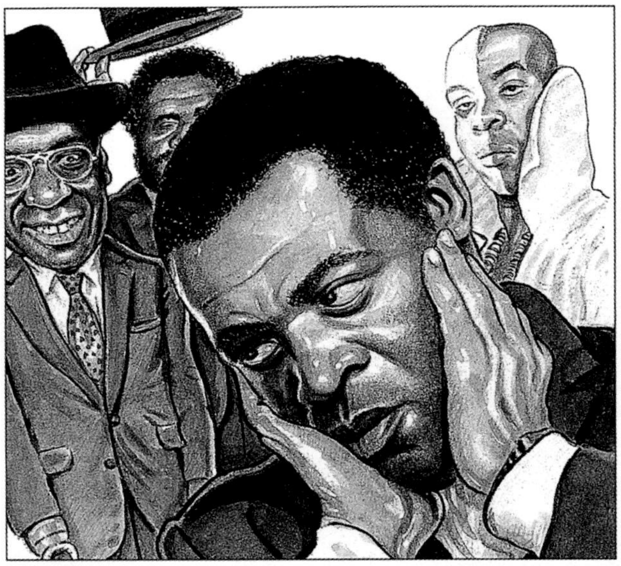

After murdering the last 15 Nobel Prize winners who have secretly worked on your weaponry, it's impossible to attract top talent anymore.

EDITOR'S PICK

AN INCONVENIENT DOOF DEPT.

Over the years, MAD has been called moronic, immature, stupid and even moronic. And we're sick of it! Which is why, to improve our image and better our situation, we've hired ten Pulitzer Prize-winning editorial cartoonists to illustrate the following article. Will this teaming smarten up MAD's image and elevate the discourse — or simply ruin the careers of ten once-respected artists? What do you *think?!?*

WHY GEORGE W. BUSH IS IN FAVOR OF GLOBAL WARMING

A MAD EXPOSÉ

WRITER: JACOB LAMBERT

Netflix sent him *An Inconvenient Truth* a few months ago — but darn it if they haven't also kept sending other, more important movies.

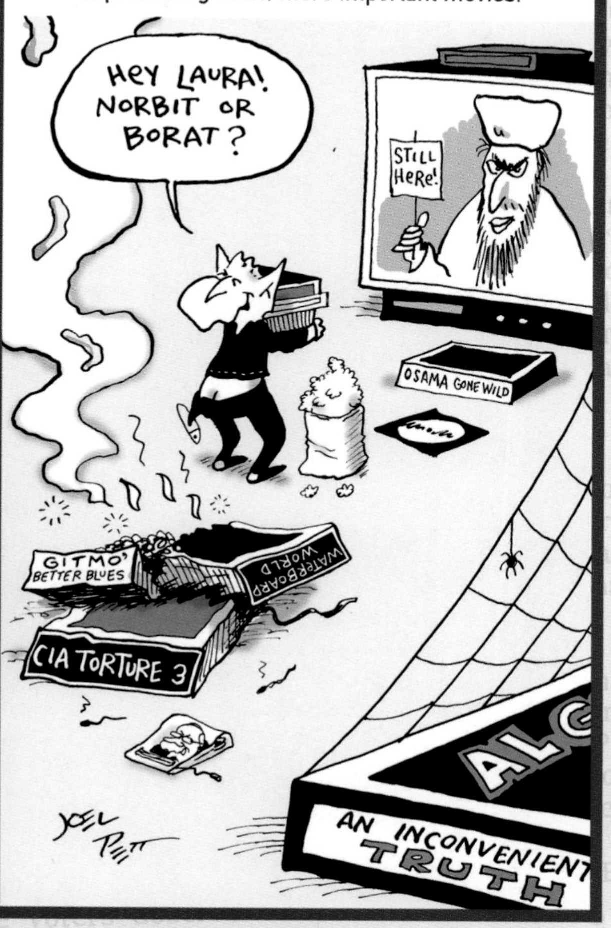
HEY LAURA! NORBIT OR BORAT?
STILL HERE!
OSAMA GONE WILD
GITMO BETTER BLUES
WATERBOARD WORLD
CIA TORTURE 3
AN INCONVENIENT TRUTH
JOEL PETT

ARTIST: JOEL PETT, LEXINGTON HERALD-LEADER PULITZER PRIZE 2000

As a devout Christian, he's doubtful about science — except, of course, when it's in the name of oil exploration, bomb-making or using satellites to spy on Americans.

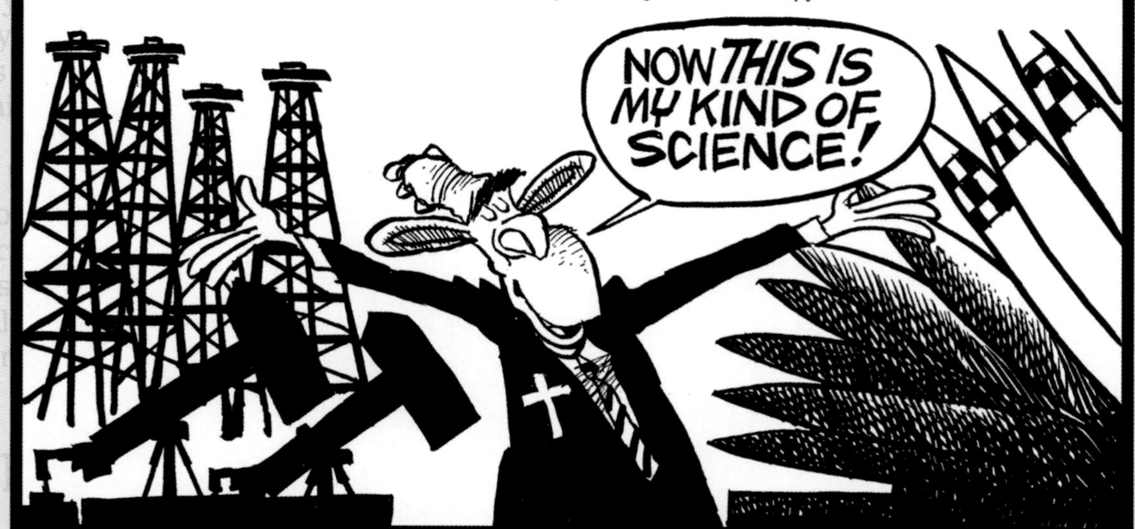
NOW THIS IS MY KIND OF SCIENCE!

ARTIST: MIKE PETERS, DAYTON DAILY NEWS PULITZER PRIZE 1981

MAD #487/MARCH 2008

One of the great things about being the editor of MAD is that you can think up crazy ideas, and then leave it to your trusted staff to sweat the pesky details. And so it was with this article. It came in just like any other MAD article, but at some point I had the idea to have each of the 10 examples in the article illustrated by a different artist. This wasn't a wholly original idea, MAD had done this several times in the past. What made my idea different was that I wanted each of the artists to be a Pulitzer Prize winning cartoonist. I thought the notion of 10 lofty and well-respected Pulitzer Prize winners contributing to a single issue of MAD, a self-proclaimed idiotic magazine, to be too absurdly delicious to pass up. Since I hadn't the vaguest idea on how to con one, let alone 10 Pulitzer Prize

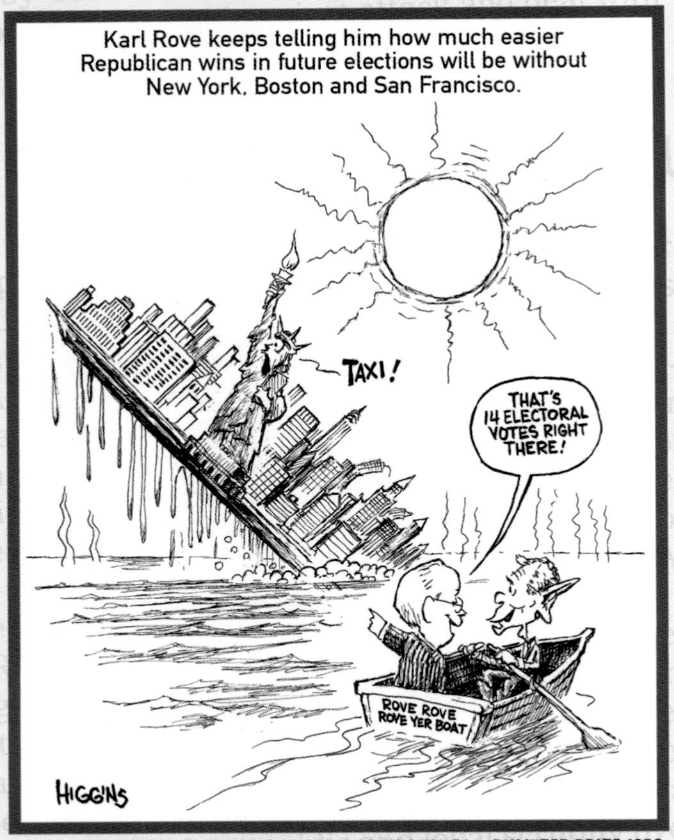
Karl Rove keeps telling him how much easier Republican wins in future elections will be without New York, Boston and San Francisco.
TAXI!
THAT'S 14 ELECTORAL VOTES RIGHT THERE!
ROVE ROVE ROVE YER BOAT
HIGGINS

ARTIST: JACK HIGGINS, CHICAGO SUN-TIMES PULITZER PRIZE 1989

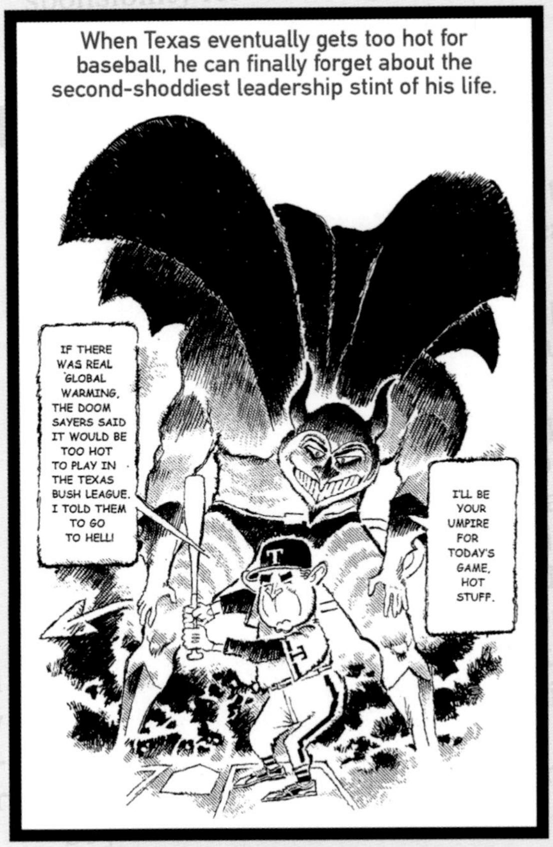
When Texas eventually gets too hot for baseball, he can finally forget about the second-shoddiest leadership stint of his life.
IF THERE WAS REAL 'GLOBAL WARMING,' THE DOOM SAYERS SAID IT WOULD BE TOO HOT TO PLAY IN THE TEXAS BUSH LEAGUE. I TOLD THEM TO GO TO HELL!
I'LL BE YOUR UMPIRE FOR TODAY'S GAME, HOT STUFF.

ARTIST: DICK LOCHER, CHICAGO TRIBUNE PULITZER PRIZE 1983

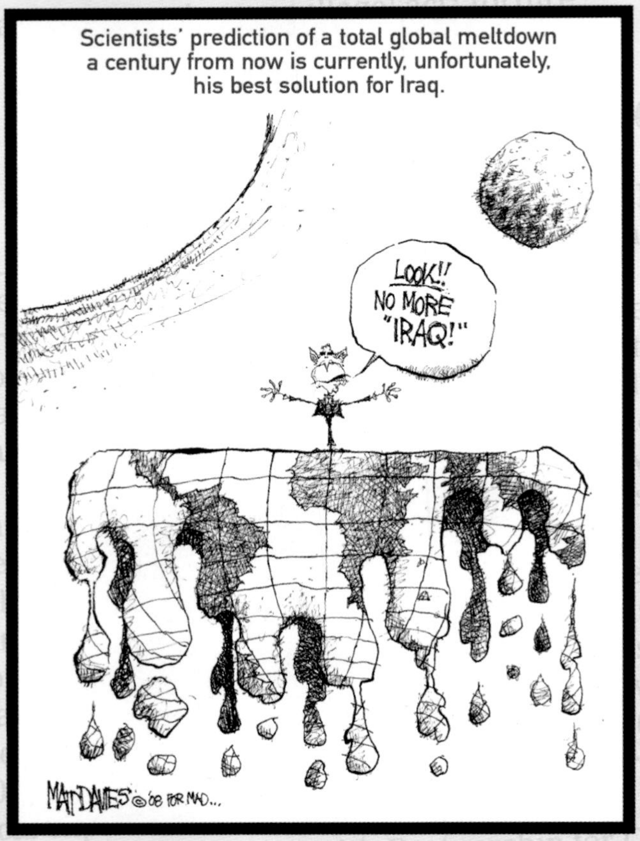
Scientists' prediction of a total global meltdown a century from now is currently, unfortunately, his best solution for Iraq.
LOOK!! NO MORE "IRAQ!"
MATDAVIES ©08 FOR MAD...

ARTIST: MATT DAVIES, JOURNAL NEWS PULITZER PRIZE 2004

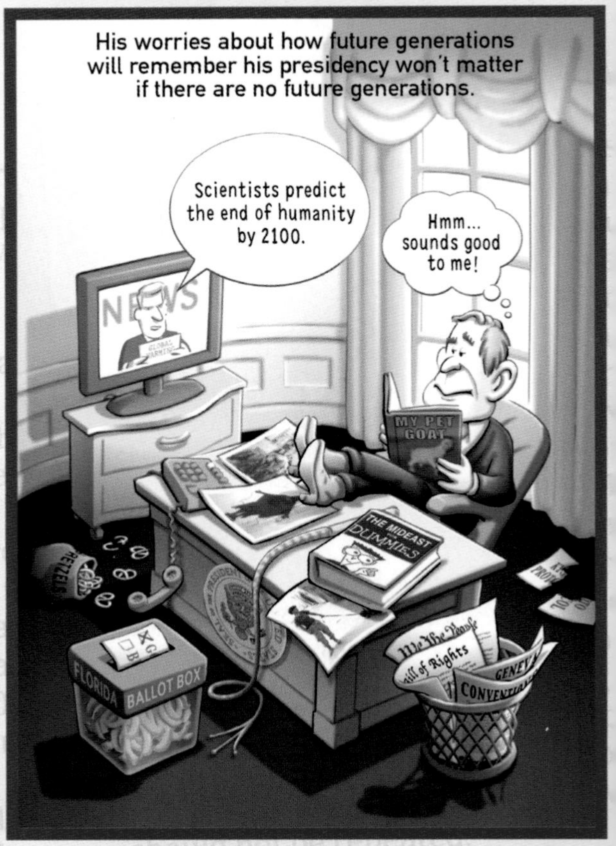
His worries about how future generations will remember his presidency won't matter if there are no future generations.
Scientists predict the end of humanity by 2100.
Hmm... sounds good to me!
NEWS
MY PET GOAT
THE MIDEAST FOR DUMMIES
FLORIDA BALLOT BOX
Bill of Rights
GENEVA CONVENTION

winners, into contributing to MAD, I called in my art director, Sam Viviano, and dropped the whole project in his lap. How Sam managed to cajole these cartoonists into risking their professional reputations by drawing for MAD, I don't want to know. I believe the legal term is "plausible deniability." But with the statute of limitations for any of these guys to be able to sue the magazine just about up, the entire, sordid story can now be told. But not by me! Sam can do it. (See what I mean about me not sweating the pesky details?) — *John Ficarra*

John neglects to mention that he came up with this brilliant idea in mid-December — and the issue was due at the printer in early January! This gave me less than a month to put this thing together. While I was acquainted with one or two Pulitzer cartoonists, I certainly didn't know ten of them. In the past 30 years, only a couple dozen cartoonists had won the Prize, several of whom had passed

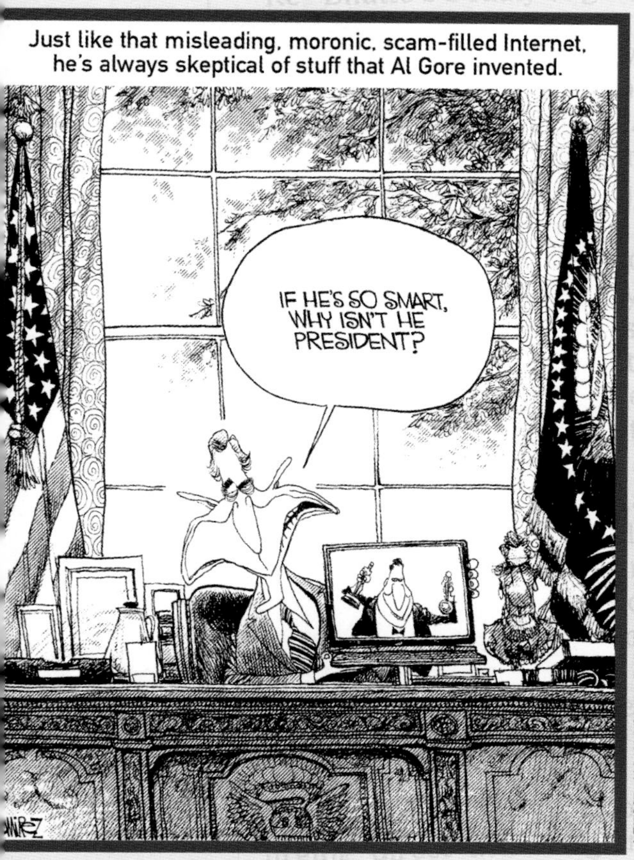
Just like that misleading, moronic, scam-filled Internet, he's always skeptical of stuff that Al Gore invented.
IF HE'S SO SMART, WHY ISN'T HE PRESIDENT?

ARTIST: MICHAEL RAMIREZ, INVESTOR'S BUSINESS DAILY PULITZER PRIZE 1994

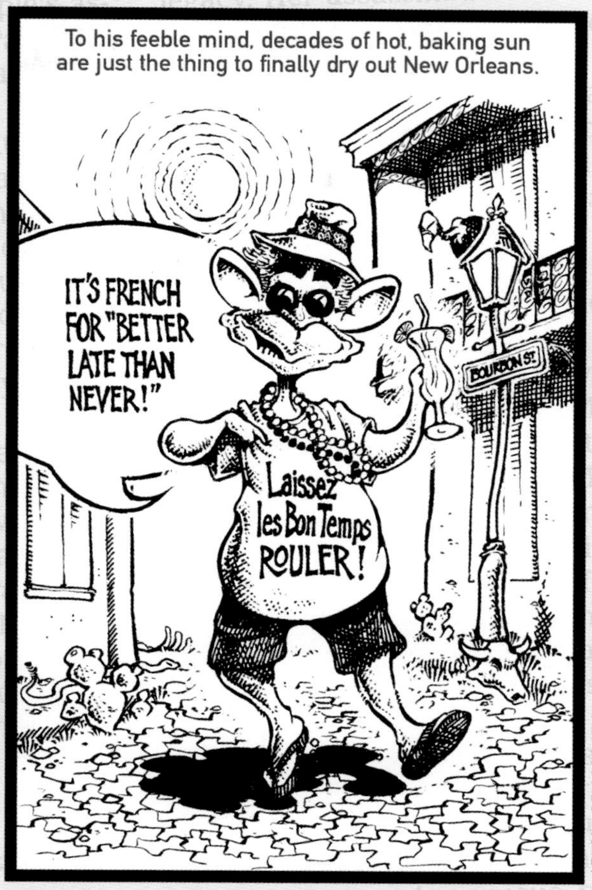
To his feeble mind, decades of hot, baking sun are just the thing to finally dry out New Orleans.
IT'S FRENCH FOR "BETTER LATE THAN NEVER!"
Laissez les Bon Temps ROULER!
BOURBON ST

ARTIST: BEN SARGENT, AUSTIN AMERICAN-STATESMAN PULITZER PRIZE 1982

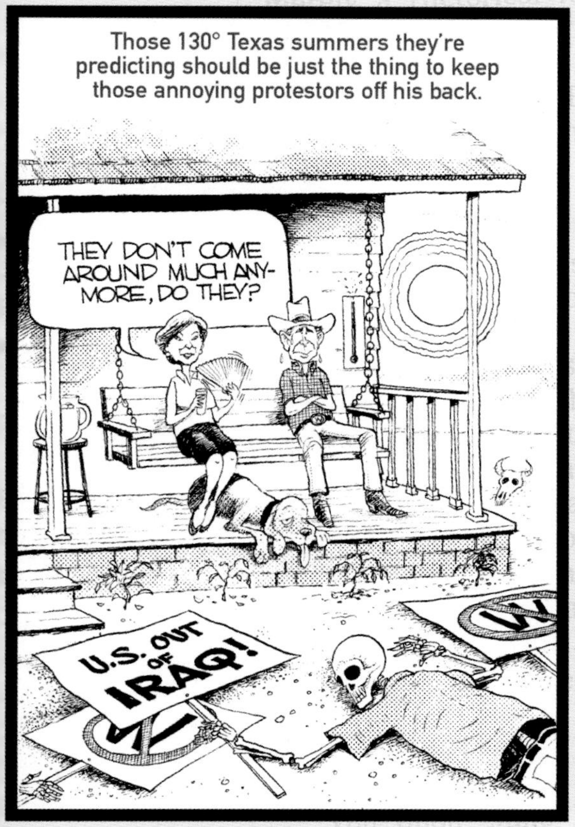
Those 130° Texas summers they're predicting should be just the thing to keep those annoying protestors off his back.
THEY DON'T COME AROUND MUCH ANY-MORE, DO THEY?
U.S. OUT OF IRAQ!

ARTIST: STEVE BREEN, SAN DIEGO UNION-TRIBUNE PULITZER PRIZE 1998

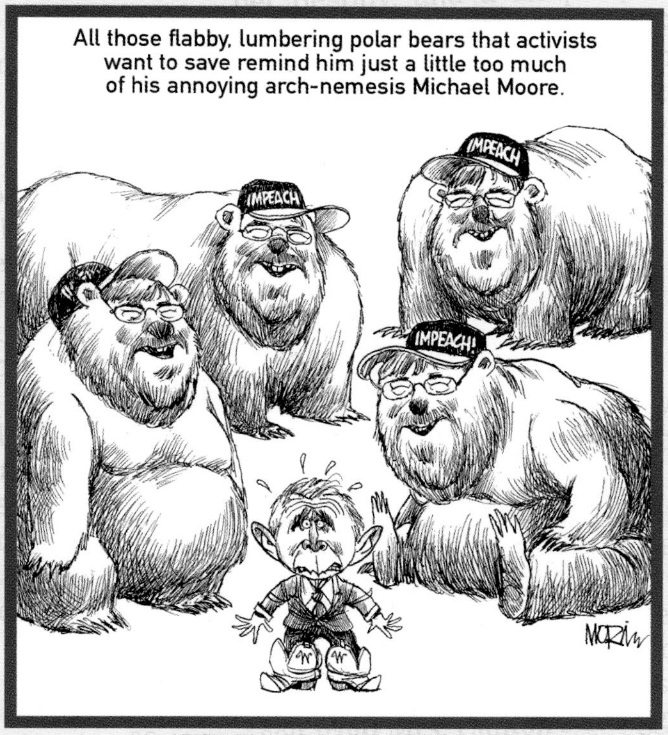
All those flabby, lumbering polar bears that activists want to save remind him just a little too much of his annoying arch-nemesis Michael Moore.
IMPEACH
IMPEACH
IMPEACH!

ARTIST: JIM MORIN, MIAMI HERALD PULITZER PRIZE 1996

away. I'd have to have a .500 batting average if this thing was to succeed. I began making calls. A few cartoonists turned me down, for various reasons, but most of them were thrilled to have a chance to contribute to MAD. By the time the Christmas break rolled around, I had nine of the ten illustrations assigned. That left one gag, and just one cartoonist sitting on the fence. If he said no, we'd have to run the article with a big hole where tenth gag was supposed to be. To make things more stressful, the one who was still mulling it over was Michael Ramirez, the most conservative of the Pulitzer winners. A few of the others assured me I'd never land him. I checked my office email from home hourly throughout the holiday break. Finally, at 1:50 pm on December 25, I received an email from Ramirez saying that yes, he would take the assignment. What a great Christmas present! All the cartoonists got their work in on time, and I made the printer's deadline with hours to spare. — *Sam Viviano*

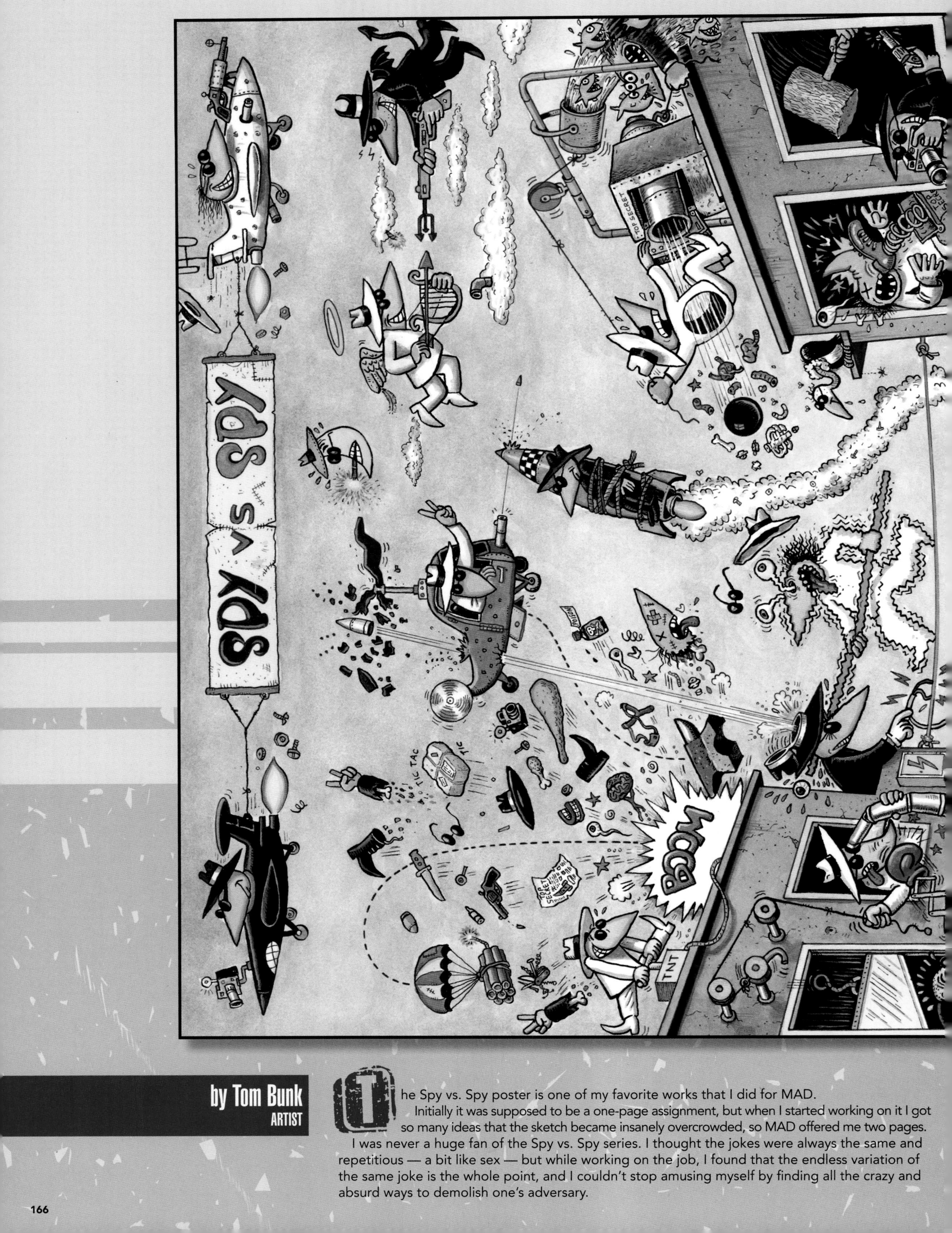
SPY vs SPY
BOOM
TNT
TOP SECRET
TIC TAC

by Tom Bunk
ARTIST

The Spy vs. Spy poster is one of my favorite works that I did for MAD.

Initially it was supposed to be a one-page assignment, but when I started working on it I got so many ideas that the sketch became insanely overcrowded, so MAD offered me two pages.

I was never a huge fan of the Spy vs. Spy series. I thought the jokes were always the same and repetitious — a bit like sex — but while working on the job, I found that the endless variation of the same joke is the whole point, and I couldn't stop amusing myself by finding all the crazy and absurd ways to demolish one's adversary.

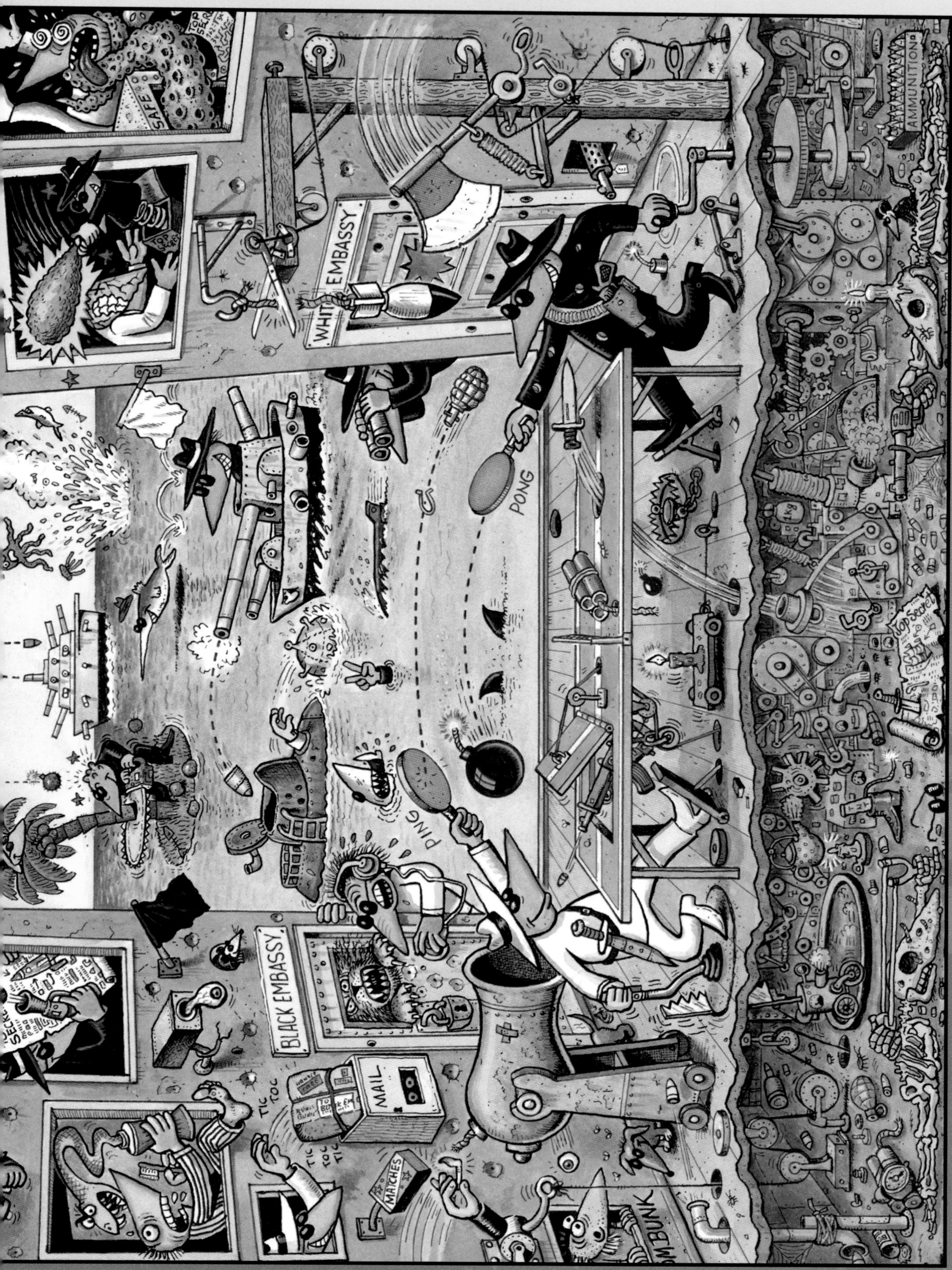
SAFE
AMMUNITION
WHITE EMBASSY
PONG
PING
BLACK EMBASSY
MAIL
MATCHES
TIC TOC
TIC TOC

MAD PRESENTS SPY VS. SPY/JANUARY 2011

In order for the activities to take place I designed an appropriate background and arranged them so that the perpetrator-Spy would become at the same time the victim, and vice versa, in a *circulus vitiosus* kind of way. Then through coloring and shading, the piece really took off and became alive. The pleasant and superb coloring is another reason why I consider this my favorite work.

When I delivered the art to MAD, everybody loved it, especially Editor John Ficarra. He said, "Bill Gaines would have loved it; he would have paid you twice, if he were alive." How convenient.

In the end, it was made into a one-piece centerfold poster and for me, that's like being paid twice.

Still, next time I go to heaven, I'll definitely check with Bill.

EDITOR'S PICK

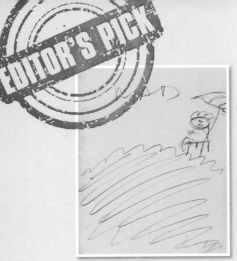

6/4/10 John Ficarra's rough sketch kicks things off

SPECIAL OIL SPILL ISSUE
MAD

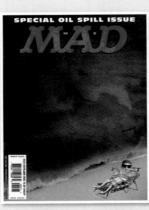

6/4/10 Sam creates a digital comp to give a feel for the final cover

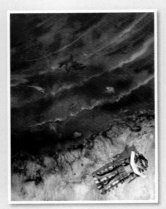

6/21/10 Mark Fredrickson starts out by trying an overhead view

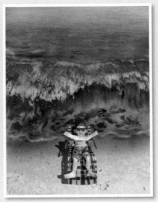

6/22/10 He then gives us a front view with Alfred facing the reader

SPECIAL OIL SPILL ISSUE
MAD

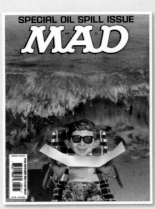

6/22/10 We see how the front view looks more closely cropped

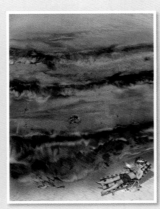

6/22/10 Mark decides to go back to our original composition.

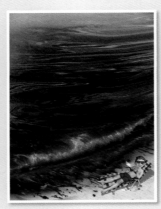

6/22/10 He revamps his rendering of the oil-soaked waves

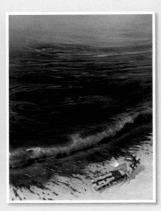

7/1/10 This version is labeled "More Progress" by Mark

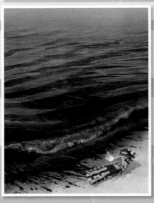

7/7/10 Waves have been added to the larger body of oily water

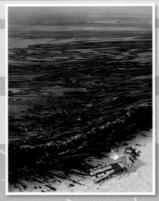

7/14/10 We receive Mark's finished art and hail it as a masterpiece...

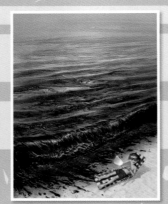

7/15/10 ...until he sends us this revamped version the next day

OUR SLICKEST ISSUE YET!
MAD

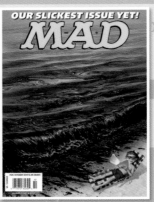

7/15/10 The final cover, with type design by Ryan Flanders

Nothing stresses me out like cover meetings. Coming up with a great cover for MAD is not an easy task, and there are instances in which we've had daily meetings for several weeks before arriving at the right idea. Even when inspiration hits quickly, there's still the intensive process of comping up the cover to iron out all the details, assigning it to an illustrator, and working with him to achieve exactly what we're looking for.

The cover of MAD #505 was inspired by the Deepwater Horizon oil spill in the Gulf of Mexico, and the basic idea came to John Ficarra pretty quickly. He pictured Alfred E. Neuman on a beach, sunning himself, as a huge wave of oil came rushing in to engulf him. I loved the idea at first sight, thinking a cover that was 80% oil with a little sunbathing Alfred in the corner would make a great design, and set off to comp it up, using photographic imagery borrowed from the internet.

Once that was given the go-ahead, I contacted Mark Fredrickson, our regular cover artist and a Photoshop wizard. He played around with the idea at first, trying different points of view, until he settled on something very close to my comp. From there it was three weeks of constant back-and-forth, as Mark labored to create a sea of petroleum that was not only convincing, but in its own oily way beautiful to look at. Hardly a day went by that we didn't receive at least one new version that was slightly different from the last.

Mark is such a perfectionist that, after we accepted his finished artwork — feeling we had a masterpiece on our hands — he worked through the night to come up with a totally overhauled (and even more impressive) rendering. It didn't stop there; after the issue had been printed and bound, Mark called me to ask if it was too late to tighten up a few details! (Yes, Mark, it was too late.) — *Sam Viviano*

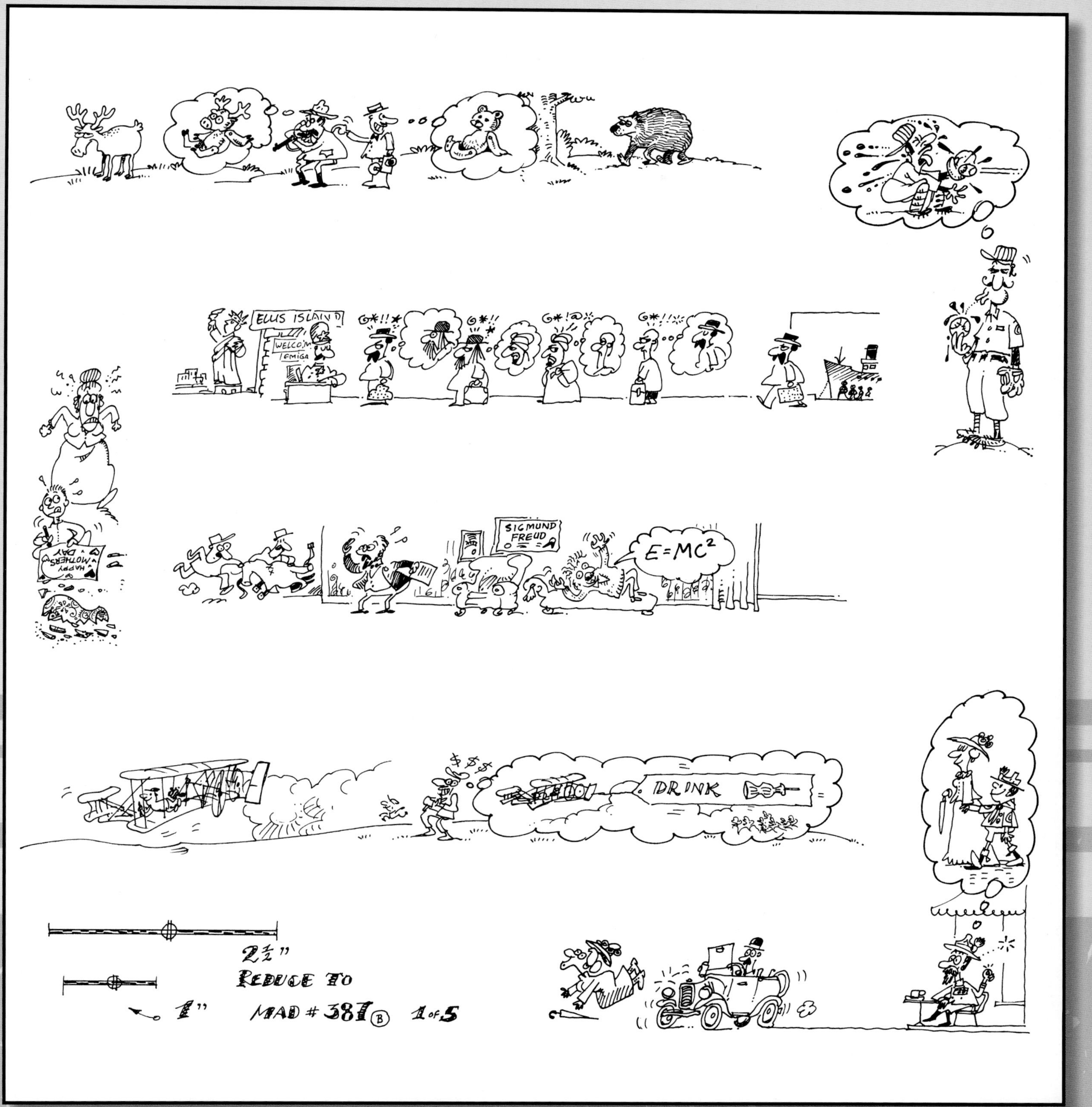

ELLIS ISLAND
SIGMUND FREUD
E=MC²
DRINK
HAPPY MOTHERS DAY
2½"
REDUCE TO
1"
MAD # 387 B 1 of 5

by Patrick Merrell
WRITER/ARTIST

One day in 1999, I was in the MAD art room when a batch of Sergio Aragonés' "MAD Marginals" drawings came in. He sends in four or five pages of these wordless drawings for each issue. At the time, Editor Nick Meglin would look them over and initial the approved cartoons. The art staff would then scatter them about the magazine wherever they fit (reduced to 60% of their original size).

This particular batch was a little different. It was destined for issue #387, which had an eight-page cover article called "MAD Regurgitates the 20th Century." All of the Marginals matched that theme, depicting famous 20th-century events.

Sergio is one of the all-time great cartoonists — the stuff just oozes out of him — and he's a master of these pantomime drawings that tell a funny story in a microscopic space with almost no words. Seeing this special batch, I decided I needed to have one of the original pages. I picked out a favorite and arranged to buy it.

Only two of these seven cartoons were used in the magazine. The E=mc² cartoon appeared on page eight and the immigration cartoon appeared on page 19. The others are making their debut in this book. Lucky you.

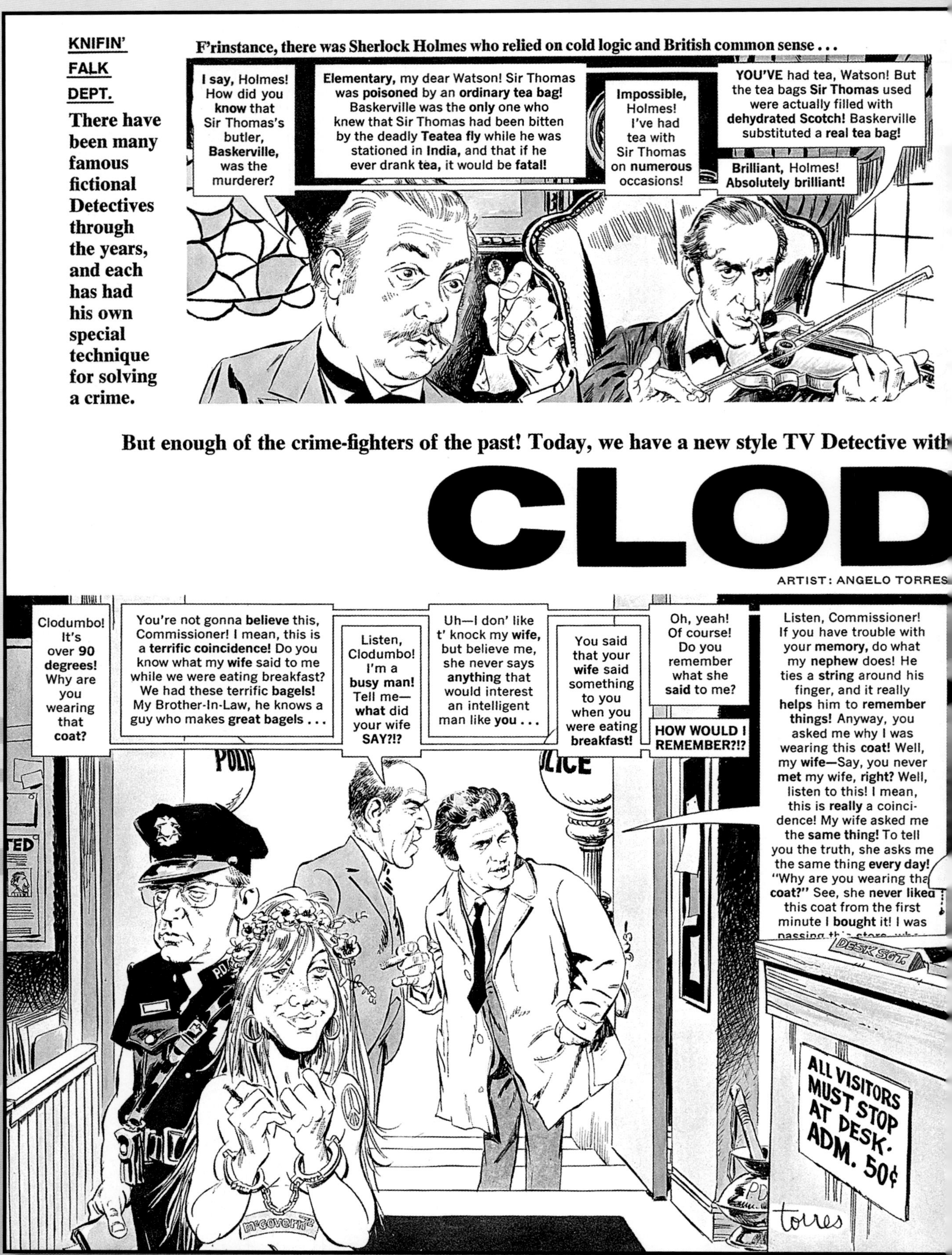
KNIFIN' FALK DEPT.
There have been many famous fictional Detectives through the years, and each has had his own special technique for solving a crime.
F'rinstance, there was Sherlock Holmes who relied on cold logic and British common sense . . .
I say, Holmes! How did you know that Sir Thomas's butler, Baskerville, was the murderer?
Elementary, my dear Watson! Sir Thomas was poisoned by an ordinary tea bag! Baskerville was the only one who knew that Sir Thomas had been bitten by the deadly Teatea fly while he was stationed in India, and that if he ever drank tea, it would be fatal!
Impossible, Holmes! I've had tea with Sir Thomas on numerous occasions!
YOU'VE had tea, Watson! But the tea bags Sir Thomas used were actually filled with dehydrated Scotch! Baskerville substituted a real tea bag!
Brilliant, Holmes! Absolutely brilliant!
But enough of the crime-fighters of the past! Today, we have a new style TV Detective with
CLOD
ARTIST: ANGELO TORRES
Clodumbo! It's over 90 degrees! Why are you wearing that coat?
You're not gonna believe this, Commissioner! I mean, this is a terrific coincidence! Do you know what my wife said to me while we were eating breakfast? We had these terrific bagels! My Brother-In-Law, he knows a guy who makes great bagels . . .
Listen, Clodumbo! I'm a busy man! Tell me—what did your wife SAY?!?
Uh—I don' like t' knock my wife, but believe me, she never says anything that would interest an intelligent man like you . . .
You said that your wife said something to you when you were eating breakfast!
Oh, yeah! Of course! Do you remember what she said to me?
HOW WOULD I REMEMBER?!?
Listen, Commissioner! If you have trouble with your memory, do what my nephew does! He ties a string around his finger, and it really helps him to remember things! Anyway, you asked me why I was wearing this coat! Well, my wife—Say, you never met my wife, right? Well, listen to this! I mean, this is really a coincidence! My wife asked me the same thing! To tell you the truth, she asks me the same thing every day! "Why are you wearing tha coat?" See, she never liked this coat from the first minute I bought it! I was
POLIC
LICE
DESK SGT.
ALL VISITORS MUST STOP AT DESK. ADM. 50¢
McGOVERN '72
torres

by Lou Silverstone
WRITER

"Yecch" is the MAD word for things that are stupid, that suck, that stink and are boring, which describes most TV shows. *Columbo* was different; it was the kind of show I would watch even if I wasn't spoofing it for MAD. Naturally, I begged and pleaded with the MAD editors to spoof it. I promised to write a masterpiece and was finally given the okay to do *Columbo*.

I said to my faithful typewriter, "Don't fail me now!" (So I talked to my typewriter, big deal! Cowboys talk to their horses and gun nuts talk to their guns, so why can't a writer talk to his

There was Charlie Chan with his inscrutable reasoning . . .

Gee, Pop! This is a **tough case!** There are **no** fingerprints on the murder weapon!

That is **correct,** Number One Son, Which reminds me of **old Chinese** proverb: "Man who wear **gloves** no leave finger smears!" Honorable **Rocky** here is **only** one wearing **gloves** . . . therefore **HE** is **murderer!**

Let's go, Rocky . . .

And there was Mike Hammer with his American approach . . .

BLAM BLAM

is own unique method of solving cases. You'll see what we mean as we take a MAD look at . . .

UMBO

WRITE: LOU SILVERSTONE

Oh-oh! It looks like the Commissioner's in **very serious trouble!**

Is he being **attacked** by a gang of hoods?

Much **worse!** He's having a conversation with **Clodumbo!**

Quick! Assign Clodumbo to a **murder case!**

There hasn't been a murder case **reported** today!

Then go out and **commit** one before we have to commit the **Commissioner!**

Good news, Captain! We just received a report of a **homicide!**

The victim was a **male Caucasian,** age 35! He was killed about an **hour** ago by a blow on the **head!**

Did **you** draw this? This is **very good!** I always **wanted** to learn to draw! But I can't even draw a **straight line!**

STOP CRIME SCENE

MAD #156/JANUARY 1973

typewriter? For you young readers, a typewriter was an instrument used for writing way back in the 1970's, B.C. — Before Computers.) But I digress.

My typewriter didn't fail me. Columbo himself, Peter Falk, and the creators of the series, Richard Levinson and William Link, loved our satire. And Angelo Torres did one hell of a job illustrating the article. He really aced it — a perfect 10!

Angelo and I worked on many TV satires together, but I always felt there was something special about our "Clodumbo." It still makes me laugh. This former member of "The Usual Gang of Idiots" picks "Clodumbo" as his all-time favorite MAD article. Excluding, of course, articles by Al Jaffee and Don Martin.

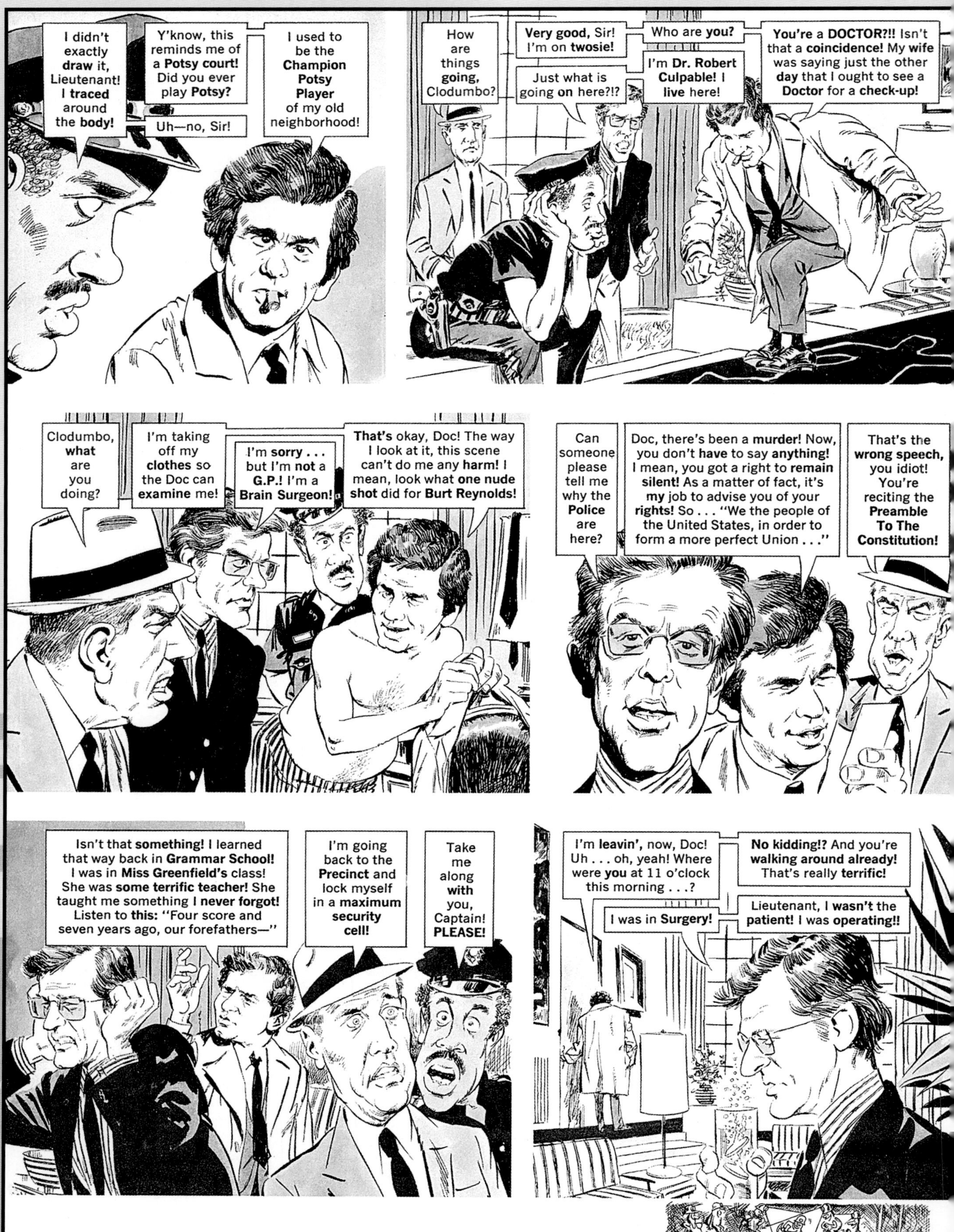
I didn't exactly **draw** it, Lieutenant! **I traced** around the **body!**
Y'know, this reminds me of a **Potsy court!** Did you ever play **Potsy?**
Uh—no, Sir!
I used to be the **Champion Potsy Player** of my old neighborhood!
How are things **going,** Clodumbo?
Very good, Sir! I'm on **twosie!**
Just what is going **on** here?!?
Who are **you?**
I'm **Dr. Robert Culpable!** I **live** here!
You're a DOCTOR?!! Isn't that a **coincidence!** My **wife** was saying just the other **day** that I ought to see a **Doctor** for a **check-up!**
Clodumbo, **what** are you doing?
I'm taking off my **clothes** so the Doc can **examine** me!
I'm **sorry . . .** but I'm **not** a **G.P.!** I'm a **Brain Surgeon!**
That's okay, Doc! The way I look at it, this scene can't do me any **harm!** I mean, look what **one nude shot** did for **Burt Reynolds!**
Can someone please tell me why the **Police** are here?
Doc, there's been a **murder!** Now, you don't **have** to say **anything!** I mean, you got a right to **remain silent!** As a matter of fact, it's **my** job to advise you of your **rights!** So . . . "We the people of the United States, in order to form a more perfect Union . . ."
That's the **wrong speech,** you idiot! You're reciting the **Preamble To The Constitution!**
Isn't that **something!** I learned that way back in **Grammar School!** I was in **Miss Greenfield's** class! She was **some terrific teacher!** She taught me something **I never forgot!** Listen to **this:** "Four score and seven years ago, our forefathers—"
I'm going back to the **Precinct** and lock myself in a **maximum security cell!**
Take me along **with** you, Captain! **PLEASE!**
I'm **leavin',** now, Doc! Uh . . . oh, yeah! Where were **you** at 11 o'clock this morning . . . ?
I was in **Surgery!**
No kidding!? And you're **walking around already!** That's really **terrific!**
Lieutenant, I **wasn't** the **patient!** I was **operating!!**

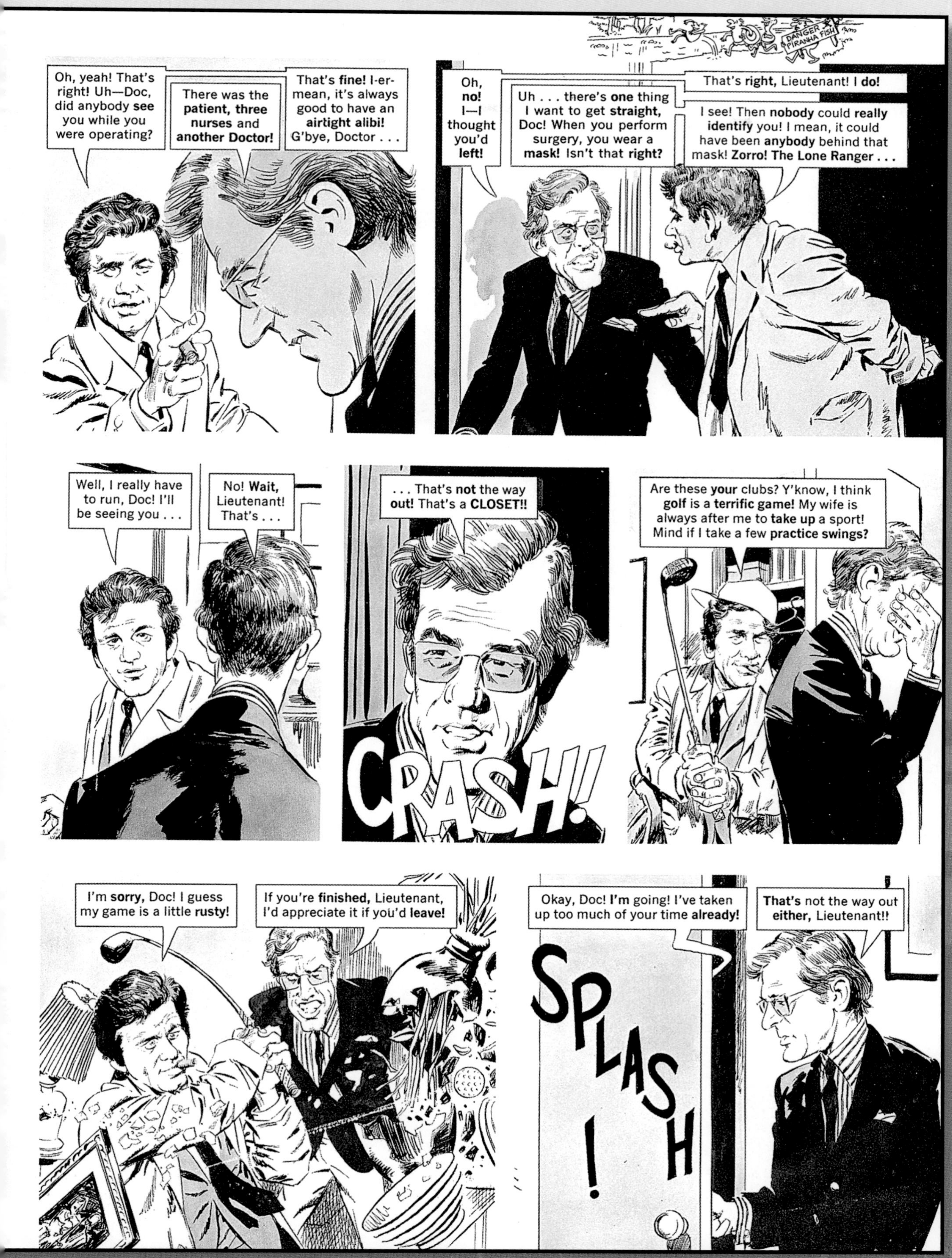
DANGER PIRANHA FISH
Oh, yeah! That's right! Uh—Doc, did anybody see you while you were operating?
There was the patient, three nurses and another Doctor!
That's fine! I-er-mean, it's always good to have an airtight alibi! G'bye, Doctor . . .
Oh, no! I—I thought you'd left!
Uh . . . there's one thing I want to get straight, Doc! When you perform surgery, you wear a mask! Isn't that right?
That's right, Lieutenant! I do!
I see! Then nobody could really identify you! I mean, it could have been anybody behind that mask! Zorro! The Lone Ranger . . .
Well, I really have to run, Doc! I'll be seeing you . . .
No! Wait, Lieutenant! That's . . .
. . . That's not the way out! That's a CLOSET!!
CRASH!!
Are these your clubs? Y'know, I think golf is a terrific game! My wife is always after me to take up a sport! Mind if I take a few practice swings?
I'm sorry, Doc! I guess my game is a little rusty!
If you're finished, Lieutenant, I'd appreciate it if you'd leave!
Okay, Doc! I'm going! I've taken up too much of your time already!
SPLASH!
That's not the way out either, Lieutenant!!

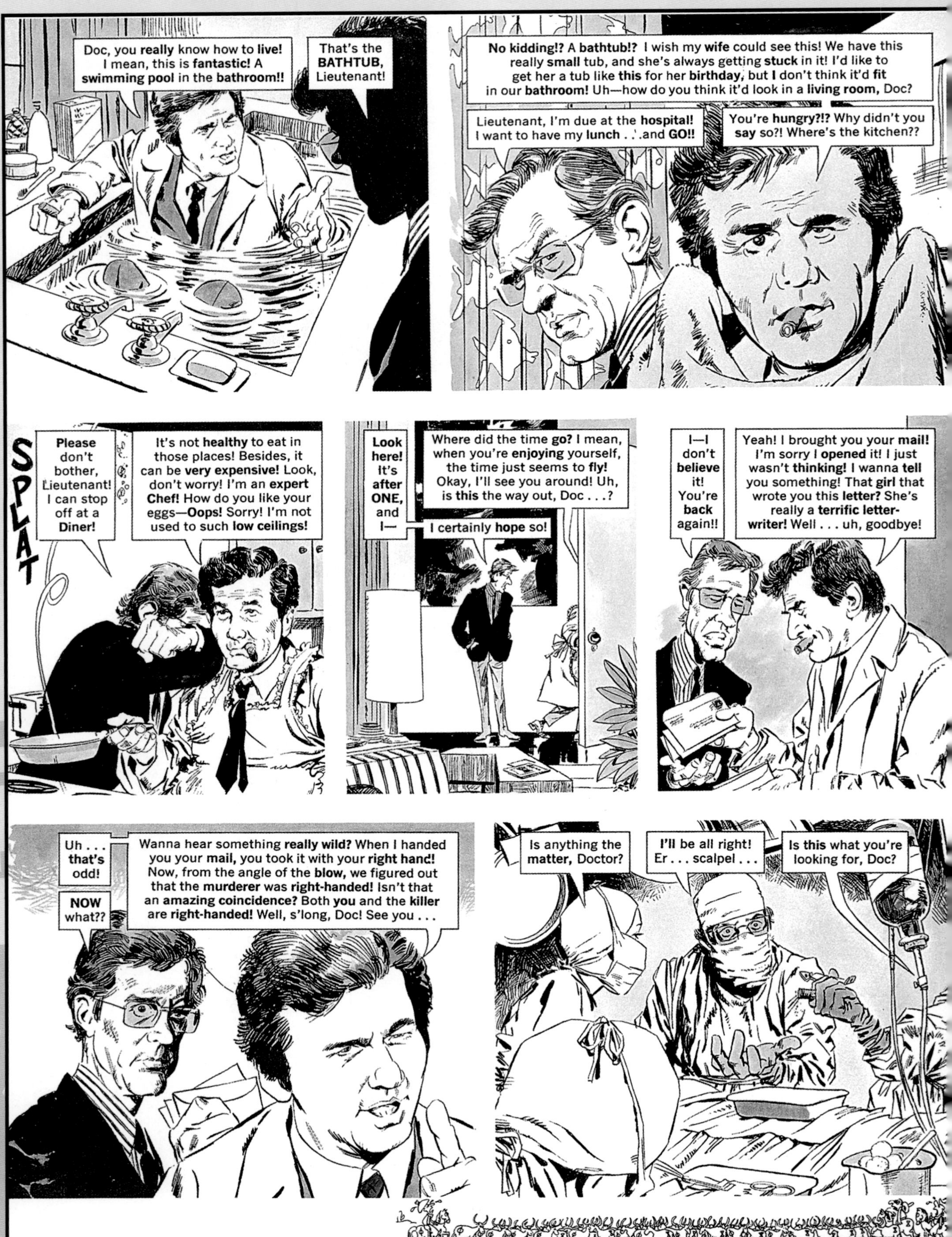

Doc, you really know how to live! I mean, this is fantastic! A swimming pool in the bathroom!!
That's the BATHTUB, Lieutenant!
No kidding!? A bathtub!? I wish my wife could see this! We have this really small tub, and she's always getting stuck in it! I'd like to get her a tub like this for her birthday, but I don't think it'd fit in our bathroom! Uh—how do you think it'd look in a living room, Doc?
Lieutenant, I'm due at the hospital! I want to have my lunch . . .and GO!!
You're hungry?!? Why didn't you say so?! Where's the kitchen??
SPLAT
Please don't bother, Lieutenant! I can stop off at a Diner!
It's not healthy to eat in those places! Besides, it can be very expensive! Look, don't worry! I'm an expert Chef! How do you like your eggs—Oops! Sorry! I'm not used to such low ceilings!
Look here! It's after ONE, and I—
Where did the time go? I mean, when you're enjoying yourself, the time just seems to fly! Okay, I'll see you around! Uh, is this the way out, Doc . . .?
I certainly hope so!
I—I don't believe it! You're back again!!
Yeah! I brought you your mail! I'm sorry I opened it! I just wasn't thinking! I wanna tell you something! That girl that wrote you this letter? She's really a terrific letter-writer! Well . . . uh, goodbye!
Uh . . . that's odd!
NOW what??
Wanna hear something really wild? When I handed you your mail, you took it with your right hand! Now, from the angle of the blow, we figured out that the murderer was right-handed! Isn't that an amazing coincidence? Both you and the killer are right-handed! Well, s'long, Doc! See you . . .
Is anything the matter, Doctor?
I'll be all right! Er . . . scalpel . . .
Is this what you're looking for, Doc?

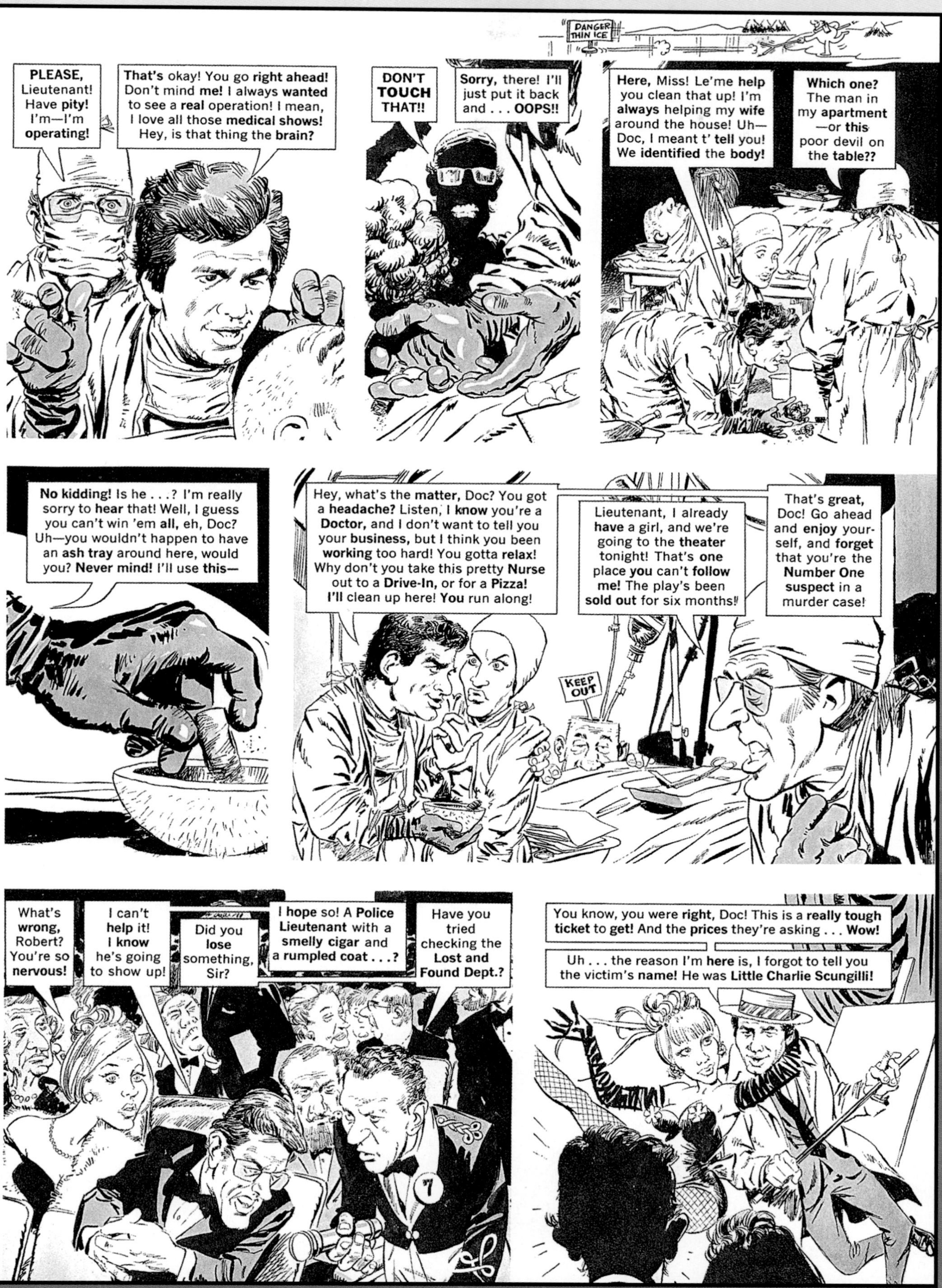

DANGER THIN ICE
PLEASE, Lieutenant! Have pity! I'm—I'm operating!
That's okay! You go right ahead! Don't mind me! I always wanted to see a real operation! I mean, I love all those medical shows! Hey, is that thing the brain?
DON'T TOUCH THAT!!
Sorry, there! I'll just put it back and . . . OOPS!!
Here, Miss! Le'me help you clean that up! I'm always helping my wife around the house! Uh—Doc, I meant t' tell you! We identified the body!
Which one? The man in my apartment —or this poor devil on the table??
No kidding! Is he . . .? I'm really sorry to hear that! Well, I guess you can't win 'em all, eh, Doc? Uh—you wouldn't happen to have an ash tray around here, would you? Never mind! I'll use this—
Hey, what's the matter, Doc? You got a headache? Listen, I know you're a Doctor, and I don't want to tell you your business, but I think you been working too hard! You gotta relax! Why don't you take this pretty Nurse out to a Drive-In, or for a Pizza! I'll clean up here! You run along!
Lieutenant, I already have a girl, and we're going to the theater tonight! That's one place you can't follow me! The play's been sold out for six months!
That's great, Doc! Go ahead and enjoy yourself, and forget that you're the Number One suspect in a murder case!
KEEP OUT
What's wrong, Robert? You're so nervous!
I can't help it! I know he's going to show up!
Did you lose something, Sir?
I hope so! A Police Lieutenant with a smelly cigar and a rumpled coat . . .?
Have you tried checking the Lost and Found Dept.?
You know, you were right, Doc! This is a really tough ticket to get! And the prices they're asking . . . Wow!
Uh . . . the reason I'm here is, I forgot to tell you the victim's name! He was Little Charlie Scungilli!

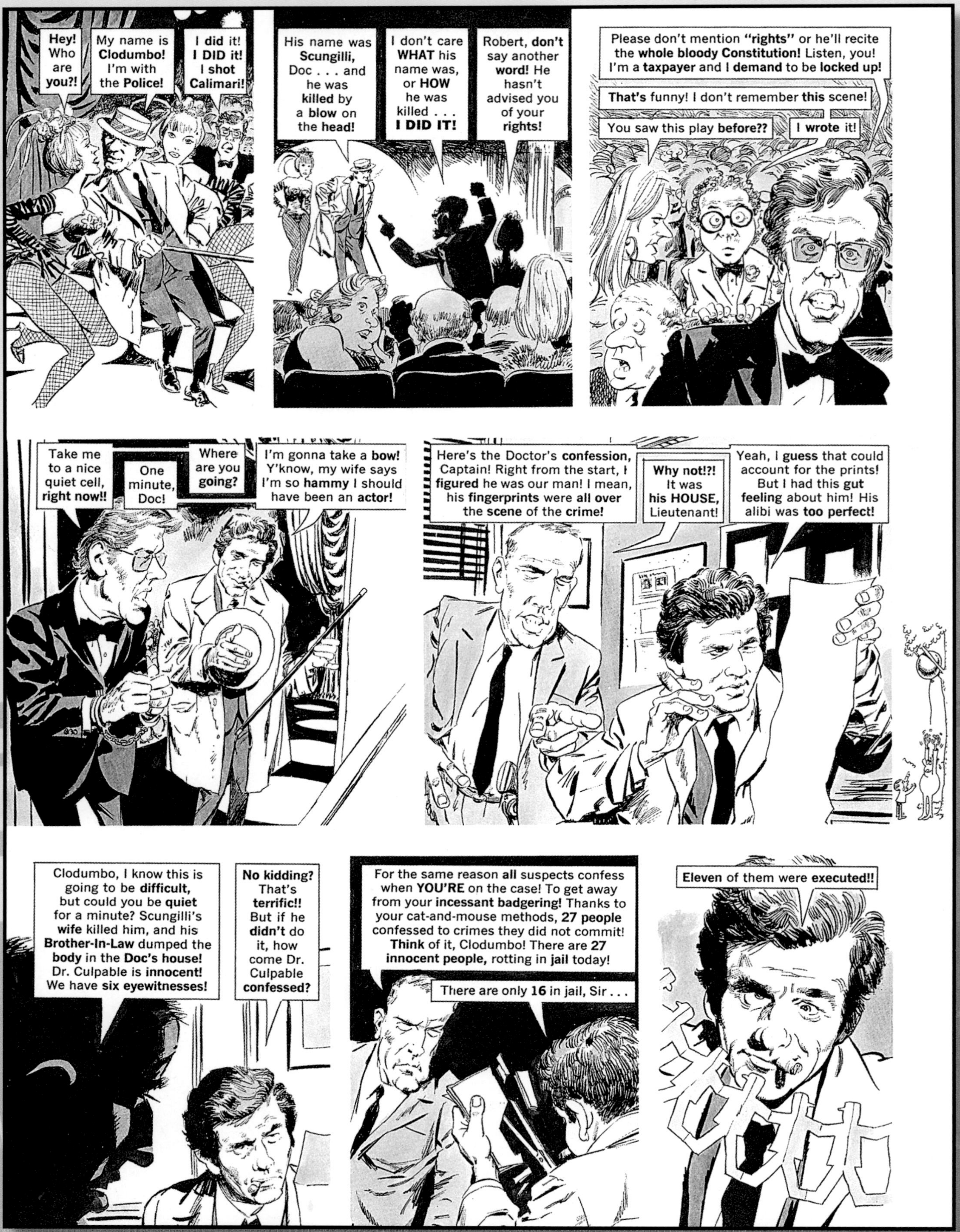
Hey! Who are you?!
My name is Clodumbo! I'm with the Police!
I did it! I DID it! I shot Calimari!
His name was Scungilli, Doc . . . and he was killed by a blow on the head!
I don't care WHAT his name was, or HOW he was killed . . . I DID IT!
Robert, don't say another word! He hasn't advised you of your rights!
Please don't mention "rights" or he'll recite the whole bloody Constitution! Listen, you! I'm a taxpayer and I demand to be locked up!
That's funny! I don't remember this scene!
You saw this play before??
I wrote it!
Take me to a nice quiet cell, right now!!
One minute, Doc!
Where are you going?
I'm gonna take a bow! Y'know, my wife says I'm so hammy I should have been an actor!
Here's the Doctor's confession, Captain! Right from the start, I figured he was our man! I mean, his fingerprints were all over the scene of the crime!
Why not!?! It was his HOUSE, Lieutenant!
Yeah, I guess that could account for the prints! But I had this gut feeling about him! His alibi was too perfect!
Clodumbo, I know this is going to be difficult, but could you be quiet for a minute? Scungilli's wife killed him, and his Brother-In-Law dumped the body in the Doc's house! Dr. Culpable is innocent! We have six eyewitnesses!
No kidding? That's terrific!! But if he didn't do it, how come Dr. Culpable confessed?
For the same reason all suspects confess when YOU'RE on the case! To get away from your incessant badgering! Thanks to your cat-and-mouse methods, 27 people confessed to crimes they did not commit! Think of it, Clodumbo! There are 27 innocent people, rotting in jail today!
There are only 16 in jail, Sir . . .
Eleven of them were executed!!

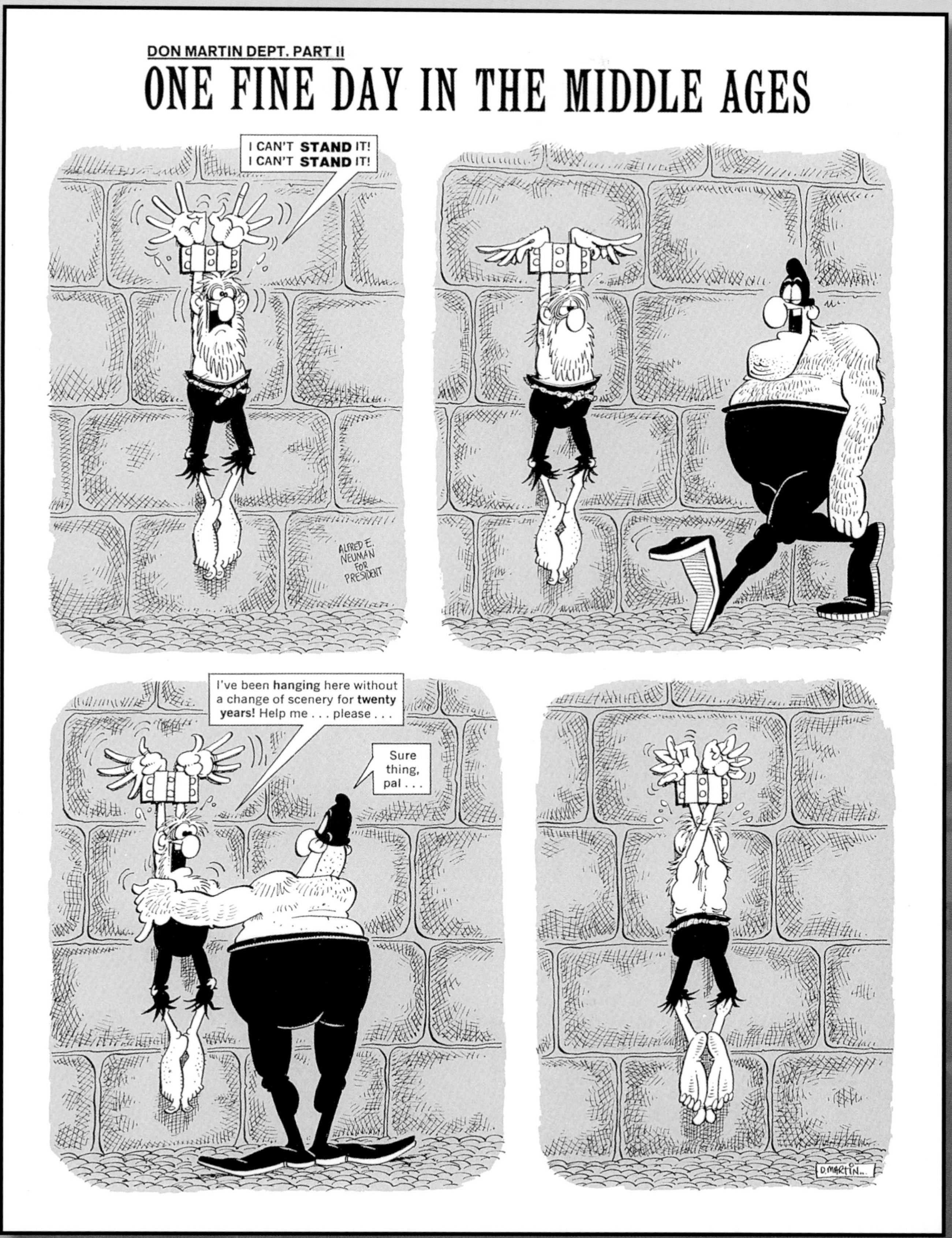
DON MARTIN DEPT. PART II
ONE FINE DAY IN THE MIDDLE AGES
I CAN'T STAND IT! I CAN'T STAND IT!
ALFRED E. NEUMAN FOR PRESIDENT
I've been hanging here without a change of scenery for twenty years! Help me . . . please . . .
Sure thing, pal . . .
D. MARTIN..

MAD #217/SEPTEMBER 1980

by Christopher Baldwin

WRITER/ARTIST

This strip. I remember reading this strip. The utter horror of it, and yet I am still laughing.

20 years of hanging from wall-mounted manacles — not only can you feel the discomfort, but the prisoner's pathetic plea of simply wanting a change of scenery…it was all so heartbreaking.

I'll never know if the prison guard was being malicious or just simpleminded, but seeing the twisted back muscles in the final panel — and knowing that for the next 20 years the prisoner would see nothing but the wall — left me in peals of laughter.

As a writer of comedy, I will never be fully comfortable with the human tendency to laugh at cruelty. I can only imagine it's a MAD part inside of us, a crazy, babbling mantra: "Thank goodness it's not me, thank goodness it's not me."

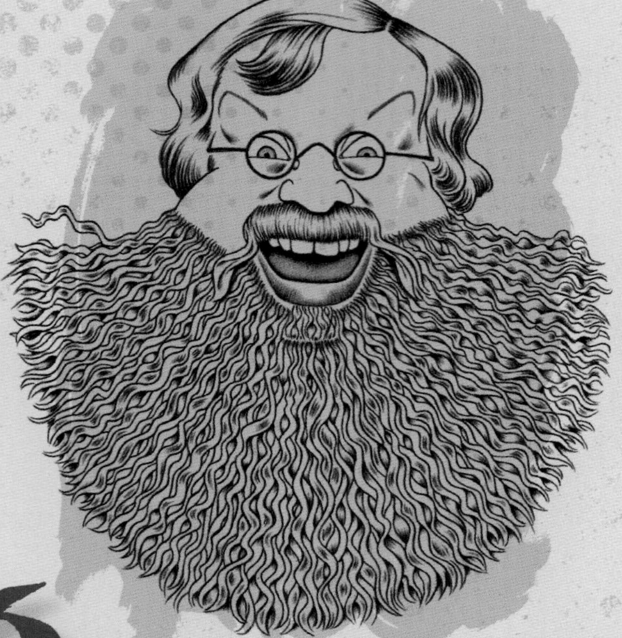

Pendleton Ward

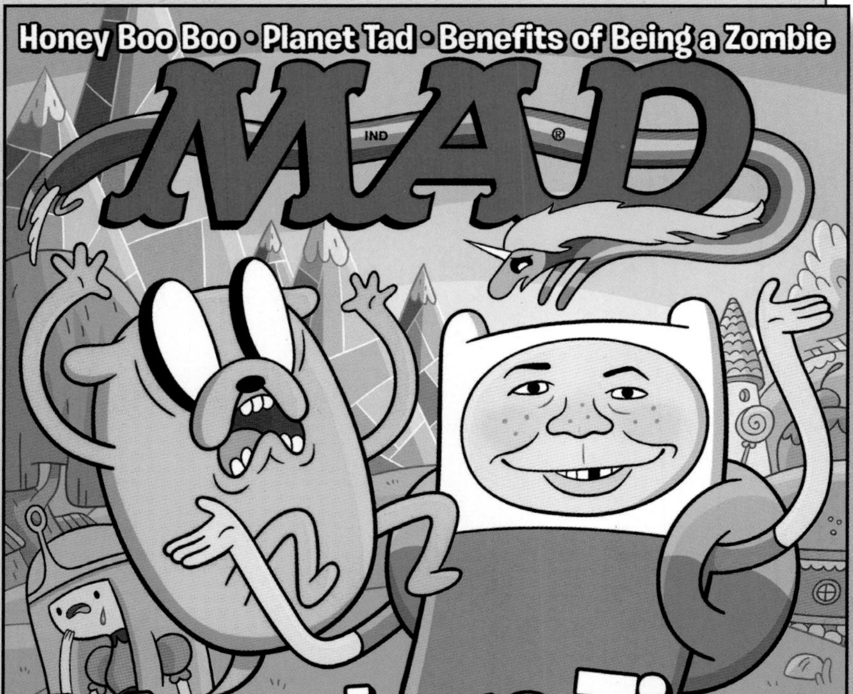
Honey Boo Boo • Planet Tad • Benefits of Being a Zombie
MAD
Adventure Time
One of the 50 Worst Things About Cartoons
#520 APRIL 2013 $5.99 CHEAP!
madmagazine.com
US / CANADA

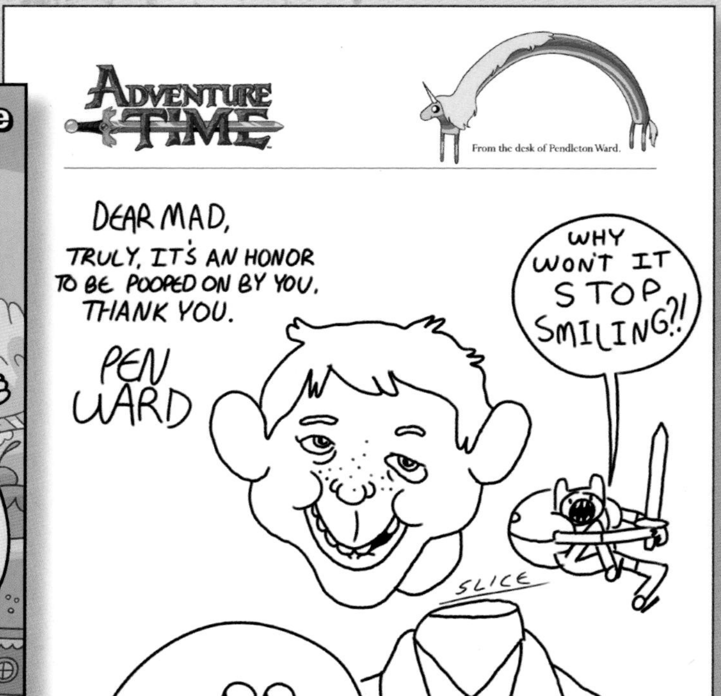
ADVENTURE TIME
From the desk of Pendleton Ward.
DEAR MAD,
TRULY, IT'S AN HONOR
TO BE POOPED ON BY YOU.
THANK YOU.
PEN WARD
WHY WON'T IT STOP SMILING?!
SLICE
IT'S A DEMON, MAN! WE GOTTA BURN IT!!
CARTOON NETWORK STUDIOS

ARTIST: CHRIS HOUGHTON

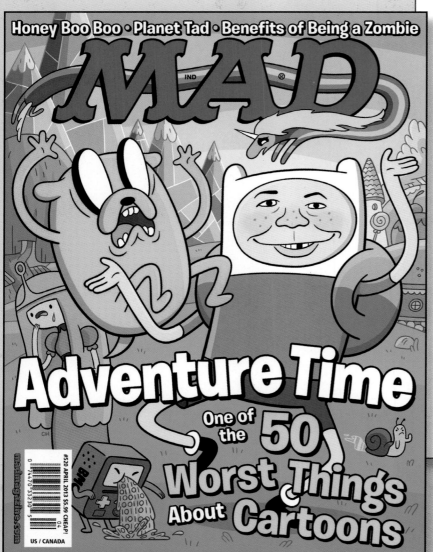

MAD #520/APRIL 2013

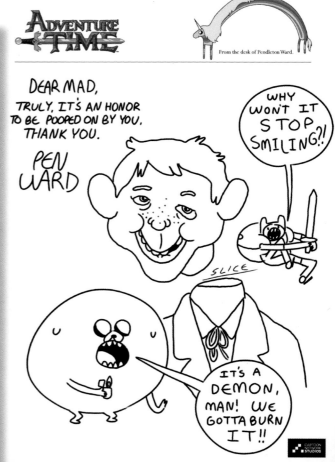

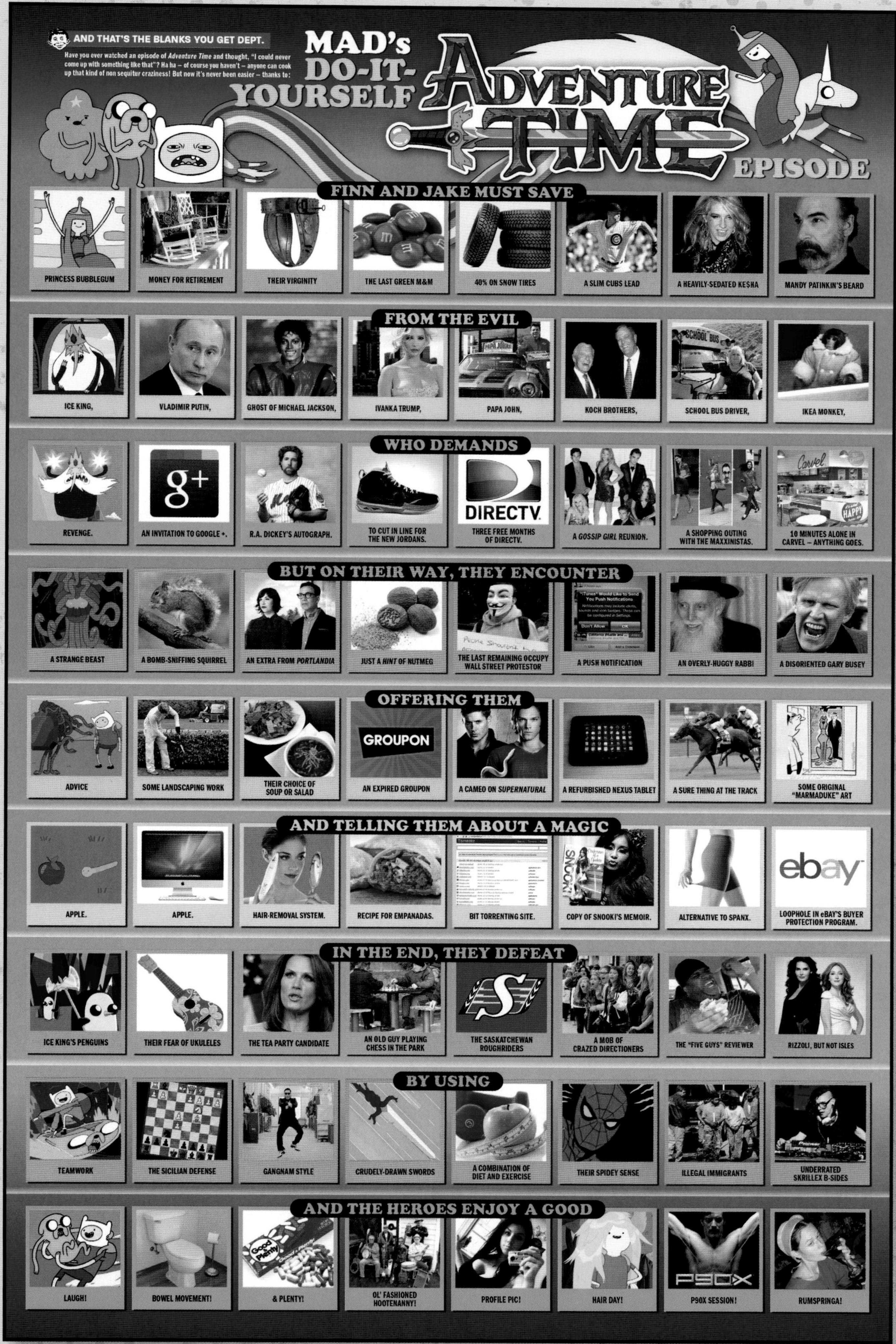
AND THAT'S THE BLANKS YOU GET DEPT.
Have you ever watched an episode of Adventure Time and thought, "I could never come up with something like that"? Ha ha – of course you haven't – anyone can cook up that kind of non sequitur craziness! But now it's never been easier – thanks to:
MAD's DO-IT-YOURSELF ADVENTURE TIME EPISODE
FINN AND JAKE MUST SAVE
PRINCESS BUBBLEGUM
MONEY FOR RETIREMENT
THEIR VIRGINITY
THE LAST GREEN M&M
40% ON SNOW TIRES
A SLIM CUBS LEAD
A HEAVILY-SEDATED KE$HA
MANDY PATINKIN'S BEARD
FROM THE EVIL
ICE KING,
VLADIMIR PUTIN,
GHOST OF MICHAEL JACKSON,
IVANKA TRUMP,
PAPA JOHN,
KOCH BROTHERS,
SCHOOL BUS DRIVER,
IKEA MONKEY,
WHO DEMANDS
REVENGE.
AN INVITATION TO GOOGLE +.
R.A. DICKEY'S AUTOGRAPH.
TO CUT IN LINE FOR THE NEW JORDANS.
THREE FREE MONTHS OF DIRECTV.
A GOSSIP GIRL REUNION.
A SHOPPING OUTING WITH THE MAXXINISTAS.
10 MINUTES ALONE IN CARVEL – ANYTHING GOES.
BUT ON THEIR WAY, THEY ENCOUNTER
A STRANGE BEAST
A BOMB-SNIFFING SQUIRREL
AN EXTRA FROM PORTLANDIA
JUST A HINT OF NUTMEG
THE LAST REMAINING OCCUPY WALL STREET PROTESTOR
A PUSH NOTIFICATION
AN OVERLY-HUGGY RABBI
A DISORIENTED GARY BUSEY
OFFERING THEM
ADVICE
SOME LANDSCAPING WORK
THEIR CHOICE OF SOUP OR SALAD
AN EXPIRED GROUPON
A CAMEO ON SUPERNATURAL
A REFURBISHED NEXUS TABLET
A SURE THING AT THE TRACK
SOME ORIGINAL "MARMADUKE" ART
AND TELLING THEM ABOUT A MAGIC
APPLE.
APPLE.
HAIR-REMOVAL SYSTEM.
RECIPE FOR EMPANADAS.
BIT TORRENTING SITE.
COPY OF SNOOKI'S MEMOIR.
ALTERNATIVE TO SPANX.
LOOPHOLE IN eBAY'S BUYER PROTECTION PROGRAM.
IN THE END, THEY DEFEAT
ICE KING'S PENGUINS
THEIR FEAR OF UKULELES
THE TEA PARTY CANDIDATE
AN OLD GUY PLAYING CHESS IN THE PARK
THE SASKATCHEWAN ROUGHRIDERS
A MOB OF CRAZED DIRECTIONERS
THE "FIVE GUYS" REVIEWER
RIZZOLI, BUT NOT ISLES
BY USING
TEAMWORK
THE SICILIAN DEFENSE
GANGNAM STYLE
CRUDELY-DRAWN SWORDS
A COMBINATION OF DIET AND EXERCISE
THEIR SPIDEY SENSE
ILLEGAL IMMIGRANTS
UNDERRATED SKRILLEX B-SIDES
AND THE HEROES ENJOY A GOOD
LAUGH!
BOWEL MOVEMENT!
& PLENTY!
OL' FASHIONED HOOTENANNY!
PROFILE PIC!
HAIR DAY!
P90X SESSION!
RUMSPRINGA!

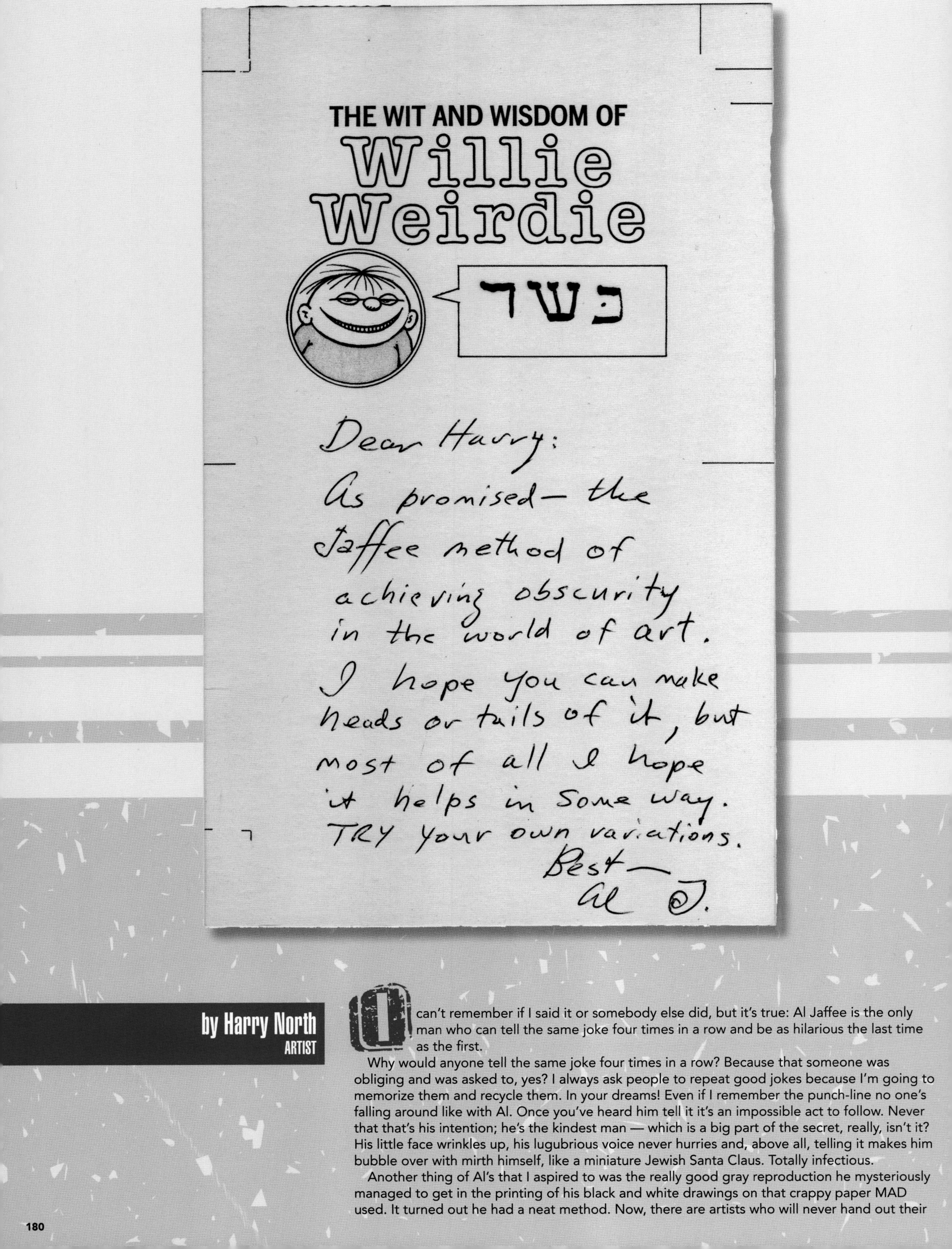
THE WIT AND WISDOM OF
Willie Weirdie
כשר

Dear Harry:
As promised— the Jaffee method of achieving obscurity in the world of art.
I hope you can make heads or tails of it, but most of all I hope it helps in some way.
TRY your own variations.
Best—
Al J.

by Harry North
ARTIST

I can't remember if I said it or somebody else did, but it's true: Al Jaffee is the only man who can tell the same joke four times in a row and be as hilarious the last time as the first.

Why would anyone tell the same joke four times in a row? Because that someone was obliging and was asked to, yes? I always ask people to repeat good jokes because I'm going to memorize them and recycle them. In your dreams! Even if I remember the punch-line no one's falling around like with Al. Once you've heard him tell it it's an impossible act to follow. Never that that's his intention; he's the kindest man — which is a big part of the secret, really, isn't it? His little face wrinkles up, his lugubrious voice never hurries and, above all, telling it makes him bubble over with mirth himself, like a miniature Jewish Santa Claus. Totally infectious.

Another thing of Al's that I aspired to was the really good gray reproduction he mysteriously managed to get in the printing of his black and white drawings on that crappy paper MAD used. It turned out he had a neat method. Now, there are artists who will never hand out their

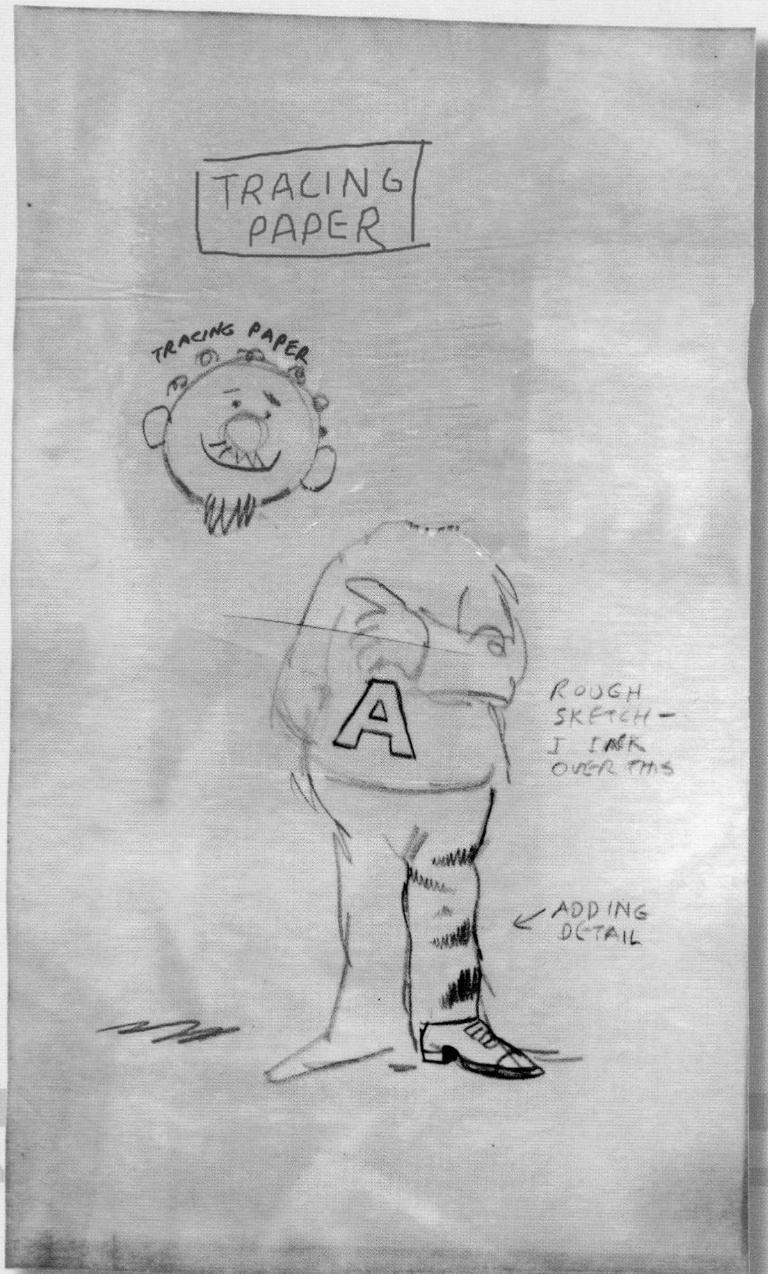
TRACING PAPER
TRACING PAPER
ROUGH SKETCH – I INK OVER THIS
ADDING DETAIL

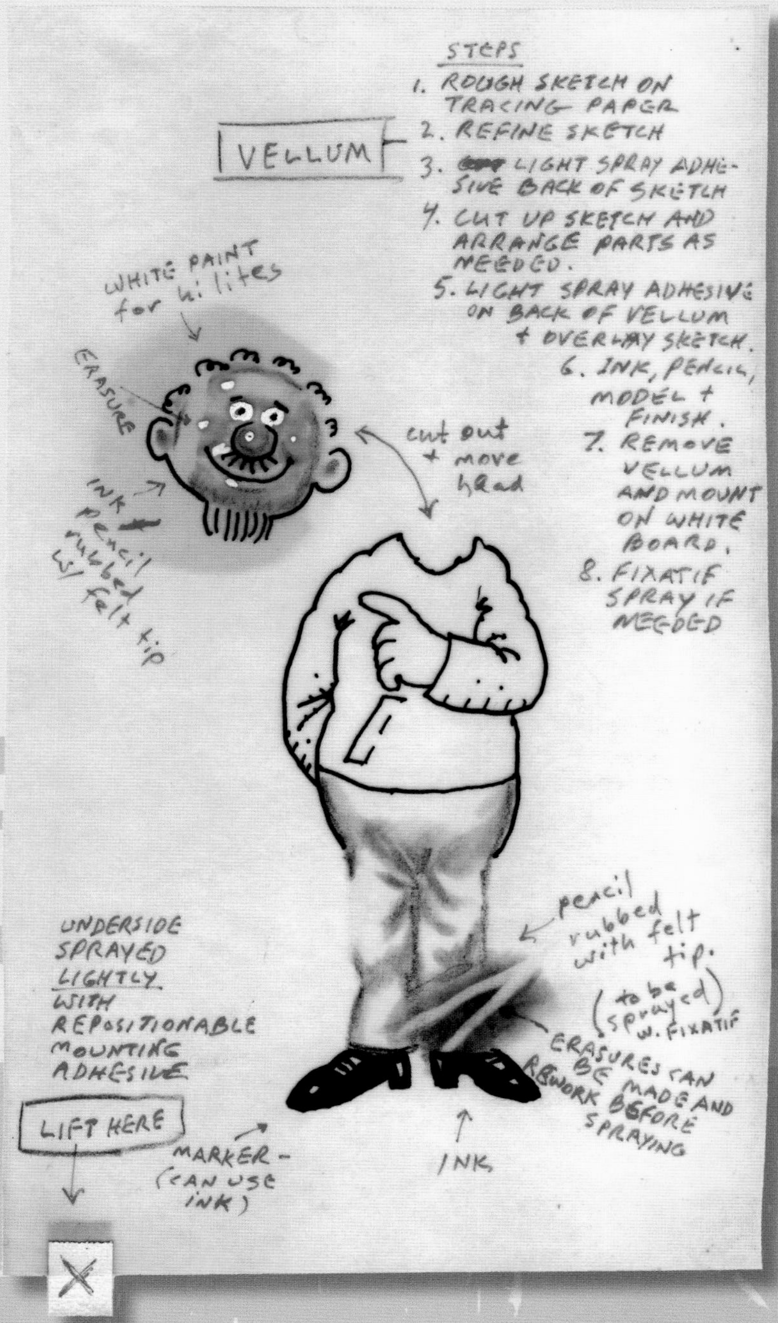
VELLUM
STEPS
1. ROUGH SKETCH ON TRACING PAPER
2. REFINE SKETCH
3. LIGHT SPRAY ADHESIVE BACK OF SKETCH
4. CUT UP SKETCH AND ARRANGE PARTS AS NEEDED.
5. LIGHT SPRAY ADHESIVE ON BACK OF VELLUM & OVERLAY SKETCH.
6. INK, PENCIL, MODEL & FINISH.
7. REMOVE VELLUM AND MOUNT ON WHITE BOARD.
8. FIXATIF SPRAY IF NEEDED
WHITE PAINT for hi lites
ERASURE
INK
pencil rubbed w/ felt tip
cut out & move head
UNDERSIDE SPRAYED LIGHTLY WITH REPOSITIONABLE MOUNTING ADHESIVE
pencil rubbed with felt tip.
(to be sprayed w. FIXATIF)
ERASURES CAN BE MADE AND REWORK BEFORE SPRAYING
LIFT HERE
MARKER – (CAN USE INK)
INK

secrets, but, as you can see above, Al went out of his way to share with me, and even though we don't as a rule send in originals these days (using Photoshop so that everything can be endlessly changed by the damned art director and editor), some of you may still be tactile enough to make use of this blending of pencil and ink technique, so here it is.

Of course, the work of Jaffee's that will be best remembered — and rightly so — is the great volume of Fold-In art from the back covers that would fill a museum. Apart from the concepts, that I hope he got some help with, the sheer illustrative working out and ingenuity was always a delight to mull over. I wonder if anyone didn't try to discern the message before folding the page. I can't imagine, it was half the pleasure. At this point, I don't recall ever actually seeing any of the original Fold-In art when it was available for view in Lenny Brenner's drawers(!). I guess that whenever I went up to the Mad office, I was too busy ogling Mort Drucker pages and begging Al Feldstein to let me draw outside the boxes a bit — that never happened, but then, if the contributors are, so to speak, the accelerator, the editor must be the brake for the bus to get you home.

MAD on TV

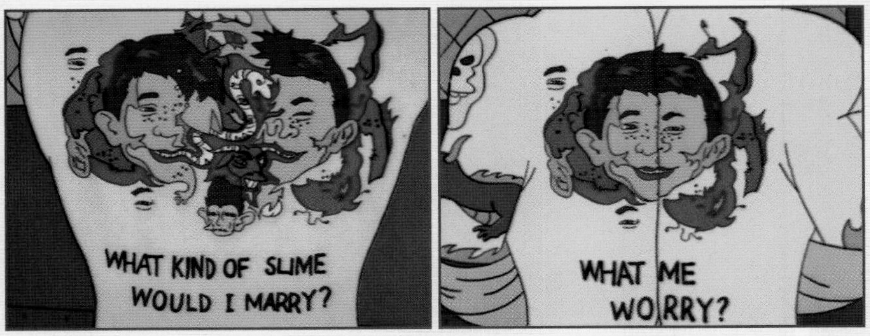
WHAT KIND OF SLIME WOULD I MARRY?
WHAT ME WORRY?

THE SIMPSONS, 1993

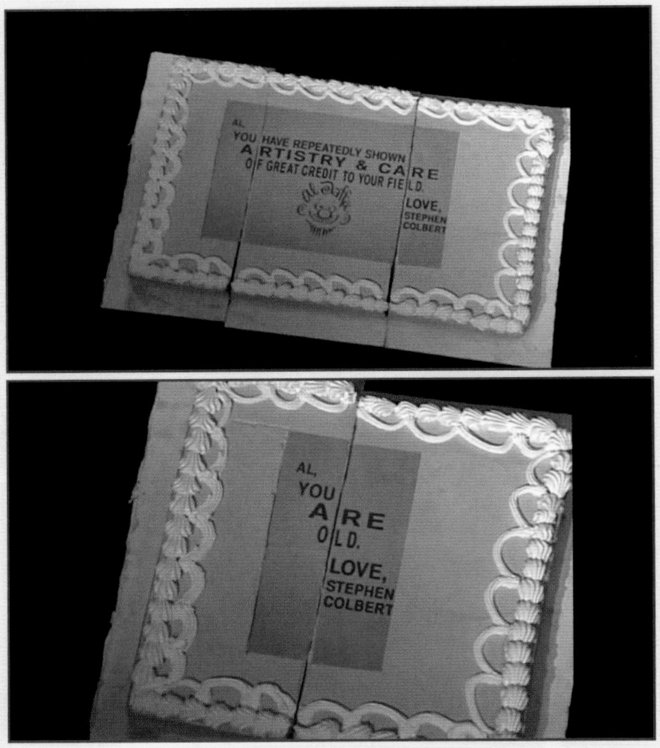
AL, YOU HAVE REPEATEDLY SHOWN ARTISTRY & CARE OF GREAT CREDIT TO YOUR FIELD.
LOVE, STEPHEN COLBERT
AL, YOU ARE OLD.
LOVE, STEPHEN COLBERT

THE COLBERT REPORT, 2006

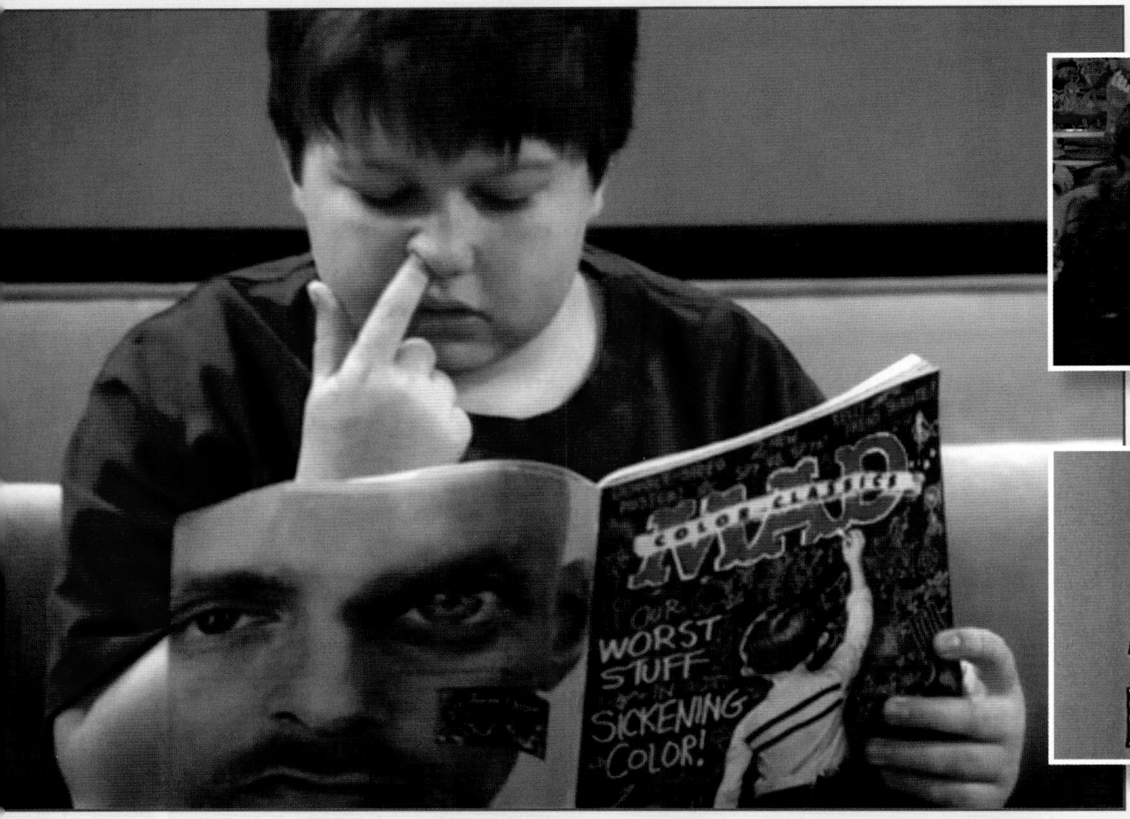
COLOR CLASSICS
MAD
OUR WORST STUFF IN SICKENING COLOR!

TWO AND A HALF MEN, 2004

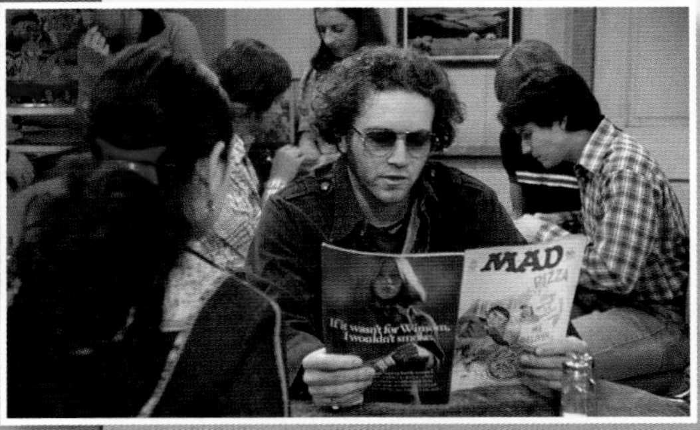
MAD

THAT '70S SHOW, 1999

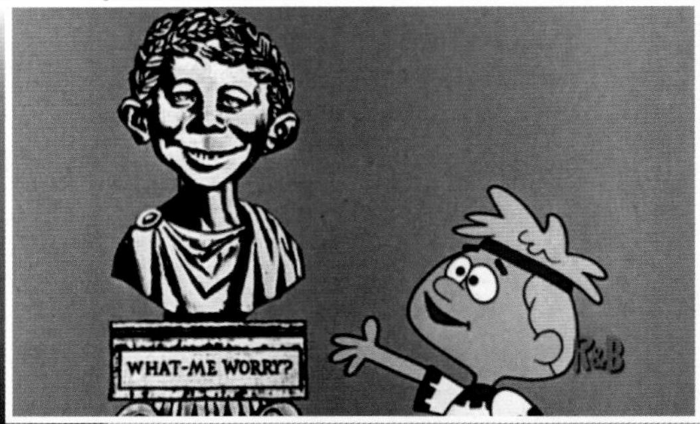
WHAT-ME WORRY?

THE ROCKY AND BULLWINKLE SHOW, 1960

THE LIGHTER SIDE OF...

THE FORCE

ARTIST & WRITER : DAVE BERG

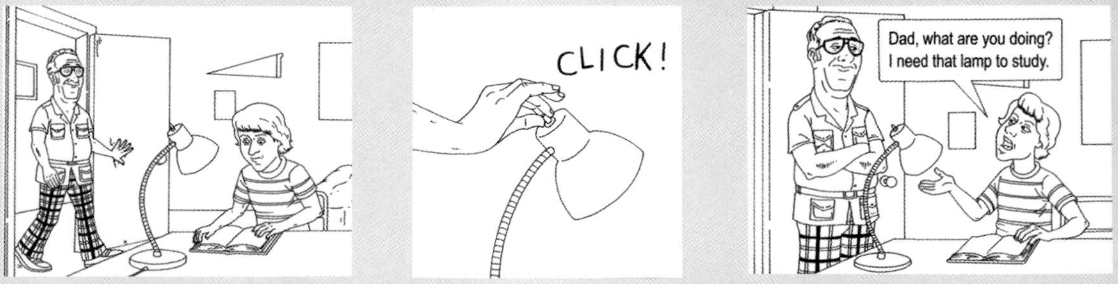
CLICK!
Dad, what are you doing? I need that lamp to study.

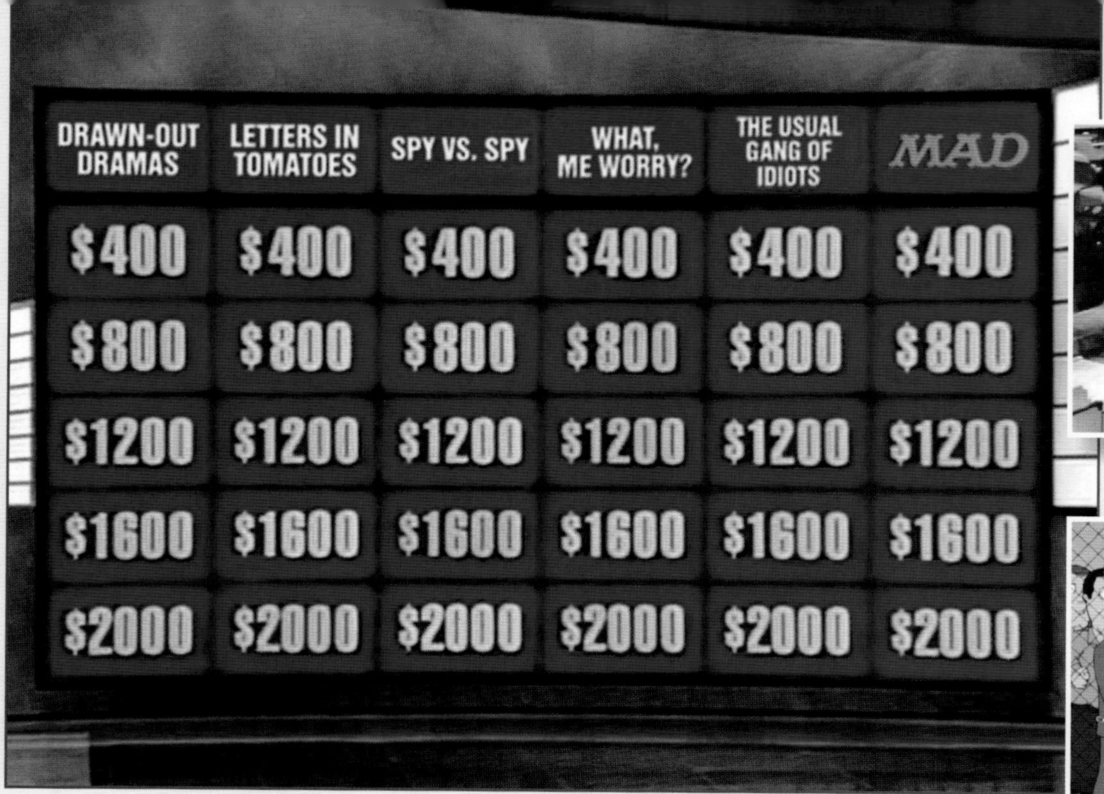

DRAWN-OUT DRAMAS	LETTERS IN TOMATOES	SPY VS. SPY	WHAT, ME WORRY?	THE USUAL GANG OF IDIOTS	MAD
$400	$400	$400	$400	$400	$400
$800	$800	$800	$800	$800	$800
$1200	$1200	$1200	$1200	$1200	$1200
$1600	$1600	$1600	$1600	$1600	$1600
$2000	$2000	$2000	$2000	$2000	$2000

JEOPARDY, 2010

21 JUMP STREET, 1989

THE WONDER YEARS, 1988

FAMILY GUY, 2009

THE DAILY SHOW, 2006

GET SMART, 1968

Sorry, son. Just trying to be a *light saver*.

FAMILY GUY, 2011

MURPHY BROWN, 1988-1998

MANY UNHAPPY RETURNS DEPT.

THE REJEC

WRITER AND ARTIST: TOM HUDSO

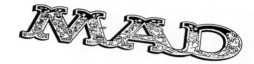

Editor
MAD Magazine
New York, New York

Dear Sir:

Upon bringing to a close my career as an unsuccessful cartoonist I find that my voluminous collection of rejection slips does not include one of yours (see sketch below).

Would you be kind enough to send me a MAD rejection slip and thus complete my collection? Thanks very much.

Sincerely,
Tom Hudson

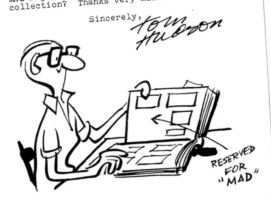

RESERVED FOR "MAD"

MAD

Dear Mr. Hudson:

We found your idea for "Rejection Slips From Various Magazines" highly amusing and have assigned the article to one of our regular writers.
We are pleased to enclose a check in payment.

Cordially,
Albert B. Feldstein
Albert B. Feldstein,
Editor

Editor
MAD Magazine
New York, New York

Dear Sir:

Thanks for the check, but please, please could you spare me one rejection slip?

As my wife would say,"Is my 'slip'showing?"

Haha. (see sketch).

Tom Hudson

MAD

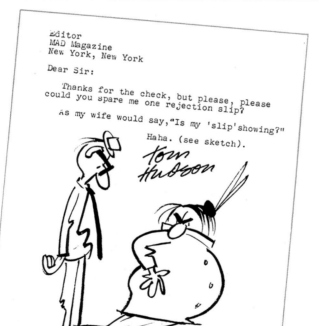

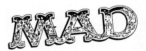

MEMO

FROM:
William M. Gaines
Publisher

TO:
Al Feldstein
Editor

Dear Al:
Just happened to run across that "slip-showing" cartoon while nosing around your desk. I think it would make a great cover painting...with Alfred standing on some big fat dame's slip at a real fancy costume ball, and looking out at the reader with his typical "What--me worry?" grin. What do you think?

Bill

P.S. Will you see that a check is sent to Hudson for this cover idea.

by Tim Carvell
WRITER

Why do I love this piece? I guess because it's hilarious, expertly paced, and a model of economy in storytelling. It's certainly not the fact that it paints the portrait of the MAD offices as a place where writers are subjected to the whims of editors who can be, by turns, arbitrary, capricious, oblivious and cruel.

TION SLIP

Editor
MAD Magazine
New York, New York

Dear Sir:

I am afraid that you have missed the point of the whole thing. My letter was a request for you to send me one of your rejection slips and not intended to be a contribution to your magazine.

I'm still looking! (see sketch)

Sincerely,
Tom Hudson

U S MAIL

MAD

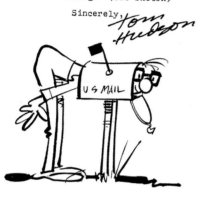

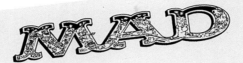

Dear Mr. Hudson:

Thank you for sending us your delightful "Mail Box" cartoon. We all enjoyed it very much, and plan to use it as the new heading for our "Letters Dept."

Enclosed, please find our check in payment.

Sincerely,
Al Feldstein
Al Feldstein,
Editor

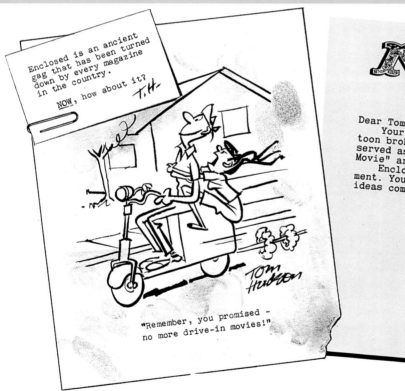

Enclosed is an ancient gag that has been turned down by every magazine in the country.

NOW, how about it?

T.H.

Tom Hudson

"Remember, you promised - no more drive-in movies!"

MAD

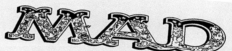

Dear Tom:

Your hilarious "Drive-In Movie" cartoon broke up the entire office, and served as a springboard for a "Drive-In Movie" article.

Enclosed please find check in payment. You're doing great! Keep those ideas coming!

MAD-ly yours,

Al

MAD #80/JULY 1963

Absolutely not.
Honest.
Nothing could be further from the truth.
What? Quit looking at me like that.

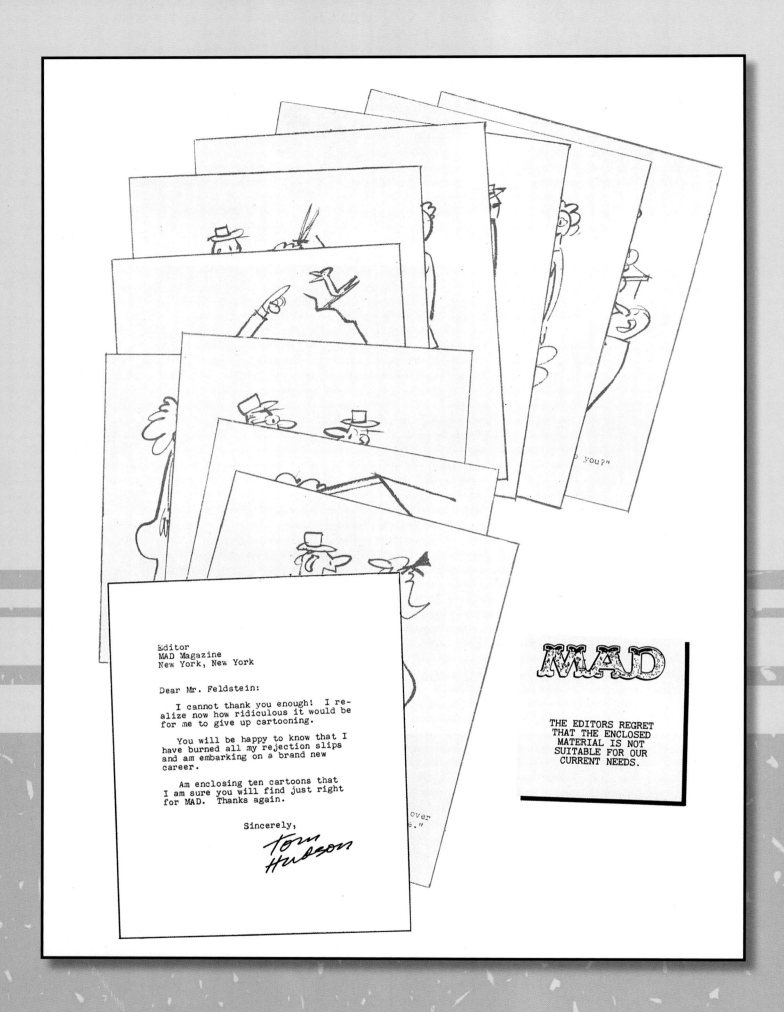

Editor
MAD Magazine
New York, New York

Dear Mr. Feldstein:

    I cannot thank you enough! I re-
alize now how ridiculous it would be
for me to give up cartooning.

    You will be happy to know that I
have burned all my rejection slips
and am embarking on a brand new
career.

    Am enclosing ten cartoons that
I am sure you will find just right
for MAD. Thanks again.

       Sincerely,

       Tom Hudson

MAD

THE EDITORS REGRET
THAT THE ENCLOSED
MATERIAL IS NOT
SUITABLE FOR OUR
CURRENT NEEDS.

PEN AND STINK DEPT.

THE STRIP CLUB

IT ONLY HURTS WHEN I LAUGH
I WONDER WHAT SHE LOOKS LIKE.
WHAT?
THE PRINCESS.
WAIT A SECOND, YOU'VE NEVER MET THIS PRINCESS AND WE'RE HERE TO RESCUE HER?
YES. YOU SEE, WE TIE THE ROPE TO THIS ARROW, YOU'LL SHOOT IT NEAR HER WINDOW WITH YOUR CROSSBOW, AND THEN WE'LL CLIMB UP AND BRING HER BACK DOWN.
AND IF YOU DON'T LIKE HER?
OF COURSE I WILL. FATE LED US HERE-IT WAS MEANT TO BE.
YEAH, SURE-SURE.
I HAVE A BETTER IDEA. HOW ABOUT WE SEND YOU UP, YOU SPEND A ROMANTIC HOUR OR TWO, AND TOMORROW, IF YOU STILL WANT HER, WE'LL COME BACK.
APPARENTLY YOU KNOW NOTHING ABOUT DESTINY.
I KNOW I'M DESTINED TO HEAR YOU BELLYACHE ABOUT YOUR AWFUL MARRIAGE FOR THE REST OF MY LIFE IF I DON'T SAY SOMETHING NOW.
DON'T YOU BELIEVE IN A SOUL MATE?
SURE! BUT WHO THE HELL FINDS HER ON THE FIRST TRY? I'VE SLEPT WITH HUNDREDS OF WOMEN AND I STILL HAVEN'T FOUND MY SOUL MATE!
YES, WELL, IT HELPS TO SLEEP WITH A MAIDEN, SOMEONE WHO'S STILL PURE.
AND YOU'VE SLEPT WITH HOW MANY MAIDENS?
WELL... NONE...
THEN HOW DO YOU KNOW?!
JUST SHOOT THE DAMN ARROW OR I'LL STAB YOU.
ALL I'M SAYING IS WHY NOT WINDOW SHOP A BIT? THERE'S A TOWER DOWN THE ROAD WITH ANOTHER MAIDEN IN IT.
HAVE SWORD, WILL STAB!
WE CAN GET THERE IN FIFTEEN MINUTES! WHAT'S FIFTEEN MINUTES?!
STABBIE-STABBIE!
YOU WERE PREMATURELY WEANED, WEREN'T YOU? IF YOU WANT TO TALK ABOUT IT, I'D BE HAPPY-
A HARD DAY'S KNIGHT
JUST SHOOT THE DAMN-
KA-TOONG!
THOONK!
AAIIEEE...
UMMM... ABOUT THAT TOWER DOWN THE ROAD...
I'LL GO SADDLE THE HORSES.
CHRISTOPHER BALDWIN '06

CHRISTOPHER BALDWIN

by Jonathan Bresman
WRITER

In 2005, Editor John Ficarra noticed that people were multi-tasking their entertainment — simultaneously reading, texting, e-mailing, web surfing, watching TV and playing games. He therefore decided to add more "bite-sized" pieces to the magazine, making it easier for people to add MAD to their mix. This led to the Strip Club, the section of the magazine that is closest to my heart. I was given the honor of recruiting cartoonists who could tell short, silly, yet cerebral stories, and I had the pleasure of inducting scores of new contributors into the Usual Gang of Idiots, including such talents as children's author Mo Willems, editorial cartoonist Ted Rall and comedy writer Simon Rich. In this Strip Club you will see Christopher Baldwin's chatty wit, Joey Alison Sayers' twisted time-travel antics, Jason Yungbluth's cosmically disastrous romance, the cutting pop-culture comedy

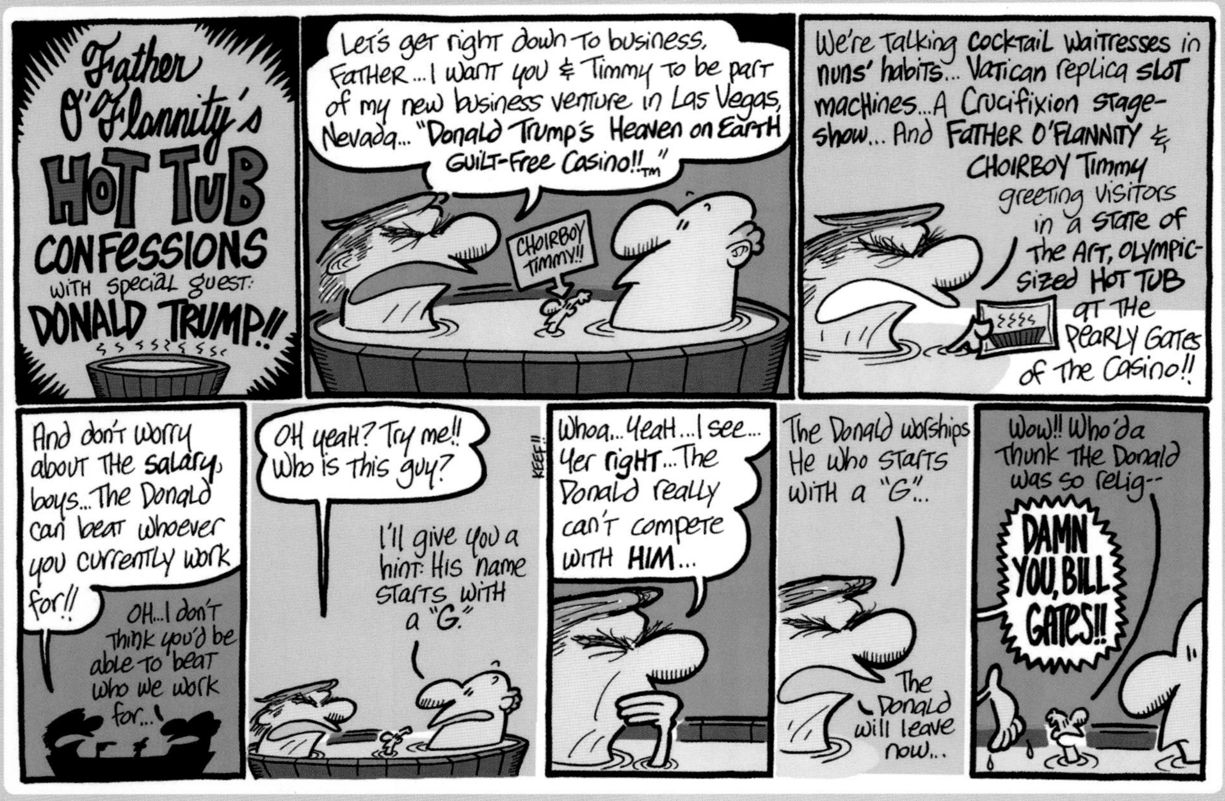
Father O'Flannity's HOT TUB CONFESSIONS with special guest: DONALD TRUMP!!
Let's get right down to business, Father... I want you & Timmy to be part of my new business venture in Las Vegas, Nevada... "Donald Trump's Heaven on Earth Guilt-Free Casino!!™"
CHOIRBOY TIMMY!!
We're talking cocktail waitresses in nuns' habits... Vatican replica slot machines... A Crucifixion stage-show... And Father O'Flannity & Choirboy Timmy greeting visitors in a state of the art, olympic-sized hot tub at the Pearly Gates of the Casino!!
And don't worry about the salary, boys... The Donald can beat whoever you currently work for!!
OH... I don't think you'd be able to beat who we work for...!
OH yeah? Try me!! Who is this guy?
I'll give you a hint: His name starts with a "G."
KEEF!!
Whoa... Yeah... I see... Yer right... The Donald really can't compete with HIM...
The Donald worships He who starts with a "G"...
The Donald will leave now...
Wow!! Who'da thunk the Donald was so relig--
DAMN YOU, BILL GATES!!

KEITH KNIGHT

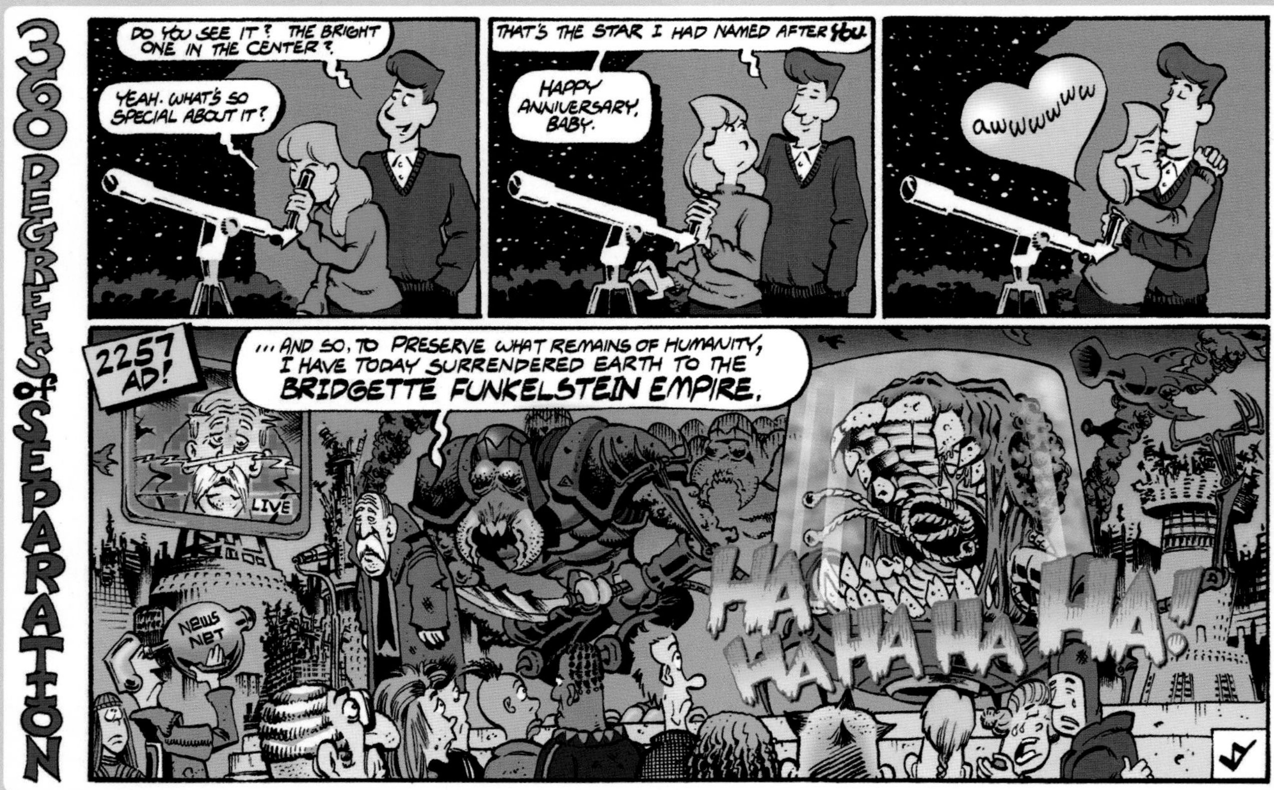
360 DEGREES of SEPARATION
DO YOU SEE IT? THE BRIGHT ONE IN THE CENTER?
YEAH. WHAT'S SO SPECIAL ABOUT IT?
THAT'S THE STAR I HAD NAMED AFTER YOU.
HAPPY ANNIVERSARY, BABY.
awwwwww
2257 AD!
...AND SO, TO PRESERVE WHAT REMAINS OF HUMANITY, I HAVE TODAY SURRENDERED EARTH TO THE BRIDGETTE FUNKELSTEIN EMPIRE.
LIVE
NEWS NET
HA HA HA HA HA!

of Keith Knight and John Kovaleski's portrayal of the limits of sock puppet loyalty. While there was only space for these strips, I hope that MAD will one day publish a Strip Club collection so that you can enjoy the work of the rest of our new Idiots while you multi-task your media consumption — further demolishing what remains of your attention span.

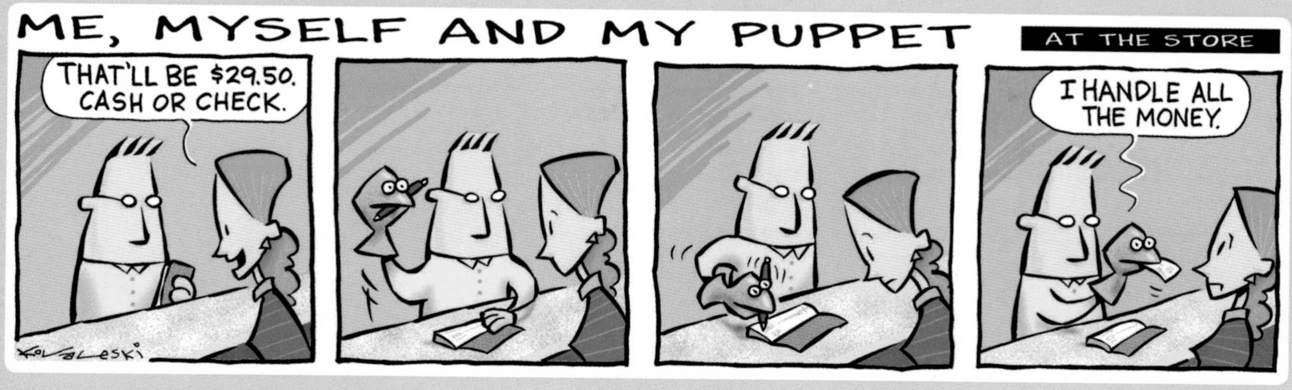
ME, MYSELF AND MY PUPPET
AT THE STORE
THAT'LL BE $29.50. CASH OR CHECK.
I HANDLE ALL THE MONEY.
KOVALESKI

JOHN KOVALESKI

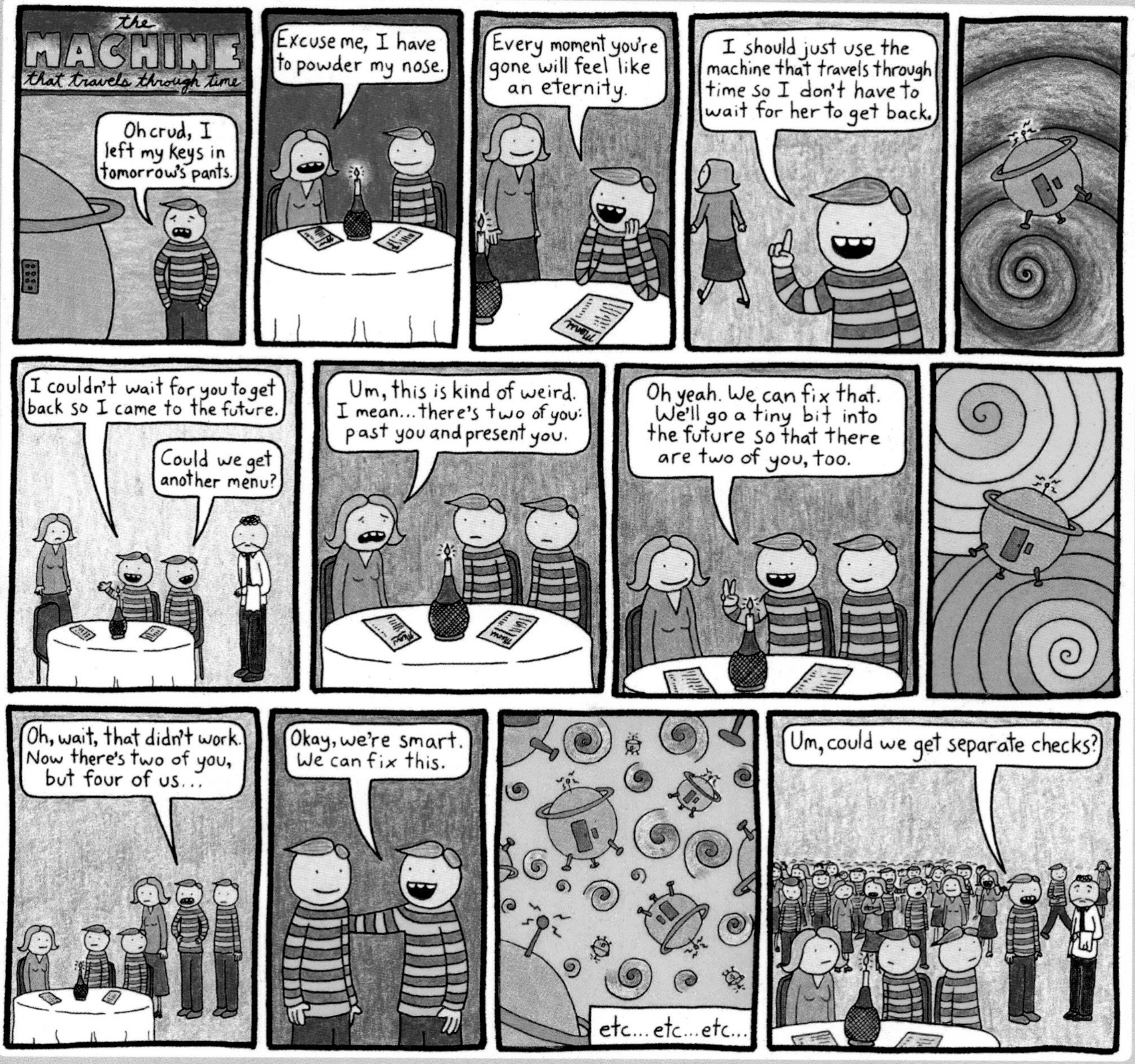
the MACHINE that travels through time
Oh crud, I left my keys in tomorrow's pants.
Excuse me, I have to powder my nose.
Every moment you're gone will feel like an eternity.
I should just use the machine that travels through time so I don't have to wait for her to get back.
I couldn't wait for you to get back so I came to the future.
Could we get another menu?
Um, this is kind of weird. I mean... there's two of you: past you and present you.
Oh yeah. We can fix that. We'll go a tiny bit into the future so that there are two of you, too.
Oh, wait, that didn't work. Now there's two of you, but four of us...
Okay, we're smart. We can fix this.
etc... etc... etc...
Um, could we get separate checks?

JOEY ALISON SAYERS

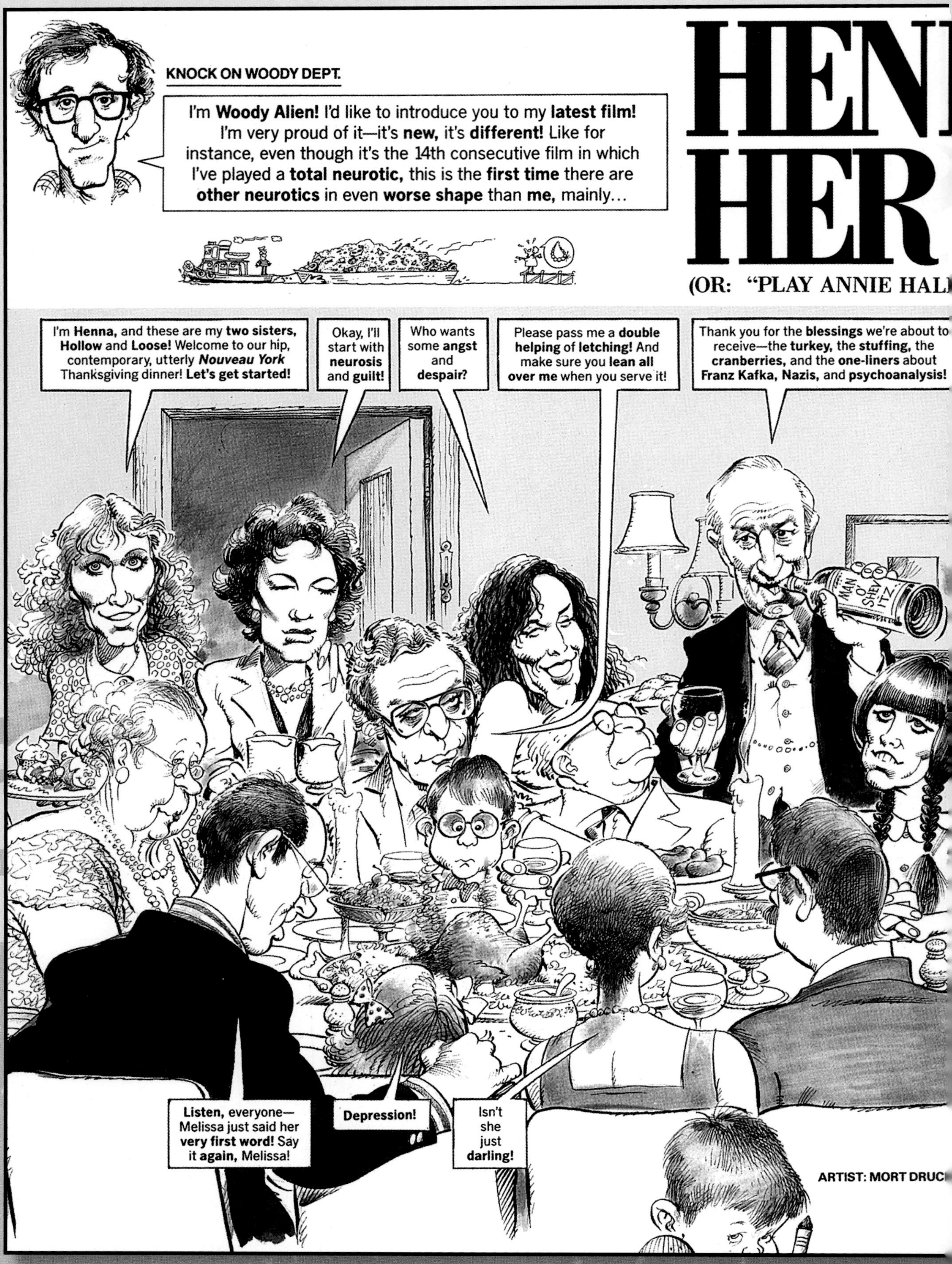

KNOCK ON WOODY DEPT.
I'm Woody Alien! I'd like to introduce you to my latest film! I'm very proud of it—it's new, it's different! Like for instance, even though it's the 14th consecutive film in which I've played a total neurotic, this is the first time there are other neurotics in even worse shape than me, mainly…
HENI
HER
(OR: "PLAY ANNIE HAL
I'm Henna, and these are my two sisters, Hollow and Loose! Welcome to our hip, contemporary, utterly Nouveau York Thanksgiving dinner! Let's get started!
Okay, I'll start with neurosis and guilt!
Who wants some angst and despair?
Please pass me a double helping of letching! And make sure you lean all over me when you serve it!
Thank you for the blessings we're about to receive—the turkey, the stuffing, the cranberries, and the one-liners about Franz Kafka, Nazis, and psychoanalysis!
Listen, everyone—Melissa just said her very first word! Say it again, Melissa!
Depression!
Isn't she just darling!
ARTIST: MORT DRUC

by Arnie Kogen
WRITER

My personal favorite MAD article of all time?

I could easily go with Tom Koch's classic "43 Man Squamish" (MAD #95). "Squamish" was the *Casablanca* of MAD articles (I actually once wrote a MAD spoof of *Casablanca*, called "Casabonkers," which, sadly, wasn't the *Casablanca* of MAD articles). Or I could go with Larry Siegel's brilliant parody of *Patton* (#140). Or, I could ignore those gems, lower the comedy bar slightly and go with one of my own articles.

Okay, I'm going with one of my own. It was written during the 1980s. People did crazy

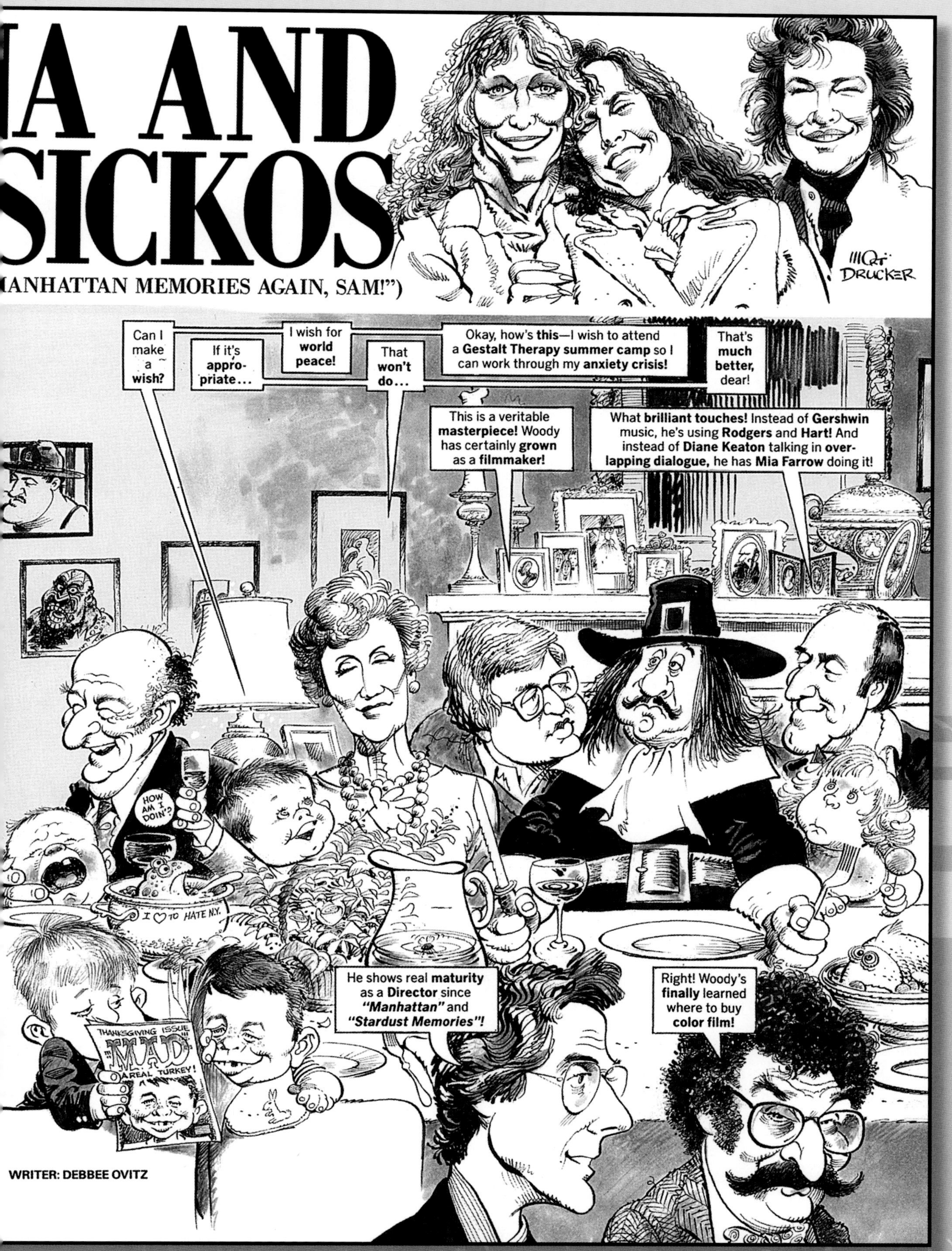
IA AND
SICKOS
ANHATTAN MEMORIES AGAIN, SAM!")
DRUCKER
Can I make a wish?
If it's appro-priate...
I wish for world peace!
That won't do...
Okay, how's this—I wish to attend a Gestalt Therapy summer camp so I can work through my anxiety crisis!
That's much better, dear!
This is a veritable masterpiece! Woody has certainly grown as a filmmaker!
What brilliant touches! Instead of Gershwin music, he's using Rodgers and Hart! And instead of Diane Keaton talking in over-lapping dialogue, he has Mia Farrow doing it!
HOW AM I DOIN'?
I ♡ TO HATE N.Y.
THANKSGIVING ISSUE
MAD
A REAL TURKEY!
He shows real maturity as a Director since "Manhattan" and "Stardust Memories"!
Right! Woody's finally learned where to buy color film!
WRITER: DEBBEE OVITZ

MAD #265/SEPTEMBER 1986

things in the eighties: they worshipped Super Mario Bros., Gummi Bears and The Beastie Boys, and actually sat through entire episodes of *The Love Boat*. Me? I wrote two MAD stories under different names: "Debbee Ovitz," which was a combination of the names of two of my agents. This, a parody of *Hannah and Her Sisters*, was one of those stories. Mort Drucker did an incredible job with this Woody Allen film, especially the opening splash. I've written around 250 articles for MAD. I think this was one of the best things I've done, and one of the best things Debbee Ovitz has done.

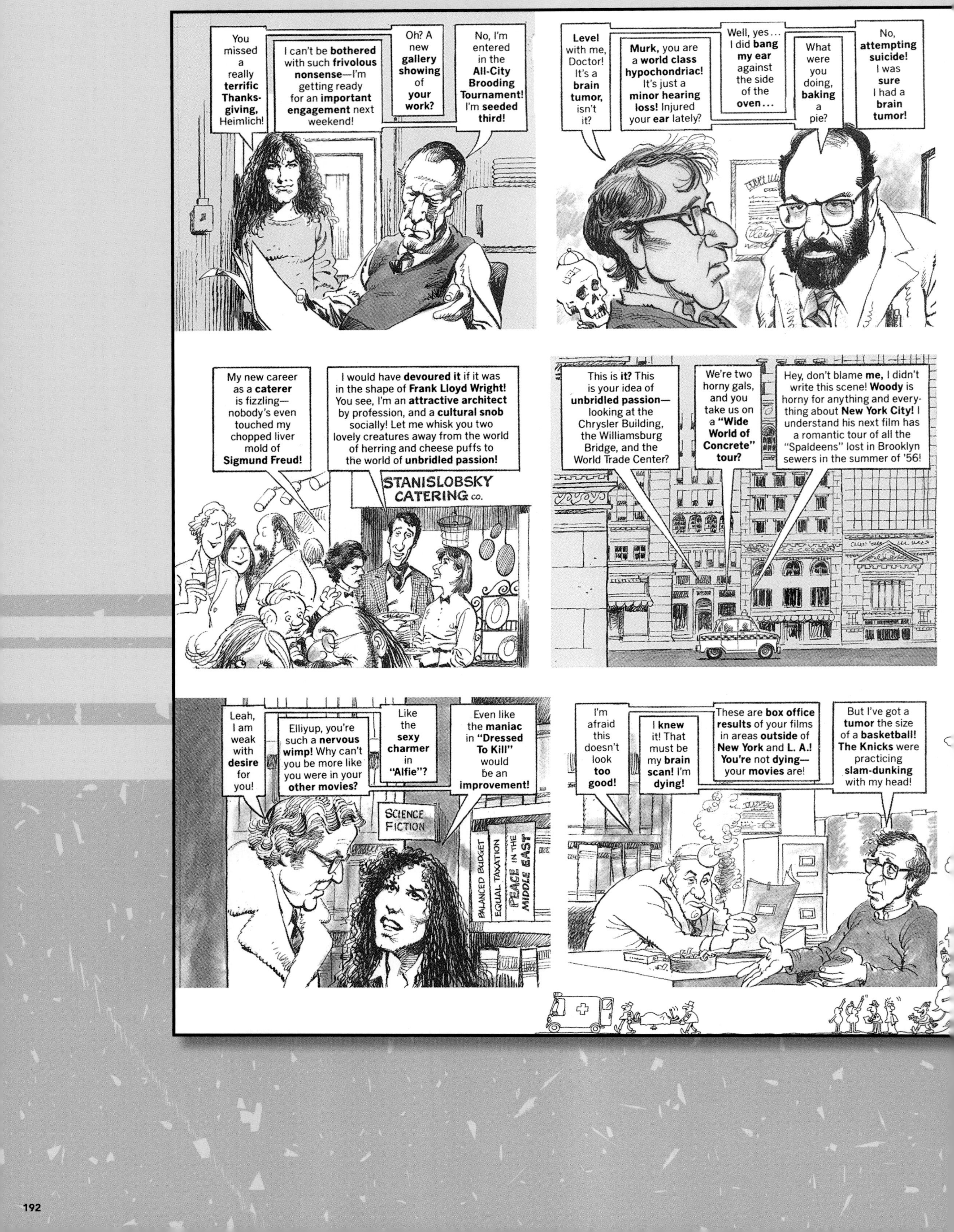
You missed a really terrific Thanks-giving, Heimlich!
I can't be bothered with such frivolous nonsense—I'm getting ready for an important engagement next weekend!
Oh? A new gallery showing of your work?
No, I'm entered in the All-City Brooding Tournament! I'm seeded third!
Level with me, Doctor! It's a brain tumor, isn't it?
Murk, you are a world class hypochondriac! It's just a minor hearing loss! Injured your ear lately?
Well, yes... I did bang my ear against the side of the oven...
What were you doing, baking a pie?
No, attempting suicide! I was sure I had a brain tumor!
My new career as a caterer is fizzling—nobody's even touched my chopped liver mold of Sigmund Freud!
I would have devoured it if it was in the shape of Frank Lloyd Wright! You see, I'm an attractive architect by profession, and a cultural snob socially! Let me whisk you two lovely creatures away from the world of herring and cheese puffs to the world of unbridled passion!
STANISLOBSKY CATERING CO.
This is it? This is your idea of unbridled passion—looking at the Chrysler Building, the Williamsburg Bridge, and the World Trade Center?
We're two horny gals, and you take us on a "Wide World of Concrete" tour?
Hey, don't blame me, I didn't write this scene! Woody is horny for anything and every-thing about New York City! I understand his next film has a romantic tour of all the "Spaldeens" lost in Brooklyn sewers in the summer of '56!
Leah, I am weak with desire for you!
Elliyup, you're such a nervous wimp! Why can't you be more like you were in your other movies?
Like the sexy charmer in "Alfie"?
Even like the maniac in "Dressed To Kill" would be an improvement!
SCIENCE FICTION
BALANCED BUDGET
EQUAL TAXATION
PEACE IN THE MIDDLE EAST
I'm afraid this doesn't look too good!
I knew it! That must be my brain scan! I'm dying!
These are box office results of your films in areas outside of New York and L. A.! You're not dying—your movies are!
But I've got a tumor the size of a basketball! The Knicks were practicing slam-dunking with my head!

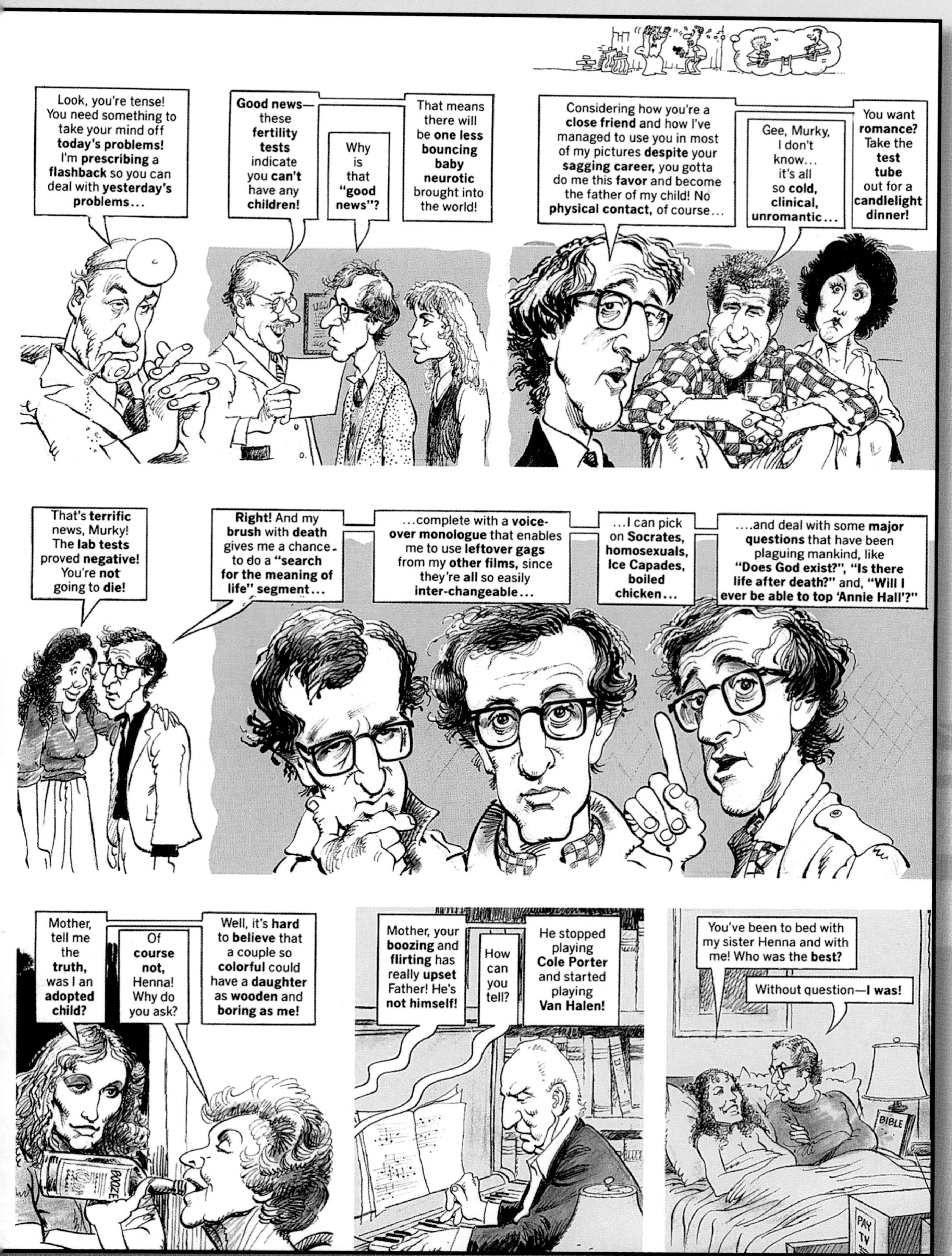

Look, you're tense! You need something to take your mind off today's problems! I'm prescribing a flashback so you can deal with yesterday's problems...
Good news—these fertility tests indicate you can't have any children!
Why is that "good news"?
That means there will be one less bouncing baby neurotic brought into the world!
Considering how you're a close friend and how I've managed to use you in most of my pictures despite your sagging career, you gotta do me this favor and become the father of my child! No physical contact, of course...
Gee, Murky, I don't know... it's all so cold, clinical, unromantic...
You want romance? Take the test tube out for a candlelight dinner!
That's terrific news, Murky! The lab tests proved negative! You're not going to die!
Right! And my brush with death gives me a chance to do a "search for the meaning of life" segment...
...complete with a voice-over monologue that enables me to use leftover gags from my other films, since they're all so easily inter-changeable...
...I can pick on Socrates, homosexuals, Ice Capades, boiled chicken...
....and deal with some major questions that have been plaguing mankind, like "Does God exist?", "Is there life after death?" and, "Will I ever be able to top 'Annie Hall'?"
Mother, tell me the truth, was I an adopted child?
Of course not, Henna! Why do you ask?
Well, it's hard to believe that a couple so colorful could have a daughter as wooden and boring as me!
BOOZE
Mother, your boozing and flirting has really upset Father! He's not himself!
How can you tell?
He stopped playing Cole Porter and started playing Van Halen!
You've been to bed with my sister Henna and with me! Who was the best?
Without question—I was!
BIBLE
PAY TV

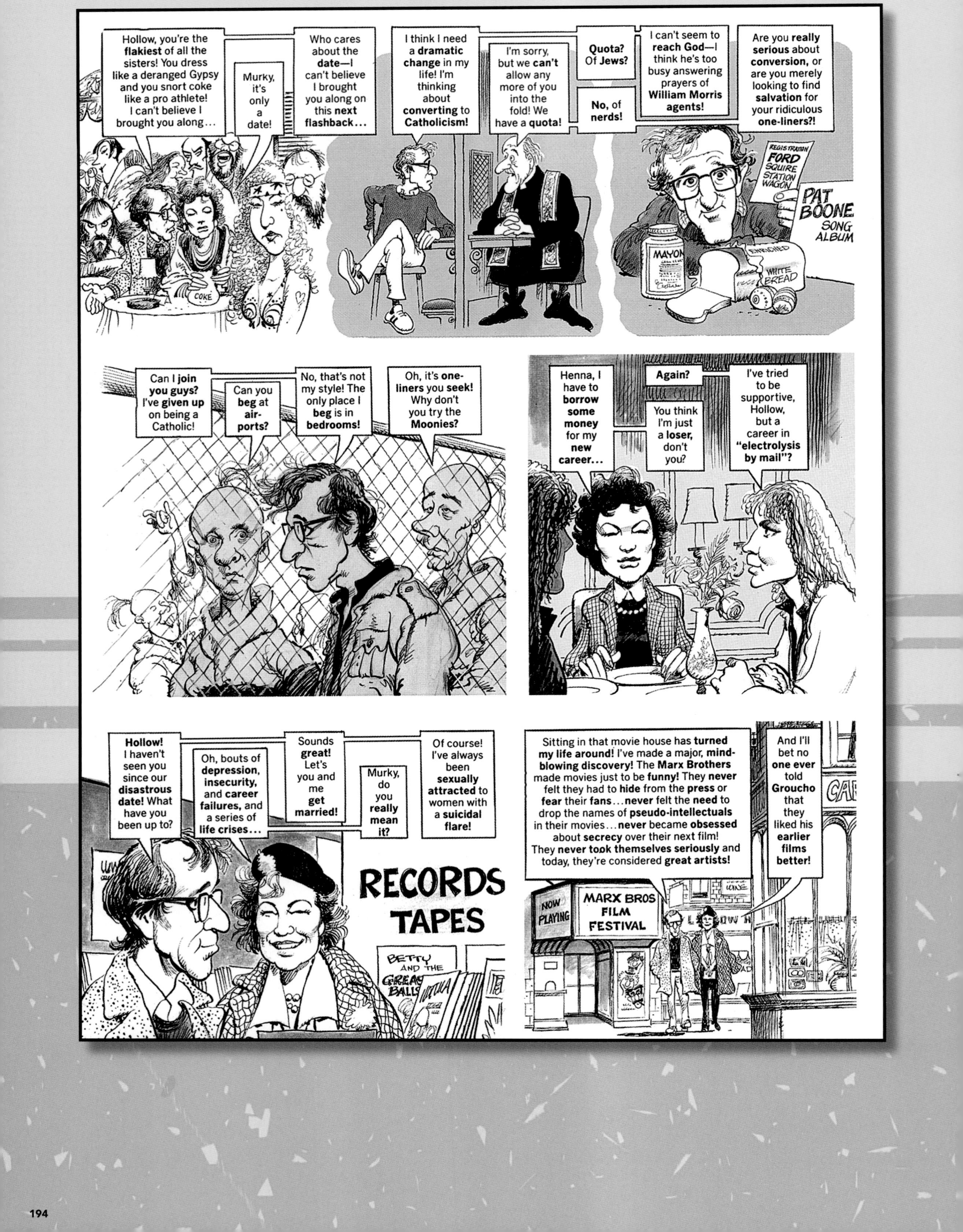
Hollow, you're the flakiest of all the sisters! You dress like a deranged Gypsy and you snort coke like a pro athlete! I can't believe I brought you along...
Murky, it's only a date!
Who cares about the date—I can't believe I brought you along on this next flashback...
COKE
I think I need a dramatic change in my life! I'm thinking about converting to Catholicism!
I'm sorry, but we can't allow any more of you into the fold! We have a quota!
Quota? Of Jews?
No, of nerds!
I can't seem to reach God—I think he's too busy answering prayers of William Morris agents!
Are you really serious about conversion, or are you merely looking to find salvation for your ridiculous one-liners?!
REGISTRATION FORD SQUIRE STATION WAGON
PAT BOONE SONG ALBUM
MAYON
ENRICHED WHITE BREAD
Can I join you guys? I've given up on being a Catholic!
Can you beg at air-ports?
No, that's not my style! The only place I beg is in bedrooms!
Oh, it's one-liners you seek! Why don't you try the Moonies?
Henna, I have to borrow some money for my new career...
Again?
You think I'm just a loser, don't you?
I've tried to be supportive, Hollow, but a career in "electrolysis by mail"?
Hollow! I haven't seen you since our disastrous date! What have you been up to?
Oh, bouts of depression, insecurity, and career failures, and a series of life crises...
Sounds great! Let's you and me get married!
Murky, do you really mean it?
Of course! I've always been sexually attracted to women with a suicidal flare!
RECORDS TAPES
BETTY AND THE GREASY BALLS
Sitting in that movie house has turned my life around! I've made a major, mind-blowing discovery! The Marx Brothers made movies just to be funny! They never felt they had to hide from the press or fear their fans...never felt the need to drop the names of pseudo-intellectuals in their movies...never became obsessed about secrecy over their next film! They never took themselves seriously and today, they're considered great artists!
And I'll bet no one ever told Groucho that they liked his earlier films better!
NOW PLAYING
MARX BROS FILM FESTIVAL

GRAND LARSON-Y DEPT.

Nowadays, the hottest comic strip in the country is Gary Larson's bizarre single-panel, "The Far Side." Far Side books are at the top of the bestseller lists and gift shops are filled with Far Side cards, mugs, posters and other stuff. With a big cash bonanza like this, it won't be long before other cartoonists jump on the bandwagon and start using Larson's approach as well. Speaking of jumping on the bandwagon, here's what we think it will be like...

When Other Comic Strips Start Using The "FAR SIDE" Formula

ARTIST: BOB CLARKE WRITER: CHARLIE KADAU

THE BLOOM COUNTY SIDE

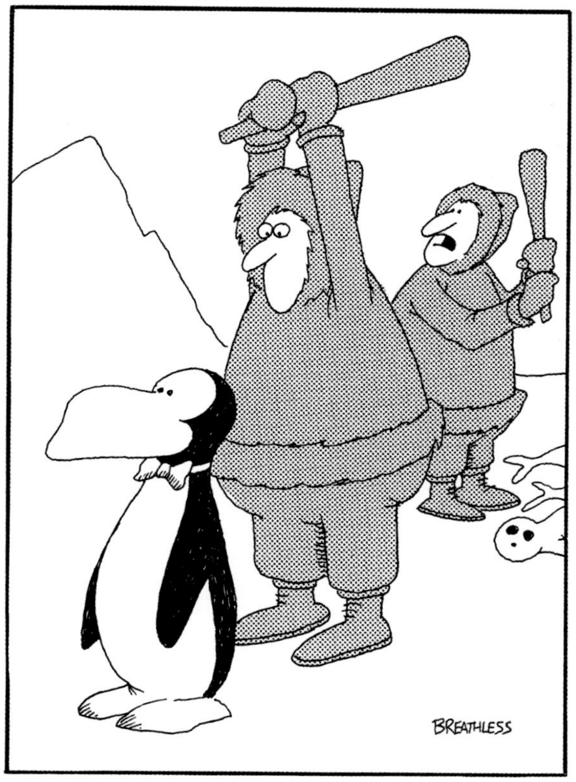
BREATHLESS

"No, Frank! The seals! Just the seals!"

THE GARFIELD SIDE

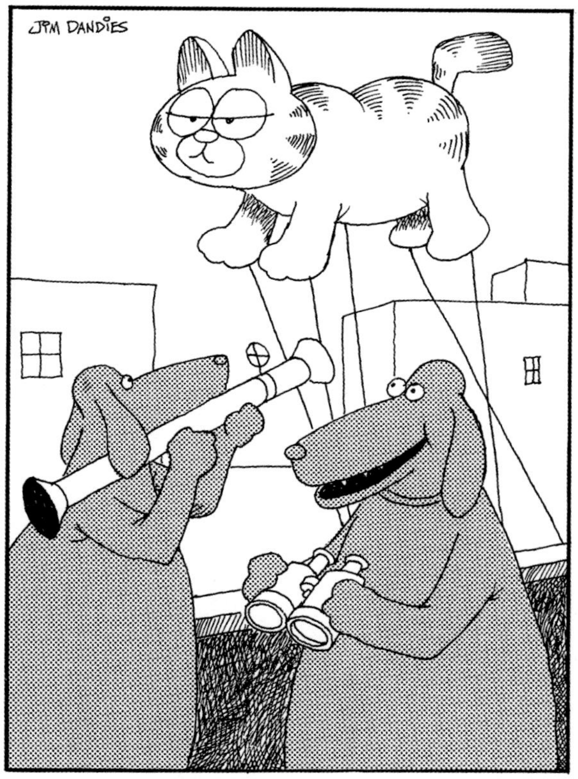
JIM DANDIES

"Okay, here it comes, here it comes...Oh, what a joy! This is one Thanksgiving Day Parade that dogs will be talking about for years to come."

MAD #280/JULY 1988

by Joe Raiola
WRITER

MAD #280 (July 1988) was a milestone issue for me and my longtime comedy-writing pal, Charlie Kadau. We'd been MAD contributors for about five years but never had more than one article in an issue. Suddenly, we had three, including our first-ever collaborations with MAD greats Al Jaffee ("Gary Hartland") and Sergio Aragonés ("A Peek Behind the Scenes at a High School Prom"). And still, Charlie managed to upstage us as a team by serving up a bona-fide MAD classic: "When Other Comic Strips Start Using 'The Far Side' Formula."

With all due respect to Charlie, he couldn't have done it without veteran MAD artist Bob Clarke, a true master of illustrative parody who perfectly captured Gary Larson's distinctive line and found a way to seamlessly integrate the style of other legendary cartoonists into the strips. That said, the concept and the writing is pure Charlie at his ridiculous best. This begs the question: Why isn't he this damn funny when he works with me?

THE BEETLE SIDE

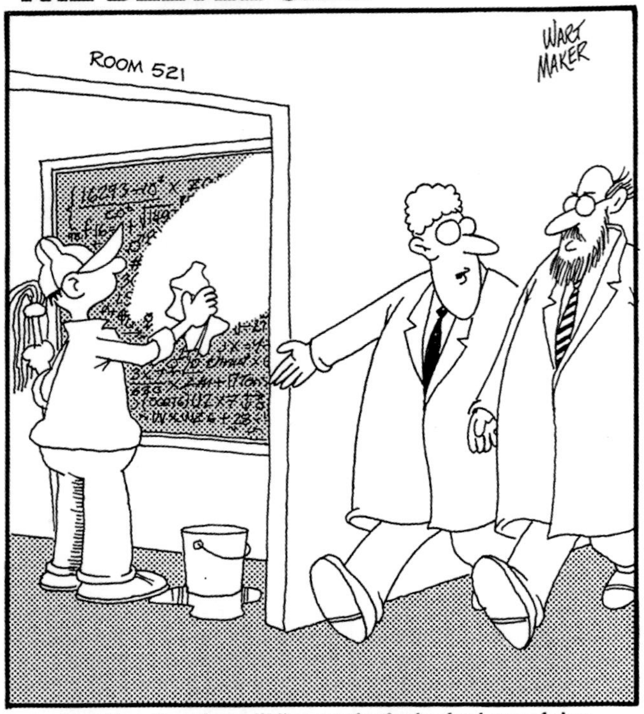
ROOM 521
WART MAKER

"Jenkins, I've done it! I've perfected a fool-proof star wars defense system! All my calculations are right in here, you must see them!"

THE CATHY SIDE

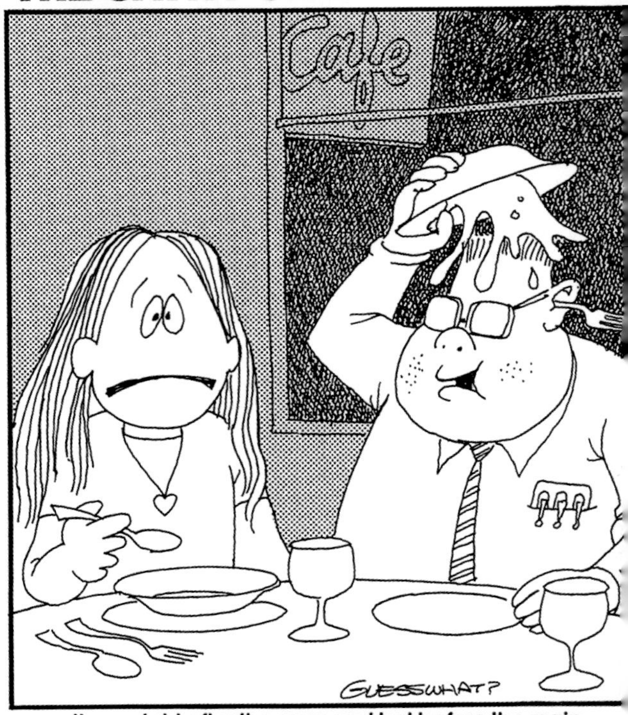
Cafe
GUESSWHAT?

It was right after the soup and just before the main course that Cathy decided she would never, under any circumstances, ever go on another blind date again. Never.

THE SPIDERMAN SIDE

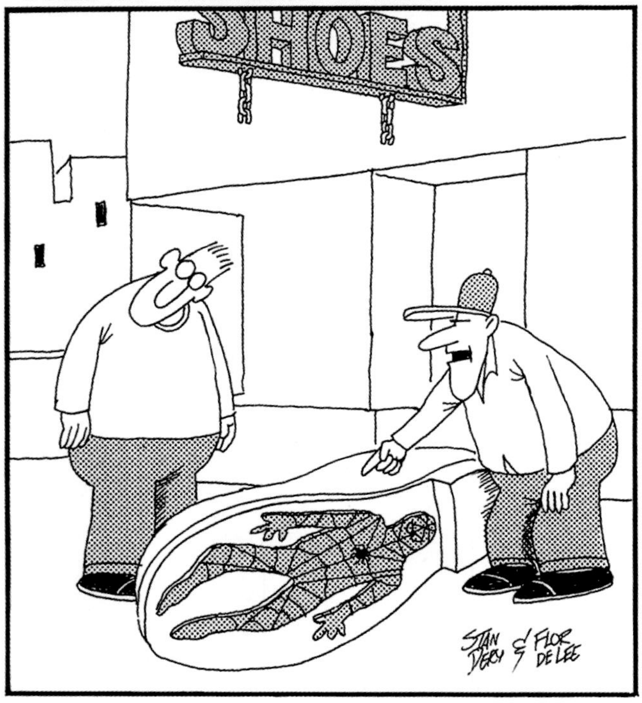
SHOES
STAN DERY & FLOR DE LEE

"It must have fallen down during the night and...Hey! Lookee what's underneath it!"

THE B.C. SIDE

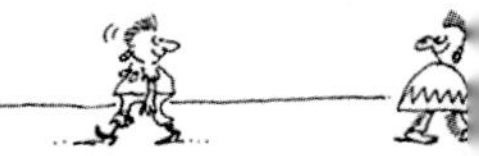

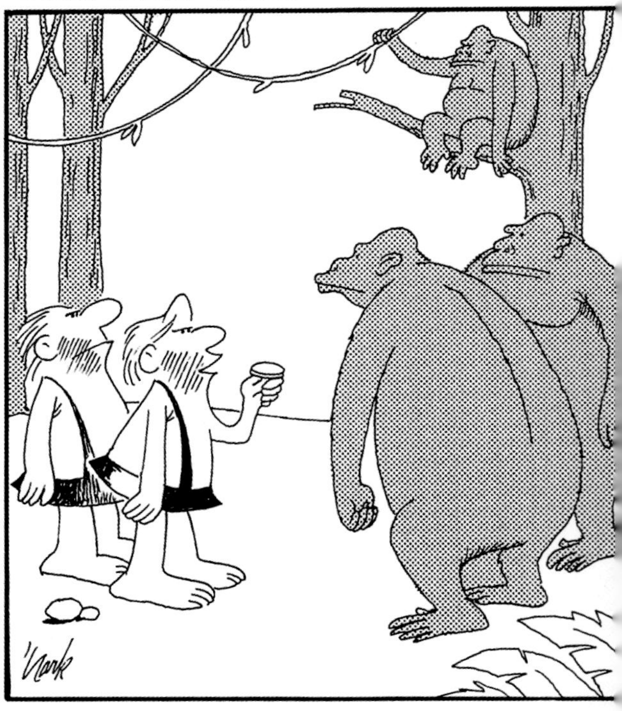

"It's agreed then: you call it in the air...winners get to lounge around in trees all day eating bananas and losers have to develop civilization and live in hot, crowded cities."

THE FAMILY CIRCUS SIDE

NO
LITTERING
PEACHY KEENE

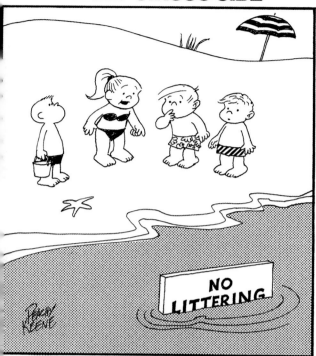

"Well, I thought this was the spot where we left daddy...I remember we buried him in the sand about an hour ago right here next to a 'No Littering' sign."

THE HAGAR SIDE

CHOC BROWNIES

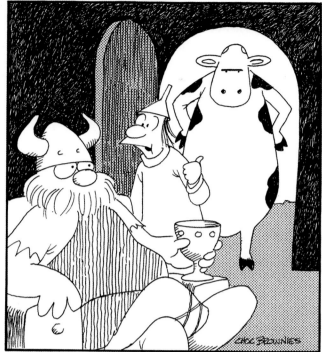

"Hagar, there's someone here who wants to speak to you about your helmet, and he doesn't look happy."

THE MENACE SIDE

Nowhell Ketch'um

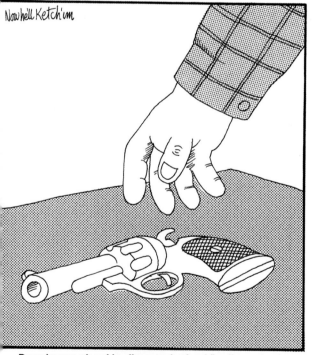

Dennis was about to discover he had finally pushed Mr. Wilson's patience just a little too far.

THE PEANUTS SIDE

DOGHOUSE
SCHULTZ

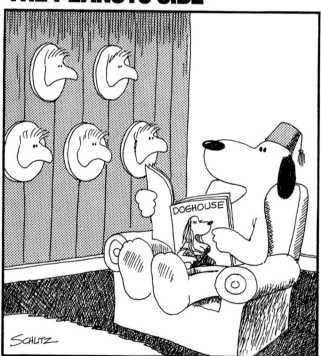

Inside Snoopy's den

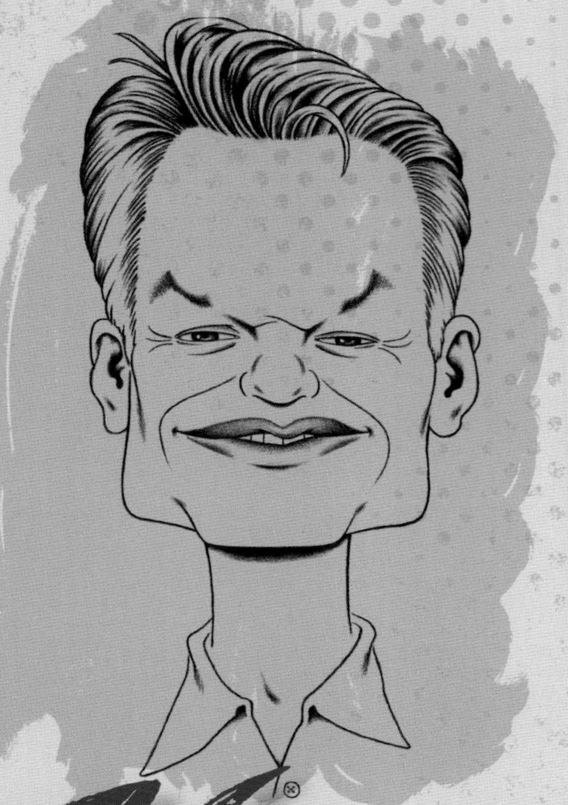

Harry Hamlin

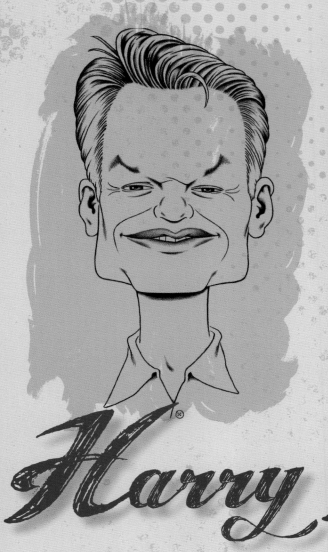

I was such a huge fan of MAD and "Spy vs. Spy" that I think it's responsible for me becoming an actor…and for my sex life, and for my son being admitted to Princeton.

I always went to the "Spy vs. Spy" pages first when I opened the magazine. I was enchanted by it. Then, when I was 11 or 12, the first James Bond movie, *Dr. No*, came out. I was intrigued, as was everyone at the time, by the phenomenon of spy movies and spy culture. I wanted to do what "Spy vs. Spy" and Sean Connery did. Coincidentally, it just so happened that I had a son with the first Bond girl ever: Ursula Andress. And she told me an interesting story of her participation in that movie. She was under contract with the studio, but didn't speak any English and hadn't made any movies and was sick and tired of the movie business. She wanted to get out of her contract so she went to the head of the studio, saying, "Let me go, please." And the guy said, "Look, your contract isn't up. We're making a completely unknown spy movie with a completely unknown actor. It's a low budget movie. We're going to make the movie and it's going to die at the box office. Then you'll have fulfilled your contract and can go on and live your life." So she did the picture and it started a whole genre. I don't know when "Spy vs. Spy" started, but I always felt that Bond film might have been the inspiration for it or vice versa.

Fast forward to when Ursula and I had our son, Dimitri. I shared MAD with him and he became a fan of the magazine, too. He's now 32, but he would have been about seven when he read the October 1987 issue when I was on the cover for the MAD spoof of *L.A. Law.* After that, Dimitri became a comic book collector and so he had MAD Magazines all over the place. He was an addict for MAD, the way he was for all comics, but MAD was front and center. In fact, it's responsible for him getting into Princeton. Because of his constant addiction, MAD educated him. It fed the evolution of his brain. He was an outside-of-the-box kid and MAD taught him to be an outside-of-the-box thinker. He's definitely an iconoclast and that's what they liked about him at Princeton.

My son was an addict for MAD... in fact, it's responsible for getting him into Princeton.

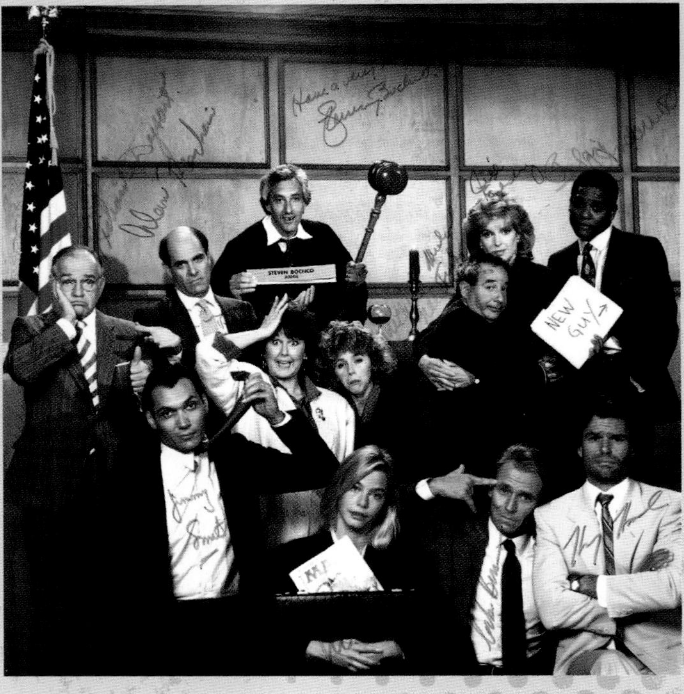
NEW GUY

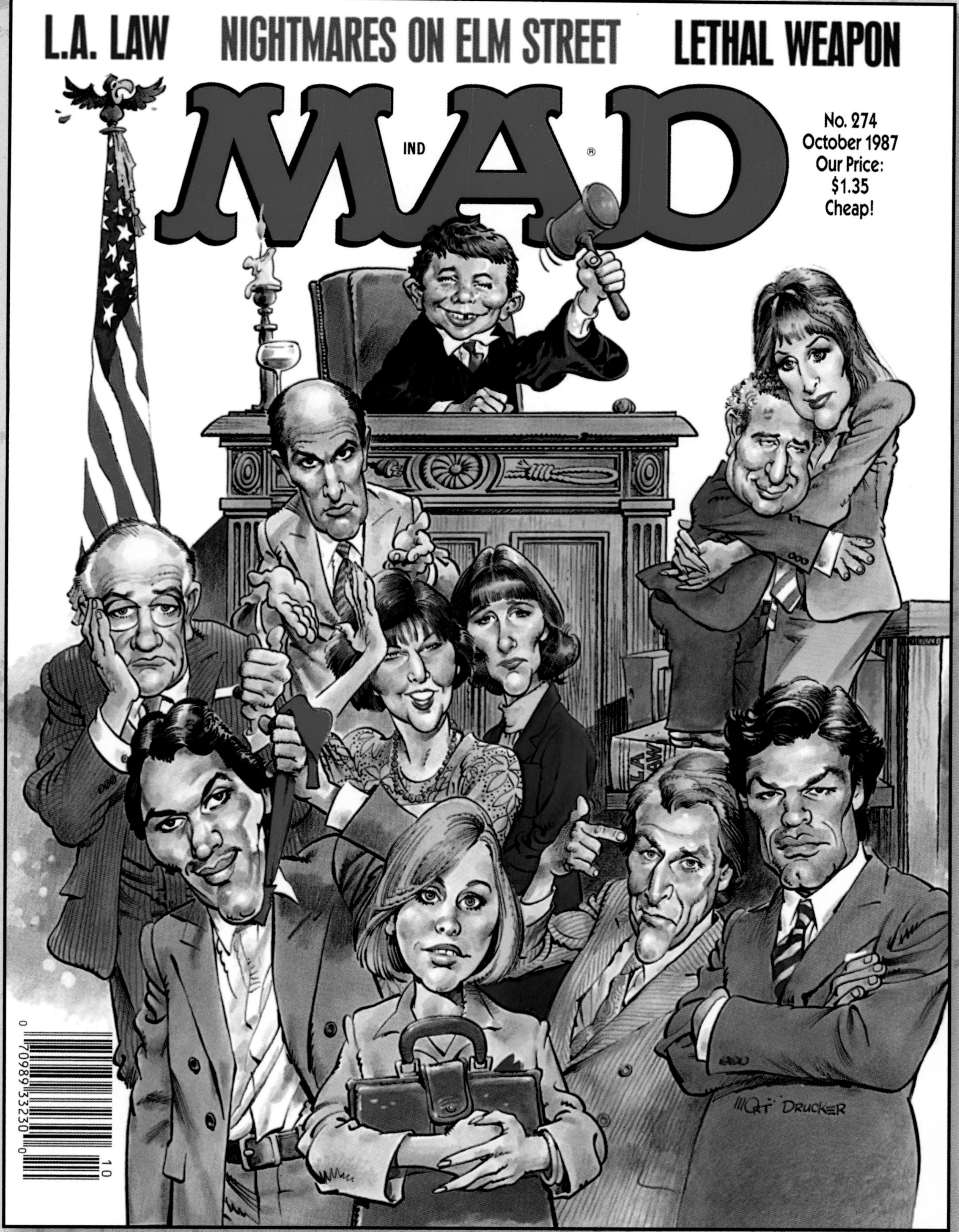
L.A. LAW
NIGHTMARES ON ELM STREET
LETHAL WEAPON
MAD
IND
No. 274
October 1987
Our Price:
$1.35
Cheap!
MORT DRUCKER

ARTIST: MORT DRUCKER

MAD #274/OCTOBER 1987

When that *L.A. Law* issue of MAD came out, I loved it. I loved it so much that I decided to take a photo of the whole cast in the same pose as the MAD cover, and send it in to the MAD editors as a joke. I clearly remember that I had to get clearance to do it. Everything requires clearance when you're doing those kinds of shows, so I had to go all the way to the top of the studio to get clearance to use the set and take the time required to set up the shot. Then I had to get all the different people in the cast there at the same time, plus our producer, Steven Bochco, to pose as Alfred E. Neuman holding a giant gavel. Then we finally took the photo after about 40 minutes to get the lighting right and get everyone posed in the right position. I was inspired to do it for some reason! I don't recall exactly why but those were my salad days.

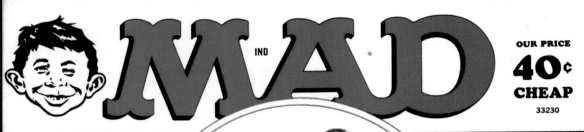

MAD
IND
OUR PRICE
40¢
CHEAP
33230
No. 171
December 1974
SUBPOENA
HOUSE OF REPRESENTATIVES
PAYOFFS
Campaign Contributions
TAX PAID
$792.81
MAD SALUTES
THE BIG CON
...Also In This Issue We Zing "THE STING"

ARTIST: NORMAN MINGO

MAD #171/DECEMBER 1974

by Dennis Snee
WRITER

"The Big Con" was then-Editor Nick Meglin's brilliant visual gag of Richard Nixon and Spiro Agnew as Paul Newman and Robert Redford's characters from the Academy Award-winning film, *The Sting*. Concept, artwork — by MAD icon Norman Mingo (the only MAD artist, according to the elders, who could render a "perfect" Alfred) — and execution combined flawlessly for the classic, deadly parody of the Nixon administration's troubles. Just brilliant. And funny. And I'm a Republican.

And if I could be permitted a "MAD Favorite 2.0"...

One day in 1980 I walked into the gym at Westchester High School in Los Angeles to meet a pal for some pickup basketball. Sitting down in the stands to wait, I noticed a guy about my age also watching the action. He looked familiar, and he should have — he was John Travolta.

I offered my standard whenever-I-meet-a-celebrity-opener, "I enjoy your work," and when he asked what I did, I felt reasonably cool saying that I was a writer and had written for Bob Hope. But Travolta wasn't interested. I added that I wrote for Rodney Dangerfield. Also not interested. Then I tossed in, "Uh, I also write for MAD Magazine..."

He flashed a 1,000-watt Vinnie Barbarino smile and laughed out loud, saying, "MAD Magazine! Man, they did the funniest parody of *Saturday Night Fever* — it was hilarious!"

He went on for five or 10 minutes, and by association I felt like an actual comedy writer. So to the estimable creative team behind "Saturday Night Feeble," Arnie Kogen and Mort Drucker: Kudos! You made Barbarino babble!

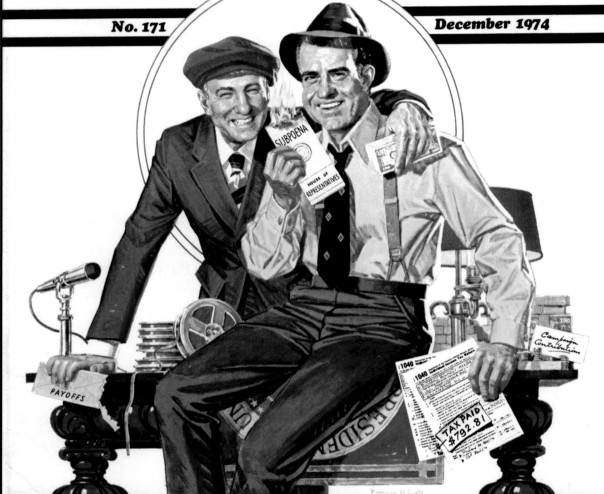

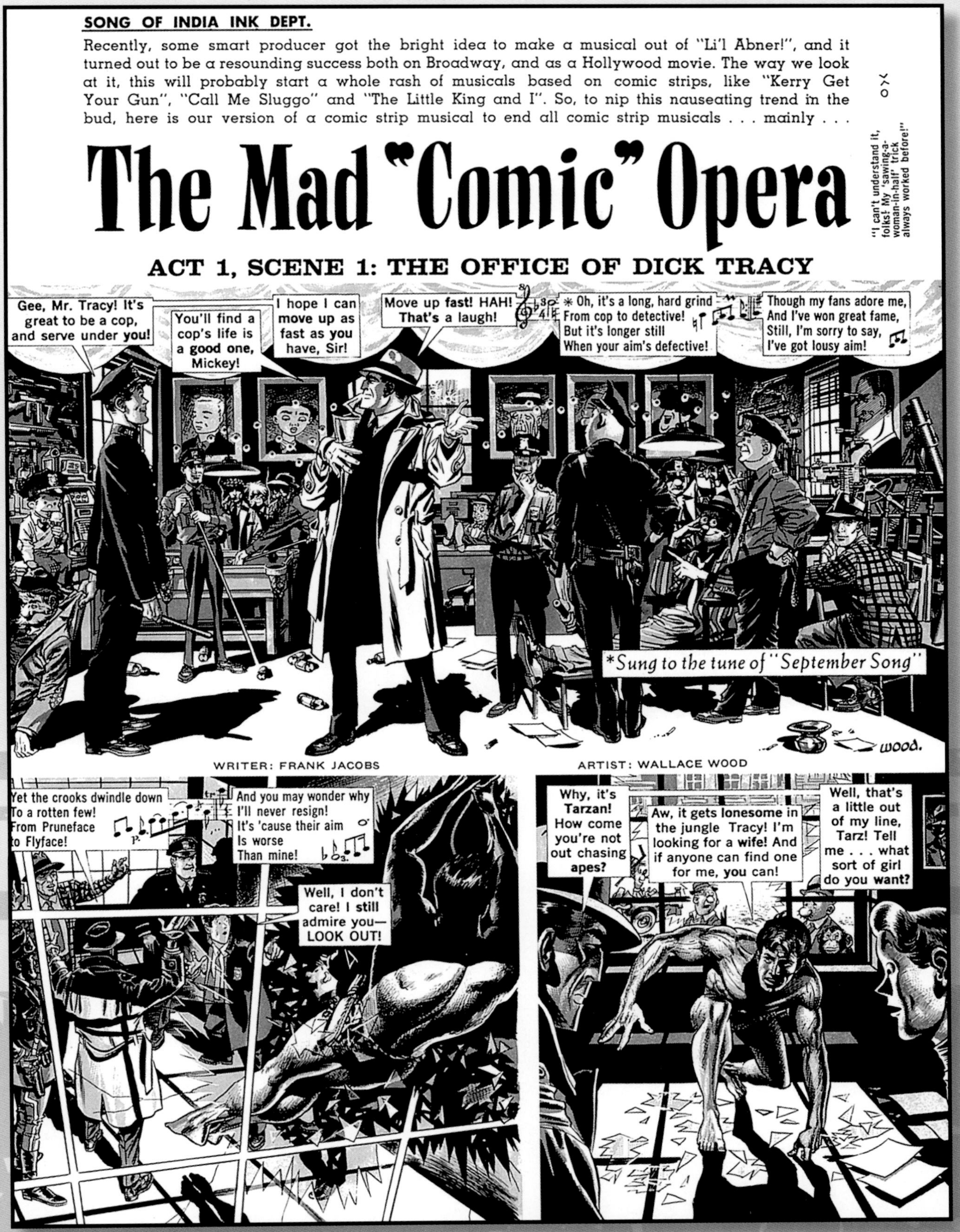
SONG OF INDIA INK DEPT.
Recently, some smart producer got the bright idea to make a musical out of "Li'l Abner!", and it turned out to be a resounding success both on Broadway, and as a Hollywood movie. The way we look at it, this will probably start a whole rash of musicals based on comic strips, like "Kerry Get Your Gun", "Call Me Sluggo" and "The Little King and I". So, to nip this nauseating trend in the bud, here is our version of a comic strip musical to end all comic strip musicals . . . mainly . . .
The Mad "Comic" Opera
"I can't understand it, folks! My 'sawing-a-woman-in-half' trick always worked before!"
ACT 1, SCENE 1: THE OFFICE OF DICK TRACY
Gee, Mr. Tracy! It's great to be a cop, and serve under you!
You'll find a cop's life is a good one, Mickey!
I hope I can move up as fast as you have, Sir!
Move up fast! HAH! That's a laugh!
* Oh, it's a long, hard grind From cop to detective! But it's longer still When your aim's defective!
Though my fans adore me, And I've won great fame, Still, I'm sorry to say, I've got lousy aim!
*Sung to the tune of "September Song"
WOOD.
WRITER: FRANK JACOBS
ARTIST: WALLACE WOOD
Yet the crooks dwindle down To a rotten few! From Pruneface to Flyface!
And you may wonder why I'll never resign! It's 'cause their aim Is worse Than mine!
Well, I don't care! I still admire you—LOOK OUT!
Why, it's Tarzan! How come you're not out chasing apes?
Aw, it gets lonesome in the jungle Tracy! I'm looking for a wife! And if anyone can find one for me, you can!
Well, that's a little out of my line, Tarz! Tell me . . . what sort of girl do you want?

MAD #56/JULY 1960

by Tom Richmond
ARTIST

Picking a favorite piece from among the many thousands published over the last 60 years in MAD is a little like picking which of your kids is your favorite — it's impossible. However, I was told I would not get paid for my last MAD job until I did just that, so...

I've always thought MAD was at its best when it took something and turned it completely on its head. They often took the realistic and serious and made it absurd and silly — but they sometimes took the absurd and silly and made it look even more so by putting it in a more realistic world. Writer Frank Jacobs and artist Wally Wood did just that in "The Mad 'Comic' Opera" in MAD #56. Frank's clever script included many of his "sung to the tune of..." song parodies, still a relatively new thing then and soon to become his iconic signature. Wally Wood's art seamlessly combined the look of simple comic strip characters into a gritty and realistic style with deep shadows and atmosphere galore. My favorite panel is the one where Dagwood's shadow is broken up by his recently acquired bullet holes...perfect art for a great story and concept.

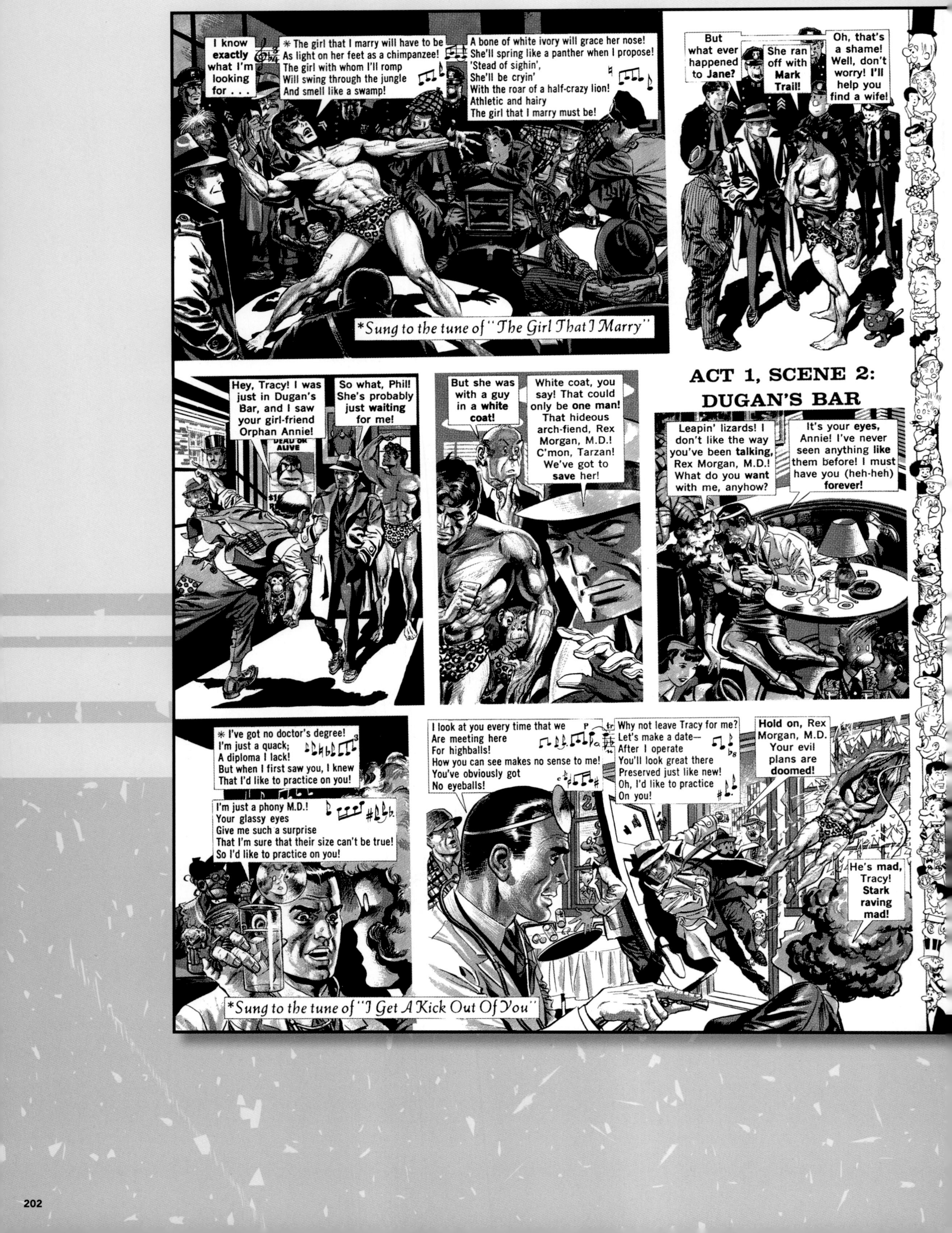

I know exactly what I'm looking for . . .
* The girl that I marry will have to be As light on her feet as a chimpanzee! The girl with whom I'll romp Will swing through the jungle And smell like a swamp!
A bone of white ivory will grace her nose! She'll spring like a panther when I propose! 'Stead of sighin', She'll be cryin' With the roar of a half-crazy lion! Athletic and hairy The girl that I marry must be!
*Sung to the tune of "The Girl That I Marry"
But what ever happened to Jane?
She ran off with Mark Trail!
Oh, that's a shame! Well, don't worry! I'll help you find a wife!
Hey, Tracy! I was just in Dugan's Bar, and I saw your girl-friend Orphan Annie!
So what, Phil! She's probably just waiting for me!
DEAD OR ALIVE
But she was with a guy in a white coat!
White coat, you say! That could only be one man! That hideous arch-fiend, Rex Morgan, M.D.! C'mon, Tarzan! We've got to save her!
ACT 1, SCENE 2: DUGAN'S BAR
Leapin' lizards! I don't like the way you've been talking, Rex Morgan, M.D.! What do you want with me, anyhow?
It's your eyes, Annie! I've never seen anything like them before! I must have you (heh-heh) forever!
* I've got no doctor's degree! I'm just a quack; A diploma I lack! But when I first saw you, I knew That I'd like to practice on you!
I'm just a phony M.D.! Your glassy eyes Give me such a surprise That I'm sure that their size can't be true! So I'd like to practice on you!
I look at you every time that we Are meeting here For highballs! How you can see makes no sense to me! You've obviously got No eyeballs!
Why not leave Tracy for me? Let's make a date— After I operate You'll look great there Preserved just like new! Oh, I'd like to practice On you!
Hold on, Rex Morgan, M.D. Your evil plans are doomed!
He's mad, Tracy! Stark raving mad!
*Sung to the tune of "I Get A Kick Out Of You"

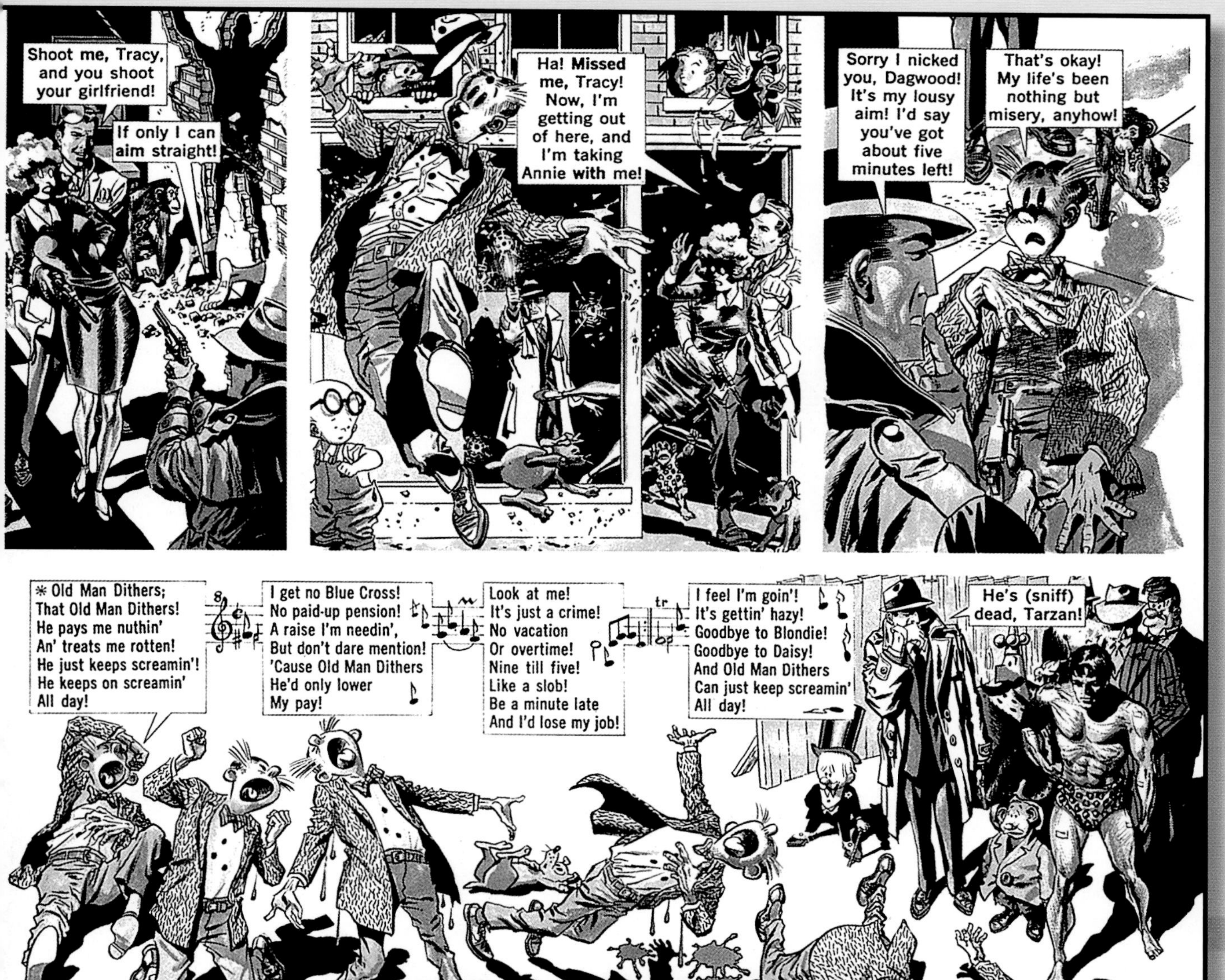

Shoot me, Tracy, and you shoot your girlfriend!
If only I can aim straight!
Ha! Missed me, Tracy! Now, I'm getting out of here, and I'm taking Annie with me!
Sorry I nicked you, Dagwood! It's my lousy aim! I'd say you've got about five minutes left!
That's okay! My life's been nothing but misery, anyhow!
* Old Man Dithers; That Old Man Dithers! He pays me nuthin' An' treats me rotten! He just keeps screamin'! He keeps on screamin' All day!
I get no Blue Cross! No paid-up pension! A raise I'm needin', But don't dare mention! 'Cause Old Man Dithers He'd only lower My pay!
Look at me! It's just a crime! No vacation Or overtime! Nine till five! Like a slob! Be a minute late And I'd lose my job!
I feel I'm goin'! It's gettin' hazy! Goodbye to Blondie! Goodbye to Daisy! And Old Man Dithers Can just keep screamin' All day!
He's (sniff) dead, Tarzan!
*Sung to the tune of "Old Man River"
Why, Tracy! You're crying! Is it because you feel sorry for killing him by mistake?
No! But I'll tell you why!
* You ask me why I sob Killing some poor slob! I of course reply When the bullets fly Something makes me cry!
True, I am just a heel! Sorrow I don't feel! Shooting the wrong guy Didn't make me cry! Smoke got in my eye!
nov shmoz ka pop
*Sung to the tune of "Smoke Gets In Your Eyes"
Why, it's Sandy! He wants us to follow him! I bet he can lead us to Orphan Annie!
Arf!

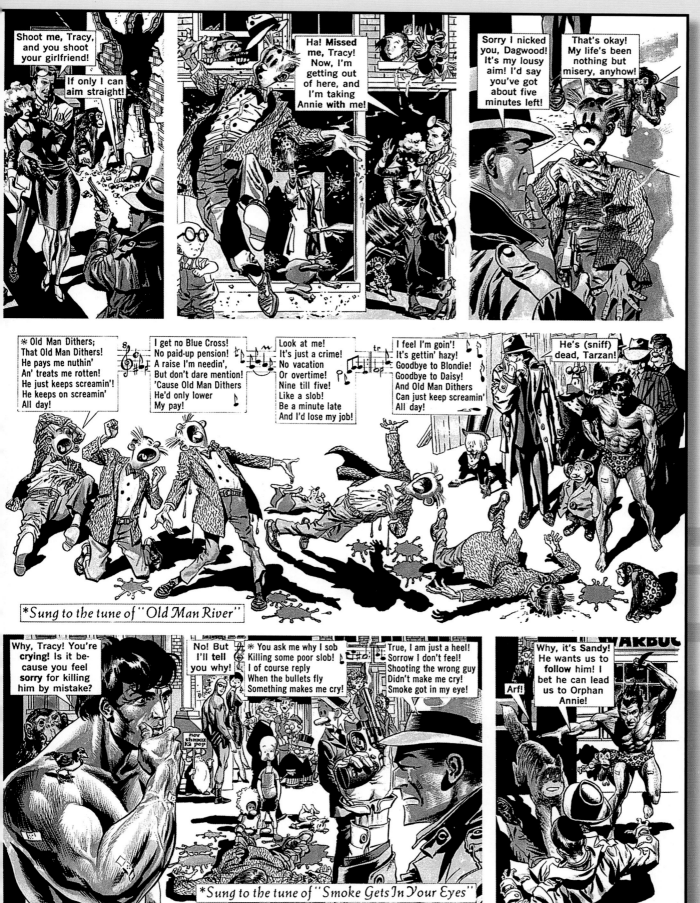

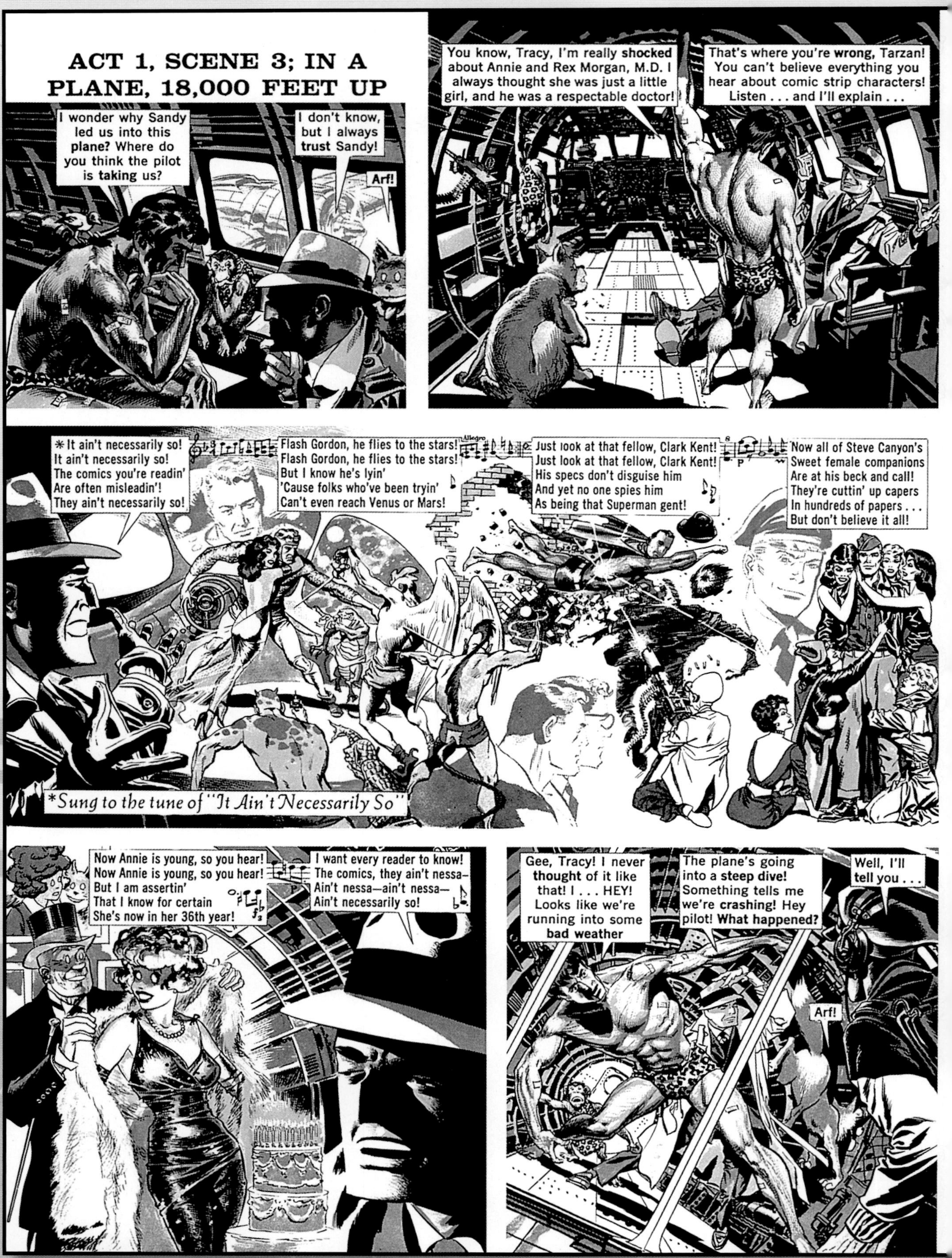
ACT 1, SCENE 3; IN A PLANE, 18,000 FEET UP
I wonder why Sandy led us into this plane? Where do you think the pilot is taking us?
I don't know, but I always trust Sandy!
Arf!
You know, Tracy, I'm really shocked about Annie and Rex Morgan, M.D. I always thought she was just a little girl, and he was a respectable doctor!
That's where you're wrong, Tarzan! You can't believe everything you hear about comic strip characters! Listen . . . and I'll explain . . .
* It ain't necessarily so! It ain't necessarily so! The comics you're readin' Are often misleadin'! They ain't necessarily so!
Flash Gordon, he flies to the stars! Flash Gordon, he flies to the stars! But I know he's lyin' 'Cause folks who've been tryin' Can't even reach Venus or Mars!
Allegro
Just look at that fellow, Clark Kent! Just look at that fellow, Clark Kent! His specs don't disguise him And yet no one spies him As being that Superman gent!
Now all of Steve Canyon's Sweet female companions Are at his beck and call! They're cuttin' up capers In hundreds of papers . . . But don't believe it all!
*Sung to the tune of "It Ain't Necessarily So"
Now Annie is young, so you hear! Now Annie is young, so you hear! But I am assertin' That I know for certain She's now in her 36th year!
I want every reader to know! The comics, they ain't nessa— Ain't nessa—ain't nessa— Ain't necessarily so!
Gee, Tracy! I never thought of it like that! I . . . HEY! Looks like we're running into some bad weather
The plane's going into a steep dive! Something tells me we're crashing! Hey pilot! What happened?
Well, I'll tell you . . .
Arf!

* It was just one of our wings! Just one of our airplane's wings! One of those breaks That bad weather brings! Just one of our wings!
It's been just one of those nights! Just one of those perilous flights! When you bail out, Count ten and pull strings! Just one of our wings!
If I'd thought a bit To the end of it, When I saw the plane was unsound! I'd have been aware Once we'd reach the air That we'd crash, smash to the ground!
So goodbye, have a nice trip! Here's hoping I've still got a strip! Now I must run, 'Cause we've got just one Of our wings!
He bailed out!
Guess we better do the same! I sure hope Sandy can count to ten . . .
Arf!
*Sung to the tune of "Just One Of Those Things"
ACT 2, SCENE 1: PENNY'S HOUSE, 18,000 FEET BELOW
I'm so glad that Penny invited you and Lowizee to dinner with us, Snuffy! Tell, me! Are you really beatniks?
Someone's at the door, Mom! I'll see who it is!
One side, Kid! The name's Morgan, M.D., and I need a hideout for Annie and me!
Run for your lives! He's mad!
Don't listen to her! She's mad herself! Just look at those staring eyes!
Pore chile's all tuckered out! Ye ailin', honey?
I'm all right! It's just that I wish Dick Tracy were here! Gosh, I miss him!
* Tra-cy! How I miss ya! How I miss ya! My dear Dick Tracy! I'd give the world to say That you were here with A—N-N-I-Even know that San-dy's Workin' for ya, barkin' for ya! He'll find me, Tracy! A happy girl I never will be Till Tracy comes an' rescues me!
Don't worry, Annie! We're here! Sandy did lead us to you!
Tracy! At last!
And now for you, Rex Morgan, M.D. Take that! And that! And . . .
Darn it! I keep missing him!
*Sung to the tune of "Swanee"

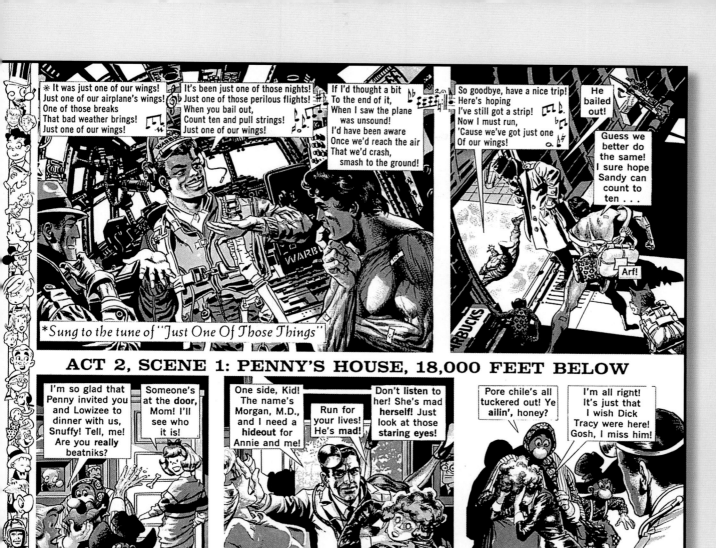

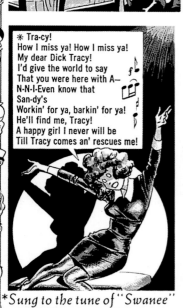

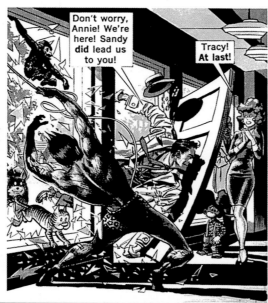

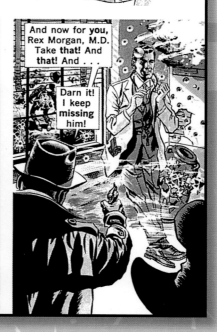

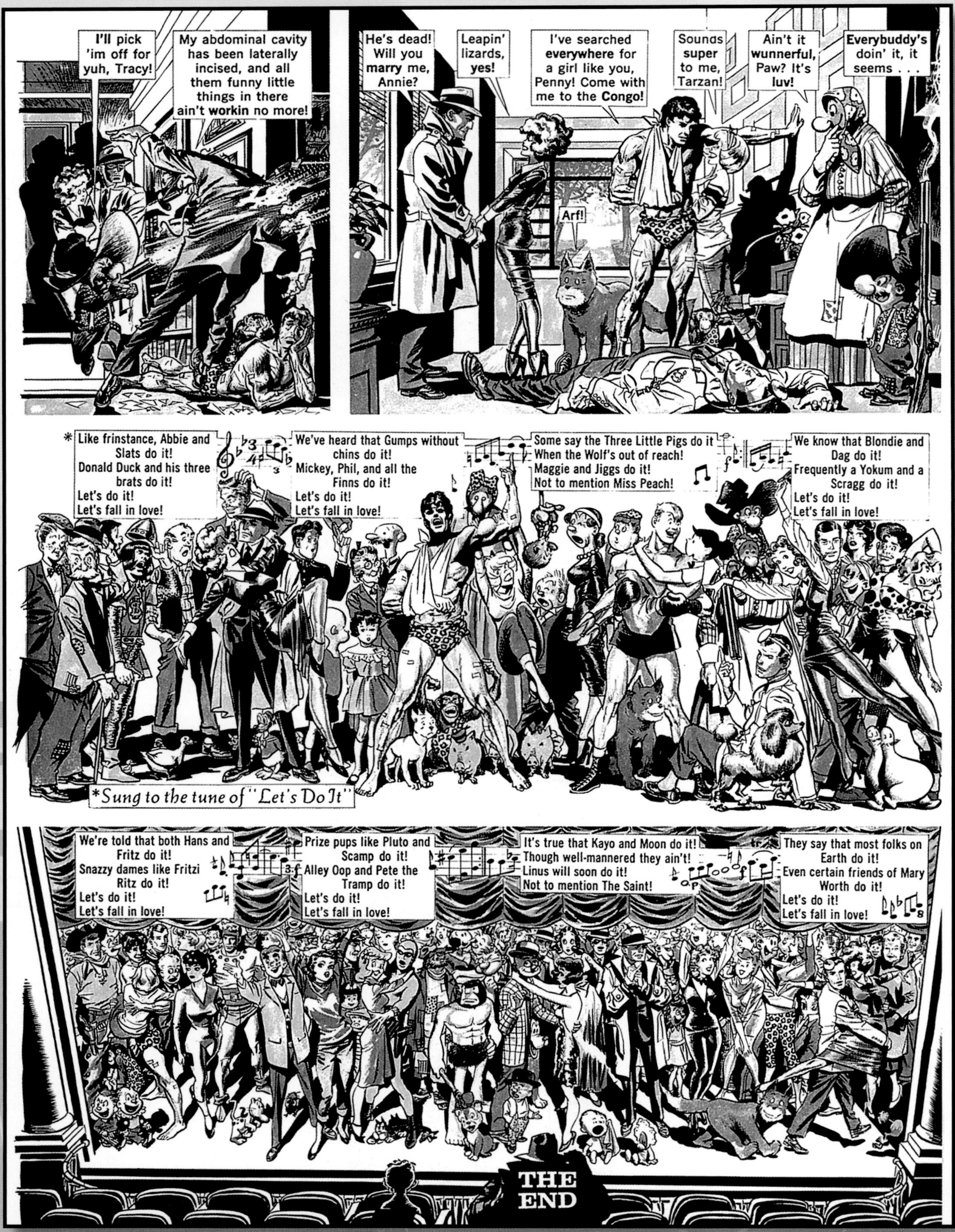

I'll pick 'im off for yuh, Tracy!
My abdominal cavity has been laterally incised, and all them funny little things in there ain't workin no more!
He's dead! Will you marry me, Annie?
Leapin' lizards, yes!
I've searched everywhere for a girl like you, Penny! Come with me to the Congo!
Sounds super to me, Tarzan!
Ain't it wunnerful, Paw? It's luv!
Everybuddy's doin' it, it seems . . .
Arf!
* Like frinstance, Abbie and Slats do it! Donald Duck and his three brats do it! Let's do it! Let's fall in love!
We've heard that Gumps without chins do it! Mickey, Phil, and all the Finns do it! Let's do it! Let's fall in love!
Some say the Three Little Pigs do it When the Wolf's out of reach! Maggie and Jiggs do it! Not to mention Miss Peach!
We know that Blondie and Dag do it! Frequently a Yokum and a Scragg do it! Let's do it! Let's fall in love!
*Sung to the tune of "Let's Do It"
We're told that both Hans and Fritz do it! Snazzy dames like Fritzi Ritz do it! Let's do it! Let's fall in love!
Prize pups like Pluto and Scamp do it! Alley Oop and Pete the Tramp do it! Let's do it! Let's fall in love!
It's true that Kayo and Moon do it! Though well-mannered they ain't! Linus will soon do it! Not to mention The Saint!
They say that most folks on Earth do it! Even certain friends of Mary Worth do it! Let's do it! Let's fall in love!
THE END

EDITOR'S PICK

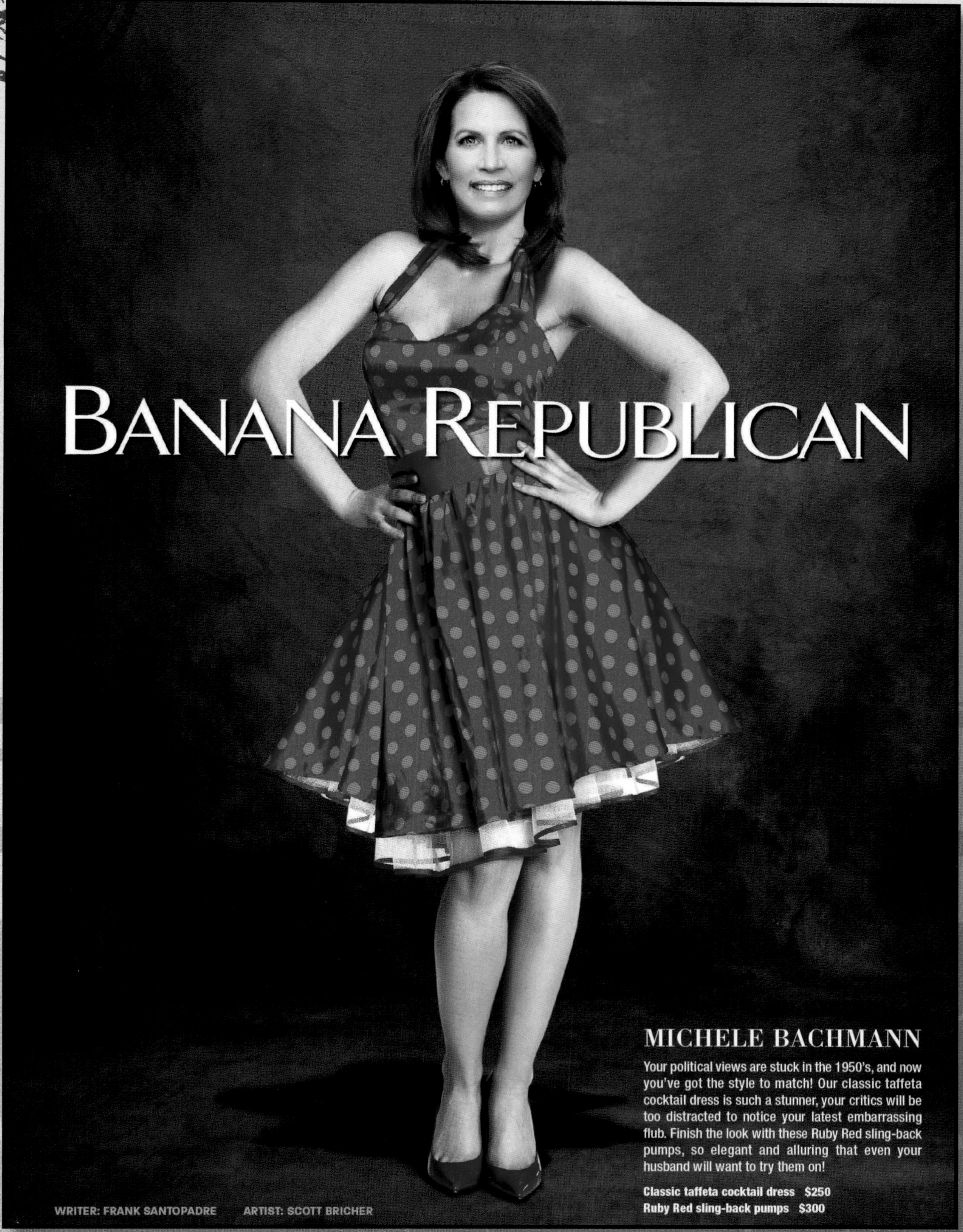
BANANA REPUBLICAN
MICHELE BACHMANN
Your political views are stuck in the 1950's, and now you've got the style to match! Our classic taffeta cocktail dress is such a stunner, your critics will be too distracted to notice your latest embarrassing flub. Finish the look with these Ruby Red sling-back pumps, so elegant and alluring that even your husband will want to try them on!
Classic taffeta cocktail dress $250
Ruby Red sling-back pumps $300
WRITER: FRANK SANTOPADRE ARTIST: SCOTT BRICHER

MAD #514/APRIL 2012

When writer Frank Santopadre first pitched the idea for a Banana Republican catalog during the 2008 presidential election, we passed on it for two reasons: 1) it was a bit late in the campaign when he pitched it and 2) it seemed like an awful lot of production work for the MAD staff. I believe our conversation to Frank went something like, "Frank, don't you have a simple idea like 'You Know You're Really Dumb When...,' with some funny examples that we can just give to Coker to illustrate and be done?" But Frank is, if nothing else, persistent and re-pitched his idea — this time very early in the 2012 presidential

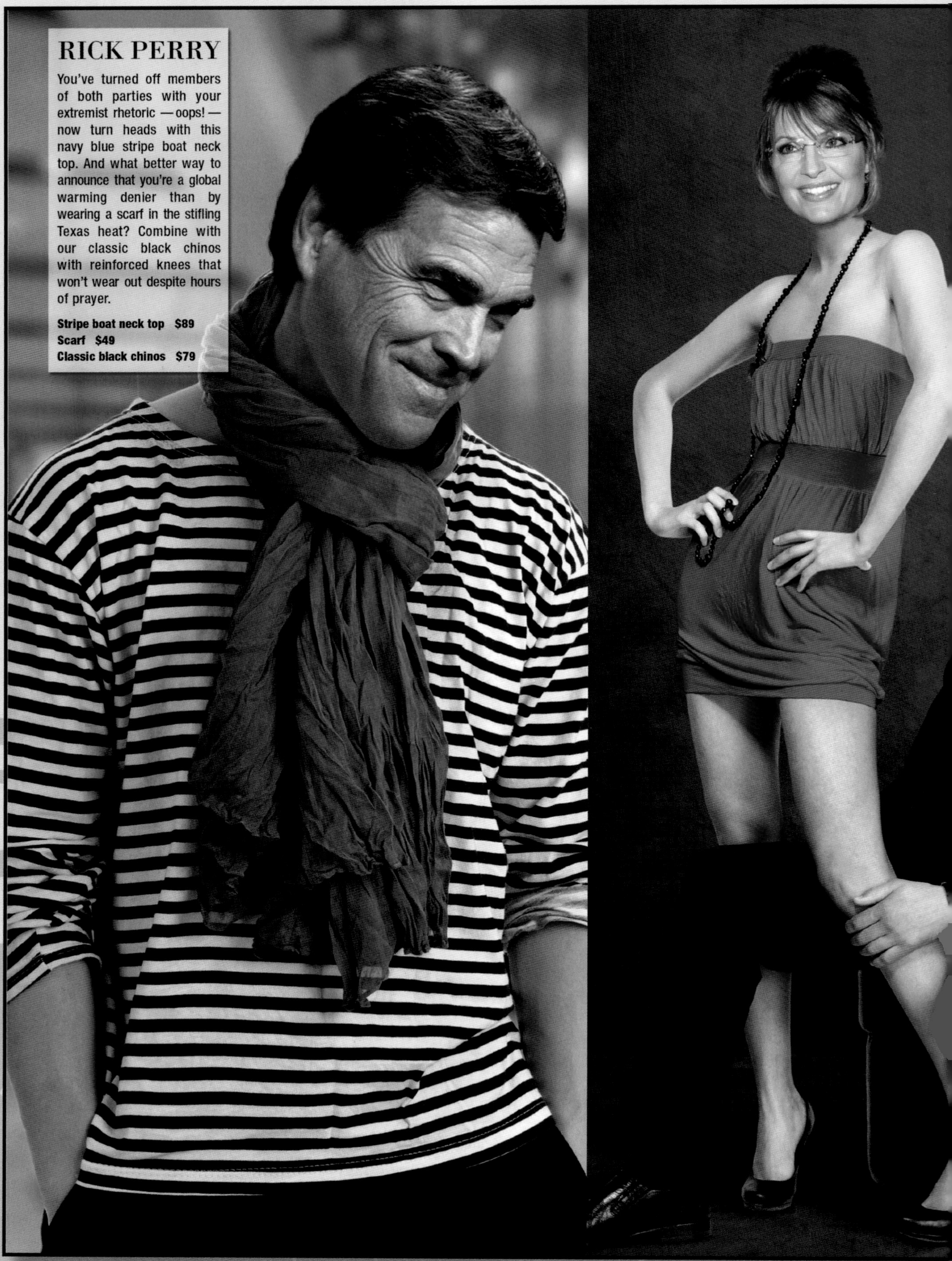
RICK PERRY
You've turned off members of both parties with your extremist rhetoric —oops!— now turn heads with this navy blue stripe boat neck top. And what better way to announce that you're a global warming denier than by wearing a scarf in the stifling Texas heat? Combine with our classic black chinos with reinforced knees that won't wear out despite hours of prayer.
Stripe boat neck top $89
Scarf $49
Classic black chinos $79

race. It still seemed like an awful lot of production work, but in a weakened moment, we gave him the green light. I'm glad we did. With a herd of GOP right-wingers in his sights, Frank brilliantly satirized their extreme positions in slick catalog-speak. Scott Bricher did some first-rate Photoshopping to visually marry the copy and candidates with the look of a Banana Republic catalog. The result, I think, was an instant MAD classic. But it was an awful lot of work… — *John Ficarra*

ARAH PALIN

an you look like a million ucks even when the GOP n't spending a million on ur wardrobe? You betcha! Our rapless tube dress is ideal r work and play, whether u're shooting down Democratic tiatives or shooting wolves om a chopper. Best of all, andex knit is both flexible and bstantial, even if you're neither.

rapless tube dress $175

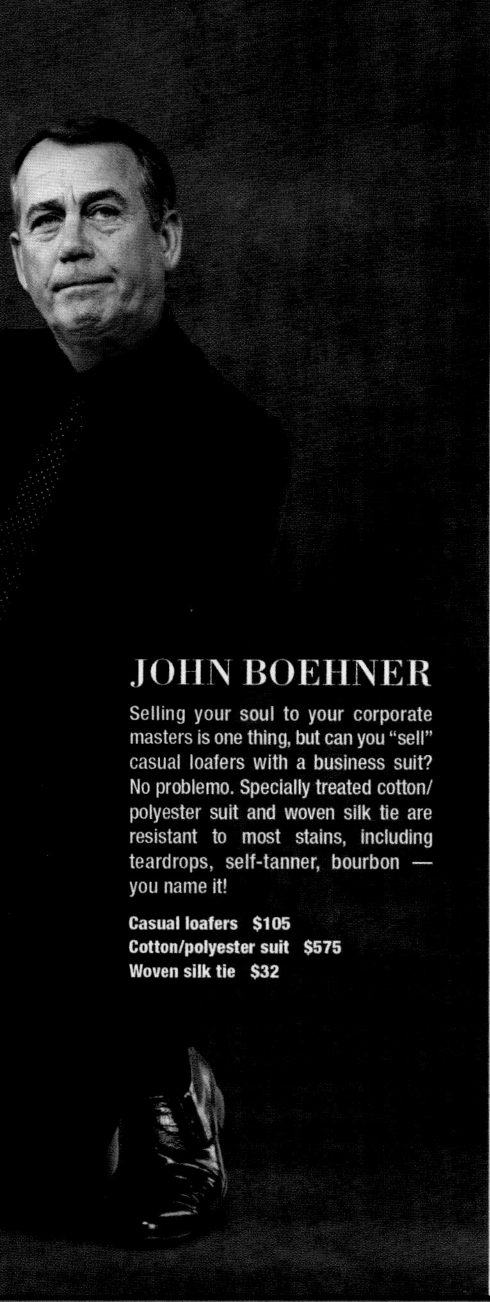

JOHN BOEHNER

Selling your soul to your corporate masters is one thing, but can you "sell" casual loafers with a business suit? No problemo. Specially treated cotton/polyester suit and woven silk tie are resistant to most stains, including teardrops, self-tanner, bourbon — you name it!

Casual loafers $105
Cotton/polyester suit $575
Woven silk tie $32

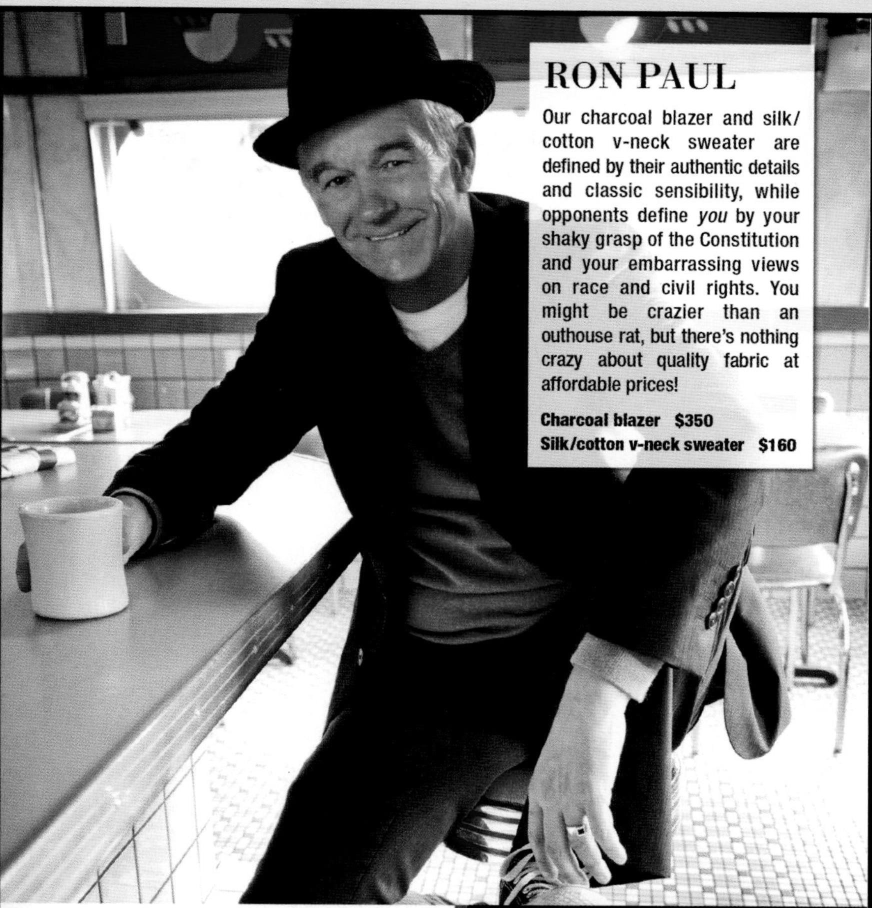

RON PAUL

Our charcoal blazer and silk/cotton v-neck sweater are defined by their authentic details and classic sensibility, while opponents define *you* by your shaky grasp of the Constitution and your embarrassing views on race and civil rights. You might be crazier than an outhouse rat, but there's nothing crazy about quality fabric at affordable prices!

Charcoal blazer $350
Silk/cotton v-neck sweater $160

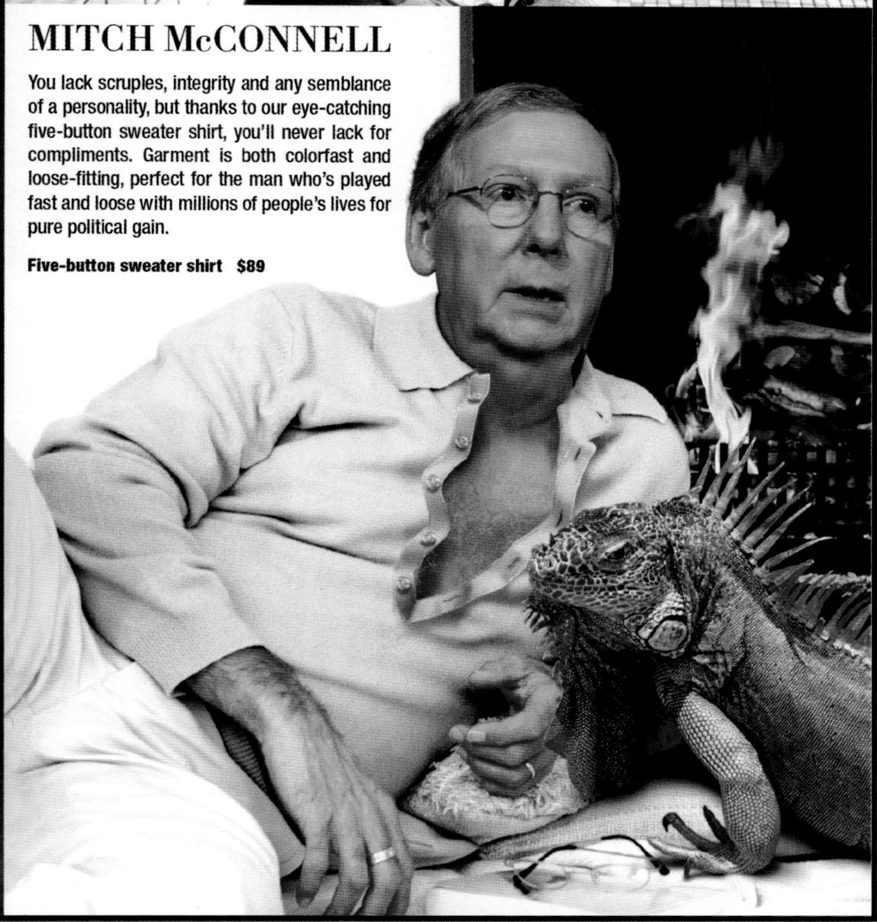

MITCH McCONNELL

You lack scruples, integrity and any semblance of a personality, but thanks to our eye-catching five-button sweater shirt, you'll never lack for compliments. Garment is both colorfast and loose-fitting, perfect for the man who's played fast and loose with millions of people's lives for pure political gain.

Five-button sweater shirt $89

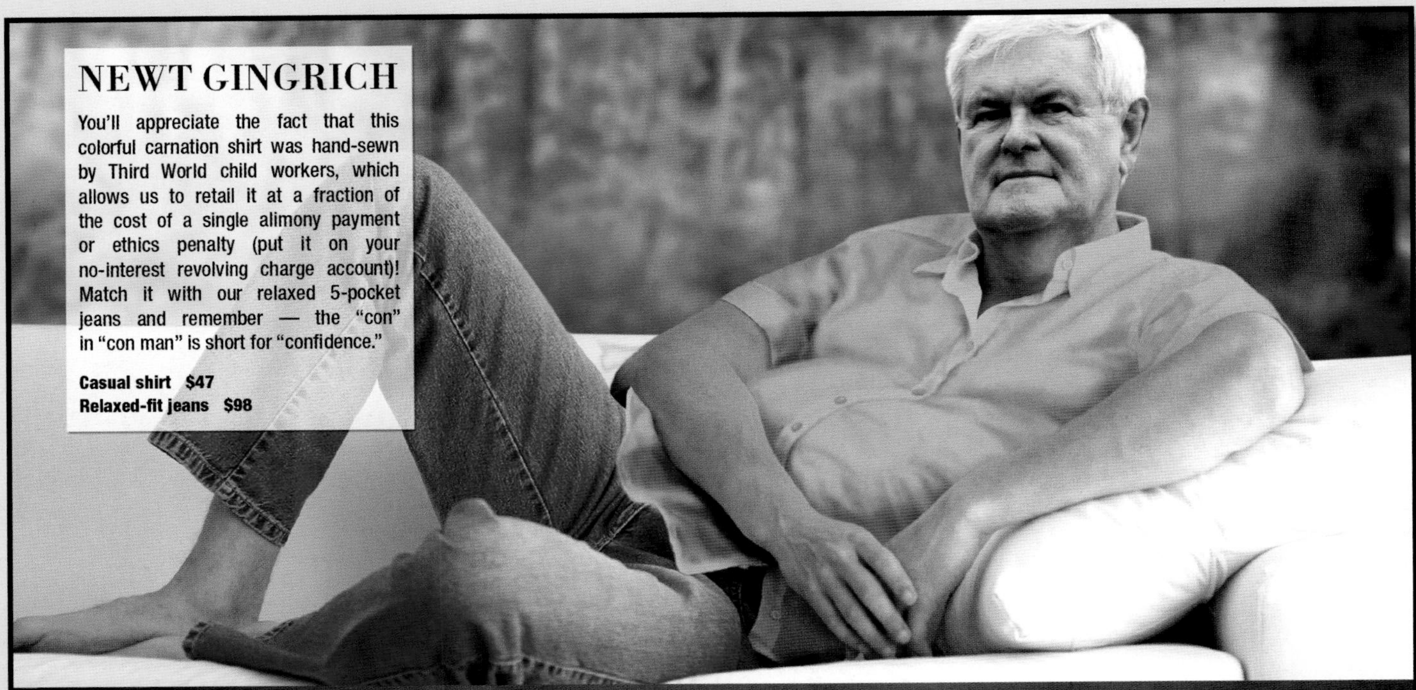

NEWT GINGRICH

You'll appreciate the fact that this colorful carnation shirt was hand-sewn by Third World child workers, which allows us to retail it at a fraction of the cost of a single alimony payment or ethics penalty (put it on your no-interest revolving charge account)! Match it with our relaxed 5-pocket jeans and remember — the "con" in "con man" is short for "confidence."

Casual shirt $47
Relaxed-fit jeans $98

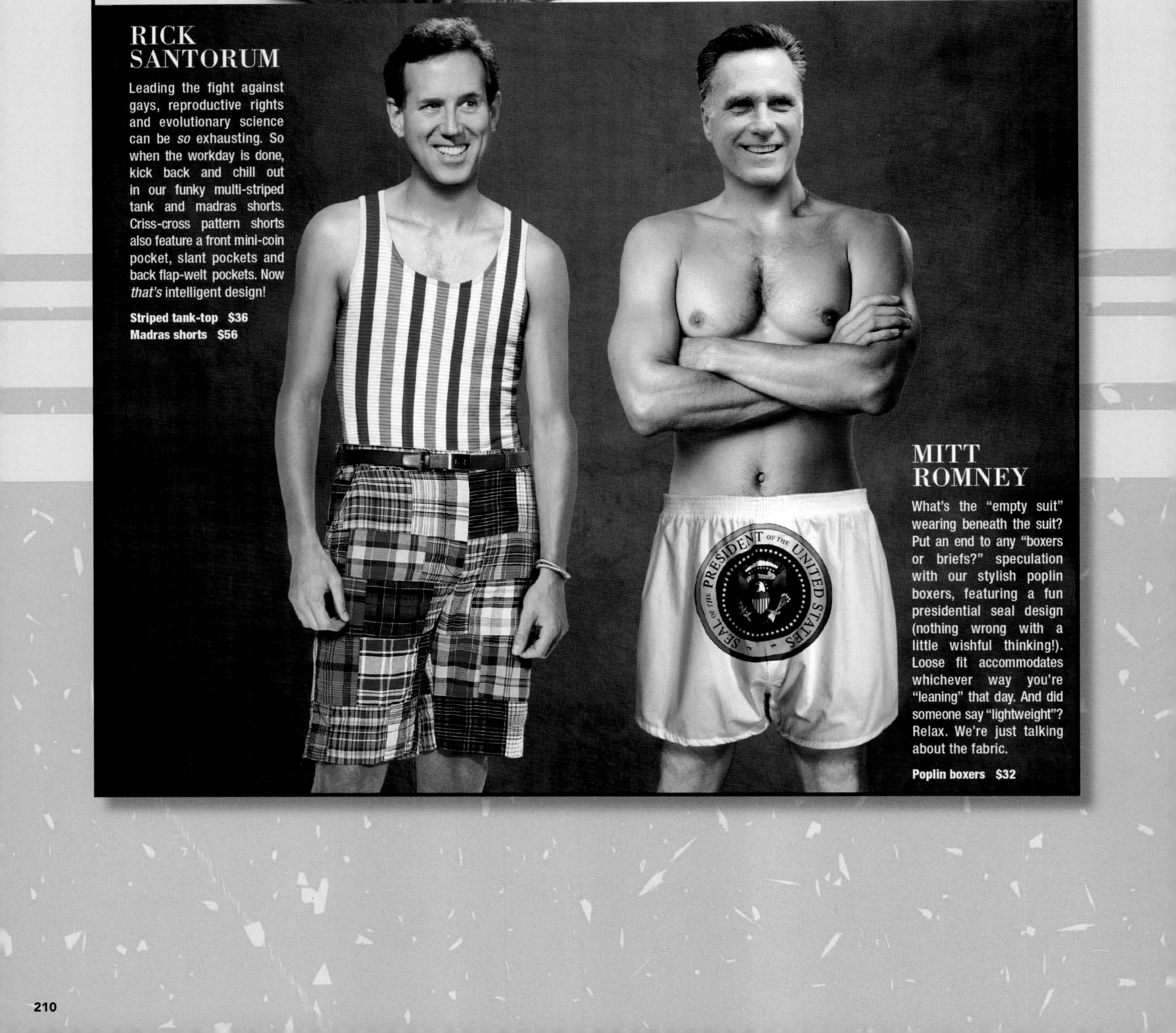
SEAL OF THE PRESIDENT OF THE UNITED STATES

RICK SANTORUM

Leading the fight against gays, reproductive rights and evolutionary science can be *so* exhausting. So when the workday is done, kick back and chill out in our funky multi-striped tank and madras shorts. Criss-cross pattern shorts also feature a front mini-coin pocket, slant pockets and back flap-welt pockets. Now *that's* intelligent design!

Striped tank-top $36
Madras shorts $56

MITT ROMNEY

What's the "empty suit" wearing beneath the suit? Put an end to any "boxers or briefs?" speculation with our stylish poplin boxers, featuring a fun presidential seal design (nothing wrong with a little wishful thinking!). Loose fit accommodates whichever way you're "leaning" that day. And did someone say "lightweight"? Relax. We're just talking about the fabric.

Poplin boxers $32

WHEN JOHNNY COMES MARCHING HOME AGAIN
hurrah, hurrah!

WELCOME HOME FROM VIETNAM JOHNNY

Thurston

MAD #149/MARCH 1972

by Peter Kuper
WRITER/ARTIST

ow many times did MAD Magazine blow my mind over the years? I tried to count once, but I ran out of fingers. A few notable pieces, however, did pop into my head when the editors of MAD asked me to answer that question.

My earliest MAD memory, after I'd given up breast-feeding (age 10), was an Al Jaffee drawing of a jackal retching. It wasn't the bent-over jackal that did it for me; it was the details. A grown man had taken the time to add the contents of the jackal's ejected stomach matter: a finger and a chicken bone along with his gacked-out dentures. But wait! In the lower right-hand corner he'd also drawn a little mouse racing away, holding a leaf over his head like an umbrella against the rain of vomit. The notion that there was a job that paid adults to sit around and draw things like this set me firmly on the path to becoming a cartoonist.

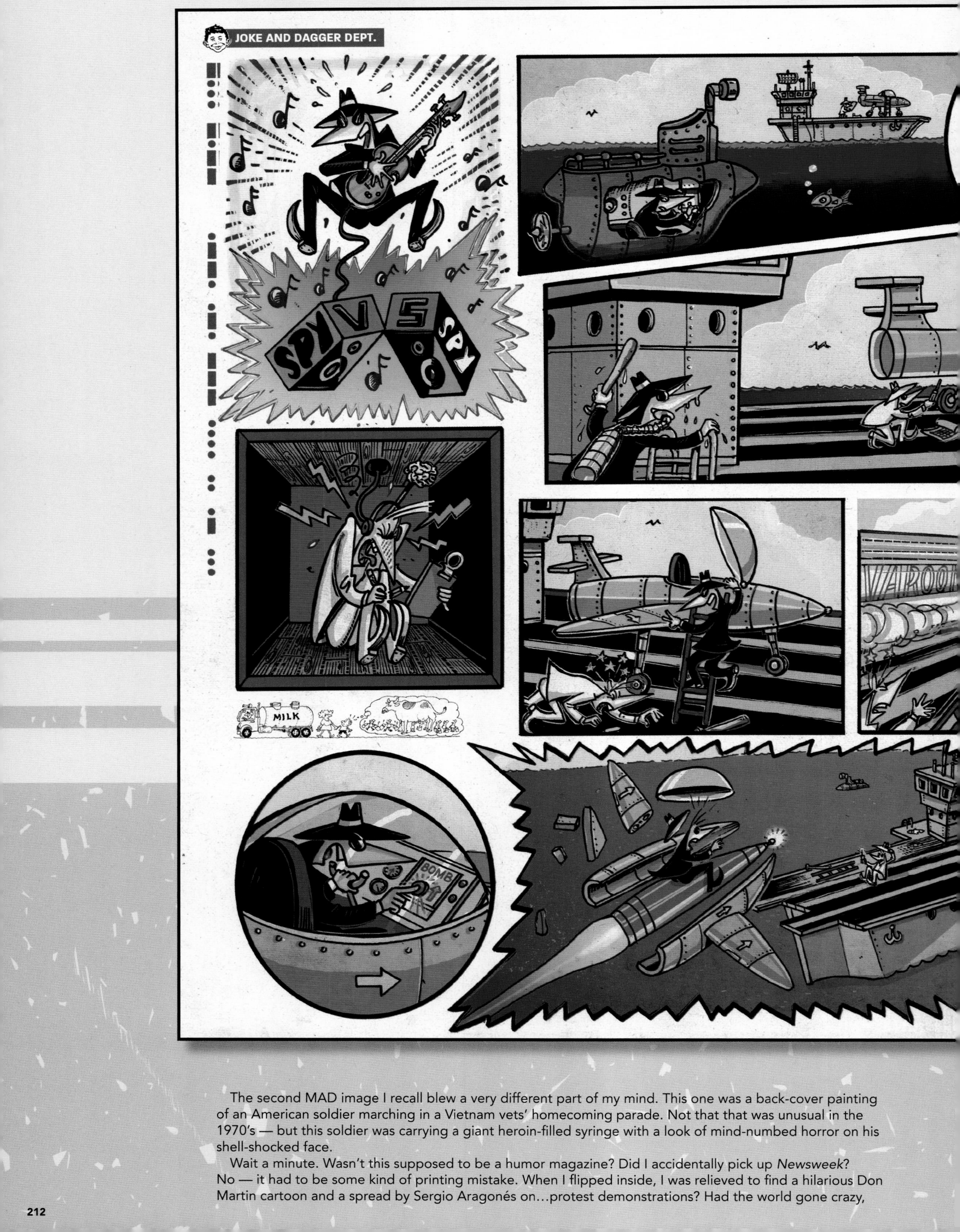
JOKE AND DAGGER DEPT.
SPY VS SPY
MILK
BOMB
VAROO

The second MAD image I recall blew a very different part of my mind. This one was a back-cover painting of an American soldier marching in a Vietnam vets' homecoming parade. Not that that was unusual in the 1970's — but this soldier was carrying a giant heroin-filled syringe with a look of mind-numbed horror on his shell-shocked face.

Wait a minute. Wasn't this supposed to be a humor magazine? Did I accidentally pick up *Newsweek*? No — it had to be some kind of printing mistake. When I flipped inside, I was relieved to find a hilarious Don Martin cartoon and a spread by Sergio Aragonés on...protest demonstrations? Had the world gone crazy,

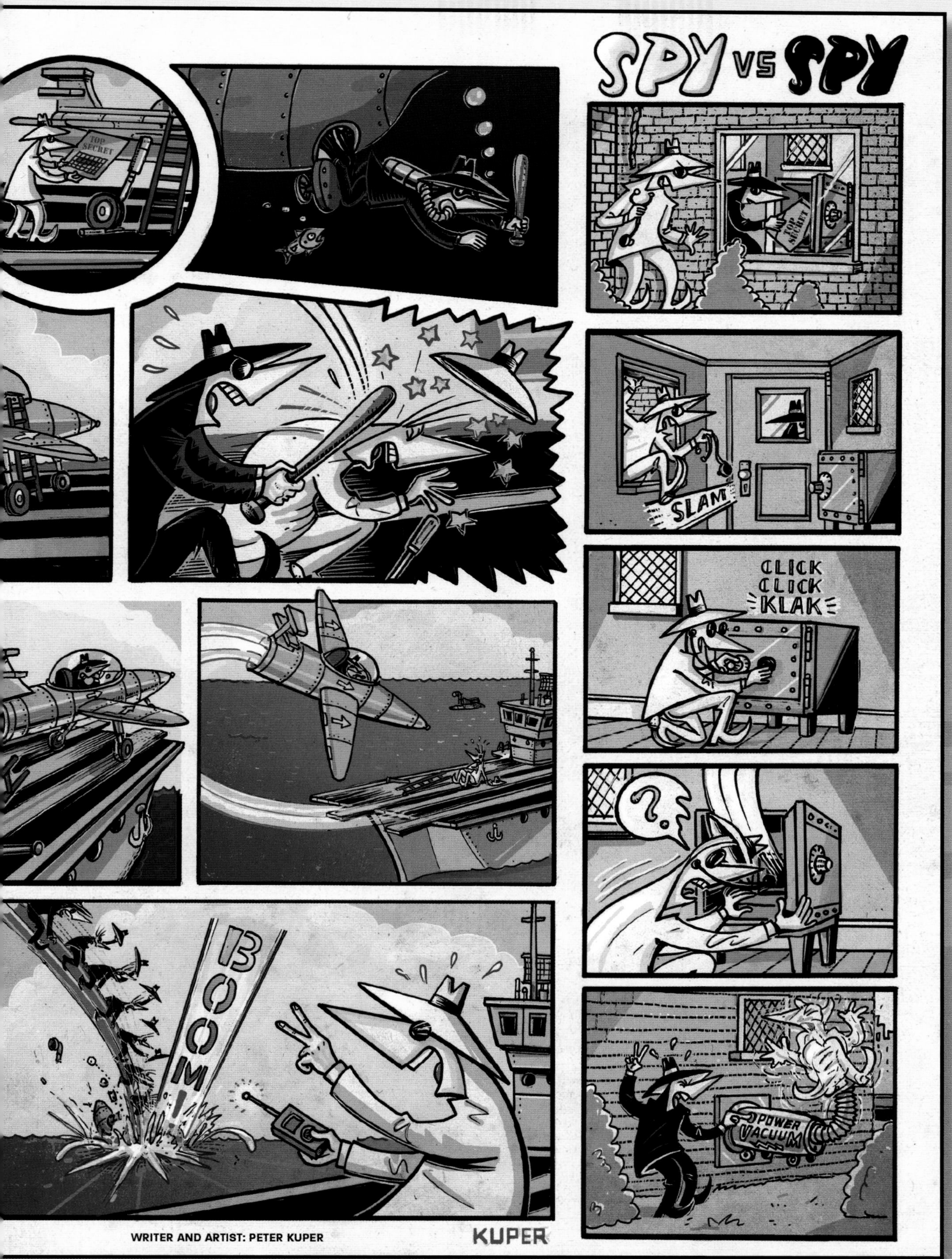
SPY vs SPY
TOP SECRET
TOP SECRET
SLAM
CLICK
CLICK
KLAK
?
BOOM!
POWER VACUUM
WRITER AND ARTIST: PETER KUPER
KUPER

MAD #513/FEBRUARY 2012

er, MAD? The answer was yes and yes. This collision of humor and politics, which MAD perfectly captured, forever altered the worldview of millions, and the direction my own cartooning would take.

And speaking of shameless segues into my own work: my entry onto the pages of MAD came thanks to a Spanish-speaking Cuban named Antonio Prohias. Little did I realize as a child, attempting to decipher the lunatic struggles of Prohias' Cold War-inspired Black and White Spies, that one day I would find myself stepping into his pointy shoes. Thanks to Prohias' elaborate Spy vs. Spy rulebook, he handed me endless ways to literally blow their minds and, hopefully, along the way, yours. Figuratively, of course.

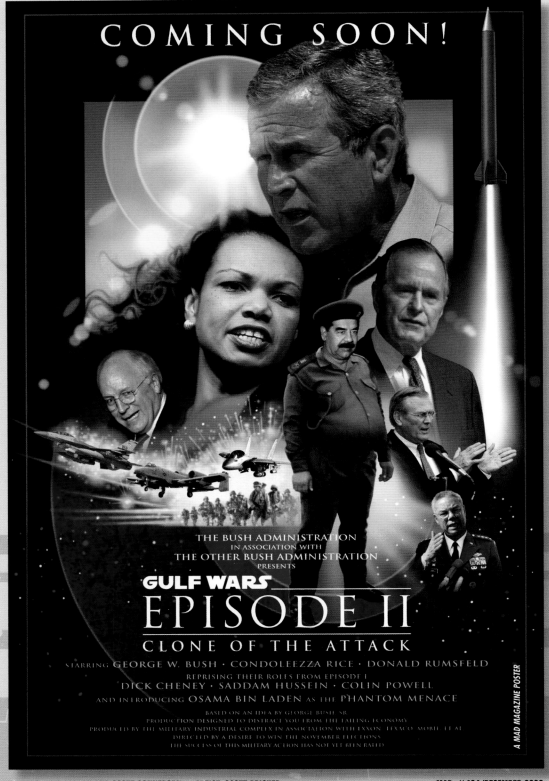

COMING SOON!

THE BUSH ADMINISTRATION
IN ASSOCIATION WITH
THE OTHER BUSH ADMINISTRATION
PRESENTS

GULF WARS
EPISODE II
CLONE OF THE ATTACK

STARRING GEORGE W. BUSH · CONDOLEEZZA RICE · DONALD RUMSFELD
REPRISING THEIR ROLES FROM EPISODE I
DICK CHENEY · SADDAM HUSSEIN · COLIN POWELL
AND INTRODUCING OSAMA BIN LADEN AS THE PHANTOM MENACE

BASED ON AN IDEA BY GEORGE BUSH SR
PRODUCTION DESIGNED TO DISTRACT YOU FROM THE FAILING ECONOMY
PRODUCED BY THE MILITARY INDUSTRIAL COMPLEX IN ASSOCIATION WITH EXXON-TEXACO-MOBIL ET AL
DIRECTED BY A DESIRE TO WIN THE NOVEMBER ELECTIONS
THE SUCCESS OF THIS MILITARY ACTION HAS NOT YET BEEN RATED

A MAD MAGAZINE POSTER

WRITERS: ARIE KAPLAN AND SCOTT SONNEBORN • ARTIST: SCOTT BRICHER

MAD #424/DECEMBER 2002

by Ward Sutton
ARTIST

When I first saw this, I had mixed feelings: on one hand, I knew it was brilliant and an instant classic. On the other, I was sad that I hadn't thought of the idea first!

Thematically, it perfectly tied in the then-new *Star Wars* film and the Iraq War. The father-son conflict in the *Star Wars* saga mirrored the Bush family drama. Saddam was depicted as a bozo here, and yet it was Bush and his cronies who represented the Empire. This was an edgy commentary at a time when Americans were being expected to mindlessly fall in line behind the war plan. I loved it.

Visually, I tend to prefer illustrated pieces, but this Photoshop image does a great job of parodying the actual *Star Wars Episode II* poster, placing Bush in the role of Anakin Skywalker, whom we all know "goes

to the dark side" by giving in to hate and violence. The "shock and awe" war machines seem straight out of Lucasfilm's dazzling special effects. And Condi nuzzling Dubya is icing on the cake.

It's worth noting that I didn't see this first in the magazine; I saw it attached to an email someone sent me. (That's how things "went viral" in the pre-social media age.) The fact that this was bouncing across the Internet and enjoyed beyond MAD's typical fan base shows how especially relevant and of-the-moment the piece was.

Just as audiences were wary of the *Star Wars* prequels, Americans were, at best, wary of a Gulf War sequel. But whatever you think of Lucas' or Bush's efforts, one thing is for sure: this hilarious MAD poster is a Mission Accomplished!

MYTH-TAKEN IDENTITIES DEPT.
Scantily-clad, buxom babes! Shirtless, sweaty hunks! Leather! Spandex! Martha Stewart's ingredients to a successful party? Well, sure! The four things that have kept Dave Berg going all these years? Absolutely! Little-known details of Mother Teresa's first year in the convent? Hey, that's sick! What the hell is the matter with you? What kind of depraved mind do you have? Why don't you seek professional help while we run our satire of...
JERKULES & ZIMA
ARTIST: ANGELO TORRES WRITER: DICK DEBARTOLO
I am Jerkules, son of Zoos! Legend has it that a lightning bolt consumed my mother and brothers, but truth be told, they abandoned me! I was the prettiest one in the family and they are a jealous bunch! But the lightning bolt thing sounds more mythological! It is said that I have more strength than most men! True! And less talent than most actors! Also true! I have a passion for righteousness, and as you can see by my outfit, an even greater passion for leather!
I'm Eagerless, Jerkules' buddy! As we roam from town to town, we beat up every corrupt and evil person we meet! It's partly for the sake of justice, and partly for our image! When two big muscle men travel around arm-in-arm, they gotta butch it up or there'll be a lotta talk in legend land!
I am Zima, the mighty princess warrior who uses all of my power and courage to really stuff a bra! Like Jerkules, I'm strong, quick to fight and slow to register any sort of emotion or acting talent! But who really cares? My Amazon legs are famous for letting me flip in the air and getting horny viewers to flip to whatever channel I'm flashing on!
I'm Zima's side-kick, Grabby! I help her battle the demons from the dark and deadly depths and take on the armies of evildoers! But my most important job is to help her handle sentences of more than five words!
POST NO BILLS
torres

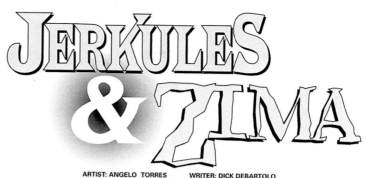

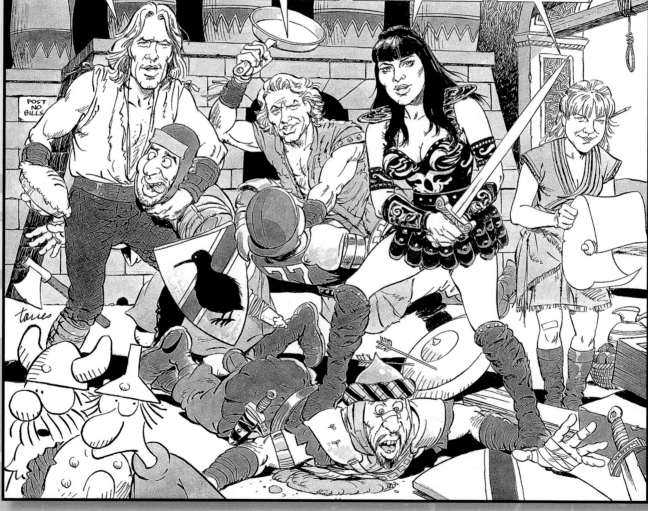

MAD #349/SEPTEMBER 1996

by Leonard Brenner
ART DIRECTOR

For me, one of the most interesting pieces of MAD Magazine trivia is that five art students attending School of Visual Arts in New York City at roughly the same time would later become close personal friends as well as professional members of MAD's Usual Gang of Idiots. The paths of Angelo Torres, George Woodbridge, Paul Peter Porges and Nick Meglin didn't cross with mine as I studied art direction and design while their courses focused on illustration and/or cartooning. I had seen Ange's work displayed from time to time in the school's award-winner exhibitions, but it wasn't until several years later when I had become MAD's assistant art director to John Putnam that we all came together to contribute our individual MADness. Nick (who was writing MAD articles while at SVA) became an editor, George soon followed as a freelance artist, then Porges (no one ever called him Paul or Peter) as a writer/artist,

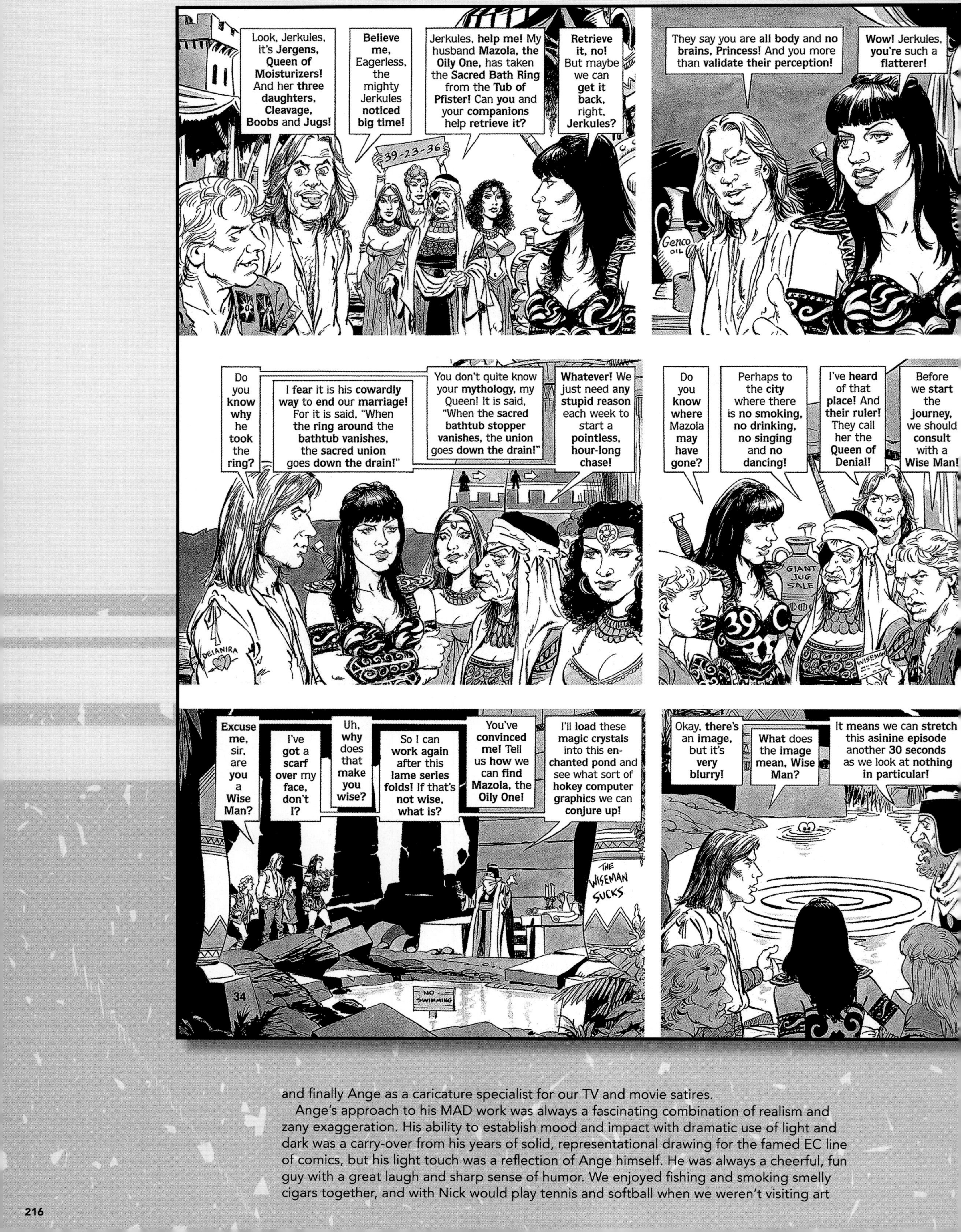

Look, Jerkules, it's Jergens, Queen of Moisturizers! And her three daughters, Cleavage, Boobs and Jugs!
Believe me, Eagerless, the mighty Jerkules noticed big time!
Jerkules, help me! My husband Mazola, the Oily One, has taken the Sacred Bath Ring from the Tub of Pfister! Can you and your companions help retrieve it?
Retrieve it, no! But maybe we can get it back, right, Jerkules?
39-23-36
They say you are all body and no brains, Princess! And you more than validate their perception!
Wow! Jerkules, you're such a flatterer!
Genco Oil
Do you know why he took the ring?
I fear it is his cowardly way to end our marriage! For it is said, "When the ring around the bathtub vanishes, the sacred union goes down the drain!"
You don't quite know your mythology, my Queen! It is said, "When the sacred bathtub stopper vanishes, the union goes down the drain!"
Whatever! We just need any stupid reason each week to start a pointless, hour-long chase!
DEIANIRA
Do you know where Mazola may have gone?
Perhaps to the city where there is no smoking, no drinking, no singing and no dancing!
I've heard of that place! And their ruler! They call her the Queen of Denial!
Before we start the journey, we should consult with a Wise Man!
GIANT JUG SALE
39
WISEMAN
Excuse me, sir, are you a Wise Man?
I've got a scarf over my face, don't I?
Uh, why does that make you wise?
So I can work again after this lame series folds! If that's not wise, what is?
You've convinced me! Tell us how we can find Mazola, the Oily One!
I'll load these magic crystals into this enchanted pond and see what sort of hokey computer graphics we can conjure up!
THE WISEMAN SUCKS
NO SWIMMING
34
Okay, there's an image, but it's very blurry!
What does the image mean, Wise Man?
It means we can stretch this asinine episode another 30 seconds as we look at nothing in particular!

and finally Ange as a caricature specialist for our TV and movie satires.

Ange's approach to his MAD work was always a fascinating combination of realism and zany exaggeration. His ability to establish mood and impact with dramatic use of light and dark was a carry-over from his years of solid, representational drawing for the famed EC line of comics, but his light touch was a reflection of Ange himself. He was always a cheerful, fun guy with a great laugh and sharp sense of humor. We enjoyed fishing and smoking smelly cigars together, and with Nick would play tennis and softball when we weren't visiting art

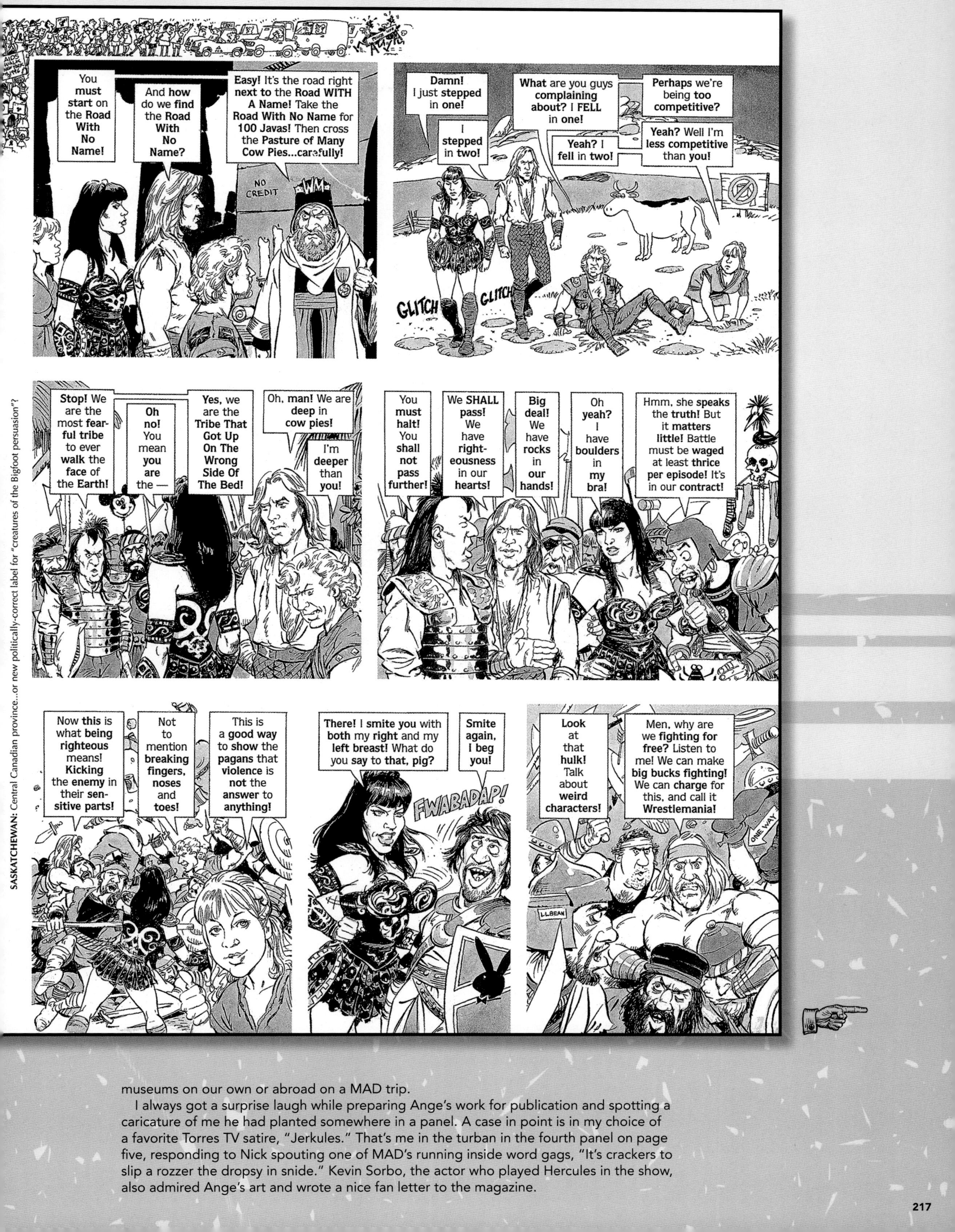
You must start on the Road With No Name!
And how do we find the Road With No Name?
Easy! It's the road right next to the Road WITH A Name! Take the Road With No Name for 100 Javas! Then cross the Pasture of Many Cow Pies...carefully!
NO CREDIT
Damn! I just stepped in one!
I stepped in two!
What are you guys complaining about? I FELL in one!
Yeah? I fell in two!
Perhaps we're being too competitive?
Yeah? Well I'm less competitive than you!
GLITCH
GLITCH
Stop! We are the most fearful tribe to ever walk the face of the Earth!
Oh no! You mean you are the —
Yes, we are the Tribe That Got Up On The Wrong Side Of The Bed!
Oh, man! We are deep in cow pies!
I'm deeper than you!
You must halt! You shall not pass further!
We SHALL pass! We have righteousness in our hearts!
Big deal! We have rocks in our hands!
Oh yeah? I have boulders in my bra!
Hmm, she speaks the truth! But it matters little! Battle must be waged at least thrice per episode! It's in our contract!
Now this is what being righteous means! Kicking the enemy in their sensitive parts!
Not to mention breaking fingers, noses and toes!
This is a good way to show the pagans that violence is not the answer to anything!
There! I smite you with both my right and my left breast! What do you say to that, pig?
Smite again, I beg you!
FWABADAP!
Look at that hulk! Talk about weird characters!
Men, why are we fighting for free? Listen to me! We can make big bucks fighting! We can charge for this, and call it Wrestlemania!
L.L.BEAN
ONE WAY
SASKATCHEWAN: Central Canadian province...or new politically-correct label for "creatures of the Bigfoot persuasion"?

museums on our own or abroad on a MAD trip.

I always got a surprise laugh while preparing Ange's work for publication and spotting a caricature of me he had planted somewhere in a panel. A case in point is in my choice of a favorite Torres TV satire, "Jerkules." That's me in the turban in the fourth panel on page five, responding to Nick spouting one of MAD's running inside word gags, "It's crackers to slip a rozzer the dropsy in snide." Kevin Sorbo, the actor who played Hercules in the show, also admired Ange's art and wrote a nice fan letter to the magazine.

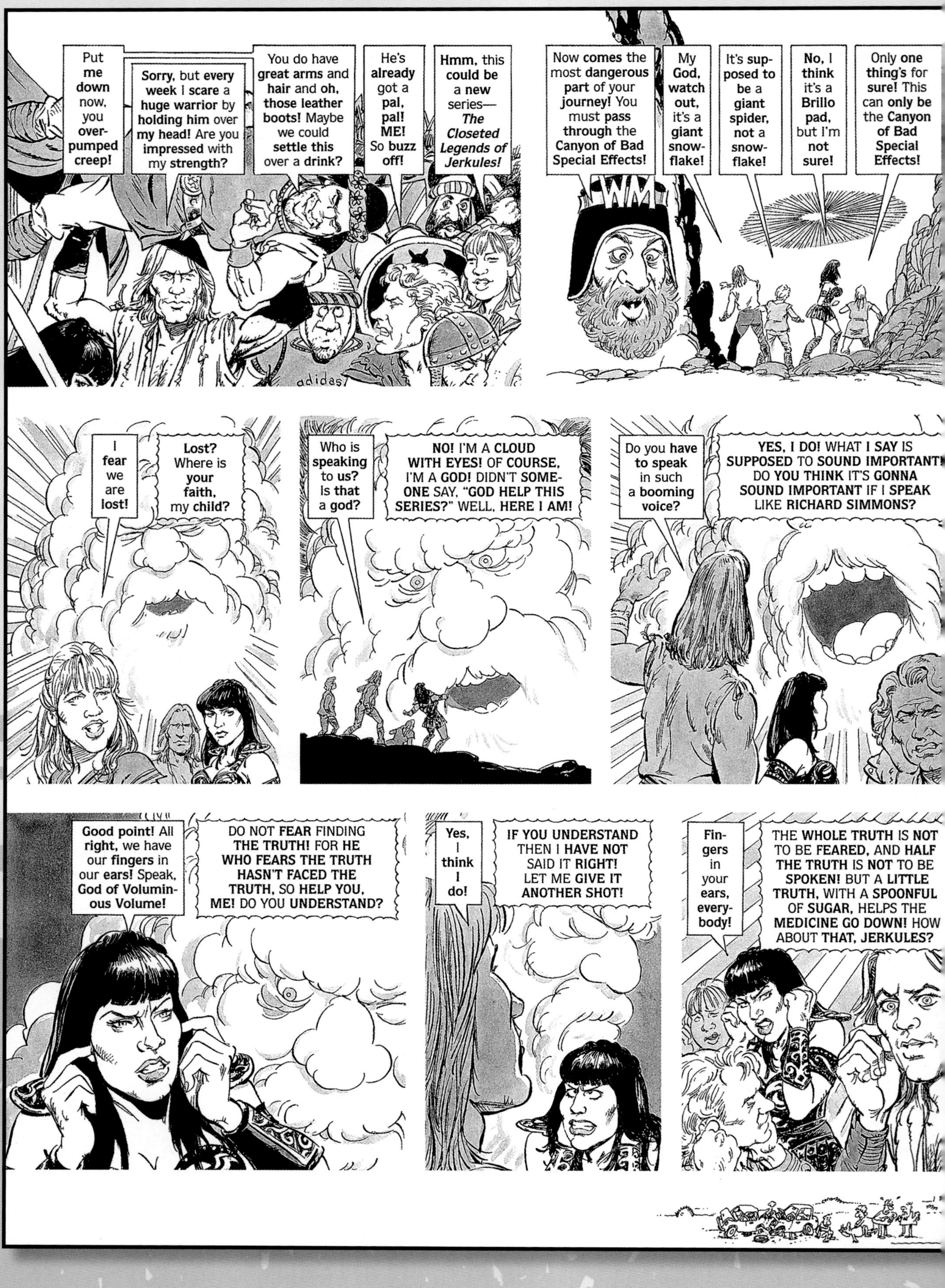

Put me down now, you over-pumped creep!
Sorry, but every week I scare a huge warrior by holding him over my head! Are you impressed with my strength?
You do have great arms and hair and oh, those leather boots! Maybe we could settle this over a drink?
He's already got a pal, pal! ME! So buzz off!
Hmm, this could be a new series— The Closeted Legends of Jerkules!
Now comes the most dangerous part of your journey! You must pass through the Canyon of Bad Special Effects!
My God, watch out, it's a giant snow-flake!
It's supposed to be a giant spider, not a snow-flake!
No, I think it's a Brillo pad, but I'm not sure!
Only one thing's for sure! This can only be the Canyon of Bad Special Effects!
I fear we are lost!
Lost? Where is your faith, my child?
Who is speaking to us? Is that a god?
NO! I'M A CLOUD WITH EYES! OF COURSE, I'M A GOD! DIDN'T SOME-ONE SAY, "GOD HELP THIS SERIES?" WELL, HERE I AM!
Do you have to speak in such a booming voice?
YES, I DO! WHAT I SAY IS SUPPOSED TO SOUND IMPORTANT! DO YOU THINK IT'S GONNA SOUND IMPORTANT IF I SPEAK LIKE RICHARD SIMMONS?
Good point! All right, we have our fingers in our ears! Speak, God of Voluminous Volume!
DO NOT FEAR FINDING THE TRUTH! FOR HE WHO FEARS THE TRUTH HASN'T FACED THE TRUTH, SO HELP YOU, ME! DO YOU UNDERSTAND?
Yes, I think I do!
IF YOU UNDERSTAND THEN I HAVE NOT SAID IT RIGHT! LET ME GIVE IT ANOTHER SHOT!
Fingers in your ears, everybody!
THE WHOLE TRUTH IS NOT TO BE FEARED, AND HALF THE TRUTH IS NOT TO BE SPOKEN! BUT A LITTLE TRUTH, WITH A SPOONFUL OF SUGAR, HELPS THE MEDICINE GO DOWN! HOW ABOUT THAT, JERKULES?

MOOKIE BLAYLOCK: Atlanta Hawks basketball player...or only string of nonsense syllables uttered by Jerry Lewis in both *The Nutty Professor* AND *The Errand Boy?*

I...I don't under-stand!
GOOD! THAT'S THE WAY THESE THINGS ARE SUPPOSED TO WORK! NOW YOU CAN GO ABOUT YOUR BUSINESS COMPLETELY CONFUSED!
Is this the City of Denial?
No, it isn't!
Can we enter?
Your entry is denied!
Call it a wild hunch, but I think this must be the place!
Go away!
Git!
No!
Scat!
Ixnay!
GO HOME
THIS WAY OUT!
Tell me, are you the one called Mazola?
No, but you're close! I'm Crisco! And the one who just fell out of the tree is Pam! He slips off everything!
I'm Mazola, and if it's the bathtub drain stopper you seek, come and get it! It's right there!
It's crackers to slip a rozzer the dropsy in snide!
I'll say!
Don't reach for that stopper! It might be a trap!
Of course it's a trap! We'll grab for it and the ceiling will cave in and the floor will fall out from under us! It's a given! S.O.P.!
By S.O.P. do you mean Standard Operating Procedure?
Nope! Stale, Old and Predict-able!
MAX KORN
GOING DOWN
The ground has collapsed under us! Eagerless, are you all right?
Yes! I'm hanging onto your finger!
That's NOT my finger!
We have rescued the bathtub stopper! But now we're falling through some sort of time tunnel!
Are you sure? Considering our usual level of special effects it looks more like we're swirling around in cotton candy!

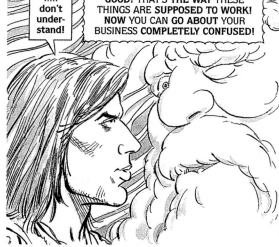

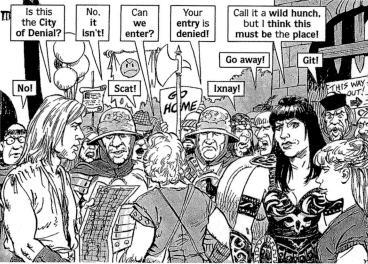

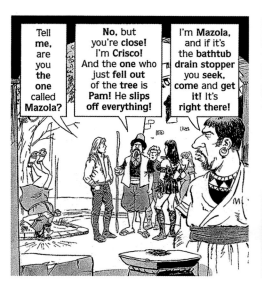

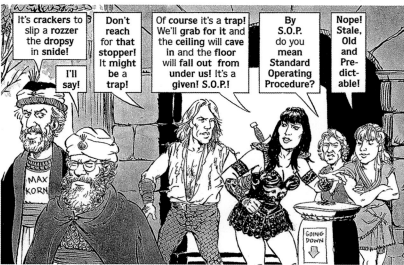

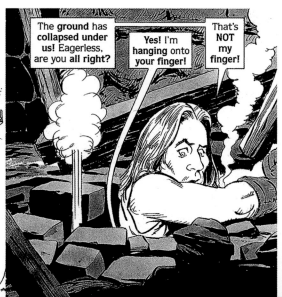

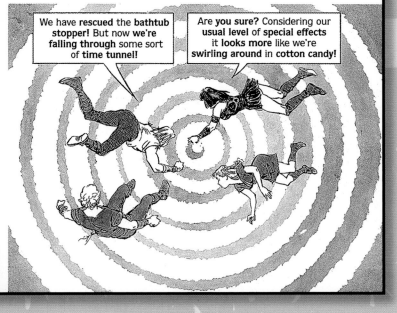

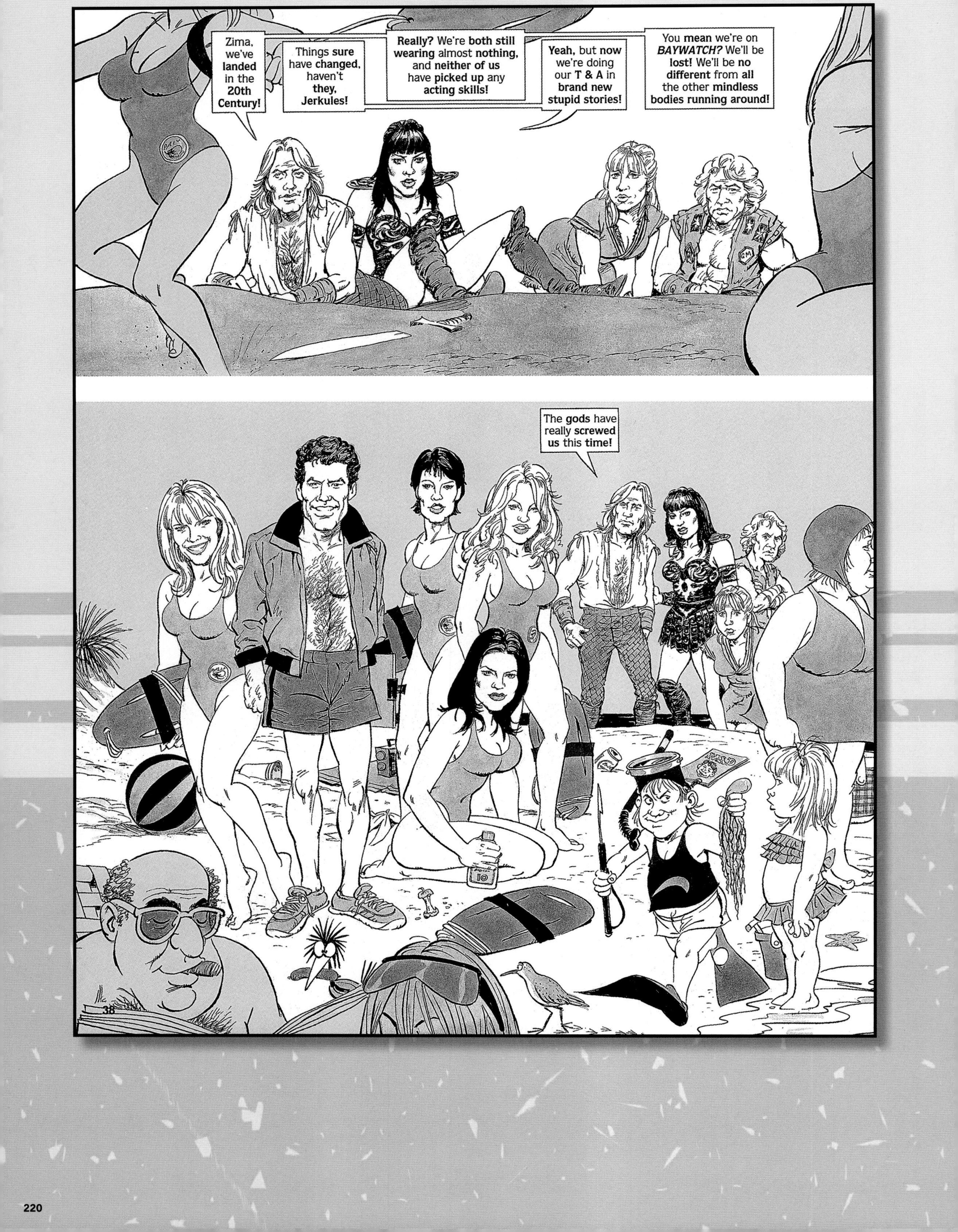
Zima, we've landed in the 20th Century!
Things sure have changed, haven't they, Jerkules!
Really? We're both still wearing almost nothing, and neither of us have picked up any acting skills!
Yeah, but now we're doing our T & A in brand new stupid stories!
You mean we're on BAYWATCH? We'll be lost! We'll be no different from all the other mindless bodies running around!
The gods have really screwed us this time!

David Lynch

The characters in MAD Magazine were like family to me.
I always considered Alfred E. Neuman as a brother.

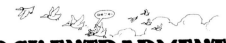

TALES FROM THE DUCK SIDE DEPT.
THE EXTRAORDINARY EULOGY ENTRAPMENT
MY BRETHEREN, WHAT CAN WE SAY ABOUT HOWARD DINKLE, A MAN WHO WAS SO LOVED BY ALL?
YOU CAN TELL THEM ABOUT HOW I ROSE FROM JUST A MAIL CLERK TO VICE PRESIDENT IN CHARGE OF SALES!
AND I'LL NEVER FORGIVE YOU FOR THAT, DINKLE! YOU TOOK MY JOB!
YEAH, YOU BACK-STABBING CREEP!
YOU ONLY MADE IT TO THE TOP BECAUSE YOU MARRIED THE BOSS'S UGLY DAUGHTER, YOU SLIMEBALL!
YOU GOT THAT RIGHT! HE MARRIED HER, BUT HE REALLY LOVED ME! BUT I WAS JUST A RECEPTIONIST--GOOD ENOUGH TO USE AS A PLAYTHING AND HAVE HIS BABY--BUT NOT GOOD ENOUGH TO MARRY! AND THAT'S WHY I POISONED YOUR COFFEE, YOU SWINE!
GREAT WORK, FATHER! YOU GOT THE MURDERER TO ADMIT TO THE CRIME! I NEVER WORKED WITH A VENTRILOQUIST PRIEST BEFORE!
ARTIST & WRITER: DUCK EDWING

MAD #293/MARCH 1990

by John Caldwell
WRITER/ARTIST

If, on a visit to the mall, you've ever been approached by some kid with a clipboard and coaxed into taking one of those "shopper surveys," then you've no doubt been asked to choose your favorite Hun. You'd be surprised how many people instinctively rattle off, "Attila." Seriously? Attila? First of all, the guy:

A) Had a wicked temper,

B) Showed no fashion sense (Unless you consider a bloody head on a spear a cool accessory) and

C) Was notoriously cheap.

For me, the favorite Hun question comes down to a dead heat between Gary The Hun, also known as the poet laureate of village ravaging, and Tiffany The Hun, considered by many to be a pioneer of modern-day pole dancing.

What, you ask, does this have to do with picking my favorite MAD article? Well, plenty,

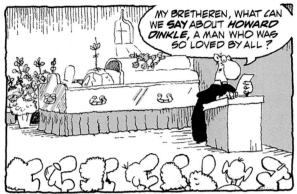

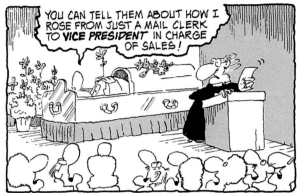

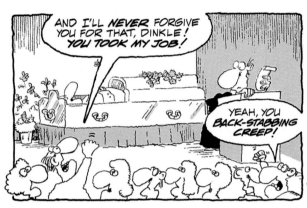

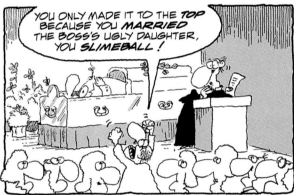

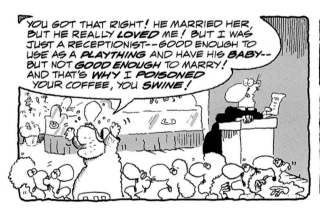

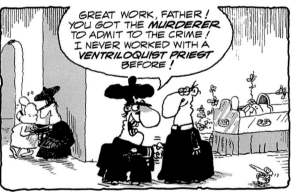

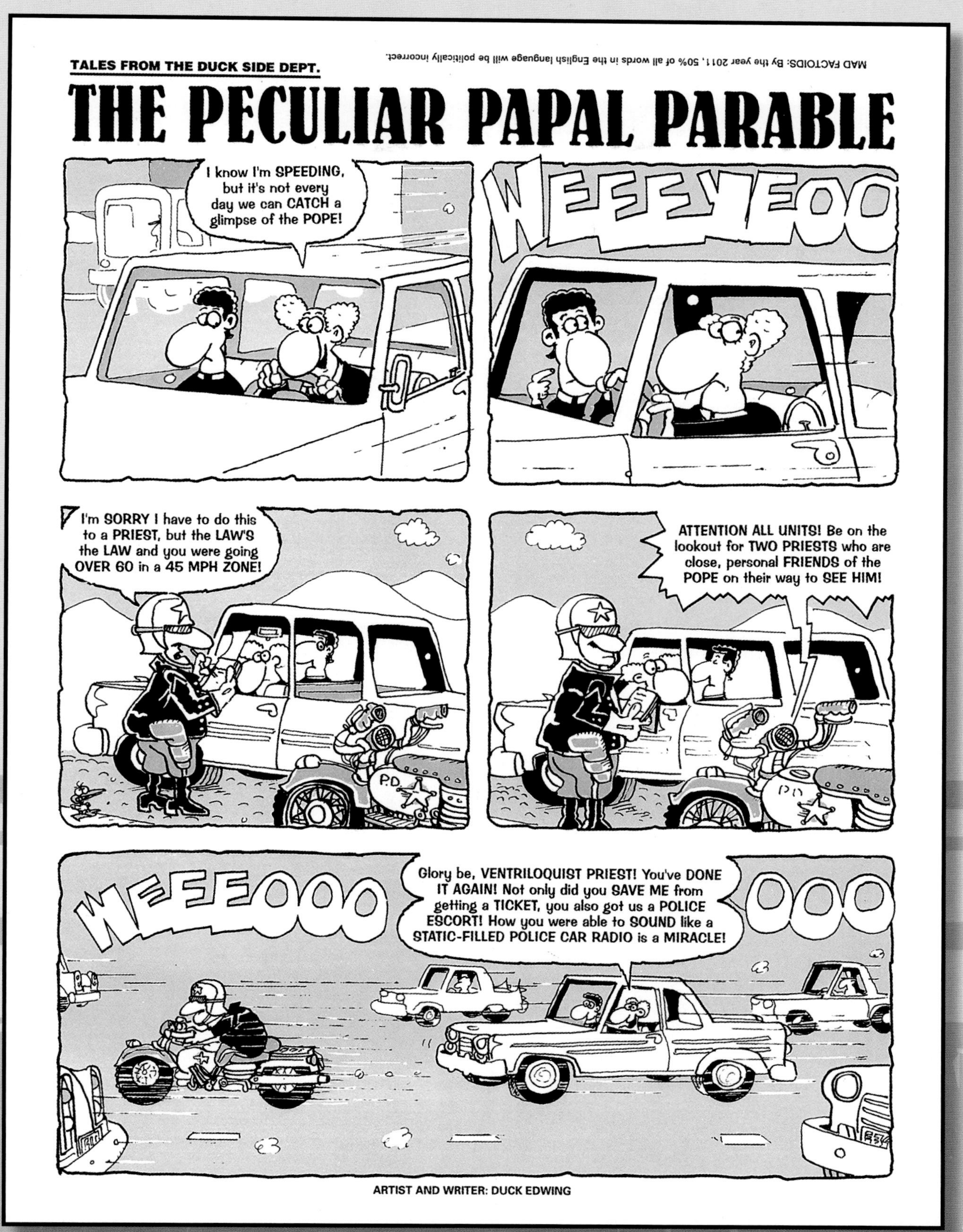
TALES FROM THE DUCK SIDE DEPT.
MAD FACTOIDS: By the year 2011, 50% of all words in the English language will be politically incorrect.
THE PECULIAR PAPAL PARABLE
I know I'm SPEEDING, but it's not every day we can CATCH a glimpse of the POPE!
WEEEYEOO
I'm SORRY I have to do this to a PRIEST, but the LAW'S the LAW and you were going OVER 60 in a 45 MPH ZONE!
ATTENTION ALL UNITS! Be on the lookout for TWO PRIESTS who are close, personal FRIENDS of the POPE on their way to SEE HIM!
WEEEOOO
Glory be, VENTRILOQUIST PRIEST! You've DONE IT AGAIN! Not only did you SAVE ME from getting a TICKET, you also got us a POLICE ESCORT! How you were able to SOUND like a STATIC-FILLED POLICE CAR RADIO is a MIRACLE!
OOO
ARTIST AND WRITER: DUCK EDWING

MAD #333/JANUARY-FEBRUARY 1995

actually. It may not be clear right now, but someday in the future, when you're pondering a tough question on a school test or, more likely, at your arraignment, you will think back on this little Hun parable and benefit from the moral of the story. Then again, knowing you, you'll just rattle off the equivalent of "Attila" because you just don't get it. Honestly, I don't know why I bother.

Anyway, my favorite MAD article turns out to be not one, but any in the "Ventriloquist Priest" series by Donald "Duck" Edwing. This very funny series appeals to me on two levels. First of all, ventriloquism is something of a hobby of mine, although I can't do it in public. The fact is I sit in a room, watch TV with the sound off and do all the voices.

Secondly, being raised Catholic, I once spent time in a Carmelite Seminary Summer Camp (no joke). I left after only four days when I realized that Larry Hopper lied about us getting to date nuns (sort of a joke). They also had a rule against visiting that second-floor "clinic" on West 42nd Street to sell our blood for beer money (not so much a joke as a thrown-in reference to a regular pastime during my art school years).

The bottom line: "Ventriloquist Priest" is my favorite MAD series and I consider Duck Edwing to be the "Gary The Hun' of present-day clergy cartooning.

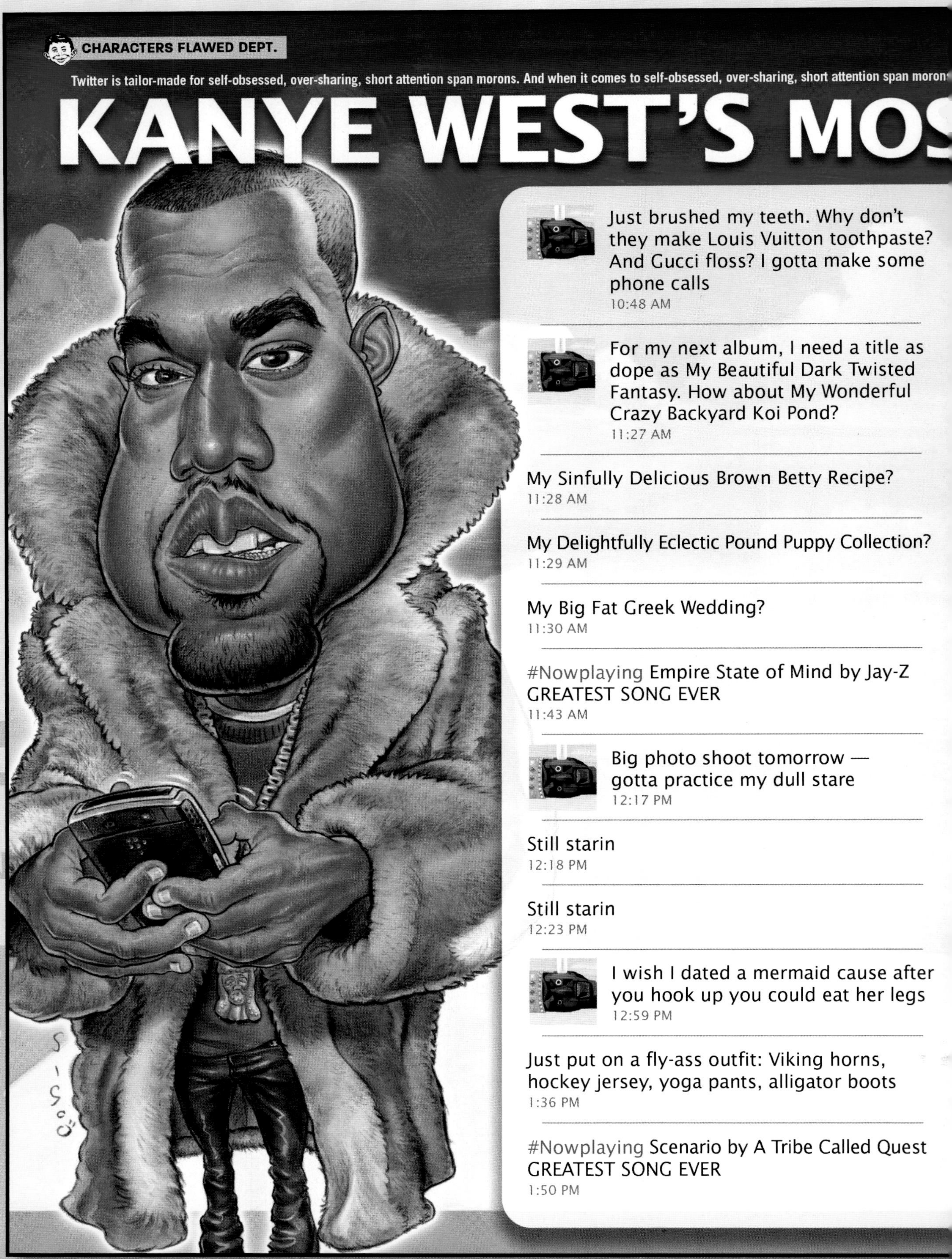
CHARACTERS FLAWED DEPT.

Twitter is tailor-made for self-obsessed, over-sharing, short attention span morons. And when it comes to self-obsessed, over-sharing, short attention span moron

KANYE WEST'S MOS

Just brushed my teeth. Why don't they make Louis Vuitton toothpaste? And Gucci floss? I gotta make some phone calls
10:48 AM

For my next album, I need a title as dope as My Beautiful Dark Twisted Fantasy. How about My Wonderful Crazy Backyard Koi Pond?
11:27 AM

My Sinfully Delicious Brown Betty Recipe?
11:28 AM

My Delightfully Eclectic Pound Puppy Collection?
11:29 AM

My Big Fat Greek Wedding?
11:30 AM

#Nowplaying Empire State of Mind by Jay-Z GREATEST SONG EVER
11:43 AM

Big photo shoot tomorrow — gotta practice my dull stare
12:17 PM

Still starin
12:18 PM

Still starin
12:23 PM

I wish I dated a mermaid cause after you hook up you could eat her legs
12:59 PM

Just put on a fly-ass outfit: Viking horns, hockey jersey, yoga pants, alligator boots
1:36 PM

#Nowplaying Scenario by A Tribe Called Quest GREATEST SONG EVER
1:50 PM

by Ryan Flanders
ASSOCIATE ART DIRECTOR

This is a modern MAD classic. It perfectly ridicules an incredible moment in history, when insanely successful celebrities are able to instantaneously broadcast their most impulsive, unstructured thoughts to anyone who will listen.

I had a great time art directing this article. I knew I'd use Kanye's real Twitter account to establish the basic look, then have one of our illustrators draw a biting caricature of the egotistical rapper. I laughed out loud every time the layout was open on my computer, no matter how often I reread the lines as I arranged them on the page. When Sam Sisco's amazing sketches came in, I knew we had something special.

Kanye West is the KING! So Kanye and Twitter is pretty much a match made in Heaven. Unfortunately, it's Hell for anyone who actually has to read....

T MORONIC TWEETS

Ever notice how hard it is to buy a decent albino rhino online? WTF??
2:22 PM

ˢO WHAT if I got a $180,000 watch that has ny face made out of diamonds on it? Who OOESN'T have a watch like that? Hobos maybe
:45 PM

ARUGULA SALAD WITH FENNEL VINAIGRETTE, BITCHES
:59 PM

'Kanyelicious" not in dictionary???!!!!!!
:24 PM

#Nowplaying Blackbird by The Beatles
GREATEST SONG EVER
:37 PM

The media's a bunch of bitches. Always wanting to build up the king so they can tear down the king. I don't need them lying-ass phonies
4:09 PM

Gotta remember to bring that up when I'm on MTV News, NPR and Regis & Kelly this week!
:10 PM

#Nowplaying Crocodile Rock by Elton John
GREATEST SONG EVER
:22 PM

People always sayin Kanye ain't street but AAAAAH! Lintball on my sweatervest!!
5:10 PM

Mila Kunis didn't get an Oscar nom?!? That **t is CRAZY!!! George Bush doesn't care about Black Swan!!!!
:47 PM

Nobody wants to play Boggle with Kanye
:03 PM

FYI critics: I prefer "fascinatingly conflicted" to "comically unfocused"
6:15 PM

How come grasshoppers hate me?
7:17 PM

#Nowplaying All Night Long by Lionel Richie
GREATEST SONG EVER
7:35 PM

I still have mad regrets about what happened with Taylor Swift. For one thing, I shoulda grabbed a boobie
8:52 PM

FOOTY PAJAMAS Y'ALL
10:57 PM

#Nowplaying Moon River by Clay Aiken
GREATEST SONG EVER
11:02 PM

Hope I have my recurring dream where I'm the president of the USA who's also a sexy half unicorn that plays for the Lakers
12:18 AM

I got a new challenge for 50 Cent: see which one of us can tie the dopest Windsor knot
12:28 AM

#Nowplaying theme song from My Two Dads
GREATEST SONG EVER
12:44 AM

Why don't hippos have wings?
COME ON, HIPPOS
1:31 AM

Are you there, God? It's me, Kanye. Seriously, I've been texting you for like THREE DAYS WTF???
2:06 AM

WRITER: JACOB LAMBERT ARTIST: SAM SISCO

MAD #509/JUNE 2011

Sam described the opportunity to mock Kanye as a "dream job." In my initial email, I suggested he give Kanye a look somewhere between "angrily defiant" and "happily crazy." Sam smartly went with "dull stare."

It's an unusual MAD piece. Unlike a movie spoof or "50 Worst" list, this is a very direct pastiche of Kanye's Twitter cadence and mindset. Jacob Lambert concocted an exquisitely spot-on parody. When MTV Geek posted a preview of the pages on their website, they thought it was a collection of actual Kanye tweets!

I told Editor Dave Croatto I picked this article for *Inside MAD*. He immediately quoted one of my favorite lines: "COME ON, HIPPOS." I later shared my choice with Jacob. He thanked me, then added: "Did I put something about a rhinoceros in there?"

A HYMN TO DISGRACE DEPT.

America, the Be

Oh, beautiful...

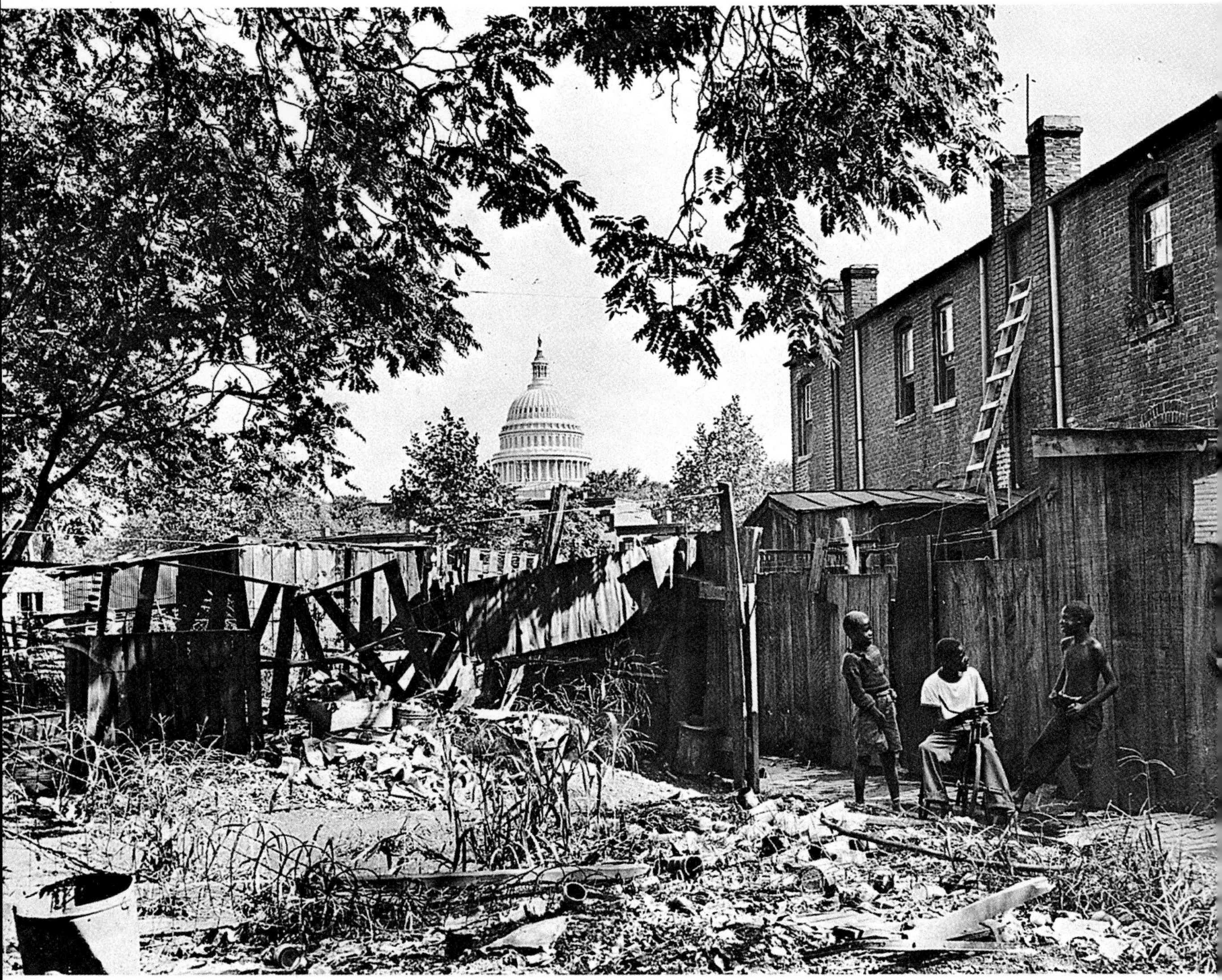

CONCEPT: FRANK JACOBS

PRODUCED BY: MAX BRANDEL

PICTURES BY: U.P.I. & W.W.

by Annie Gaines
LOGISTICS

There are so many laugh-out-loud, outrageously funny articles from MAD that if I had to pick my favorite funny article, I'd be in big trouble. My favorite MAD article is more of a serious, wake-up-America piece, and the reason it's my favorite is that it literally changed my life!

In 1969 I was a student at Penn State, and I had an assignment to do a class project on absolutely anything I wanted. I decided to do a pollution-cartoon scrapbook. The world was waking up to the fact that the air and water everywhere were becoming

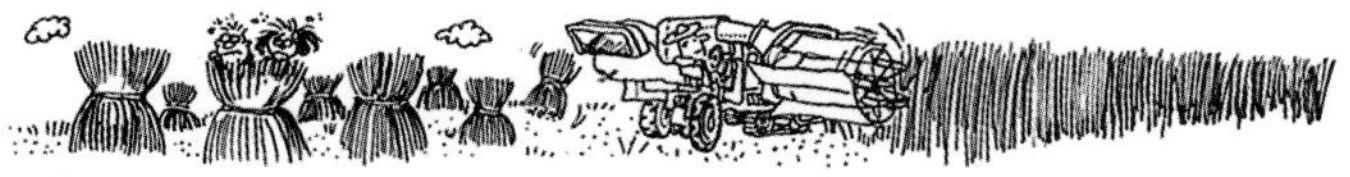

autiful - Revisited

for spacious skies...

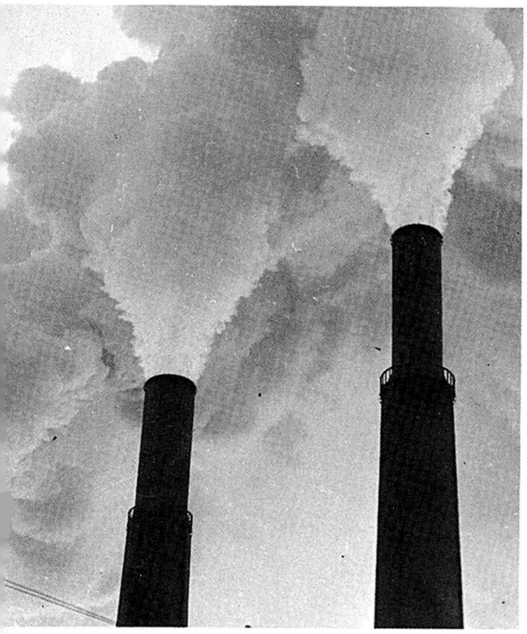

for amber waves of grain...

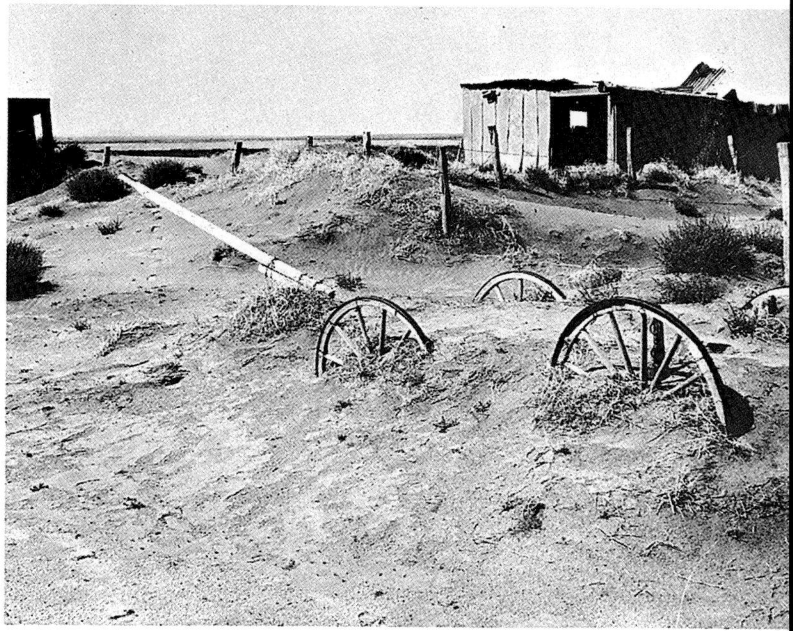

for purple mountain majesties...

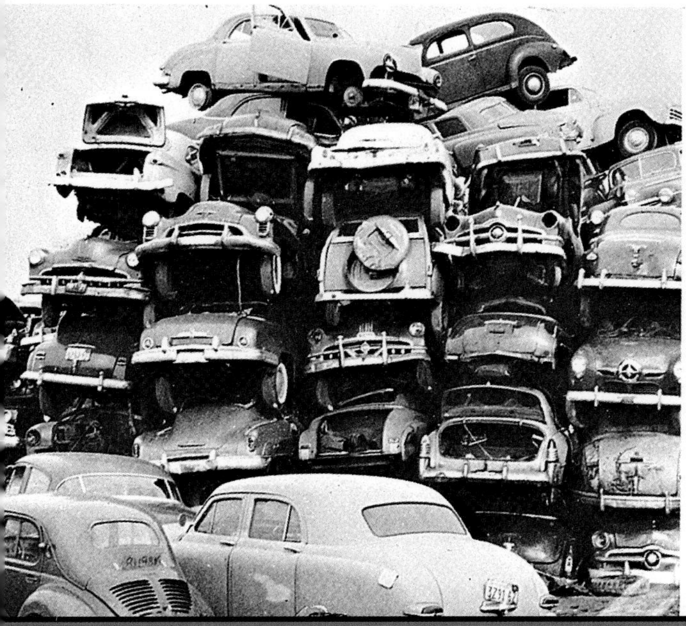

above the fruited plain...

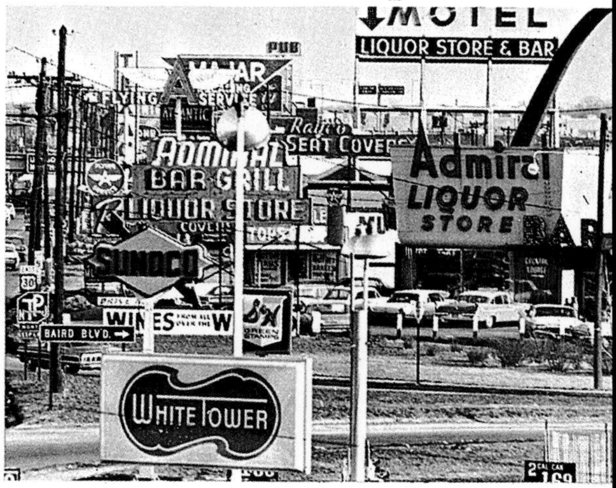

MOTEL
LIQUOR STORE & BAR
ADMIRAL
BAR GRILL
LIQUOR STORE
Admiral
LIQUOR
STORE
SUNOCO
WINES
BAIRD BLVD.
WHITE TOWER

MAD #113/SEPTEMBER 1967

polluted, and our highways and city streets were littered with trash. There were loads of anti-pollution cartoons everywhere — in newspapers, magazines, and of course, in MAD. On one of my weekends home, I scoured all the various magazines we had, paying special attention to our family's collection of MADs. But I couldn't find one MAD article I remembered and really wanted to include in the scrapbook — "America the Beautiful — Revisited." So I decided to write to the publisher, William M. Gaines, to ask for a reprint of the article. He sent it to me. We began a correspondence, which, a few years later, blossomed into love and a two-decades-long

America, America...

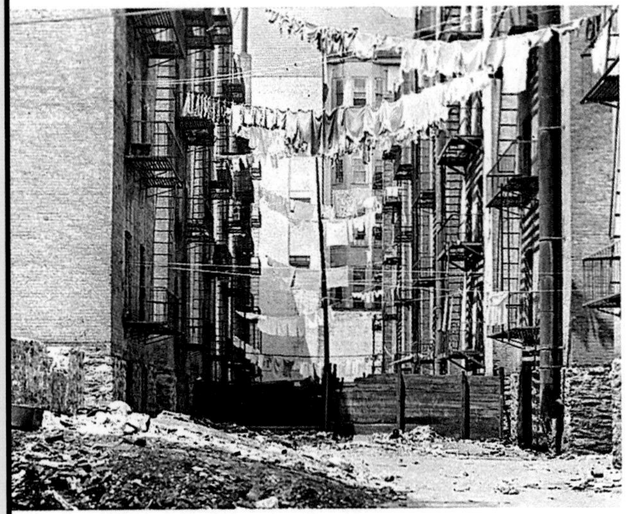

God shed His grace on thee...

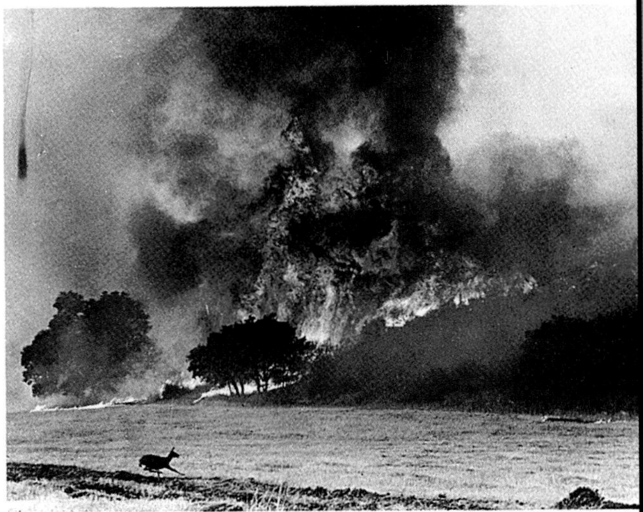

and crown thy good with brotherhood...

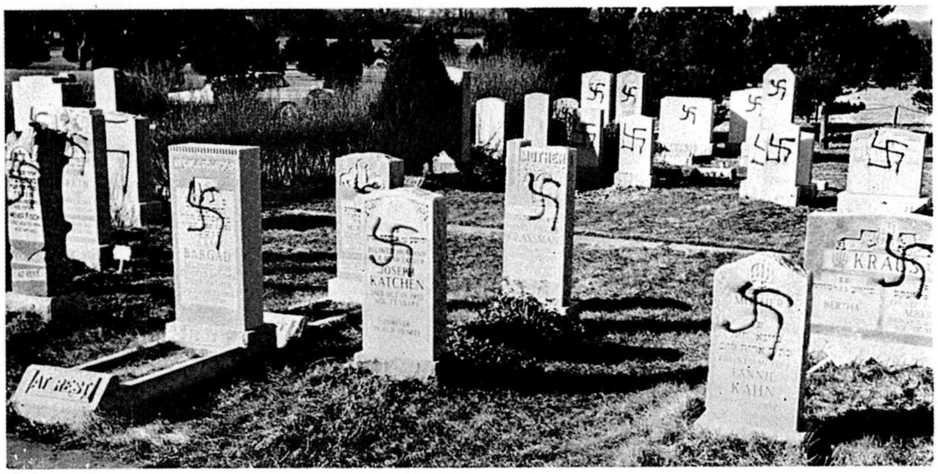

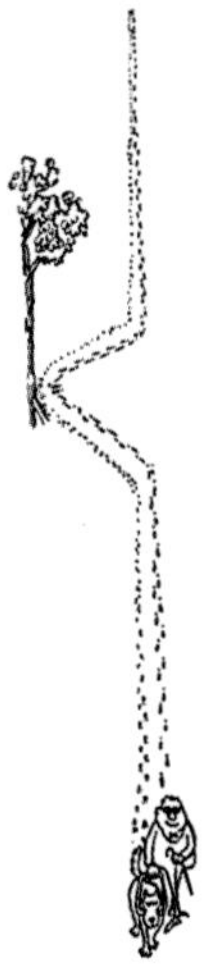

from sea to shining sea.

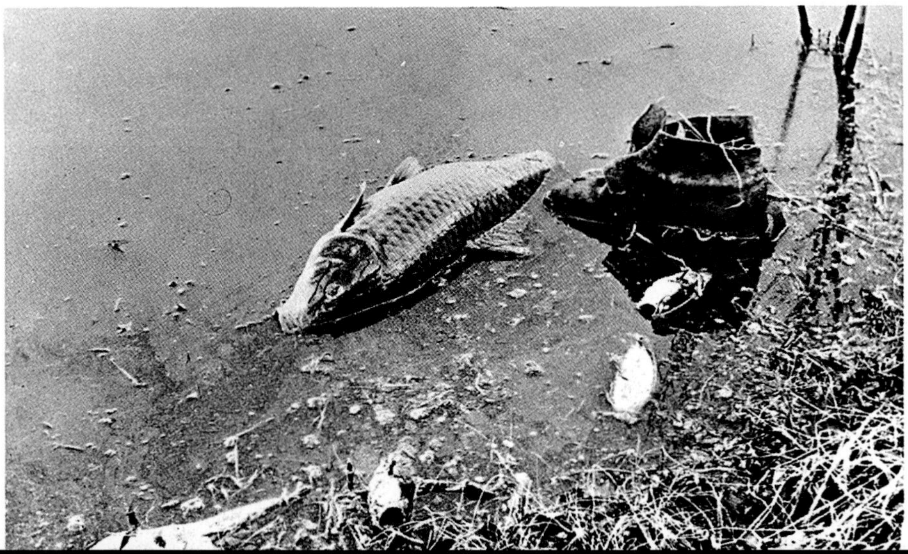

whirlwind adventure of romance, travel, laughter, the best foods and wines, a job at MAD and marriage! Bill treated me like a queen and we had a marvelously happy life together. A year after Bill died, I flew to Kansas City to attend the wedding of MAD artist Paul Coker, and Paul's bride Rosemary introduced me to the man who would become my second husband! Don and I have a happy marriage, a lovely home and beautiful twin daughters — and it's all because I wanted that article from MAD for a silly cartoon scrapbook and took the time to write a letter to Bill Gaines.

I love MAD Magazine. It's the only magazine made by idiots for idiots, which explains why I'm still a subscriber. MAD is emblematic of what I value as an artist, which is "think for yourself."

I first encountered MAD Magazine when I was 11 years old. My sister broke her leg, and my parents bought it for her while she was convalescing. So of course I took it, started reading, and soon became a glutton for MAD. I bought all the books. I would go to the movies and think, "What is MAD going to write about that?" I wrote letters to my parents like those letters to MAD, but I never sent anything in to the magazine because I was not organized enough to figure out how to get a stamp. MAD even inspired me to draw, but I drew conquistadors, not cartoons. I must have been a pretentious kid, because at the time I was mostly into Renaissance portraits of guys on horseback. But I still loved MAD.

One of the things I enjoyed the most about MAD was that it was so busy. The differing styles of the artists and the drawings in the margins were so engaging. When I read it now, I revert back to being 13 years old. And while I didn't know half the songs that MAD was parodying or a lot of the political references, it made me want to dig up information on all of them. MAD inspired me to learn and to try to figure out who, or what, Alfred E. Neuman was.

Matthew Weiner

MAD was the only place where you'd see anything anti-smoking. Or making fun of alcoholism. Or making fun of racism. Or sexism.

MAD was the first thing I ever saw that made fun of the world. And I didn't just like that because I grew up in a house of Nixon haters — MAD made fun of everybody. They were a mysterious group of adults satirizing the duplicity of the "important" people, and that took fearlessness. MAD was brave.

MAD was a big influence on *Mad Men*. I had gotten into the MAD book compilations and started reading about the high '50s. That's where I witnessed MAD's complete contempt for advertising and the people who do it, and I started to get a picture of this drunken, callow, glib, self-serving ad man. But there was a little glamour to the way the world of advertising was depicted as well, and that glamour stuck with me.

MAD Magazine made a physical appearance on *Mad Men* too. In Season 1 the character of Paul Kinsey writes a play and puts it in his desk drawer. The play is experimental and caustic and kind of an autobiographical fantasy of vengeance, as many first plays are. But what I love is that also in that desk drawer is a copy of MAD Magazine. We put it there because it cut the pretension of the play in half. It basically said: "You work in an ad agency and you're reading MAD, which means you're definitely not a complete boob."

Those early issues of MAD attacked the hypocrisies of a 1950s society that perceived itself as normal. MAD was the only place where you'd see anything anti-smoking, and it wasn't afraid to make fun of alcoholism or sexism or racism. Which are all things I've targeted in *Mad Men*. MAD Magazine not only shaped my worldview, it taught me the crucial lesson that, when it comes to art, there are no boundaries.

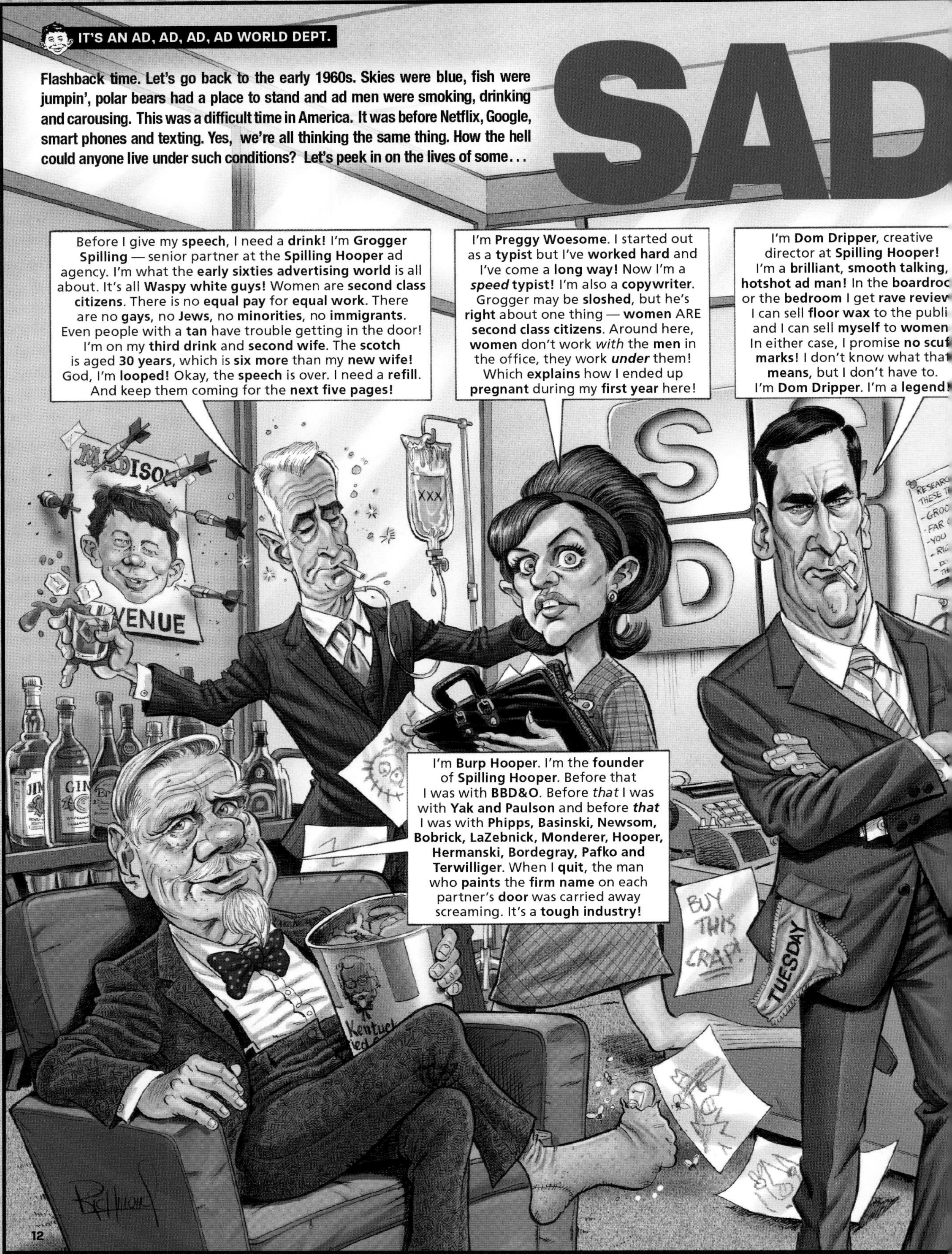

IT'S AN AD, AD, AD, AD WORLD DEPT.
Flashback time. Let's go back to the early 1960s. Skies were blue, fish were jumpin', polar bears had a place to stand and ad men were smoking, drinking and carousing. This was a difficult time in America. It was before Netflix, Google, smart phones and texting. Yes, we're all thinking the same thing. How the hell could anyone live under such conditions? Let's peek in on the lives of some...
SAD
Before I give my speech, I need a drink! I'm Grogger Spilling — senior partner at the Spilling Hooper ad agency. I'm what the early sixties advertising world is all about. It's all Waspy white guys! Women are second class citizens. There is no equal pay for equal work. There are no gays, no Jews, no minorities, no immigrants. Even people with a tan have trouble getting in the door! I'm on my third drink and second wife. The scotch is aged 30 years, which is six more than my new wife! God, I'm looped! Okay, the speech is over. I need a refill. And keep them coming for the next five pages!
I'm Preggy Woesome. I started out as a typist but I've worked hard and I've come a long way! Now I'm a speed typist! I'm also a copywriter. Grogger may be sloshed, but he's right about one thing — women ARE second class citizens. Around here, women don't work with the men in the office, they work under them! Which explains how I ended up pregnant during my first year here!
I'm Dom Dripper, creative director at Spilling Hooper! I'm a brilliant, smooth talking, hotshot ad man! In the boardroc or the bedroom I get rave review I can sell floor wax to the publi and I can sell myself to women In either case, I promise no scuf marks! I don't know what tha means, but I don't have to. I'm Dom Dripper. I'm a legend!
I'm Burp Hooper. I'm the founder of Spilling Hooper. Before that I was with BBD&O. Before that I was with Yak and Paulson and before that I was with Phipps, Basinski, Newsom, Bobrick, LaZebnick, Monderer, Hooper, Hermanski, Bordegray, Pafko and Terwilliger. When I quit, the man who paints the firm name on each partner's door was carried away screaming. It's a tough industry!
MADISON AVENUE
XXX
BUY THIS CRAP!
TUESDAY
12

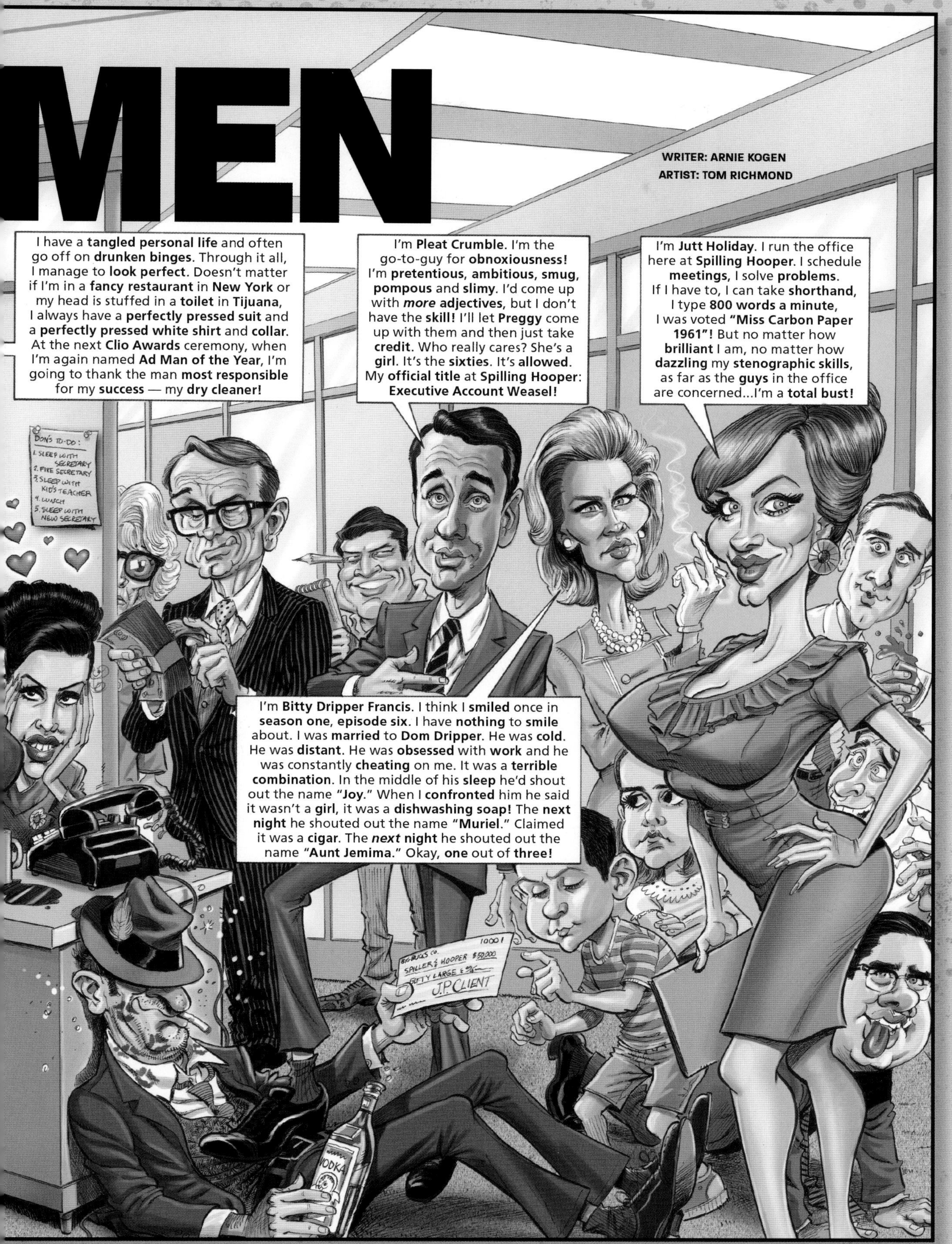
MEN
WRITER: ARNIE KOGEN
ARTIST: TOM RICHMOND
I have a **tangled personal life** and often go off on **drunken binges**. Through it all, I manage to **look perfect**. Doesn't matter if I'm in a **fancy restaurant** in **New York** or my head is stuffed in a **toilet** in **Tijuana**, I always have a **perfectly pressed suit** and a **perfectly pressed white shirt** and **collar**. At the next **Clio Awards** ceremony, when I'm again named **Ad Man of the Year**, I'm going to thank the man **most responsible** for my **success** — my **dry cleaner!**
I'm **Pleat Crumble**. I'm the go-to-guy for **obnoxiousness!** I'm **pretentious, ambitious, smug, pompous** and **slimy**. I'd come up with ***more* adjectives**, but I don't have the **skill!** I'll let **Preggy** come up with them and then just take **credit**. Who really cares? She's a **girl**. It's the **sixties**. It's **allowed**. My **official title** at **Spilling Hooper**: **Executive Account Weasel!**
I'm **Jutt Holiday**. I run the office here at **Spilling Hooper**. I schedule **meetings**, I solve **problems**. If I have to, I can take **shorthand**, I type **800 words a minute**, I was voted **"Miss Carbon Paper 1961"!** But no matter how **brilliant** I am, no matter how **dazzling** my **stenographic skills**, as far as the **guys** in the office are concerned...I'm a **total bust!**
DON'S TO-DO: 1. SLEEP WITH SECRETARY 2. FIRE SECRETARY 3. SLEEP WITH KID'S TEACHER 4. LUNCH 5. SLEEP WITH NEW SECRETARY
I'm **Bitty Dripper Francis**. I think I **smiled** once in **season one, episode six**. I have **nothing** to **smile** about. I was **married** to **Dom Dripper**. He was **cold**. He was **distant**. He was **obsessed** with **work** and he was constantly **cheating** on me. It was a **terrible combination**. In the middle of his **sleep** he'd shout out the name **"Joy."** When I **confronted** him he said it wasn't a **girl**, it was a **dishwashing soap!** The **next night** he shouted out the name **"Muriel."** Claimed it was a **cigar**. The ***next* night** he shouted out the name **"Aunt Jemima."** Okay, **one** out of **three!**
J.P. CLIENT
VODKA

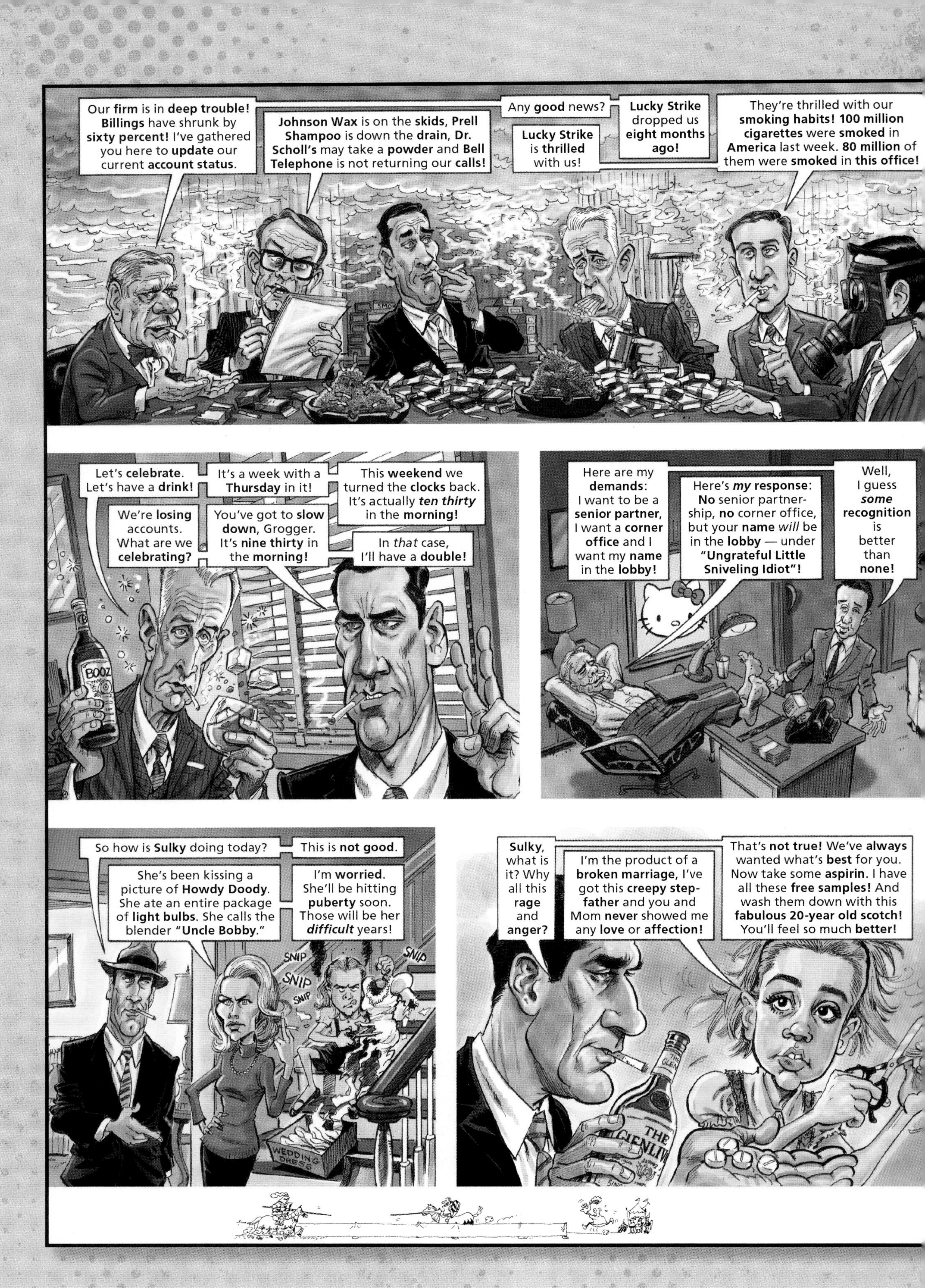
Our firm is in deep trouble! Billings have shrunk by sixty percent! I've gathered you here to update our current account status.
Johnson Wax is on the skids, Prell Shampoo is down the drain, Dr. Scholl's may take a powder and Bell Telephone is not returning our calls!
Any good news?
Lucky Strike is thrilled with us!
Lucky Strike dropped us eight months ago!
They're thrilled with our smoking habits! 100 million cigarettes were smoked in America last week. 80 million of them were smoked in this office!
Let's celebrate. Let's have a drink!
We're losing accounts. What are we celebrating?
It's a week with a Thursday in it!
You've got to slow down, Grogger. It's nine thirty in the morning!
This weekend we turned the clocks back. It's actually ten thirty in the morning!
In that case, I'll have a double!
BOOZ
Here are my demands: I want to be a senior partner, I want a corner office and I want my name in the lobby!
Here's my response: No senior partnership, no corner office, but your name will be in the lobby — under "Ungrateful Little Sniveling Idiot"!
Well, I guess some recognition is better than none!
So how is Sulky doing today?
She's been kissing a picture of Howdy Doody. She ate an entire package of light bulbs. She calls the blender "Uncle Bobby."
This is not good.
I'm worried. She'll be hitting puberty soon. Those will be her difficult years!
SNIP
SNIP
SNIP
SNIP
WEDDING DRESS
Sulky, what is it? Why all this rage and anger?
I'm the product of a broken marriage, I've got this creepy stepfather and you and Mom never showed me any love or affection!
That's not true! We've always wanted what's best for you. Now take some aspirin. I have all these free samples! And wash them down with this fabulous 20-year old scotch! You'll feel so much better!

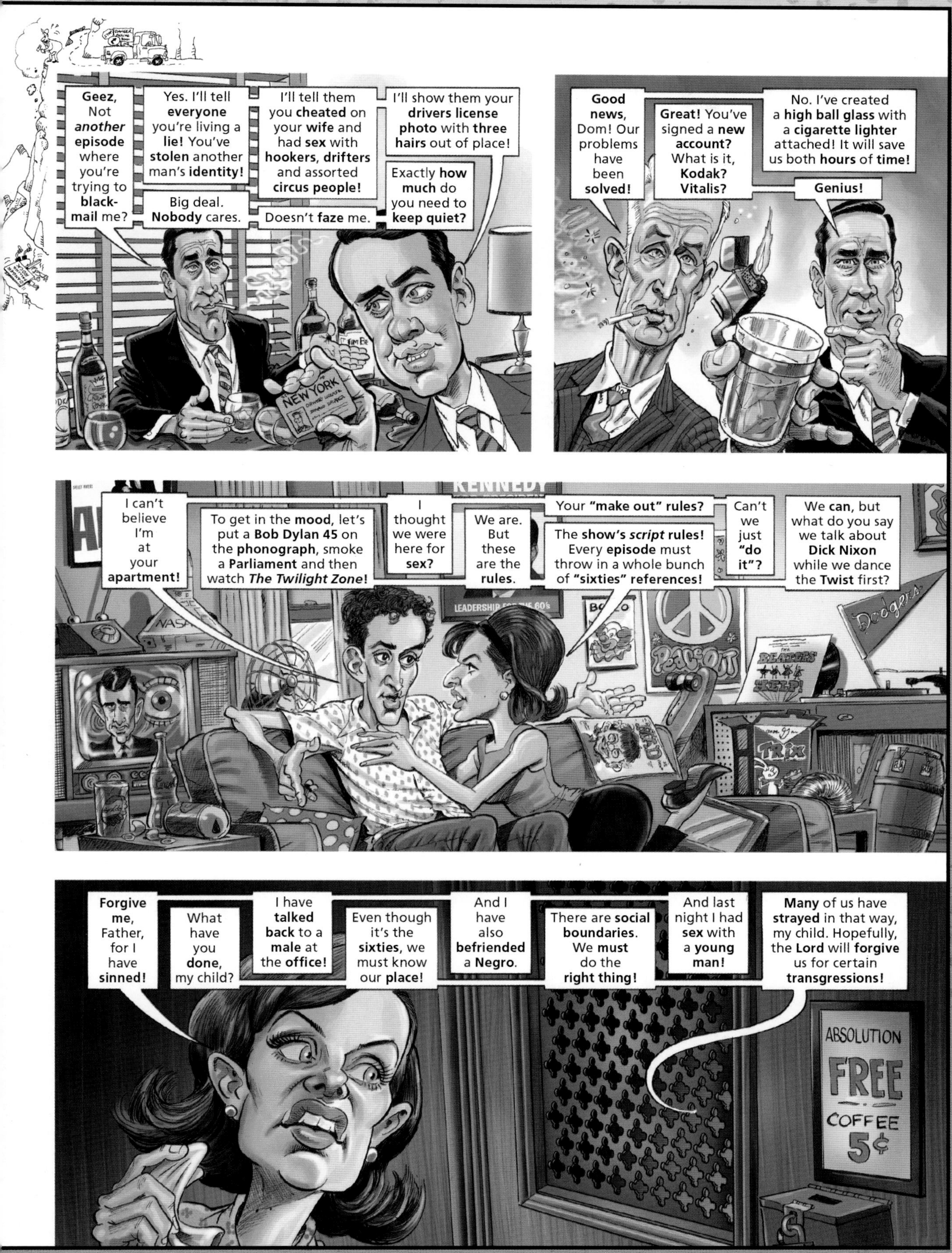

Geez, Not another episode where you're trying to black-mail me?
Yes. I'll tell everyone you're living a lie! You've stolen another man's identity!
Big deal. Nobody cares.
I'll tell them you cheated on your wife and had sex with hookers, drifters and assorted circus people!
Doesn't faze me.
I'll show them your drivers license photo with three hairs out of place!
Exactly how much do you need to keep quiet?
NEW YORK
Good news, Dom! Our problems have been solved!
Great! You've signed a new account? What is it, Kodak? Vitalis?
No. I've created a high ball glass with a cigarette lighter attached! It will save us both hours of time!
Genius!
KENNEDY
I can't believe I'm at your apartment!
To get in the mood, let's put a Bob Dylan 45 on the phonograph, smoke a Parliament and then watch The Twilight Zone!
I thought we were here for sex?
We are. But these are the rules.
Your "make out" rules?
The show's script rules! Every episode must throw in a whole bunch of "sixties" references!
Can't we just "do it"?
We can, but what do you say we talk about Dick Nixon while we dance the Twist first?
LEADERSHIP FOR THE 60's
NASA
Dodgers
Peace Out
HELP!
TRIX
Forgive me, Father, for I have sinned!
What have you done, my child?
I have talked back to a male at the office!
Even though it's the sixties, we must know our place!
And I have also befriended a Negro.
There are social boundaries. We must do the right thing!
And last night I had sex with a young man!
Many of us have strayed in that way, my child. Hopefully, the Lord will forgive us for certain transgressions!
ABSOLUTION FREE
COFFEE 5¢

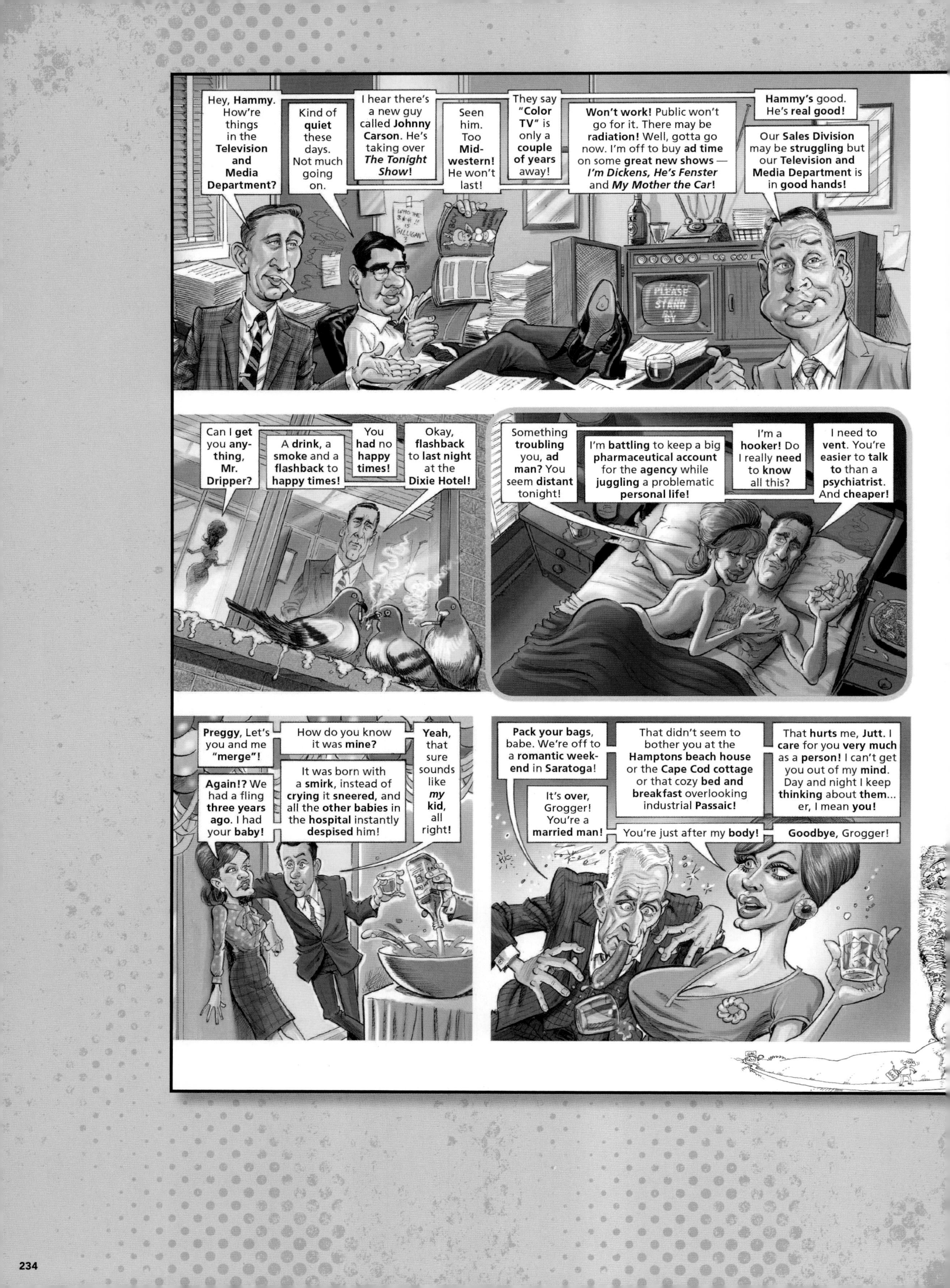

Hey, Hammy. How're things in the Television and Media Department?
Kind of quiet these days. Not much going on.
I hear there's a new guy called Johnny Carson. He's taking over The Tonight Show!
Seen him. Too Mid-western! He won't last!
They say "Color TV" is only a couple of years away!
Won't work! Public won't go for it. There may be radiation! Well, gotta go now. I'm off to buy ad time on some great new shows — I'm Dickens, He's Fenster and My Mother the Car!
Hammy's good. He's real good!
Our Sales Division may be struggling but our Television and Media Department is in good hands!
PLEASE STAND BY
Can I get you any-thing, Mr. Dripper?
A drink, a smoke and a flashback to happy times!
You had no happy times!
Okay, flashback to last night at the Dixie Hotel!
Something troubling you, ad man? You seem distant tonight!
I'm battling to keep a big pharmaceutical account for the agency while juggling a problematic personal life!
I'm a hooker! Do I really need to know all this?
I need to vent. You're easier to talk to than a psychiatrist. And cheaper!
Preggy, Let's you and me "merge"!
Again!? We had a fling three years ago. I had your baby!
How do you know it was mine?
It was born with a smirk, instead of crying it sneered, and all the other babies in the hospital instantly despised him!
Yeah, that sure sounds like my kid, all right!
Pack your bags, babe. We're off to a romantic week-end in Saratoga!
It's over, Grogger! You're a married man!
That didn't seem to bother you at the Hamptons beach house or the Cape Cod cottage or that cozy bed and breakfast overlooking industrial Passaic!
You're just after my body!
That hurts me, Jutt. I care for you very much as a person! I can't get you out of my mind. Day and night I keep thinking about them... er, I mean you!
Goodbye, Grogger!

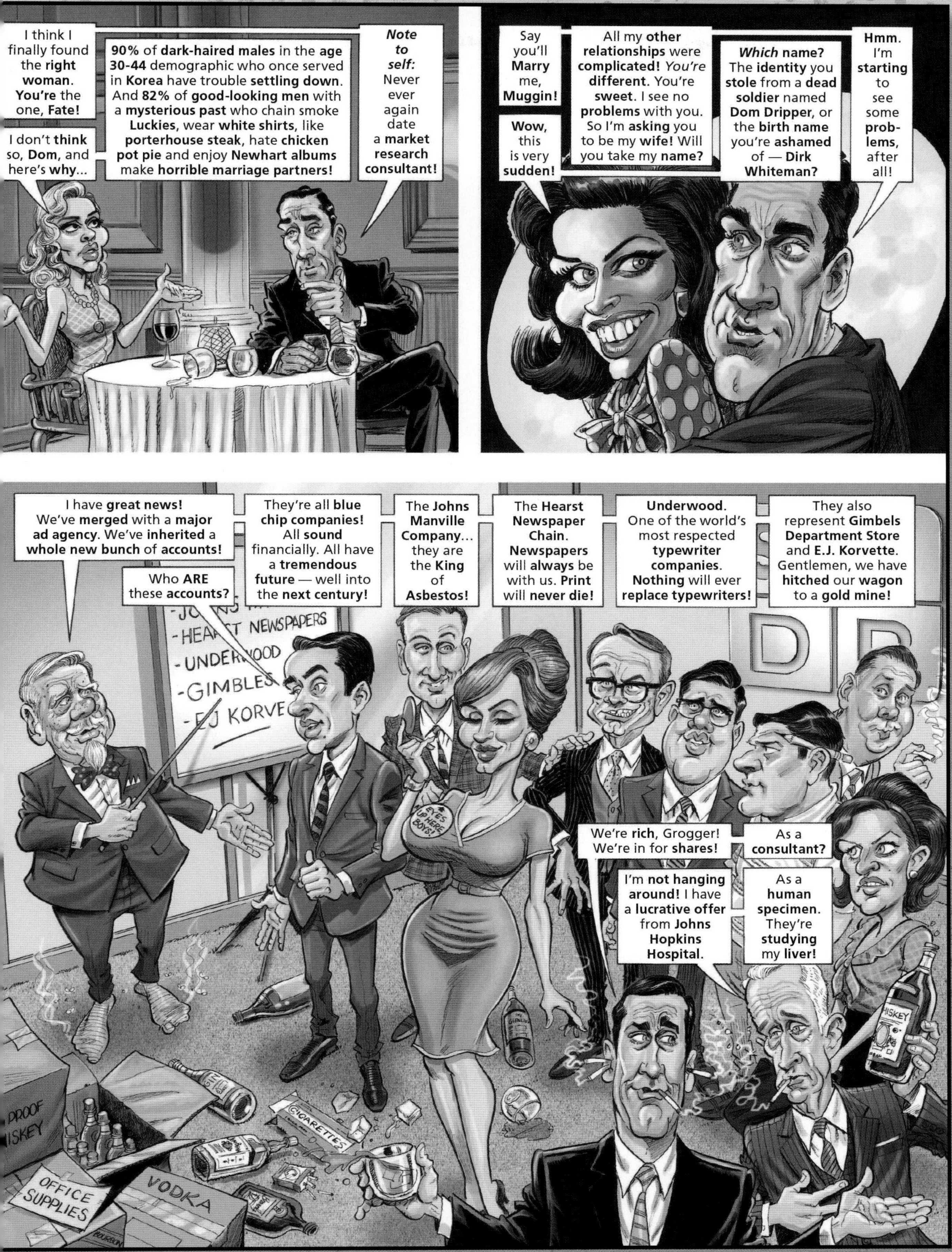
I think I finally found the **right woman**. **You're** the one, **Fate!**
I don't **think** so, **Dom**, and here's **why**...
90% of **dark-haired males** in the **age 30-44** demographic who once served in **Korea** have trouble **settling down**. And **82%** of **good-looking men** with a **mysterious past** who chain smoke **Luckies**, wear **white shirts**, like **porterhouse steak**, hate **chicken pot pie** and enjoy **Newhart albums** make **horrible marriage partners!**
Note to self: Never ever again date a **market research consultant!**
Say you'll **Marry** me, **Muggin!**
Wow, this is very **sudden!**
All my **other relationships** were **complicated!** *You're* **different**. You're **sweet**. I see no **problems** with you. So I'm **asking** you to be my **wife!** Will you take my **name?**
***Which* name?** The **identity** you **stole** from a **dead soldier** named **Dom Dripper**, or the **birth name** you're **ashamed** of — **Dirk Whiteman?**
Hmm. I'm **starting** to see some **prob-lems**, after all!
I have **great news!** We've **merged** with a **major ad agency**. We've **inherited** a **whole new bunch** of **accounts!**
Who **ARE** these **accounts?**
They're all **blue chip companies!** All **sound** financially. All have a **tremendous future** — well into the **next century!**
The **Johns Manville Company**... they are the **King** of **Asbestos!**
The **Hearst Newspaper Chain**. **Newspapers** will **always** be with us. **Print** will **never die!**
Underwood. One of the world's most respected **typewriter companies**. **Nothing** will ever **replace typewriters!**
They also represent **Gimbels Department Store** and **E.J. Korvette**. Gentlemen, we have **hitched** our **wagon** to a **gold mine!**
-HEARST NEWSPAPERS
-GIMBLES
EYES UP HERE BOYS!
We're **rich**, Grogger! We're in for **shares!**
As a **consultant?**
I'm **not hanging around!** I have a **lucrative offer** from **Johns Hopkins Hospital**.
As a **human specimen**. They're **studying** my **liver!**
CIGARETTES
OFFICE SUPPLIES
VODKA

John Slattery

I couldn't wait for the new MAD to come out. I loved everything about it. I had a whole cartooning phase as a result, trying to draw like Jack Davis and Don Martin. Everything, Spy vs. Spy, Sergio Aragonés. I'd take it with me until I either lost it, or one of my friends stole it. I think I actually subscribed for a while, which, given the general lack of organization in my life then, is saying a lot.

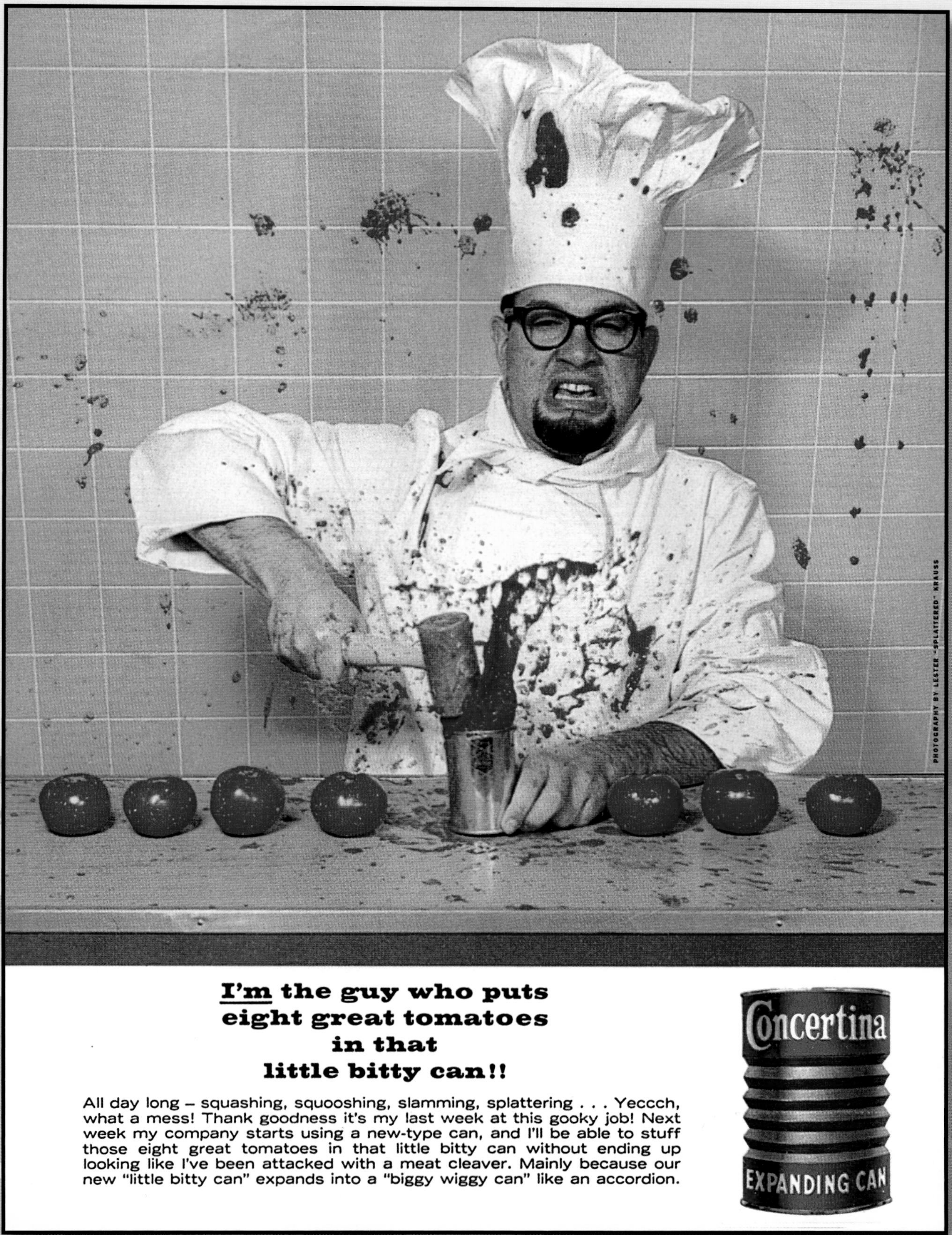
PHOTOGRAPHY BY LESTER "SPLATTERED" KRAUSS
I'm the guy who puts eight great tomatoes in that little bitty can!!
All day long – squashing, squooshing, slamming, splattering . . . Yeccch, what a mess! Thank goodness it's my last week at this gooky job! Next week my company starts using a new-type can, and I'll be able to stuff those eight great tomatoes in that little bitty can without ending up looking like I've been attacked with a meat cleaver. Mainly because our new "little bitty can" expands into a "biggy wiggy can" like an accordion.
Concertina
EXPANDING CAN

MAD #84/JANUARY 1964

by Stan Sinberg
WRITER

That for many years MAD, singularly among all newsstand publications, didn't accept advertising (or, as I secretly suspected, couldn't attract advertisers) bestowed upon it a certain level of integrity. Not beholden to anyone, it was free to go after powerful, behemoth targets that no one else would dare touch. Like Contadina, a tomato paste company that asked, in their catchy jingles, who put "eight great tomatoes in that itty-bitty can?" (The answer was "Contadina.") Really, Contadina? Eight? And "great?" And the can *was* small, but "itty-bitty?" No. It took a fearless publication like MAD to expose the lies and obfuscations behind this patently absurd claim. Plus, by pounding the &%$% out of the tomatoes in the ad parody, and making a total mess, the result was unbridled hilarity and chaos! (And for a burgeoning satirist, it was my first realization that TV commercials basically just lie to us — a notion that caused me to turn away from a potentially lucrative career on Madison Avenue and slave away for MAD.) So yeah — thanks, MAD.

WE ALL HAVE OUR BLUE CROSS TO BEAR DEPT.
While the bozos in Washington D.C. continue prattling over health care reform, more and more Americans are turning to the wonderful world of the Health Maintenance Organizations (HMOs). You know, those little companies that enable people to get somewhat adequate medical help for cheaper prices. (But you remember what your mom said about getting what you pay for, right?) With the market flooded with these organizations it can be an ordeal just choosing one, so here's MAD's sure-fire way...
HOW TO TELL IF YOU'VE SELECTED A BAD HMO
ARTIST AND WRITER: JOHN CALDWELL
Every time the doctor writes a prescription, he brags, "I used to fee these to Elvis like they were M&Ms."
You're the only human waiting to be treated.
Prior to a minor surgical procedure, the doctor asks if you'd mind filling out a toe tag.
The dental coverage only includes spinach removal.
The doctor loses it every tim he examines your symptoms

by Andrew J. Schwartzberg

WRITER

Editors are not really supposed to say they have a favorite artist or writer. It's kind of akin to a parent admitting they have a favorite kid. You just don't do it, unless you're a heartless idiot. But, since I haven't been on MAD's editorial staff for almost 20 years, I'm thinking this rule no longer applies to me. So now I can scream from the mountaintops that John Caldwell was my favorite artist/writer. (Of course, I live in a relatively flat area and I'm too lazy to drive to a

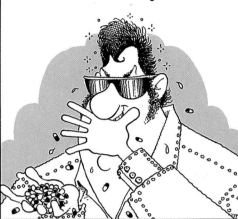

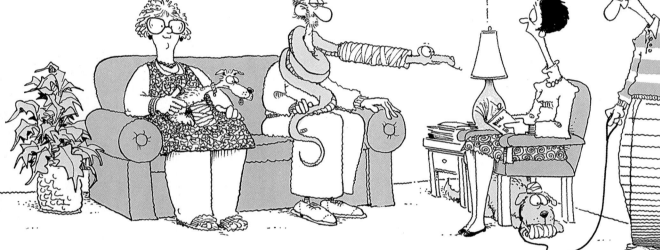

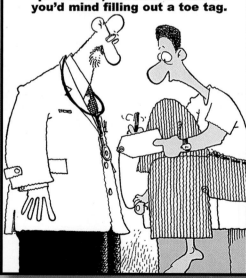

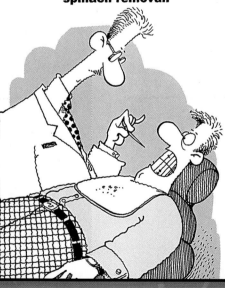

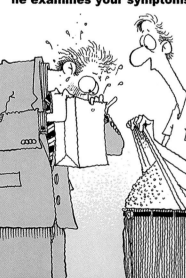

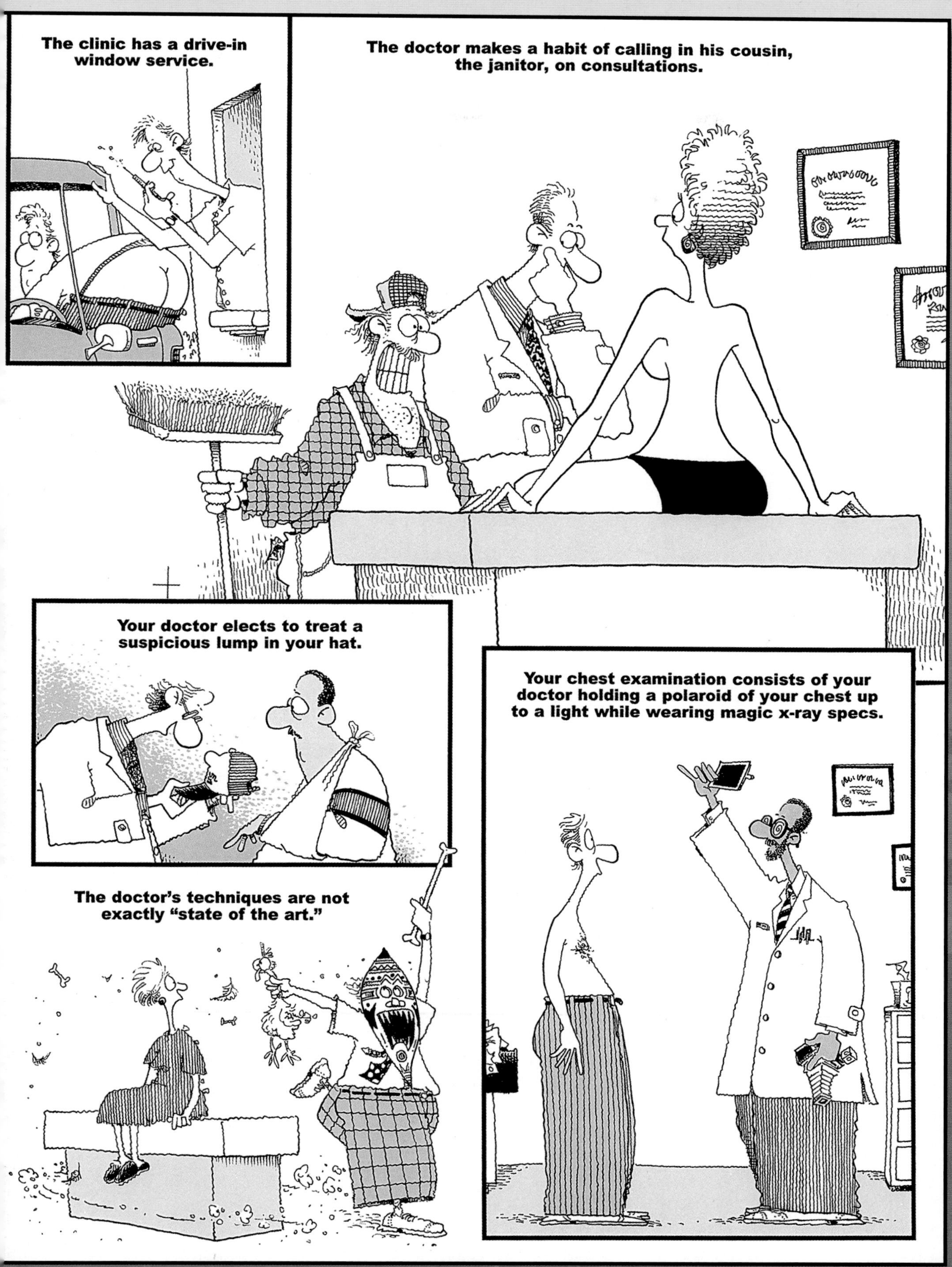
The clinic has a drive-in window service.
The doctor makes a habit of calling in his cousin, the janitor, on consultations.
Your doctor elects to treat a suspicious lump in your hat.
Your chest examination consists of your doctor holding a polaroid of your chest up to a light while wearing magic x-ray specs.
The doctor's techniques are not exactly "state of the art."

MAD #341/DECEMBER 1995

mountaintop, so I won't actually do it.) In any event, his work consistently made me laugh out loud and I eagerly awaited every new piece he sent in. The last article of his that I got to review before I left MAD was "How to Tell if You've Selected a Bad HMO," so I've always had a soft spot for it. There are some great lines in there and, to this day, whenever I see a doctor whose advice I question I think to myself, "What are you going to do next — treat the suspicious lump in my hat?"

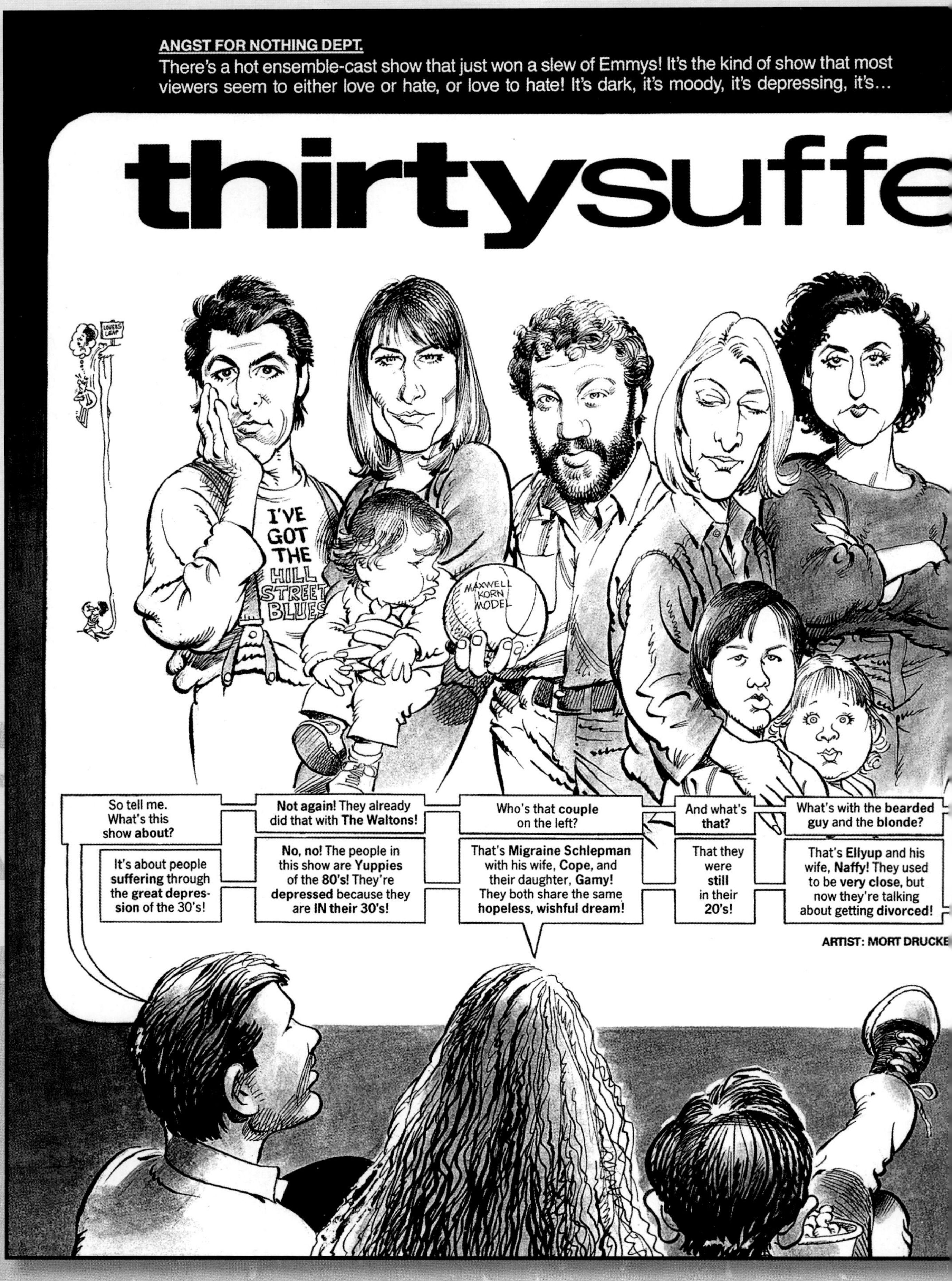
ANGST FOR NOTHING DEPT.
There's a hot ensemble-cast show that just won a slew of Emmys! It's the kind of show that most viewers seem to either love or hate, or love to hate! It's dark, it's moody, it's depressing, it's...
thirtysuffe
LOVERS LEAP
I'VE GOT THE HILL STREET BLUES
MAXWELL KORN MODEL
So tell me. What's this show about?
It's about people suffering through the great depression of the 30's!
Not again! They already did that with The Waltons!
No, no! The people in this show are Yuppies of the 80's! They're depressed because they are IN their 30's!
Who's that couple on the left?
That's Migraine Schlepman with his wife, Cope, and their daughter, Gamy! They both share the same hopeless, wishful dream!
And what's that?
That they were still in their 20's!
What's with the bearded guy and the blonde?
That's Ellyup and his wife, Naffy! They used to be very close, but now they're talking about getting divorced!
ARTIST: MORT DRUCKE

by Nick Meglin
EDITOR

Choosing to parody the popular *thirtysomething* TV show was as much an aesthetic choice as it was a personal highlight for me as a MAD editor. Like all new TV shows that garnered a strong following early on, we initially watched it for its satire potential. But unlike most network offerings, this one was brilliantly written and got many of us hooked, including MAD writer Frank Jacobs.

Frank submitted a strong premise and was assigned the script. The choice of Mort Drucker to illustrate it was a no-brainer — each talented member of the show's cast

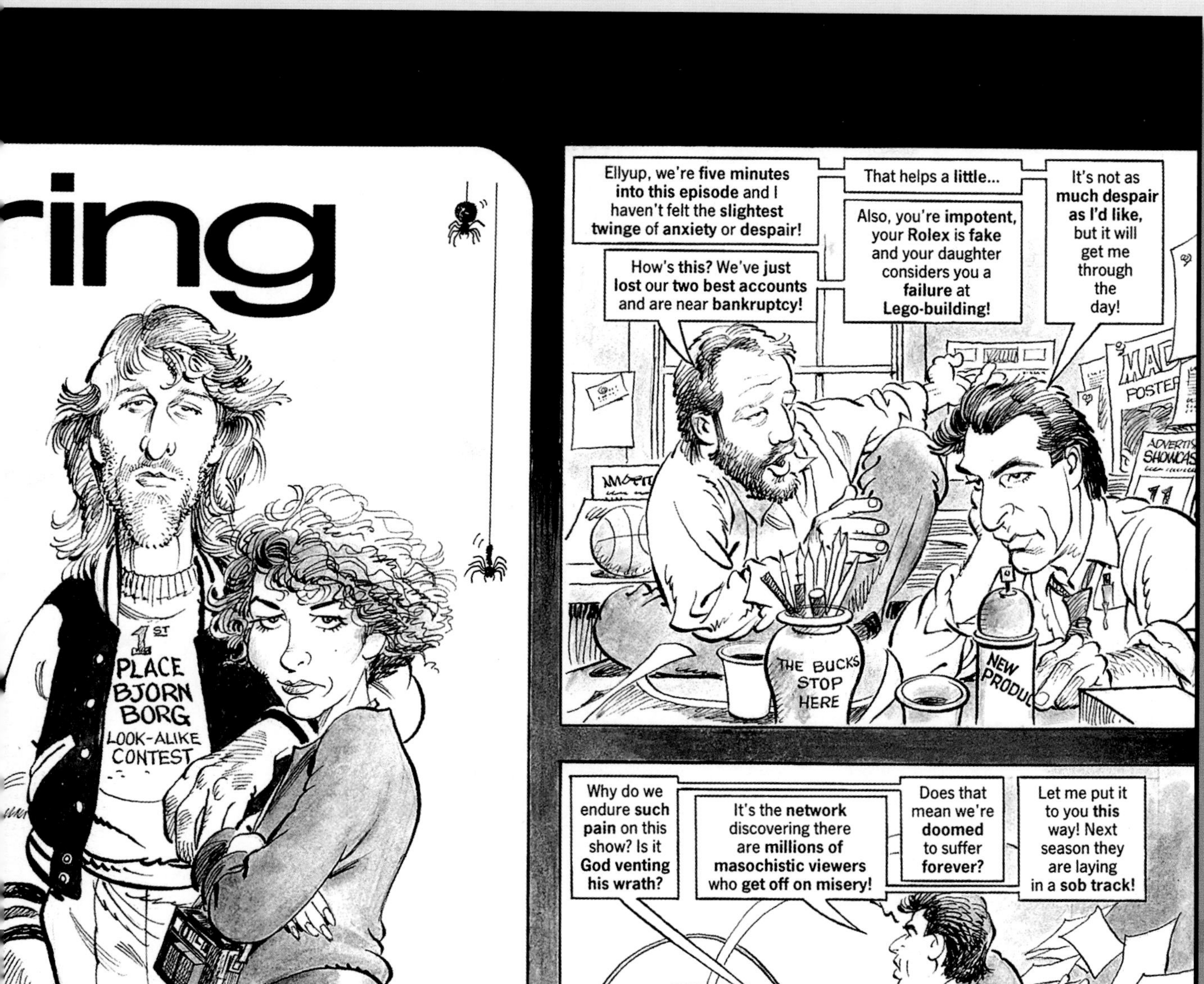
ring
1ST PLACE BJORN BORG LOOK-ALIKE CONTEST
hat happened? Did ey both suddenly iscover there was omeone they loved more than each other?
eah, themselves!
Who are the three on the right?
That's Ailin and Hairy and Meshugga—the supporting cast! They're all single! Being around the two couples has given them a purpose!
And what is that?
To stay single!
ITER: FRANK JACOBS
Ellyup, we're five minutes into this episode and I haven't felt the slightest twinge of anxiety or despair!
That helps a little...
It's not as much despair as I'd like, but it will get me through the day!
How's this? We've just lost our two best accounts and are near bankruptcy!
Also, you're impotent, your Rolex is fake and your daughter considers you a failure at Lego-building!
THE BUCKS STOP HERE
NEW PRODU
POSTER
Why do we endure such pain on this show? Is it God venting his wrath?
It's the network discovering there are millions of masochistic viewers who get off on misery!
Does that mean we're doomed to suffer forever?
Let me put it to you this way! Next season they are laying in a sob track!
DRUCKER
WANNA PLAY?

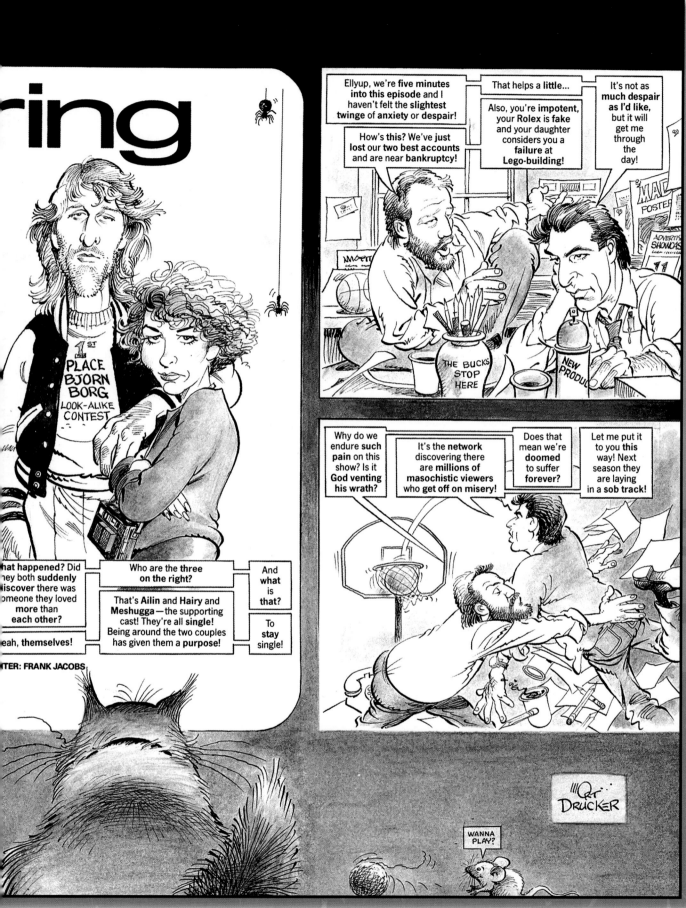

MAD #286/APRIL 1989

had wonderful facial qualities that were sure to inspire this great caricaturist. Two of the show's top writers, Joe Dougherty and Ann Hamilton, were big-time MAD fans and called me soon after the issue was published, requesting prints of the original art to present to the show's producers. The art department sent them off and a "thank you" call from Joe and Ann included a personal invitation for me to visit the *thirtysomething* set the next time I traveled to L.A. for creative meetings with MAD talents who lived in that area. As it turned out, many of the show's stars were also MAD fans and

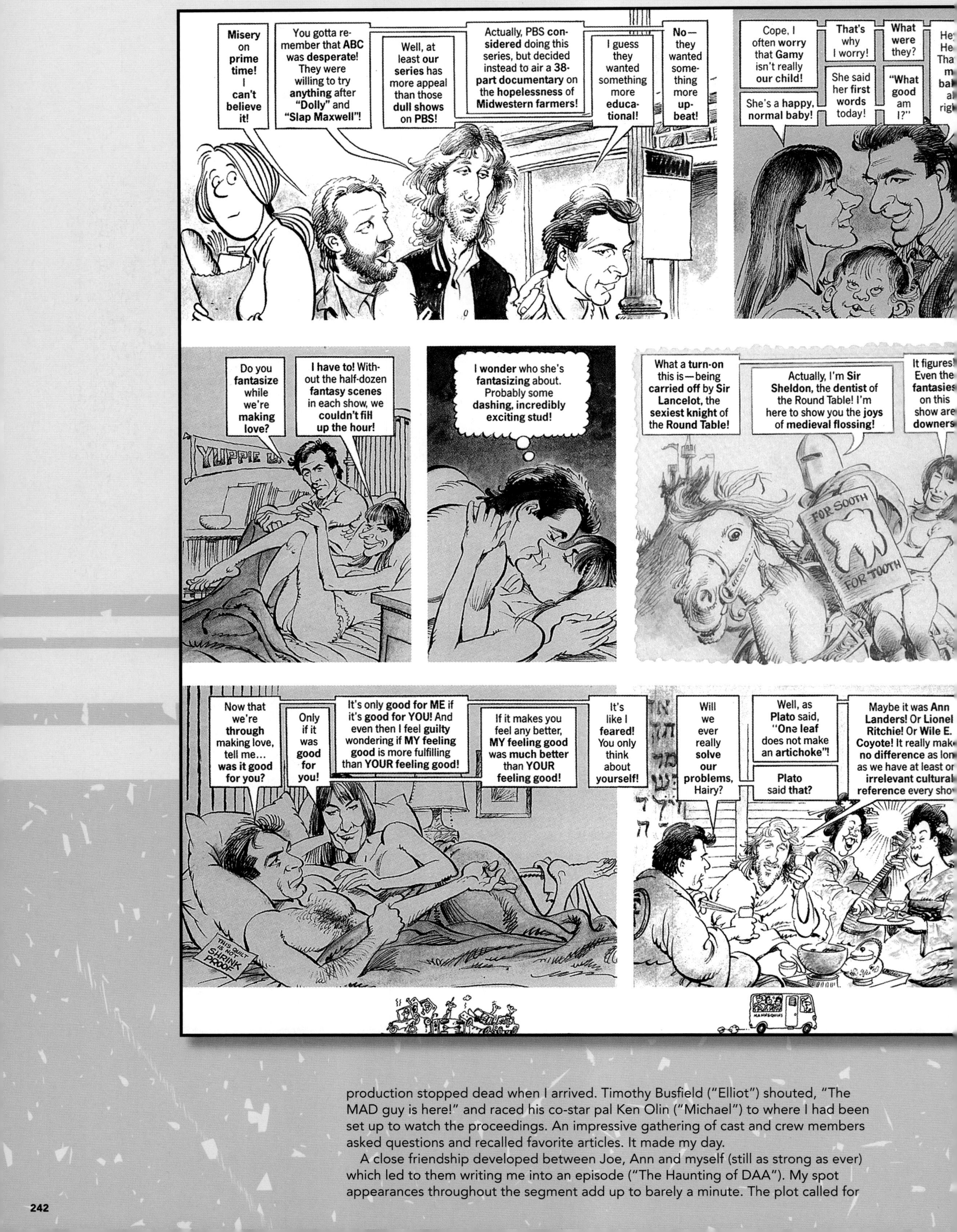
Misery on prime time! I can't believe it!
You gotta remember that ABC was desperate! They were willing to try anything after "Dolly" and "Slap Maxwell"!
Well, at least our series has more appeal than those dull shows on PBS!
Actually, PBS considered doing this series, but decided instead to air a 38-part documentary on the hopelessness of Midwestern farmers!
I guess they wanted something more educational!
No—they wanted something more upbeat!
Cope, I often worry that Gamy isn't really our child!
She's a happy, normal baby!
That's why I worry!
She said her first words today!
What were they?
"What good am I?"
Do you fantasize while we're making love?
I have to! Without the half-dozen fantasy scenes in each show, we couldn't fill up the hour!
YUPPIE U.
I wonder who she's fantasizing about. Probably some dashing, incredibly exciting stud!
What a turn-on this is—being carried off by Sir Lancelot, the sexiest knight of the Round Table!
Actually, I'm Sir Sheldon, the dentist of the Round Table! I'm here to show you the joys of medieval flossing!
It figures! Even the fantasies on this show are downers
FOR SOOTH
FOR TOOTH
Now that we're through making love, tell me... was it good for you?
Only if it was good for you!
It's only good for ME if it's good for YOU! And even then I feel guilty wondering if MY feeling good is more fulfilling than YOUR feeling good!
If it makes you feel any better, MY feeling good was much better than YOUR feeling good!
It's like I feared! You only think about yourself!
THIS QUILT IS NOT SHRINK PROOF
Will we ever really solve our problems, Hairy?
Well, as Plato said, "One leaf does not make an artichoke"!
Plato said that?
Maybe it was Ann Landers! Or Lionel Ritchie! Or Wile E. Coyote!
MANNEQUINS

production stopped dead when I arrived. Timothy Busfield ("Elliot") shouted, "The MAD guy is here!" and raced his co-star pal Ken Olin ("Michael") to where I had been set up to watch the proceedings. An impressive gathering of cast and crew members asked questions and recalled favorite articles. It made my day.

A close friendship developed between Joe, Ann and myself (still as strong as ever) which led to them writing me into an episode ("The Haunting of DAA"). My spot appearances throughout the segment add up to barely a minute. The plot called for

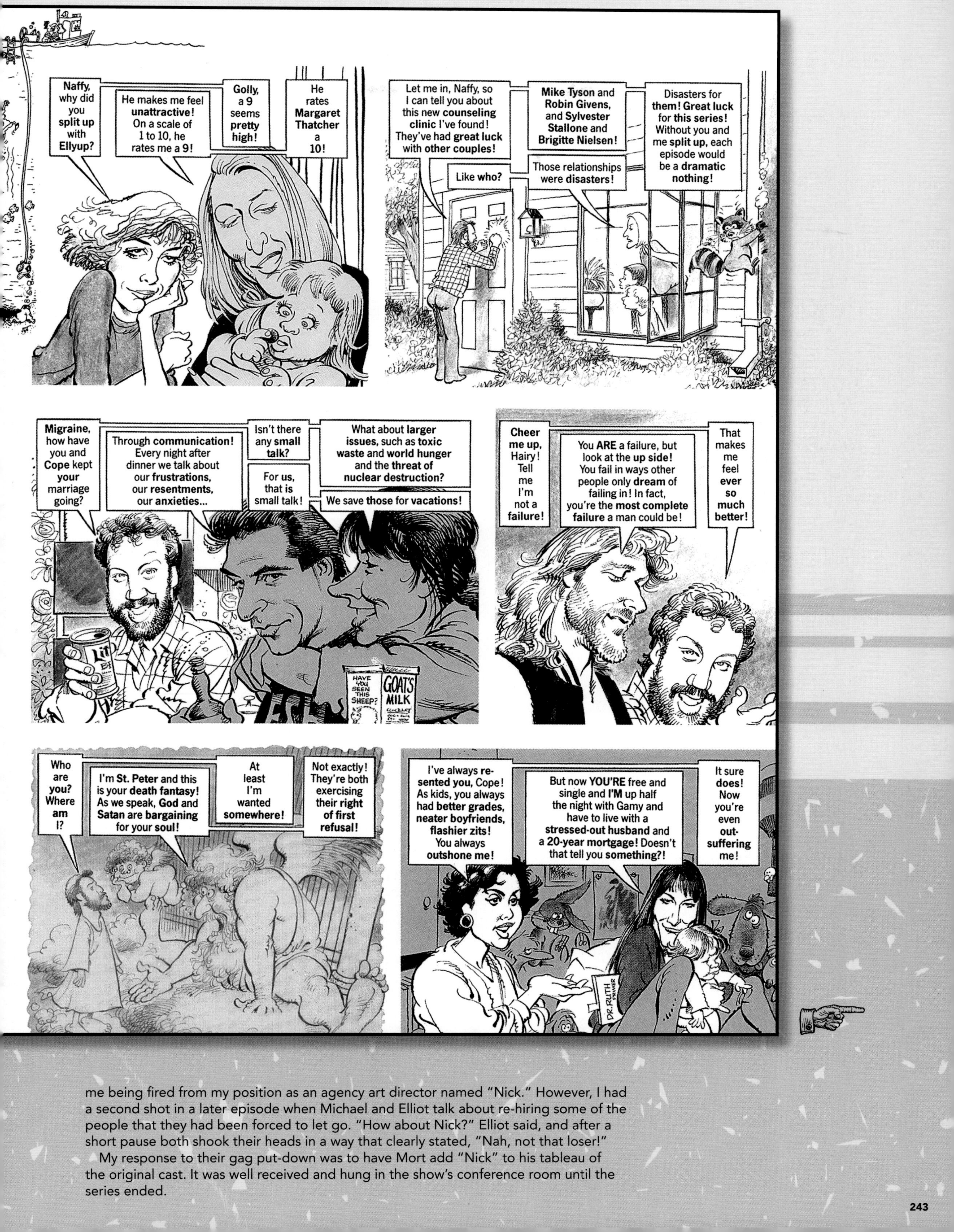

Naffy, why did you split up with Ellyup?
He makes me feel unattractive! On a scale of 1 to 10, he rates me a 9!
Golly, a 9 seems pretty high!
He rates Margaret Thatcher a 10!
Let me in, Naffy, so I can tell you about this new counseling clinic I've found! They've had great luck with other couples!
Like who?
Mike Tyson and Robin Givens, and Sylvester Stallone and Brigitte Nielsen!
Those relationships were disasters!
Disasters for them! Great luck for this series! Without you and me split up, each episode would be a dramatic nothing!
Migraine, how have you and Cope kept your marriage going?
Through communication! Every night after dinner we talk about our frustrations, our resentments, our anxieties...
Isn't there any small talk?
For us, that is small talk!
What about larger issues, such as toxic waste and world hunger and the threat of nuclear destruction?
We save those for vacations!
HAVE YOU SEEN THIS SHEEP?
GOAT'S MILK
Cheer me up, Hairy! Tell me I'm not a failure!
You ARE a failure, but look at the up side! You fail in ways other people only dream of failing in! In fact, you're the most complete failure a man could be!
That makes me feel ever so much better!
Who are you? Where am I?
I'm St. Peter and this is your death fantasy! As we speak, God and Satan are bargaining for your soul!
At least I'm wanted somewhere!
Not exactly! They're both exercising their right of first refusal!
I've always resented you, Cope! As kids, you always had better grades, neater boyfriends, flashier zits! You always outshone me!
But now YOU'RE free and single and I'M up half the night with Gamy and have to live with a stressed-out husband and a 20-year mortgage! Doesn't that tell you something?!
It sure does! Now you're even out-suffering me!
DR. RUTH PRIMER

me being fired from my position as an agency art director named "Nick." However, I had a second shot in a later episode when Michael and Elliot talk about re-hiring some of the people that they had been forced to let go. "How about Nick?" Elliot said, and after a short pause both shook their heads in a way that clearly stated, "Nah, not that loser!"

My response to their gag put-down was to have Mort add "Nick" to his tableau of the original cast. It was well received and hung in the show's conference room until the series ended.

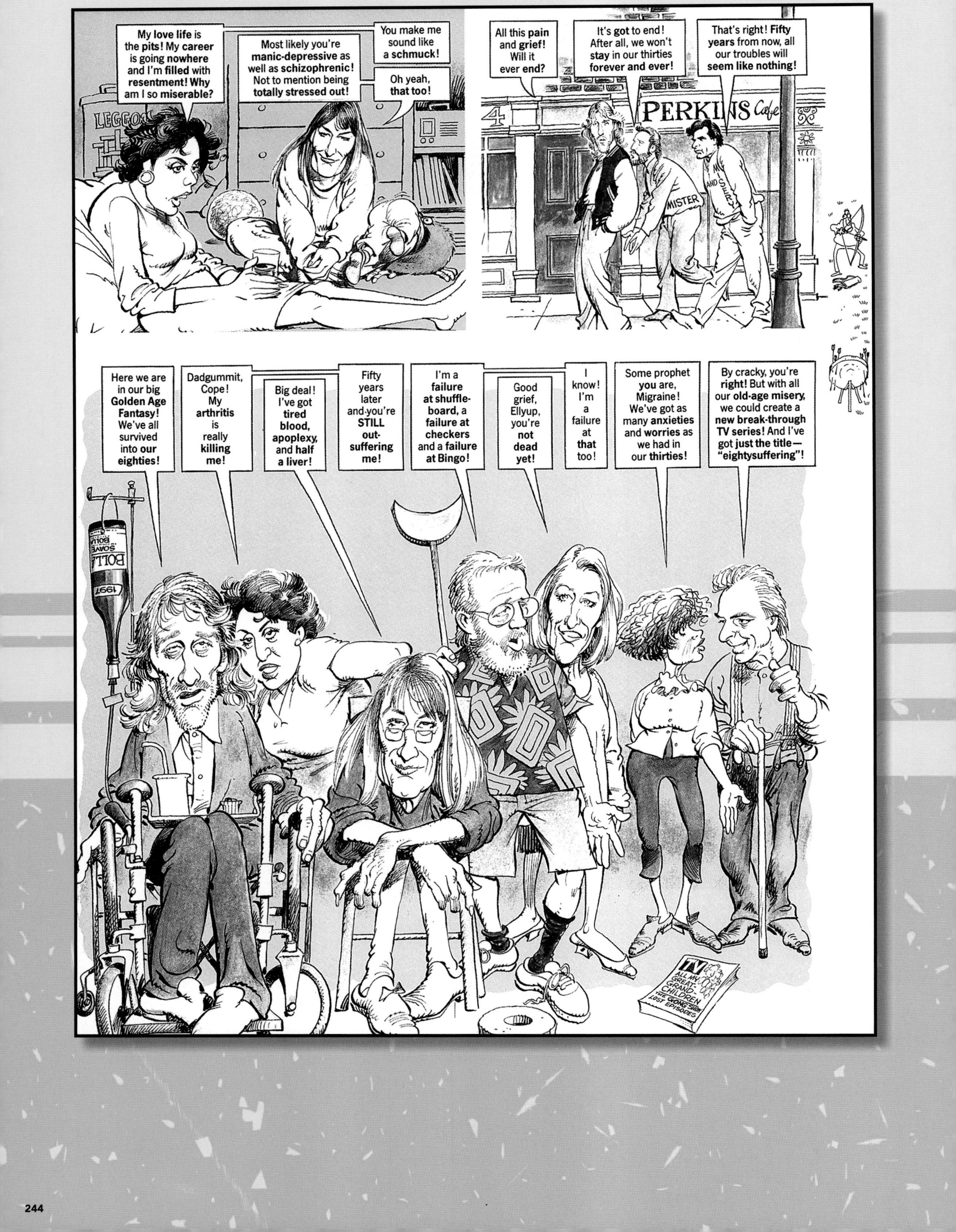
My love life is the pits! My career is going nowhere and I'm filled with resentment! Why am I so miserable?
Most likely you're manic-depressive as well as schizophrenic! Not to mention being totally stressed out!
You make me sound like a schmuck!
Oh yeah, that too!
All this pain and grief! Will it ever end?
It's got to end! After all, we won't stay in our thirties forever and ever!
That's right! Fifty years from now, all our troubles will seem like nothing!
PERKINS Cafe
MISTER
Here we are in our big Golden Age Fantasy! We've all survived into our eighties!
Dadgummit, Cope! My arthritis is really killing me!
Big deal! I've got tired blood, apoplexy, and half a liver!
Fifty years later and you're STILL out-suffering me!
I'm a failure at shuffle-board, a failure at checkers and a failure at Bingo!
Good grief, Ellyup, you're not dead yet!
I know! I'm a failure at that too!
Some prophet you are, Migraine! We've got as many anxieties and worries as we had in our thirties!
By cracky, you're right! But with all our old-age misery, we could create a new break-through TV series! And I've got just the title—"eightysuffering"!
BOLLA
SOAVE
1997
TV
ALL MY GREAT-GRAND-CHILDREN
THE GONG SHOW LOST EPISODES

As long as we can remember, Safety Songs have always played an important part in the education of children. Grammar school teachers are constantly leading their classes in the singing of tunes which tell kids how to live safely amidst the many and varied pitfalls of life. However, a thought recently occurred to us : mainly

CHILDREN's SAFETY SONGS
ARE USUALLY BASED ON OLD-FASHIONED SUBJECTS

ARTIST: JOE ORLANDO   WRITER: LARRY SIEGEL

...like playing with matches:

BAD, BAD MATCHES
(to the tune of "Frère Jacques")

Bad, bad matches,
  Bad, bad matches,
I touched you,
  I touched you.
You made quite a fire,
  There goes brother Meyer . . .
Toodle-ooo,
Toodle-oo.

...and touching nasty plants:

MY BODY HAS CALAMINE LOTION
(to the tune of "My Bonnie Lies Over The Ocean")

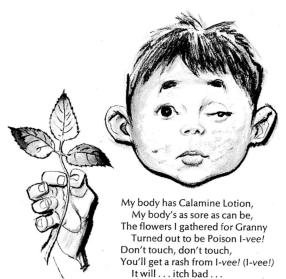

My body has Calamine Lotion,
  My body's as sore as can be,
The flowers I gathered for Granny
  Turned out to be Poison I-vee!
Don't touch, don't touch,
  You'll get a rash from I-vee! (I-vee!)
    It will . . . itch bad . . .
  And it looks worse than ac-nee!

...and fooling around in medicine cabinets:

YOU FUNNY IODINE
(to the tune of "My Darling Clementine")

In the chest there, in the bathroom,
  O'er the sink whose faucets shine,
Stands a funny little bottle,
  And we call it iodine.

Oh you funny, oh you funny,
  Oh, you funny iodine.
You don't taste good with a cookie
  But for booboos you're just fine.

MAD #92/JANUARY 1965

by Larry Siegel
WRITER

After nearly 40 years atop MAD's idiotic writing heap, purveying explosive insanity to young readers, it may sound strange that when I was asked to contribute one of my favorite pieces to this book, I bypassed film and TV satires of mine such as "Flawrence of Arabia" and "Gall in the Family Fare" for, of all things, a song parody of a childhood-type school primer. One of the many things I always loved about this (pardon the expression from a MAD penman) "literary" form is that a primer can hit its target with soft streams of childlike innocence and gentle sprays of kindergarten-like chatter rather than "in-your-face" seltzer-bottle spritzes of gross idiocy. As I once said in a newspaper interview, "I never write down to my young readers. I always bring them up to me."

Unfortunately, my house is now infested with 63 MAD fans, and frankly, I don't know how the hell to get rid of them!

Now we realize, of course, that playing with matches and drinking iodine and touching poison ivy and crossing in the middle of the block always have been and always will be dangerous. But we feel that,

UP-TO-DATE SAFETY

WHEN THE BOMB COMES FALLING DOWN
(to the tune of "London Bridge Is Falling Down")

When the Bomb comes falling down,
Falling down, falling down,
When the Bomb comes falling down,
There'll be fallout.

Cover up your face and head,
Face and head, face and head,
Then put on your suit of lead,
'Cause there's fallout.

Do not stop to talk or play,
Talk or play, talk or play,
Find your shelter right away,
'Cause there's fallout.

Just admit your nearest kin,
Nearest kin, nearest kin,
Shoot down neighbors who want in,
'Cause there's fallout.

Wait until they sound All Clear,
Sound All Clear, sound All Clear,
Don't drink milk till late next year,
'Cause there's fallout.

IT'S A GRAND OLD BAG
(to the tune of "You're A Grand Old Flag")

It's a grand old bag,
    It's a nice plastic bag,
And we find them on all of our clothes.
    Oh a kid can play
The livelong day
    With *them* everywhere that he goes.
They are lots more fun
    Than a doll or a gun,
You can wave them around like flags.
    But should old acquaintance be forgot,
Keep your head out of plastic bags.

ROAD-RAVAGED VALLEY
(to the tune of "Red River Valley")

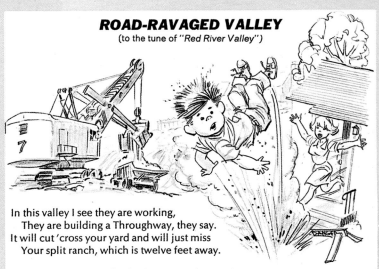

In this valley I see they are working,
    They are building a Throughway, they say.
It will cut 'cross your yard and will just miss
    Your split ranch, which is twelve feet away.

Do not play by the craters they're digging,
    For the craters are big and they're deep.
If you fall into one you'll be buried,
    And you don't really need all that sleep.

Do not touch all those funny explosives,
    Do not play with that dynamite cap.
Otherwise you will find, like the Throughway,
    You'll be spread out all over the map.

as times change, we should add **new** Safety Songs to Grammar school repertoires. Songs which are in keeping with more **modern** safety problems in the Soaring Sixties. And so here are some suggested . . .

SONGS FOR CHILDREN

I'VE GOT TO STOP SMOKING
(to the tune of "On Top Of Old Smoky")

I've got to stop smoking,
  My doctor has said,
Or else when I'm seven,
  I'm sure to be dead.

Cigarettes can cause cancer,
  And that makes no sense.
So I must stop stealing
  My dear Daddy's Kents.

Now here in the 60's,
  When going with chicks,
Cigarettes can bring status
  To a boy who is six.

But I must live clean now;
  At six life is ripe.
Cigarettes I will give up—
  And switch to a pipe!

NORTH SIDE, SOUTH SIDE
(to the tune of "East Side, West Side")
North Side, South Side,
  All around the Square,
The fact'ry smoke is polluting
  Every cubic inch of air.
Cars and trucks together
  Spew exhaust up and down;
Let's dance and pla-ay in gas masks
  On the sidewalks of our town.

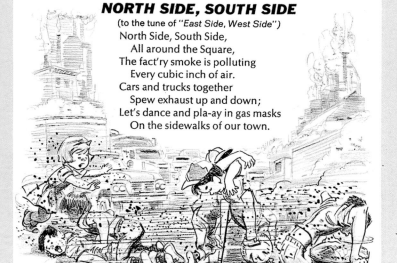

BUCKLE UP YOUR HELMET STRAP
(to the tune of "Button Up Your Overcoat")

Buckle up your helmet strap,
  Hide behind a tree;
There's a riot again
  Down at P.S. 3.

Don't go near the picket line,
  That's no place to be;
They may fracture your skull
  Down at P.S. 3.

Beware of roughneck nuts *(mmm-mmm)*
  Switchblade cuts *(mmm-mmm)*
Trooper's mutts *(mmm-mmm)*
  You'll get a bite in your tummy-tum-tum-tum . . .

Keep away from flying rocks,
  They may break your knee;
Life at school nowadays
  Is like World War III.

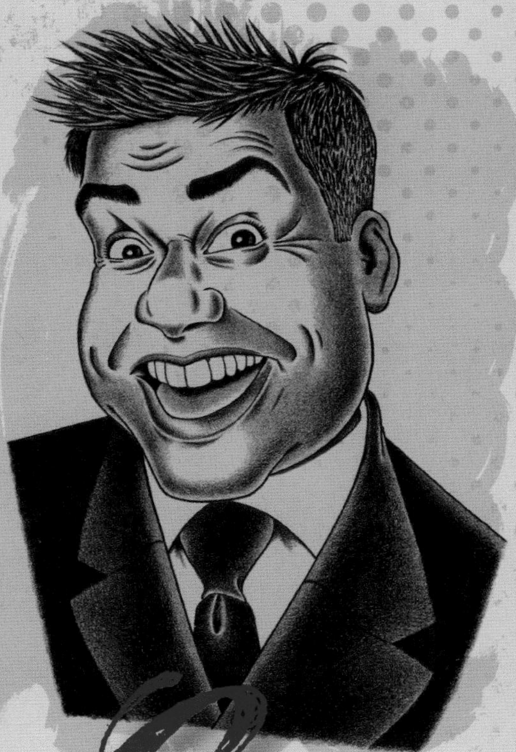

George Lopez

All I had to do is see a couple recent magazine covers to refresh my memories of MAD. It was very easy to remember how MAD first made a huge impact on my life.

I remember the very first time I ever saw MAD. I was seven years old, and it was on the magazine stand at the Thrifty Drug Store near my house in San Fernando, California. It jumped out at me. It really stood out because back then there really wasn't parody. Not on TV, not in the movies, and there was no Internet. There wasn't the abundance of comedy that there is now. Now there are thousands of comedians, and thousands of hours of comedic programs. But not then. For me, MAD was the entire history of comedy. It was my only source of laughs. My house was bleak! So I remember this vividly: the drugstore had the magazine rack on the right, with the checkout counter into the store a little bit. So at the cash register I would turn and see MAD Magazine and start laughing — every time — because it was a dead-on satire of *Star Wars* or *Rocky* or *Jaws* or whatever was happening at the time. It was great! I would run over there and grab it, but then that walk from picking up a copy to walking over to ask my Grandmother if I could buy it was the longest walk ever. When the answer was "no" I'd sit there and read it. I might have lifted a few of 'em. I had to have it, so I would just grab it and walk out the door.

No crap: MAD lined my birdcage

MAD was a huge influence on me. Look, if you didn't look at those sketches in the margins by Sergio Aragonés and then try to draw like that dude, you weren't really looking. The caricatures — and especially drawings by Aragonés and "Spy vs. Spy" by Antonio Prohias — looked simple to draw. You might think, "What's so hard about that?" until you try to do it yourself. You can't do it. I know, because I tried. It looks easy: three little lines for hair, hands on two sticks for arms. I would sit and draw and draw and draw, but it never looked the same. And then try and draw a story like they did — without words! Impossible. I distinctly remember an old Aragonés piece from way back. It was a drawing of New York City in the background, and in the foreground in the water was a drawing of a shark swimming, with graffiti on its side as if the shark had been tagged like a subway train. Incredible. And, like "Spy vs. Spy," it was drawn by a Latino. Amazing. That really spoke to me.

MAD was central to my life for another reason, too. As young Latino kids, we all knew somebody who looked like those characters in "Spy vs. Spy." A skinny kid with a long nose. We used to call him "Spy vs. Spy." And all the Latino kids in my neighborhood knew somebody who looked like Alfred E. Neuman. We called him "Mad." Truthfully, I felt like everybody in MAD Magazine looked like somebody I went to school with.

As great as MAD's artists have always been, the writers are what has always made MAD so consistent. The writing was always good, the parody was always right on target. And because MAD did it first, and was the only one doing it for so long, I would always end up waiting for the next issue, meanwhile wearing out the last one by reading and rereading it again and again.

I always wanted to draw because MAD encouraged me to draw, but that's only the beginning of how it inspired me. What MAD did was take a dead battery — me — and gave it a jump. It charged my creativity. It gave me insight. I was an only child, raised by my grandparents in a tough house to grow up in. I was a bird locked in a cage and MAD Magazine was the lining to my cage. MAD was my open door. Without MAD I never would have learned to fly. It was like that briefcase in *Pulp Fiction* where light poured out when you opened it. MAD was the only thing in my life that gave me comedic vision or even a comedic thing to do. It made me laugh, and that was a very precious thing.

JOKE AND DAGGER DEPT.

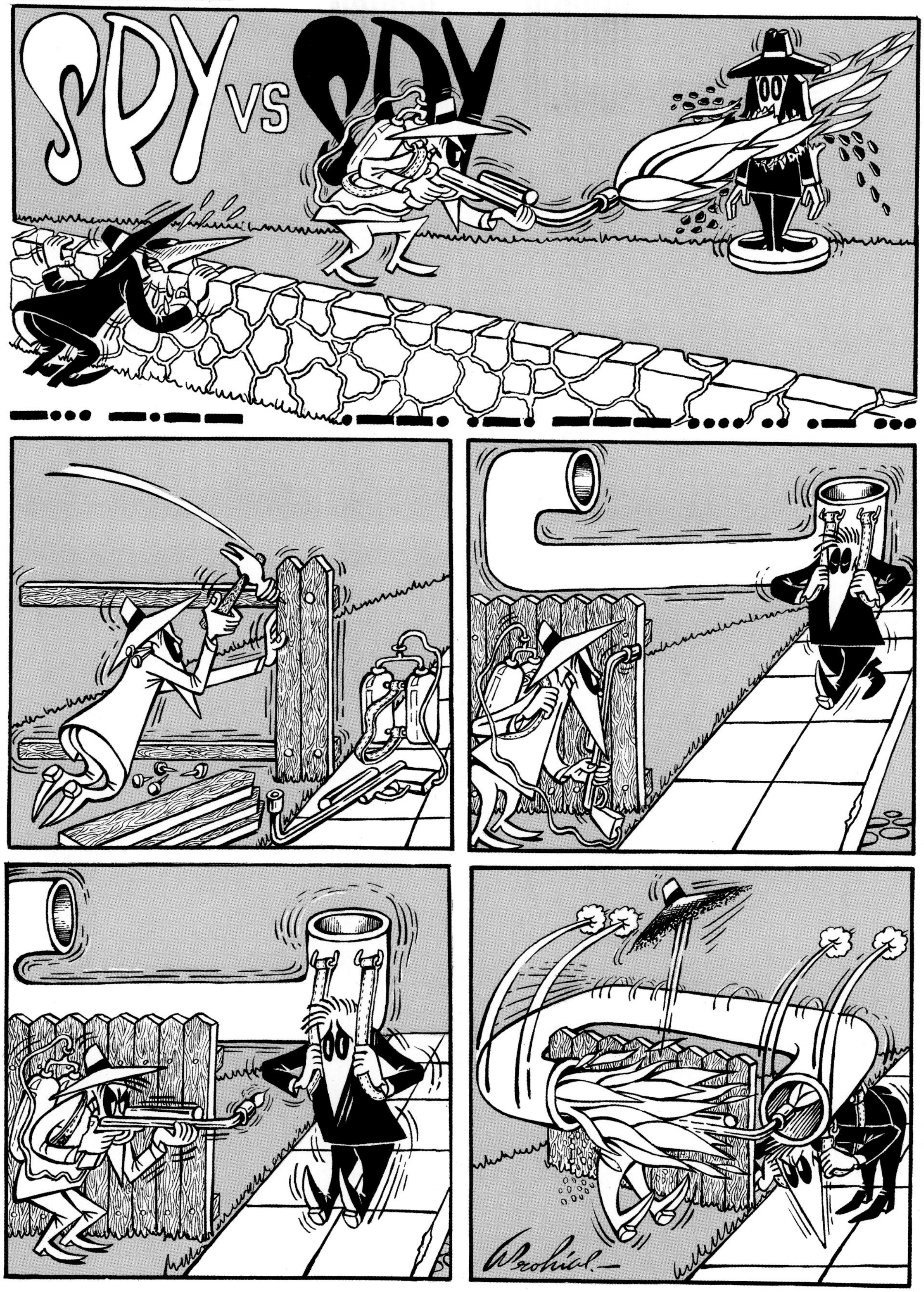
SPY vs SPY
Prohias

WRITER AND ARTIST: ANTONIO PROHIAS

MAD #181/MARCH 1976

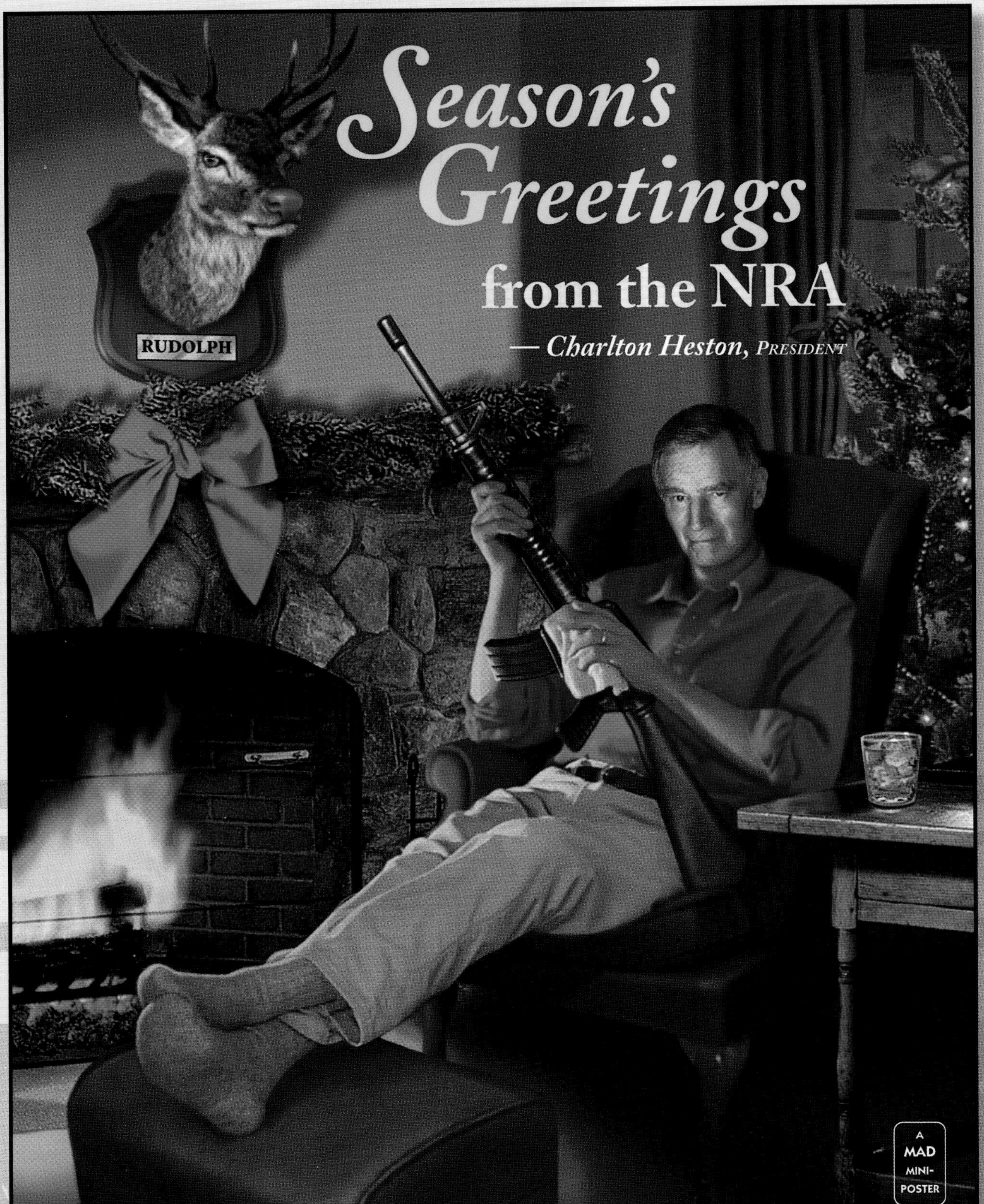
Season's Greetings from the NRA
— Charlton Heston, PRESIDENT
RUDOLPH
A MAD MINI-POSTER

MAD #377/JANUARY 1999

by Scott Bricher
ARTIST

The NRA back cover, issue #377, ushered in a new era of digital art for MAD. The editors wanted a very realistic painting on a tight deadline. MAD had a preference for traditional art media, so I did sketches on the computer and finals with paint. I photographed my friend Mark as Charlton Heston's body double and set about creating a reference image in Photoshop

CHARLTON HESTON

January 26, 1999

Dear Mr. Ficarra:

Thanks for the copies of MAD: as I wrote
your letters editor, I feel I've finally succeeded
now that I made the back cover. I have truly
enjoyed your magazine over the years. Thanks for
keeping your standards.

My gratitude and best wishes to you in all
that you do.

Cordially,

[signature]

to paint from. I got as far as transferring the image to a board and starting
to oil paint when I had an epiphany: "What they really want is a photo, not a
painting!" I returned to Photoshop and everyone was happy with the result,
including, as I am told, Mr. Heston. (My father is a hunter and this piece is his
favorite. I grew up among stuffed deer heads.)

Call us crazy, but it seems that the characters in *Star Wars Episode II: Attack of the Clones* are beginning to remind us of television's most popular family — no, not the Osbournes, Ewok head, the Bradys! There's the handsome Greg Brady type who's always getting into trouble (Anakin), the pretty Marcia Brady type who's always changing her outfits (Padmé), the well-meaning but kind of dull dad Mike Brady type (Obi Wan), and even the funny-looking, wrinkly Alice the maid type (Yoda)! So we decided to kick off this special section of six *Star Wars* articles with a theme song borrowed (well, okay, stolen) from that other bunch! Sing along as we introduce...

The Jedi Bunch

(SUNG TO THE TUNE OF...GOOD LORD, DO WE *REALLY* HAVE TO TELL YOU?)

Here's the story,
Of a sexy girl queen,
Living in a galaxy
  far, far away
When she was almost
  Killed by rival forces
She knew she
  couldn't stay

Here's the story,
Of a young Skywalker
Who was learn-ing The
  Force both night and day
Taught by three Knights,
  playing with Light Sabers
It all seemed Kind of gay

Then the people and their
  robots and the muppet
Got together and decided
  over brunch
That this group, must
  somehow fight the Dark Side
That's the way they all
  became the Jedi Bunch,

The Jedi Bunch -
(You'll lose your lunch!)
That's the way -
  they became
  the Jedi Bunch!

ARTIST: SAM SISCO   WRITER: CHARLIE KADAU

MAD #419/JULY 2002

by Sam Sisco
ARTIST

This is the first piece I ever did for MAD. Art Director Sam Viviano gave me the juicy task of parodying several contemporary *Star Wars* characters to be placed inside *Brady Bunch*-style TV frames. Of the eight small pieces, the most interesting turned out to be the ultra-bulbous, bald, shiny-headed Mace Windu character played by Samuel L. Jackson. The best part was delivering the piece to Sam and getting his exuberant reaction: "What

are they putting in the water up there in Canada?" This, of course, filled my previously miniscule ego to the brim.

This set the standard for me as a contributing Idiot for every piece after that. I haven't always hit that mark, but I still have that little memory which keeps me loving every moment that I get to really be an Idiot. For those of you who don't know this, the guys and gals who hire us artists are a great mix of demanding and caring. They can be hard to please, but that's what keeps us pushing ourselves to reach new lows. Being part of the MAD family has been a wonderful journey and, for me, working with great people makes it the best gig going for any illustrator with at least one screw loose.

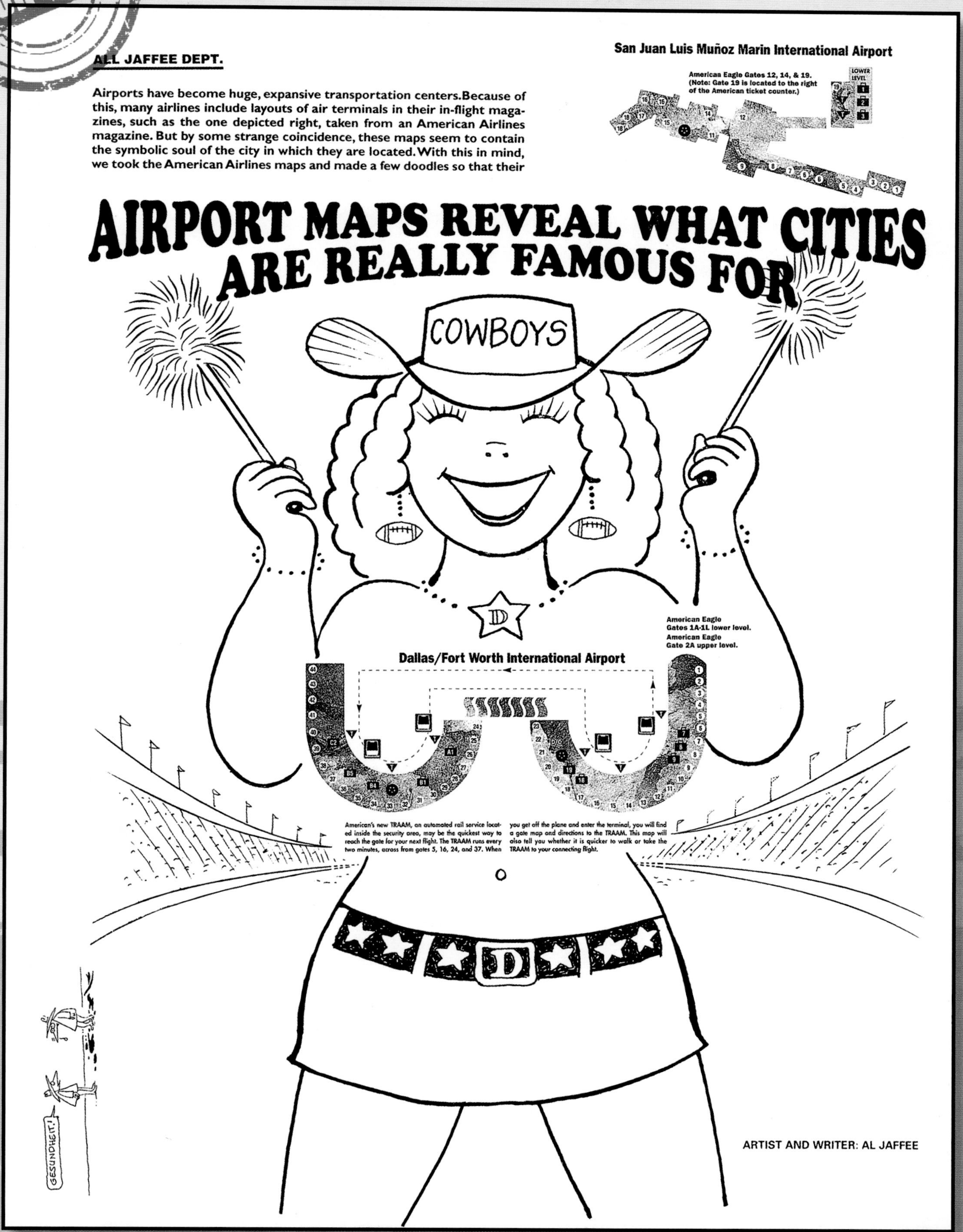
ALL JAFFEE DEPT.
Airports have become huge, expansive transportation centers. Because of this, many airlines include layouts of air terminals in their in-flight magazines, such as the one depicted right, taken from an American Airlines magazine. But by some strange coincidence, these maps seem to contain the symbolic soul of the city in which they are located. With this in mind, we took the American Airlines maps and made a few doodles so that their
San Juan Luis Muñoz Marin International Airport
American Eagle Gates 12, 14, & 19. (Note: Gate 19 is located to the right of the American ticket counter.)
LOWER LEVEL
AIRPORT MAPS REVEAL WHAT CITIES ARE REALLY FAMOUS FOR
COWBOYS
D
American Eagle Gates 1A-1L lower level.
American Eagle Gate 2A upper level.
Dallas/Fort Worth International Airport
American's new TRAAM, an automated rail service located inside the security area, may be the quickest way to reach the gate for your next flight. The TRAAM runs every two minutes, across from gates 5, 16, 24, and 37. When you get off the plane and enter the terminal, you will find a gate map and directions to the TRAAM. This map will also tell you whether it is quicker to walk or take the TRAAM to your connecting flight.
D
GESUNDHEIT!
ARTIST AND WRITER: AL JAFFEE

MAD #331/OCTOBER-NOVEMBER 1994

The idea for this article came to Al Jaffee as he was flipping through an American Airlines in-flight magazine, trying to pass the time sitting on the tarmac while his flight was delayed. It's classic, visually-inventive Jaffee, using the layouts of various cities' air terminals to comment on the state of the cities themselves. American Airlines was not amused. Within days, MAD received a letter from American's attorney. "While American Airlines is not without a sense of humor," the attorney wrote, "these images are not what American Airlines wishes to project to the public." The letter went on to request that "MAD Magazine

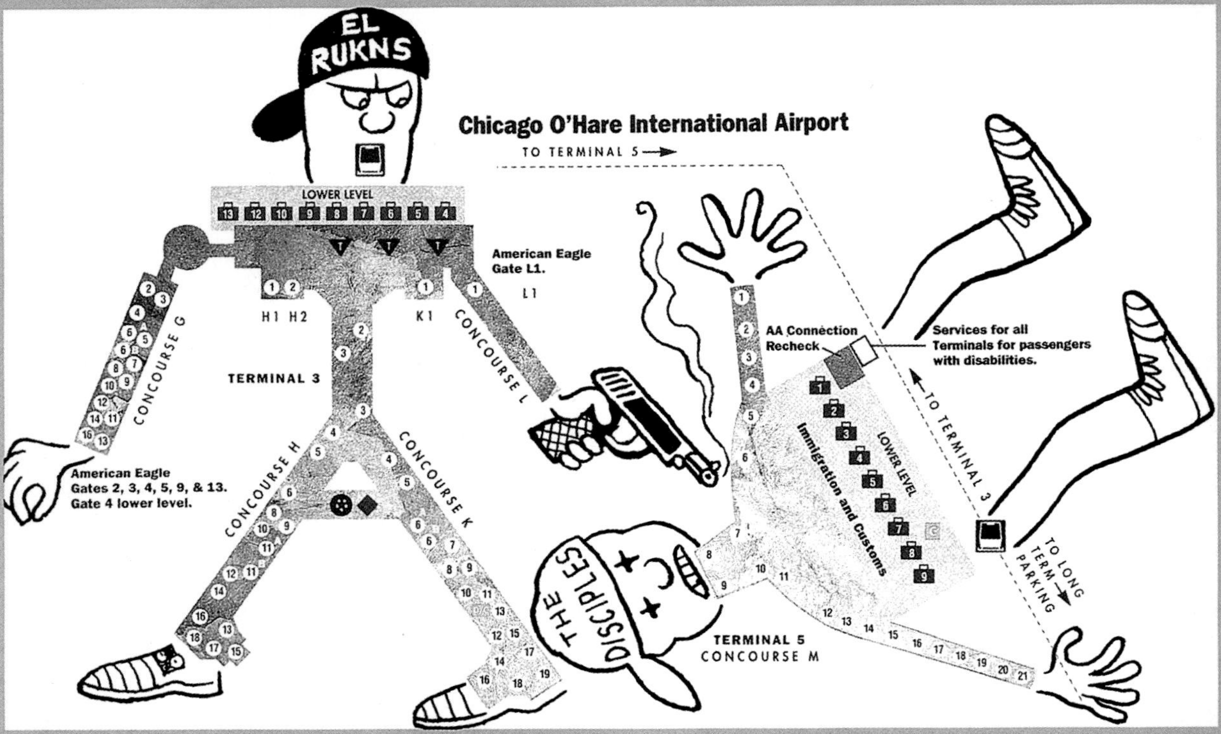
EL RUKNS
Chicago O'Hare International Airport
TO TERMINAL 5
LOWER LEVEL
American Eagle Gate L1.
L1
H1 H2
K1
CONCOURSE G
CONCOURSE L
TERMINAL 3
CONCOURSE H
CONCOURSE K
American Eagle Gates 2, 3, 4, 5, 9, & 13. Gate 4 lower level.
AA Connection Recheck
Services for all Terminals for passengers with disabilities.
TO TERMINAL 3
Immigration and Customs
LOWER LEVEL
TO LONG TERM PARKING
THE DISCIPLES
TERMINAL 5
CONCOURSE M

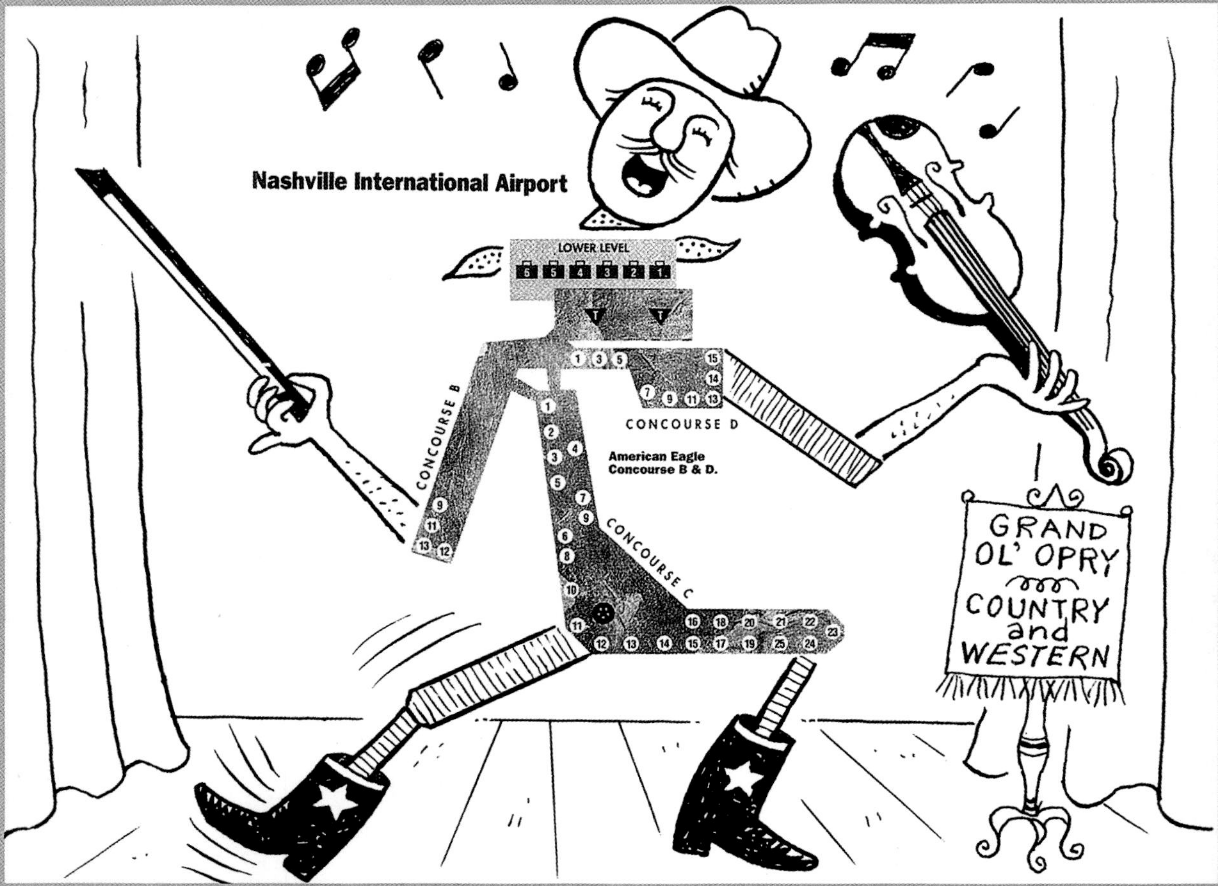
Nashville International Airport
LOWER LEVEL
CONCOURSE B
CONCOURSE D
American Eagle Concourse B & D.
CONCOURSE C
GRAND OL' OPRY
COUNTRY and WESTERN

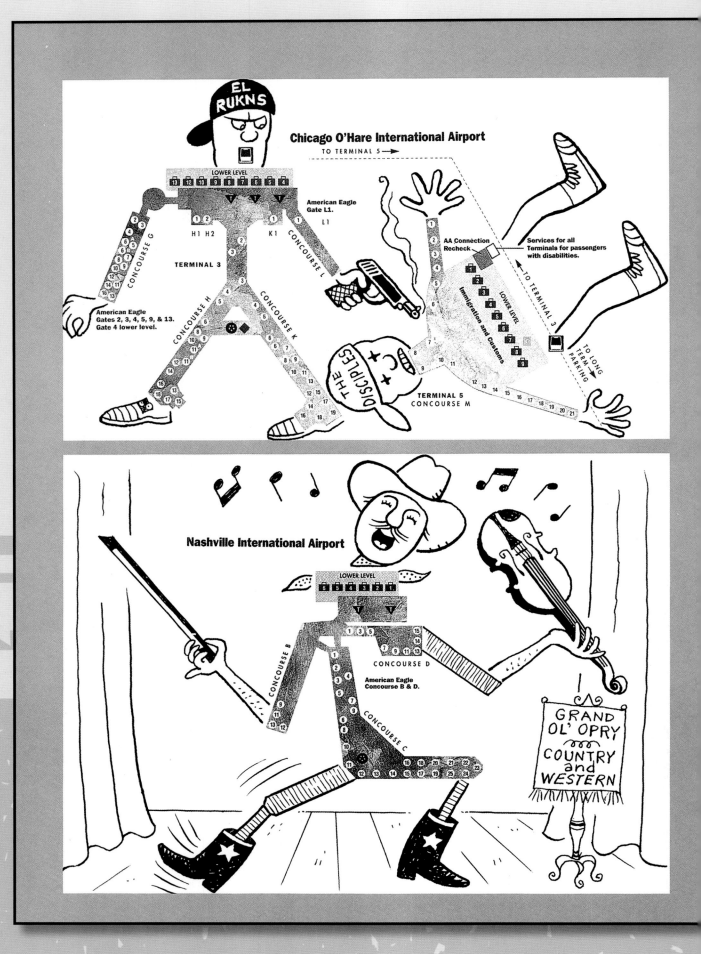

offer their guarantee and assurances that they will not in the future run other cartoons and/or articles of this ilk on American Airlines without first contacting American Airlines and requesting approval from the Public Relations department." In his response, longtime MAD attorney Jack Albert pointed out that MAD had a lengthy publishing history satirizing various institutions of American culture. "There are no sacred cows — politics, business, the media are all fair game for

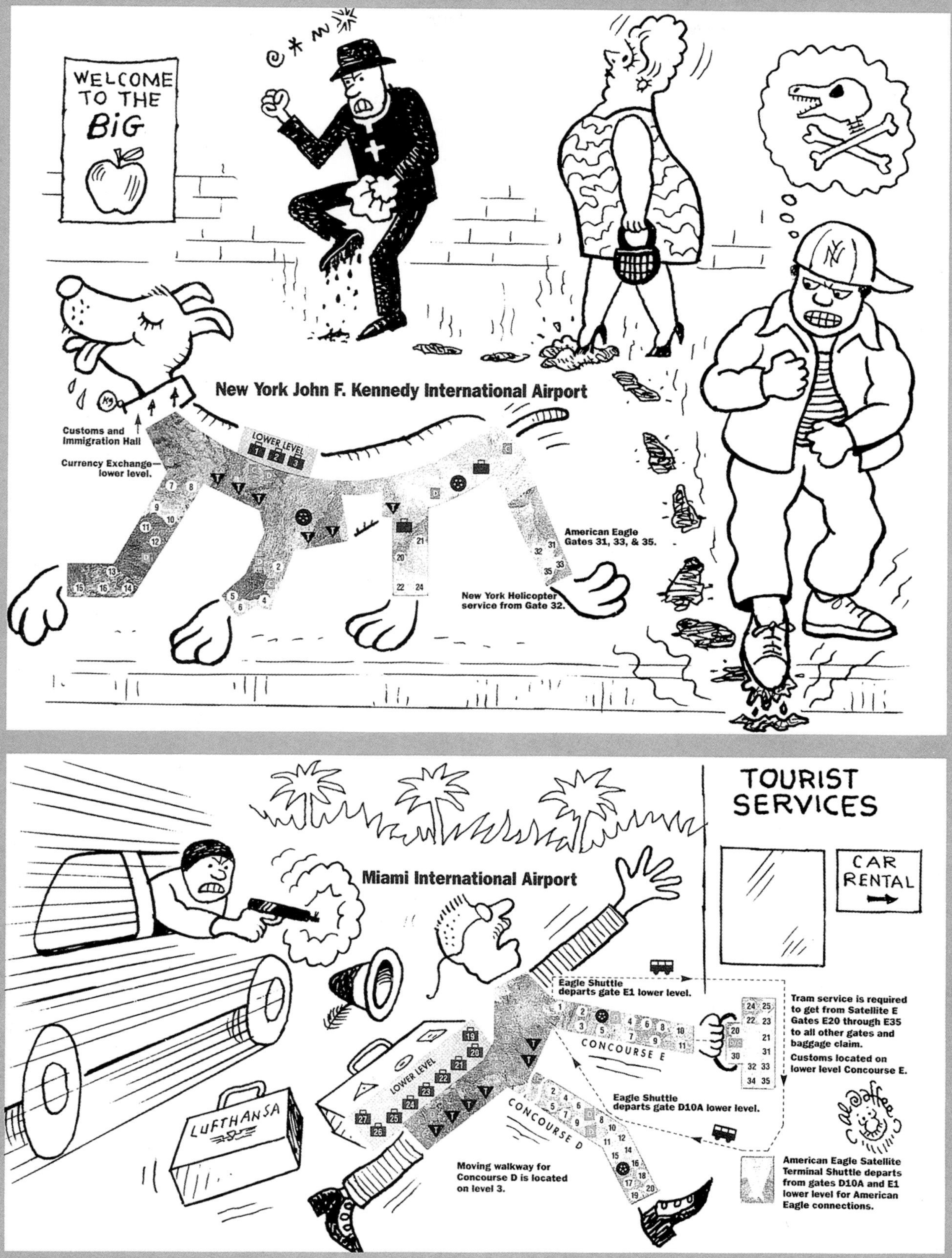
WELCOME TO THE BiG
New York John F. Kennedy International Airport
Customs and Immigration Hall
Currency Exchange—lower level.
LOWER LEVEL
American Eagle Gates 31, 33, & 35.
New York Helicopter service from Gate 32.
TOURIST SERVICES
CAR RENTAL
Miami International Airport
Eagle Shuttle departs gate E1 lower level.
Tram service is required to get from Satellite E Gates E20 through E35 to all other gates and baggage claim.
Customs located on lower level Concourse E.
CONCOURSE E
LOWER LEVEL
Eagle Shuttle departs gate D10A lower level.
CONCOURSE D
LUFTHANSA
Moving walkway for Concourse D is located on level 3.
American Eagle Satellite Terminal Shuttle departs from gates D10A and E1 lower level for American Eagle connections.
al jaffee

such comment," Albert wrote. "It is not MAD's policy to publish a disclaimer such as you request or to issue a guarantee that it will seek permission from any future possible subject of it artists' and writers' parodies." Albert concluded his letter by inviting American Airlines to submit a letter to the editors which briefly set forth its position for publication consideration. Just like an unlucky airline passenger's luggage, no letter ever arrived. — *John Ficarra*

When I was a kid, I wanted to be funny. MAD Magazine was my training manual. It was a portable classroom that came into my possession eight times a year. Its arrival on the newsstand was celebrated like the reappearance of a missing loved one. Every page was devoured and taken to heart like a religious scripture. I remember the smell of the printed pages as I turned each one for the first time. I remember the delicate care I took folding the back page to reveal the hidden joke, which was sometimes funny and sometimes scarily political, which then taught me that comedy could be used not solely to make people laugh.

My parents and I always thought MAD was a kids' magazine, but the humor wasn't for kids. MAD spoke to me like an adult. MAD made jokes I couldn't believe they made. More often than I care to admit, MAD made jokes I didn't get, jokes I then had to consult with my friends on — sometimes embarrassingly so — to understand. MAD took me out of the kid-jokes world of riddles and puns and showed me how grown-ups — truly funny grown-ups — made other people laugh.

Paul Feig

MAD Magazine made me the man I am today (in other words, it's their fault)

Don Martin, Dave Berg, Sergio Aragonés, Mort Drucker, Al Jaffee. These guys were my Beatles. To me, they didn't walk on this Earth. They had to exist in some other universe and send their work down to us from on high. They lived in a place where adults weren't so serious, where they weren't so hung up on protocol and respect and reverence for the way things are. But they also weren't the 1960s hippies and the radicals on my TV who were scarily telling me that my friends and I should rebel against my parents and the world around us. The MAD guys were fighting the system and tearing down idols and making fun of it all from inside its walls, all while making me laugh the entire time.

MAD Magazine made me who I am today: a middle-aged, paunchy and occasionally sober man. It also showed me what funny is and gave me the inspiration to create my own comedy. I try every day to live up to their standards. I strive to make them proud and I pray with all my heart they will make fun of my work.

For me, it's not "What Would Jesus Do?" It's "What Would MAD Do?" And right now, I think they'd just tell me to shut up and stop embarrassing them.

And so I will. Thanks again, MAD.